ACCESSORIES IN PRIVATE LAW

Accessory liability is an often neglected, but very important, topic across all areas of private law. By providing a principled analytical framework for the law of accessories and identifying common themes and problems that arise in the law, this book provides much-needed clarity. It explains the fundamental concepts that are used to impose liability on accessories, particularly the conduct and mental elements of liability: 'involvement' in the primary wrong and (generally) knowledge. It also sets out in detail the specific rules and principles of liability as these operate in different areas of common law, equity and statute. The authors undertake a comparative study across the common law and criminal law, and across a number of jurisdictions, including the United States, with a focus on Anglo-Australian law. The book sheds new light on what is and what is not accessory liability.

Joachim Dietrich is a professor at the Faculty of Law, Bond University, Queensland, where his research and teaching interests range across the spectrum of private law.

Pauline Ridge is an associate professor at the Australian National University, where she is also Director of the Centre for Commercial Law. She researches and teaches in equity, restitution, contract and property law, and the regulation of religion by private law.

ACCESSORIES IN PRIVATE LAW

JOACHIM DIETRICH AND PAULINE RIDGE

CAMBRIDGE
UNIVERSITY PRESS

CAMBRIDGE
UNIVERSITY PRESS

University Printing House, Cambridge CB2 8BS, United Kingdom

Cambridge University Press is part of the University of Cambridge.

It furthers the University's mission by disseminating knowledge in the pursuit of education, learning and research at the highest international levels of excellence.

www.cambridge.org
Information on this title: www.cambridge.org/9781107063440

First published 2015

A catalogue record for this publication is available from the British Library

Library of Congress Cataloguing in Publication data
Dietrich, Joachim, author.
Accessories in private law / Joachim Dietrich and Pauline Ridge.
pages cm
ISBN 978-1-107-06344-0
1. Liability (Law) 2. Joint tortfeasors. 3. Correality and solidarity. 4. Accomplices.
5. Liability (Law) – English-speaking countries. I. Ridge, Pauline, author. II. Title.
K579.L5D54 2015
346–dc23
2015023033

ISBN 978-1-107-06344-0 Hardback

For Birgit, Melanie and Dominik
and
For David, Geraldine, Alice, Emily and Lucy

CONTENTS

FOREWORD

For some years now I have had the hope that Joachim Dietrich and Pauline Ridge, both former students of mine, would address together this greatly under-analysed, but practically very significant, subject. It has now come to pass. Their's is an important publication, and a much needed one. It obviously required mastery of major parts of the common law, equity and statute. It warranted – and received – considerable comparative treatment of the laws of other common law jurisdictions (beyond England and Australia), and especially of the United States. From these it is apparent they derived both helpful insights and, I venture, reassurance. As I anticipated, the authors have displayed an informed understanding of the methodology, the inspirations and the inevitable complexities of judge-made law. This saved their work from the allure of over-simplification, a common vice when one is seeking to bring cohesion and harmony to judicial utterances drawn from disparate bodies of law. I will return to this last theme below.

Beyond the criminal law of accessory liability (to which a chapter usefully is devoted), Anglo-Australian common law has displayed little by way of explicit acceptance, let alone development, of a jurisprudence focused on accessory liability for civil wrongs as such. There is not, for that reason, a readily available common language to which the authors could turn. Yet at the peripheries of quite some number of bodies of law – be they common law, equity-related or statutory – there has been the recognition that, at least in some circumstances, a third party's involvement in another's civil wrongdoing (be it a particular tort, a breach of contract, an equitable wrong, a misuse or misappropriation of property, or a breach of statutory duty) could result in that person being held liable to an injured plaintiff for, or on account of, that other's wrong. But as the authors acknowledge, accessory liability by no means provides the sole basis for imposing liability on a third party.

Necessarily they needed to give considerable explanation of what differentiates accessory liability from other species of third party-liability.

Much of this, I should add, required them to differentiate a variety of possible third-party liabilities which can arise particularly in tort law, and in equity. The tort of conspiracy and claims against third-party recipients of trust property, or of equitable interests in property, demonstrate why this is necessary. To complicate matters, as the authors accept, a possible difficulty here is that in some settings the same facts can give rise to several distinct possible liabilities (of which accessory liability can be one), for which there may be little by way of difference in the remedies that are available.

Over the last three decades or so, some number of judges and scholars have asserted with greater or lesser confidence that at least some of the disparate forms of third-party liability do, or else could be said to, display at least a general uniformity of legal themes, if not in fact far greater coherence than merely this. In short, they have heralded recognition of a body of accessory liability law having its own distinctive function. The important question, though, is this: to what extent will such a body of law continue to reflect the values, the compromises and characteristics of the separate and distinct bodies of law which have accepted in some degree an accessory-like form of liability?

It is in answering this question that the authors have revealed what I consider to be both a great virtue of this book and the breadth and perceptiveness of their own scholarship.

They have recognised what is immanent in the case law itself. While accessory liability in its various manifestations shares a deceptively simple analytical framework, there is in their view no single cause of action for this liability. As they put it, '[the] legal rules that determine accessory liability across private law are too complex and varied, even as to the form of the liability itself, for that to be the case'. This conclusion might disappoint those who wish for simplicity in all things. But it is intuitively correct. It does, incidentally, conform with my own experience with, at least, equity jurisprudence.

Nonetheless, the authors go on to suggest that the analytical framework of accessory liability depends upon three indispensable factors: the commission of a civil wrong by a primary wrongdoer; the accessory's involvement, through his or her own conduct, in that wrong; and the accessory's mental state at the time of such involvement.

The first of these – a primary wrongdoing by another – is a precondition. Without it, there can be no possibility of accessory liability. The other two factors – the accessory's own conduct and, to put it shortly, the mental state required at the time of the accessory's involvement – are necessary to found liability. Nonetheless, the content required of each (and hence the reach of accessory liability itself in a given setting) is a function of the purposes, values and historical development of the primary wrong in question.

What may seem to complicate matters more is that the law takes two quite different approaches to how it formulates an accessory's liability. In some cases, it is formulated as being for the primary wrongdoer's wrong, that is, as a secondary liability for the same wrong. In other cases, accessories are held liable on the basis of an independent cause of action. The tort of inducing a breach of contract is an easy example of the latter. The authors, as one would expect, have discussed in detail with each species of accessory liability, the remedies and defences which are available. I will not enlarge on these.

Of the many particular matters dealt with in this book, there are three I should emphasise. The first relates to wrongs involving companies and the possible accessory liability of the company (as an artificial legal person) and, distinctly, of directors as accessories. I simply note, because of its significance for Australian law, that the authors conclude that, as in the United Kingdom, the principles that determine the liability of ordinary persons as either primary wrongdoers or accessories apply equally to company directors and to companies themselves. They emphasise that there are no cogent reasons why directors deserve special immunity from liability for wrongs; nor why the principles of accessory liability, properly understood, should not provide just outcomes.

The second matter is that one chapter deals specifically with accessory liability and infringement of statutory intellectual property rights. The present challenges for the law come in part from technological innovations, particularly on the internet, which enable widespread and repeated infringements by numerous individual infringers. Here their use of comparative law is instructive.

The third matter is of particular importance to an Australian audience. This relates to those statutory schemes, such as the misnamed Australian Consumer Law (it is not limited to consumer transactions), which create obligations the contravention of which can give rise to a wide range of remedies against primary wrongdoers, but which also impose civil liability on accessories, that is, parties involved 'in the contravention' of a statutory obligation. Legislation of this variety has revolutionised the private law of obligations in Australia. Again, a separate chapter has been devoted to such legislative schemes, and to the obvious affinity these have with the analytical framework which supports accessorial liability more generally.

In sum, Joachim Dietrich and Pauline Ridge have made a very considerable contribution to the law. They have created from previously opaque and much neglected case material a coherent body of civil law which can stand alongside other major areas of the law as providing sources of liability in its own right. Judges, practising lawyers and scholars alike have every reason to be grateful for the authors' endeavours. It is not often that we can witness the unearthing of a distinct and credible category of the law for what, after all, is a form of civil liability of such practical significance. I congratulate them on their achievement.

Paul Finn

PREFACE

This book owes its origins and inspiration to Paul Finn, former Justice of the Federal Court of Australia. Paul suggested, too many years ago, that accessory liability was one of the last great unexplored areas of private law and was worthy of deeper analysis. He was undoubtedly correct in his view. The size and complexity of the topic made us initially reluctant to take on the task, although we individually wrote and researched on various aspects of accessory liability. This convinced us even more of the merit of Paul's idea and we decided to take up his challenge. This book is our attempt to do so. Our many citations of Paul's judgments and academic scholarship throughout the book demonstrate his leadership in this area of law. We are honoured that he has agreed to write the Foreword.

We hope that this book does not disappoint in seeking to meet the challenge of exploring accessory liability (and its boundaries) in its many guises, but we are mindful that we have, perhaps, taken on a far larger task than we initially envisaged. Not only have we sought to explore accessory liability across a range of topics in private law, we have also considered accessory-related doctrines and criminal law; nor have we ignored statutory accessory liability. Further, the book ranges across a number of common law jurisdictions, although the focus is on English and Australian law. Although we took primary responsibility for some of the chapters, the book is the result of our joint efforts. Joachim took primary responsibility for Chapters 4–6 and 9–10. Pauline took primary responsibility for Chapters 7–8. Fortunately, despite robustly criticising each other's writing and methodology and arguing at length over our ideas, we have remained good friends.

This book could not have been achieved without the assistance of many people. We are grateful to those who have given up their time and been happy to share their wisdom. We apologise to anyone that we may have overlooked in the note of thanks here.

First, we would like to thank the friends and colleagues who have read parts of the draft manuscript and/or discussed our ideas with us. They are Malcolm Barrett, Rick Bigwood, Joel Butler, Peter Cane, John Farrer, Iain Field, the Honourable Paul Finn, the Honourable William Gummow AC (former Justice of the High Court of Australia), Harold Luntz, Tom Middleton, Jane Stapleton and Michael Tarlowski. We are also very grateful to the Obligations Group at Melbourne University Law School, especially Elise Bant, Michael Bryan, Matthew Harding and Katy Barnett, for their generous support and encouragement of private law scholars across Australia. They provided feedback on our work on at least three occasions. Pauline also thanks the Asian Law Institute, National University of Singapore, for providing a visiting fellowship for work related to this book.

Joachim would like to thank in particular Joel Butler, whose steadfast willingness to listen and to discuss ideas was always greatly appreciated. Only a friend could have put up with so much without complaint. Joachim would also like to thank Iain Field in particular for his thoughtful comments provided in short time frames. Pauline would like to thank her colleagues at the ANU, particularly Dennis Pearce for his support and friendship, and Michael Tarlowski.

A number of research assistants have provided valuable assistance over many years. We thank them for their thorough research and attention to detail. They are Radhika Chaudhri, Rouslun Churches, Michael Cole, Susie Forder, Rupert Holden, Tonya Roberts, Michael Tarlowski, Stephen Webster and Kim Weinert. In addition, Alison Gurr generously shared her research on equitable accessory liability in the United States.

Most importantly, we would like to thank our families, to whom this book is dedicated. Joachim would like to thank Birgit, Melanie and Dominik for their love and support. Birgit had to live with and put up with Joachim's many mood swings, particularly during the emotionally difficult last few months of the project, and did so with love and understanding. When Melanie was told that the book was about 'accessories', she responded positively: 'Great, it's about handbags and jewellery.' Her assumption has been corrected – at least she will no longer have any unmet expectations on that front. Dominik always showed great concern for his dad's well-being. Pauline thanks her daughters, Alice, Emily and Lucy, for their patience and many kindnesses during this project. Most of all, she thanks David and her mother, Geraldine, for their unfailing support and unconditional love.

TABLE OF CASES

Australia

Canada

European Union

Hong Kong

New Zealand

Singapore

United Kingdom and Privy Council

United States

Table of legislation

Australia

Commonwealth

Australian Capital Territory

New South Wales

Northern Territory

Queensland

South Australia

Tasmania

Victoria

Western Australia

New Zealand

United Kingdom

United States legislation

PART I

General principles

1

Introduction

1.1 An organising principle of accessory liability

When a person commits a civil wrong, other persons may in some circumstances also be held legally liable for some or all of the consequences of that wrong despite not having personally satisfied all its elements. Legal concepts that explain such liability include vicarious liability as an employer or a principal; attribution to a principal of the acts of agents or alter egos; breach of non-delegable duties; receipt of benefits or property as a consequence of the wrong; and accessory liability. This book considers the last of these concepts.

Specifically, this book concerns whether there is an organising principle of accessory liability discernible throughout private law. We argue that there is indeed such a principle and seek to explain its elements and operation. Our claim is not novel. Many judges and commentators have suggested that this might be so, although there is no consensus regarding how such a principle might operate or what its contents might be.[1]

At its core, the notion of an accessory is intuitively simple: an accessory is someone who is wrongfully involved in another's wrong. As with many concepts, however, legally defining 'accessory liability' and drawing the precise boundaries between it and other, perhaps related, concepts is not easy. We argue that there are three key elements of accessory liability in its various manifestations throughout private law, namely:

(1) a primary wrong committed by another;
(2) involvement, through conduct by the accessory, in that wrong; and

[1] See, e.g., R. P. Austin, 'Constructive Trusts' in P. D. Finn (ed.), *Essays in Equity* (Sydney, Law Book Company, 1985) 196, 200 n. 22; Philip Sales, 'The Tort of Conspiracy and Civil Secondary Liability' (1990) 49 *Cambridge Law Journal* 491; Peter Birks, 'Civil Wrongs: A New World' in *The Butterworth Lectures 1990–91* (London, Butterworths, 1992) 101; Paul S. Davies, *Accessory Liability* (Oxford, Hart, 2015). We were not able to read Paul Davies' book before submitting our own manuscript for publication.

(3) a requisite mental state on the part of the accessory, generally knowledge of the other's wrong.

The contents of each element of the organising principle are fleshed out by specific doctrines within the common law, equity and statute. Ultimately, the question of liability is a normative one of whether a person is sufficiently involved in the primary wrong with sufficient knowledge such that it is appropriate to hold him or her liable for the primary wrong of the primary wrongdoer. The answer depends on the primary wrong that has been committed, particularly in light of the purposes and values promoted by the law proscribing that wrong, and the factual context in which that wrong came about. In simple terms, accessory liability is justified by the accessory's own wrongful conduct that contributes to the commission of the primary wrong. These matters form the subject matter of our book.

1.2 The objectives of the book

This book explores the variety of forms in which accessory liability manifests itself throughout private law; we do not ignore statute in that exercise. This book also explores the question of whether liability rules can be characterised as accessorial or not. Our objectives are threefold:

(i) to explain why we consider that there is an organising principle of accessory liability operating across private law;
(ii) to provide a principled analytical framework for accessory liability in private law according to which common themes and problems can be identified and coherent solutions to those problems suggested; and
(iii) to set out in detail the specific rules and principles of accessory liability as they currently operate in private law.

Objectives (i) and (ii) form the basis of Part I of this book. Objective (iii) forms the basis of Part II. We intend Part II to be a useful resource for those seeking information on the substantive law. This book not only focuses upon Anglo-Australian law, but also refers to other common law jurisdictions. We use US law as a useful point of comparison and insight in relation to some areas of accessory liability, but we do not claim to provide a comprehensive or authoritative treatment of that country's various jurisdictions.

Describing accessory liability in isolation from the contexts in which it operates would be to present a distorted, inaccurate picture of the law. Furthermore, in order to understand what accessory liability *is*, it is crucial to understand what accessory liability *is not*. Hence, Part II includes discussion of some related rules that also impose liability on third parties to a primary wrong and which have considerable affinity with accessory liability. We have taken this approach, for example, in relation to equity by including discussion of persisting property claims and recipient liability; and in intellectual property law by including 'indirect' liability rules. These bases of liability must be disentangled from what we consider to be, conceptually, accessory liability. We also do not wish to disrupt settled groupings of liabilities that make sense on other grounds. For example, equitable accessory liability and recipient liability form part of a broader 'participatory' liability in equity; it would be misleading to imply that the courts treat equitable accessory liability in isolation.

1.3 The methodology and general approach of the book

Extracting a concept of accessory liability from case law and legislation has the potential to be a circular process, given that such a task presupposes a prior understanding of the concept. Chapter 2 identifies what 'accessory' could mean in a legal sense and demonstrates that our understanding of the concept is consistent with actual usages of the term 'accessory' in private and criminal law. We then explain that, regardless of the terminology, the same concept exists in different guises across private law. Chapter 2 also explains the rationales for accessory liability and distinguishes it from other concepts. In Chapter 3, we present a conceptual framework of accessory liability that is based upon our conclusions in Chapter 2 and that draws upon the substantive law discussed in Part II.

In formulating our understanding of civil accessory liability, we draw upon the well-developed (albeit complex and uncertain) criminal law jurisprudence. There are obvious parallels between accessory liability in private and criminal law, but equally there are dangers in too readily analogising between the two legal systems. Chapter 4 provides an overview of accessory liability in criminal law and explains how it may help us understand civil accessory liability.

1.4 An analytical framework, not a uniform test or rigid taxonomy

As accessory liability describes rules that are evident throughout private law, does this mean that there is a single coherent test for, or determinative standard of, liability that uniformly applies across different areas of law? It would be surprising if this was so and that is the conclusion that this book has reached. The elements that we set out in Chapter 3 are formulated too generally to operate as uniform tests of liability; these elements merely provide a starting point for analysis. It is necessary to consider the specific legal principles and rules as set out in Part II in order to gain an accurate understanding of how accessory liability operates in its respective contexts.

This book does not advocate a rigid taxonomy of accessory liability. Exceptional or borderline cases of liability exist that may share some, but not all, of the characteristics of accessory liability. We are mindful of the dangers of a categorisation that is too rigid. As Thomas has stated,

> Instead of analysing the law as it actually exists, as a product of piece-meal (often haphazard) historical development, with all its uncertainties and inconsistencies, there seems to be a passion for re-ordering and re-classifying it as commentators would wish it to be. . . . Many areas of law might, perhaps, be better arranged and rendered more logical if one were starting with a blank canvas.[2]

Overzealously promoting one classificatory scheme may distract attention from equally important, yet inconsistent, commonalities. To do so may also distort the law through oversimplification. Similarly, we do not intend to reject alternative classificatory frameworks that encompass all or some of the principles that we include in our accessorial scheme. We do not see how any classificatory scheme can claim to be the sole and exclusive means of organising the law. With such qualifications in mind, however, the analytical framework set out in Chapter 3 is nonetheless intended to illuminate and clarify the current law.

1.5 Terminology

We refer to the claimant, or C, as the party to whom liability, accessorial or otherwise, is owed, and we refer to the party who has personally committed the wrongful conduct to which accessory liability attaches as the 'primary wrongdoer' (PW or, if a company, PW Co). In the context

[2] Geraint Thomas, *Thomas on Powers*, 2nd edn (Oxford University Press, 2012) *x*.

of criminal law, that party is referred to as the 'principal offender' or PO. When the liability is indisputably accessorial and no confusion arises, we refer to the accessory as A; otherwise, we generally refer to third parties involved in the wrongful conduct without having personally committed it as the 'defendant' or D. Purely for reasons of style and convenience, A is assumed to be male and PW is assumed to be female.

Accessory liability is described by a proliferation of terms in specific legal contexts, but there are few terms that adequately describe accessory liability as a generic concept. 'Accessory liability' itself is often associated with criminal liability. Conversely, in the United States (US), 'aiding and abetting' liability is widely used, even outside of its core operation in criminal and tort law, but does not naturally encompass all forms of accessorial conduct such as procurement. In Anglo-Australian law, one widely used generic term is 'secondary liability'. To the extent that 'secondary' means derivative or 'ancillary'[3] liability, that is dependent on, or subsidiary to, the commission of a wrong by another person, that label is useful. Nonetheless, we prefer the generic label 'accessory' to 'secondary' or, for that matter, 'ancillary' and consider that 'secondary liability' is best avoided for the following reasons.

The term 'secondary liability' is sometimes used to refer to non-accessory liabilities, such as vicarious liability, and is therefore too wide for our purposes.[4] It is also used by some commentators to mean that the accessory must be liable for the same wrong as that committed by PW and that the same remedies must therefore apply against the accessory as those available against PW.[5] This issue goes to the heart of our understanding of accessory liability and is explored fully in Chapter 2. Here, it suffices to note that 'secondary' in this sense is inaccurate where A is liable for what is a different wrong, as is the case in equity [Chapter 8], and the tort of inducing breach of contract [Chapter 6], for example. Necessarily, that party is subject to potentially different remedies.[6] Furthermore, accessory

[3] See *Williams* v. *Central Bank of Nigeria* [2014] UKSC 10; [2014] 2 WLR 355 [9] (Lord Sumption); *Hasler* v. *Singtel Optus Pty Ltd* [2014] NSWCA 266; (2014) 101 ACSR 167 [72] (Leeming JA).

[4] See, e.g., Sales, 'The Tort of Conspiracy', 502–503.

[5] See in the context of liability for assistance in a breach of trust or fiduciary duty, Steven Elliott and Charles Mitchell, 'Remedies for Dishonest Assistance' (2004) 67 *Modern Law Review* 16.

[6] It should be added that debates about which remedies are available against an accessory and whether such remedies are duplicative of those available against PW, ought not to turn on whether we label such liability as 'secondary' or as a discrete wrong.

liability need not necessarily duplicate the remedies available against PW (though it usually does) even where A's liability is for the same wrong as PW [2.6]. Finally, the term 'secondary liability' might be confused with the term 'secondary rights', which is used to denote remedial rights arising from the breach of legal duties and which differ from the 'primary' rights that have been infringed.[7] For these reasons, 'accessory liability', rather than 'secondary liability', is used in this book as a generic label. Both 'accessory' and 'accessorial' can be used as an adjective; we have chosen for convenience the term 'accessory liability', and in all other adjectival contexts we use 'accessorial'.

Finally, by 'private law' we mean the case law and statutes that regulate the interactions of private actors, and we use 'wrong' in the conventional sense of breach of a legal duty that leads to remedial outcomes. In private law, a wrong encompasses breach of common law duties (torts and breach of contract), breach of equitable duties (including breach of trust, fiduciary duty and confidence) and breach of privately actionable statutory duties (for example, concerning misleading conduct by persons engaged in trade or commerce). Equity has a broader understanding of wrongful conduct, the various permutations of which are encapsulated in the general concept of unconscionability or unconscientous conduct, and which we also consider in this book.

1.6 The structure of the book

Part I of this book is concerned with identifying and explaining the organising principle of accessory liability that operates in private law. Chapter 2 identifies and describes the general features of the principle, explains its rationales and distinguishes it from other forms of liability. Chapter 3 explores the analytical framework of accessory liability with reference to the substantive law detailed in Part II. Chapter 4 concludes Part I with an overview of criminal accessory liability that explains its relevance to accessory liability in private law.

Chapters 5–10 of Part II of this book are ordered according to the respective jurisdictions of private law: common law, equity and statute. The very particular questions that arise across private law in determining accessory liability in the context of wrongs involving companies are discussed separately in Chapter 11. The chapter headings in Part II

[7] See, e.g., Robert Stevens, *Torts and Rights* (Oxford University Press, 2007), particularly 285 onwards, which explains the distinction between primary and secondary rights.

generally refer to the primary wrong that has been committed by PW, but the content of these chapters (with the exception of Chapter 7) focuses on the accessory liability rules that apply to determine who are accessories to those wrongs. This focus generally matches the chapter headings, but it does lead to some unavoidable overlap in coverage. Specifically, intellectual property infringements are statutory torts and, consequently, the courts have applied both general accessory rules, from tort law, as well as specific statutory accessory rules to intellectual property infringements. Consequently, the primary wrongs of intellectual property infringements are considered both in the chapter dealing generally with torts [Chapter 5] and the chapter dealing specifically with infringement of statutory intellectual property rights [Chapter 9]. The subject matter of Chapter 7, which deals with infringement of equitable property rights, is unusual in that it concerns non-accessory liabilities that are closely related to equitable accessory liability and that need to be clearly distinguished from it. It forms a necessary prelude to the discussion of equitable participatory liability (including both accessory and recipient liability) in Chapter 8. Chapter 12 contains our brief concluding observations.

2

Identifying accessory liability in private law

2.1 Overview

This chapter identifies – by drawing upon first principles, the substantive principles of private law and, to a lesser extent, the criminal law – a form of liability that is appropriately characterised as accessory liability and that arises across private law. The chapter explains when a liability can be appropriately characterised as accessorial, regardless of whether it is formulated as an independent wrong or as a 'secondary' liability to the primary wrong of the primary wrongdoer (PW), and irrespective of the actual terminology used to describe that concept. The chapter explores the rationales of accessory liability and when it is needed in the law: that is, why it serves an important function in some areas of law and not in others. It explains why accessory liability is derivative upon another person committing a primary wrong, but need not duplicate, or replicate, PW's liability. Finally, this chapter distinguishes other forms of liability and explains why it is necessary to consider some non-accessorial, but related, liabilities in more depth, specifically ones concerning the protection of equitable property rights, recipient liability and the protection of statutory intellectual property (IP) rights.

2.2 Identifying accessory liability in private law

In simple, non-legal terms, 'accessory' means something that is additional to, or contributes to, something else. The core legal understanding of accessory accords with this meaning: an accessory is someone who is linked to another's wrongdoing in such a way as to be made responsible for its consequences. Such a generic statement, however, hides a range of more specific possible meanings. At its broadest, 'accessory' could encompass all situations in which the commission of a primary wrong is a prerequisite to another's liability and could, for example, therefore include vicarious liability [2.8.1], [5.3.1]. But such a meaning would be unhelpfully wide. A narrower meaning is one that focuses on wrongful conduct that *contributes* to the commission of another's primary wrong. It is this idea that forms the basis of our identification of accessories because, where such contribution exists, a number of common and overlapping rationales justify this narrower form of liability [2.4]. Furthermore, those rationales do not equally apply to any broader 'accessory' concept.

Consistent with this narrower understanding of 'accessory', we identify three common features of accessory liability, specifically:

(1) a primary wrong committed by PW;
(2) some involvement by the accessory, A, in PW's commission of the wrong (the conduct element); and
(3) such involvement is accompanied by a requisite mental state, generally knowledge by A of PW's conduct or intended conduct that constitutes the wrong (the mental element).

The combination of A's conduct and knowledge creates a 'participation' link between A and PW's wrong.

As with many other legal concepts that defy precise definition, the elements as set out here are intended by way of description, rather than being definitive. The elements are formulated too generally to operate as uniform tests of liability. They therefore provide merely a starting point for analysis. The detailed content of these three elements is discussed in Chapter 3.

Liability that accords with this description arises in criminal and private law, but is described by an over-proliferation of terms, some of which have the same, similar or overlapping meanings.[1] Such terms include 'aiding and abetting', 'authorisation', 'common design', 'conspiracy', 'constructive trusteeship', 'contributory liability', 'counselling', 'inducing or procuring', 'dishonest and knowing assistance', 'being "knowingly concerned"' in and 'secondary liability'. In the law of torts, accessory liability is subsumed under the label of 'joint tortfeasors' [5.1.2]. No doubt, the many different labels reflect the fact that accessory liability has developed independently in different areas of private law, but they also obscure its existence and potentially create confusion, since related ideas are at work.

[1] At times the label 'accessory' may be used to describe liability that is not, conceptually, accessorial as we have defined it. An example is 'accessory' after the fact: see [3.3.4], [4.3].

Regardless of the terminology used to describe accessory liability and the confusion this can create, accessory liability, as we have described it, exists for breaches of various private law obligations: for torts; for breaches of contract via the independent tort of inducing breach of contract; for breach of equitable duties, as well as, possibly, for more broadly defined equitable 'wrongdoing'; for infringements of IP rights, via both statutory and common law concepts; and for statutory wrongs more generally.[2]

2.3 Accessory liability can be 'secondary' to the primary wrong or an independent wrong

2.3.1 'Secondary' or independent liability?

One of the challenges in identifying accessory liability is that the law takes two quite distinct approaches as to how it formulates an accessory's liability. In some cases, such liability is formulated as being for PW's primary wrong, that is, as 'secondary' to the same liability as that of PW. In other cases, the law holds accessories liable on the basis of an independent cause of action. Whichever of these two formulations is used, however, should not change the characterisation of the substance of the liability rule.

2.3.2 Liability as an accessory for the same wrong as that committed by PW

Where the liability of A is not for an independent wrong, A is considered liable for PW's wrong, that is, as if A is also a primary wrongdoer of that wrong. For example, in tort, the accessory is liable as a joint tortfeasor for PW's tort; in criminal law, accessories are liable as if they were principal offenders (POs). Although A is liable for the same wrong as that committed by PW, such liability is still based on A's own wrongful conduct [2.4]. Importantly, the elements that need to be established against A are different to those that need to be established against PW: PW's liability depends on proof of the elements of the primary wrong, whereas A's liability is determined by proof of very different facts and a different set of

[2] Whether the tort of inducing breach of contract is appropriately characterised as protecting contracts from third-party accessories to breaches is contested. We explain and defend our characterisation of it as accessorial in [6.2.2].

(accessorial) elements, namely, in general terms, knowing involvement in PW's wrong.[3]

One consequence of holding A 'secondarily' liable for the same wrong as that committed by PW[4] is that A will usually be liable for the same remedies as PW; however, this need not be so. Courts may distinguish between the respective culpability of the parties and award different remedies; that is, A's and PW's liability need not be identical and A's liability therefore is not duplicative [2.6]. Indeed, analogously, in criminal law, A may be liable for a different, either lesser or more serious, offence than PO [4.5.1].

2.3.3 *Liability as an accessory for an independent wrong*

Some examples of accessory liability take the form of independent causes of action. Examples include equitable accessory liability [Chapter 8], inducing breach of contract [Chapter 6] and authorisation of IP infringements [9.2.2]. In equity, for example, an accessory is liable for his own independently wrongful conduct that constitutes a distinct wrong. Indeed, in equity, there may have been an evolution in the understanding of the nature of A's liability from being a form of secondary liability to an independent basis of liability.[5] It follows from this approach that different remedies to those available against PW are potentially available against A.[6]

Where accessory liability takes the form of an independent wrong, liability is still accessorial as it depends on some primary wrong being committed by a party other than A. PW's wrong is a prerequisite for, and element of, A's liability. Further, the conduct that renders A liable must be accessorial in nature: that is, knowing involvement in the commission

[3] E.g., if PW enters C's land without C's consent, proof that PW consciously crossed the boundaries means that the elements of trespass are made out against PW. However, if C should sue A, who did not enter C's land, then absent any vicarious liability, C would need to prove very different matters against A than those against PW in order to establish A's liability: that A procured, or acted in furtherance of a common design with, PW to commit the tortious act.

[4] Note, however, that A may in some circumstances be liable even when PW is not [2.6].

[5] See, e.g., the evolving understanding of an accessory in equity's liability as constructive trustee [8.1.7].

[6] See, e.g., *Michael Wilson & Partners Ltd* v. *Nicholls* [2011] HCA 48; (2011) 244 CLR 427 [106] (*Michael Wilson*), and [2.6]. Indeed, a converse process of reasoning may be at work: because different remedies may or do apply, A's liability is described as distinct.

of PW's primary wrong so as to create a participation link to that primary wrong.

The development of accessory liability in some areas of law as a distinct cause of action may be the result of conceptual barriers to the 'accessory' being liable for the same wrong as that committed by PW. For example, in the context of the tort of inducing breach of contract, it was conceptually and historically difficult for the common law of contract to develop accessory liability principles within the doctrinal confines of contract law itself, for reasons explained in [6.1]; see also in equity [8.2]. Since non-contracting parties could not be liable as if they themselves had breached the contract, other doctrinal tools were needed if the law was to provide protection to a claimant (C) against A's involvement in PW's breach of her contract with C. The tort of inducing breach solved the difficulties by establishing an independent wrong. That wrong shares many of the characteristics of other forms of accessory liability, but the 'accessory' is never liable for the same wrong as the contract breaker.

2.3.4 Doctrines that redress accessorial conduct without constituting accessory liability

Some liability rules, in their application, *factually* involve, and are directed to, accessorial conduct and give rise to liability against parties that often could be described as accessories, but the rules nonetheless do not fit our description of accessory liability. This is because the liability rules themselves do not contain the three necessary elements of accessory liability as set out in our framework. Nonetheless, the function of those liability rules is primarily concerned with attaching liability to accessories. Examples are recipient liability, noted in [2.8.2] and discussed in Chapters 7 and 8, and the tort of conspiracy. For the tort of conspiracy, most defendants against whom the tort is alleged are also accessories, but the rule operates beyond that scope, so that the rule as a whole cannot be characterised as accessorial [5.3.2]. Not surprisingly, such wrongs have rationales that overlap with those for accessory liability.

2.4 Rationales for accessory liability

2.4.1 Possible rationales

There are a number of rationales that underpin either accessory liability in general or specific examples of it. We consider four of these in detail, though there may, of course, be more specific rationales and policy factors that apply to particular primary wrongs. It should be added that the underlying rationales for particular accessory rules may not always be clearly articulated.[7]

First, accessory liability redresses the accessory's own wrongful conduct that is linked to PW's wrong. Secondly, it vindicates the rights of claimants and the obligations of primary wrongdoers by extending the protection of claimants via claims against parties other than PW. Thirdly, accessory liability may act as a deterrent against future wrongs being committed. Related to this third rationale are economic efficiency goals, which may also underlie the second rationale. Finally, a property-protection rationale may apply. Although this could be seen as a manifestation of the vindication of rights more generally, courts have identified this rationale as justifying some species of accessory liability.

2.4.2 The accessory's wrongful conduct that is linked to the primary wrong

In our view, the fundamental rationale for accessory liability is that A should be held responsible for culpable conduct that interferes in the rights of C and that is linked to breach of the corresponding obligations owed by PW (the primary wrong). It is the combination of A's involvement in PW's wrong with a requisite mental state that creates the link with PW's wrong and makes A's conduct culpable. When such a link exists, the risk of wrongdoing is enhanced and A ought not to be able to hide behind the fact that he did not himself, *commit* the primary wrong.[8] A's own wrongful conduct of itself justifies liability to remedy the consequences of PW's wrong.

Not all interference in the rights of C vis-à-vis PW is legally wrongful, that is, actionable. Whether it is or not depends on the purposes, values

[7] E.g., for statutory accessory liability for breaches of financial regulation in the United Kingdom, Eva Lomnicka, '"Knowingly Concerned"? Participatory Liability to Regulators' (2000) 21(4) *Company Lawyer* 120, 121, has stated that:

> The rationale for the liability has never been articulated, Scott LJ in [*SIB* v. *Pantell SA (No. 2)* [2004] EWHC 3255 (Ch)] finding "the legislative policy . . . difficult to discern". However, it would seem to comprise a combination of discouraging such involvement, encouraging a degree of self-policing by those involved in the relevant financial sector and providing alternative, deep-pocket defendants.

[8] *Cf.* discussion in Chapter 4 at n. 23.

and historical development of the primary wrong in question as well as the operation of the applicable accessory rules. For example, for inducing breach of contract, A's conduct probably needs to be a 'but for' cause of PW's decision to commit the wrong or commission of the wrong; whereas in other areas of law, even quite minor contributions to the commission of the primary wrong may suffice [3.3.3]. The narrow range of actionable interference permitted by the tort of inducing breach of contract reflects contract law's reluctance to unduly inhibit commercial dealings. Further, what is the minimum culpable mental state also varies in different contexts.

2.4.3 Providing enhanced protection and further vindicating existing rights

Accessory liability performs the pragmatic function of spreading the net of obligation beyond PW, thereby enhancing the protection of the victims of wrongs[9] and further vindicating their rights. It may be easier for C to proceed against an accessory; this may be so, for example, if PW has disappeared, or if A has deeper pockets.[10] Importantly, the scope of any additional protection afforded depends on the specific primary wrong committed. Rights that warrant special protection, perhaps because the holders of such rights are particularly vulnerable, are better protected by more broadly operative accessorial rules. There is no better illustration of this than equity's protection of the beneficiary of a trust, and the broad-ranging liability rules and remedies that enhance the beneficiary's rights against a range of parties, including accessories and even innocent parties.[11] Equity's accessory rules provide C with an alternative means of recourse, thereby increasing C's chances of a successful claim [8.1.1], [8.1.3].[12]

Similarly, in copyright law, in *Metro Goldwyn Mayer Studios, Inc,* v. *Grokster Ltd*,[13] the US Supreme Court noted that for widespread and multiple infringements, the impossibility of effectively enforcing rights against direct (primary) infringers may mean that the only practical

[9] See, e.g., *Consul Development Pty Ltd* v. *DPC Estates Pty Ltd* (1975) 132 CLR 373 (HCA) 397 (Gibbs J).

[10] *Cf.* Lomnicka, '"Knowingly concerned"?' 121.

[11] E.g., as a result of a persisting property claim against an innocent recipient of property [7.5]. This is not to suggest that such generous protection is warranted.

[12] *Royal Brunei Airlines Sdn Bhd* v. *Tan* [1995] 2 AC 378 (PC) 386–387.

[13] 545 US 913, 929–930; 64 IPR 645 (2005).

alternative is to pursue parties for 'secondary' liability. The potential to seek relief against 'secondary' infringers enhances the means by which copyright owners can protect their rights.[14] Similar ideas are at play in the context of IP infringements more generally.

This rationale is related to deterrence, because one way of protecting claimants is to deter future breaches; that is, liability rules may have a prophylactic purpose.

2.4.4 *Deterrence*

Accessory liability, especially if it is for the full extent of C's losses or A's gains, provides a disincentive for potential accessories to involve themselves in the wrongs of others and may therefore lead to fewer wrongs.

The deterrence rationale is particularly evident in equitable accessory liability.[15] It reflects the importance attached to equitable obligations of trust and confidence and the historically strong prophylactic function of equity's jurisdiction over trusts and other fiduciary relationships.[16]

In the context of IP infringements, the deterrence idea is sometimes expressed by reference to 'gatekeepers'. Particularly from the perspectives of IP right holders, it may be desirable to require some 'intermediaries' (such as internet service providers, ISPs) to act as 'gatekeepers'.[17] Gatekeepers may in part be identified on economic efficiency grounds,[18] 'based on who is in the best position to prevent the harm in question', such that the question of liability is treated as partly one of 'cost allocation'.[19] Economic efficiency grounds reflect the protection and

[14] *Cf. Roadshow Films Pty Ltd* v. *iiNet Ltd* [2012] HCA 16; (2012) 248 CLR 42 [110] (Gummow and Hayne JJ) quoted n. 18 below (*Roadshow*).

[15] See, e.g., *Zhu* v. *Treasurer (NSW)* [2004] HCA 56; (2004) 218 CLR 530 [121](*Zhu*).

[16] P. Finn, 'The Liability of Third Parties for Knowing Receipt or Assistance' in D. Waters (ed.), *Equity, Fiduciaries and Trusts* (Toronto, Carswell, 1993) 195, 197.

[17] See generally, Renier Kraakman, 'Gatekeepers: The Anatomy of a Third Party Enforcement Strategy' (1986) 2 *Journal of Law, Economics and Organisation* 53.

[18] As was noted by Gummow and Hayne JJ in *Roadshow* [2012] HCA 16; (2012) 248 CLR 42 [110]:

> Liability as a secondary infringer of copyright has been said to have an economic rationale similar to that of the tort of inducing breach of contract, namely a lower cost of prevention of breach of the primary obligation.

They cite William M. Landes and Richard A. Posner, *The Economic Structure of Intellectual Property Law* (Harvard University Press, 2003), 118–119.

[19] Katja Weckström, 'Liability for Trademark Infringement for Internet Providers' (2012) 16 *Marquette Intellectual Property Law Review* 1, 39.

deterrence rationales, rather than being a distinct rationale for liability.[20] A gatekeeper who is in the best position to prevent infringements may be able to deter future infringements, and if he fails to do so, may also be the most cost-efficient defendant – it being easier to bring a legal claim against a single third party rather than against multiple infringers.[21]

However, economic efficiency arguments do not of themselves justify liability. Although on the one hand, some persons may be well placed to detect and deter misconduct, on the other hand, doing so imposes business costs and, clearly, imposing liability is less desirable if it substantially interferes with legitimate activity.[22] As Landes and Posner have noted, whether liability in a given case should be imposed on grounds of promoting economic welfare involves difficult balancing questions that may be impossible to answer.[23] Further, any liability justified by efficiency may be disproportionate to the degree of culpability.

Economic efficiency arguments may support widening the meaning of culpable conduct. Taken too far, however, attaching liability to conduct that can no longer realistically be considered wrongful means that such liability becomes less accessorial and is more likely to be driven by policy rather than a fault-based rationale.[24] Overall, however, it is probably fair to conclude that in the IP context, fault-based accessorial concepts may not be adequate for the task of meeting the many challenges posed by widespread IP infringements, at least from the perspectives of rights holders [9.1.2].[25] Policy and economic deterrence goals may therefore lead to further legislative liability rules, including ones that impose obligations on some parties to take positive steps to stop infringements

[20] The economic efficiency language of who is the 'cheapest cost avoider' (Megan Richardson, 'Why Policy Matters: *Google Inc v Australian Competition and Consumer Commission*' (2012) 34 *Sydney Law Review* 587, 592) covers both deterrence and protection.

[21] *Metro Goldwyn Mayer Studios, Inc,* v. *Grokster Ltd* 545 US 913, 929–930; 64 IPR 645 (2005).

[22] See Robert Burrell and Kimberlee Weatherall, 'Before the High Court: Providing Services to Copyright Infringers: *Roadshow Films Pty Ltd* v. *iiNet Ltd*' (2011) 33 *Sydney Law Review* 801, 829–830.

[23] Landes and Posner, *Economic Structure*, 119–121.

[24] Richardson, 'Why Policy Matters', 593–594, commenting in the context of statutory liability, suggests that courts in Australia have resisted a wide accessorial regime aimed at making certain parties gatekeepers, but that in some jurisdictions, expanding liability may be based on a broader policy of discouraging infringement [9.1.2].

[25] *Cf. Roadshow* [2012] HCA 16; (2012) 248 CLR 42 [79] (French CJ, Crennan and Kiefel JJ): accessorial concepts 'not readily suited to enforcing the rights of copyright owners in respect of widespread infringement'.

before they occur. Some of these provisions are distinguished from accessory liability in Chapter 9.

2.4.5 *Property protection*

Accessory liability may protect property rights against interference by third parties. A property-protection rationale is particularly evident in equity and supports broad participatory (including accessory) liability, particularly in protecting the property interests of trust beneficiaries.[26] Property protection may give rise to liability beyond that which is accessorial or even wrong-based. The distinctions between the various property-based claims in equity are discussed in Chapter 7 and the classification of one such claim, recipient liability, is considered in [7.6].

Similarly, according to the High Court of Australia, one justification for the tort of inducing breach of contract is the protection of quasi-proprietary rights, that is, that contract rights are 'a species of property'[27] protected by limited rights against non-contracting parties.[28] The Court considered this to be the most important rationale for liability, alongside more general accessorial rationales of deterring and remedying A's wrongdoing.[29]

2.4.6 *Countervailing policies that limit accessory liability*

Where countervailing concerns are at play, the law may limit accessory liability. For example, in the tort of inducing breach of contract, the broader the liability, the more the tort may stifle commercial competition.[30] The law therefore needs to balance the interests of defendants in freedom of action against the interests of claimants in the security of their

[26] *Zhu* [2004] HCA 56; 218 CLR 530 [121]–[122].

[27] See Kitto J's analysis in *Attorney-General for New South Wales* v. *Perpetual Trustee Co. (Ltd)* (1952) 85 CLR 237, 294–295 (also describing the rights as *in rem*).

[28] *Zhu* [2004] HCA 56; 218 CLR 530 [124]–[135], the joint judgment (Gleeson CJ, Gummow, Kirby, Callinan and Heydon JJ) strongly endorsing a property analysis. The Court noted the obvious resonances with the need to protect equitable property interests (at [121]–[122]).

[29] See *ibid.* [121], in which the court described the tort as another instance in which 'the law grants remedies against a third party who interferes in the legal relations between two other persons'. The Court then proceeded to cite a number of examples of clearly accessory liability.

[30] D. Howarth, 'Against *Lumley* v. *Gye*' (2005) 68 MLR 195, 202.

contracts. A consequence of these competing policy objectives is that inducing breach of contract is one of the narrowest forms of accessory liability, requiring generally both actual knowledge by A – that A's deliberate inducing conduct is highly likely to lead to conduct by PW that amounts to a breach of contract [6.3.4][31] – and an act of involvement (inducing the breach) that is causative of the primary wrong [6.3.3]. Another example of how policy may militate against accessory liability arises in the context of whether breach of a director's duty to exercise discretionary powers for proper purposes and in the best interests of the company should attract such liability [8.3.1.2].

2.5 Distinguishing accessory liability from primary liability

2.5.1 It may be difficult to determine, factually, whether a person has committed a primary wrong

If a person has committed a primary wrong then that person cannot be an accessory to *that* primary wrong.[32] It is simply unnecessary to consider accessory principles. Whether a person is a primary wrongdoer depends on whether all of the elements of the primary wrong in question can be proved against that person. It may in some cases, however, be difficult to determine as a matter of fact whether a defendant has committed all the elements of a primary wrong and is therefore a primary wrongdoer, perhaps jointly alongside others, or whether the only possible liability is as an accessory.[33] One example is where a defendant uses a third party as a means to an end without that third party committing any wrong because he or she lacks an essential mental state.[34] This issue arises, for example, in some cases of fraud [5.1.3], [5.2.2].

[31] A's reckless indifference to that possibility suffices for the purpose of the liability rule.

[32] Of course, as noted, some accessory liability takes the form of independent causes of action and in that sense can be described as a distinct 'primary' wrong.

[33] This difficulty should not be mistaken for the semantic point common in many areas of the law, in which the accessory is described as being liable 'as if a principal' (including in criminal law [4.2]), or as a 'joint tortfeasor' [5.1] or 'constructive trustee' [8.1.7]. We criticise such language at relevant points where it obscures the essentially accessorial nature of the liability rules.

[34] E.g., if D physically pushes X onto C's land, or hypnotised her to enter C's land, then X has not committed the primary wrong of trespass (no intentional act) and D cannot be an accessory. X is an innocent agent, or the means by which D achieves his goals. D is a primary wrongdoer – the element of the direct incursion onto C's land is made out against D – albeit that incursion was via the use of a 'tool' or intermediary. See also the

If a defendant has *contributed* to the conduct elements of a wrong and satisfies any required mental element, then such a defendant is a primary wrongdoer or joint primary wrongdoer. Although one needs to be cautious in applying criminal law concepts to private law [4.1], the criminal law draws the distinction on the basis of whether parties have each contributed *by their own acts*,[35] 'as distinct from anything done by [PO] with [A's] advice or assistance', to the *actus reus*.[36] If they have, then they are primary offenders (or wrongdoers). A defendant is also liable as a primary offender where the conduct elements giving rise to the commission of a wrong are only fulfilled by *the combined acts* of several parties, again so long as each satisfies any mental element. An example is where X and Y separately administer poison to C – only the combined dosage of which is enough to kill. A better analysis here is that neither X's nor Y's liability for C's death is as an accessory.[37] These principles seem equally applicable to private law.

The fact that a person is a party to an agreement, common design or conspiracy[38] to commit a wrong with others (a basis of liability that does not generally arise in equity) does not make them a primary wrongdoer as such; they are liable as accessories for the wrongs committed by the other parties (and also liable primarily for any wrongs personally committed by themselves). Being a party to an agreement is merely one means of involving oneself in a wrong (provided that some act in furtherance of the scheme has been committed). There is, however, one

discussion of innocent agency in criminal law and for which the perpetrator can only be liable as a PO [4.5.1].

35 The person's conduct will be the cause of an act or omission 'if it was the last human conduct before the result': Andrew Ashworth, *Principles of Criminal Law*, 6th edn (Oxford University Press 2009) 105.

36 David Ormerod, *Smith and Hogan's Criminal Law*, 13th edn (Oxford University Press, 2011) 190. See also Lord Kerr (in dissent on the facts) in *R* v. *Gnango* [2011] UKSC 59; [2012] 1 AC 827 [129]: joint principal must contribute 'to the cause of the *actus reus*'. The PO is, therefore, the party who fulfils the elements of the offence 'most directly and immediately': K. J. M. Smith, *A Modern Treaties on the Law of Criminal Complicity* (Oxford, Clarendon Press, 1991), 27–28. A person may also be one of several principals for the one wrong or offence if each separately satisfies the elements of it.

37 See, e.g., A. P. Simester, J. R. Spencer, G. R. Sullivan and G. J. Virgo, *Simester and Sullivan's Criminal Law Theory and Doctrine*, 4th edn (Oxford, Hart Publishing, 2010) 207. Each of their acts must pass a minimal threshold of contribution: see Ashworth, *Principles of Criminal Law*, 105. In other words, each party's acts contribute to causing the conduct elements of an offence and the acts together fulfil such conduct elements (404–405).

38 The terms are here used interchangeably. Conspiracy is not here a reference to the tort of that name.

significant difference between a co-conspirator on the one hand and an accessory who procures or merely assists without being *ad idem* with PW on the other, namely that an assistant is liable for the wrongs of PW, whereas PW would not be liable for wrongs committed by the assistant, absent a finding of agreement.[39]

2.5.2 Categorising liability rules as accessory or primary: dual categorisation

Some elements of some causes of action are broadly defined so as to capture a wide range of actors as potential primary wrongdoers. One consequence of this is that the application of such liability rules may give rise to liability that may be characterised as both primary and accessorial. In other words, a dual classification may be possible; see, for example, breach of a duty of confidence [8.4.1], defamation [5.5.4] and the discussion in [2.7].

The characterisation of liability rules is not always easy as some statutory liability rules for IP infringements illustrate; see [9.4]. An example is provided by copyright provisions imposing 'indirect' liability. These have considerable affinity with accessory liability, since they are intended to curb acts that will almost invariably lead to primary infringement. Further, where primary infringements do occur, the defendant's conduct will have contributed to those infringements. However, it is not a prerequisite to liability that a primary infringement has taken place. If the commission of a primary wrong is not a prerequisite for a particular liability rule, then such a liability rule is not accessorial. Nonetheless, indirect liability shares many of the rationales for accessory liability, namely deterring primary infringements and protecting the interests of rights holders, and we consider some examples in Chapter 9.[40]

2.6 Accessory liability is derivative, not duplicative

The analysis of the case law across the different areas of private law in Part II demonstrates that accessory liability is *derivative* upon the commission of a primary wrong by PW, but A's liability is nonetheless

[39] See in US tort law, *Halberstam* v. *Welch* 705 F2d 472, 478 (DC Cir, 1983).

[40] Further examples include statutory contributory infringements in patents law for the supply of an unpatented product or means that can be used as part of a patented method or to produce a patented product [9.4.2].

grounded in his own wrongdoing.[41] One consequence of this is that the remedies that are available against A need not duplicate those against PW, that is, be identical to them. Of course, this goes without saying where accessory rules constitute an independent wrong, given that A will not be liable for the same wrong; but this conclusion applies equally to 'secondary' liability for PW's primary wrong. Further, A may be liable in private law in some circumstances in which PW is not liable. For example, A might be liable even if PW has a personal excuse that is not available to the accessory, though there are few cases on point. That is the position in equity [8.6.2], probably inducing breach of contract [6.3.2] and perhaps tort law.

Non-duplicative accessory liability is most obviously evidenced where it takes the form of an independent wrong, such as the tort of inducing breach of contract. The remedy and the relevant rules for assessing the tort and contract remedies (against A and PW, respectively) necessarily differ. For example, exemplary damages are potentially available for the tort, but not against the contract breaker.[42] Further, accessorial *tort* liability for the *contractual* wrong may arise even where the breach of contract is not actionable, such as where PW is not liable because she has contractually excluded the obligation to pay damages.[43]

Outside the context of independent accessorial wrongs, accessories are generally liable for the same remedy or remedies as applied against PW. For example, where persons are found to be joint tortfeasors, each is responsible as a 'principal' for the same tort and therefore liable for the full, 'single' damage caused to C. There are, however, exceptions to this general position: more recent Australian decisions have held that damages against various defendants need not be the same where aggravated and exemplary damages are at issue [5.7.1]: damages need not always be single and indivisible. That conclusion is to be welcomed and is consistent with the approach to remedies, other than compensation, in equitable accessory liability.

It is in the context of non-independent accessory liability that the label 'secondary' is used. It is sometimes argued that this means that A is liable for the same wrong as that committed by PW and that the same

[41] See, e.g., in the context of equity, *Michael Wilson* [2011] HCA 48; (2011) 244 CLR 427 [106].

[42] *Pratt* v. *British Medical Association* [1919] 1 KB 244; *Hospitality Group Pty Ltd* v. *Australian Rugby Union Ltd* [2001] FCA 1040 (FC).

[43] See Robert Stevens, *Torts and Rights* (Oxford University Press, 2007) 277, citing *Merkur Island Shipping Corp.* v. *Laughton* [1983] 2 AC 570.

remedies must apply to A as apply to PW.[44] In other words, liability is parasitic or duplicative of PW's liability rather than merely derivative. This is the view of some commentators on equitable accessory liability [8.1.5].[45] Once a link is established between A's conduct and the primary wrong, it is argued, A *becomes* PW for remedial purposes. This approach is not persuasive and leads to unjust outcomes, particularly if it were to be applied to profit-based remedies, so as to make A liable, for example, for gains obtained by PW, or vice versa.[46] To avoid injustice, each wrongdoer should only be liable for the profits each has received, other than in exceptional circumstances, such as where A uses PW as a vehicle for A's enrichment [8.1.5], [8.7.3].

A similar debate has occurred in the criminal law context. Although A is generally treated as having committed the same crimes as PO, the criminal law cases and many theorists have rejected a restriction that requires A's liability always to be identical to that of PO.[47] A criminal accessory can be guilty of more or less serious offences than PO (because of A's different mental states), and may be found guilty even where PO is not found guilty [4.5.1].

To conclude, there are no persuasive reasons why A may not be liable for a different, greater or lesser, remedy than PW, since it is A's own wrongdoing that grounds liability. Where both PW and A are liable, the remedy against each ought to be considered separately to reflect each wrongdoer's culpability and its consequences. Of course, if the only remedies being sought are compensatory, then A will be liable for the same loss caused by PW's wrong [8.8.1]. If, however, for example in tort, PW has a

[44] See, e.g., Stevens, *Torts*, 277. Of course, the label 'secondary' is apt if it is used in the sense that A's liability is dependent upon there being a primary wrong committed by PW.

[45] Steven B. Elliott and Charles Mitchell, 'Remedies for Dishonest Assistance' (2004) 67 MLR 16, cited with approval in *Ultraframe (UK) Ltd* v. *Fielding* [2005] EWHC 1638 (Ch); [2006] FSR 16 [1600]. The argument was subsequently revised in Charles Mitchell and Stephen Watterson, 'Remedies for Knowing Receipt' in Charles Mitchell (ed.), *Constructive and Resulting Trusts* (Oxford, Hart Publishing, 2009) 115, 150–153.

[46] Elliott and Mitchell, 'Remedies for Dishonest Assistance', accept this point.

[47] Care must be taken with terminology, however. In criminal law, 'derivative' liability is often used to describe the view that A's liability is identical to that of PO, that is, it is used to mean 'duplicative' in the way we use that term. See, e.g., Jain, *Perpetrators and Accessories*, 104–108, noting however that broader derivative theory focuses on the 'objectively harmful wrong perpetrated' by PO, rather than the specific crime committed such that even on that theory, A need not be found guilty of the identical offence. In any case, 'derivative' theory (duplicative theory in our terminology) does not reflect the outcomes of criminal law [4.5.1] and is challenged by commentators. See Jain's summary, 155–158.

state of mind that differs from that of A, as where only one acts maliciously, this may perhaps justify exemplary damages against that party. This does not detract from the accessorial nature of liability. If anything, it is reflective of a general approach in the general law and statute that uncouples remedy from the cause of action, requiring a separate assessment of remedial issues once liability, on whatever basis, has been established.[48]

2.7 When is accessory liability needed?

In some areas of law, accessory liability serves an important role that is performed by well-recognised rules. In other areas, accessory liability is obscured or even non-existent. What explains the importance or otherwise of accessory liability in different areas of law? Factors that impact on the scope of accessory liability include the underlying purposes and values of the primary wrong. Consider, for example, the prophylactic functions of equity's panoply of rules aimed at protecting beneficiaries of trusts, and the consequent wide reach of equitable liability rules and remedies, accessorial or otherwise.

Another significant factor that may influence the importance of accessory liability is whether the elements of the primary liability itself are cast restrictively or widely. This requires explanation.

Where a primary wrong is formulated in restrictive or narrow terms, such as where a duty is held only by a narrow class of persons, or liability requires specific conduct, then only a limited number of persons can be found liable as primary wrongdoers. It is in such legal contexts that accessory liability has developed most broadly; it becomes essential in order to prevent wrongdoers from escaping liability merely because they do not personally hold a duty or have not personally committed the requisite acts. For example, a third party involved in a breach of trust or fiduciary duty by another is not, thereby, a trustee or a fiduciary and has not breached those duties.[49] This is one reason why accessory liability plays such an important role in equity in order to protect beneficiaries against wrongs committed with the aid of, or at the behest of, third parties.

[48] This is a desirable state of affairs, though some commentators have argued against it and debate continues. For a discussion of the broader issues, see, e.g., Simon Evans, 'Defending Discretionary Remedialism' (2001) 23 *Sydney Law Review* 436.

[49] *Cf.*, however, the liability of a trustee de son tort [7.2].

Primary liability may also be restrictive because it requires personal conduct for the elements of the wrong to be made out, such as a direct interaction between PW and C. For example, trespass requires a tortfeasor personally to commit a direct act (of contact, for example, for battery). Therefore, if PW hits C, then A has not personally committed the tort. One mechanism by which A can nonetheless be held liable is via an accessorial link between A and PW's wrongdoing. Accessory liability plays a more important role in trespass cases than many other torts [5.2].

Where, however, primary wrongs are formulated widely, so that even peripheral players or indirect actors may satisfy all of the 'acts' (conduct elements) that constitute the wrong, then there is limited need for accessory liability. This means that a wide-range of potential defendants may be liable as primary wrongdoers and claimants will rarely need to rely upon accessory liability.[50] For example, equity's well-developed accessory principles are rarely used to remedy breaches of confidence, because a duty of confidentiality can easily arise against anyone involved in PW's breach of confidence who obtains confidential information in circumstances where they know or ought to know of its confidential nature [8.4]. Such parties are liable as primary wrongdoers (alongside others, perhaps) because they will have personally breached the duty [8.4.1].

A further example is that, unlike trespass actions, most torts do not have a restrictive element of 'directness'. In defamation law, a person is liable if they publish defamatory matter. Publication is not limited to those parties who actually communicate the matter to third parties [5.5.4], that is, it does not require the defendant to be the 'immediate' or 'direct' publisher. Such a broad definition captures multiple persons as primary wrongdoers, including persons who have not personally communicated matter, but authorised others to do so. There is therefore less need to rely on accessorial concepts.[51]

[50] Another example is provided by statutory accessory liability to a statutory misleading conduct claim in Australian law. Establishing liability of a person as primary wrongdoer for misleading conduct is relatively easy since it is strict and requires no direct interaction between PW and C, and therefore accessory provisions have not been widely used [10.4.1].

[51] There is, however, considerable potential for overlap, in terms of possible analysis in defamation law, between treating a person as being held liable either as a primary wrongdoer or as an accessory.

2.8 Distinguishing accessory liability from related concepts

2.8.1 Vicarious liability

It is necessary to differentiate accessory liability from other types of liability such as vicarious liability. Vicarious liability of an employer for its employees' torts arises from the status of the employer's relationship with the employee and is imposed despite the (usual) innocence of the employer. Although vicarious liability is sometimes described as a form of 'secondary liability', it is important to stress that such liability is imposed independently of any wrongful involvement by the employer in the employee's tort. Liability is strict and not based on fault. For vicarious liability, the employees' wrongs are attributed to the employer, as if they had committed the tort, whereas an accessory is a wrongdoer.[52] Although the distinction is conceptually clear enough, there are some contexts, namely the vicarious liability of agents, where drawing a clear distinction with accessory liability is more problematic [5.3.1.2].[53]

2.8.2 Property-based liabilities

A number of overlapping equitable causes of an action may arise as a result of the receipt of, or dealing with, property in which C asserts an equitable interest or legal interest (for example, company assets in hands of directors). Such claims are at the intersection of accessorial and non-accessorial claims. It may be difficult to disentangle them for accessory liability purposes because they share a property-protection objective, they overlap in their requisite elements and they were not conceived of with such classificatory concepts in mind. The various non-accessorial property-based claims are explained and distinguished in Chapter 7. For the most part, they can be distinguished from accessory liability on the basis that wrongful involvement in PW's wrong is not an element of, or even necessarily a factual aspect of, liability. In some cases, liability may be primary, despite being triggered by another's wrong. For example, where a trustee or a beneficiary pursues a persisting property claim [7.5] against a third party recipient of trust property, the rationale for liability is overwhelmingly concerned with the protection of C's proprietary

[52] See N. J. McBride and R. Bagshaw, *Tort Law*, 3rd edn (England, Pearson Education Ltd, 2008) 649–650.

[53] Vicarious liability is distinguished from attribution of liability in Chapter 11.

rights. The liability is self-evidently primary rather than accessorial even though in this context it is triggered by another's wrong (breach of trust). D is not liable because of D's involvement in that wrong, but because C's proprietary rights have priority over D's proprietary rights.[54]

Recipient liability has considerable affinity and overlap with accessory liability and is considered in detail in Chapter 8 along with equitable accessory liability. The two liabilities form part of a broader principle of participatory liability in equity.

2.8.3 Criminal accessory liability

The criminal law on accessories differs in many respects from the various manifestations of accessory liability in private law, which themselves are not, of course, uniform. It has been suggested that it is not desirable to compare accessory principles of criminal law with those of private law or to use the former to inform the latter. We consider such arguments in [4.1] and conclude, to the contrary, that criminal law offers some useful insights to aid in the understanding of accessory liability in private law.

[54] Similarly, some liability rules may sometimes involve there being a primary wrong, but not necessarily so: e.g., knowing dealing with trust property [7.3].

3

An analytical framework for accessory liability

3.1 Introduction to the framework and its operation

In order to establish accessory liability it is necessary to show that the following three elements are present:

(1) a primary wrong committed by a person other than the accessory;
(2) involvement, through conduct, by the accessory in that wrong;[1] and
(3) a requisite mental state, generally established by reference to the accessory's knowledge of the primary wrongdoer's (PW's) wrong.

These three elements form the analytical framework of accessory liability in private law. Ultimately, the question of liability is a normative one: was A sufficiently involved in the primary wrong, with sufficient knowledge, such that he should be held liable for the primary wrong in light of the purposes and values of that primary wrong? Once A's liability is established, it is necessary to consider which defences may be available to A and which remedies are available against A.

The elements of the framework are not discrete; their doctrinal content and judicial application in individual cases are influenced by the content and significance of the other two elements. Of particular importance is the combination of the accessory's conduct and mental state that creates a 'participation link' to the primary wrong and justifies the accessory being liable for some or all of the consequences of the primary wrong. This 'participation link' is generally the most important factor in determining liability. The dynamic and relational operation of the framework is discussed further in [3.5].

The dynamic, relational operation of the three elements of the framework may be more accurately portrayed as in Figure 3.1, rather than as a list of discrete requirements.

The form of A's liability, that is, whether A's liability is for an independent wrong or for the same wrong as that committed by PW, is not an

[1] In exceptional circumstances, inaction may constitute involvement: [3.3.6].

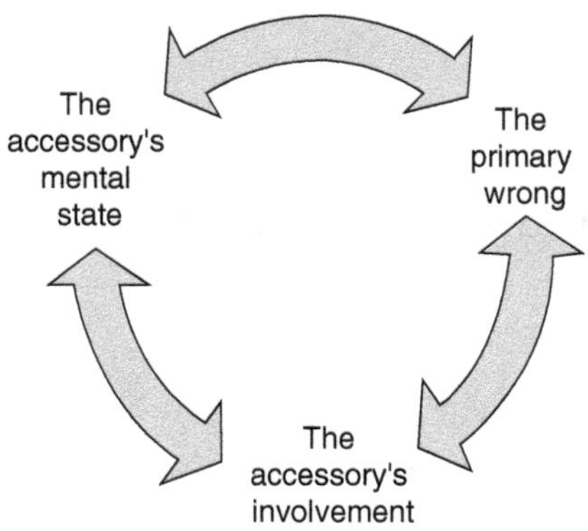

Figure 3.1 The dynamic operation of the analytical framework.

element of the analytical framework because it does not determine or influence A's liability in any principled way [2.3]. The three elements of accessory liability remain the same; it is only the means by which accessory liability is imposed that differs, and such differences can be explained by jurisdictional and historical factors. Hence, it is not necessary for the purposes of the framework to posit that A's liability is for the same primary wrong as that committed by PW or for a different wrong. Neither outcome precludes A's liability being accessorial.

Our construction of the framework is largely (and designedly) a descriptive exercise based upon the substantive law detailed in Part II. It accurately replicates in a more abstract format most, but not necessarily all, of that law as it is currently expressed. We would go further, however, and argue that in some areas of private law where the elements of our framework are not necessarily adverted to by the courts, those elements are in fact relevant. As such, the framework has a further, explicitly normative, function in that it may assist in resolving uncertainties in the law by suggesting conceptually coherent solutions.

The framework is expressed at a high level of generality and does not, nor is it intended to, supply a definitive test for liability or the template for a generic cause of action. The doctrinal content of the three elements of the framework is determined in all but one case by the purposes and values of the substantive law of the primary wrong in question, namely tort, equity or the particular statute. The exception is the tort of inducing breach of contract, where the purposes and values of both contract and tort are reflected in the content of the doctrine.

Different areas of law can, coherently, have different accessory liability rules, depending on the purposes and values of the law of the primary wrong and, in particular, the nature of the primary right of the claimant (C) (and the corresponding duty of PW) with which A interferes. These determine what interests are sought to be protected; how narrow or broad such protection should be; and what countervailing interests are relevant. In other words, the purposes of the relevant body of law are critical in determining the scope of accessory liability and the extent of protection provided to C.[2]

As Hazel Carty notes, different examples of 'secondary' (accessory) liability:

> reveal that different 'links' to the primary wrongdoer are demanded by these *separate* examples of secondary liability: such liability in the civil law involves a list of disparate doctrines. . . . [T]here does not exist a standardized approach to 'secondary' liability in the civil law, parallel to secondary criminal liability, that applies the same test of secondary liability to tort, contract breach and breach of trust/fiduciary duty . . .[3]

To the extent that 'standardized approach' means a single test of accessory liability, we agree that this does not exist.[4] If, however, Carty is denying the value of a common framework for analysis and of exploring commonalities that exist with respect to different types of accessories, we disagree. In our view, our analytical framework brings greater clarity to understanding and developing the law despite its generality, because it enables a consistent set of questions to be asked and coherent answers proposed. Through such a process, greater clarity can be brought to accessory liability in its many manifestations and examples of incoherence can be identified and either justified or eliminated.

It should be noted that in relation to at least one form of accessorial involvement, courts have countenanced the possibility of a generic cause of action. They have relied upon broad statements of principle by Erle J in *Lumley* v. *Gye*, the seminal case on inducing breach of contract, to the effect

[2] See *Zhu* v. *Treasurer (NSW)* [2004] HCA 56; (2004) 218 CLR 530 [121]–[122] (*Zhu*).

[3] Hazel Carty, *An Analysis of the Economic Torts*, 2nd edn (Oxford University Press, 2010) 306 (emphasis in original). See also at 307. Indeed, even for wrongs within a single (albeit broad) 'category', such as tort law, different accessorial rules are applied.

[4] Perhaps contra Peter Birks, 'Civil Wrongs: A New World' in *The Butterworth Lectures 1990–91* (London, Butterworths, 1992) 101: 'We need one law on the civil liability of accessories.'

that the 'procurement of the violation' of a right is a cause of action.[5] A generic liability rule for procurement would potentially apply to the violation of any actionable wrong such as breach of an actionable statutory duty.[6] Such a generic principle has not developed beyond the embryonic stage and is probably unnecessary. Cases of procurement continue to be decided within the specific contexts within which they arise and may generate different liability rules.[7] Further, any appropriate remedy would still be determined by reference to the specific doctrinal context of the primary wrong. Nonetheless, it is clear that cases of accessory liability for procuring a wrong do show significant commonalities [3.3.5], [3.4.3.6].

Finally by way of introduction and overview, the analytical framework is not presented as the only means of analysis for the bodies of law in question. The law that we discuss in Part II may concurrently form part of other conceptual groupings.[8] Nor is it possible to be definitive in all cases as to whether liabilities are accessorial or non-accessorial. There are areas where it is better to talk of accessorial themes being present even where liability is not necessarily full-blown accessory liability (for example, some instances of equitable participatory liability as discussed in [7.6.2] and [8.5], and some instances of intellectual property (IP) law as discussed in [9.4]). This does not mean, however, that the framework does not helpfully illuminate an organising principle of accessory liability in private law.

The content and operation of the three elements of the framework are discussed in the remainder of this chapter by reference to the substantive law detailed in Part II. For the sake of completeness, the chapter concludes with a brief discussion of defences and remedies.

[5] (1853) 2 E & B 216, 232; 118 ER 749, 755. The principle was approved by Dixon J in *James* v. *The Commonwealth* (1939) 62 CLR 339, 370; Dixon J's views are cited, seemingly with approval, in *Zhu* [2004] HCA 56; (2004) 218 CLR 530 [116]. The generality with which the principle was expressed in *Lumley* v. *Gye* was acknowledged by Lord Nicholls in *OBG* v. *Allen* [2007] UKHL 21; [2008] 1 AC 1 [169]–[171]. *Lumley* v. *Gye* has also been used to support the recognition of a 'tort' of knowing assistance. See [8.1.6].

[6] E.g., *Associated British Ports* v. *TGWU* [1989] 1 WLR 939 (HL) 959. In *Law Debenture Trust Corp.* v. *Ural Caspian Oil Corporation* (1993) 1 WLR 138, a claim for procuring a violation of a secondary right to a remedy arising from the tort of inducing breach of contract was held to be arguable by Hoffmann J. The case is not referred to by Lord Hoffmann in *OBG* v. *Allen* [2007] UKHL 21; [2008] 1 AC 1.

[7] As this book explains, the rules on procuring a breach of contract probably operate differently to, and are certainly much more developed than, the equitable rules on procuring breach of trust: [Chapter 6], [8.3.2.1].

[8] E.g., such as equitable 'participatory' liability [8.3.5].

3.2 The primary wrong

3.2.1 A primary wrong must have been committed

Liability as an accessory in private law is necessarily premised upon the commission of a wrong by another person.[9] If no primary wrong has been committed, then it is not possible for a defendant to be an accessory. For example, one cannot induce a breach of 'contract' if such 'contract' is void.[10]

While it must be shown that the elements of the primary wrong are made out, it is not always necessary that PW be found liable or even be sued.[11] An important rationale for accessory liability in areas of private law, such as equity, where the rights of C vis-à-vis PW are given high priority, is that it provides C with alternative means of redress where PW has absconded or is otherwise unable to satisfy her liability; in other words, where it is not feasible to hold PW liable [8.1.3]. Nonetheless, at least in equity, PW should still be made a party unless 'unavailable to be sued'.[12]

The position is more complicated when a 'defence' justifies an otherwise prima facie infringement. In such cases, no primary wrong has occurred and neither PW nor A are liable. For example, C's consent to, or acquiescence in, the primary wrong will constitute a defence to both PW and A: there is, in effect, no primary wrong.[13] In some cases, however, PW is excused from liability for reasons personal to PW. In such cases, there is still a primary wrong and thus A may still be accessorily liable. Whether A's liability does survive in such cases is a matter for the particular doctrine and the 'defence' in question [3.6] (see, e.g., torts [5.6.2], inducing breach of contract [6.3.2], equity [8.6.2]).

9 *Cf.* inchoate offences in criminal law [4.3].

10 *News Limited* v. *Australian Rugby Football League Ltd* (1996) 64 FCR 410, 516.

11 Contra the common law position in criminal law (attainder of the principal offender was required), reversed by nineteenth-century legislative reforms: *Likiardopoulos* v. *R* [2012] HCA 37; (2012) 247 CLR 265 [26].

12 *Yeshiva Properties No. 1 Property Ltd* v. *Marshall* [2005] NSWCA 23; (2005) 219 ALR 112 [77], giving as examples that PW 'cannot be found, is insolvent, [or] has a bankruptcy discharge.' Contra the position in tort law, see, e.g., *Mitchell* v. *Tarbutt* (1794) 5 TR 649; 101 ER 362.

13 *Blackwood* v. *Borrowes* (1843) 4 Dr & War 441; 65 RR 729. See also *Jyske Bank (Gibralter) Limited* v. *Spjeldnaes* (CA, 29 July 1999).

3.2.2 The primary wrong determines the doctrinal content of the accessory liability rules

There is no generic cause of action for accessory liability [3.1]; instead, it is necessary to focus on the particular wrong that PW has committed. Specific wrongs activate specific liability rules, the explanation for which are to be found in the purposes, values and historical development of the primary wrong in question. An obvious example is equity which has very generous, claimant-favouring accessory liability rules for breach of trust and fiduciary duty that reflect, inter alia, the importance and vulnerability of equitable property interests and, more broadly, relationships of trust and confidence [8.1.3]. By comparison, breach of contract is generally not viewed in such absolute terms as a breach of equitable duty and there is a corresponding reluctance to impose accessory liability for conduct beyond procurement or inducement. Policy considerations also play a significant role in IP law and have resulted in quite complex legislative schemes that incorporate both accessory and accessory-like liabilities and, sometimes, irreconcilable case law (Chapter 9).

3.2.3 The meaning of primary wrong

We use 'wrong' in the conventional sense of breach of a legal duty that leads to remedial outcomes.[14] In private law, a wrong in this sense encompasses breach of common law duties (torts and breach of contract), breach of equitable duties (including breach of trust, fiduciary duty and confidence) and breach of privately actionable statutory duties (for example, misleading and deceptive conduct by persons engaged in trade or commerce [Chapter 10]). Equity has a broader understanding of wrongful conduct, the various permutations of which are included in the general concept of unconscionability or unconscientious conduct, and which we also consider in this book [8.1.2] and [8.5].

The labelling of PW's wrong as 'primary' is not intended to suggest that A's liability is 'secondary' in any sense other than that it is derivative of, or ancillary to, the former's wrong. The 'primary' wrong is important because A's liability is contingent upon its commission and

14 See, e.g., Peter Birks, *An Introduction to the Law of Restitution* (Oxford, Clarendon Press, 1985) 313: '[The word 'wrong'] is used to cover all conduct, acts or omissions, whose effect in creating legal consequences is attributable to its being characterised as a breach of duty.'

because it determines the scope and content of the specific accessory liability rules. It is not 'primary' in the sense of necessarily being more significant or egregious than A's wrong; indeed, A may be the 'main player' in the commission of the primary wrong and PW an unsuspecting tool.[15]

3.3 A's involvement in the primary wrong: the conduct element

3.3.1 A's conduct

There must be an act or acts by A that involve A in the primary wrong.[16] This is the conduct element of the analytical framework. In the US criminal law context, it has been said that an 'accomplice's' 'act must have something to do with why, how, or with what ease the legally prohibited result was brought about by someone else'.[17] This also usefully describes the gist of 'involvement' in private law accessory liability that requires that A's conduct contribute to the successful commission of the primary wrong [3.3.3].

A's involvement can vary considerably from A being the 'puppeteer' that 'pulls the strings'[18] and instigates the wrong by PW to being a reluctant lackey or an obtuse professional agent who takes only a minor role in a wrongful enterprise. Where A instigates the wrong or is a genuine equal partner or co-conspirator in it, the parties having a 'joint purpose',[19] A's involvement is clear. Assistance also often suffices for accessorial conduct, although there are exceptions to this (tort law [5.4.2.3], [5.5.1], including inducing breach of contract [Chapter 6]). Merely watching another commit a wrong, or mere passive acquiescence in it, however, does not give rise to accessory liability other than in some exceptional circumstances [3.3.6].

In many areas of private law, a wide range of conduct will satisfy the conduct element. Some statutory schemes of accessory liability,

[15] E.g., in equity a fiduciary is strictly liable for breach of the conflict of interest and profit prohibitions and so may have acted in complete good faith: *Boardman* v. *Phipps* [1967] 2 AC 46 (HL).

[16] The attribution of conduct to companies is discussed in Chapter 11.

[17] Michael S. Moore, 'Causing, Aiding, and the Superfluity of Accomplice Liability', (2008) 156 *University of Pennsylvania Law Review* 395, 401. The author's comments were made by way of introduction to a more complex and sophisticated analysis of criminal accessory liability.

[18] *Allen* v. *Flood* [1898] AC 1 (HL) 152 (Lord Macnaghten).

[19] *Clark* v. *Newsam and Edwards* (1847) 1 Ex 130, 140; 154 ER 55, 59.

in particular, apply a broadly encompassing conduct element [10.4.3]. Even quite minor acts of involvement, facilitating some aspects of another's wrongdoing, will satisfy the minimum conduct element. The purpose of such legislation seems to have been to cast a very wide net. Importantly, however, even if the requisite act of involvement encompasses a wide range of conduct, this will not necessarily equate to broad accessory liability. Instead, it appears to be the case across private law that the mental element of accessory liability, when considered in combination with A's conduct, is the key to establishing wrongdoing on the part of A and restrains liability to prevent overreach [3.5.1]: The mental element protects the 'innocent'.[20]

3.3.2 The terminology used to describe accessorial conduct

The terminology used across private law to describe accessorial conduct is varied. References to A's conduct often form part of the description of the accessory liability rules themselves, as in: aiding and abetting, authorisation, common design, conspiracy, counselling, inducing or procuring, knowing or dishonest assistance, being knowingly concerned and (sometimes) being a joint tortfeasor. 'Procurement' is ubiquitous [3.3.5]. Some statutory schemes of accessory liability incorporate criminal ('aid, abet, counsel, or procure') and common law labels (such as inducement and conspiracy) of accessorial conduct, as well as introducing generic terms such as 'knowingly concerned' [Chapter 10]. Others, such as the various schemes protecting IP rights, use more specific terms such as 'authorise' [9.2]. The legal definitions of these terms are discussed in the relevant chapters of Part II.

In some areas of accessory liability, the courts tend not to place much weight on the meaning of individual descriptive terms [8.3.2.2]. A similar broad-brush approach can be seen in criminal law [4.4.1]. Much more attention has been paid to the meaning of the specific terms used in the context of inducing breach of contract [Chapter 6]; presumably, this is because less active forms of conduct than procurement or inducement will never suffice for liability.

Although there appears to be some consistency in the meaning attributed to some terms used across private law, it would be misleading to

[20] See, e.g., *New Zealand Bus Ltd and Infratil Ltd* v. *Commerce Commission* [2007] NZCA 502 [118]–[119] (Hammond J, Wilson J agreeing, in the context of pecuniary penalties for anti-competitive mergers).

suggest that the terms are, in fact, always used consistently. In the context of statutory accessory liability, in particular, it will be necessary to comply with the principles of statutory interpretation, rather than assuming that a universal meaning can be attributed to a word used in a statute. One particular instance where difficult statutory interpretation questions arise is where criminal terms have been imported into statutes that confer private rights of action.[21] Nonetheless, explanations of the meaning of terms used also in other areas of private, rather than criminal, law may assist in determining their meaning within a particular doctrine.

3.3.3 The causal relationship between A's conduct and the primary wrong

There are two ways in which A's conduct may be causally connected to PW's wrong; it could be a 'but for' cause or a 'contributing' cause. Further, A's conduct can relate to either PW's *decision* to commit the wrong or PW's *commission* of the wrong

First, A's conduct might be a 'but for' causal factor. It could be a 'but for' cause of either PW's decision to or capacity to commit the wrong. In the former scenario, PW would not have decided to commit the wrong 'but for' A's actions. This suggests a very strong causal link. In the latter scenario, A's conduct may provide assistance to PW without which PW *could* not have committed the wrong in the way that she did.[22] Given PW's independent decision to commit such wrong, however, even if 'but for' causation is satisfied in relation to the specific wrong committed, it could be described as a 'weaker' form of causation because, for example, PW may have found other means to commit the wrong.[23]

Despite the courts' inconsistent use of 'but for' causal language, it is reasonably clear that a 'but for' causal link between A's conduct and PW's decision or capacity to commit the primary wrong (that is, 'but for' A's conduct, PW would not have decided to or been able to commit

21 See, e.g., *Yorke* v. *Lucas* (1985) 158 CLR 661 (HCA).

22 See Philip Sales, 'The Tort of Conspiracy and Civil Secondary Liability' (1990) 49 *Cambridge Law Journal* 491, 507. It is, however, conceivable that PW may not in some circumstances have decided to commit the tort without A's assistance.

23 *Cf. ibid.* Consider also this scenario: A drives PW to C's house in order for her to beat C. Had A not offered to drive, PW would have walked to C's house. Has A's conduct caused the tort against C? The circumstances that in fact occurred would not have occurred 'but for' A's driving, but C would still have been injured even if A had not driven PW.

the wrong) is generally not necessary (and would be hard to prove in any event). In equity [8.3.3] and tort law common design liability [5.4.2.1], for example, A's conduct need not be a 'but for' cause of PW's wrong.

One exception, probably, is inducing breach of contract where the courts appear to require a 'but for' connection to PW's decision to breach the contract, but infer this from the circumstances [6.3.3]. More generally, it is reasonable to assume that a 'but for' causal connection to PW's decision to commit the wrong may also be required wherever A procures (or induces) the primary wrong [3.3.5]. Given that procurement means to 'bring about' the primary wrong, this implies that a strong causal connection to PW's decision is required, such that without 'his [A's] persuasion, [PW's wrong] would or might never have been committed'.[24]

Secondly, A's conduct might be a contributing causal factor. Here, the causal connection is that A's conduct contributed to PW's decision to commit, or the actual commission of, the primary wrong, but was not essential in the sense that the decision would have been made or the primary wrong would have occurred even without A's contribution. Jane Stapleton has coined the term 'contributing cause' to describe causes that contribute to an outcome, without being 'but for' causes of that outcome.[25] If A's actions contributed to the commission of the wrong, we can see it as causally relevant. For example, if PW intends to commit a wrong for various reasons, including, but not only, because A agreed to assist PW in her plan, then A's conduct is a contributing cause even though PW would still have decided to continue with her plan without A. A's assistance is also a contributing cause if it contributed to PW carrying out her plan, although PW had capacity to do so even absent A's involvement.[26]

[24] *Allen* v. *Flood* [1898] AC 1 (HL) 106–107 (Lord Watson) citing Erle J's judgment in *Lumley* v. *Gye* (1853) 2 E & B 216, 232; 118 ER 749, 755 with approval.

[25] See generally Jane Stapleton, 'Unnecessary causes' (2013) 129 *Law Quarterly Review* 39.

[26] *Ibid.*, particularly the examples at 43–45 and 47–48, including the example where three persons independently, but simultaneously, lean on a car, causing it to topple over a cliff. If the force of one was insufficient to propel the car, but the force of two was sufficient, then no individual was necessary for the damage to the car occurring. As Stapleton, 45–46, points out, it is in the context of human decision-making that causation is often 'over-subscribed', i.e., not a necessary but a contributing factor. Causation would also be established where A's conduct is one of several equally sufficient factors for the outcome, e.g., if PW requires only one assistant and two persons volunteer to help. See *Allianz Australia Ltd* v. *Sim* [2012] NSWCA 68 [139].

In most circumstances, the courts appear to require that A's conduct be at least a contributing cause to PW's decision or capacity to carry out a wrong.[27] Certainly, the language of the courts in many accessory cases is consistent with that approach, for example, tort law [5.4.2.1].[28] Similarly, in areas of law that recognise assistance as sufficient accessorial conduct, such as equity, the requisite causal connection is generally not expressed in 'but for' terms. It will not matter that PW might have been able to commit the wrong even if A had not assisted, so long as A's conduct can be shown to '"make a difference" and forward or advance the [primary wrong] in some way'.[29] See [8.3.3]. A contributing cause must be more than trivial see, for example, [5.4.2.1].

Having said this, the courts have rarely concerned themselves with questions of causation in any accessorial context, including in cases where causation may not be self-evident. Further, the issue is one that may be forensically difficult or even impossible to determine without resort to presumptions as to what the impact of A's actions were on PW's decision or capacity to commit the wrong.

3.3.4 *The timing of A's conduct*

In order for conduct to 'involve' A in the primary wrong, it must have a temporal immediacy to the wrong. At common law, it is clear that A's conduct must either be before (for example, procuring PW to breach her contract with C) or during (for example, by assisting a fiduciary to exploit a business opportunity that should have been offered to C) the commission of the primary wrong. The same is true of statutory forms of accessory liability [10.4.3].[30]

The timing of A's conduct appears not to have been the subject of discussion in equity.[31] In that context, it may be that conduct by A that

[27] Consider, however, e.g., whether even a contributing cause exists where A encourages PW to continue in a wrong she has already commenced.

[28] The statutory concept of 'authorisation' of an IP infringement, which overlaps to an extent with the concept of procurement, also has inherent within it a causative element [9.2.4]. Again, the courts have not spelt out precisely what causation requires here, however, a 'but for' requirement is unlikely.

[29] *Re-Engine Pty Ltd (in liq.)* v. *Fergusson* [2007] VSC 57 [120] *(Re-Engine)*.

[30] See *ASIC* v. *Australian Investors Forum Pty Ltd (No 2)* [2005] NSWSC 267; (2005) 53 ACSR 305 [114]–[118].

[31] The following comments are directed to liability for knowing assistance, rather than equitable recipient liability, although they also have ramifications for that liability: see [7.6.2].

contributes to the successful outcome of the primary wrong may constitute involvement in it even if occurring after its commission. So, for example, financial service providers, or lawyers, who knowingly facilitate the money laundering of funds misappropriated in breach of fiduciary duty may be liable for dishonest assistance in the breach of fiduciary duty regardless of whether that breach is considered complete at the time of the misappropriation, rather than disposal, of the funds in question.[32] In such scenarios, it may be that the requisite temporal connection with A's involvement is to the scheme as a whole, rather than specifically to the primary wrong committed within that scheme. Alternatively, it could be argued that, if the primary wrong involves trust funds, the breach of trust or fiduciary duty will be ongoing until those funds are restored; hence, A's conduct is still 'during' the commission of the wrong. Another possible explanation, depending upon the particular facts, is that A's prior agreement to participate in the primary wrong (through disposing of the proceeds, for example) with any more active role deferred until after the primary wrong has been completed, satisfies the temporal connection.

The requirement that A's conduct has contributed to the primary wrong in the sense that it is temporally and 'causally' linked to it (that is, that A be involved in the wrong) reflects our understanding of how accessory liability operates in private law. This understanding is not undermined by the presence in criminal law of 'accessory' after the fact liability [4.3]. An accessory after the fact is guilty of assisting the principal offender (PO) to escape justice. The offending conduct clearly occurs after the commission of the principal offence. The basis of liability, however, is not that A has contributed to the commission of the primary offence, but instead reflects fundamental concerns and objectives of the criminal law that are not present in civil law.

3.3.5 *Procuring a wrong*

Procuring or inducing another to commit a wrong is recognised across the private law as culpable conduct that renders A liable for the consequences of the primary wrong.[33] It is the strongest form of accessorial

[32] See, e.g., the facts of *Barlow Clowes International Ltd (in liquidation)* v. *Eurotrust International Ltd* [2005] UKPC 37; [2006] 1 WLR 1476; and *Attorney General of Zambia* v. *Meer Care and Desai* [2008] EWCA Civ 1007; [2008] Lloyd's Rep FC 587 (accessory liability not found on the facts).

[33] Indeed it has been suggested that there should be a generic cause of action for procurement 'of the violation' of a right: *Lumley* v. *Gye* (1853) 2 E & B 216, 232; 118 ER 749, 755: [3.1].

conduct and has distinctive features that warrant special mention (see in relation to the requisite mental element and the possibility of strict liability [3.4.3.6], [3.4.3.7]). Outside the law on inducing breach of contract, however, there have been few successful claims founded on procuring, and few attempts to explain what that concept entails other than in superficial terms.

Procuring or inducing means 'to bring about'; it implies a causal connection such that 'but for his [A's] persuasion, [PW's wrong] would or might never have been committed'; see [3.3.3].[34] It suggests positive conduct – 'to produce by endeavour' – that aims at achieving a particular outcome.[35] The meaning of procure as 'to bring about' appears to be consistent with how the term is used in private law [5.4.1.2], [6.3.3], [8.3.2.1].

Although there have been some suggested definitions that draw subtle distinctions between the meaning of procure and induce,[36] the terms are generally, including in this book, used interchangeably.[37] There are no obvious differences as to the legal consequences that flow based on whether conduct is labelled as procuring or inducing.[38]

One of the reasons why procurement is rarely the basis of accessory liability being found is that in many areas of law (excepting again, inducing breach of contract), lesser conduct on the part of A may suffice

[34] *Allen* v. *Flood* [1898] AC 1, 106–107, Lord Watson, citing Erle J's judgment in *Lumley* v. *Gye* (1853) 2 E & B 216, 232; 118 ER 749, 755 with approval.

[35] See in the context of criminal law, *Attorney-General's Reference (No 1 of 1975)* [1975] 1 QB 773, 779 (Lord Widgery CJ): 'You procure a thing by setting out to see that it happens and taking the appropriate steps to produce that happening.'

[36] See, e.g., *National Foods Milk Ltd* v. *McMahon Milk Pty Ltd* [2008] VSC 208 [277] (Hargrave J) (dictionary meaning): although 'induce' may carry with it a suggestion of pressure or persuasion, both terms mean 'to bring about', albeit procuring includes 'especially by unscrupulous or indirect means'. 'Inducing' connotes 'some act of compulsion by force or threat of force or some act of persuasion or stimulation aimed at ensuring that an act is committed which constitutes a contravention'. *Yorke* v. *Lucas* (1983) 49 ALR 672 (FCAFC) 681. The High Court of Australia in *Farah Constructions Pty Limited* v. *Say-Dee Pty Limited* [2007] HCA 22; (2007) 230 CLR 89 [161] referred to 'immediately procure or knowingly induce', thereby perhaps implying some difference in meanings.

[37] See, e.g., *CBS Songs Ltd* v. *Amstrad Consumer Electronics plc* [1988] AC 1013, 1058 (Lord Templeman): procure by 'inducement, incitement or persuasion'; and Sales, 'Conspiracy' 503. *Cf.* the meaning of 'counsel', which is said to be 'probably equivalent to "instigate"': *Yorke* v. *Lucas* (1983) 49 ALR 672 (FCAFC) 681.

[38] This does not mean that the law of the particular wrong in question may not differ as to the requirements of procuring and as to its consequences, but this is not a product of different labels being used.

to establish liability; for example, knowing assistance in equity, and assistance done in furtherance of a common design in tort.

A finding that A has procured the primary wrong creates the requisite 'involvement' in the primary wrong for accessory liability. The conduct element contained within procurement is clear, namely, any intentional (deliberate) conduct that successfully brings about PW's wrong (see the various examples in [6.3.3]).

3.3.6 Can A's inaction constitute sufficient involvement?

For A to be involved in PW's primary wrong generally requires there to be some act or acts by A either before or during the commission of the primary wrong; that is, inaction will not suffice. The concept of 'inaction' in the context of accessory liability appears to have been understood in two senses by the courts. The first sense is that of A being merely present at the commission of the primary wrong. The second sense is that of A's silence before or during the commission of the primary wrong, despite A having knowledge of the intended or actual wrong that could be imparted to C, thereby preventing or ending the commission of PW's wrong. Inaction in these two senses, without anything more, is generally insufficient to satisfy the conduct element of accessory liability; see in relation to criminal law [4.4.1], torts [5.4.2.2], equity [8.3.2.2], and statutory wrongs [10.4.3].[39] Nonetheless, there are exceptional circumstances where inaction, in either sense, might constitute sufficient involvement in PW's wrong.

Where A is merely present at the commission of the primary wrong, but A's presence is attributable to a prior agreement with PW or if A intended thereby to facilitate the primary wrong, then, in principle, A's inaction could suffice for liability.[40] There is some support for this; see torts [5.4.2.2] and equity [8.3.2.2].

[39] See, e.g., in the context of tort: 'the mere presence of a person at the time a tort is committed by another person does not render that person responsible for that tort', *Pringle* v. *Everingham* [2006] NSWCA 195 [94] (Hunt AJA, Mason P and Santow JA agreeing); and equity: 'Mere passive acquiescence in the breach would not, in the ordinary case, suffice to establish liability on the ground of assistance.' *Re-Engine Pty Ltd* [2007] VSC 57; (2007) 209 FLR 1[120] (Dodds-Streeton J).

[40] See, e.g., *Pringle* v. *Everingham* [2006] NSWCA 195 [94] where it was held that a policeman's mere presence at the scene of his fellow officer's battery did not render him accessorily liable for the tort of battery because the facts did not show an agreement with PW or intention by A to commit the battery.

Where A remains silent despite knowing of the intended or ongoing primary wrong, there are at least three scenarios in which A's inaction may still suffice for liability. The first is that just discussed. The second is where A is under a duty to speak (for example, because A is C's lawyer and the relevant matter is within the scope of A's retainer) [8.3.2.2].[41] But accessory liability appears otiose here, given that A may be subject to a separate liability for breach of duty in any event. The third possible scenario of silence leading to liability is where A has a special status in, or control over, the events constituting the primary wrong, although not necessarily owing a duty to C.[42]

3.4 A's knowledge: the mental state

3.4.1 Overview

Generally, A must 'know', broadly speaking, of the primary wrong or intended primary wrong at the time of A's involvement in that wrong.[43] It is A's knowledge of the primary wrong, in conjunction with A's conduct, that determines whether A's involvement is sufficiently wrongful to justify liability for the consequences of the primary wrong.[44] Knowledge of the primary wrong at the time of involvement is therefore crucial in colouring the moral quality of A's conduct.

This much, and this much only, is clear regarding the necessary mental state for accessory liability. Furthermore, even the above paragraph must be qualified in a number of ways. 'Knowledge' is a malleable concept in accessory liability. It encompasses both knowledge of a present state of affairs as well as predictions as to the likelihood of future events; and although subjective, or 'actual', knowledge is emphasised, sometimes objective knowledge suffices. These distinctions are not always made clear in the cases. Further undermining any clarity in this area, exceptionally, even knowledge of the essential features of PW's conduct that make it a wrong may not be required and A will be strictly liable as an accessory [3.4.3.7]. Particular difficulties also arise in

[41] See, e.g., *KPERS* v. *Kutak Rock* 44 P3d 407; 273 Kan 481 (2002).

[42] Under statutory accessory liability, see [10.4.3]. For tort, see further [5.4.2.2].

[43] Knowledge subsequently acquired does not make A an accessory: some other basis of liability must be found unless, perhaps, A's involvement is ongoing and continues after knowledge of the primary wrong is acquired. See, e.g., [8.4.1.2].

[44] See, e.g., [9.2.5] and *University of New South Wales* v. *Moorhouse* (1975) 13 CLR 1 (HCA) 12–13.

relation to the requisite mental state for procurement; these are discussed in [3.4.3.6].

There are two main sources of uncertainty. The first concerns the requisite 'content' of A's knowledge in the sense of the facts that A must know regarding PW's conduct or intended conduct (the 'essential matters'). The second concerns the 'degree' of A's knowledge, that is, whether anything less than actual knowledge of the requisite content will suffice for liability. These two broad questions have proved to be the most doctrinally complex and uncertain aspects of accessory liability in private law. The resulting case law has, in some areas, reached the 'zenith of complexity'.[45] The complexity and uncertainty have been exacerbated by overspecification of what is required, that is, by the 'proliferation and refinement of various categories of "knowledge"'.[46]

The analytical framework for accessory liability is particularly useful here. It illuminates the recurrence and similarities of the knowledge questions across private law, and it demonstrates that what is required by way of the necessary mental element of the analytical framework is influenced by the other two elements: A's conduct and the primary wrong. This suggests further that the question of A's mental state and whether it suffices for liability is best framed as one of broad principle to be applied in a contextual fashion to the facts, taking into account all the circumstances, including the relationship of the conduct and primary wrong elements of the framework. The courts have also emphasised that such questions are always ones of fact. In essence, broadly expressed principles, coupled with trust in the courts' ability to apply them to specific facts, is the key to reducing the complexity and uncertainty of the 'knowledge question' for accessory liability [8.3.4.4].[47]

[45] J. D. Heydon and M. J. Leeming, *Jacobs' Law of Trusts in Australia*, 7th edn (Australia, LexisNexis Butterworths, 2006) [1335].

[46] *Imobilari Pty Ltd* v. *Opes Prime Stockbroking Ltd* [2008] FCA 1920; (2008) 69 ACSR 235 [28]. See also *Royal Brunei Airlines Sdn Bhd* v. *Tan* [1995] 2 AC 378 (PC) 391 (Lord Nicholls) *(Royal Brunei Airlines)*: '"knowingly" is inapt as a criterion when applied to the gradually darkening spectrum where the differences are of degree and not kind.'

[47] *Cf.*, in the context of equitable accessory liability, *Mortgage Express Ltd* v. *S Newman & Co* [2000] Lloyd's Rep PN 745 [40].

3.4.2 *The content of A's knowledge*

3.4.2.1 Overview

Accessory liability rules generally require that A knows what PW is doing, or intends to do, at the time of A's involvement.[48] The requisite content of A's knowledge (the facts concerning PW's actual or intended conduct that A must know *of*) is often assumed, and the existing judicial discussions are not always very clear. Perhaps explaining this lack of attention and clarity is that the question of the content of A's knowledge may blur into the question of the degree of A's knowledge; for example, whether A must have actual knowledge of the requisite facts.[49]

3.4.2.2 Identifying the facts of which A must know: the 'essential matters'

At a minimum, A must know of the facts that are essential to establish the primary wrong, that is, the core features of the primary wrong committed by PW that make it a wrong. What A must know therefore depends on the court's articulation of the essence of the primary wrong.[50]

The language used in the criminal law to describe this requirement is that A must know of the 'essential matters' that make up the crime [4.4.3], [10.4.4.1]. 'Essential matters' here means that A must have knowledge of the type of crime intended by PO, although not necessarily the precise offence.[51] Determining what A must be proven to have known requires 'close' consideration of the essential matters going to the offence, but these essential matters 'must not be characterised in too narrow a fashion',[52] that is, A need not know all of the details of the offence and information pertaining to it, nor that the conduct is unlawful.[53]

The criminal law's approach has been incorporated into some Australian private law statutory schemes. Accordingly, in that context,

[48] There are some exceptional circumstances of strict accessory liability where A's knowledge of the quality of PW's conduct that makes it a wrong may not be relevant [3.4.3.7].

[49] See, e.g., *Yeshiva Properties No. 1 Property Ltd* v. *Marshall* [2005] NSWCA 23; (2005) 219 ALR 112 [22], where the court formulated what A needed to know in objective terms as whether 'the known facts would communicate to a reasonable person a general understanding that there was a fraud, breach of trust or breach of fiduciary duty'.

[50] *Cf. Rafferty* v. *Madgwicks* [2012] FCAFC 37 [253].

[51] *Giorgianni* v. *R* (1985) 156 CLR 473, 500, 506 and, e.g., *R* v. *Bainbridge* [1959] 3 WLR 656, discussed in [4.4.3].

[52] See *HIH Insurance Ltd (in liquidation)* v. *Adler* [2007] NSWSC 633 [49] (citing *James Andrew Sweeney* v. *State of Western Australia* [2006] WASCA 118) and generally [48]–[51].

[53] *HIH Insurance Ltd (in liquidation)* v. *Adler* [2007] NSWSC 633 [51].

it has been said that A need not know or 'appreciate'[54] that PW's conduct amounts to infringing conduct: it suffices that A knows of the conduct that amounts to the infringement.[55] Thus, ignorance of, or mistakes as to, the law or the legal effect of PW's conduct do not excuse A from liability. For example, in the context of the primary wrong of misleading and deceptive conduct (a statutory infringement), A must know that PW's statement to C is false, but not necessarily that to make a false statement in the particular circumstances is unlawful.[56] Similarly, in relation to torts other than inducing breach of contract, A need not be aware of the unlawfulness of PW's conduct; it suffices for A to know that PW is committing or intends to commit the acts that constitute the tort [5.4.3.2].

We consider 'essential matters' to be a helpful description of the requisite content of A's knowledge more broadly in private law accessory liability, but it should only ever be understood as shorthand for whether A knows enough about PW's conduct or intended conduct such that A's knowledge renders his involvement in that conduct wrongful. In particular, the following qualifications apply.

First, both inducing breach of contract (fairly clearly) and equitable accessory liability (less clearly) go beyond the 'essential matters' requirement and may require some appreciation of the legal significance of the facts [3.4.2.3].

Secondly, the 'essential matters' approach is less helpful where the elements of the primary wrong are complex [10.4.4.1]. Sometimes the 'essential matters' will be reasonably self-evident, but not always.

Thirdly, nor is it clear how a court should determine the level of specificity of the requisite facts: need they relate to the specific wrong or, more broadly, wrongs of that general type, for example? It is clear that in criminal law A need not know of the precise offence, but in private law, the level of specificity required must surely depend upon the purposes and values of the primary wrong in question.

[54] *ACCC* v. *Grant* [2000] FCA 1564 [13].

[55] This does not necessarily involve actual subjective knowledge of a contravention. It is 'conceivable' that an accessory can still be acting in good faith. See *Dimension Data Australia Pty Ltd* v. *Kepper* [2000] FCA 218 (Full Court). See also *Wheeler Grace and Pierucci Pty Ltd* v. *Wright* [1989] FCA 127; (1989) 16 IPR 189; (1989) ATPR ¶40–940, 50,255–50,257.

[56] See, e.g., *ACCC* v. *Grant* [2000] FCA 1564 (director of a corporation liable as accessory, having had knowledge of the falsity of the statements he made on behalf of the corporation).

Fourthly, in some contexts, such as tort accessory liability for mass IP infringements, the question of content may depend in part on how detailed A's knowledge is regarding the likelihood of infringements [5.4.3.2], [9.2.6.4], [9.2.7].

Finally, also relevant, we would suggest, is the degree of A's knowledge [3.4.3] and the nature of A's conduct, that is, it would be artificial to consider the content of A's knowledge in isolation from the interplay of the three elements for accessory liability as a whole. In any event, a measure of judicial discretion is inevitable if the essential matters approach is accepted more widely.

3.4.2.3 Must A ever know the legal significance of the essential matters?

In two areas of private law accessory liability it seems that A must know not only of the essential matters concerning the actual or intended primary wrong, but also their legal complexion. A's ignorance of, or mistakes as to, the relevant law may preclude liability.

In the tort of inducing breach of contract, an accessory who has a subjective mistaken belief as to the legal position, for example, that the desired outcome can be achieved without a breach of contract by PW, or a genuine belief that PW's conduct would not amount to a breach of contract, will probably not be held liable [6.3.4.1]. This can be explained specifically by reference to the requirement that A must intend the primary wrong (breach). That is only possible if A knows enough to be able accurately to predict that PW will not comply with her obligations if A's inducement is successful.[57] The stricter approach to the content of A's knowledge also accords with the purposes and values of contract law.

In relation to the second exception, equitable accessory liability, the position is less clear [8.3.4.2]. Generally, there need not be a 'full appreciation of the legal analysis of the transaction',[58] that is, A need not recognise a breach of trust or fiduciary duty, for example. But, it is clear that an appreciation of the unlawfulness of PW's conduct at a more general level (for example, that there is a 'misappropriation of

[57] See Simon Deakin and John Randall, 'Rethinking the Economic Torts' (2009) 72(4) *Modern Law Review* 519, 539–540.

[58] *Twinsectra Ltd* v. *Yardley* [2002] UKHL 12; [2002] 2 AC 164 [24] (Lord Hoffmann). See also [135] (Lord Millett).

money')[59] is required, although the courts have not been consistent in their approach and the issue is not often discussed.

3.4.2.4 Predictions as to future events

'Knowledge' – what we 'know' – obviously includes observable facts and current states of affairs. However, the term 'knowledge' is often also used, at times confusingly, to refer to future events, even though in one sense, we cannot 'know' the future, but can only predict (to a greater or lesser degree of certainty) what will likely occur as a result of certain actions. We 'know' that something *will* happen because, from the facts, we *predict* with (near) certainty that something will happen.[60] Knowledge in this sense must necessarily be in question when liability for procuring or inducing or for similarly intentional conduct directed towards achieving an outcome is in issue: in such scenarios, the primary wrong is necessarily yet to occur and A's 'knowledge' concerns the likelihood of future events. The word 'knowledge' is used by the courts to include that sense as well, that is, 'prospectively knowing',[61] and this book does likewise, although sometimes it is useful to distinguish the two senses.[62]

Finally, it should be noted that where the law requires actual knowledge by A of PW's intended act (which will be a wrong) that act does not need to be certain to follow. For example, PW may only intend to commit the wrongful act if certain eventualities arise; see tort [5.4.3.2], [5.5.1] and criminal law [4.4.3].[63]

3.4.2.5 Knowledge of an alleged primary wrong

Is it sufficient for liability that A knows only of an allegation by C that a primary wrong is being, or will be, committed? In such scenarios, the

[59] *Barlow Clowes International Ltd (in liquidation)* v. *Eurotrust International Ltd* [2005] UKPC 37; [2006] 1 WLR 1476 [28].

[60] In the words of Holmes J, such 'foresight of consequences' is 'a picture of a future state of things called up by knowledge of the present state of things, the future being viewed as standing to the present in the relation of effect to cause'. Mark DeWolfe Howe (ed.), Oliver Wendell Holmes, *The Common Law* (London, Macmillan, 1968) 45, quoted in *Director of Public Prosecutions* v. *Smith* (1961) AC 290 (HL) 327.

[61] *New Zealand Bus Ltd and Infratil Ltd* v. *Commerce Commission* [2007] NZCA 502 [129].

[62] The term 'intention' is sometimes also used in the sense of prediction: see, e.g., *Allstate Life Insurance Company* v. *Australia and New Zealand Banking Group Ltd* (1995) 58 FCR 26, 37.

[63] See, e.g., *R* v. *Gnango* [2011] UKSC 59; [2012] 1 AC 827 [14] (endorsing *R* v. *A* [2010] EWCA Crim 1622; [2011] QB 841 [27]: it is sufficient that A foresees that PO might carry out the actual offence).

courts consider how A should have acted in response to C's claim and, in particular, whether A should have taken further steps to ascertain its veracity [8.3.4.2], [9.4.3.2]. Where the question has arisen in equity, there has been a legitimate reluctance to impose a duty upon a professional agent, such as a solicitor or banker, to take further steps to investigate C's claim given that this may conflict with such agent's duties to his or her principal, the alleged PW. Requiring agents to inquire into C's claim might also unduly impede the conduct of commercial dealings.[64]

Other than in the professional agency context, if C's claim is detailed and consistent with the surrounding circumstances, there is time to make an informed decision as to the claim's veracity before pursuing A's own interests further, and A will not suffer any detriment from so doing, A may be fixed with knowledge of the primary wrong: [8.3.4.2], [9.4.3.2].

3.4.3 *Degrees of knowledge*

3.4.3.1 Overview

States of mind relevant to accessory liability can be classified according to the following spectrum of culpability, keeping in mind that this is indeed a 'spectrum', rather than a list of distinct categories and that mental states are not susceptible to precise classification:[65]

- Intention
- Actual knowledge
- Recklessness
- Objective knowledge

It is also necessary to add to this spectrum the possibility of strict liability, that is, where A is liable for actively bringing about an outcome (that is a wrong) but without having a culpable state of mind [3.4.3.6].

Generally speaking, actual knowledge of the primary wrong is required in many areas of accessory liability. But it is dangerous to generalise. What the courts are prepared to recognise as constituting actual

[64] See, e.g., *US International Marketing* [2004] 1 NZLR 589 (NZCA) [6]; *Nicholson v. Morgan (No 3)* [2013] WASC 110; 8 ASTLR 277 [67].

[65] In formulating this spectrum, we have drawn upon *Imobilari* [2008] FCA 1920; (2008) 69 ACSR 235 [28] (Finkelstein J referring to categories of *mens reas* for the purpose of simplifying the knowledge requirement for knowing assistance and knowing receipt in equity). We have substituted 'objective knowledge' for 'carelessness' (which is not a category of mental state, but rather culpability). *Cf.* the *Baden* scale of knowledge sometimes used in equity and criticisms of it: [8.3.4.3].

knowledge and whether lesser degrees of knowledge or culpability are recognised as sufficing for liability, depends very much upon the purposes and values of the particular doctrine or statutory provision.[66] Furthermore, the requisite content of A's knowledge cannot be completely divorced from this inquiry.

As in any area of law, ascertaining a defendant's knowledge for the purposes of liability is bound to be challenging and it is inevitable that courts will resort to a variety of aids:

> It is not always easy for a court to decide whether, at some time in the past, a person knew something ... The apparently irresistible urge to classify "knowledge" by the use of epithets like "actual", "constructive", "imputed", or by the use of metaphors like "Nelsonian knowledge" emphasises that the task can be difficult.[67]

Ascertaining A's knowledge is further complicated where A is 'an inanimate legal construct' such as a company [Chapter 11] or in the overlapping scenario where A is the principal in an agency relationship.[68]

3.4.3.2 Intention

Accessory doctrines in private law generally do not require that A have a particular intention at the time of the primary wrong in order to be liable. But in some instances the courts have suggested that a mental state of intention is necessary; that is, A must 'intend' the primary wrong. What might this mean? It certainly means that A's conduct must be deliberate and conscious,[69] but this does not add much, since there is little scope realistically for non-deliberate or involuntary conduct in the accessory context. For example, in the tort of inducing breach of contract, the act of involvement at issue, namely to induce or procure, already connotes within it the sense of deliberate conduct that seeks to achieve a particular outcome [6.3.3].

[66] E.g., statutory accessory schemes that borrow from criminal accessory law do not accept anything less than actual knowledge and are cautious regarding terms such as 'wilful blindness': *Richardson & Wrench (Holdings) Pty Ltd* v. *Ligon No 174 Pty Ltd* (1994) 123 ALR 681, 693.

[67] *Permanent Trustee Australia Limited* v. *FAI General Insurance Company Limited (In Liquidation)* [2003] HCA 25; (2003) 214 CLR 514 [76] (Gummow and Hayne JJ) (citations omitted).

[68] Legal techniques for aggregating the knowledge of various personnel for the purposes of determining the knowledge of a company and attributing an agent's knowledge to a principal are discussed in the context of companies and accessory liability in Chapter 11.

[69] See Peter Cane, *Responsibility in Law and Morality* (Oxford, Hart Publishing 2002) 79.

Beyond deliberate and conscious conduct, then, could 'intention' further require that A must intend to harm or that A intend that PW commit the act that is the wrong? The first possible intention, to harm (or 'malice'), on current law is not a requirement for accessory liability (unless perhaps where malice is an element of the primary wrong itself). In relation to the second possibility (that A must have intended the wrong), it appears that any such intention is inferred from A's actual knowledge. This is borne out by the cases on inducing breach of contract. As is explained in [6.3.4.1], knowledge, rather than intention, appears to be the crucial question in determining A's liability here. If A knows of the contract between C and PW, and that certain acts by PW will be in breach of it, but still pursues that outcome knowing (in the sense of predicting) that it is highly likely that the breach will eventuate, then intention is inferred. In other words, intention connotes a very strong level of actual knowledge both of present facts and future outcomes. The accessory cannot intend a breach without knowledge of the contract; knowledge is the prerequisite for intention. It is the cognitive platform upon which the higher mental state is built.

Other instances where intention is required, such as in the Australian statutory accessory schemes [10.4.2],[70] are consistent with these conclusions. Knowledge is the predominant concern: 'the necessary intent being based upon knowledge of the essential elements of the [primary wrong]'.[71] Thus, we suggest, references to intention, where they exist in private law, generally mean deliberate and conscious conduct with sufficient knowledge.

In equity, the relationship between intention and knowledge is not much discussed and courts apply the same criterion of fault, whether that be knowledge or dishonesty [8.3.4.1], regardless of the form of accessorial conduct involved (procurement or assistance). This may be because procurement of breach of trust was not treated as a distinct form of liability until relatively recently [8.3.4]. Nonetheless, procurement was always actionable in equity, although under the rubric of assistance, and this supports our suggestion that knowledge, rather than intention, is generally an adequate criterion of fault. The mental element for procurement is further discussed in [3.4.3.6].

[70] These incorporate criminal accessory law's requirement of intention as well as knowledge; see also Chapter 4.

[71] *Yorke* v. *Lucas* (1983) 49 ALR 672 (FCAFC) 670.

3.4.3.3 Actual knowledge

For many forms of accessory liability in private law, A must have actual knowledge of the primary wrong. This is particularly so where the liability is closely related to criminal accessory liability (as it is for some statutory wrongs: Chapter 10). In some areas of accessory liability, the determination of the mental element appears to present little difficulty because actual knowledge is generally clear on the facts. In others, the courts have gone to extraordinary lengths to formulate descriptors of what equates to actual knowledge.

A finding of actual knowledge is not limited to where there is direct evidence of such knowledge (for example, an admission by A that he knew of the primary wrong). Actual knowledge of the primary wrong may be inferred (in the manner of a jury question) from evidence of what A did in fact know.[72] Because inferred knowledge is still actual knowledge, the inference drawn by the court must be as to what A knew, rather than what a reasonable person in A's position would have known.[73]

A pervasive image in the context of inferred knowledge is that of chosen 'blindness' [8.3.4.3], [8.3.4.4], [8.5.2] and [10.4.4.2].[74] Thus, the courts refer, for example, to A's 'wilful ignorance', 'wilful blindness', 'blind-eye knowledge', 'Nelsonian knowledge', 'wilfully shutting one's eyes to the obvious'[75] and 'contrived ignorance'.[76] The concept of inferred knowledge comes from the common law and relates to actual knowledge. It was explained by Lord Esher MR:

> When a man has statements made to him, or has knowledge of facts, which do not expressly tell him of something which is against him, and he abstains from making further inquiry because he knows what the result

[72] *The English & Scottish Mercantile Investment Co Ltd* v. *Brunton* [1892] 2 QB 700 (CA) 707–708.

[73] In the context of copyright infringement and third parties see, *RCA Corporation* v. *Custom Cleared Sales Pty Ltd* (1978) 19 ALR 123 (NSWCA) 126: 'the court is not concerned with the knowledge of a reasonable man but is concerned with reasonable inferences to be drawn from a concrete situation as disclosed in the evidence as it affects the particular person whose knowledge is in issue.'

[74] Sometimes this includes deafness: 'Nor does an honest person ... deliberately close his eyes and ears, or deliberately not ask questions, lest he learn something he would rather not know' (*Royal Brunei Airlines* [1995] 2 AC 378 (PC) 389).

[75] Level (ii) on the *Baden* scale in equitable accessory liability: *Baden* v. *Société Générale pour Favoriser le Développement du Commerce et de l'Industrie en France SA* [1993] 1 WLR 509 (Ch) 575–576. See further [8.3.4.3].

[76] See generally, *Manifest Shipping Co Ltd* v. *Uni-Polaris Insurance Co Ltd* [2001] UKHL 1; [2003] 1 AC 469; *Richardson & Wrench (Holdings) Pty Ltd* v. *Ligon No 174 Pty Ltd* [1994] FCA 1222; (1994) 123 ALR 681.

> would be–or, as the phrase is, he "wilfully shuts his eyes"–then judges are in the habit of telling juries that they may infer that he did know what was against him. It is an inference of fact drawn because you cannot look into a man's mind, but you can infer from his conduct whether he is speaking truly or not when he says that he did not know of particular facts. There is no question of constructive notice or constructive knowledge involved in that inference; it is actual knowledge which is inferred.[77]

Particularly where accessorial rules in private law have derived from criminal accessory liability, the courts have been careful to emphasise that a finding of 'wilful blindness' is potentially ambiguous and is only relevant where it shows actual knowledge:

> the fact of exposure to the obvious may warrant the inference of knowledge. The shutting of one's eyes to the obvious is not, however, an alternative to the actual knowledge which is required as the basis of intent to aid, abet, counsel or procure.[78]

3.4.3.4 Recklessness

In some accessory liability contexts, the courts will accept lesser degrees of knowledge than actual knowledge, that is, alternatives to actual knowledge, that are as good as actual knowledge for the purposes of liability in the particular context.[79] 'Recklessness', the mental state that accompanies risk-taking conduct, is the main example; see, for example, [6.3.4.2], [8.3.4] and [9.2.7].

Recklessness has been usefully defined as 'awareness of a risk that certain consequences will result from conduct, and indifference to that risk'.[80] The risk must be so substantial, as to have been an unreasonable one to take,[81]

[77] *The English & Scottish Mercantile Investment Co Ltd* v. *Brunton* [1892] 2 QB 700 (CA) 707–708.

[78] *Giorgianni* v. *R* (1985) 156 CLR 473 HCA 507–508 (Wilson, Deane and Dawson JJ), quoted in *Richardson & Wrench (Holdings) Pty Ltd* v. *Ligon No 174 Pty Ltd* (1994) 123 ALR 681, 693. *Cf.*, in the context of inducing breach of contract, *Allstate Life Insurance Company* v. *Australia and New Zealand Banking Group Ltd* (1995) 130 ALR 469 (FCA) 479, and discussion in [6.3.4.2].

[79] The term 'surrogate' is used to describe lesser degrees of knowledge that are acceptable substitutes for actual knowledge in *Grimaldi* v. *Chameleon Mining NL (No 2)* [2012] FCAFC 6; (2012) 200 FCR 296 [261] (*Grimaldi*) (in the context of objective knowledge for the purposes of equitable accessory liability).

[80] See A. Ashworth, *Principles of Criminal Law*, 3rd edn (Oxford University Press, 1999) 184–185, cited in Peter Cane, '*Mens Rea* in Tort Law' (2000) Oxford Journal of Legal Studies 533, 535.

[81] Cane, '*Mens Rea*', 535, and Cane, *Responsibility*, 80: the required knowledge of the actor is of a risk that, *because of the likelihood* of its outcome, is unreasonable to take; and see also

that is, there must be a 'conscious disregard of a substantial and unjustifiable risk'.[82] These descriptions combine subjective and objective elements: the person's actual knowledge of the facts, combined with the reasonable predictions that could be drawn from those facts, leads to a finding of reckless indifference. Both subjective and objective elements are included in the definition of 'recklessness' given in the *Restatement (Third) of Torts: Liability for Physical & Emotional Harm* § 2:

> (a) the person knows of the risk of harm created by the conduct or knows facts that make the risk obvious to another in the person's situation, and (b) the precaution that would eliminate or reduce the risk involves burdens that are so slight relative to the magnitude of the risk as to render the person's failure to adopt the precaution a demonstration of the person's indifference to the risk.[83]

One needs to be careful with such definitions, however, since recklessness in the context of accessory liability usually refers to A's disregard for the risk that PW is committing or is likely to commit a primary wrong when actively involving himself in PW's acts, and therefore the reference to precautions has less relevance.

Reckless indifference to the consequences of one's actions, determined objectively on the basis of facts that A actually knew, suffices as the necessary mental element in equitable accessory liability. Under the traditional equitable framework, this is formulated in explicitly objective terms: 'wilfully and recklessly failing to make such inquiries as an honest and reasonable man would make' [8.3.4.3].[84] Under the reformed equitable framework reference is made to '[a]cting in reckless disregard of others' rights or possible rights . . . ' [8.3.4.4].[85]

3.4.3.5 Objective knowledge

Generally speaking, 'objective knowledge' is not a sufficiently culpable mental state for accessory liability.[86] By 'objective knowledge', we mean

Jim Evans, 'Choice and Responsibility' (2002) 27 *Australian Journal of Legal Philosophy* 97, 106.

82 *Imobilari Pty Ltd* v. *Opes Prime Stockbroking Ltd* [2008] FCA 1920 [28] (Finkelstein J).

83 American Law Institute (2005).

84 *Baden* v. *Société Générale pour Favoriser le Développement du Commerce et de l'Industrie en France SA* [1993] 1 WLR 509 (Ch) 572–573 (Peter Gibson J) (level iv knowledge).

85 *Royal Brunei Airlines* [1995] 2 AC 378 (PC) 390. The question here is whether A is dishonest and this is determined objectively with regard to A's actual knowledge of the facts. See also [3.5.2].

86 This is clear in the Australian statutory accessory liability schemes that incorporate criminal law concepts of accessory liability [10.4.4.2]. See, e.g., Foster J's finding of no

a state of mind attributed to A that is determined according to an objective standard – that of the reasonable person – and in contradistinction to A's actual knowledge (including wilful blindness) or reckless indifference.

'Objective knowledge' is not a legal term of art. In equity, where various forms of objective knowledge are recognised in particular contexts,[87] it is described as 'constructive knowledge' or 'constructive notice', although the meaning ascribed to those terms is not always consistent, see [7.5], [8.3.4.3]. More generally in the law, objective knowledge is described in terms of 'carelessness' or 'negligence', although these descriptions may be misleading given that they connote a normative evaluation of conduct, rather than a mental state per se.

Although, generally, objective knowledge does not suffice for accessory liability, courts using the traditional framework of equitable accessory liability accept as sufficiently culpable, one form of objective knowledge. This is the knowledge that 'an honest and reasonable'[88] person in A's position would deduce from facts actually known to A [8.3.4.3]. This form of objective knowledge has been described in terms of 'moral obtuseness'[89] and as 'an understandable, objective, default rule' that is 'the surrogate of actual knowledge'.[90] It is a pragmatic acknowledgement that there is no bright-line distinction between inferred actual knowledge (a question of fact) and objective knowledge (a question that adds to the question of fact normative factors: what A *should* have known if A were a reasonable person given the facts that A actually knew). Its acceptance can be explained by reference to the purposes and values underpinning equitable primary wrongs, but it is controversial and does not satisfy the culpability test of 'dishonesty' adopted by the reformed framework for equitable accessory liability [8.3.4.4]; see also [8.3.5].

liability in *Inchcape Financial Services (Aust) Pty Ltd* v. *Classic Automobiles Pty Ltd* [1999] NSWSC 895 [118] in the context of the statutory primary wrong of misleading and deceptive conduct: although, 'undoubtedly, [A] should have been aware of what was going on in the [relevant transaction], he was not. He left it to [PW] to make sure that the deals were safe and proper'.

87 *The English & Scottish Mercantile Investment Co Ltd* v. *Brunton* [1892] 2 QB 700 (CA) 707.

88 *Baden* [1993] 1 WLR 509 (Ch) 572–573 (Peter Gibson J).

89 *Consul Development Pty Ltd* v. *DPC Estates Pty Ltd* (1975) 132 CLR 373, 397 (Gibbs J); *Farah Constructions Pty Limited* v. *Say-Dee Pty Limited* [2007] HCA 22; (2007) 230 CLR 89 [177].

90 *Grimaldi* v. *Chameleon Mining NL (No 2)* [2012] FCAFC 6; (2012) 200 FCR 296 [261] (Finn, Stone and Perram JJ).

Exceptionally, and admittedly in a borderline category, objective knowledge in an even broader form may be relevant to 'indirect infringement' of IP rights [9.4.3.2]. The various statutory formulations of objective knowledge, such as 'obvious to a reasonable person' for example, do not make it clear whether the objective assessment is based on A's actual knowledge or whether the test is purely objective and equates to carelessness and includes facts a reasonable person may have discovered. The case law is confused, but the weight of authority rightly favours the former approach.

3.4.3.6 Mental states and procurement

One of several difficulties with the concept of procurement is that the term of itself does not spell out the precise mental element for liability. To procure a wrong suggests that A must have actual knowledge of the wrong, that is, of the essential matters of PW's conduct that make it a wrong.[91] In a handful of equity cases, courts appear to assume that A must have such actual knowledge [8.3.4.3]. And the law of inducing breach of contract requires either actual knowledge of PW's breach or a reckless indifference to that possibility, albeit recklessness here requires a subjective awareness of that risk.[92] Procuring a seemingly innocent act by PW does not give rise to liability.

More difficult questions as to the requisite knowledge arise where A procures acts or outcomes, not in themselves wrongful, but wrongs flow as a consequence of those acts or PW uses wrongful means to achieve those outcomes. In a perhaps related context, namely cases on authorising a nuisance, some cases appear to have held that an authoriser may be liable for wrongs that arise 'in the natural course of things' [5.5.3]. It is not clear whether this requires some knowledge on A's part, or is based merely on objective assessments of risks.[93] If the latter,

[91] See *Yorke* v. *Lucas* (1985) 158 CLR 661, 670 in the context of statutory accessory liability and the meaning of 'inducing', which 'clearly' requires 'intent based upon knowledge'. Similarly, in that case in the Federal Court (1983) 49 ALR 672, 681–682, it was said that 'something more than innocent participation by the defendant is involved in the notion of inducing'. Admittedly, the statutory scheme in question is based on criminal law concepts and the court was applying criminal law notions.

[92] This is in contrast to the general meaning of recklessness we have adopted above as extending to serious risks that are objectively determinable from the facts of which A actually (subjectively) knows.

[93] In any case, care must be taken with authorisation cases in nuisance, since authorising appears to extend beyond procuring conduct to merely permitting certain acts to be carried out.

it could be justified on the basis that we are presumed to intend the natural and reasonable consequences of our actions.[94] In other words, the law deems A to know, indeed, perhaps even to intend, such consequences.

Finally, one further complexity arises in procuring cases. Some authorities have held in some limited contexts that A may be liable for procuring some strict liability wrongs even if A has no knowledge of the essential matters of PW's conduct that make it a wrong. In other words, A might be strictly liable, even where A is innocently unaware that a wrong is being committed by PW. If such strict liability has a widespread operation (which we doubt), then procuring becomes an anomalous and potentially harsh source of liability. The issue is discussed in the following section.

3.4.3.7 The requisite mental state for strict liability primary wrongs

It has correctly been stated that where a primary wrong incorporates a particular mental element that needs to be satisfied, then any person charged with being an accessory must also possess such a mental state. The liability of the accessory 'cannot be more extensive than that of the individual who personally did the [wrongful] act'.[95] Therefore, for a wrong such as the tort of deceit, which requires a particular intentional element or *mens rea* on the part of PW (dishonesty), A must also possess that 'necessary intention'.[96]

This does not mean, however, that A's mental state needs to merely equate with any mental state, or absence thereof,[97] that is necessary to

[94] It is 'a principle of the law ... that people are presumed to intend the reasonable consequences of their acts': *South Wales Miners Federation* v. *Glamorgan Coal Co. Ltd* [1905] AC 239, 244 (Lord Halsbury). See also *Palmer-Bruyn and Parker Pty Ltd* v. *Parsons* [2001] HCA 69; 208 CLR 388 [73] (Gummow J) (similarly Gleeson CJ at [13]). See also Spigelman CJ (Mason P and Grove JA concurring) in *TCN Channel Nine Pty Ltd* v. *Anning* [2002] NSWCA 82; (2002) 54 NSWLR 333 [100], who states: 'Although [*Palmer-Bruyn*] involved [the tort of] injurious falsehood, the High Court's reasoning is of more general application to intentional torts'.

[95] *C Evans & Sons Ltd* v. *Spritebrand Ltd* [1985] 2 All ER 415, 424, Slade LJ's observation being made in the context of director's liability for company torts.

[96] See *Johnson Matthey (Aust) Ltd* v. *Dascorp Pty Ltd* [2003] VSC 291; (2003) 9 VR 171, 195 [150], also made in the context of directors' liability.

[97] *Cf.* the rejection in criminal law of parallelism (that is, the argument that the mental element for PO and A must be the same): [4.4.3] [4.5.1]. Some criminal lawyers have argued that A's mental state need merely parallel that of PO's in criminal law in order to

find PW liable. If PW is liable for a strict liability wrong, and therefore potentially liable even absent any culpable mental state, it does not follow that A is also necessarily strictly liable. On the contrary, A must generally be knowingly and culpably involved in PW's wrong, that is, with the knowledge of the essential quality of PW's conduct that makes it a wrong, even for primary wrongs for which PW herself may be strictly liable.

This is the position throughout much of private law as well as criminal law [4.4.3] and applies even where A procures the very act of PW that is a wrong. In equity, for example, a knowing assistant or procurer is not liable absent knowledge of features of a trustee's or fiduciary's conduct that constitutes the breach, despite the fact that such trustee or fiduciary might be liable absent proof of any 'fault'.[98] The same applies under statutory accessory rules in Australia that apply to misleading conduct liability. To take a simple example, A must know of the falsity of PW's statement even if PW does not [Chapter 10]. The issue has not been fully explored in torts, but one would assume the same position holds. For example, a nurse who hands a scalpel to a surgeon, both wrongly believing that the patient has consented to the operation, ought not to be an accessory to trespass to person, even though the surgeon is strictly liable.[99]

This is the general position, but there are some exceptions. It has been held that for some strict liability wrongs (some torts, and statutory IP torts) and particularly in some contexts (directors' liability for company wrongs), A may be liable for *procuring* wrongs even if A has no knowledge of the essential matters of PW's conduct that make it a wrong. In other words, A might be strictly liable, even where A is innocently unaware that a wrong is being committed. Thus, in *Johnson Matthey (Aust) Ltd* v. *Dascorp Pty Ltd*,[100] company directors were liable as

be liable, but that approach leads to injustice where PO is liable for a strict liability offence, and has been rejected as a general approach. Even for strict liability or limited fault offences, A must generally have a culpable mental state. See [4.4.3] and M. Barrett and J. Dietrich, 'The Knowledge Element for Accessories to Strict Liability and Limited Cognition Offences: Revisiting *Tabe* v. *R*' (2014) 38 *Criminal Law Journal* 197. There are resonances of such parallel knowledge arguments in *C Evans & Sons Ltd* v. *Spritebrand Ltd* [1985] 1 WLR 317; [1985] 2 All ER 415, and *Johnson Matthey (Aust) Ltd* v. *Dascorp Pty Ltd* [2003] VSC 291; (2003) 9 VR 171, discussed in detail in Chapter 11.

98 This is also the case for breach of contract and inducing breach [Chapter 6].

99 Of course, the nurse ought to be liable if he or she knows that the patient has not consented, even if the surgeon does not. Query where the nurse's belief as to no consent is unreasonable? What ought to be the position as to the liability of a person who procures the surgeon to commit the operation?

100 [2003] VSC 291; (2003) 9 VR 171.

accessories to their company's conversion of goods, even absent any knowledge on their part (and therefore the company's part) of the seller's lack of title and C's rights. The issue has arisen most often for IP infringements generally[101] and particularly when made by companies. For example, if A procures PW to copy certain materials, A may be liable even if he is innocently unaware of the subsistence of copyright, especially if A is a director of PW Co [Chapter 11]. The view that A may be the instigator of PW's conduct that is the wrong, PW being merely A's 'tool', may underlie the perceived need for broader liability.[102]

In the IP context, the statutory test of 'authorising' an infringement has been used to impose strict liability in some circumstances,[103] but the problem is that that test extends to conduct of A that is less active than procuring. The role of knowledge ought to be given more prominence within the law on 'authorising' and the issues are discussed in [9.2.5]–[9.2.7].

Similarly, for directors' liability for company wrongs, the 'direct or procure' test could extend to less targeted conduct than procuring, such as where directors permit or 'direct' certain outcomes, thereby potentially yielding broader strict accessory liability. Most cases in that context, are consistent, however, with knowledge being a relevant and important consideration. The issues are discussed in Chapter 11.

Given the importance generally attached in accessory liability to knowledge and related states of consciousness, doctrines or statutory provisions that permit liability where A's knowledge merely relates to the commission of certain acts, but which acts A may believe to be innocent – in other words, strict liability – should be exceptional.

[101] It was in that context that Mustill LJ stated: there is no 'need for a common design to infringe. It is enough if the parties combine to secure the doing of acts which in the event prove to be infringements.' See *Unilever plc* v. *Gillette (UK) Ltd* [1989] RPC 583, 609 (infringement of patents). But this statement is ambiguous. It may merely mean that A cannot plead ignorance of IP law, but it could also mean that A is liable even if ignorant of the existence of the IP rights over the particular matter. The latter interpretation is problematic since the comment was made for 'common design' and not a procuring basis of liability.

[102] A is liable according to the character of the act that A has procured. See, e.g., *Keller* v. *LED Technologies Pty Ltd* [2010] FCAFC 55; (2010) 185 FCR 449 [383] (Jessup J): 'if the director had instructed a clerk to take a copy of the [copyrighted] work . . . the director would be liable because, in essence, the act of photocopying was his or her own. The role of the clerk would be purely instrumental.'

[103] Of course, where A is PW's employer, vicarious liability in any case arises, but courts may be imposing vicarious-like liability for 'lesser' relationships by using accessorial concepts such as 'authorising' a tort or nuisance where A merely has some authority over PW. See [5.3.1.2], [5.5.3].

Certainly, they ought to be limited to situations in which A seeks to bring about the very conduct of PW that is a wrong and only then for some primary wrongs and in limited contexts.

3.5 The operation of the analytical framework

3.5.1 The interplay of the three elements determines A's culpability

Culpable involvement in another's wrong is both the main rationale for, and defining characteristic of, accessory liability [2.4.2]. A is culpable because A's involvement (accessorial conduct) in combination with A's mental state, generally knowledge of PW's wrongdoing, links A to PW's wrong. Accessory liability therefore requires both a conduct element and a mental element, the combination of which constitutes a 'participation link' between A and PW thereby justifying A's liability in relation to the primary wrong. Whether a person is liable as an accessory therefore depends (at a conceptual level, at least) on the *interplay* between the conduct and mental elements as well as, less significantly, the egregiousness of the primary wrong and the purposes and values that underpin that primary wrong. As a general rule, and accepting that this need not apply to all species of accessorial liability, the more active A is in bringing about the primary wrong, the less he may need to know about PW's planned wrongdoing in order to be liable; the less active A is, then the more detailed information A will probably need to know and to a higher degree in order to be liable. Where both elements are weak, the case for liability is also weak.

Ultimately, the question of liability is a normative one of whether a party is sufficiently involved in PW's wrong with sufficient knowledge such that it is appropriate to hold him liable for PW's wrong; the answer is determined holistically taking into account the purposes and values of the primary wrong that has been infringed. The analytical framework for accessory liability thus operates at the conceptual level in a relational and dynamic fashion.

3.5.2 Should A's culpability be further defined: 'dishonesty' and other labels

Is it preferable to describe A's culpability by reference to a general standard, rather than by separate reference to the three elements of the analytical framework? This would be difficult to do at a general level across private law, given that the content of the three elements of the framework will differ according to the different accessorial rules. It would seem most feasible in relation to procurement, given the similarities that exist in relation to that form of accessory liability across the law [3.1], [3.3.5] and [3.4.3.6]. But the question is also relevant in relation to specific accessorial doctrines. For example, under the dominant framework for breach of trust and fiduciary duty, liability is now determined by reference to a general criterion of 'dishonesty' [8.1.4.2].[104]

The criterion of dishonesty as used in equitable accessory liability reflects the operation of our analytical framework: whether A was dishonest involves a normative judgment upon A's conduct (the conduct element) in all the circumstances, including, particularly, A's knowledge (the mental element). Dishonesty is determined objectively, but with reference to A's actual knowledge at the time of the primary wrong. This is said to reflect the purposes and values of the law of trusts (the primary wrong).[105]

The criterion of dishonesty was intended to simplify the complexity of the law concerning the requisite mental element for equitable accessory liability. It has some merit in that it makes explicit the normative and contextual nature of the inquiry and that what needs to be shown is A's independently culpable conduct. But such labels are misleading. They are conclusory. They do not assist in determining when such culpability actually exists and add a (perhaps unnecessary) rhetorical gloss to the underlying analytical framework of accessory liability. As evidenced by the subsequent history of the dishonesty requirement in equitable accessory liability, the meaning of the term was not self-evident and still required legal explication in the particular liability context. Crucially, it could not circumvent the necessary inquiry into A's mental state, including whether A had actual knowledge or behaved recklessly. Indeed, it has been suggested that, once the requisite mental element is properly understood, there is no need for the additional label of 'dishonesty'.[106] For these reasons, we do not consider that culpability 'labels' are required.

[104] *Royal Brunei Airlines* [1995] 2 AC 378 (PC). 'Unconscionability' has been similarly proposed as the culpability standard for recipient liability: *Bank of Credit and Commerce International (Overseas) Ltd* v. *Akindele* [2001] Ch 437 (CA) 455; [8.3.4.4]. In *Royal Brunei Airlines* at 392, Lord Nicholls rejected the suitability of 'unconscionability' as a description of the threshold for liability because in his view it did not have an obvious meaning in this context. With respect, the same could be said of 'dishonesty' (and many other legal 'labels').

[105] This is described in terms of what trust beneficiaries can reasonably expect of persons interacting with their trustees. See *Royal Brunei Airlines* [1995] 2 AC 378 (PC).

[106] *Twinsectra Ltd* v. *Yardley* [2002] UKHL 12; [2002] 2 AC 164 [134] (Lord Millett dissenting).

3.5.3 Can the framework operate at the level of judicial determination of liability?

The dynamic and relational operation of the framework can sometimes be seen at the doctrinal level where it explains why the requirements of particular accessorial rules are formulated as they are.[107] But is the operation of the framework also relevant to the 'lower' level of judicial determination of accessory liability in individual cases? We are not suggesting here that existing accessorial liability rules be jettisoned in favour of a holistic inquiry in which the significance and weighting of each element of the framework is at large. But, within the parameters of the existing rules, is it possible to illuminate and simplify the process of judicial determination of liability by more explicit reference to the dynamic interplay of the three elements of the framework?

There is support in equity for an approach that considers all relevant factors, as part of an overall assessment as to whether A's conduct in all the circumstances is culpable. As discussed in [3.5.2] in relation to the culpability 'label' of dishonesty, the English judicial methodology for determining equitable accessory liability reflects the operation of the analytical framework at the conceptual level as we have described it. Furthermore, the methodology involved appears to have been fully embraced by the English courts [8.3.4.4]. A similar methodology is implied in the Federal Court of Australia's description of equitable participatory liability in *Grimaldi*, albeit perhaps at the doctrinal, rather than judicial determination, level.[108] The Court's description presages a judicial methodology by which the three elements of the framework are considered in a context-specific fashion and given varying weight accordingly.

> [P]articipatory liability as it evolved in equity . . . was not based on inflexible formulae. Given the variety of circumstances in which, and bases on which, a third party could be characterised as a wrongdoer in equity . . . varying importance has been given to three matters: (i) the nature of the actual fiduciary or trustee wrongdoing in which the third party was a participant; (ii) the nature of the third party's role and participation, eg as alter ago, inducer or procurer, dealer at arm's length, etc; and (iii) the extent of the

[107] E.g., according to the equitable doctrine of knowing *assistance*, the requisite primary wrong of breach of trust or fiduciary duty must be particularly egregious ('a dishonest and fraudulent design'); whereas, if A *procures* the primary wrong (that is, A's involvement has greater import), *any* breach of trust suffices [8.3.1.4]. See also, *Grimaldi* v. *Chameleon Mining NL (No 2)* [2012] FCAFC 6; (2012) 200 FCR 296 [247].

[108] *Grimaldi* [2012] FCAFC 6; (2012) 200 FCR 296 [247].

> participant's knowledge or, assumption of the risk of, or indifference to, actual, apprehended or suspected wrongdoing by the fiduciary.[109]

Thus, support can be found across the jurisdictions for a judicial methodology in equitable accessory liability that reflects the dynamic and relational operation of the analytical framework. Further, the case law on authorisation of copyright can be interpreted as demonstrating this relationship, without expressly adopting such reasoning [9.2.6], [9.2.7].

Should such judicial methodology be confined to the more 'discretionary' context of equitable decision-making? It is difficult to find explicit examples of the same or similar methodologies in common law accessory liability; nor can it be necessarily countenanced in statutory contexts, absent legislative warrant. In the US context of accessory liability for torts, the courts have sometimes applied a 'sliding scale' or 'tandem' approach to establishing liability [5.4.4]. The sliding scale analysis proposes that the elements of knowledge and 'substantial assistance' required for civil aiding and abetting liability be analysed in tandem, or 'relative to one another'.[110] Under this approach, where there is a high level of involvement by A in PW's wrong, a lower minimum threshold of knowledge may suffice for A to be held culpable and vice versa. While a number of qualifications are necessary in relation to the merits of the US approach (for example, it does not incorporate the nature of the primary wrongdoing, see [5.4.4]) it does provide some support at least for a judicial methodology in common law accessory liability that reflects the conceptual operation of the analytical framework.

To summarise, it is clear that the particular accessorial rule in question must set the parameters for judicial determination of the three elements of accessory liability. This is particularly so in relation to statutory accessory liability. But, we would argue, there is otherwise scope for greater acknowledgement of the dynamic interplay of those elements in determining A's liability. Judicial determination of accessory liability in a way that conforms to the conceptual operation of our analytical framework has already been implemented to good effect in the context of dishonest assistance liability in equity and a similar methodology could be adopted more widely. This would have particular advantages in determining the sufficiency of the conduct and mental

[109] *Ibid.*

[110] *Metge* v. *Baehler* 762 F2d 621, 624 (8th Cir, 1985), citing *Stokes* v. *Lokken,* 644 F2d 779, 784 (8th Cir, 1981).

elements of accessory liability (the 'participation link') that justify A becoming liable for PW's wrong.

3.6 Defences

As a general rule, the defences available to A are determined by the jurisdiction (torts or equity) or legislation governing A's accessory liability. The available defences are not limited to defences that PW (or other accessories) can establish; that is, A can plead all defences potentially available, even where PW may not be able to establish all the elements of such defence. For example, where PW is disbarred from a defence because she has a certain state of mind, this will not defeat a defence by a joint wrongdoer, such as A, who does not have that state of mind. A will not be barred by the disentitling conduct of PW. This principle applies in torts law [5.6.1] and should apply more generally, but the issue has not often arisen.

Questions arise as to whether A can still be held liable where PW has successfully pleaded a 'defence'. It is clear that A will not be liable if PW's defence justifies what would otherwise constitute a wrong, for example, where C has consented to, or acquiesced in, the primary wrong [3.2.1], [8.6.2].[111] Here, PW's successful defence effectively means that there was no primary wrong and, hence, must also operate to preclude A's accessory liability: [3.2.1]. But PW's defence may be personal to PW such as where a court excuses a trustee or fiduciary pursuant to exculpatory legislation [8.6.2]. In such cases, the primary wrong and, consequently A's accessory liability, may survive.[112] Where C has undertaken not to sue PW, A's liability also will survive, given that the primary wrong has not been extinguished and PW is still prima facie liable. But A may seek contribution from PW, despite the undertaking, where contribution is otherwise available [5.6.2], [8.6.2] and [8.8.3].

The most difficult question is whether A's liability survives where PW is prima facie liable, but has been released from liability by C. That issue has arisen in relation to joint tortfeasors [5.6.2] and in equity [8.6.2] and is discussed in those chapters.

111 Strictly speaking, it is a contested point as to whether consent is merely a defence or whether C has not established a necessary element of the primary wrong itself; however, courts often use the language of 'defence' more loosely to encompass the latter scenario as well.

112 See *Farah Constructions* [2007] HCA 22; (2007) 230 CLR 89 [184] n. 264.

3.7 Remedies

The remedies available against A are generally determined according to the operative remedial rules of the primary wrong, except in the case of inducing breach of contract where the remedies are those available in tort law, rather than contract law. Remedies are determined according to A's own culpability and by reference to the consequences of the primary wrong for C and A, respectively. The remedies need not duplicate those available against PW because accessory liability is based upon A's own, independently culpable, conduct. The non-duplicative nature of accessory liability and implications for the remedies available against A are discussed in depth in [2.6] and in relation to torts [5.7.1] and equity [8.1.5], [8.7]. The non-duplicative nature of A's liability also means that A may be subject to a greater range of remedies than PW.

4

Accessories in criminal law

4.1 The relevance of criminal law to private law

There has been some debate as to whether the criminal law can be used to elucidate the private law of accessories. After considering the arguments, we conclude that there are similarities between the two areas of accessory law. Consequently, this book draws on the criminal law where it appears relevant and, to that end, provides a general overview of criminal law.

Although there are obvious parallels between accessory liability in private and criminal law, the question is whether the well-developed (albeit complex and uncertain) criminal law jurisprudence can further our understanding of civil accessory liability. Some judges assert, without necessarily full substantiation, the view that the criminal law is in a problematic state and therefore perhaps unhelpful as a source of guidance.[1] Further, and undeniably, there are some fundamental differences between civil liability and liability as an accessory to a crime. These include the following.

First, criminal law seeks to deter and punish unacceptable social behaviour, whereas civil law is focused on who, as between the accessory (A) and claimant (C), ought to bear a particular loss, or benefit from a particular gain.[2] Indeed, in civil claims, C will often seek remedies against an accessory because of practical impediments to pursuing claims against the primary wrongdoers (PWs) (such as their insolvency). In criminal law, by way of contrast, the moral quality of A's

[1] See, e.g., *Sea Shepherd* v. *Fish and Fish Ltd* [2015] UKSC 10 [20] (Lord Toulson); see also [39] (Lord Sumption). *Cf.* the more detailed discussion of the criminal law in the Court of Appeal: [2013] EWCA Civ 544; [2013] 1 WLR 3700 [41]–[45].

[2] In the very different context of the defence of self-defence in torts, compare the comments of Lord Scott in *Ashley* v. *Chief Constable of Sussex Police* [2008] UKHL 25; [2008] AC 962 [18], noting that tort law needs to strike a balance between 'conflicting rights' of the claimant and defendant, whereas the criminal law does not and serves a different purpose. *Cf.* also Lord Carswell at [76].

conduct – whether it is sufficiently antisocial and culpable – is the overriding concern. Peter Cane has encapsulated the differences in terms of mental fault and conduct being the main focus of criminal law, whereas causation and the consequences of particular conduct are the focus of civil law.[3] Of course, this does not mean that causation and consequences are not also important in criminal law, and that personal culpability is not important in civil liability.

Secondly, it can be argued that the opprobrium of being found guilty of a crime as an accessory and the consequent punishment is more severe than being found liable as a civil accessory.[4] Interestingly, where a conviction for a serious crime is at issue, one might therefore expect that the law is restrained in extending accessory liability too far. Yet perhaps anomalously, criminal liability in some circumstances is potentially very wide-ranging [4.5.2].[5] It cannot be assumed that criminal law liability is necessarily narrower than civil liability. For example, somewhat surprisingly, English law acknowledges the seemingly counter-intuitive conclusion that tort liability may be more restrictive than criminal liability:

> the consequence is that selling a person a gun knowing that person will use it to kill someone else will make the seller an accessory to the murder but will not in itself make him liable in tort.[6]

Conversely, in the US, it has been held that parties who may not be criminal accessories (say, to murder), may be *civilly* liable as accessories

[3] Peter Cane, *Responsibility in Law and Morality* (Oxford, Hart Publishing, 2002) Ch. 3. For further fundamental differences between criminal and tort law, see Peter Cane, '*Mens Rea* in Tort Law' (2000) *Oxford Journal of Legal Studies* 533, 553–555: e.g., criminal law is focused on the accused's state of mind and is more 'agent focused', whereas tort law is more concerned with consequences for victims.

[4] Perhaps in some circumstances at least, being held fully liable for C's (perhaps substantial) losses may have even more serious consequences for a civil accessory than suffering a criminal penalty. E.g., accessories under statutory liability regimes may potentially be subject to civil remedies, but also liable for contravention of criminal offences and civil penalty provisions. If losses are substantial, civil liability could eclipse any civil penalty or even criminal punishment. It has been noted that where civil liability requires a finding of dishonesty (or a similarly pejorative conclusion) the law may also be reluctant to draw that conclusion. See Lord Millett in *Twinsectra Ltd* v. *Yardley* [2002] UKHL 12; [2002] 2 AC 164 [115]–[117].

[5] The view that criminal activity in groups poses a greater social threat than individually committed crimes may underlie this readiness to impose criminal liability; the same threat does not arise from concerted civil wrongs.

[6] *Fish and Fish Ltd* v. *Sea Shepherd UK* [2013] EWCA Civ 544; [2013] 1 WLR 3700 (Beatson LJ, McCombe and Mummery LJJ concurring) [42], citing the 'well-known' example of Devlin J in *National Coal Board* v. *Gamble* [1959] 1 QB 11, 23.

to a wrongful death; indeed, the assumption appears to be that establishing tort liability is less onerous than criminal responsibility.[7]

Finally, civil liability raises the question of what remedies are available against an accessory; this is not, of course, an issue in criminal law.[8]

All this suggests a need for caution,[9] but does it mean that it 'is a mistake to compare crime and [civil accessory liability]', as was asserted by Lord Templeman in *CBS Songs Ltd* v. *Amstrad Plc*, in the context of tort accessory liability?[10] Certainly, it is prudent to highlight any idiosyncratic or anomalous features of criminal law and, where relevant, to acknowledge differences that are the product of differing policy goals. As Dowsett J remarked in *Temple* v. *Powell* on the possible differences between criminal and tort accessory liability, 'there may be dangers in seeking to apply decisions as to common law accessorial liability in crime when considering accessorial liability in tort'.[11]

Such comments are animated by a justifiable resistance to *transplanting* specific rules, principles or interpretations from one sphere of law to another.[12] Such transplantation may not be justified even from one sphere of private law to another. Comparison with related areas of

[7] See, e.g., *Rice* v. *Paladin Enterprises, Inc* 128 F3d 233, 251 (4th Cir, 1997). *Cf.* the US Supreme Court in *Rosemond* v. *US* 575 US 1, 12 n. 8 (2014), leaving this question open.

[8] Where, however, criminal contempt of court is found, including against someone who has aided another in that contempt, e.g., for breach of an injunction, such a finding may be an indirect means of rectifying a breach. See, e.g., *Avery* v. *Andrews* (1882) 51 LJ Ch 414.

[9] The need for caution is in part borne out by the difficulties that arose after the *Twinsectra Ltd* v. *Yardley* [2002] UKHL 12; [2002] 2 AC 164, in which a test of 'dishonesty' was adopted for equitable accessory liability. See the discussion in [8.3.4.4].

[10] [1988] 1 AC 1013, 1059. For other statements resistant to the use of the criminal law analogously in civil law, given the different policy objectives of the criminal law, see *Credit Lyonnais Bank Nederland NV* v. *Export Credit Guarantee Department* [1998] 1 Lloyd's LR 19, particularly at 42–46, and *Credit Lyonnais Bank Nederland NV* v. *Export Credit Guarantee Department* [2000] 1 AC 486, 499–500. Hazel Carty, 'Joint Tortfeasance and Assistance Liability' (1999) 19 *Legal Studies* 489, also rejects such analogies.

[11] (2008) 169 FCR 169; [2008] FCA 714 [44].

[12] Specific doctrinal differences have led some commentators quite rightly to reject the utility of resorting to criminal law to *flesh out gaps* in the civil law. See, e.g., Mark Bartholomew, 'Cops, Robbers and Search Engines: The Questionable Role of Criminal Law in the Contributory Infringement Doctrine' (2009) 4 *Brigham Young University Law Review* 783, 785, discussing intellectual property and patents law: 'Contributory infringement and its criminal law counterpart . . . have evolved in different directions because they are animated by different principles.' Nonetheless, Bartholomew accepts that criminal law 'offers insights into the current functioning and normative goals of contributory infringement law'.

law, however, is necessary in order to identify common problems that arise and the concepts that may be useful in resolving those problems,[13] and without which one cannot determine whether reasoning by analogy is justified or not. For example, two conceptual difficulties observable both in criminal and civil law concern, first, the determinative role of knowledge in establishing liability (particularly, the question of what, precisely, A must know – the content of knowledge – to establish liability); and secondly, whether A can be liable, where PO or PW is not, or for different offences or remedies than PO or PW, respectively.

There are, of course, specific doctrinal differences between criminal and civil accessory liability (as, indeed, there are between different areas of civil law). But differences ought not to be overstated, either; they need not always be matters of substance, but rather may be matters of terminology. In particular, the criminal origins of tort law have been stressed in numerous cases, and it has been stated by the courts that those two areas of law are 'greatly intermingled' so that there is no 'sharp cleavage' between the public policy of two areas.[14]

To conclude, it is justifiable to look to the criminal law in a book about private law liability. Where relevant, significant similarities and differences in approach between criminal and (all or some areas of) civil law will be noted. Our purpose in considering criminal law is a limited one of highlighting the key concepts utilised to resolve questions of accessory liability, as well as to distinguish accessory liability from other forms of liability.

[13] Similarly, see Eva Lomnicka, '"Knowingly concerned"? Participatory liability to regulators' (2000) 21(4) *Company Lawyer* 120, 123, who considers civil statutory provisions that use the concept of 'knowingly concerned'. She concludes that, given the civil context, 'it would seem that criminal law approaches are unlikely to be regarded as the more helpful in interpreting "knowingly concerned". But it would be too narrow an attitude to ignore completely this vast body of case law ... [particularly since] criminal liability may arise concurrently when the underlying wrongdoing (which gives rise to the regulatory liability at issue) is itself criminal ... [so that] the parallels ... will be obvious and ... relevant.'

[14] See *Gray* v. *Motor Accident Commission* [1998] HCA 70; (1998) 196 CLR 1, 7–8 [16] (Gleeson CJ, McHugh, Gummow and Hayne JJ) (and see also at 5–6 [8]–[12]), approving statements of Windeyer J in *Uren* v. *John Fairfax & Sons Pty Ltd* (1966) 117 CLR 118, 149–150. Admittedly, those statements were made in the context of the availability of exemplary damages for torts. Those sentiments are not limited to that context; however, see e.g., *Regie Nationale Des Usines Renault SA* v. *Zhang* [2002] HCA 10; (2002) 210 CLR 491, 510–511 [46].

4.2 Overview of criminal law accessories

Notwithstanding its ancient origins, the liability of an accessory for a crime committed by another[15] remains 'one of the most uncertain and controversial fields of legal doctrine'.[16] The uncertainty in the law is all the more problematic given the serious consequences of being held criminally responsible as an accessory: for example, a party who assists another to commit grievous bodily harm (gbh) in a minor way, perhaps even hoping that the other fails in her endeavour, may be found guilty of murder.[17]

An accessory[18] in criminal law is someone who has not committed the acts that constitute the offence, the *actus reus*,[19] but is held criminally responsible *as if* A had committed that offence,[20] because A was a party to a joint enterprise to commit the offence, or otherwise encouraged, assisted or participated in the offence committed by PO or POs.[21] Three elements – conduct, intention and knowledge – must exist [4.4]. If these elements are satisfied, it is necessary to consider the principal offence that PO has committed with A's involvement and knowledge, and whether A may be held criminally responsible for a 'greater' or 'lesser' offence, or for further offences that PO has committed [4.5].

An accessory's criminal responsibility is said to be derivative or parasitic in nature.[22] Such terms are misleading, however, to the extent that

[15] We have drawn significantly on a collaborative piece of one of the authors: J. Dietrich and M. Barrett, 'The Knowledge Element for Accessories to Strict Liability and Limited Cognition Offences: Revisiting *Tabe* v. *The Queen*' (2014) 38 *Criminal Law Journal* 197.

[16] A. Simester, 'The Mental Element in Complicity' (2006) 122 *Law Quarterly Review* 578, 578.

[17] See, e.g., The Bureau of Investigative Journalism, Report, *Joint Enterprise: An investigation into the legal doctrine of joint enterprise in criminal convictions* (2014) highlighting some of the anomalies in outcomes, the potential arbitrariness and injustice of some decisions, and the uncertainties in UK law. The report is available at www.thebureauinvestigates.com.

[18] The label 'accessory' is also applied to 'accessories after the fact' who are not true accessories as described here, see below.

[19] Or, at the very least, it is not provable that A has committed such acts.

[20] In some circumstances, A may be liable for a different offence to that committed by PO, albeit constituted by the same conduct elements, e.g., if A has a different mental state to PO. See [4.5].

[21] *Cf.* in the US, *Rosemond* v. *US* 575 US 1, 5 (2014): 'a person may be responsible for a crime he has not personally carried out if he helps another to complete its commission'.

[22] K. J. M. Smith, *A Modern Treatise on the Law of Criminal Complicity* (Oxford, Clarendon Press, 1991) 3.

they imply the attribution of PO's liability to A; that is, that the liability of A is identical and 'duplicative'.[23] An accessory does not have PO's criminal responsibility attributed to him. Instead, A's responsibility is *dependent* on PO having committed the offence and A having assisted or encouraged that commission.[24] The principle of derivation is therefore primarily concerned with the physical or *actus reus* requirements of an offence. And since A need not be held responsible for the *same* offence [4.5], his liability is not *duplicative* of PO's liability.

In the UK,[25] general accessory liability (outside specific legislative provisions) is based on Section 8 of the Accessories and Abettors Act 1861.[26] This section provides that a person who shall 'aid, abet, counsel, or procure the commission of any indictable offence . . . shall be liable . . . as a principal offender'.[27] The section incorporates common law concepts and the interpretation and meaning of those terms is therefore

[23] Sandford H. Kadish, 'Complicity, Cause and Blame: A Study in the Interpretation of Doctrine' (1985) 73 *California Law Review* 323, 349. As Neha Jain, *Perpetrators and Accessories in International Criminal Law: Individual Modes of Responsibility for Collective Crimes* (Oxford, Hart Publishing, 2014) 104–108, notes, however, broader derivative theory focuses on the 'objectively harmful wrong perpetrated' by PO, rather than the specific crime committed such that even on that theory, A need not be found guilty of the identical offence. In any case, 'derivative' theory (duplicative theory in our terminology) does not reflect the outcomes of criminal law (see [4.5] and [4.4.3]) and is challenged by commentators. See Jain's summary, 155–158. As Jain points out, in criminal law there are at least three different rationales that explain the accessory's liability for criminal prosecution, even despite the independently causal decision of PO to commit the offence. Two of these, either that A made *some* causal contribution to the crime, or that the actions of PO are attributed to A on the basis of some agency notions (a sort of fictional deemed agency) command little support among criminal law theorists or the courts. The theory that has been widely accepted is that A's independently wrongful conduct enhances *the risk* of wrongdoing occurring in general, and therefore endangers potential victims. As Jain has concluded in that context (at 157):

> The liability of the accessory no longer flows from his contribution to the offence committed by the primary party but is contingent on his own conduct towards the offence he intended or contemplated. This suggests a move towards a risk or endangerment rationale for accessorial responsibility.

[24] Kadish, 'Complicity', 349.

[25] We have placed significant reliance on David Ormerod, *Smith and Hogan's Criminal Law*, 13th edn (Oxford University Press, 2011), and Justice Hooper and David Ormerod (Gen. Eds) *Blackstone's Criminal Practice* 2012 edn (Oxford University Press) in our summary of English law in this section.

[26] As amended by the Criminal Law Act 1977.

[27] See also Magistrates' Courts Act 1980, s. 44.

determined by common law.[28] In essence, the inquiry is whether A knowingly and intentionally assisted or encouraged PO's crime.[29]

In Australia, there is no uniformly applicable criminal law. The Commonwealth Criminal Code deals with some criminal offences, but most criminal law falls within state and territory jurisdiction. The law in the majority of states and territories is codified (though not uniformly) but the criminal law in New South Wales, South Australia and Victoria is based on common law, albeit with extensive additions contained in legislation.

Given the complexity of the law concerning criminal accessory liability, it is neither practical nor necessary for current purposes to set out for each jurisdiction the detailed statutory sections or common law rules. Instead, this chapter provides a broad overview of the key concepts and the essential principles upon which accessories are held criminally responsible for the purposes of comparison and possible illumination of the civil law position.

4.3 Principal offender or accessory?

Pursuant to section 8 of the Accessories and Abettors Act 1861, accessories may be held criminally responsible *as* a PO, that is, as *if* they had committed the offence themselves. Similarly, statutory provisions in each of the Australian jurisdictions ensure that accessories are tried and punished as POs;[30] in short, they are deemed to be murderers, burglars, etc. This does not mean that the distinction between principals and accessories is somehow obsolete. It 'is still necessary to distinguish between different modes of participation in crime',[31] since the liability

[28] See *R* v. *Gnango* [2011] UKSC 59; [2011] UKSC 59; [2012] 1 AC 827 [13]; and J.C. Smith, 'Aid, Abet, Counsel, or Procure', in R. Glazebrook (ed.), *Reshaping the Criminal Law: Essays in Honour of Glanville Williams* (London, Stevens & Sons, 1978) 125. For an extensive and detailed summary of the English law, see Law Commission Report No. 305, *Participating in Crime* (2007) Part 2 and Appendix B.

[29] Complex provisions of the Serious Crime Act 2007, dealing with 'encouragement and assistance', are not considered here since those offences are, for the most part, inchoate. There is some overlap with accessory liability, however, see, e.g., s. 49(1). For detailed consideration, see R. Fortson, *Blackstone's Guide to the Serious Crime Act 2007* (Oxford University Press, 2008) Ch. 6, and D. Ormerod and R. Fortson, 'Serious Crime Act 2007: The Part 2 Offences' (2009) *Criminal Law Review* 389.

[30] See, e.g., Criminal Code 1995 (Cth) s. 11.2, Crimes Act 1990 (NSW) s. 346, Criminal Code 1899 (Qld) s. 7, Criminal Law Consolidation Act 1935 (SA) s. 267, and Criminal Code Act 1924 (Tas) s. 3, Crimes Act 1958 (Vic) s. 323, and Criminal Code 1913 (WA) s. 7.

[31] J. C. Smith, 'Aid', 121.

of A is proven on a different basis and perhaps on different evidence than is the liability of PO, namely that A assisted, etc., PO.[32] In the words of Darling J, '[a]n accessory does not cease to be an accessory although he may be charged as a principal'.[33]

Nonetheless, confusion in labelling is rife in this area of the law. At common law in Australia, a person who is at the scene of the crime pursuant to an express or tacit agreement to commit an offence – a joint enterprise or a common purpose – is prosecuted and described as a *joint* PO where a crime is committed by another pursuant to that common purpose (for example, to murder X).[34] Even on this approach, however, it can be argued that liability is still accessorial, even if not clearly articulated as such. If only PO has committed the acts that constitute the crime (the *actus reus*) pursuant to a common purpose or agreement, it is artificial to say that the other party to the plan (A) is liable on exactly the same conceptual basis as PO. For example, unlike PO, A must be shown to be a party to a common purpose. It should be added that even on this approach, if A is charged on the basis of merely assisting or encouraging a crime and not as part of a joint enterprise, then A is always liable as an accessory and not as a joint principal.

The Australian common law approach has been rejected in English common law[35] and under the State ('Griffith') Code jurisdictions in Australia.[36] There, parties are only joint principals if they have each

[32] Such assistance etc. may be as a party to an agreed joint enterprise with PO.

[33] *Gould & Co. Ltd* v. *Houghton* [1921] 1 KB 509, 522.

[34] See *Osland* v. *The Queen* [1998] HCA 75; (1998) 197 CLR 316, 342, and *Lowery* v. *King (No 2)* [1972] VR 560, 560. This form of responsibility is also referred to as acting in concert (or 'joint commission': Criminal Code 1995 (Cth) s. 11.2A(1)(a)(i) and (2)). One plausible justification for the common law approach is that it avoids difficulties of proof that would otherwise exist in the not uncommon situation where it is not possible to prove which party was the PO and which was the A, by ensuring that all present and involved at the scene of the crime are convicted as POs. This problem can be avoided by other means, see n. 36 below.

[35] See Ormerod, *Smith and Hogan's*, 190.

[36] For convenience, the Code jurisdictions are collectively encompassed by the label 'Griffith Code'. Under the Griffith Code, criminal responsibility (as joint principals) based on acting in concert has been rejected as common law 'heresy': *R* v. *Sherrington and Kuchler* [2001] QCA 105 [11] and [139]. Consequently, a person who commits the elements of the offence can be convicted as a PO while participants who do not commit all the elements of the offence but who assist or encourage at the scene, whether as parties to an agreement or not, must be convicted as accessories (see also *R* v. *Graham and Alliston* [2011] QCA 187). The problem of proof of who is the PO has been avoided, as the courts do not always require identification of any PO where it is not possible to prove who committed the elements of the offence, e.g., where several people engage in a fight in which one

contributed by their own acts, 'as distinct from anything done by [PO] with [A's] advice or assistance', to the *actus reus*.[37] The English approach is preferable because labels do matter: it is preferable to call an accessory an accessory and not a joint principal.

The English approach has been made less certain, however, by the decision of *R* v. *Gnango*[38] in which President Lord Brown and Lord Clark (of the majority) considered that a joint principal approach was open on the basis of the existence of a joint enterprise.[39] The other majority judges, Lords Phillips, Judge and Wilson, applied the more orthodox accessory analysis: where a crime is committed by PO pursuant to a joint enterprise, other parties to the enterprise are liable as accessories for 'aiding' and 'abetting' the acts done pursuant to that joint enterprise. However, their Lordships endorsed the view that 'the distinction between a joint principal and an abettor is sometimes difficult, and unnecessary, to draw'[40] and they considered that the difference in approach 'is not a difference of substance'.[41]

This is not correct for the reasons already noted. Further, it is analytically important to distinguish accessories from genuine (joint) POs who have contributed to the commission of the conduct elements of an offence. For example, in *R* v. *Kennedy (No 2)*,[42] the House of Lords held that preparing and supplying (but not administering) a loaded

(unknown) party delivers a fatal knife wound. Therefore, a point of difference between the Code and English common law on the one hand, and Australian common law on the other, is that on such identical facts, two or more individuals would under the latter be prosecuted as POs, whereas under the former they would be convicted as accessories without the necessity that anyone be convicted as a PO.

37 Ormerod, *Smith and Hogan's*, 190. See also Lord Kerr (in dissent on the facts) in *R* v. *Gnango* [2011] UKSC 59; [2012] 1 AC 827 [129]: joint principal must contribute 'to the cause of the actus reus'. Even though a joint enterprise may be readily found, so that even two parties acting together to commit the same offence, e.g., to beat V, can be deemed to be engaged in a joint enterprise that can be inferred from their conduct, such conduct is an example of accessory liability and subject to the same principles: *R* v. *Mendez and Thompson* [2010] EWCA Crim 516.

38 [2011] UKSC 59; [2012] 1 AC 827.

39 *Ibid.* [69]–[71], [81]. Lord Kerr (in dissent) strongly disagreed and re-affirmed the English orthodoxy: *ibid.* [127]–[130].

40 [2011] UKSC 59; [2012] 1 AC 827 [62]. They cite *Archbold: Criminal Pleading, Evidence and Practice*, 2011 edn, (UK, Sweet & Maxwell) [18.6]. *Cf.* Lord Dyson at [104]–[105].

41 *Ibid.* [62]. Interestingly, since in *Gnango* the joint enterprise was to be shot at, A was held to be an accessory to the crime to cause serious injury or death *to himself*, albeit he was held liable for the accidental shooting of V, on the basis of transferred malice. The case was not one for extended parasitic accessory liability, discussed in [4.5.2].

42 [2008] 1 AC 269. See also, e.g., *Burns* v. *R* [2012] HCA 35; (2012) 246 CLR 334.

drug syringe to another was not the cause of that other's death from overdose, such as to render the accused liable for manslaughter. The accused had not contributed to the act that led to the deceased's death and was not a joint principal; further, since negligently killing oneself by injection is not a crime, the accused could not be held liable as an accessory since no principal offence had been committed at all.[43] Absent the commission of a principal offence, there can be no accessorial involvement.

This does not mean, however, that the prosecution always needs to prove who PO was. As long as an offence was committed and the accused was in some way involved in that offence,[44] the prosecution may proceed by charging *all* members of a group as accessories (the English common law and Griffith Code approach).[45] A may be found liable even if it is not provable who committed the offence as principal (perhaps even A did so).

Accessory liability must also be distinguished from attempts, conspiracy and incitement,[46] collectively referred to as inchoate offences,[47] and from accessories after the fact. Criminal responsibility for inchoate offences is based on an accused's conduct in agreeing to, encouraging or taking action towards, the commission of a substantive offence. Unlike accessory liability, however, an inchoate offence does not require proof that the offence was committed[48] and it generally does not result in a conviction for the commission of the substantive offence.[49] Accessories after the fact likewise commit a separate offence and are not convicted of the original substantive offence. Their conviction is not based on assisting in PO's offence but helping PO to escape punishment. Therefore,

43 These principles do not necessarily translate to all private law wrongs. It depends upon how the elements of the wrong are formulated and understood. If the accused in *Kennedy* [2008] 1 AC 269 had been sued in the tort of negligence, then one would conclude that his acts were a cause of the death, whereas if he was sued in trespass, we would conclude that no trespass occurred and therefore the death was not caused by that wrong.

44 See, e.g., *R* v. *Giannetto* [1997] 1 Cr App R 1 (CA); *Likiardopoulos* v. *R* [2012] HCA 37; (2012) 247 CLR 265; Ormerod, *Smith and Hogan's,* 185–186.

45 See above, nn. 34 and 36. In Australian common law, as noted, members of the group would all be charged as joint principals.

46 Incitement has been abolished in the UK and replaced by the specific offences contained in the Serious Crime Act 2007. It is an inchoate offence in all Australian jurisdictions except Queensland.

47 Smith, *Complicity*, 8, refers to such forms of liability as being genealogically, operationally and in appearance related to accessory liability.

48 Ormerod, *Smith and Hogan's*, 186.

49 There are, however, statutory exceptions to this, e.g., s. 245 of the Criminal Code 1899 (Qld).

inchoate and 'accessory after the fact' offences lack the derivative characteristic of accessory liability. Of course, if a conspiracy is carried into effect, the parties to that conspiracy may also be liable as accessories to the substantive offences committed.[50] Since civil law does not recognise inchoate wrongs such as attempts or conspiracies (that are not carried into effect) they are not further considered here.

4.4 Elements of accessory liability

4.4.1 Conduct

In order for A to be found criminally responsible, A must be 'linked in purpose with the person actually committing the crime', such that his 'words or conduct [do] something to bring about, or [render] more likely' the commission of the offence.[51] This is a low threshold test. This element is concerned with identifying conduct at the time, or before, the offence is committed or completed, that in some way involves A in PO's offence, such as by assisting or encouraging PO in those acts, inciting them, etc. A need not assist in every conduct element of the offence.[52]

The law uses a variety of terms to describe the nature of the assistance or involvement in the crime (the precise terminology depends on the jurisdiction). Recurring, however, are terms such as 'aid', 'abet' or 'enables', and 'counsel', 'procure'[53] or 'instigates'. For the purpose of

[50] It is possible to be an accessory to an inchoate offence. E.g., in Canada a person may aid and abet a conspiracy. See *JF* v. *R* [2013] SCC 12; [2013] 1 SCR 565. This is a concept of limited utility, however. Since membership of a conspiracy can be inferred by conduct, there would appear to be little need for such a remote source of criminal responsibility, though see the US example cited at [41] (A brings parties together to allow them to reach agreement, to conspire, without A's participation in that conspiracy). Nonetheless, liability as accessories to inchoate offences is a plausible source of responsibility in English law (see J. C. Smith, 'Secondary participation and inchoate offences' in *Crime, Proof and Punishment* (London, Butterworths, 1981) 21, 28–29; Ormerod, *Smith and Hogan's*, 187), and under legislation in some Griffith Code states in Australia.

[51] *R* v. *Russell* [1933] VLR 59, 67, per Cussen ACJ, approved by Gibbs CJ and Mason J in *Giorgianni* v. *R* (1985) 156 CLR 473, 480, 493. A must act for the purpose of making the commission of the offence more likely. Accordingly (with the possible exception of where A has procured another), it is not necessary to prove that A's actions had the desired effect (see *Howell* v. *Doyle* [1952] VLR 128, 144 and *R* v. *B, EG; R* v. *S, BD* [2012] SASC 157 [30], and see Smith, *Complicity*, Ch. 3 on the role of causation in accessory liability).

[52] See *Rosemond* v. *US*, 575 US 1, 7–8 (2014): A can be convicted as aider and abettor without proof that A 'participated in each and every element of the offence'. But A must intend to facilitate the whole crime, that is, with knowledge of all essential elements.

[53] See Accessories and Abettors Act 1861 s. 8; Criminal Code 1995 (Cth) s. 11.2; Criminal Code 2002 (ACT) s. 45; Crimes Act 1900 (NSW) s. 351B; Criminal Law Consolidation Act

describing the relevant events, the courts often distinguish between those involved before the fact and those involved at the facts but there is little or no distinction between these various forms of involvement in terms of the fault element or the offence for which A can be convicted. Indeed, it is not unusual for a case to consider evidence of more than one, if not all, of the bases of involvement, or for courts to use the shorthand 'assist' or 'encourage'. For the most part, then, courts have not distinguished between the meanings of the individual terms, which are often used interchangeably.[54] In some cases, however, judges have sought to define individual terms, in particular as to the meaning of 'procure'.[55]

With the exception of procuring, A's relevant acts need not be shown to be causative – whether a 'but for' cause or otherwise – of the offence, or PO's decision to commit the offence.[56] Indeed, aiding does not even require a consensus between A and PO, since PO may not even be aware of the assistance A gives (for example, by stopping a police officer from intervening to prevent the crime).[57] Unlike the other forms of

1935 (SA) s. 267; and Crimes Act 1958 (Vic) s. 323, all retaining the common law terms of aid and abet, and counsel or procure. Other Australian jurisdictions adopt very similar language, but use the word 'enables' rather than 'abets'. See Criminal Code Act 1983 (NT) s. 12; Criminal Code 1899 (Qld) s. 7; and Criminal Code 1913 (WA) s. 7.

[54] See, e.g., J. C. Smith, 'Aid', 125, and *Tabe* v. *R* [2005] HCA 59; (2005) 225 CLR 418 [93] (Hayne J) and [151] (Callinan and Heydon JJ), and *R* v. *Graham and Alliston* [2011] QCA 187 [31], where the term 'abetted' or 'abetter' is used in reference to the Criminal Code 1899 (Qld) even though the term is not used in the Code. *R* v. *Russell* [1933] VLR 59, 67 (Cussen ACJ), approved in *Giorgianni* v. *R* (1985) 156 CLR 473, 480 (Gibbs CJ); 493 (Mason J). Stephen Odgers, *Principles of Federal Criminal Law*, 2nd edn (Australia, Thomson Reuters, 2010) 163, argues that the terms 'should be considered as a compendious phrase, descriptive of a single concept'. The lack of concern for differences in language can be attributed to the fact that the statutory language is declaratory of the common law, see, e.g., *Wyles; Ex parte A-G* [1977] Qd R 169, 175–176.

[55] See, e.g., *AG's Reference (No. 1 of 1975)* [1975] QB 773, 779.

[56] See, e.g., *R* v. *Kennedy (No. 2)* [2007] UKHL 38; [2008] Crim LR 223 [17]; Ormerod, *Smith and Hogan's*, 194; *R* v. *Luffmann* [2008] EWCA Crim 1752. E.g., A may assist while PO has already started to commit the offence. Even where A is responsible for PO's decision to commit the offence, A is not considered to have caused the criminal conduct, given the intervening cause of PO's independent decision to commit the crime. See Andrew Ashworth, *Principles of Criminal Law*, 6th edn (Oxford University Press, 2009) 105–111. If, however, 'A' has personally caused the *actus reus* of the principal offence, then 'A' is a PO.

[57] Ormerod, *Smith and Hogan's*, 192; J. C. Smith, 'Aid', 133–134, but contra Fortson, *Blackstone's*, 65, relying on *Attorney-General's Reference (No 1 of 1975)* [1975] 1 QB 773, 779, without any analysis of the issue. Procuring, like aiding, does not necessarily require consensus with PO, and therefore in *AG's Reference*, A was held liable for PO's act of drink-driving even though PO may not have been aware of having had his drink spiked by A.

conduct, however, procuring does suggest some success in achieving the outcome: 'To procure means to produce by endeavour. You procure a thing by setting out to see that it happens and taking the appropriate steps to produce that happening.'[58]

Finally, and to simplify, an *omission* may amount to a sufficient act of encouragement of unlawful conduct if A has a duty to act, or has a right *and* capacity/power to control the actions of PO and deliberately refrains from exercising the power, in circumstances where such inactivity amounts to encouragement.[59] Absent such duty/power, mere passive presence alone generally does not suffice, unless perhaps done in a deliberate way so as to encourage the illegal activity, for example, by attending an organised illegal event, with foreknowledge, and remaining for some time.[60]

4.4.2 *Intention*

A's encouragement or assistance must be intentional.[61] This concept is closely related to knowledge. It is not possible to intend to assist or encourage in the absence of knowledge of PO's plan, and knowledge without intent to assist, etc., is not culpable. Therefore, a person who has knowledge of PO's plan to commit an offence and who takes action intended to defeat the plan has not encouraged or assisted PO even if the person's actions have the opposite effect to that intended. Nonetheless, 'intention' generally only requires *deliberate* conduct by A with knowledge, not that A intends that PO be successful in committing the crime.[62] A may be liable even if indifferent to that outcome's success,

[58] *Attorney-General's Reference (No 1 of 1975)* [1975] 1 QB 773, 779 (Lord Widgery CJ). See also *R* v. *Menniti* [1985] 1 Qd R 520, 532.

[59] See *Blackstone's*, 78 [A4.13]; contrast Ormerod, *Smith and Hogan's*, 197, 'power *or* right to control', which statement is problematic since a mere power without any lawful right to exercise it probably does not suffice.

[60] *Cf. R* v. *Coney* (1882) 8 QBD 534 (mere presence at an illegal prize fight insufficient to amount to aiding or abetting, absent further evidence).

[61] Ormerod, *Smith and Hogan's*, 191. See, e.g., *Johnson* v. *Youden* [1950] 1 KB 544, 546–547. Similarly, in relation to the Code jurisdictions see, e.g., *Wilson* v. *Dobra* (1955) 57 WALR 95, and *R* v. *Beck* [1990] 1 Qd R 30.

[62] In the US, see *Rosemond* v. *United States* 575 US 1, 11 (2014), quoting Learned Hand J in *United States* v. *Peoni*, 100 F2d 401, 402 (2d Cir, 1938): intention requires that A participate in the venture 'as something that he wishes to bring about [and] seek by his actions to make succeed'. However, that intent requirement is satisfied 'when a person actively participates in a criminal venture with full knowledge of the circumstances constituting the charged offence'. (*Rosemond*, 11–12).

or even if preferring that PO were not to succeed.[63] In short, A need only act consciously, in a way that A knows will assist PO, that is, for the purpose of aiding, etc.

Stating the element in this way does mean, however, that seemingly innocent conduct may give rise to criminal responsibility.[64] As Duff notes, not all persons consciously providing assistance that they know may facilitate an offence ought to be held liable as accessories:[65] for example, the doctor who supplies contraceptives to a minor, thereby facilitating an unlawful carnal knowledge offence against that minor.[66] Duff concludes that conscious conduct by A that A knows will facilitate the commission of an offence should not *always* suffice for liability, but nor should it *never* suffice. Duff considers that the law might adopt presumptions either for or against liability, and then indicate factors that support or militate against such liability.[67]

Leaving aside the issue of whether and when conscious assistance or encouragement should suffice, to summarise: even though courts formulate liability in terms of intention, intent is essentially a requirement of

[63] See, e.g., *National Coal Board* v. *Gamble* [1959] 1 QB 11; *Rosemond* v. *US*, 575 US 1, 15 (2014) (the law does not care whether A participates 'with a happy heart or a sense of foreboding'); *R* v. *Beck* [1990] 1 Qd R 30.

[64] See, e.g., Fortson, *Blackstone's* [A4.4] 68.

[65] R. A. Duff, '"Can I help you?" Accessorial liability and the intention to assist' (1990) 10 *Legal Studies* 165. *National Coal Board* v. *Gamble* [1959] 1 QB 11 is an example of a decision that is open to criticism for imposing responsibility on too broad a basis.

[66] *Cf. Gillick* v. *W Norfolk & Wisbech Area Health Authority* [1986] 1 AC 112, such doctor if acting bona fide in clinical judgment is not (190, Lord Scarman, 194, Lord Bridge of Harwich) or is unlikely to be (174–175, Lord Fraser of Tullybelton) an accessory to the commission of an offence. Consider also the example left open in *Rosemond* v. *US*, 575 US 1, 12 (2014) n. 8, of someone who 'incidentally facilitates a criminal venture rather than actively participates in it', such as where a gun shop owner sells firearms to a criminal, 'knowing but not caring how the gun will be used'.

[67] Duff, 'Can I help you?', particularly at 177. One factor that Duff does not allude to, that seems critical to criminal liability where A acts consciously with knowledge, is how detailed and specific A's knowledge is about the 'who, what, where, and when' of an offence. To take the doctor example: obviously there are mitigating policy factors against such doctor being liable, e.g., that a doctor is exercising bona fide clinical judgment; and the fact that the patient is herself the likely 'willing' victim of the offence and cannot be a perpetrator: *Gillick* v. *W Norfolk & Wisbech Area Health Authority* [1986] 1 AC 112, 174–175 (Lord Fraser of Tullybelton). Putting those aside, however, such a doctor is also unlikely to have *specific* knowledge about any likely sexual offence that is to be committed against the young patient. If, however, a doctor were at the scene of a prospective unlawful carnal knowledge, and handed the male perpetrator a condom, then such doctor probably ought to be liable. Similarly, a shopkeeper who sells tools capable of use for break and entry to a known burglar ought generally not to be held liable, but we might conclude otherwise if PO has confided in the shopkeeper the details of the proposed heist.

conscious conduct – in the sense of awareness by A that A's conduct assists – which conscious conduct is done with knowledge of PO's planned or intended offence. Knowledge is critical.

4.4.3 *Knowledge*

Given the limited role of intention, the key element that must be proven against A apart from a conduct link is that he must have knowledge of the 'essential matters of the offence'[68] (and see [3.4.2.2]). In other words, A must know of the facts and circumstances that make PO's conduct criminal, though not necessarily all the details of the offence and information pertaining to it. It is not necessary that A know that what is to transpire is proscribed by law (since ignorance of the law is no excuse); however, A must know of the specific aspects of PO's intended conduct that renders her activity unlawful.[69] This means that the essential matters may require A to know PO's mental state (*mens rea*) if that is an element of the offence. Although the term 'essential matters' is inherently vague,[70] such vagueness is in part an unavoidable product of the essentially fact-based nature of the inquiry.

A's culpable involvement in PO's conduct must be with sufficient knowledge of the essential matters going to the offence. This is a question of how to characterise the conduct of PO or, in the language of the courts, what are the essential matters? This requires consideration of what PO did or intended to do. In some cases, this involves a simple reference to *unlawful* behaviour, for example, that PO stabbed the victim. The result of such behaviour, although determinative of the offence for which A (and PO) are charged, is not necessarily an essential matter.[71] In other

[68] The leading authority is *Johnson* v. *Youden* [1950] 1 KB 544, 546, where Goddard LJ stated that an aider or abettor 'must at least know the essential matters which constitute the offence'. See also *Giorgianni* v. *R* (1985) 156 CLR 473, 487–488 (Gibbs CJ), 494 (Mason J), 503 (Wilson, Deane and Dawson JJ), and *R* v. *Jeffrey* [2003] 2 Qd R 306, 310, and *R* v. *Jervis* [1993] 1 Qd R 643, 648.

[69] *Giorgianni* v. *R* (1985) 156 CLR 473, 480 (Gibbs CJ), 500–501 (Wilson, Deane and Dawson JJ). In *Johnson* v. *Youden* [1950] 1 KB 544, 546, Lord Goddard CJ stated that an accessory 'need not actually know that an offence has been committed, because he may not know that the facts constitute an offence and ignorance of the law is not a defence'.

[70] See Brent Fisse, *Howard's Criminal Law*, 5th edn (Australia, Thomson Reuters, 1990) 336, who accordingly advocates for rules that make it unnecessary to consider the essential matters of an offence; and see Simon Bronitt, 'Defending Giorgianni – Part One: The Fault Requirement For Complicity' (1993) 17 *Criminal Law Journal* 242, 254–256.

[71] To convict A of manslaughter it is not necessary to prove that A knew that the result of PO's act of stabbing would be death. If such knowledge existed, then A would be guilty of

cases, it is necessary additionally to refer to a prescribed circumstance, and/or prescribed mental element and/or prescribed result, for example, robbery when armed with a dangerous weapon (rather than 'robbery'). In that respect, the offence committed by PO dictates the characterisation of the behaviour that A is said to have encouraged or assisted, etc. The behaviour, however, is not simply the elements of the offence, but rather the essential facts that constitute the offence.

Although the requirement is put in terms of A's actual 'knowledge' of essential elements, this can be misleading. 'Knowledge' here refers both to existing facts, but also refers to what A can be said to know – in the sense of being able to predict – about the likelihood of a future event, namely that an offence will or might be committed.[72] It suffices if A actually knows that PO *might* do certain acts (or with a certain state of mind) when A assists, encourages, etc.[73] There need not be any certainty about that outcome.

The prosecution need not prove that A knew the precise nature of PO's criminal intent, but nor does it suffice that A merely knows that PO is to engage in some form of criminal conduct. For example, A cannot be convicted of aiding in the possession of a dangerous drug,

murder not manslaughter. Similarly, to convict A of dangerous driving causing death, the Crown need only prove that A assisted or encouraged PO in dangerous driving and accordingly it is not required to prove knowledge by A of the death. See *R* v. *Millward* [1994] *Criminal Law Review* 527 (CA), *Giorgianni* v. *R* (1985) 156 CLR 473, and *R* v. *Jervis* [1993] 1 Qd R 643, 650.

72 *Cf.* Ormerod, *Smith and Hogan's*, 206–208: know 'in practical terms means foresee'; realising the possibility suffices; A must merely foresee the likelihood of the essential matters.

73 See, e.g., *R* v. *Gnango* [2011] UKSC 59; [2012] 1 AC 827 [14] (realising crime 'may' be committed; foresees that PO might carry out offence); *R* v. *Hyde* [1991] 1 QB 134 (CA) (A need not tacitly agree to that outcome, but merely contemplate it); *R* v. *Powell: R* v. *English* AC [1999] 1 AC 1, 27 (Lord Hutton: sufficient if A realised that PO *might* act with certain intention etc.; i.e., it need only be possible, not probable). Although this language is particularly widespread in the context of extended, 'parasitic accessorial liability' arising from a joint enterprise, it is clear, however, particularly from *Hyde*, that this low-level predictability requirement is not limited to where A acts under an actual agreement with PO. In other words, it is not limited to common purpose cases, but applies equally to cases involving mere assistance and encouragement. See Fortson, *Blackstone's*, 70–71 [A4.6], and *Hui Chi-ming* v. *R* [1992] 1 AC 34 (PC). A is liable if A *assists* PO, merely contemplating the possibility that PO might commit the offence; it need not be certain that PO will commit the offence. One might therefore tentatively suggest that extended parasitic liability [4.5.2] is largely an unnecessary concept: A will be liable, irrespective of whether within or outside a joint enterprise, for the possible consequences when involving himself in PO's venture. Indeed, if anything, the terms of any joint enterprise may be a means of *limiting* A's liability, if certain conduct was precluded.

merely because A knew PO possessed something that is illegal to possess, such as counterfeit coins or an unlicensed firearm. To hold otherwise would be inconsistent with the decisions that limit A's responsibility to offences of the same type or that were actually contemplated by A.[74] Nonetheless, determining the 'essential matters' is problematic where there is some uncertainty from the outset about the specific offence that PO will commit, such that it may be difficult to pin down in what offence A has involved himself. In *R* v. *Bainbridge*,[75] the English Court of Appeal held that A must be proven to have known of the *type* of crime intended to be committed by PO. It was not sufficient that he knew that the equipment that A had sold to PO would be used for some kind of unspecified illegal activity. It was not necessary, however, that A knew of the precise details of the offence. In *Bainbridge*, A had sold oxygen cutting equipment to PO who used it six weeks later to break into a bank. The court held that if the Crown established that A knew that the equipment might be used to commit break and enter and theft, the fact that he did not know details such as the precise bank was not an impediment to A's liability.[76]

The exact limits of decisions such as *Bainbridge* remain unclear. The courts have not provided clear guidance as to how to identify the essential matters that A must know in order to determine whether the offence committed also included the same essential matters and therefore was the same *type* of offence. The question could be formulated in this way: given what A knows about the essential matters of PO's conduct and intentions (that is, the elements of the offence), what are the range of offences caught by those essential matters that PO might realistically (as opposed to, say, fancifully) commit; and does the offence PO actually committed fall within that range?[77]

[74] It would also undermine the joint enterprise/common purpose doctrine because it would render its requirements redundant.

[75] (1960) 1 QB 129.

[76] A had maintained that he thought the equipment may be used for some illegal purpose such as melting down stolen goods. *Bainbridge* was followed in the Queensland case of *R* v. *Ancuta* [1991] 2 Qd R 413, 418: the Crown need not prove that the aider knew precisely which offence was to be committed, but it was not sufficient simply to prove that A knew that some illegal activity was to be committed. A's conviction for aiding in the unlawful possession of a motor vehicle was upheld where A handed over vehicle compliance plates knowing that PO intended to use them to commit an offence related to motor vehicles. A knew of the *type* of offence actually committed, even absent A's knowledge that PO would attach the plates to stolen vehicles.

[77] *Cf. DPP for Northern Ireland* v. *Maxwell* [1978] 3 All ER 1140. In Barrett and Dietrich, 'The Knowledge Element', this issue was considered within the discussion of extended common purpose liability, but on further reflection, it is an aspect of the knowledge element.

Some commentators and judges have advocated the view that A's *mens rea*, or mental state, must equate to, or be parallel to, the mental state of PO, that is, that A must share the same fault requirement as PO. This view has been diversely labelled as parallelism, equivalence or the link principle.[78] According to this view, A's fault element and the fault element of PO must be equivalent. The courts have categorically rejected this view. To be sure, in many circumstances, A and PO will share the same fault element. But this common factual coexistence should not be transformed into a principle that determines A's criminal responsibility.

One critic of parallelism, Smith, states that the application of the principle in the context of strict liability offences would too broadly cast the net of accessory liability, whereas its application in the context of *mens rea* offences such as murder would produce an overly restricted application of accessory liability.[79] Consistently with Smith's arguments, parallelism for strict liability offences has authoritatively and rightly been rejected by the courts.[80] Absent A's knowledge of the aspects of PO's conduct that render it an offence, no basis for imposing criminal responsibility on A as an accessory arises,[81] even if PO may be held criminally responsible absent such knowledge. Further, as seen in [4.5.1] parallelism has also been rejected for offences requiring *mens rea*.[82]

[78] Competing views in the debate are evidenced by, e.g., Bronitt, 'Defending Giorgianni', 251–252, and Smith, *Complicity*, 5–6, on one side, and on the other, Brent Fisse, 'Complicity in Regulatory Offences' (1968) 6 *Melbourne University Law Review* 278 and Fisse, *Howard's*, 335–337.

[79] Smith, *Complicity*, 5–6. As is noted below, the reason for this conclusion is that where, e.g., A knows that PO intends to kill or cause grievous bodily harm to V, and assists PO in that act, A should be liable as an accessory to murder even if, e.g., PO is not criminally responsible for reasons of insanity (see *Matusevich* v. *R* (1977) 137 CLR 633).

[80] E.g., *Johnson* v. *Youden* [1950] 1 KB 544, *Giorgianni* v. *R* (1985) 156 CLR 473. That is also the prevailing rule in the US: see, e.g., Wayne R. La Fave, *Substantive Criminal Law*, 13.2(c), 2nd edn (Eagan, Thomson/West, 2003), cited by Mark Bartholomew, 'Cops, Robbers and Search Engines: The Questionable Role of Criminal Law in the Contributory Infringement Doctrine' (2009) 4 *Brigham Young University Law Review* 783, 803–804: A must intend to aid proscribed activity, even if PO is liable absent such intent.

[81] This conclusion may be contrary to that reached in the High Court in *Tabe* v. *R* [2005] HCA 59; (2005) 225 CLR 418, albeit a case interpreting specific statutory provisions. In that case, the accused was convicted as an accessory to the offence of possession of a dangerous drug, an offence against s. 9 of the Drugs Misuse Act 1986 (Qld). In that statutory context, it was held that where an intent to commit the acts that constitute the crime, or knowledge of some essential fact, are not necessary elements needing to be proved against PO, then it is also unnecessary to prove such mental state against A. The decision is critiqued in Barrett and Dietrich, 'The Knowledge Element'.

[82] A may be held liable for an offence if A has the requisite *mens rea*, even if PO does not.

4.5 The offences for which the accessory may be liable

4.5.1 Accessory's liability for a different offence to the principal offender

Historically, accessory liability was seen as 'derivative' (meaning duplicative in our terminology [2.6]) and this meant that PO had to be convicted before proceedings could be brought against A in respect of his assistance or encouragement of PO's offence.[83] This rule has been abandoned,[84] such that the criminal responsibility of accessories is no longer dependent on the criminal responsibility of PO. Accordingly, A may be convicted of a lesser offence than PO when that is all that can be established.[85] Historically, it was also argued on the basis of the 'derivative' principle that A could only be convicted of a more serious offence than PO in exceptional circumstances such as where PO could rely on a partial defence to murder of provocation or diminished responsibility that was not available to A.[86] Nowadays, however, there is no rule against A being convicted of a more serious offence than PO.

In 2012, the High Court of Australia in *Likiardopoulos* v. *R* held that A could be convicted as an accessory to murder in circumstances where the Crown had accepted a guilty plea to manslaughter from the POs.[87] In the case against A, the Crown adduced evidence that one or more of the POs had committed murder and, accordingly, A was convicted of encouraging the more serious offence.[88] Although in *Likiardopoulos*,

[83] See *Likiardopoulos* v. *R* [2012] HCA 37; (2012) 247 CLR 265, 274–276 [24]–[26] and S. Bronitt and B. McSherry, *Principles of Criminal Law*, 3rd edn (Australia, Lawbook Co., 2010) 382–384.

[84] *Likiardopoulos* v. *R* [2012] HCA 37; (2012) 247 CLR 265, 274–276 [24]–[26].

[85] E.g., PO will be convicted of murder in circumstances where she intends to kill or, depending on the jurisdiction, intends to inflict grievous bodily harm (e.g., Crimes Act 1900 (NSW) s. 18(1)(a); Criminal Code 1899 (Qld) s. 302(1)(a)) or 'serious harm' (Crimes Act 1900 (ACT) s. 12(1)(c); Criminal Code Act 1983 (NT) s. 156(1)(c)), or 'bodily harm' (Criminal Code Act 1924 (Tas) s. 157(1)(b); Criminal Code 1913 (WA) s. 279(1)(b)). However, A may be convicted only of manslaughter if all that can be proven is that A knowingly encouraged or assisted in the commission of lesser harm. See, e.g., *Brennan* v. *R* (1936) 55 CLR 253, *Kwaku Mensah* v. *R* [1946] AC 83, 91, and *R* v. *Jervis* [1993] 1 Qd R 643, 650.

[86] Fisse, *Howard's*, 325–326. The language of the Criminal Code 1995 (Cth) s. 11.2(1) and the Criminal Code 1983 (NT) s. 43BG(1) suggests that A cannot be convicted of a more serious offence than PO: see Odgers, *Federal Criminal Law*, 166.

[87] [2012] HCA 37; (2012) 247 CLR 265, 275.

[88] *Ibid.* 275 [24], [20] (Gummow, Hayne, Crennan, Kiefel and Bell JJ, with whom French CJ agreed), and 283 [45] where Heydon J stated: 'The key question was thus: was the evidence at the trial of the appellant capable of establishing that the alleged principals committed murder? It was.'

the Crown could prove that the POs had murderous intent,[89] A can also be convicted of the more serious offence if A knows it will occur and assists or encourages its commission, even though PO does not share the fault element for the more serious offence and is therefore convicted of a lesser offence.[90]

An accessory can also be convicted of an offence even where PO is not or cannot be convicted of any offence.[91] The PO could be dead or unknown,[92] or she could be a child or could be insane and therefore not criminally responsible,[93] or PO may not have had the requisite knowledge or awareness that rendered her conduct unlawful.[94] There are different theories as to why this should be so. For example, it has been argued (correctly in our view) that if an offence has objectively been committed, then the person can be liable as an accessory, even if PO has a 'defence' personal to her alone.[95]

[89] The High Court based its decision on all parties to the common purpose being (deemed) joint principals: [2012] HCA 37; (2012) 247 CLR 265 [27]. The High Court did not consider the position where A is liable in the absence of a common purpose, i.e., as a mere accessory: the joint judgment proceeded on the basis that, 'accepting that liability on the accessorial case was purely derivative [i.e., duplicative]', murder had been committed by the POs (and therefore A could be held liable for murder). The same conclusions have been reached in England, however, where the parties are liable as accessories, and not as joint principals. *Cf.* the hypothetical example in *R* v. *Howe* [1987] 1 AC 417, 458; *R* v. *Millward* [1994] *Criminal Law Review* 527 (CA). One can entertain doubts about the latter decision, given that A was held liable for reckless driving causing death, despite only having knowledge of the defective state of the vehicle. *Cf.* Fortson, *Blackstone's* [A4.11] 76.

[90] E.g., *Warren* v. *R* [1987] WAR 314, 323–324. A is liable for more serious offence than PO where A has a requisite mental state that PO does not: e.g., A assists PO to attack V, knowing that V has an 'egg-shell' skull and that the attack may cause gbh. A is liable for murder, even if PO acted only with an intent to wound, such that PO is only liable for manslaughter if V dies.

[91] In Australia, the rule is given statutory expression in the Crimes Act 1900 (ACT) s. 45(6); Criminal Code 1995 (Cth) s. 11.2(5); Crimes Act 1900 (NSW) ss 346 and 347; and Criminal Code Act 1983 (NT) s. 43BG(6), but it applies equally at common law.

[92] See, e.g., *R* v. *Lopuszynski* [1971] QWN 33 (A can be convicted of rape in circumstances where the victim is able to identify A but not the PO).

[93] See, e.g., *Matusevich* v. *R* (1977) 137 CLR 633, 636.

[94] See, e.g., *R* v. *Cogan and Leak* [1976] QB 217, in which Cogan convinced his intoxicated friend Leak to have sexual intercourse with Cogan's wife, who did not struggle out of fear of her husband. The court held Leak not to be criminally responsible as he may have honestly believed that the victim was consenting. Nonetheless, the court upheld Cogan's conviction as an accessory as he knew the victim was not consenting and even though Leak had been acquitted. The decision and the accessorial reasoning is correct, but some of the further reasoning is questionable (see below).

[95] If PO merely is excused, it is appropriate to consider that an offence has been committed, even if PO is not criminally responsible for it. See, e.g., *R* v. *Millward* [1994] *Criminal Law*

One further complexity is that in some cases, a person may be guilty of an offence when acting through an innocent agent. It has been argued that accessories must be distinguished from POs who have used innocent agents to perpetrate offences. The precise boundaries between cases of innocent agency and accessory liability are unclear and some difficult distinctions are being drawn here.[96] Innocent agency is not a defined legal concept and is of limited utility. All it really means is that the conduct elements of an offence can be established against a person (as a PO), even though he has used another, the innocent agent, as an intermediary to carry out certain acts. That agent, as the label 'innocent' suggests, has not committed any offence at all. An obvious example is where Z gives poison to X to deliver to the victim, X not being aware that it is poison. Z is not *an accessory* to murder, but is the PO, indeed, is the only PO, since X is innocent of any crime.[97] Where, however, a person procures an insane person to kill or injure another, this is better seen as accessory liability. Objectively speaking, a crime has been committed by the insane person against the victim; the fact that the direct perpetrator is not criminally responsible ought not to preclude such a finding.[98]

In any case, 'innocent agency' has limited explanatory value because for some offences – such as rape, bigamy or driving offences – innocent agency is not analytically convincing. Such offences are ones in which a person can only be a PO if she has a certain status or capacity[99] or need personally to have performed certain acts. To take rape as an example,

Review 527 (CA); Fortson, *Blackstone's* [A4.11] 75, and G. Williams, 'Theory of Excuses' (1982) *Criminal Law Review* 732, particularly 735–738. Williams defines an excuse as a defence (which can include the denial of an element of the offence) that denies a proscribed state of mind or negligence or affirms that the accused was not a free, responsible and hence accountable agent (735). Excuses do not take away the underlying wrongfulness of an act, whereas justifications (e.g., self-defence) do. Ormerod, *Smith and Hogan's*, 235, is sceptical, however, and considers it 'doubtful that [the distinction] sheds any greater light on the issue'.

[96] Problematic to classify is where Z procures a child to commit an act, the nature of which it understands but the child nonetheless does not have criminal capacity. Is Z a principal offender or an accessory to the child's crime? Williams, 'Excuses', 735, classifies it as a matter of excuse and not something that denies the wrongfulness of the act.

[97] *Anon* (1634) Kel 53; 84 ER 1079. X lacks any relevant mental state or intention to harm (let alone kill) the victim.

[98] Williams, 'Excuses'. See contra, *Anon* (1634) Kel 53; 84 ER 1079 (Z giving sword to a 'madman' to kill V; Z is the perpetrator as PO and not an accessory to the 'madman's' crime), and Ormerod, *Smith and Hogan's*, 188–189 [8.3.1] who categorises this example in the same way.

[99] As Williams, 'Excuses', 737, puts it, '[a] person cannot intelligibly be said to bugger, rape or drive a vehicle by the instrumentality of another'. For rape, a person cannot use an

even if the person committing sexual intercourse is found not guilty, a perpetrator who procured PO to engage in intercourse (or, we suggest, aided or abetted it) knowing that V was not consenting, can be held liable as an accessory to PO's 'crime'.[100] A can be an accessory as long as the *actus reus* of an offence has been committed and the person committing the *actus reus* is merely excused because of some factors personal to her.[101] We have seen above that A may be liable for a 'greater' offence than PO, so it would be odd if A could not be found liable where PO is not criminally responsible for any offence at all.[102]

Accordingly, PO's and A's responsibility can differ. A's liability is therefore not *duplicative*, as A is not necessarily guilty of the same offences as PO or deemed to share the same mental state as PO.[103]

4.5.2 *Extended joint enterprise liability*

One issue that has proved difficult is determining the circumstances in which A may be liable for other offences committed in furtherance of the parties' common purpose or joint endeavour. If A and PO have a common intention to commit crime 1, and PO commits crime 2 as an

innocent agent to commit the offence, and therefore be liable as a PO, because such person has not 'had intercourse' (J. C. Smith, 'Aid', 134–135), or may lack a penis (if penile penetration is required for the offence) or may be in an exempted category (e.g., a husband prior to abolition of the 'no rape in marriage' rules). Contrast, however, *R* v. *Cogan and Leak* [1976] QB 217, (n. 94 above) in which the Court of Appeal suggested that the accused could be found liable as a PO, using an innocent agent, alongside the court's finding of liability on accessory principles. The latter explanation is more persuasive.

100 Contra Ormerod, *Smith and Hogan's*, 189 [8.3.1], who accepts that innocent agency is not an appropriate analysis, but consider that accessory liability is also problematic as an explanation: if the 'PO' is not criminally responsible, no primary offence has been committed. Instead, Ormerod argues that there should be a substantive offence of procuring the commission of an *actus reus* (235 [8.7.2]). Williams, 'Excuses', 737, reaches the same conclusion but considers that such an offence can only plausibly be introduced via legislation ('"accessory" must be made guilty of an offence of his own' rather than as an accessory to a 'spectral crime'). Fortson, *Blackstone's* disagrees, and prefers the simpler, if not entirely logical, accessorial analysis, as do we. Indeed, Williams, 736, accepts that the accessory analysis is 'acceptable as a matter of policy, and would be workable in many cases'.

101 See *R* v. *Howe* [1987] 1 AC 417, 458 (reduced charge for PO for 'some reason special to himself' does not reduce the charge of accessories).

102 And equally, the reverse would also be odd: *cf.* Fortson, *Blackstone's* [A4.12] 77, citing *R* v. *Howe* [1987] 1 AC 417, itself affirming that A may be liable where PO is not guilty by reason of duress; and see also *R* v. *Bourne* (1952) 36 Cr App R 125.

103 A's liability is still dependent, however, in that it is necessary that PO commits the relevant acts constituting the offence.

incident of or in the course of committing crime 1, the existence of A and PO's joint endeavour may be a mechanism to extend liability.[104] This is a complex topic. Although the issue only rarely arises in the private law context, it is worthwhile briefly outlining the relevant legal principles because similar issues have arisen in tort law[105] and may arise in other contexts.

Whether A's liability may extend to crimes that diverge in some ways from that which was agreed or envisaged raises the question of the types of variations in result from A and PO's unlawful purpose. It is dealt with in law under the related concepts of common unlawful purpose,[106] joint enterprise liability, or 'parasitic accessorial liability'.[107] The question concerns how and when criminal responsibility for the additional, non-targeted, offence that is outside the scope of the joint enterprise is attributable to A?[108] The requisite fault element in respect of the non-targeted offence is complex, subject to considerable differences of opinion, and varies according to jurisdiction. In non-Code jurisdictions, A will be liable for any further offences that A subjectively foresees or realises that PO *may* commit as a possibility of carrying out, or in furtherance of, their unlawful purpose.[109] In three of the Australian Griffith Code jurisdictions, the fault element differs from that of the common law in that it is objectively determined by whether the offence

104 *R* v. *Gnango* [2011] UKSC 59; [2012] 1 AC 827 [42]; see also [14]–[15].

105 See [5.4.5].

106 In the Griffith Code jurisdictions, this is one area of accessory liability where a distinction is made between the various forms of involvement. See, e.g., Criminal Code 1899 (Qld) s. 8, Criminal Code Act 1924 (Tas) s. 4, and Criminal Code 1913 (WA) s. 8 (aiders or enablers (abettors)). Compare the Criminal Code 1899 (Qld) s. 9, the Criminal Code Act 1924 (Tas) s. 5, and the Criminal Code 1913 (WA) s. 9 (counsellors).

107 *R* v. *Gnango* [2011] UKSC 59; [2012] 1 AC 827 [14]–[15].

108 Simester, 'The Mental Element', 592–593. Despite the views of A. Simester, J. R. Spencer, G. R. Sullivan and G. J. Virgo, *Simester and Sullivan's Criminal Law Theory and Doctrine*, 4th edn (Oxford, Hart Publishing, 2010) 242–243, that joint enterprise liability is distinguishable from ordinary accessory liability, we agree with Ormerod, *Smith and Hogan's*, 228–230, that this is merely an example of accessory liability: liability arises from A's culpable involvement in the original, targeted offence, and that liability for the non-targeted offence derives from aiding, abetting, etc. the original offence, where it was foreseeable that the further offence might be done in furtherance of that offence. See also *ABCD* [2010] EWCA Crim 1622 [37].

109 *R* v. *A* [2010] EWCA Crim 1622; [2011] QB 841, approved in *R* v. *Gnango* [2011] UKSC 59; [2012] 1 AC 827 [14]. This may include foreseeing that PO might commit acts with a specific mental element. See also *McAuliffe* v. *R* [1995] HCA 37; (1995) 183 CLR 108 115–119, *Gillard* v. *R* [2003] HCA 64; (2003) 219 CLR 1 [112], and Criminal Code 1995 (Cth) s. 11.2A(1)(a)(ii) and (3)).

was committed in the prosecution of the common unlawful purpose and was an objective probable consequence of it.[110]

One possible consequence of this extended liability is that an accessory might be found liable on more easily satisfied tests than the principal: an accessory must merely have foreseen a possibility of a particular offence, say, a victim being killed with intent (to kill or cause gbh) to be guilty of murder, whereas persons committing the acts that cause a death will not be liable for murder where they have merely foreseen the possibility of death or gbh.[111] Although this characterisation somewhat simplifies the ground on which a PO may be found liable,[112] it has led some to suggest that liability is based on 'reckless accessoryship'; indeed, recklessness that is established by mere possibilities that have been foreseen.[113]

The cases are also difficult where A has foreseen the possibility of a certain offence, but the offence is committed in a different way to that which was contemplated. Such deviation relates to matters such as timing, method, or what Hayne J in *R* v. *Keenan* describes as 'what was done, how it was to be done and who was to do what to bring about the intended purpose'.[114] Here,

[110] See Criminal Code 1899 (Qld) ss. 8 and 9, Criminal Code (Tas) ss. 4 and 5, and Criminal Code 1913 (WA) ss. 8 and 9. Although probability suggests a higher threshold of likelihood, it is, however, an objective test. See *R* v. *Barlow* (1997) 188 CLR 1, 20.

[111] In the UK see authorities cited n. 73 above. In Australia, see, e.g., *McAuliffe* v. *R* [1995] HCA 37; (1995) 183 CLR 108, 118 (for a critical note, see Stephen Odgers, 'Criminal Cases in the High Court of Australia: McAuliffe and McAuliffe' (1996) 20 *Criminal Law Journal* 43); *Gillard* v. *R* [2003] HCA 64; (2003) 219 CLR 1 [112]; *Clayton* v. *R* [2006] HCA 58; (2006) 231 ALR 500 [17]. This is a subjective test, but potentially very easy to meet and consequently broad. See Stephen Gray, '"I Didn't Know, I Wasn't There": Common Purpose and the Liability of Accessories to Crime' (1999) 23(4) *Criminal Law Journal* 201.

[112] This is because in most jurisdictions, POs may be held liable in various ways for what is generally called 'constructive murder', e.g., for acts done in prosecution of an unlawful purpose which acts are likely to endanger human life. See, e.g., Criminal Code 1899 (Qld) s. 302(1)(b).

[113] See Odgers, 'Criminal Cases', particularly at 45–47, who considers that it will result in conviction for 'constructive murder'. See also Kirby J in his dissenting judgment in *Clayton* v. *R* [2006] HCA 58; (2006) 231 ALR 500 [87] onwards, rejecting such broad liability, at [87]. Contrast the majority joint judgment of Gleeson CJ, Gummow, Hayne, Callinan, Heydon and Crennan JJ at [15]–[21] and particularly at [17]. The extended liability is persuasively defended by the House of Lords in *R* v. *Powell; R* v. *English* [1999] 1 AC 1, 13–15. The policy reasons that might justify such a broad liability are discussed by Simester, 'The Mental Element', particularly at 598–600; and J. C. Smith, 'Criminal Liability of Accessories: Law and Law Reform' (1997) 113 *Law Quarterly Review* 453, particularly at 464, who points out that A must be reckless as to whether a murder is committed, and '[r]ecklessness whether murder be committed is different from, and more serious than, recklessness whether death be caused by an accident'.

[114] [2009] HCA 1; (2009) 236 CLR 397, 424 [87].

the question is what extent of variation may occur and yet still come within conduct that was 'known' by A. This depends on how the essential element of the crime is characterised. The issue therefore overlaps considerably with the 'knowledge' of essential matters element discussed in [4.4.3]. Uncertainty as to, and variations and changes to, the timing, location or method used to perpetrate the planned offence are generally not a bar to a successful prosecution,[115] unless such variation means that the type of offence was not foreseeable (at common law) or was not objectively a probable consequence (under the Codes). The courts have at times drawn difficult distinctions here, particularly in cases where a certain outcome was contemplated, but where PO has used a different weapon to that which was contemplated (a gun or a knife instead of a baseball bat, for example). The focus ought to be on whether the conduct that constitutes the offence was an *offence* of such a nature that it was foreseen (at common law) or a probable consequence (Griffith Code jurisdictions),[116] and not as the House of Lords held,[117] whether the specific type of act itself was foreseen or a probable consequence.

[115] See *R* v. *Ancuta* [1991] 2 Qd R 413, 417, in which the Court of Criminal Appeal approved the statement that '[i]t was not necessary to show knowledge of the particular date and premises concerned'. See also, e.g., *R* v. *Da Costa* [2005] QCA 385: conviction of appellant who knew that victim was to be struck with a sword; in fact the victim was wounded by means of a knife. *Cf. R* v. *English* [1999] 1 AC 1, below n. 117.

[116] See *R* v. *Keenan* [2009] HCA 1; (2009) 236 CLR 397, 431 [114] onwards, a case concerning the objective test of probable consequence from Criminal Code 1899 (Qld), but the same test appears equally helpful under the foreseeability test.

[117] See *R* v. *Powell; R* v. *English* [1999] 1 AC 1, 28, and contrast the High Court decision in *R* v. *Keenan* [2009] HCA 1; (2009) 236 CLR 397, concerning the test of objectively probable consequences, although the reasoning translates equally to the foreseeability test, in our view. In *Keenan*, it was held that where A participated in a violent attack intended to cause gbh, to be carried out by at least one of the parties with a baseball bat, A was equally culpable for gbh caused by use of a gun. Importantly, the Court considered that the *offence* had to be a probable consequence, rather than the particular type of conduct. As the majority found at 434 [123], 'it would be an odd result if the respondent could be criminally responsible for [gbh] inflicted by means of a baseball-type bat but not by means of a gun, when the level of harm intended was achieved'. Similarly, see at 434 [124]: courts in England appear to have retreated somewhat from the *English* decision. See Fortson, *Blackstone's* [A4.7] 71–72; *R* v. *Rahman* [2009] 1 AC 129; and Ormerod, *Smith and Hogan*, 219–225.

PART II

Accessory liability in private law

5

Torts

5.1 Introduction

5.1.1 Overview of chapter

The liability of an accessory to a primary tortfeasor's tort has not been the focus of much analysis. There are a number of possible reasons for this. In part, accessory liability is obscured in tort law because it is subsumed under the label of 'joint tortfeasors', a concept that encompasses other grounds for liability [5.1.2]. All joint tortfeasors are said to be liable as 'principals' for the same tort,[1] though this can only mean that they are liable *as if they* were 'principals' (primary tortfeasors) if accessorial concepts are used to render them joint tortfeasors. More importantly, accessorial concepts are only applied and relevant to some torts (for reasons explained in [5.2.1]). Finally, some examples of accessory liability have themselves developed into, or are found within, discrete wrongs: for example, in our view, the tort of inducing breach of contract [Chapter 6] and many circumstances in which the tort of conspiracy is alleged [5.3.2].[2] Even where liability arises as part of an independent tort, if the defendant's (A's) liability is determined on the basis of some tort (or other wrong) having been committed by a third party, the primary wrongdoer (PW), against a claimant (C) and A's

1 This led in some early cases at least to the denial of the existence of 'accessory liability': 'there being no accessories in trespass the [party] must either be guilty as a principal or not at all': *Barker* v. *Braham and Norwood* (1773) 3 Black W 866, 868; 96 ER 510, 511 (De Grey CJ) (reference omitted).

2 The tendency to treat cases of accessory liability as independent torts can also be seen in the suggestion that to procure an infringement of a *statutory right* is a distinct and separate tort. See *Belegging-en Exploitatiemaatschappij Lavender BV* v. *Witten Industrial Diamonds Ltd* [1979] FSR 59, 66, cited in *MCA Records Inc* v. *Charly Records* [2001] EWCA Civ 1441; [2002] ECDR 37 (*MCA Records*). See also *TS and B Retail Systems Pty Ltd* v. *3Fold Resources Pty Ltd (No 3)* [2007] FCA 151 [179]–[187] (distinct tort of procurement of a civil wrong). But this approach has been doubted: see *MCA Records* [2001] EWCA Civ 1441; [2002] ECDR 37 [33], relying on *CBS Songs Ltd* v. *Amstrad Consumer Electronics plc* [1988] AC 1013 (*CBS Songs*); *cf.* however, at [52].

knowing involvement in that wrong, then A's liability is derivative upon PW's wrong and is therefore accessorial. The liability is not, however, duplicative; that is, A need not be liable for the same wrong or necessarily always for the same remedy as PW [5.7.1], [2.6].

Accessory liability has not been widely recognised in tort law; indeed it has been questioned whether accessory liability truly exists at all [5.1.3]. Accessory liability continues to be under-analysed and largely inconspicuous, a fact that is reflected in the small volume of commentary on this topic.[3] The view expressed about US law, that the theory of civil accessory liability remains very 'underdeveloped' and that 'courts apply different tests and often obfuscate their analyses',[4] probably applies equally to Anglo-Australian law.

Different tests have been articulated for establishing when a person is a 'joint tortfeasor' on accessorial principles. One accepted test for accessory liability is where a party procures or induces[5] another to commit a wrong.[6] A second well-established test is that of common design, where

[3] Even Glanville Williams' seminal work on joint tortfeasors devotes only seven pages to accessory liability: *Joint Torts and Contributory Negligence*, (London, Stevens, 1951). For the most part, the work considers procedural consequences of joint liability and contribution rights. There have also been few articles, but see, e.g., Phillip Sales, 'The Tort of Conspiracy and Civil Secondary Liability' (1990) 49 *Cambridge Law Journal* 491; Hazel Carty, 'Joint Tortfeasance and Assistance Liability' (1999) 19 *Legal Studies* 489; Paul S. Davies, 'Joint tortfeasance and common design' (2013) 129 *Law Quarterly Review* 495; and, with a more narrow focus, Neil Foster, 'Personal Liability of Company Officers' (2008) 16 *Torts Law Journal* 20. Textbook writers often give the topic scant treatment: e.g., Michael A. Jones (ed.), *Clerk and Lindsell on Torts*, 20th edn (London, Sweet and Maxwell, 2010) (*Clerk and Lindsell*) devote merely two paragraphs to this category of 'joint tortfeasors', [4–04]–[4–05]; R. Balkin and J. L. R. Davis, *Law of Torts*, 4th edn (Australia, LexisNexis Butterworths, 2009) (one paragraph, [29.25]) (Balkin and Davis); Carolyn Sappideen and Prue Vines (eds.), *Fleming's The Law of Torts*, 10th edn (Australia, Lawbook Co., 2011) (three pages) (*Fleming's*).

Similarly, in the US, Warren Freedman, *Joint and Several Liability: Allocation of Risk and Apportionment of Damages* (Massachusetts, Butterworths Legal Publishers, 1987), concerns procedural matters and contribution.

[4] See N. I. Combs, 'Civil Aiding and Abetting Liability' (2005) 58 *Vanderbilt Law Review* 241, 249 and 246. See also *Central Bank of Denver* v. *First Interstate Bank of Denver*, 511 US 164, 188–189 (1994) (Kennedy J): decisions are made on an 'ad hoc basis, offering little predictive value'. Indeed, in one case it was said, perhaps tongue in cheek, that the '[p]recedent, except in the securities [fraud] area, is largely confined to isolated acts of adolescents in rural society'. See *Halberstam* v. *Welch*, 705 F2d 472, 484 (DC Cir, 1983) (Wald, Bork and Scalia JJ).

[5] The terms in this context are generally, and are here, used interchangeably; *cf.* Sales, 'Conspiracy', 503, and see [3.3.5].

[6] *Lumley* v. *Gye* (1853) 2 E & B 216, 232; 118 ER 749, 755 (Erle J): 'he who procures the wrong is a joint wrongdoer, and may be sued, either alone or jointly with the agent, in the appropriate action for the wrong complained of'.

two persons 'agree to common action, in the course of, and further to which, one of them commits a tort'.[7] Acts done by one party to further the common design makes the assistant 'liable for the tortious acts of the primary actor'.[8] Although the weight of more recent authority is against the proposition that conduct in the nature of assistance in or facilitation of a tort suffices (absent a common design) to generate liability as an accessory, the question is not closed in Australian law, at least. In the US, liability on the basis of assistance is indisputably accepted [5.4.1.4]. In our view, for some torts, particularly trespass torts, assistance ought to be recognised as sufficient to constitute involvement in another's tort and, provided that such assistance is accompanied by a sufficiently culpable mental state, could give rise to accessory liability.

It is implicit in the two tests[9] that a primary wrong has been committed (by PW) and that the elements of such tort cannot be established personally against the alleged accessory. Problematically, however, the tests do not clearly and separately identify the requisite involvement and mental state of A that establish accessory liability, that is, the conduct and mental elements. These may differ according to the factual context and the primary tort that has been committed. It is necessary, therefore, to separately consider how accessory liability concepts are specifically applied to different torts [5.5]. Nonetheless, one can draw some general conclusions on the requisite conduct and mental states, namely:

(1) Tort law generally requires a high degree of involvement by A in PW's tort, either in actively seeking to bring about an outcome (procuring), or agreeing in the commission of the tort (a common design). Although, for common design, even relatively minor acts that contribute to the commission of the tort suffice, provided they further the common design, a finding of common design in some circumstances ought not to be necessary and is artificial [5.5.1].
(2) The requisite mental state, what A must know, will vary according to the tort in question, the facts of the case, and the extent of A's involvement. In many cases, A will have actual knowledge that a

[7] *The Koursk* [1924] P 140 (CA) 155 (Scrutton LJ). As such, the parties' 'shares in the commission of the tort are done in furtherance of a common design'. See 156 (Scrutton LJ) and 159 (Sargent LJ), both quoting from *Clerk and Lindsell on Torts*, 7th edn, 59–60.

[8] *Sea Shepherd (UK)* v. *Fish & Fish Ltd* [2015] UKSC 10; [2015] 2 WLR 694 [38] (Lord Sumption dissenting on the fact) (*Sea Shepherd*).

[9] *Ibid.* [19], [20] (Lord Toulson describing them as different categories of liability).

specific tortfeasor is committing or intends to commit particular types of acts that are tortious; but less detailed knowledge may suffice, such as reckless indifference to the substantial likelihood of a wrong being committed, particularly where A's conduct serves no other purpose than to facilitate or induce tortious conduct [5.4.3].

A further question that needs to be considered, one that has arisen in US law but is rarely addressed explicitly in Anglo-Australian law, is whether A's liability extends to other wrongs that are the foreseeable consequences of the wrong in which A is knowingly involved [5.4.5].

The structure of this chapter is as follows. It explains why accessory liability is important in some torts and not in others [5.2]. Further, it compares accessory liability to related tort concepts such as vicarious liability [5.3]. In [5.4] it sets out the necessary requirements for establishing accessory liability. This section considers the judicial tests used to establish liability and organises the discussion according to the requisite conduct and mental elements. The chapter then considers in detail the operation of accessory concepts in specific torts [5.5] and, finally, defence-related and remedial issues [5.6], [5.7]. The structure adopted involves some repetition, but this is inevitable given that there are two major distinct tests and that their application (alongside other tests) differs considerably according to the specific (and often unrelated) torts in issue.

5.1.2 Accessory liability is often subsumed under 'joint tortfeasors' label

Accessory liability is often subsumed under the concept and label of 'joint tortfeasors', a term that William Prosser described as 'one of those unhappy phrases of indeterminate meaning, whose repetition has done so much to befog the law'.[10] Parties are joint tortfeasors if they are all responsible for the same wrongful act, leading to the same damage, though there is some circularity in that statement.[11] The general principles relating

[10] Prosser's classic article, 'Joint Torts and Several Liability' 25 *California Law Review* 413 (1936–37), did much to dispel the fog. Prosser also stated (413) that 'much of the existing confusion is due to an entire failure to distinguish the different senses in which the term is used; . . . and [which] have very little in common'.

[11] It has also been said that parties are joint tortfeasors if the same evidence would support the claim against each of them: see *Brunsden* v. *Humphrey* (1884) 14 QBD 141, 147, but this has been described as unhelpful and inaccurate by Robert Stevens, *Torts and Rights* (Oxford University Press, 2007) 245, since further and different evidence needs to be brought against, e.g., a party procuring the tort.

to joint tortfeasors are well set out by Gleeson CJ and Callinan J in *Baxter* v. *Obacelo Pty Ltd*:[12]

> Joint tortfeasors are responsible for the same wrongful act leading to single damage. ... Several concurrent tortfeasors are independent tortfeasors whose separate acts combine to produce damage. In their case, 'concurrence is exclusively in the realm of causation'.[13] In *Thompson* v. *Australian Capital Television Pty Ltd (Thompson)*,[14] Brennan CJ, Dawson and Toohey JJ said:
>
> > ... As was said in *The 'Koursk'*, for there to be joint tortfeasors 'there must be a concurrence in the act or acts causing damage, not merely a coincidence of separate acts which by their conjoined effect cause damage'. Principal and agent may be joint tortfeasors where the agent commits a tort on behalf of the principal, as master and servant may be where the servant commits a tort in the course of employment. Persons who breach a joint duty may also be joint tortfeasors. Otherwise, to constitute joint tortfeasors two or more persons must act in concert in committing the tort.

Clearly, the generic label of joint tortfeasors attaches to conceptually distinct circumstances in which liability is imposed and treats them as instances of the same phenomenon.[15] Of the categories noted by their Honours in *Thompson*, only 'acting in concert' identifies accessory liability.[16]

Each joint tortfeasor, being responsible as a 'principal' for the same tort, is generally liable for the full, 'single' damage caused to C.[17] Exceptions to this rule now arise under statutes that impose proportionate liability in some contexts and in some jurisdictions. Further, exceptions to the single and indivisible damages rule also apply in relation to aggravated and exemplary damages, so that not all joint tortfeasors need to be treated identically [5.7.1]. This is to be welcomed. Accessory liability is derivative on PW's primary wrong, but need not always duplicate PW's liability [2.6].

[12] [2001] HCA 66; (2001) 205 CLR 635 [24].

[13] Glanville Williams, *Joint Torts and Contributory Negligence* (London, Stevens & Sons, 1951) § 1, 1.

[14] [1996] HCA 381; (1996) 186 CLR 574, 580–581.

[15] *Cf.* Prosser, 'Joint Torts', 413.

[16] *Cf. Roadshow Films Pty Ltd* v. *iiNet Ltd* [2012] HCA 16; (2012) 248 CLR 42 [100] (Gummow and Hayne JJ) noting that joint liability as joint tortfeasors is imposed on the basis of 'agency', 'vicarious liability' or 'common design'. In our view, the fact that such joint tortfeasors are treated in law as if they are primary tortfeasors does not alter the accessorial nature of the liability. Contra Stevens, *Torts*, 257, discussed in [5.1.3].

[17] *Baxter* v. *Obacelo Pty Ltd* [2001] HCA 66; (2001) 205 CLR 635 [24]. It is not necessary that a claimant join all joint tortfeasors: see, e.g., *Mitchell* v. *Tarbutt* (1794) 5 TR 649; 101 ER 362.

Where the term 'joint tortfeasor' is used in contexts involving accessories, this can lead to semantic confusion,[18] especially where 'joint tortfeasor' is used without the user clearly identifying whether the party's liability is as an accessory or on some other basis. The preferable approach is to specifically identify, where such is the case, liability that is accessorial and based on A's involvement in PW's tort, and to avoid describing accessories as 'joint tortfeasors'[19] other than when describing the consequences of liability. Similarly, other confusing labels such as describing the 'actual perpetrator', PW, as the 'agent' of the other party to the common design, A,[20] are misleading, since it is not a true agency, but is instead established by reference to the concept of a 'common design'.

'Accessory liability' usefully encompasses the disparate concepts and labels that are used to describe the same phenomenon,[21] namely wrongful involvement in another's commission of a wrong where A has not personally satisfied the elements constituting that wrong. Furthermore, 'accessory liability' appropriately distinguishes such liability from that of other types of joint tortfeasors.

5.1.3 Arguments against accessory liability in tort law

Partly for terminological reasons, but also for substantive reasons, some judges and commentators either reject the label 'accessory liability' or go further and deny that accessory liability exists at all in tort law. One line of argument is semantic and equates accessory liability with liability rules in criminal law that catch 'aiders and abettors' as accessories and,

[18] E.g., in *Hoath* v. *Connect Internet Services* [2006] NSWSC 158, White J noted that the plaintiff's statement of claim 'is hard to follow'. In some cases, the labels 'accessory' and 'joint tortfeasor' are still used interchangeably; e.g., *Johnson Matthey (Aust) Ltd* v. *Dascorp Pty Ltd* [2003] VSC 291; (2003) 9 VR 171.

[19] Finn J adopts the preferable approach in *Oakley Inc* v. *Oslu Import and Export Pty Ltd* [2001] FCA 385 [5], concluding that the evidence in that case was sufficient to 'justify a finding of secondary tortious liability [of A] for [PW's] primary wrong as infringer'.

[20] See, e.g., *Fish & Fish Ltd* v. *Sea Shepherd UK* [2013] EWCA Civ 544; [2013] 1 WLR 3700 [42] (*Fish*), overturned on appeal on the application of the law to the facts, in *Sea Shepherd* [2015] UKSC 10; [2015] 2 WLR 694.

[21] In the US, accessory liability ('aiding and abetting liability') is described by an overproliferation of terms of similar meaning. Accessory liability is known as 'secondary liability', 'accomplice liability', 'concerted action', 'conspiracy' and, most commonly, 'aiding and abetting liability'. The label 'accessorial' is used in some contexts, mostly in connection with the *Alien Tort Statute*, 28 USC § 1350. Confusingly, the label vicarious liability is also sometimes used. See also Combs, 'Civil Aiding' 259–260.

as part of the rejection of liability for mere assistance, similarly rejects the label 'accessory liability' in tort law.[22] The label 'accessory' does not of itself, however, dictate the accepted grounds for liability. Even a person procuring or entering a common design with PW to commit a wrong is still an accessory to it. That person's liability is not founded on proof of the same elements necessary to establish PW's wrongdoing: very different facts need to be proved against that person.[23] The UK Supreme Court has now accepted that accessory liability appropriately describes parties to a common design as being accessories to the 'primary' actor's tortious acts.[24]

A more sustained challenge to the recognition of accessory liability in tort law comes from Robert Stevens' rights theory. In brief, this is the theory that tort law enforces obligations generated by the infringement of primary rights. In expounding his theory, Stevens has argued that it is doubtful that 'a more general principle of [civil] secondary liability for wrongs committed by others exists. According to Stevens, if there was such a principle, then the various species of such liability would be 'expected to share the same characteristics', which is countered by the fact that the forms of purported accessory liability 'have different features'.[25] This statement is not inconsistent with our conclusion in [1.4], and [3.1], that there is *no single* test for accessory liability across private law. Instead, we argue for a consistent and stable analytical framework for determining liability.

Stevens goes further, however. He considers that the various joint tortfeasor scenarios are all explicable in terms of attribution of one person's acts onto the other party to the tort; for example, 'procuring a trespass ... involves the attribution of action' and is not 'a form of secondary liability, analogous to secondary participation in a crime'.[26]

Stevens makes a number of different arguments in support of these conclusions, most of which relate specifically to the tort of inducing

[22] See, e.g., *Fish* [2013] EWCA Civ 544; [2013] 1 WLR 3700, particularly [40]–[45], and also *Belhaj and Boudchar* v. *Straw* [2014] EWCA Civ 1394 [75]. See also Simon Deakin and John Randall, 'Rethinking the Economic Torts' (2009) 72(4) *Modern Law Review* 519, who rightly reject an accessorial analysis of the economic torts in general, but also in particular, deny that inducing breach of contract and unlawful act conspiracy are accessorial. They do so on the basis that mere assistance does not suffice for liability. They also therefore appear to equate accessory liability with assistance liability.

[23] See n. 11 above.

[24] *Sea Shepherd* [2015] UKSC 10; [2015] 2 WLR 694, e.g., [38] (Lord Sumption dissenting on the facts); [21] (Lord Toulson).

[25] See 256–257, 275, and generally Ch. 11 and 12.

[26] *Ibid.* 275–276.

breach of contract and are discussed in that context [Chapter 6]. More generally, however, Stevens stresses that the law holds a joint tortfeasor 'liable as a principal, not as an accessory' for the same wrong as another.[27] This observation is by the way: it describes the consequences of liability but does not mean that such liability is not founded on accessorial concepts. Criminal law similarly treats accessories as being liable *as* 'principals' but they are accessories nonetheless.[28]

Perhaps Stevens' strongest argument in favour of liability on the basis of the attribution of acts, and against liability on the basis of participation in another's wrong, is that, in some cases, a (joint) tortfeasor may be liable even if the person committing the relevant act is not.[29] One such situation is where the party personally performing the acts does not have the requisite state of mind to satisfy the elements of the tort, and yet the person procuring or authorising those acts does have a requisite state of mind. Stevens gives the example of a party who authorises an innocent agent to make an untrue statement that the authoriser knows to be untrue. There is no 'joint tort' here at all, as Steven points out. Clearly, such cases are not examples of accessory liability: the elements of the tort can be made out against the authorising party who is liable as a primary tortfeasor,[30] since there is no requirement for the tort of deceit that a fraudster must make false statements *directly* to the victim [5.2.2].[31]

[27] *Ibid.* 257.

[28] See Chapter 4. The criminal law does not ignore, and tort law should not ignore, the critical '*as*' component of that conclusion and the very different basis for it. Similarly, Stevens, *ibid.* 256, notes that there is no inchoate liability in torts, whereas there is in criminal law. But since inchoate liability is conceptually distinct from accessory liability in any case [4.3], its absence in private law tells us nothing about accessory liability in torts or more generally.

[29] Stevens, *Torts,* 254–255.

[30] The conclusion that liability is primary does not detract from our analysis of those cases in which all the elements of a wrong *cannot* be made out against the alleged, 'accessorial', wrongdoer. It is also open to debate whether the primary liability is on the basis of attribution of the agent's acts. If D grabs X's arm and hits C we do not attribute X's actions to D, but instead conclude that D has used an intermediary as a means to an end.

[31] The second situation is where 'PW' has a 'defence' that is not available to 'A', such that 'PW' is not liable. Can liability be accessorial in such circumstances? This situation is likely to be very rare in tort law. Most defences justify 'PW's' infringement of C's rights, and C has no claim against anyone, e.g., C having consented to 'PW's' act. There would be few situations in which C's rights have been infringed, but 'PW' has a personal excuse that answers C's claim. Where this does arise no doubt the pragmatic solution that A is liable as an 'accessory' raises some intractable logical problems, but consistently with similar conclusions in inducing breach of contract [6.3.2] and equity [Chapter 8], we can still

Based on the view that tort law is rights-based, Stevens concludes:

> it is only the person who infringed the claimant's right who has liability imposed upon him. We cannot take the benefit of rights which we do not have, and we cannot be burdened by duties to which we are not subject.[32]

This conclusion asserts what it seeks to prove. Even accepting a rights-based explanation of tort law, our rights could include a right that others do not procure (or otherwise involve themselves in), infringements of our primary rights. Such a 'right' and A's corresponding liability are still dependent upon proof of a commission of a primary wrong by PW.

The differences between accessory liability and Stevens' notion of 'attribution' may be partly semantic. As Stevens states, 'the necessary link between the actor and the person to whom the actions are attributed [is established] through the latter's participation in the action'.[33] The analytical framework in this book helps in determining what is *sufficient* involvement; and what is sufficient may differ according to different wrongs.

5.2 When is accessory liability needed in tort law?

5.2.1 *Limited use and relevance of accessory liability concepts*

There are a number of reasons that explain why accessory liability is relatively rare in the law of torts. One reason is that tort law has alternative avenues of redress against parties who are not the 'main' actors in the commission of a tort: vicarious liability is readily established in many contexts [5.3.1]. Further, primary liability is also often readily established, even in relation to more peripheral actors. This second point requires some detailed explanation.

describe the third party as an accessory. On this view, a wrong has been committed by another, to which A can be an accessory, albeit the primary wrong is not an *actionable* wrong. Similarly, in criminal law, an accessory may be convicted even if the principal offender is excused and, further, accessories may be convicted of different offences to those of which the principal is convicted. See the more detailed discussion in [4.5]. Further, agency and attribution ideas, that the acts of a perpetrator are attributed to the accessory, have generally been rejected in criminal law. See, e.g., for a good summary of the English legal position, Neha Jain, *Perpetrators and Accessories in International Criminal Law: Individual Modes of Responsibility for Collective Crimes* (Oxford, Hart Publishing, 2014) 155–158.

32 Stevens, *Torts*, 275. Indeed, at 281, Stevens describes accessory liability in equity as based on a 'right against everyone else that they do not assist a trustee or fiduciary in breaching his duty'. Although the liability is thus described in terms of rights infringements, it is still a very different liability, analytically, from that of PW.

33 *Ibid.* 246.

A defendant who has committed the primary wrong is a primary wrongdoer. However, whether a defendant's conduct satisfies all of the elements of a primary wrong depends on how, precisely, those elements are formulated. Do the elements require particular conduct (for example, direct, personal or positive) or a particular status? As was noted in [2.7], whether accessorial concepts play an important function in an area of law depends in part on how restrictively the elements of the primary cause of action are formulated. If they are formulated restrictively, then accessory liability may provide an important mechanism that attaches liability to third parties involved in another's wrongdoing. Many torts, however, are not so formulated: there is no requirement that a defendant hold a narrowly confined status or directly engage with C. This means that accessory liability is redundant (or largely so) in some torts, while having a more important function in others.

5.2.2 Torts in which there is wide-ranging primary liability

The tort of conversion provides a good example of a tort in which primary liability predominates. Conversion is the 'unauthorised dealing with the claimant's chattel so as to question or deny his title to it'[34] or, in the words of Douglas, 'the exclusion of the claimant from the use or possession of his goods'.[35]

Conversion has been described as an 'idiosyncratic' tort,[36] in that the tort may be constituted not only by intentional conduct that is an infringement of a C's rights, but also by conduct that is not blameworthy at all, such as where a converter mistakenly and reasonably believes she is entitled to deal with the goods in the way that she has, but is nonetheless liable.[37] The liability is strict, since a party may be liable without fault, there being no intention to harm or even carelessness.[38] Strict liability

[34] See *Clerk and Lindsell*, [17–06] 1115.

[35] S. J. Douglas, 'The Nature of Conversion' [2009] 68 *Cambridge Law Journal* 198.

[36] *Johnson Matthey (Aust) Ltd* v. *Dascorp Pty Ltd* [2003] VSC 291; (2003) 9 VR 171, 195 (Redlich J) citing A. Tettenborn 'Damages in Conversion – the Exception or the Anomaly?', (1993) 52(1) *Cambridge Law Journal* 128, 128 and 137.

[37] This is barring statutory defences, e.g., purchasers of goods are protected in some contexts under the Sale of Goods Acts.

[38] See, e.g., *National Australia Bank Ltd* v. *Nemur Varity Pty Ltd* (2002) 4 VR 252, 276–277 [58], in which Batt JA describes conversion as a tort:

> to be found at the lower or less culpable end of what Lord Steyn in *Smith New Court* [*Securities Ltd* v. *Scrimgeour Vickers (Asset Management) Ltd* [1997] AC 254 at 279] called 'the sliding scale from strict liability to intentional wrongdoing'.

means that it is relatively easy for claimants to establish all the elements of the tort against a variety of persons who deal with the property. Each new act of conversion is actionable, giving rise to primary liability. Consequently, accessory principles are not usually relied on.[39]

Another example is provided by defamation. A wide definition of the element of publication in defamation law means that accessory principles are largely redundant; defendants can be found liable as primary wrongdoers. This approach has given rise, however, to possibly overly wide primary liability. Such wide primary liability also leads to confusion as to whether different knowledge requirements should apply to some seemingly more remote 'primary' tortfeasors than apply generally. Therefore, there is also considerable potential for overlap in terms of possible analysis between a person being held liable as a primary wrongdoer, or as an accessory. These difficulties mean that defamation law warrants more detailed discussion [5.5.4].

Other torts, such as deceit, do not require that PW deal directly with C in order to be liable: for example, innocent agents (who have not themselves committed a wrong) can be used to commit wrongs. Many cases in deceit concern whether a principal is responsible for an agent's fraud. Outside the realm of vicarious liability, if the principal authorises the agent to make a statement that the principal, but not the agent, knows to be false, then the principal is liable for fraud,[40] though not on accessorial principles. The principal is liable as PW: authorising of an act so as to thereby use the agent as an intermediary to achieve one's ends satisfies the elements of deceit.[41] If, however, an agent has made a false statement, but not knowingly so, the principal is not liable unless she has authorised the statement (knowing it to be false).[42] The courts in these

[39] In any case, subsequent converters of the same property need not be involved in, or linked at all with, the earlier acts of conversion. One example of accessory principles being applied to conversion, involving directors' liability for a company's conversion, is *Johnson Matthey (Aust) Ltd* v. *Dascorp Pty Ltd* [2003] VSC 291; (2003) 9 VR 171, discussed Chapter 11, and see also *White* v. *Withers LLP* [2009] EWCA Civ 1122; [2010] 1 FLR 859.

[40] E.g., *Krakowski* v. *Eurolynx Properties Ltd* (1995) 183 CLR 563 (HCA).

[41] According to Stevens, this is based on the attribution of agents' acts to the principal (see discussion in [5.1.3]), but equally it can be described as the principal using indirect means to achieve her goal.

[42] See, e.g., *Krakowski* v. *Eurolynx Properties Ltd* (1995) 183 CLR 563 (HCA). There are statements seemingly to the contrary in *London County Freehold and Leasehold Properties Ltd* v. *Berkeley Property and Investment Co Ltd* [1936] 2 All ER 1039, and *S Pearson and Son Ltd* v. *Dublin Corporation* [1907] AC 351 (HL), but the former case has been interpreted as involving a fraudulent agent and therefore consistent with vicarious liability principles. See, e.g., *Armstrong* v. *Strain* [1952] 1 KB 232, and *Anglo-Scottish*

types of cases have quite rightly refused to combine the acts of one person (the agent in making the statement) with the mental state of another (the principal's knowledge of its falsity) to conclude that there is fraud.[43] Since neither party has individually committed fraud, no fraud can be found. Nor would accessorial principles justify any contrary conclusion, since no primary wrong has been committed.[44]

As a more general observation, tort law accepts that a party may have caused harm to C, even despite the fact that the immediate cause of the harm may have been the independent conduct of some intermediary.[45] A defendant may be liable in negligence, for example, for omissions, where the direct cause of the harm was the negligent or even deliberate wrongdoing of another. Further, if a person's wrongful conduct causally *contributes* to a harm that is the result of the combined acts of several parties, without being on its own *sufficient* to constitute that harm; such person may still be liable for the primary tort.[46] For these and perhaps other reasons, accessory liability is not needed in the tort of negligence. Negligence is nonetheless considered further below because some cases have utilised accessorial concepts in relation to that tort, particularly in the US. We conclude that such use is conceptually misconceived [5.5.5].

Beet Sugar Corporation Ltd v. *Spalding Urban District Council* [1937] 2 KB 607, 621, 623–627.

43 *Krakowski* v. *Eurolynx Properties Ltd* (1995) 183 CLR 563; *Awaroa Holdings Ltd* v. *Commercial Securities and Finance Ltd* [1976] 1 NZLR 19; *Armstrong* v. *Strain* [1952] 1 KB 232; *Anglo-Scottish Beet Sugar Corporation Ltd* v. *Spalding Urban District Council* [1937] 2 KB 607; *Cornfoot* v. *Fowke* (1840) 6 M & W 358; 151 ER 450. Contrast *Vettese* v. *Kemp* (2000) 77 SASR 53.

44 See, e.g., *Armstrong* v. *Strain* [1952] 1 KB 232.

45 This is one difference between tort law and criminal law. In criminal law, the prevailing position is that the independent decision of a party to commit an offence is an intervening event. Any person who merely plays a part in that decision is therefore said not to have caused the primary offence (unless that person's conduct also contributed to the conduct elements constituting the offence). Such a party will need to be charged as an accessory. See [4.3].

46 See generally Jane Stapleton, 'Unnecessary Causes' (2013) 129 *Law Quarterly Review* 39, and [3.3.3] and [5.4.2.1]. In nuisance, for example, liability has been found on the basis of *concerted action* in which the parties have independently committed wrongful acts, albeit where their breach *in combination with others* is what causes the harm (e.g., pollution by the cumulative effect of several polluters' acts). See also *Strong* v. *Woolworths Ltd* [2012] HCA 5; (2012) 246 CLR 182 [22]. At times, courts have resorted to accessorial reasoning, but this is unpersuasive and unnecessary. See *Moses* v. *Town of Morgantown* 133 SE 421 (NC 1926) 423 (Clarkson J), a case concerning joint tortfeasors for nuisance: 'Where all have knowledge of the independent acts that create the result and continue the independent acts with knowledge, this ipso facto creates a concert of action and makes a common design or purpose.'

5.2.3 *Torts in which accessory liability is significant*

From the above discussion, it therefore remains to identify those torts in which accessory liability has frequently been used and in which it serves an important legal function, including the following, which are considered in more detail in [5.5].

(1) Trespass actions, since such actions generally require a defendant to have personally committed some act of interference in C's rights (vicarious liability aside) [5.5.1].
(2) Infringement of statutory intellectual property (IP) rights.[47] Much of the law concerning accessory liability in tort law generally, has arisen in the context of these statutory torts. Importantly, the common law rules operate alongside specific statutory tests of accessory liability. Cases that apply common law tort principles to infringements of IP rights are generally discussed here [5.5.2]. Cases of liability based on IP statutory provisions are discussed in Chapter 9. There is an obvious overlap between the two.
(3) The tort of nuisance in which accessorial concepts have played some role. There is considerable confusion, however, as to the application of primary, vicarious and accessory liability principles in this area and the courts have not always drawn clear distinctions [5.5.3].
(4) The tort of conspiracy, many examples of which are accessorial. The relationship between that tort and accessory liability more generally is explained in [5.3.2].
(5) The liability of directors for company torts and wrongs more generally. That topic warrants separate consideration and is covered in Chapter 11.

5.3 Accessory liability compared to other tort concepts

5.3.1 *Accessory liability and vicarious liability*

5.3.1.1 Employer–employee relationship

In simple terms, one way of differentiating vicarious liability from accessory liability is that vicarious liability is based on a relationship

[47] Policy concerns that arise in the IP context may have influenced the articulation of accessory liability principles generally, leading to an unduly narrow approach. See [5.5.2].

link between the parties, whereas accessory liability is based on a 'participation' link between A and PW, as a result of A's culpable conduct.[48]

Vicarious liability of an employer for its employees' torts arises from the status of the employer's relationship with the employee and is imposed despite the (usual) innocence of the employer.[49] Vicarious liability is based on policy grounds – the precise nature of which, and hence the precise scope of vicarious liability, are the subject of ongoing debate.[50] These matters are not the concern of this chapter.[51] Although vicarious liability is sometimes described as a form of 'secondary liability',[52] it is important to stress that such liability is imposed independently of any culpable involvement by the employer in the employee's tort. Liability is strict and not based on fault. For vicarious liability, the employees' wrongs are attributed to the employer, as if it had committed the tort, whereas an accessory is a wrongdoer.[53]

There are borderline cases. For example, in the tort of nuisance [5.5.3] and cases involving agents [5.3.1.2], where liability has been imposed on defendants for 'authorising' certain acts of third parties, it is not clear whether the liability is vicarious or accessorial (or even primary).

48 See Carty, 'Joint Tortfeasance', 490.

49 See, e.g., *Bazley* v. *Curry* [1999] 2 SCR 534; (1999) 174 DLR 4th 45 (vicarious liability for sexual abuse of children). See generally, *Clerk and Lindsell*, Ch. 6; Balkin and Davis, Ch. 26; H. Luntz, D. Hambly, K. Burns, J. Dietrich and N. Foster, *Torts Cases and Commentary,* 7th edn (Australia, LexisNexis Butterworths, 2013) Ch. 17 (Luntz et al); K. Barker, P. Cane, M. Lunney and F. Trindade, *The Law of Torts in Australia*, 5th edn (Australia, Oxford University Press, 2012) Ch. 17, (Barker et al., *Torts*).

50 *Sweeney* v. *Boylan Nominees Pty Ltd* [2006] HCA 19; (2006) 226 CLR 161 [11].

51 For more on the concept of vicarious liability, see Paula Gilikar, *Vicarious Liability in Torts: A Comparative Perspective* (Cambridge University Press, 2010), and Christine Beuermann, 'Tort Law in the Employment Relationship: A Response to the Potential Abuse of an Employer's Authority' (2014) 21 *Torts Law Journal* 169.

52 See, e.g., Sales, 'Conspiracy', 502–503, who stresses, however, that vicarious liability is based on 'policy factors concerning the imposition of liability where it can best be borne'. Confusingly, in the US, 'vicarious liability' is also sometimes used to describe aiding and abetting.

53 See N. J. McBride and R. Bagshaw, *Tort Law*, 3rd edn (England, Pearson Education Ltd, 2008) 649–650. This means that it is possible for an employer to be vicariously liable for an employee's accessory liability, so long as all of the actions that render the employee liable occur in the course of employment: see 672–673, and *Credit Lyonnais Bank Nederland NV* v. *Export Credit Guarantee Department* [2000] 1 AC 486.

5.3.1.2 'Agents'

More difficult to differentiate from accessory liability are the circumstances in which 'vicarious liability' arises for the acts of 'agents'. Such liability will generally arise in at least three circumstances:

(1) where the agent is in fact an employee;
(2) if the principal procures or 'authorises' the tort of the agent ('authorises' is commonly used in this context); or
(3) where the principal holds the agent out as having authority to engage in such conduct.[54]

The scope of the third circumstance may be quite narrow and limited largely to cases of fraudulent and, perhaps, negligent statements.[55] The first two circumstances are not limited to agency cases: they involve the application of general principles concerning authorising wrongs that apply irrespective of whether the term 'agent' is used. In these situations, it is therefore uncertain whether the label 'agent' has any legal significance and, indeed, how it is being defined. The better view may therefore be that '[a]part from cases of fraud [that is, the third circumstance] the category of "agent" seems, as such, to have no relevance in the law of torts' and that there are no special rules peculiar to principal and agent.[56] Nonetheless, given references to 'agency' by the courts, and the acknowledged role of the concept of authority, it is necessary to explore liability for agents further. We will take the three situations in turn.

(1) In the first situation, an agent may be an employee, an independent contractor, or neither. If the agent is an employee, then liability for the acts of the agent is vicarious, irrespective of whether the test is one of scope of employment or, more likely,[57] scope of authority.[58]

[54] See Balkin and Davis, [26.12]–[26–15], 726–728.

[55] See *Kooragang Investments Pty Ltd* v. *Richardson and Wrench Ltd* [1982] AC 462 (PC). There are other anomalous situations in which vicarious liability for agents may arise, but the courts have generally been careful to confine these: see, e.g., *Scott* v. *Davis* [2000] HCA 52; (2000) 204 CLR 333.

[56] *Clerk and Lindsell*, [6–79], 398. See also Balkin and Davis, 727, [26.12]: 'categorisation' as agent will not 'generally be a relevant criterion'. *Cf.* Barker et al., *Torts*, [17.7], 775–777: 'broader use of agency as a means of imposing vicarious liability'.

[57] See the discussion in Peter Watts, 'Principals' tortious liability for agents' negligent statements – is "authority" necessary?' (2012) 128 *Law Quarterly Review* 260.

[58] The latter is used specifically in the context of agents and is, perhaps, narrower, and is particularly apt in the context of liability for fraudulent or negligent statements, where the identity of the employee as agent is critical. See situation (3) below, and see also Christine Beuermann, 'Dissociating the Two Forms of So-called "Vicarious Liability"' in

(2) The second situation involves accessory liability as we conceive it, at least to the extent that 'authorising' a tort is equivalent to procuring it.[59] In such a case, it would not matter whether the party authorised to commit wrongful acts is an employee or independent contractor or, indeed, an agent as well. Liability would arise even in the absence of a pre-existing relationship.[60] An authoriser is liable for all the damage that ordinarily arises from the authorised wrongful acts. For example, if a person authorised 'agents' to commit trespass by entering and searching C's premises without consent, then such person would be liable for all the specific trespasses committed by the agents while doing the wrongful acts, including presumably any negligently caused damage to the property.[61]

One difficulty that has arisen in the context of nuisance has been determining what precisely must have been authorised: the nuisance itself, or acts as a result of which the nuisance was a natural, likely, or merely foreseeable, consequence. If a party has authorised acts that could have been performed lawfully, then it appears much more doubtful that any liability imposed is based on accessorial principles.[62] The 'authoriser' is not

Stephen G. A. Pitel, Jason W. Neyers and Erika Chamberlain (eds.), *Tort Law: Challenging Orthodoxy* (Oxford, Hart Publishing, 2013) 463.

59 The concept of 'authorising' applies to more than just procuring conduct: see Chapter 9.

60 See *Ellis* v. *Sheffield Gas Consumers Co* (1853) 2 El and Bl 767, 770; 118 ER 955 (Lord Campbell CJ) involving a contractor: it would be 'monstrous if party causing another to do a thing were exempted from liability for that act merely because there was a contract' between the parties. The case is discussed in [5.5.3].

61 *Cf. Schumann* v. *Abbot* [1961] SASR 149. That case concerned the liability of the agents and not the principal who had authorised the entry into his wife's premises to search for 'evidence of adultery'. It seems clear, however (though note some doubts expressed at 155), that the principal would have been liable as an accessory not just for trespass in general, but for all the specific torts committed in the course of the authorised act. In such a case, it is not unrealistic to say that the principal has authorised the specific torts if they were contemplated within the general, authorised, wrongful act. See also *Restatement (Second) of Torts* 294 (1979) illustration 2; and discussion in [5.4.5].

62 E.g., authorising a contractor to destroy rabbits is a task that could, presumably, be done without committing a nuisance by starting fires, though the court thought otherwise in *McInnes* v. *Wardle* (1931) 45 CLR 548 (HCA). Unless one is convinced by that factual conclusion, the decision is not justifiable on principles of accessory liability (since no wrongful act has been authorised) and instead, the decision appears either to apply vicarious liability for the contractor's tort, or else it could be seen as resting on the ultimate control of the occupier of land. See [5.5.3] and the discussion of the authorisation of nuisances created by independent contractors, e.g., in *Clerk and Lindsell* [20–71]–[20–74], 1313–1315.

procuring a wrong. The authorities are far from clear and the issue is discussed further in [5.5.3].

(3) The third situation (agents committing torts while acting within their actual or ostensible authority) is best seen as an extension of vicarious liability principles,[63] rather than as based on any genuine and independent fault on the part of the principal. The liability is not accessorial in nature because authorised acts may give rise to liability even where they could and should have been done non-tortiously and where the agent acts against the interests of the principal.[64] The cases for the most part concern liability for an agent's fraud and whether the fraud falls within the scope of the agent's actual or ostensible authority, and may be peculiar to that context.[65]

A more difficult question is whether there is a fourth situation in which liability for agents arises, which involves overlapping principles of authorisation and vicarious liability, so that liability extends beyond cases of representations in the third category. Should a principal who *authorises* an 'agent' (or even anyone acting in a representative capacity) to act in a lawful way nonetheless become liable for that agent's torts if they are committed in the furtherance of, or in the course of, such actions?[66] If any such liability arises, it is best seen as a relationship-based liability, rather than as accessorial.[67]

[63] See, e.g., Barker et al, *Torts*, 775; *Clerk and Lindsell*, [6–49]–[6–52], 381–384.

[64] E.g., *Colonial Mutual Life Assurance Society Ltd* v. *Producers and Citizens Co-Operative Assurance Co of Australia Ltd* (1931) 46 CLR 41 (HCA) (principal held liable for defamatory statements of agent authorised to speak on behalf of the principal, even where agent prohibited from making defamatory statements).

[65] *Armagas Ltd* v. *Mundogas (The Ocean Frost)* [1986] 1 AC 717 (HL). Where an agent who is not an employee negligently causes personal injury, then vicarious liability does not arise for such wrong. See Watts, 'Principals' tortious liability'.

[66] Perhaps *McInnes* v. *Wardle* (1931) 45 CLR 548 (HCA), above n. 62, might be a case in point. For example, if P authorises an agent to dig at spot X, which is lawful, and the agent leaves rubble on the highway, or does so negligently and damages pipes, should P be liable, in public nuisance or negligence, and should the relationship of 'agency', however that may be defined, have any impact on that conclusion? *Ellis* v. *Sheffield Gas Consumers Co* (1853) 2 El and Bl 767; 118 ER 955 [5.5.3], presumably would answer this question as 'no', though the principal tortfeasors were not 'agents' in that case.

[67] If it were accessorial, then liability is being imposed for a lower level of culpability than is generally required; that is, even in the absence of any knowledge by A of the wrong [5.4.3]. See also the discussion in [5.5.3] on nuisance.

5.3.1.3 Non-delegable duties

The precise scope of, and rationale for, liability for breach of non-delegable duty is far from clear and is the subject of debate.[68] Cases that impose liability for breach of a non-delegable duty of care can be characterised in one of at least two ways: either, as a (less transparent) mechanism for imposing vicarious liability[69] or, secondly (and less commonly), as a genuine fault-based form of liability, where the act of delegating a particular task is done in a careless manner, or the delegation is not justified and the responsibility for the task rests with the holder of that duty.[70] Neither form of 'non-delegable' liability involves accessory liability.

5.3.2 Accessory liability and the tort of conspiracy

In some situations, tort law designates conduct that is a form of accessory liability as itself constituting a distinct tort. Some forms of the economic tort of conspiracy are an example.[71] Conspiracy captures certain conduct that is often akin to accessory liability, and designates it as a (primary) wrong. This has the effect of hiding many examples of what may also be seen as accessory liability.

Leaving aside lawful act conspiracy, which is not accessorial,[72] conspiracy is established where two or more parties combine to commit an

[68] See, e.g., the differing views of the members of the High Court in *New South Wales* v. *Lepore* [2003] HCA 4; (2003) 212 CLR 511.

[69] See, e.g., *Scott* v. *Davis* [2000] HCA 52; (2000) 204 CLR 333 [248]; *Leichardt Municipal Council* v. *Montgomery* [2007] HCA 6; (2007) 230 CLR 22 [6]–[8]. Contra Stevens, *Torts*, 122–123. Such a view of non-delegable duty may inform the introduction of the cryptically worded s. 5Q Civil Liability Act 2002 (NSW) (breach of non-delegable duty to be determined 'as if [it] were vicarious liability'; *cf.* s. 61(1) Wrongs Act 1958 (Vic)), and see *Withyman* v. *State of New South Wales and Blackburn* [2013] NSWCA 10 [132], and Commonwealth of Australia, *Review of the Law of Negligence: Final Report (Ipp Report)* [11.15]–[11.16]. For an excellent attempt at rationalisation of non-delegable duty liability arising in employment relationships, see Christine Beuermann, 'Tort Law in the Employment Relationship: A Response to the Potential Abuse of an Employer's Authority' (2014) 21 *Torts Law Journal* 169; and see also Beuermann, 'Vicarious Liability and Conferred Authority Strict Liability: *Woodland* v. *Swimming Teachers' Association* [2012] EWCA Civ 239' (2013) 20 *Torts Law Journal* 265.

[70] *Clerk and Lindsell*, [6–57], 386–387, appear to characterise it as fault-based.

[71] See generally, Hazel Carty, *An Analysis of the Economic Torts*, 2nd edn (Oxford University Press, 2010), Ch. 6; Balkin and Davis, [21.43]–[21.56], 613–620. See also Sales, 'Conspiracy'.

[72] Conspiracy by *lawful* means is where parties combine with the predominant intention to cause damage by the doing of acts that, if done by one person alone, would be lawful. Since the acts committed by the conspirators to carry out their ends are lawful, such

unlawful act with the intention to harm C's economic interests. Agreement alone is not, however, sufficient. There must be some act to carry the agreement into effect. It is unimportant which party carried out the specific acts.

Many claims for unlawful act conspiracy could equally be brought on the basis of the parties being accessorial 'joint tortfeasors', at least where the conspiracy is one to commit torts. For example, a conspiracy to harm C's business by making threats against his or her clients might be carried out by PW making the actual threats and/or trespassing on C's land, with A providing physical support. In such a case, PW may have committed the torts of assault (against C's clients) and intimidation and trespass (against C). And A could be seen as an accessory to all of these torts. One can certainly conclude, therefore, that if there is an agreement, and parties 'have acted in concert to commit a tort it is immaterial whether they (or any one or more of them) are sued as joint tortfeasors of that other tort or the action is framed as one of conspiracy to commit that other tort'.[73]

In England, however, the House of Lords in *Total Network SL* v. *Her Majesty's Revenue and Customs* (*Total*)[74] has recently rejected the view that unlawful means conspiracy is a form of accessory liability. In doing so, the House of Lords rejected the argument of a number of commentators that unlawful means conspiracy could either be subsumed under the tort of the intentional infliction of economic loss by unlawful means, or that it adds 'nothing to the existing secondary [accessorial] tort liability'.[75] On this argument, conspiracy is a tort of narrow operation with

means do not therefore constitute a tort or other wrong to which the conspirators can be accessories. It is, it should be added, a less common form of conspiracy and has almost always been argued without success, including in those cases that authoritatively establish the existence of the tort. In England, see *Crofter Hand Woven Harris Tweed Co Ltd* v. *Veitch* [1942] AC 435 (HL); in Australia, see *McKernan* v. *Fraser* (1931) 46 CLR 343 (HCA). See, however, exceptionally, *Huntley* v. *Thornton* [1957] 1 All ER 234.

73 Balkin and Davis, [21.51]–[21.52], 664–665. See also *Sorrell* v. *Smith* [1925] AC 700 (HL) 716; *Ward* v. *Lewis* [1955] 1 WLR 9, 11; *Rookes* v. *Barnard* [1964] AC 1129 (HL) 1204; and *TS and B Retail Systems Pty Ltd* v. *3Fold Resources Pty Ltd (No 3)* [2007] FCA 151; (2007) 239 ALR 117 [191] (Finkelstein J):

> Joint tortfeasors are not necessarily conspirators. . . . On the other hand, when persons are engaged in wrongful conduct in concert, it is difficult to avoid the conclusion that as well as being conspirators they also are joint tortfeasors.

74 [2008] UKHL 19; [2008] 1 AC 117. This rejection has been described as controversial by Pey-Woan Lee, 'Inducing Breach of Contract, Conversion and Contract as Property' (2009) 29 *Oxford Journal of Legal Studies* 511, 522.

75 Carty, *An Analysis of the Economic Torts*, 25, and see also Sales, 'Conspiracy'. Carty cites Stevens, *Torts*, 248–251, for the contention that there is no independent tort of unlawful

'unlawful means' being limited to means that are *actionable* by C against the persons committing such acts. The House of Lords rejected this limitation and reaffirmed that unlawful means used to injure C need not be actionable by C against the conspirators. It suffices that the unlawful means are a crime or a breach of contract against third parties.[76] Lord Walker's reasoning bears repeating:[77]

> If an unlawful means conspiracy is indeed a form of secondary liability for a civil wrong then the need for the unlawful means to be actionable as a civil wrong would be self-evident.
>
> However the premise is in my opinion mistaken. . . .
>
> In short, and with great respect to those who take a different view, any suggestion that the unlawful means conspiracy is a form of secondary liability, and must therefore have an actionable wrong as an essential ingredient, seems to me to be a circular argument which assumes what it sets out to prove.[78]

With respect, we agree with the House of Lords' view of conspiracy as being *wider* than actionable unlawful means and thus encompassing more than just accessory liability.[79] This view follows logically once it is

means conspiracy. See also Carty's criticisms of *Total* in Ch. 2, 6, 8 and 13. Carty views unlawful means conspiracy as analogous to accessory liability (170) whereas Sales, 'Conspiracy', considers it an instance of general accessory liability principles.

[76] See *Total* [2008] UKHL 19; [2008] 1 AC 117, e.g., [41]–[45] (Lord Hope), [56] (Lord Scott of Foscote); [89]–[104] (Lord Walker of Gestingthorpe), [116] (Lord Mance); [227] (Lord Neuberger). The House of Lords overruled the English Court of Appeal in *Powell* v. *Boladz* [1998] Lloyd's Rep Med 116. This is so long as the unlawful acts 'are indeed the means by which harm is intentionally inflicted on the claimant (rather than being merely incidental to it)'. See at [93] (Lord Walker). *Cf.* Lord Hope, who considered that the unlawful means have to be directed at the claimants who have suffered the loss; where the unlawful means are directed against other parties, Lord Hope left the question open [43]. Therefore, in *Total*, the Commissioners of Customs and Excise were entitled to bring a claim against the defendant who was party to a conspiracy in the form of a complex fraudulent scheme (a 'carousal fraud') whereby other parties to the scheme (the co-conspirators) had, by criminal means, obtained tax credits to which they were not entitled.

[77] *Total* [2008] UKHL 19; [2008] 1 AC 117 [101]–[104] and also at [66], rejecting Carty, *An Analysis of the Economic Torts* (2001) 22, and Sales, 'Conspiracy'. See also Lord Mance at [116] and Lord Neuberger (dissenting on other grounds), agreeing at [225]. See also Lord Scott (at [56]) who agrees with Lord Walker on the unlawful means point, though he does not expressly deal with the issue of conspiracy as a form of accessory liability.

[78] Carty has reiterated her narrow conception of conspiracy as limited to actionable unlawful means, and therefore sharply criticises the decision in *Total*, in the second edition of *An Analysis of the Economic Torts*. See in particular, Ch. 2, 6, 8 and 13. Other commentators are more favourably disposed to *Total*, e.g., Janet O'Sullivan, 'Unlawful Means Conspiracy in the House of Lords' (2008) 67(3) *Cambridge Law Journal* 459.

[79] This is therefore a rejection of the view of Stevens, *Torts*, 249, that unlawful means conspiracy is 'otiose' (see *Clerk and Lindsell*, [4–04], 274). *Cf.* also Deakin and Randall, 'Rethinking the Economic Torts', 542–544.

accepted that unlawful means do not need to be *actionable* by C against the parties committing such acts. If the conspiracy is one to commit a statutory wrong where no civil liability attaches to such wrong or a criminal offence, then the notion of (accessorial) 'joint torts' is obviously inapplicable. As was stated in *Total*, where no independent tort claim is available to C, then the conspirators to the unlawful act cannot be sued as 'joint tortfeasors' and '[t]his is a gap that needs to be filled'.[80]

Nonetheless, many cases of conspiracy are examples of accessory liability and could be analysed, and liability imposed, accordingly. We consider that the House of Lords' view is reconcilable with that position, since there is no reason why conspiracy cannot have a broader operation and cover territory that is not covered by accessory liability.[81]

5.4 Establishing accessory liability

5.4.1 *Judicial tests for liability*

5.4.1.1 Introduction

Some of the earliest cases on joint tortfeasors stated the basis of liability for involvement in another's tort very broadly. In *Petrie* v. *Lamont*, for example, it was said that '[a]ll persons in trespass who aid or counsel, direct, or join, are joint trespassers'.[82] Such broad statements were cited with approval in numerous subsequent cases, particularly in the early 1900s,[83] but in more recent cases two fairly narrow tests dominate as

80 *Total* [2008] UKHL 19; [2008] 1 AC 117 [44](Lord Hope dissenting on other grounds). In any case, even if conspiracy were narrowly formulated and limited to actionable wrongs, it still adds, theoretically at least, an extra dimension to liability beyond accessory liability. For example, if the tortious acts are committed against third parties, but no tort (other than conspiracy) is committed against C, then C would have no claim against 'A' as an accessory to any tort against C. Another situation where this might be so is given by Sales, 'Conspiracy', 511.

81 Similarly, the House of Lords' view is not necessarily inconsistent with the observations of Finkelstein J above, n. 73, and others which, as general observations focused on *tortious* unlawful means, are correct. It should be added that the debate about the precise limits of the conspiracy tort forms part of an inconclusive and complex debate as to the precise limits of and interrelationship between the various economic torts: see Carty, *An Analysis of the Economic Torts*, Ch. 8.

82 (1841) Car and M 93, 96; 174 ER 424, 426 (Tindal CJ).

83 E.g. *Pratt* v. *British Medical Association* [1919] 1 KB 244, 254; *The Koursk* [1924] P 140, 159–160, (Sargent LJ, quoting *Clerk and Lindsell on Torts*, 7th edn, 59–60); see also at 152 (Bankes LJ). See even more generally *De Crespigny* v. *Wellesley* (1829) 5 Bing 392, 404 (Best CJ), concerning republishing a libel or slander: 'it is a principle of our law, that whoever wilfully assists in the doing of an unlawful act, becomes answerable for all the

general judicial tests of accessory liability, namely procuring another to commit a wrong, or participating in a common design. We begin by outlining the general features of these tests in this section, and then consider their application to specific torts in [5.5]. As a general observation, procurement and common design are often considered together in the cases and if C fails to make out a common design, procurement may be difficult to establish.[84]

These two tests of 'joint' tort liability conflate, and do not separately refer to, the conduct and mental elements necessary for liability. Nonetheless, consideration of these two elements is inherent in much of the reasoning in the case law, at least where the two elements are not self-evident, and we draw some general conclusions about each element in [5.4.2], [5.4.3].

Although these two tests operate generally in torts (at least in those contexts in which accessory liability is relevant), they are not the only ones. For example, a further test of liability is used in nuisance cases, namely whether a nuisance is 'authorised'. There is little analysis, however, as to the meaning of authorisation at common law and, in particular, whether this means something different to procuring.[85] In this section, we also briefly introduce the US approach to establishing accessory liability in tort law; US case law is referred to in this chapter where relevant.

It must be stressed that establishing accessory liability is a question of fact and requires a close analysis of the facts.[86] It has been said for this reason that reference to previous authority for the purpose of determining a new case at hand is of limited value.[87] However, one needs to be cautious about taking this view too far. Obviously, establishing the requisite principles of liability is a *legal* question that requires consideration of existing authorities.

consequences of such act'. For a more extensive list of authorities, see Sales, 'Conspiracy', 504, fn. 39. Note also, the early case law supporting accessory-after-the-fact type liability [5.4.2.2].

84 *Cf. L'Oreal SA* v. *eBay International AG* [2009] EWHC 1094 (Ch) [2009] ETMR 53 [359].

85 We define the concept by reference to decisions on authorisation in IP statutory contexts noted elsewhere [9.2]. That concept, as well as others, has also been used to establish liability of directors for company wrongs, and is also considered in that context. See Chapter 11 for the various tests and see, e.g., *Sabaf SpA* v. *Meneghetti SpA* [2002] EWCA Civ 976; [2003] RPC 14 [59], below, n. 216.

86 See, e.g., *Sea Shepherd* [2015] UKSC 10; [2015] 2 WLR 694 [37], [56].

87 See, e.g., *Sepracor inc* v. *Hoechst Marrion Roussel Limited* [1999] FSR 746; (1999) 22 (4) IPD 22,034 [28] (Laddie J): 'Each case turns on its own facts. . . . Extensive reference to [other authorities] in court will normally not be productive.' *Cf. Unilever plc* v. *Gillette (UK) Ltd* [1989] RPC 583, 608.

The problems inherent in considering the appropriate limits of accessory liability can be illustrated by the following scenario: 'A' (an alleged accessory) supplies a baseball bat *knowing* that PW is obtaining it for the particular purpose of beating C (or members of the class of which C is a member), but A does not procure that tort.

A critical question for the law, and one that challenges the borders of liability, is whether this scenario ought to give rise to liability. Is A's involvement in this scenario sufficiently linked to PW's commission of the tort, and does A have sufficient knowledge or intention in relation to PW's acts such that A's conduct is sufficiently culpable? Is liability justified only if we construe the facts to find that A has entered into a common design with PW to that end? Does that finding add anything? The answer on current English authority is that, absent a common design, no liability should arise in tort law. Somewhat surprisingly, English law acknowledges the seemingly counter-intuitive conclusion that tort liability may be more restrictive than criminal liability:

> the consequence is that selling a person a gun knowing that person will use it to kill someone else will make the seller an accessory to the murder but will not in itself make him liable in tort.[88]

That conclusion is challenged in this chapter. Compare the above scenario with one in which A merely supplies a potential weapon (that it is lawful to sell) that foreseeably is used by some of the purchasers for committing wrongs. In this scenario, liability clearly does not arise: merely foreseeing such risks does not suffice.[89]

5.4.1.2 Procuring or inducing tortious acts or wrongs

Outside the law on inducing breach of contract [Chapter 6], there has been little attempt in the cases to define procuring (or inducing) [3.3.5][90] or to explain what, precisely, needs to be proved. Whether there has been procurement is essentially a question of fact and many of the cases do not

[88] *Fish* [2013] EWCA Civ. 544; [2013] 1 WLR 3700 (Beatson LJ, McCombe and Mummery LJJ concurring) [42], citing the 'well-known' example of Devlin J in *NCB* v. *Gamble* [1959] 1 QB 11, 23.

[89] Compare, however, the extension of liability in some US cases to other wrongs that are the foreseeable *consequences* of PW's wrong in which A was a knowing participant [5.4.5]. If, therefore, the example were stated as A supplies a baseball bat to PW, *knowing* that PW intends to use it to commit burglaries, then A may be liable for the beating of C if that is a foreseeable consequence of carrying out burglaries.

[90] *Cf. CBS Songs* [1988] AC 1013 (HL) 1058 (Lord Templeman): procure by 'inducement, incitement or persuasion'.

elaborate on the concept. The language of 'procurement' identifies conduct that clearly constitutes a sufficient involvement in PW's tort, namely, some positive acts aimed at bringing about PW's acts that are wrongs. It also implicitly suggests a sufficient mental state: A 'intends and procures and shares a common design that infringement shall take place'.[91] Procuring is therefore unequivocally linked with PW's wrong: both in terms of A's actions and A's intentions and therefore actual knowledge of the intended consequences.

For liability to arise, procurement must be of an act that is a *wrong*. Where A brings about or 'authorises' a lawful act, one would assume that A is not liable for any wrong committed by PW in performing that act; but should liability extend even where the commission of a wrong is merely a natural or inevitable consequence of that act? Similarly, if A procures an outcome that could have been achieved by lawful or unlawful means, A is probably not liable[92] unless A knew, or presumably, was recklessly indifferent to, the likelihood of PW using unlawful means to achieve the outcome. These issues have rarely been explored, and difficult questions of liability arise.

5.4.1.3 Common design

In order for a party to be liable on the basis of a common design, that party must, first, 'have assisted the commission of an act by the primary tortfeasor; secondly, . . . pursuant to a common design [with that person] that the act be committed; and, thirdly, the act must constitute a tort as against the claimant'.[93] There is therefore a conduct element since a party must have taken some more than *de minimis* or minimal steps[94] in furtherance of the commission of the tort;[95] agreement alone does not

[91] *Ibid.* 1058, though this statement does conflate procuring with common design.

[92] See *Sea Shepherd* [2015] UKSC 10; [2015] 2 WLR 694 [60].

[93] See *Sea Shepherd* [2015] UKSC 10; [2015] 2 WLR 694 [55] (Lord Neuberger); and see [37] (Lord Sumption); *cf.* the two elements of Lord Toulson [21], merging the second and third elements. See also *The Koursk* [1924] P 140 (CA), 156 and 155 (Scrutton LJ) and 159 (Sargent LJ), both quoting from *Clerk and Lindsell on Torts*, 7th edn, 59–60.

[94] See *Sea Shepherd* [2015] UKSC 10; [2015] 2 WLR 694 [57] (Lord Neuberger:'substantial' assistance); [49] (Lord Sumption: 'material' assistance), but both define these negatively as more than trivial, etc.

[95] *Unilever Plc* v. *Gillette (UK) Ltd* [1989] RPC 583, 609. A need not have 'joined in doing the very act constituting the tort': *Sea Shepherd* [2015] UKSC 10; [2015] 2 WLR 694 [38] (Lord Sumption dissenting on the facts). Where the tort of one person merely enables another to commit a tort, such parties will not be joint tortfeasors as there is no common design. *Clerk and Lindsell*, [4–04], 275, give the example of the negligence of a parent enabling a child to tortiously injure another: the parent may be independently, concurrently liable. They cite *Bebee* v. *Sales* (1916) 32 TLR 413; *Newton* v. *Edgerley* [1959] 1 WLR 1031.

suffice.[96] There must also be a mental element (agreeing to a 'common end'). This is in part established by the knowledge of A; and generally requires some knowledge by A of PW's acts or intended acts[97] that constitute a tort. Since, however, the authorities have stressed that assistance with knowledge is not sufficient for liability [5.4.2.3], [5.5.1], something more is required. Yet the authorities do not identify more precisely what a 'common design' or a 'common end' entails.[98] Of course, if there is evidence of express agreement, this suffices, but it is accepted that a 'common design' can arise even in the absence of a prior agreement and on the basis of tacit agreement.[99] As Mustill LJ stated in *Unilever plc* v. *Gillette (UK) Ltd*, in relation to 'common design' or 'concerted action':

> They all convey the same idea. The idea does not . . . call for any finding that the secondary party has explicitly mapped out a plan with the primary offender. Their tacit agreement will be sufficient.[100]

In Australia, it has been said that joint tortfeasors 'must act in concert in committing the tort'.[101] Subsequent courts have interpreted this statement, which appears ambiguous, in restrictive terms, as effectively requiring a common agreement or design. There must be 'at least an *understanding* between them as to their common purpose or object'.[102]

96 *Unilever Plc* v. *Chefaro Proprietaries Ltd* [1995] 1 All ER 587; [1994] FSR 135.

97 See *Sea Shepherd* [2015] UKSC 10; [2015] 2 WLR 694 [65]–[66] (Lord Neuberger) suggesting that knowledge of PW's intention to commit, or the inevitability of PW committing, the tortious acts, as necessary for a common design. Oddly, Lord Neuberger at [60] considers what A must have known about PW's conduct or intended conduct when discussing the third element of common design. *Cf.* Lord Toulson who seems to suggest that A must intend that PW commit the tortious act.

98 *Cf.* in the US, in *Halberstam* v. *Welch* 705 F2d 472, 478 (DC Cir, 1983) (Wald, Bork and Scalia JJ) 'conspiracy' (i.e., common design liability) is said to include the following four distinct factors: '(1) An agreement between two or more persons; (2) to participate in an unlawful act or a lawful act in an unlawful manner; (3) an injury caused by an unlawful overt act performed by one of the parties to the agreement; (4) which overt act was done pursuant to and in furtherance of the common scheme.'

99 Examples include *Sea Shepherd* [2015] UKSC 10; [2015] 2 WLR 694, and *Shah* v. *Gale* [2005] EWHC 1087, discussed [5.5.1]. See also *Credit Lyonnais Bank Nederland NV* v. *Export Credit Guarantee Department* [1998] 1 Lloyd's LR 19, 36. That further element is not intention.

100 [1989] RPC 583, 609. Mustill LJ also warned against construing as statutory terms the various expressions used to convey the same essential idea.

101 *Thompson* v. *Australian Capital Television Pty Ltd* [1996] HCA 381; (1996) 186 CLR 574, 581 (Brennan CJ, Dawson and Toohey JJ). Their Honours note that '[t]orts of all kinds may be joint and defamation is no exception'.

102 *Adsteam Building Industries Pty Ltd* v. *Queensland Cement and Lime Company Ltd (No 4)* [1985] 1 Qd R 127, 132 (McPherson J, emphasis added) (although this was not an accessory liability case). See also *Louis Vuitton Malletier SA* v. *Toea Pty Ltd* [2006] FCA

The content of the agreement determines the liability of A. Not only must A have taken more than some *de minimis* steps in furtherance of the common design, but the torts committed by PW must also have been done in furtherance of that design. In *Downham* v. *Bellette*,[103] the first defendant, A, was not liable to C for the significant assault and batteries committed by the second and third defendants. Although A had asked them to keep a look out for a person who had previously trespassed (by leaving, among other things, excrement on A's driveway) in order to *apprehend* the culprit (C), and was therefore liable for the false imprisonment when they did so, he was not party to a common design to commit batteries of the nature that had been committed.

5.4.1.4 'Aiding and abetting' in United States law

Although the theory and structure of US accessory law is unhelpful, as some courts in the US themselves have acknowledged,[104] some consideration of US tort law is nevertheless instructive in informing our law and drawing the boundaries of liability. Significantly, liability in the US extends to assistance and many of the seminal cases, it is suggested, are correctly decided.[105] In addition, borderline cases, in which liability *may* have been justifiable on the facts, provide useful factual scenarios that test the limits of liability in an Anglo-Australian context.

Tort law in the various US jurisdictions applies two main and overlapping concepts for determining whether a person is liable as an accessory, namely, acting 'in concert' (or common design) and 'aiding and abetting'. The former is in essence similar to liability on the basis of a common design in Anglo-Australian law, requiring acts done in accordance with an agreement. It is not discussed further here.[106] Of more

1443; (2006) 237 ALR 118 [148]–[164]; and in the context of defamation cases, e.g., *Commisso* v. *United Telecasters Sydney Pty Ltd* [1999] NSWSC 51 [63] (Levine J):

> It is not merely 'participation' or 'connection' or 'involvement' in the commission of a tort which renders a person liable as a joint tortfeasor. It is acting in concert or concurrence to achieve a common end which is required.

[103] (1986) Aust Torts Reports 80–038. [104] See references above n. 4.

[105] This is so at least outside of the securities context, the case law on which is too complex and diverse to be able to generalise.

[106] This type of liability is also described as conspiracy, though it is uncertain what the relationship is between this source of liability and a separate tort of conspiracy, if any such tort should exist. See, e.g., J. Whitson, 'Civil Conspiracy: A Substantive Tort?' (1979) 59 *Boston University Law Review* 921. Courts in the US have been less willing than those in Anglo-Australian jurisdictions to accept a concept of lawful act conspiracy. See, e.g., *Cohen* v. *Bowdoin* 288 A2d 106, 110 (Me 1972) (Wernick J: 'no liability for

interest is aiding and abetting liability. The *Restatement (Second) of Torts* §876(b) (1979) provides:

> For harms resulting to a third person from the tortious conduct of another, one is subject to liability if he. . .
>
> (b) knows that the other's conduct constitutes a breach of duty and gives substantial assistance or encouragement to the other so to conduct himself;[107]

These elements reflect the broad structure adopted in this book, namely, the commission of a primary wrong and involvement ('substantial assistance') in that wrong with knowledge of the 'breach of duty' or wrongdoing (the mental state). However, there is considerable confusion apparent in the cases about what these concepts encompass; some courts have considered that the elements are too widely stated.[108] Consequent to the perceived shortcomings of the *Restatement* when applied to financial transaction and securities cases, courts have developed the 'judicial test' for civil aiding and abetting, which *appears* to be different in some important regards,[109] stressed in the words emphasised:

conspiracy absent the actual commission of some independently recognized tort; and when such separate tort has been committed, it is that tort, and not the fact of combination, which is the foundation of the civil liability'). See also [5.3.2].

[107] See also §876(c), person liable if he: 'gives substantial assistance to the other in accomplishing a tortious result and his own conduct, separately considered constitutes a breach of duty to the third person'. This is an oddly expressed principle, and appears to capture persons who have themselves committed a primary breach of a duty. It does not appear to be a form of accessory liability. Further, most of the illustrations given in the *Restatement* are examples in which no liability arises at all. See *Restatement (Second) of Torts Appendix §§ 841 to End*, 121 (1977).

See also § 877 of the *Restatement*, 'Directing or Permitting Conduct of Another', which sets out a number of other grounds for liability confusingly grouped together. However, much of this falls within the main body of negligence liability, a point seemingly acknowledged in the comments to the *Restatement* 321.

[108] For example, it has been assumed by some courts and commentators that knowledge of some general unlawful conduct may satisfy the knowledge element. See, e.g., *Woodward* v. *Metro Bank of Dallas* 522 F2d 84, 94–95 (5th Cir, 1975). In *Woodward*, the court appeared to assume (albeit in a cryptic judgment) that facilitating *the business* of a wrongdoer may satisfy the assistance requirement under the *Restatement* test, rather than the test requiring assistance by A *in* the actual wrong committed by PW. *Cf.* at 95 (and see generally 95–96). Seemingly suggesting that such knowledge might suffice, see *Metge* v. *Baehler* 762 F2d 621, 630 (8th Cir, 1985). See also the absurd examples given by Combs, 'Civil Aiding', 274–278, albeit rejecting liability in such cases, but seemingly suggesting that current tests could capture such 'accessories'; and see at 286.

[109] At times, however, the courts cite both tests together without comment: e.g., *Re Temporomandibular Joint (TMJ) Implants Products Liability Litigation*, 113 F3d 1484 (8th Cir, 1997).

> (1) the primary actor must commit a wrongful act that causes an injury; (2) the aider and abettor *must be generally aware of his role* in the overall wrongful activity at the time assistance is provided; and (3) the aider and abettor must *knowingly* and substantially assist the wrongful act.[110]

The notion of 'substantial assistance' is relevant to the discussion of involvement; less helpful is US law on the knowledge requirement. The status and role of knowledge in the judicial test is confused, in part because the judicial test has two references to knowledge and it is not clear what separate role these play.[111]

5.4.2 Conduct

5.4.2.1 Is there a need for a causal link between A's involvement and PW's wrongdoing?

For accessory liability, as we have conceptualised it, there must be some conduct by A that establishes a link with the tort committed by PW, that is, that involves A in PW's wrongful acts. Does A's conduct, however, need to be *causally* connected to the commission of PW's tort and thereby to C's loss? As we concluded in [3.3.3] the accessory's conduct in most areas of accessory liability does not need to be a 'but for' cause of either PW's decision or capacity to commit the wrong, though procuring a wrong is an exception to this. For example, if A2 joins A1 and PW in a common design to commit a tort, such conduct ought to give rise to liability even if A1 and PW had already decided to, and had the capacity to, carry out such design regardless of A2's participation. We cannot dismiss liability merely because there is no 'but for' causative connection.[112] Instead, A's conduct generally only needs to be a contributing

[110] *Ibid.* 1495 (8th Cir, 1997). *Cf. Gould* v. *American Hawaiian* 535 F2d 761 (1976), citing *Rochez Brothers, Inc.* v. *Rhoades (Rochez II)* 527 F2d 880, 886 (3d Cir, 1975). A fourth element, that the alleged substantial assistance must be the 'proximate cause' of the plaintiff's harm (the harm must be within the scope of A's liability) is noted in [5.4.5].

[111] See Combs, 'Civil Aiding', 267: the two concepts seem almost indistinguishable. See also 289–291.

[112] Stevens, *Torts*, 254, has pointed out that no causal link is necessary where there is a conspiracy or common design to carry out a tort (or where a tort has been 'authorised' by another): that is, liability will follow even if the tort would have been carried out in any event; Sales, 'Conspiracy', 510, 509, fn. 62, in advocating a broad accessory liability regime that extends to assistance liability, seems to agree.

factor (as explained in [3.3.3]) towards PW's decision or capacity to commit the wrong. This ought also to be the position in tort law.[113]

These general propositions appear to be consistent with the case law. In applying the common design test, Lord Neuberger in *Sea Shepherd* stated that C does not 'need to establish that the tort would not have been committed, or even that it would not have been committed in the precise way that it was, without the assistance of the defendant'.[114] The act done merely needs to be more than a '*de minimis*' or trivial contribution to the tort. Of course, this poses the question of what *de minimis* means here, although Lord Neuberger noted that assistance may be more than *de minimis* even if it is relatively minor or indirect in terms of its contribution to the tortious act.[115]

US case law also supports the conclusion that A's conduct need not be a 'but for' cause of PW's decision, or capacity, to commit the tort such that in the absence of A's conduct C would have escaped harm; the act must merely 'be *a* factor in the resulting harm'.[116] For example, in *Rael* v. *Cadena*,[117] the defendant, who had given verbal

[113] This conclusion compares with the view of Paul Davies, arguing that there must be 'some causal link' between assistance and the commission of the primary tort and absent such causal relationship there is no basis for liability: 'Accessory Liability for Assisting Torts' (2011) 70 *Cambridge Law Journal* 353, 360. See also at 359: 'the need for a causal link should not be ignored'. It is not entirely clear whether Davies is suggesting that 'but for' causation needs to be established, though reading the comments in context, it appears not and that Davies merely intends by such terminology to exclude trivial or *de minimis* conduct by A. See at 359–360 (connections between assistance and tort 'less strong' than for inducement, but in both cases, are 'necessarily attenuated') and 355–336. We agree with that general conclusion, contrary to earlier views expressed by one of the authors: J. Dietrich, 'Accessory Liability in the Law of Torts' (2011) 31 *Legal Studies* 231.

[114] See *Sea Shepherd* [2015] UKSC 10; [2015] 2 WLR 694 [57]. See also at [49] (Lord Sumption): 'the assistance [need not] have been indispensable to the commission of the tort'. Contrast the reference in *Credit Lyonnais Bank Nederland NV* v. *Export Credit Guarantee Department* [1998] 1 Lloyd's LR 19, 36, to whether A's conduct was an 'essential part' of PW's wrong. In *Fish* [2013] EWCA Civ 544; [2013] 1 WLR 3700 [55], such reference was explained away, and the court reiterated the absence of such element in formulations by, e.g., Glidewell LJ in *Unilever Plc* v. *Chefaro Proprietaries Ltd* [1995] 1 All ER 587; [1994] FSR 135, and Hobhouse LJ in *Credit Lyonnais* at 46.

[115] See *Sea Shepherd* [2015] UKSC 10; [2015] 2 WLR 694 [57].

[116] See N. I. Combs, 'Civil Aiding and Abetting Liability' (2005) 58 *Vanderbilt Law Review* 241, 293, citing Dan B. Dobbs, *The Law of Torts* (2000) § 171, 415. Liability is limited by reference to the 'proximate cause' concept (or extent of liability) discussed in [5.4.5].

[117] 93 NM 684; 604 P2d 822 (1979). The court noted that mere presence at the scene would not be sufficient for liability. Of course, if encouragement occurs before the unlawful venture has commenced, then it may not only have been a significant factor in PW's decision, it could easily shade into a 'but for' inducement.

encouragement ('Kill him!' and 'Hit him more!') to an assailant, but had not physically assisted in a battery, was culpable without proof that the injury had directly resulted from the encouragement. The court found that the fact of encouragement was enough to create joint liability for the battery even absent a finding of action in concert.[118] The preponderance of US authorities merely requires that any assistance must be 'substantial'.[119]

In summary, 'but for' causation of either PW's decision to commit or PW's manner of carrying out the tortious acts is not required for A's liability. This means that as a general principle, any conduct that materially (that is, not trivially) contributes to PW's decision or capacity to commit the wrong, and that thereby increases the likelihood of the commission of the wrong, could potentially suffice as an act of involvement.[120] A's conduct needs to be *a* relevant factor, in the sense that A's conduct is more than a minimal step in furtherance of the wrong (and therefore C's harm) but need not be a necessary condition of it.

5.4.2.2 The type of conduct that constitutes involvement

A variety of conduct can constitute involvement in a wrong.[121]

Procuring has been defined as conduct directed at PW that seeks to bring about a particular outcome. In the tort of inducing breach of

[118] The court cited the *Restatement* § 876(b). Some US cases have stated the requirement in terms of proof that the aider 'caused the harm on which the primary liability is predicated'. See, e.g., *Cromer Financial Ltd* v. *Berger* 137 FSupp 2d 452, 470 (SDNY 2001). See also Mark Bartholomew and Patrick F. McArdle, 'Causing Infringement' (2011) 64 *Vanderbilt Law Review* 675, 698 onwards, stating the requirement in tort as one requiring a causal link. Again, this is presumably not a reference to 'but for' causation.

[119] It should be noted, however, that the notion of 'substantial' is not exclusively limited to the causal impact of the assistance. See below n. 195.

[120] A must 'have done something or put himself in a position which ... does expose the rights of others to risk and danger', to quote Harrison Moore, 'Misfeasance and Non-feasance in the Liability of Public Authorities' (1914) 30 *Law Quarterly Review* 276, 278, in a different context. *Cf.* the low threshold test from criminal law: whether A's conduct or words do something to render more likely the contravention. See *Giorgianni* v. *R* [1985] HCA 29; (1985) 156 CLR 473, 492.

[121] That conduct must be linked to the jurisdiction in which action is brought. An accessory's conduct may be actionable and governed by the law of a jurisdiction even if it occurred outside of the jurisdiction, so long as the primary tort occurred in the jurisdiction. See *Morton-Norwich Products Inc* v. *Intercen Ltd* [1978] RPC 501, 515, approved in *Apotex Pty Ltd* v. *Les Laboratoires Servier (No 2)* [2012] FCA 748 [24]. Further, claims may be brought against accessories within a jurisdiction for torts committed outside of a jurisdiction. See, e.g., *Sea Shepherd* [2015] UKSC 10; [2015] 2 WLR 694.

contract, such conduct may include threats, payments, persuasion, etc. [6.3.3]. Outside of the breach of contract context, procuring has been held to include telling or asking others to commit a wrong. A solicitor who tells his client to obtain documents belonging to her husband is potentially liable for the trespass or conversion committed.[122] A defendant who sends out his hounds and servants to hunt, having been given notice not to enter C's land, is liable for the trespasses and all damage committed by other gentlemen he has invited to hunt with him, even if he does not enter the land himself.[123]

For participating in a common design, the courts have not as clearly identified the types of conduct (the acts) that constitute accessory liability. Although it is clear that quite minor acts of assistance can give rise to liability *if* the parties are in a common design, it is not clear what further conduct factors are necessary to establish a common design, particularly a tacit agreement. For example, if A tells PW that C lives at a certain address, this seems harmless enough. But what if A knows that PW intends to beat C?[124] Should A be liable for PW's commission of the tort? Presumably, even a tacit agreement must include within it an (albeit unstated) knowledge requirement. Lord Sumption in *Sea Shepherd (UK)* v. *Fish & Fish Ltd* (*Sea Shepherd*) said that the evidence of a common design in some cases was 'thin', but more problematically, none of the Law Lords identified what evidence is required.

One thing is certain, however, passive observers, without more, are not liable for the torts committed by others in their presence,[125] a position that is consistent with other areas of accessory liability [3.3.6]. Consistently with the law's general objection to rendering persons liable for omissions, it has been said that cases of liability 'in tort for pure omission are in truth rare . . . [t]he common law . . . looks askance at . . . liability . . . merely upon the omission to do something which would have prevented the mischief'.[126] Therefore, for example, a police officer is not

[122] *White* v. *Withers LLP* [2009] EWCA Civ 1122; [2010] 1 FLR 859 (strikeout application).

[123] *Baker* v. *Berkeley* (1827) 3 C & P 32; 172 ER 310.

[124] *Cf. Gale* v. *Shah; Gale* v. *Grant and Others* [2005] EWHC 1087 (QB).

[125] *Pringle* v. *Everingham* [2006] NSWCA 195 [94]. See also *McFadzean* v. *CFMEU* [2004] VSC 289 [138], where Ashley J notes that according to Glanville Williams, 'a tortfeasor does not become a joint tortfeasor only because he knows that a similar tort is being committed by another at the same time'.

[126] Moore, 'Misfeasance' (1914) 30 *Law Quarterly Review* 276, 278, cited with approval in *Roadshow* [2012] HCA 16; (2012) 248 CLR 42 [108]. See also, e.g., *Stovin* v. *Wise* [1996] AC 923 (HL) 943–944 (Lord Hoffmann giving reasons for the law's reluctance to impose liability for omissions).

liable for a battery committed in his presence by an accompanying officer where the first did not share the intention to commit the battery. However, if the battery were 'contemplated . . . as a possible incident of the joint enterprise to arrest and subdue the plaintiff', then presumably liability would follow.[127] The more difficult question is whether mere presence suffices if there already exists an express agreement to commit the tort? One would assume so. Even though the participants to a joint enterprise must act 'in furtherance of such an agreement',[128] standing by when the tort is committed ought to suffice where a common design has been entered into by the watcher.[129] Liability for passive conduct might also arise if A's presence *and status* as an actor in the specific drama facilitates (albeit passively) another's wrong.[130]

Liability does not arise for conduct by a person *after* the commission of a wrong since it cannot satisfy the requirement of wrongful involvement *in* the wrong.[131] There are, however, some early English cases[132] and some anomalous US cases that appear to support liability in these circumstances.[133] Such liability would be too broad and is contrary to a

[127] *Pringle* v. *Everingham* [2006] NSWCA 195 [94]. [128] *Ibid.* [93].

[129] See *ibid.* [93]–[94], implicitly supporting such a conclusion, in interpreting and qualifying a statement by John Fleming in the 9th edn of *The Law of Torts* (Australia, LBC, 1998) 289: 'Knowingly assisting, encouraging or merely being present as a conspirator at the commission of the wrong would suffice.'

[130] At least some early cases have suggested that liability extends to someone who, by standing by, assents to the acts of others, especially where such party has some control over the situation. See *M'Laughlin* v. *Pryor* (1842) 4 Man and G 48; 134 ER 21. Similarly, it has been said that liability for the fraud of a co-director of a company might arise if the fellow directors 'wilfully and with a view to enable him to do this abstain from interfering where they ought to have interfered'. See *Cargill* v. *Bower* (1878) 10 Ch D 502, 514–515 (Fry J). Such an approach is consistent with criminal law; *cf.*, e.g., *Randall and Farmer* v. *R* [2004] TASSC 42.

[131] *Cf.* the liability of a principal for the ratification of an agent's earlier wrongful actions, e.g., in *Hilbery* v. *Hatton* (1864) 2 H and C 822; 159 ER 341. This is not accessory liability, but is based on the authority of an agent and the binding nature of the agent's acts upon the principal.

[132] E.g., *Petrie* v. *Lamont* (1841) Car and M 93, 96; 174 ER 424, 426 (Tindal CJ) suggesting that business partners may be liable for a trespass committed by another partner, by 'evidence afterwards that they concurred and received the benefit of it'. The claim arose from the ejectment of the plaintiff from his premises, and the seizure of his goods. Similarly in *Barker* v. *Braham and Norwood* (1773) 3 Black W 866, 868; 96 ER 510, 511, De Grey CJ stated that a joint trespasser includes one 'who assents afterwards'.

[133] See, e.g., *Little* v. *Tingle*, 26 Ind. 168 (1866), in which the defendant was held liable for encouraging and assisting battery, including for injuries incurred *before* that assistance took place; and see *Stull* v. *Porter* 196 Pac 1116, 1118 (1921) (liability for wrongful act done for A's benefit, 'and that he approved it').

principled analysis, since such acts do not contribute to the commission of that wrong.

5.4.2.3 Assistance does not suffice for liability?

The modern English view that mere assistance of a tort, not being in pursuance of a common design or procuring the tort, does not suffice for accessory liability is said to follow from Lord Templeman's judgment in *CBS Songs*,[134] and is categorically put by Hobhouse LJ in *Credit Lyonnais Bank Nederland NV* v. *Export Credit Guarantee Department*:[135]

> the authorities ... show ... that knowing assistance is not enough to found tortious liability. ...
>
> Accordingly, in my judgment there is no second category [of aiding and abetting] in the law of tort. Mere assistance, even knowing assistance, does not suffice to make the 'secondary' party jointly liable as a joint tortfeasor with the primary party. What he does must go further.[136]

The rejection of assistance liability has recently been affirmed by the UK Supreme Court in *Sea Shepherd*,[137] which is discussed in relation to trespass in [5.5.1].

In Australian law, there are cases in which broader formulations are seemingly endorsed, so that it is arguable that the courts are open to a broader test for liability.[138] It must be conceded, however, that in the

[134] [1988] 1 AC 1013. See also Carty, 'Joint Tortfeasance', 503–504.

[135] [1998] 1 Lloyd's Rep 19.

[136] *Ibid.* 46. There is no shortage of supporting authorities: *PLG Research Ltd* v. *Ardon International Ltd* [1993] FSR 197, 238–239, (albeit dealing with director's liability for a patent infringement); *Unilever Plc* v. *Gillette (UK) Ltd* [1989] RPC 583, 608–609; *The Proctor and Gamble Co* v. *Reckitt Benckiser (UK) Ltd* [2006] EWHC 2872 [17]; *MCA Records* [2002] EMLR 1 [51]. Supporting commentators include Carty, 'Joint Tortfeasance'. Contra, see Sales, 'Conspiracy', and Davies, 'Accessory Liability'.

[137] [2015] UKSC 10; [2015] 2 WLR 694.

[138] There are a number of ambiguous judicial statements that could be seen as supporting liability for 'mere' assistance. E.g., in *Thompson* v. *Australian Capital Television Pty Ltd* [1996] HCA 381; (1996) 186 CLR 574, 600 (Gummow J), (Gaudron J agreeing at 580) citing Sargant LJ's broad statement in *The 'Koursk'*, accepting the proposition that persons are joint tortfeasors when their 'respective shares in the commission of the tort are done in furtherance of a common design' so that those who 'aid or counsel, direct, or join' in commission of the tort are joint tortfeasors. Admittedly, Gummow J's statement appears to limit the reference to aid or join to the earlier phrase, 'in furtherance of a common design', but in *Temple* v. *Powell* [2008] FCA 714 [43]–[44], Dowsett J noted the possible ambiguity: 'It was not necessary for his Honour to consider whether there was any inconsistency between the two propositions or to state any preference as

context of IP cases, and in particular patent infringement cases,[139] Australian courts have generally accepted the UK courts' preclusion of assistance liability.[140]

When considering trespass torts, we challenge the conclusion that 'assistance is not enough to found tortious liability' because such an approach leads to artificial reasoning and is conceptually unnecessary,

between them'. See also *TS and B Retail Systems Pty Ltd* v. *3Fold Resources Pty Ltd (No 3)* [2007] FCA 151; (2007) 239 ALR 117 [178].

Similarly, in *McFadzean* v. *CFMEU* [2004] VSC 289 [137] (references deleted), Ashley J quoted with approval broad but ambiguous statements in John G. Fleming, *The Law of Torts*, 9th edn (Sydney, LBC Information Services, 1998), and stated that the law on the issue 'is clear':

> Broadly speaking, says Fleming, 'This means a conspiracy with all participants acting in furtherance of the wrong, though it is not necessary that they should realise they are committing a tort'. As to the extent of required involvement, Fleming proposes that there should be included not only the perpetrator of an act but also 'anyone who "aids and abets" whether or not he actively intervenes. Knowingly assisting, encouraging or even being present as a conspirator at the commission of the wrong would suffice'.

Are the concepts of 'knowing assistance' and 'encouragement' limited by the phrase 'as conspirators' and by earlier references to participation in a conspiracy? The statement is repeated in the 10th edn of Fleming. *McFadzean* concerned accessory liability for false imprisonment, assault and battery, the intentional infliction of harm ('*Wilkinson* v. *Downton*' liability), and public nuisance, arising out of conflicts between anti-logging protestors and loggers. Joint liability was held to exist on the basis of *Wilkinson*, and public nuisance, but not on other grounds. See also on appeal: *McFadzean* v. *Construction, Forestry, Mining & Energy Union* [2007] VSCA 289; (2007) 20 VR 250 (CA), SLR [2008] HCATrans 213 (23 May 2008).

139 In our view, special policy considerations may justify a restrictive approach excluding liability for knowing facilitation in the specific context of patents and other IP cases [5.5.2.4]. Outside of patents, many of the cases rejecting liability for assistance are explicable and consistent with the denial of liability on other grounds, namely that the requisite content of knowledge was not present. E.g., *CBS Songs* [1988] AC 1013 [5.5.2].

140 E.g., in *Murex Diagnostics Australia Pty Ltd* v. *Chiron Corporation & Ortho Diagnostic Systems Inc* (1995) 30 IPR 277, 288–289; 55 FCR 194, Burchett J approved the following, quoting from *Mölnlycke AB* v. *Procter and Gamble Ltd* [1992] 1 WLR 1112, 1118 (Dillon LJ, Woolf and Leggatt LJJ agreeing):

> A person who merely facilitated, but did not procure, the infringement was not a joint tortfeasor with the infringer and so was not liable if, for instance, he sold articles which could be used for infringing or non-infringing purposes even though he knew that they would probably be used and were intended to be used for the infringing purposes.

Burchett J considered the UK decisions to be consistent with the High Court's decision in *Walker* v. *Alemite Corp* (1933) 49 CLR 643, discussed in [5.5.2.4]. See also, e.g., *Cooper* v. *Universal Music Australia Pty Ltd* [2006] FCAFC 187; (2006) 156 FCR 380 [173]; *Louis Vuitton Malletier SA* v. *Toea Pty Ltd* [2006] FCA 1443; (2006) 237 ALR 118 [163] and [164].

at least in some torts cases. That conclusion need not apply to all torts: the law in relation to different torts may continue to adopt a narrow or broader approach to the conduct element of accessory liability. Significantly, liability for assistance need not of itself be broader than existing liability since the work of confining liability can be done by reference to A's mental state, that is, by application of a rigorous knowledge requirement.[141]

5.4.3 *Mental element: A's knowledge*

5.4.3.1 Overview

It is necessary to consider A's mental state when A involves himself in PW's wrongdoing: what must A know at the time of such involvement? Without some wrongful involvement, there is no basis for sheeting home responsibility to A for the tort of another. This section addresses the general principles and issues relevant to knowledge, but what A must have known in order to be liable is discussed in more detail in relation to the case law on specific torts [5.5]. Liability is a question of fact and the requisite knowledge depends on the wrong being committed and may vary according to the extent of A's involvement in that wrong. It is therefore difficult to draw general conclusions here. The interrelationship between knowledge and involvement has been considered in US law and is addressed further in [5.4.4].

Three broad questions arise in relation to A's knowledge. The first two concern the requisite content of A's knowledge [3.4.2] (and, consequently, the scope of A's liability). The third question concerns the requisite degree of A's knowledge [3.4.3].

First, how precise and detailed must A's knowledge be? For example, must A know who the precise tortfeasor is, or merely of the class of possible tortfeasors (the who question); must A know when and where the wrongs take place (the when/where question)? This problem may arise, for example, when A facilitates mass infringements of IP rights by numerous tortfeasors via the internet [5.5.2].

[141] *Cf.*, e.g., David S. Ruder, 'Multiple Defendants in Securities Law Fraud Cases: Aiding and Abetting, Conspiracy, In Pari Delicto, Indemnification and Contribution' (1972) 120 *University of Pennsylvania Law Review* 597, 630. This approach is consistent with the approach in other areas of law, such as statutory civil accessory liability, where a broad range of conduct suffices as involvement, including aiding and abetting and even encouraging the commission of a wrongful act [Chapter 10], but the knowledge requirement constrains liability.

Secondly, does it suffice if A merely knows of the generic type of wrongdoing that PW intends (the 'which tort' question)? This requires a consideration of the 'essential matters' [3.4.2.2] of the tort committed by PW and also goes to the scope of A's liability, a difficult issue rarely expressly addressed in civil law [5.4.5].

Thirdly, does something less than actual knowledge suffice? For example, what if A is recklessly indifferent to PW committing certain acts that are tortious? This is the *degree* of knowledge question.

Importantly, the requisite mental state may vary according to the tort in question. For example, it is difficult to prove accessory liability for the tort of deceit. For the commission of a tort that has a *mens rea* element such as dishonesty, liability can only be imposed on accessories who procure such conduct with the same mental state. The parties must have the required state of mind in common;[142] A must either have the same dishonest intention or – and it amounts to the same thing – deliberately participate in PW's scheme knowing that PW has such dishonest intention.[143]

5.4.3.2 Content of knowledge

The following discussion considers in general terms the possible content of knowledge that may suffice for liability, that is, what are the 'essential matters' going to the wrong. The issue is addressed in detail when considering the individual torts.

One point that the courts have stressed irrespective of which test of liability is applied is that A need not be aware of the unlawfulness of PW's conduct; it suffices for A to know that PW is committing or intends to commit the acts that are wrongful and that constitute the tort. There is 'no need for the common design to be to commit the tort. It suffices that the parties have combined to secure the doing of acts which in the event prove to be tortious'.[144]

[142] See *Gardiner* v. *Moore* [1969] 1 QB 55, 91(comments were made in the context of a case on absence of malice and defamation, but the principles are stated in more generally applicable terms). See also *Johnson Matthey (Aust) Ltd* v. *Dascorp Pty Ltd* [2003] VSC 291; (2003) 9 VR 171, 195 [150].

[143] If two parties do have a common fraudulent state of mind, however, then the precise role each party had in the fraudulent scheme is by the way. The briber of an agent and the agent are both liable for a fraud committed against the principal; it would not matter which party dealt with the principal. See *Salford Corporation* v. *Lever* [1891] 1 QB 168; see also *Mahesan* v. *Malaysian Housing Society* [1979] AC 374 (PC).

[144] See, e.g., *Sea Shepherd* [2015] UKSC 10; [2015] 2 WLR 694 [60]; *Fish* [2013] EWCA Civ 544; [2013] 1 WLR 3700 [66], citing *Unilever plc* v. *Gillette (UK) Ltd* [1989] RPC 583, 609.

In relation to procurement, the question of A's mental state is implicit: where A procures PW to commit a tortious act, although knowledge is not specifically alluded to, A clearly knows that PW may do so, and probably even *intends* that PW do so,[145] although any 'intention' is satisfied by A's deliberate conduct to bring about PW's wrong.[146]

Less obvious is what A needs to know in order to be in a common design with PW. It is clearly sufficient if A knows that a specific tortfeasor (or a class of tortfeasor) is committing or intends to commit specific types of acts (that prove tortious) (though such precise knowledge is not always necessary).[147] For example, it is in circumstances such as where A is present at the scene of the tort and therefore is fully aware of what is going on (for example, a battery by PW on C) that US cases such as *Rael* v. *Cadena*[148] [5.4.2.1] have imposed liability for relatively 'minor' acts of involvement such as encouragement after a battery has already begun. No doubt, Anglo-Australian law would find a tacit agreement in such circumstances. It is not necessary, however, that the tortious acts be certain to follow, for example, if PW was merely prepared to use tortious means in some circumstances, or such means were inevitable in certain eventualities.[149]

Where A's conduct is targeted towards facilitating infringement and has no plausible, legitimate purpose other than to encourage unlawful conduct at large, then A may be liable even absent precise knowledge as to the circumstances of the infringements. Liability may be justified because infringements are inevitable or highly likely. The cases on 'joint' tortfeasor liability for IP torts bear out these conclusions [5.5.2]. A similar approach to liability in the absence of precise knowledge may

Similarly, see e.g., *McFadzean* v. *CFMEU* [2004] VSC 289 [137] (parties need not realise they are committing a tort).

145 The point is made by Lord Templeman in *CBS Songs Ltd* [1988] AC 1013, 1058, in describing a procurer: 'he intends and procures and shares a common design that infringement shall take place'.

146 A need not even necessarily know of the wrongful quality of that conduct. See discussion on IP in Chapter 9 and Chapter 3. *Cf.* inducing breach of contract, where A must know that PW's conduct is a breach [Chapter 6].

147 See *Sea Shepherd* [2015] UKSC 10; [2015] 2 WLR 694 [60] (Lord Neuberger): C does not need to show 'that the defendant knew that a specific act harming a specific defendant was intended.' *Cf.* Beatson LJ in the Court of Appeal in *Fish* [2013] EWCA Civ 544; [2013] 1 WLR 3700 [44]: A must have 'actual knowledge of the intent [by PW] to commit the specific tort' in order to be liable.

148 93 NM 684, 604 P2d 822 (1979). See also *Little* v. *Tingle*, 26 Ind 168 (1866).

149 See *Sea Shepherd* [2015] UKSC 10; [2015] 2 WLR 694 [27], [48].

also be seen, even in trespass cases, in the US [5.5.1].[150] Absent inevitable or highly likely infringements, however, it is difficult to justify liability.

5.4.3.3 Degrees of knowledge

Turning to the degree of A's knowledge, it seems that the courts have rejected a requirement that A must intend the wrong:[151] intent is not a necessary ingredient of civil, as opposed to criminal, liability.[152] Clearly, however, it would suffice for liability if such intent were present, coupled with conduct to carry out that intent. Beyond this, the courts have rarely considered the requisite degree of knowledge and the common law tests do not allude to it. Clearly, actual knowledge by A of PW's intended actions will suffice, but some cases are also consistent with A being liable where he is recklessly indifferent to the substantial likelihood of PW committing a wrong, especially where A is more active in the overall wrongdoing. This appears to be so particularly in the IP tort cases [5.5.2], nuisance cases [5.5.3][153] and in US case law. Mere negligence is not sufficient to make A liable as a culpable participant in PW's tort.[154] Were it otherwise, parties could be accessories to torts merely for failing to foresee that PW may commit such torts. Such liability could be broader than that of PW and would also circumvent the tort of negligence.[155]

[150] This is especially so where the conduct is done for the (economic) benefit of the assistant. See *Rice* v. *Paladin Enterprises, Inc* 128 F3d 233 (4th Cir, 1997). See also *Halberstam* v. *Welch* 705 F2d 472, 482 (DC Cir, 1983).

[151] *Sea Shepherd* [2015] UKSC 10; [2015] 2 WLR 694, supports that conclusion implicitly, there being no stated element of intent; see, e.g., at [60] (Lord Neuberger); note, however, that at [41] Lord Sumption (dissenting on the facts) suggests that A must intend that PW commit the tortious act.

[152] See *TS and B Retail Systems Pty Ltd* v. *3Fold Resources Pty Ltd (No 3)* [2007] FCA 151; (2007) 239 ALR 117 [178], though it should be noted that intent is generally established in criminal law by the deliberate or conscious conduct of A done with actual knowledge of the wrong.

[153] It has been suggested in one case in nuisance that a lesser mental element should perhaps suffice: see n. 257.

[154] See also obiter in *Grimme Maschinenfabrik Gmbh and Co KG* v. *Scott* [2010] EWCA Civ 1110 [106], that negligence is an insufficient knowledge requirement of intentional torts.

[155] See, e.g., *Paterson Zochonis and Co Ltd* v. *Merfarken Packaging Ltd* [1986] 3 All ER 522, in which claims were brought against a supplier of printed matter used by another to commit the tort of passing off. The English Court of Appeal struck out claims based on the party being unknowingly 'privy' to such tort, or an accessory to such tort, merely on the basis of a negligent failure to inquire and the foreseeability of damages flowing from the use made by the third party of the printed materials. Although these claims were framed in the tort of negligence, and the Court ruled that no duty of care arose in the circumstances, the judgments also stressed that such a claim would in effect render the

5.4.4 *The relationship between the conduct and mental elements*

As already noted, it is difficult to draw general conclusions as to the required content and degree of knowledge that justifies liability. This is one reason why this book advocates that a flexible approach to liability is needed. In particular, it appears that what A must know and the degree to which A must know it may depend on how actively A was involved in the wrong. When considered together, alongside other factors such as the tort committed, A's involvement and A's knowledge determine whether A's conduct is wrongful such as to justify liability. In short, the greater A's involvement in the commission of a wrong, the less knowledge A need have about the particular parties committing the torts and the circumstances in which the tort is committed; the more detailed A's knowledge is about the torts being committed, the parties committing them and the circumstances in which they are committed, the less involvement on A's part may justify liability.

There are parallels to this approach in US tort law, where the courts have developed a framework for determining accessory liability that is called the 'sliding scale' or 'in-tandem' approach. The sliding scale analysis proposes that the elements of knowledge and substantial assistance comprised within the test for civil aiding and abetting be analysed in tandem, or 'relative to one another'.[156] For example, in *Re Temporomandibular Joint (TMJ) Implants Products Liability Litigation*, the court stated:

> We evaluate the [knowledge] and [substantial assistance] requirements in tandem – the stronger the evidence of [the defendant's] general awareness of the alleged tortious activity, the less evidence of the defendant's substantial assistance is required.[157]

Similarly, in *Metge* v. *Baehler*:

innocent party an accessory to another's tort. See particularly the judgment of Oliver J at 526, 529. At 530, Oliver J puts the question in terms of whether the 'innocent but ... careless supply of such materials' to the party engaging in passing off can be a 'ground of liability'.

[156] *Metge* v. *Baehler* 762 F2d 621, 624 (8th Cir, 1985), citing *Stokes* v. *Lokken*, 644 F2d 779, 784 (8th Cir, 1981). It has been suggested by Combs, 'Civil Aiding', 268, that the 'sliding scale' has been proposed as a way of dealing with the 'difficulty' of proving knowledge and substantial assistance as elements (citing Josephine Willis, 'To (B) or Not to (B): The Future of Aider and Abettor Liability in South Carolina' 51 *South Carolina Law Rev* 1045, 1056 (2000). 'Difficulty', Combs notes, refers to the inconsistencies in the formulations of the various tests.

[157] 113 F3d 1484, 1495 (8th Cir, 1997), citing *Metge* v. *Baehler* 762 F2d 621, 624 (8th Cir, 1985).

> Practically speaking, this means that 'where there is a minimal showing of substantial assistance, a greater showing of scienter is required.' ... Thus the two factors vary inversely relative to one another and where, as here, the evidence of substantial assistance is slim, the requirement of knowledge or scienter is enhanced accordingly.[158]

The converse also seems to apply; that is, if knowledge is minimal, then more substantial 'assistance' or involvement would need to be proven.

The sliding scale analysis has been the subject of criticism. In the view of Combs, for example, the fundamental basis for aiding and abetting liability is that the defendant *both* (1) knows of the primary actor's wrongful conduct, and (2) substantially assists or encourages PW to so act. Combs argues that where there is complete knowledge, almost any degree of assistance would attract liability under the sliding scale approach, which undermines the requirement of 'substantial assistance'. Combs therefore concludes that the logical approach is to analyse the defendant's knowledge and assistance independently and that both need to be satisfied.[159] The basic criticism made by Combs has validity. One reason is that, undeniably, the law may require minimum thresholds of conduct or knowledge before any potential liability arises. Although the sliding scale approach has some similarity to the broad and flexible process as adopted in this book, it is a more simplistic approach.

5.4.5 Extent of liability

One issue that has rarely been addressed in Anglo-Australian civil law, but arises commonly in criminal law [4.5.2] and has also been considered in US civil law, is the question of the extent of A's liability. For example, if A and PW agree to a common design to beat up C, is A liable if C is killed, or C's house is burnt down, as a result of the plan being put into effect?[160] Such extension of liability for further torts committed *may* be justifiable where A and PW act to achieve an *unlawful* outcome, as long as the tort committed is a foreseeable consequence of their plan. For example, once A has actual knowledge of PW's intention to carry a gun while

[158] *Metge* v. *Baehler* 762 F2d 621, 624 (8th Cir, 1985), citing *Stokes* v. *Lokken* 644 F2d 779, 784 (8th Cir, 1981), citing in turn *Woodward* v. *Metro Bank of Dallas* 522 F2d 84, 95 (5th Cir, 1975).

[159] See Combs, 'Civil Aiding', 267 onwards.

[160] See *Restatement (Second) of Torts* § 876 (1979) comment (d) illust. 10, 318, and *cf.* the facts of *American Family Mutual Insurance Co* v. *Grim* 440 P2d 621 (Kan 1968), a questionable decision that is discussed below.

committing a robbery, then A may be liable for the foreseeable consequences of such unlawful plan, namely that some persons may be shot.[161]

In Anglo-Australian law, the issue comes within the requirement that PW's actions must be done in furtherance of the common design or come within the scope of the agreement.[162] Once a party has acted in concert with others in pursuit of a common design with knowledge of its general objects, such party is liable for what occurs in pursuit of those general objects, 'even though as to some of the incidents [A] may not have anticipated that they would happen'.[163] Presumably, if PW acts to further their plan, A's liability for such acts ought to be limited by some concept of reasonableness or foreseeability, though there are few cases to support this conclusion.

In the US, the issue has been addressed in the courts under both 'conspiracy' (common design) and aiding and abetting heads of liability. Where acts are done in furtherance of or in pursuance of the common design, a 'conspirator' can be liable 'even if he neither planned nor knew about the particular overt act that caused the injury, so long as the purpose of the act was to advance the overall object of the conspiracy'.[164] For aiding and abetting liability, the issue is addressed under the concept of 'proximate cause'. Under both concepts, liability is probably limited to foreseeable consequences.[165]

An example is provided by *Halberstam* v. *Welch*,[166] a difficult case that pushes the boundaries of liability. Welch killed the plaintiff's husband during a burglary. The plaintiff brought a wrongful death

[161] Once A knows that PW intends to commit an unlawful act, the law does not frame the issue of A's extended liability in terms of A's (actual) knowledge that PW intends to commit further and different wrongs in the course of such unlawful conduct. By way of contrast, if A participates in PW's *lawful* conduct, any liability for wrongs committed in the course thereof is determined by A's higher-level knowledge of such wrongs, not merely their foreseeability. The difference is implicit in *Halberstam* v. *Welch*, 705 F2d 472, 485 (DC Cir, 1983) fn 14, where the court accepted that liability for mere recklessness is controversial under the heading of whether A 'knowingly assists in the violation' (i.e. does A know of the violation?) but readily accepted liability for foreseeable consequences where A knew of PW's *unlawful* plans (to commit property offences at night, probably while carrying a weapon).

[162] See *Downham* v. *Bellette* (1986) Aust Torts Reports 80-038, discussed [5.4.1.3].

[163] *Schumann* v. *Abbott and Davis* [1961] SASR 149, 155, 157: agents of husband agreed to trespass on wife's premises to search for 'evidence of adultery'. Even though one of the agents knew only the general objects of the enterprise and may have been little more than an onlooker who did not participate in some of the others' high-handed and insolent acts, nonetheless he was equally liable for all the torts committed.

[164] *Halberstam* v. *Welch* 705 F2d 472, 487 (DC Cir, 1983).

[165] *Ibid.* 484–485, 487–489.

[166] *Ibid.* 482.

action against both Welch and his live-in companion of five years, Hamilton. It was held that Hamilton was liable both for acting in concert with and for aiding and abetting Welch. Hamilton knew that Welch's criminal activity was the source of their wealth and she acted in concert with Welch in his burglary enterprise by helping him dispose of stolen property and serving as his banker, bookkeeper and secretary over a five-year period. Hamilton was also liable as an aider and abettor because she provided substantial assistance to Welch, knowing that Welch's conduct was tortious. Although not a participant to the actual burglary that resulted in the murder, Hamilton was held civilly liable as an accomplice to the murder. Liability did not depend upon Hamilton being aware of the precise type of criminal behaviour (here burglary); it was enough that she knew Welch was involved in some type of property crime at night – and violence and killing was a foreseeable risk of this type of enterprise.[167]

Where A is merely involved in *lawful* conduct, however, the same arguments do not apply and liability ought not to extend to foreseeable wrongful consequences.[168] Having said that, some nuisance cases lend support, albeit not definitive, to the view that that where A authorises (or presumably procures) PW to commit certain lawful acts, A may be liable for the natural or inevitable wrongful consequences of such acts [5.5.3].[169]

5.5 The application of accessorial principles to specific torts

5.5.1 Trespass

Many early accessory cases in tort involved trespass to person, battery, assault and the like.[170] This no doubt reflects the criminal law origins of

[167] Interestingly, it is questionable whether Hamilton could have been found liable as a criminal accessory to murder as she probably did not have sufficient knowledge of, and therefore intent to assist in, the specific crimes committed.

Another US decision, *American Family Mutual Insurance Co* v. *Grim* 440 P2d 621 (Kan 1968), may extend liability too far (defendant involved in burglary liable for fire damage to building from unextinguished torches, despite absence of knowledge and despite the fire not being the result of deliberate wrongs committed by the co-conspirators in furtherance of their plan).

[168] See *Tetley* v. *Chitty* [1986] 1 All ER 663, 668–671 [5.5.3].

[169] See also *Ellis* v. *Sheffield Gas Consumers Co* (1853) 2 El and Bl 767; 118 ER 955, and [5.5.3].

[170] E.g., *Heydon's Case* (1612) 11 Co Rep 5a, 5b; 77 ER 1150; *Smithson* v. *Garth* (1691) 3 Lev 323, 324; 83 ER 711.

both tort law and of accessory concepts [4.1].[171] Accessory liability has also been applied to trespass to land.[172] Given the element of direct interference, accessorial principles are generally necessary to hold a defendant liable for the acts of trespass of another, in the absence of vicarious liability or a non-delegable duty. A trespass committed by a contractor will not be attributed to the party for whom work is done unless that party ordered, authorised or directed the act that constitutes the trespass, or some act that comprises the trespass or which by 'physical necessity' leads to the trespass.[173] This looks like liability for procurement.[174]

Accessory concepts play an important role in trespass cases for at least two reasons. First, courts have generally been more reluctant to impose vicarious liability for intentional wrongdoing than for negligence.[175] Secondly, trespass requires a *direct* act by the tortfeasor (of contact etc.). Therefore, if PW hits C, then it is not possible to prove that A has committed the tort and one mechanism by which A can be held liable is by establishing that A is an accessory to PW's wrongdoing. Other torts do not have such a restrictive element of 'directness'. Interestingly, in false imprisonment claims the element of directness has been more broadly interpreted. The courts have held that a person who promotes or causes the arrest of another using, say, the intermediary of the police, nonetheless satisfies the 'directness' element, provided that the police have not

171 Interestingly, two of the ground-breaking US cases that have analysed aiding and abetting are both relatively recent and involve wrongful death claims: see *Rice* v. *Paladin Enterprises, Inc* 128 F3d 233 (4th Cir, 1997); *Halberstam* v. *Welch* 705 F2d 472 (DC Cir, 1983).

172 E.g., in *Hume* v. *Oldacre* (1816) 1 Starke 351; 171 ER 494. See also *Schumann* v. *Abbot* [1961] SASR 149.

173 See *Stoneman* v. *Lyons* [1975] HCA 59; (1975) 133 CLR 550, 574, citing *Sharrod* v. *London and Northern Railway Co* (1849) 4 Exch 580, 585; 154 ER 1345, 1347-8, and *Darling Island Stevedoring and Lighterage Co Ltd* v. *Long* [1957] HCA 26; (1957) 97 CLR 36, 64-5.

174 More difficult to characterise are cases in which a defendant landowner causes or permits tenants, employees or agents to repeatedly trespass on a claimant's (neighbouring) land, or allows a trespass to continue. Liability in these instances is said to arise on similar principles to those that apply to an occupier of land continuing a nuisance [5.5.3]. See, e.g., *Field Common Ltd* v. *Elmsbridge Borough Council* [2008] EWHC 2079 (Ch); (2008) All ER (D) 141, citing *Sefton* v. *Topham* [1967] 1 AC 60, and see the discussion of authorities in *SSYBA Pty Ltd* v. *Lane* [2013] WASC 445.

175 There have, however, been many more recent cases in which claimants have sought to impose vicarious liability for intentional wrongs, such as for PW's sexual assault of C, or for PW's beating, as a nightclub bouncer, of C. See, e.g., *Mattis* v. *Pollock* [2003] EWCA Civ 887; [2003] 1 WLR 2158; *Starks* v. *RSM Security Pty Ltd* (2004) Aust Torts Reports 81-763; *Ryan* v. *Ann St Holdings Pty Ltd* [2006] QCA 217; [2006] 2 Qd R 486.

exercised an independent discretion to make the arrest.[176] Hence, resort to accessory liability is largely unnecessary.

Anglo-Australian law, but not US law, requires a finding of a common design to render A liable for PW's trespass against C, though a tacit agreement may be inferred. Presumably, this could be established from the mere fact that A assists or encourages PW while engaged in a trespass, say an attack on C.[177] Certainly, English courts have accepted liability in cases that appear little different to 'mere' assistance, where A's even quite minor acts that further PW's wrong may be used to infer 'tacit' 'common designs'. Thus, in *Shah* v. *Gale*,[178] where A pointed out the residence of a man whom the primary tortfeasors had informed A they intended to 'beat up', A was a joint tortfeasor to the battery, being implicated in a 'common design',[179] perhaps on very 'thin' evidence.[180]

In *Sea Shepherd*,[181] the UK Supreme Court considered in some depth the relevant accessory principles in the context of trespass claims, in particular reiterating that assistance only gives rise to liability if a common design exists.[182] In *Sea Shepherd*, C sought to establish the liability (for procedural purposes) of Sea Shepherd UK (SSUK), the UK arm of an international charity called Sea Shepherd Conservation Society (SSCS), for the trespass to goods and property damage caused by SSCS. SSCS had rammed a vessel and damaged cages owned by C, releasing tuna, while it

176 See, e.g., *Coles Myer Ltd* v. *Webster* [2009] NSWCA 299; (2009) Aust Torts Reps 82-033; *Myers Stores* v. *Soo* [1991] 2 VR 597 (VSC); *Dickinson* v. *Waters Ltd* (1931) 31 SR (NSW) 593 (FC); *Aitken* v. *Bedwell* (1827) Mood & M 68. Contrast where the defendant merely provides information to police: *Davidson* v. *Chief Constable of North Wales* [1994] 2 All ER 597 (CA). If the law required direct physical acts of restraint by defendants for primary liability in false imprisonment, then defendants in these scenarios would need to be held liable as accessories for procuring the imprisonment. *Cf. Restatement (Second) of Torts* § 45A (1979): liability of persons who instigate or participate in an unlawful confinement, which does not specify whether liability is as a primary tortfeasor or on the basis of accessorial concepts.

177 *Cf.* in the US, *Rael* v. *Cadena* 93 NM 684; 604 P2d 822 (1979).

178 [2005] EWHC 1087 (QB).

179 A was rightly held liable because she had actual knowledge of the general malicious intentions of the PWs against a specific victim, though she was not liable for the death of the victim, killed with a knife the existence of which she was unaware. If a common design is seen as reflecting the fact that the parties are all 'pursuing the same goal' (*cf. Halberstam* v. *Welch* 705 F2d 472, 478 (DC Cir, 1983) 48, discussed [5.4.5]), inferring it on the facts of *Shah* appears artificial.

180 See *Sea Shepherd* [2015] UKSC 10; [2015] 2 WLR 694 [38] (although surely Lord Sumption was not suggesting that the case was wrongly decided).

181 [2015] UKSC 10; [2015] 2 WLR 694.

182 The Supreme Court therefore affirmed the Court of Appeal's rejection of assistance liability: e.g., *ibid.* [21], [41]–[42], [57].

was engaged in a campaign to stop allegedly illegal tuna fishing. SSUK's alleged acts of involvement in the torts committed by SSCS were that it had transferred a small amount of funds specifically for the tuna campaign, had liaised with two volunteers who went to France to assist in preparing the boat used for the campaign, and had made some payments for maintenance and repairs, for which SSUK was usually reimbursed by SSCS.[183]

The Supreme Court by majority allowed an appeal from the Court of Appeal, but all judges in the Supreme Court broadly concurred in their statements as to the relevant principles of law, which were broadly similar to those stated by the Court of Appeal;[184] the differences concerned the application of those principles to the facts. The Supreme Court agreed with the Court of Appeal that SSUK was party to a common design and that it had sufficient knowledge of the intention on the part of SSCS to commit the specific types of torts in the circumstances that arose. The Supreme Court found, however, contrary to the Court of Appeal, that SSUK's involvement in furtherance of the common design was trivial or *de minimis* contributions to those tortious acts.

The decision on its facts is, with respect, correct. The assistance provided was a *de minimis* contribution to the specific wrongs committed; SSUK's fundraising activities were instigated by SSCS, albeit using SSUK's name and bank details, and SSUK merely passed those funds on.[185] Even that assistance was for the purposes of aiding SSCS's *general* cause, and was not targeted at the specific strategy of engaging in violent confrontations.

A number of questions, however, are left unanswered by the Supreme Court's decision. It is not clear on what basis the Supreme Court inferred that a common design existed. The issue was not the focus of the judgments, but Lord Toulson considered that 'the acts were done in pursuit of a campaign of which the appellant approved with knowledge that the campaign involved a preparedness ... to use violent intervention'.[186] In short,

183 Although the ship used by SSCS was registered in the name of SSUK, SSCS had possession and control of the vessel and was its beneficial owner.

184 *Fish* [2013] EWCA Civ 544; [2013] 1 WLR 3700.

185 Even the dissenting judges considered the fundraising as being no more than trivial. Lord Mance did not expressly exclude the activities in sending two volunteers as being a sufficient contribution, but only considered those fundraising activities.

186 [2015] UKSC 10; [2015] 2 WLR 694 [27]. Presumably, the Supreme Court broadly agreed with the Court of Appeal which found a common design from the support provided, in combination with the encouragement and moral support provided to

apart from 'approval', nothing further than knowing assistance is identified as sustaining the common design.[187]

More generally, the rejection of liability for mere assistance need not give rise to potential liability that is broader than that of parties to common designs,[188] as the decision of the Court of Appeal and the dissentients in the Supreme Court, illustrate. On either approach, A's assistance must be more than trivial, A must know of PW's conduct or intended conduct, and there must be a high likelihood that tortious acts will be committed. Unfortunately, although knowledge features prominently in most of the judgments, these do not spell out under which of the elements of liability ([5.4.1.3]) it is relevant. More explicit reference to the requisite mental element would assist in analysing liability. It allows for a focus on what A must know in order to be liable, given the *extent* of A's contribution to the wrong actually committed.

Further, in many trespass cases, A's acts of assistance may even be a significant factor in PW's decision or capacity to carry out the wrong. An example is where A provides PW with a baseball bat as PW is punching C, which PW uses to hit C.[189] In such cases, since sufficient knowledge by A is established (A knows what PW is doing), A *should* be liable. And under current authorities, liability almost certainly would arise in any case, but it would be rationalised on the basis that A implicitly entered into a common design with PW to beat C.[190] This suggests that any dividing

SSCS, as evidenced in SSUK's campaign literature and emails: *Fish* [2013] EWCA Civ 544; [2013] 1 WLR 3700 [59]–[69].

187 One difficulty with this conclusion is that, presumably, SSUK's public supporters may have given moral and even financial support to SSCS's campaign and tactics, without thereby making themselves parties to a common design; indeed, those supporters donated funds, whereas SSUK merely transferred them.

188 *Cf.* Paul S. Davies, 'Joint tortfeasance and common design' (2013) 129 *Law Quarterly Review* 495. *Cf. Fish* [2013] EWCA Civ 544; [2013] 1 WLR 3700 [44], in which the reasons more generally given for the difference in approach between tort law and other areas of law in which assistance suffices, are unconvincing. The Court also suggested at [50], that rejecting assistance liability was consistent with cases that had rejected the inference of a common design, though the examples given are either ones where no assistance was in any case provided (looking on with approval while another makes plans or being a related entity to the tortfeasor) or such assistance was provided in the context of patent infringements, where special policy considerations apply [5.5.2.4].

189 See the example in W. V. H. Rogers et al., *Winfield and Jolowicz on Tort,* 18th edn (London, Sweet & Maxwell, 2010) [21–23], n. 30. As the authors conclude, it is difficult to say that there is any procurement or common design in such circumstances. Indeed, surely liability is justified here even if PW does not use the bat to complete her beating of C.

190 *Cf. Shah* v. *Gale* [2005] EWHC 1087 (QB).

line between assistance on the one hand, and procuring or participation in a common design on the other, is in some cases 'so fine as to be non-existent'.[191] We agree that '[t]here is much to be said for keeping the law in this area as simple as possible', but with respect to Lord Toulson, that is better achieved if determination of liability is not hidden behind an opaque tacit agreement, the terms of which have not been expressly spelt out by the parties.[192] The courts have not identified what further evidence, beyond knowing assistance, substantiates a finding of common design.

In the US, assistance has been held to suffice for aiding and abetting liability[193] and the case law demonstrates the dangers of precluding liability for 'mere' assistance in trespass cases.

It has been held that 'assistance' extends beyond actual presence during the commission of a tort or practical aid lent in that endeavour, and may include advice, encouragement or countenance given to the wrongdoer.[194] It must be more than trivial conduct; the conduct must be 'a substantial factor in causing the resulting tort' to qualify as assistance.[195]

191 Sales, 'Conspiracy', 507. If A knows that PW intends to commit a wrong against a specific party, and assists, is there such a fundamental difference between the culpability of A so as to preclude liability, from cases of inducement or common design, for which A is liable? As Sales points out, 'Often the offering of assistance is itself an inducement to the third party to act wrongfully'.

192 [2015] UKSC 10; [2015] 2 WLR 694 [20]. Discussion of this requirement in cases searching for a common design at times is little different to an inquiry as to whether A was involved in PW's wrong by assisting it in some way. See, e.g., *Mead Corporation* v. *Riverwood* [1993] FSR 484, 489-90.

193 Criminal law definitions of assistance, such as that of Learned Hand J in *United States* v. *Peoni* 100 F2d 401, 402 (2nd Cir, 1938), have often been cited as equally applicable in civil cases, e.g., in *SEC* v. *Apuzzo* 689 F3d 206, 212 (2nd Cir, 2012).

194 Some early cases include *Daingerfield* v. *Thompson* (1880) 33 Grat (Va) 136; *Hilmes* v. *Stroebel* (1883) 59 Wis 74, 17 NW 539; *Bird* v. *Lynn* 10 B Mon (Ky 1850) 422; and *Brown* v. *Perkins* (1861) 1 Allen (Mass) 89. According to the *Restatement (Second) of Torts* 317 (1979), liability is imposed because encouragement is tantamount to 'moral support', which embroils the advisor in the wrong as much as someone who gives physical assistance.

195 *Landy* v. *Federal Deposit Ins Corp* 486 F2d 139, 163 (3rd Cir, 1973). The *Restatement (Second) of Torts* § 876(b) (1979) lists factors that are to be weighed up in determining whether A's participation is so slight that A should not be deemed to have assisted. These include: the nature of the act encouraged; the amount of assistance given by the defendant; the defendant's presence or absence at the time of the tort; the defendant's relation to the principal tortfeasor; the defendant's state of mind. Unfortunately, the last factor confuses the elements of liability, since it is concerned with A's mental state. *Halberstam* v. *Welch* 705 F2d 472, 484 (DC Cir, 1983), perhaps the most influential case on aiding, added a sixth factor – 'duration of the assistance provided' – to the original five. See also *Re Temporomandibular Joint (TMJ) Implants Products Liability Litigation*, 113 F3d 1484, 1496 (8th Cir, 1997), applying those factors.

Of significance in this regard is the body of cases that are not explicable in terms of implied agreements or common designs.[196] It would not be convincing to argue that all such cases are wrongly decided or that they are explicable on the basis of a tacit agreement, as the following case illustrates.

In the fascinating and tragic case of *Rice* v. *Paladin Enterprises, Inc.*[197] the defendant was a publisher of a book called 'Hit Man', containing detailed instructions on how to commit murder. A contract killer carried out murders after meticulously studying the book and following its instructions. The relatives of the three murdered people launched a civil claim against the defendant for aiding and abetting the wrongful death by publishing the book. As the court noted, the book did not merely detail how to commit murder; 'through powerful prose in the second person and imperative voice, it encourages its readers in their specific acts of murder'.[198] Further, the publisher had conceded that it intended the book to be used by criminals to commit murders for hire.[199] Importantly, the publisher was not able to raise anything other than 'implausible' examples as to any lawful or legitimate purposes for which the book may be used;[200] the detailed instructions had only one purpose. The Court of Appeals held that a summary judgment in the defendant's favour in the lower court ought not to have been entered and remitted the matter for trial.[201]

The decision in this case is a legitimate extension of (potential) liability despite the absence of any common design between the publisher and the as-yet-unknown tortfeasors who might use the book (or any procurement).[202] Further, the decision is justified even though the defendant did

[196] As noted in *Halberstam* v. *Welch* 705 F2d 472, 477 (DC Cir, 1983): '[i]n some situations, the trier of fact cannot reasonably infer an agreement from substantial assistance or encouragement.' There is a qualitative difference between an agreement to participate and knowing action that aids tortious conduct. See also at 478.

[197] 128 F3d 233 (4th Cir, 1997). See also *Rael* v. *Cadena*, 93 NM 684; 604 P2d 822 (1979).

[198] 128 F3d 233, 252 (4th Cir, 1997). [199] *Ibid.* 253. [200] *Ibid.* 255.

[201] Another classic example is *Hirschman* v. *Emme* 83 NW 482 (Minn 1900), in which one of the defendants, Emme, was an active participant in a 'hazing' attack on the plaintiff that escalated when the defendant's nephew struck the plaintiff on the head with a club, badly and permanently injuring him. The court found that 'none of the parties intended to injure the plaintiff when the hazing commenced'; but nonetheless found that one act induced and was followed by another, culminating in the serious battery. The defendant was held liable, justifiably, on the basis of encouragement and assistance.

[202] The case cannot be explained by resort to procurement, whereby A intends that PW commit a wrong and seeks to bring about that outcome. No doubt, the publisher may well have preferred that no one actually took up its advice.

not know of the precise circumstances in which the wrongs might be committed, or by whom.[203]

5.5.2 *Intellectual property torts*

5.5.2.1 General principles

Infringements of IP rights are treated as statutory 'torts'. Perhaps somewhat controversially, the courts have therefore applied general tort law principles to determine whether a party is an accessory (or 'joint tortfeasor') to a primary statutory infringement by another.[204] As Mustill LJ noted in *Unilever Plc* v. *Gillette (UK) Limited* when discussing relevant cases in the context of patents and copyright law:

> [this line of authority] concerns persons who are said to have jointly infringed a patent. Essentially this takes a situation where [PW] is an infringer, and adds to it (via the authorities on joint tortfeasors) the possibility that [A] may also have infringed, not through any act which he himself has done, but by virtue of a common design with [PW]. This also is a bold step, since it applies a common law doctrine to the interpretation of a statute. Nevertheless, in the light of *CBS Songs* v. *Amstrad Consumer Electronics* [1988] 2 W.L.R. 1191 the principle is firmly established . . .[205]

The courts have generally tended to find accessory liability only in very clear-cut and narrowly defined situations; this follows from the rejection of liability for mere assistance or facilitation,[206] as well as from a

[203] Such knowledge is normally required when one provides assistance that, at least *in the absence of* knowledge of what it is that a specific wrongdoer intends, is seemingly harmless – for example, selling guns, e.g., for sport or hunting. *Cf. Hamilton* v. *Beretta USA Corp* 750 NE2d 1055, 1059 (NY 2001). In any case, the defendant had targeted a specific group of likely purchasers because they might *use* the book. Less precise knowledge suffices where A makes available the means that will be used almost solely for the commission of wrongs, usually in order for A to profit for itself, i.e., A's facilitation is targeted, meaning there is no real *legitimate* purpose or use for the facilitating act. There are parallels in Anglo-Australian law, where cases on internet IP infringements have extended liability to defendants whose knowledge is comparable [5.5.2].

[204] The statutory tort claims may also arise alongside common law torts such as passing off. For an early case on passing off see *Lever* v. *Goodwin* (1887) 4 RPC 492, 498.

[205] [1989] RPC 583, 602; cited with approval by Chadwick LJ (Tuckey and Simon Brown LJJ agreeing) in *MCA Records* [2001] EWCA Civ 1441; [2002] ECDR 37 [31]; in Australia, see, e.g., *Ward Group Pty Ltd* v. *Brodie and Stone plc* [2005] FCA 471; (2005) 143 FCR 479 (trademark infringements).

[206] Denying liability in many of the cases appears to be based on broader policy grounds. If the courts had wished to find liability, in some cases, a tacit common design could easily have been found, e.g., where a defendant sells products to others knowing that they will

restrictive application of the two recognised grounds of liability (procurement and common design).

5.5.2.2 Procurement of specific torts

Minimal judicial attention has been given to what, precisely, must be proved in order to establish 'procurement'. The courts have tended to find that defendants procured torts only if, by their conduct, they sought to bring about specific acts that are infringements. Conduct that could have resulted in some unspecified infringements being committed by some unspecified party or parties has generally not sufficed. Inducement to infringe 'must be by a defendant to an *individual infringer* and must *identifiably* procure a *particular* infringement'.[207] Therefore, in *CBS Songs*,[208] a supplier of sophisticated recording technology that made the high-speed copying of copyrighted materials by its users easier or more likely was not liable, despite the fact that, in the absence of such technology, very little pirate recording would or could take place. As the equipment could have been used for a range of legitimate purposes,[209] the defendant could not have known when, where or to what extent infringements would take place.[210]

use them to infringe patents [5.5.2.4]. A common design could be said to be present in such circumstances no less so than in *Sea Shepherd* [2015] UKSC 10; [2015] 2 WLR 694.

207 *CBS Songs* [1988] 1 AC 1013, 1058 (emphasis added). Unhelpfully, Lord Templeman appears to suggest knowledge of an individual infringer and of a particular infringement is always a legal requirement for liability, rather than something that will inevitably be present merely in cases of 'inducing'.

208 [1988] AC 1013.

209 In the US, on similar facts, the substantial non-infringing use to which equipment could be put precluded liability in *Sony Corp of America* v. *Universal City Studios Inc.* 464 US 417 (1984). If a device used solely to infringe is implanted into a product that may have non-infringing use, liability is not precluded: see *Ricoh Co, Ltd* v. *Qanta Computer Inc.* 550 F3d 1325 (Fed Cir, 2008). *Cf.* liability for internet infringements in *Metro-Goldwyn-Mayer Studios, Inc.* v. *Grokster, Ltd* 545 US 913 (2005), and in *Twentieth Century Fox Film Corporation* v. *Newzbin Ltd* [2010] EWHC 608; [2010] ECC 13 (*Newzbin*).

210 Therefore, even if the court had accepted the possibility of liability for merely assisting, the absence of more precise knowledge in the circumstances of *CBS Songs* justified the end result, since the defendant would only be able to predict that *some* unknown tortfeasors *might* infringe, whereas some buyers could put the equipment to perfectly lawful uses.

In the context of authorisation of copyright infringement, the absence of any control over the primary infringers is significant in precluding liability. *Cf. Australian Tape Manufacturers Association Ltd* v. *Commonwealth* [1993] HCA 10; (1993) 176 CLR 480, 497–498 (no authorisation by seller of blank tapes as no control over purchasers' use), and contrast *University of New South Wales* v. *Moorhouse* (1975) 133 CLR 1 (HCA) discussed Chapter 9.

A broader approach, however, has been adopted, correctly in our view, where the acts of a party by their very design are intended to promote and encourage, indeed, considerably simplify, the process of carrying out inevitable multiple infringements by numerous (primary) tortfeasors. In *Twentieth Century Fox Film Corporation* v. *Newzbin Ltd* (*Newzbin*),[211] an internet search engine for 'Usenet' (an electronic internet message board) provided sophisticated indexing to movies and television programmes, and provided users with the means to download and reassemble the multiple digital component parts (files) of infringing materials posted by other users. The provider of the search engine was held liable as a joint tortfeasor for the multiple infringements. Importantly, the defendant profited considerably from these activities. The inability of Cs to identify particular infringements by particular users was because the defendant did not keep records.[212]

[211] [2010] EWHC 608; [2010] ECC 13. In the US, see *A and M Records Inc* v. *Napster, Inc* 239 F3d 1004 (9th Cir, 2001), and *Metro-Goldwyn-Mayer Studios, Inc* v. *Grokster, Ltd* 545 US 913 (2005). In *Grokster*, liability arose despite the fact that the website was also used for non-infringing conduct, since the defendant intended that infringements occur, i.e., induced them: see at 938–940. In *Napster*, injunctive relief was granted against a website providing peer-to-peer file sharing technology; the Court held (at 1022) that the preliminary injunction was justified, even if some non-infringing use was made of the technology, since 'Napster has *actual* knowledge that *specific* infringing material is available using its system, that it could block access to the system by suppliers of the infringing material, and that it failed to remove the material.' Similarly, in *Perfect 10* v. *Amazon.com Inc*, 508 F3d 1146 (9th Cir, 2007), Google Inc. was potentially liable if its search engine directed users to infringing websites, making available the plaintiff's images in breach of copyright. 'Google could be held contributorily liable if it had knowledge that infringing Perfect 10 images were available using its search engine, could take simple measures to prevent further damage to Perfect 10's copyrighted works, and failed to take such steps' (at 1172). 'Intent' that infringements occur could be imputed from the knowledge of past infringements and failure to take simple steps. Contrast *Perfect 10* v. *Visa International Services Association* 494 F3d 788 (9th Cir, 2007), finding that a credit card payment systems provider could not be held liable, even if possessing the same knowledge, since its conduct was not a materially contributing factor to infringement (796–800). The two cases are difficult to distinguish other than on the basis of policy distinctions: see Bartholomew and McArdle, 'Causing Infringement', 710–711.

[212] [2010] EWHC 608; [2010] ECC 13 [111]. Although attempts were made to conceal the purpose of the search engine and to warn users against infringing or illegal acts, these were 'entirely cosmetic and . . . neither intended to be nor in fact acted upon'; see at [42]. See also *In re Aimster Copyright Litigation* 334 F3d 643 (7th Cir, 2003): website that allowed file exchanges using software provided, held liable, despite the use of encryption features that prevented website owner from knowing which files were being traded; the encryption software supported a finding of wilful blindness (and in any case, the court noted that constructive knowledge may be sufficient for liability).

Although the case held that there had been procurement, the better view is that this was a case of assisting others to infringe. This is because the facilities were provided to users *for their own* purposes, many (but not all) of which infringed IP rights.

Providers of facilities that allow persons to purchase and sell goods, such as the owner of eBay, an internet market place,[213] like the operator of a real-life market,[214] is not liable as an accessory for trademark infringements by some sellers. In the case of eBay, it was held that eBay owed no positive duty to prevent *some* users from infringing, even where it knew some infringements had occurred and were likely to continue to occur. Importantly, it could not 'be said that the facility is one which inherently leads to infringement'.[215]

5.5.2.3 Common design: a close link between infringing acts and a defendant's conduct

The cases have given greater guidance as to the meaning of common design. Again, in applying this concept, the courts have insisted on a close link between the primary infringing act or acts and the alleged accessory's conduct. Some cases have expressed this connection restrictively in terms of the 'accessory' making the primary infringing acts 'his' own.[216] For example, in a case of database rights infringements where the joint tortfeasor made internet links available to customers that directed them to infringing databases that they were encouraged to use, it was held that

[213] *L'Oreal SA* v. *eBay International AG* [2009] EWHC 1094 (Ch); [2009] ETMR 53. At most eBay is only a 'facilitator'.

[214] *Louis Vuitton Malletier SA* v. *Toea Pty Ltd* [2006] FCA 1443 (2006) 237 ALR 118 (counterfeit goods sold by stallholders).

[215] *L'Oreal SA* v. *eBay International AG* [2009] EWHC 1094 (Ch); [2009] ETMR 53 [382] and [360]-381] (Arnold J). A similar outcome was reached in the US in *Tiffany (NJ) Inc* v. *eBay, Inc* 600 F3d 93 (2nd Cir, 2010), affirming *Tiffany, Inc* v. *eBay, Inc* 576 FSupp 2d 463 (SDNY 2008). Notice by the claimant, Tiffany Inc, that infringements were occurring was not sufficient, since it merely informed the defendant of Tiffany's belief that infringing conduct was occurring; it did not prove knowledge of specific infringements by specific sellers (FSupp at 515). General knowledge that some infringements might be occurring was not sufficient (F3d at 107, 114). Significant here was the lack of control by eBay over the infringing conduct and that eBay had taken major steps to uncover fraud and prevent it.

[216] E.g., *Sabaf SpA* v. *Meneghetti SpA* [2002] EWCA Civ 976; [2003] RPC 14 [59] (Peter Gibson, Jonathan Parker, Longmore LJJ): 'the joint tortfeasor has been so involved in the commission of the tort as to make himself liable for the tort. ... [and] made the infringing act his own'. This test was applied in *Football Dataco Ltd* v. *Sportradar GMBH* [2012] EWHC 1185 Ch [79], where the parties to the case 'focussed on the way the test was put' in *Sabaf*.

the service was provided 'in pursuance of a common design with their customers ... [such that the service providers] adopt the acts of extraction which their customers will perform and make them their own'.[217] Such statements appear conclusory; the more focused reasoning on knowledge in *Newzbin* is preferable.[218] This formulation of the connection between the primary infringing act or acts and the alleged accessory's conduct has also been rightly criticised on the basis that is 'ultimately circular',[219] and it has been suggested that the 'common design' test is 'rather more helpful'.[220]

The courts have generally refused to find accessory liability where a party merely sells materials that are then used by others to infringe copyright, trademarks or patents (the last raises particular policy concerns [5.5.2.4]). For example, a manufacturer who sells goods in one jurisdiction, subject to trademarks held by C in another jurisdiction, is not liable for the offering for sale of those goods on the internet by the persons acquiring them, even in C's jurisdiction (whether for trademark infringement or, potentially, passing off). In order to be liable, the manufacturer must knowingly equip or intend to equip any purchaser with an 'instrument' or 'badge' of fraud or deception.[221] In other words, the manufacturer must put the means of deceiving others into the hands of the purchaser.[222] The fact that C has informed the manufacturer that infringing sales are taking place does not convert lawful conduct into unlawful conduct.[223]

The mere fact that a parent company has a close relationship with and overall control over a subsidiary does not of itself mean that the parent company is an accessory to the subsidiary's infringement;[224] in such circumstances, it must be shown either that acts were done in furtherance

[217] *Football Dataco Ltd* v. *Sportradar GMBH* [2012] EWHC 1185 Ch [84] (Floyd J). The case appears to have been decided on the basis of both procurement and common design, though this is not entirely clear.

[218] [2010] EWHC 608; [2010] ECC 13.

[219] *Sea Shepherd* [2015] UKSC 10; [2015] 2 WLR 694 [59] (Lord Neuberger); *cf.* at [24] (Lord Toulson: not separate test, but merely underlying concept that A has combined with others).

[220] See *Fabio Perini SpA* v. *LPC Group Plc* [2010] EWCA Civ 525 [104], [105] (Lord Neuberger MR, Hughes and Jackson LJJ agreeing).

[221] *Ward Group Pty Ltd* v. *Brodie and Stone plc* [2005] FCA 471; (2005) 143 FCR 479 [61]. See also *Cadbury Ltd* v. *Ulmer GmbH* [1998] FSR 385, regarding trademarks and the tort of passing off.

[222] *Ward Group Pty Ltd* v. *Brodie and Stone plc* [2005] FCA 471 [60], citing *Lever* v. *Goodwin* (1887) 4 RPC 492, 498.

[223] *Ibid.* [62].

[224] *Apotex Pty Ltd* v. *Les Laboratoires Servier (No 2)* [2012] FCA 748 [26], citing *Mead Corporation* v. *Riverwood Multiple Packaging* [1997] FSR 484, 490 (Laddie J).

of a common design or that one company procured the other to infringe.[225]

5.5.2.4 Patent infringements

Many cases concern patent infringements where a vendor sells goods that are then imported into a jurisdiction where they infringe patents. Some decisions are based on the fact that a seller can legitimately be indifferent to how the purchased materials are used. For example, in *Sabaf SpA* v. *Meneghetti SpA*[226] it was held that selling goods to a purchaser who resells in another jurisdiction in infringement of a patent does not amount to 'joint tortfeasance', even where the seller arranges for carriage of the goods to that jurisdiction. The seller 'was merely acting as a supplier of goods to a purchaser which was free to do what it wanted with the goods'.[227] Knowledge that the purchaser *is intending* to use the product so as to infringe does not alter this conclusion. In effect, a party is entitled to sell goods outside of the jurisdiction in which a patent is held, even if the purchaser intends to import them into that jurisdiction.[228] Otherwise, the geographic limits of the monopoly would not be maintained.

A related situation arises in cases concerning sellers of goods that are able to be used as part of an infringing process or product. The cases have held that defendant suppliers who have not supplied a whole combination (where the patent is over a combination)[229] are not liable. It matters not that 'the manufacturer or vendor knows perfectly well that the

[225] *Unilever Plc* v. *Chefaro Proprietaries Ltd* [1995] 1 WLR 243; [1994] FSR 135. A number of factors may be considered to determine whether the parent company had an active role in the infringement. See *Apotex Pty Ltd* v. *Les Laboratoires Servier (No 2)* [2012] FCA 748.

[226] [2002] EWCA Civ 976; [2003] RPC 14. *Cf. Fabio Perini SPA* v. *LPC Group Plc* [2010] EWCA Civ 525: a defendant is not an accessory for merely selling and installing machinery that is used in infringement of a patented *method* to operate the machinery by the purchaser, even if it knows some infringement will take place. If the seller goes further, however, for example, by ensuring that the machinery runs using the particular method, and trains staff as to its continued use, then the seller is liable as a joint infringer. See at [102]–[109]. *Cf.* no liability for copyright infringement in *Navitaire Inc* v. *easyJet Airline Co Ltd (No. 2)* [2005] EWHC 282 (Ch); [2006] RPC 4.

[227] [2002] EWCA Civ 976; [2003] RPC 14 [58].

[228] *Generics (UK) Ltd* v. *H Lundbeck A/S* [2006] EWCA Civ 126; *Fabio Perini SPA* v. *LPC Group Plc* [2010] EWCA Civ 525.

[229] If they have supplied the combination in components or as a kit, then there will be liability if there is no other use to which it can be put or if it is supplied with assembly instructions: see, e.g., obiter comments in *Great Western Corporation Pty Ltd* v. *Grove Hill Pty Ltd* [2001] FCA 423 [30], approved *Grove Hill Pty Ltd* v. *Great Western Corporation Pty Ltd* (2002) 55 IPR 257, 341.

separate elements are destined eventually to be combined so as to constitute an infringement',[230] unless the supplier has merely omitted some link that the purchaser 'can easily furnish'.[231] Dixon J summarised the position in *Walker* v. *Alemite Corp,* citing substantial English authority, as follows:[232]

> [I]t is settled law that the exclusive property in a combination invention is not infringed upon by the sale of the components . . .; that selling articles to persons to be used for the purpose of infringing a patent is not an infringement of the patent . . .; and that sale with a knowledge that the purchaser will use the articles for infringement is not itself an infringement . . . [T]he vendor must have made himself a party to the act of infringement.

Importantly, these principles in the patent cases are based on *sui generis* policy reasons that support a narrower and more restrictive accessory liability than might otherwise be justified. According to Dixon J, this 'narrow . . . view' as to what 'constitutes participation' is based on the policy that if a sold item is not itself subject to patent, then it can be lawfully sold for whatever purpose it may be used by the purchaser: 'whatever is not included in the monopoly granted is *publici juris* and may be freely used as of common right'.[233]

One negative consequence of these perhaps justifiable policy concerns is that the reasoning in the cases, focused on the rejection of liability for 'mere' assistance, has impacted on the understanding of accessory liability principles in tort law more generally. Interestingly, this restrictive interpretation of the law by the courts has led (ironically) to a legislative broadening of liability in the IP context – considered in Chapter 9. These provisions significantly lessen the relevance of common law (joint tortfeasor) principles.

5.5.3 *Nuisance*

In nuisance, liability has in some cases been imposed on defendants for acts of nuisance committed by others. In part, this is determined by

230 *Walker* v. *Alemite Corporation* (1933) 49 CLR 643 (HCA) 657 (Dixon J, McTiernan J concurring), quoting *Terrell on Patents*, 7th edn (1927), 161.

231 *Ramset Fasteners (Aust) Pty Ltd* v. *Advanced Building Systems Pty Ltd* (1999) 44 IPR 481, 500 (FCAFC). The same conclusion applies where someone has not performed all of a process (where the patent is over a method).

232 (1933) 49 CLR 643 (HCA) 657-8, references to cases omitted.

233 *Ibid.* 658. This was cited with approval by Crennan J in *Northern Territory* v. *Collins* [2008] HCA 49; (2008) 235 CLR 619 [104].

asking whether the defendant authorised the nuisance, though some examples of authorisation are probably not cases of accessory liability but rather primary liability or even, in some cases, vicarious liability (see also [5.3.1.2]).

In order to be liable in nuisance as a primary tortfeasor, a defendant must either have created a nuisance or have 'adopted or continued' a nuisance.[234] For creators of nuisances, liability can be strict, irrespective of whether it is foreseeable that their conduct will result in a nuisance.[235] Most cases of private nuisance involve nuisances that emanate from the defendant's land, though this is not an essential element of the tort.[236] All elements of the tort can generally be established against occupiers where they have created the nuisance, or adopted or continued the nuisance (or potential nuisance), even where the acts causing the nuisance were initially carried out by others, or are the deliberate ongoing acts of others.[237] This is not accessory liability, because the occupier, even if continuing a nuisance, is also committing the tort. There is a justifiable logic in treating occupiers as principal duty holders responsible for ensuring that no nuisance emanates from their land.[238]

More difficult to categorise are cases of authorisation. Accessory liability concepts potentially come into play where a person authorises certain acts of persons (other than employees), which acts result in a private or public nuisance. The authorities are in a confused state, however, as to what exactly must be authorised – the nuisance itself, or perhaps merely some lawful acts of which the nuisance is a consequence. In the latter case, how predictable must that consequence be?

An early example is *Ellis* v. *Sheffield Gas Consumers Co*,[239] in which the defendant (A) contracted with another party (PW) to tear

234 As to the fault elements necessary to be proved, see generally Luntz et al., *Torts*, [14.2.1] 749–750.

235 See, e.g., *Barr* v. *Biffa Waste Services Ltd* [2012] EWCA Civ 312; [2013] QB 455 [46] (Carnwath LJ, Arden and Patten LJJ concurring): no requirement for claimant to prove negligence.

236 See, e.g., *Hargrave* v. *Goldman* (1963) 110 CLR 40 (HCA) 60; *Jones (Insurance Brokers) Ltd* v. *Portsmouth City Council* [2002] EWCA Civ 1723; [2003] 1 WLR 427; and *Fennel* v. *Robson Excavation Pty Ltd* [1977] 2 NSWLR 486.

237 See, e.g., *Sedleigh-Denfield* v. *O'Callaghan* [1940] AC 880; *Lippiatt* v. *South Gloucestershire CC* [1999] EWCA Civ 1151; [2000] QB 51.

238 This is unlike defamation [5.5.4], where we question the logic of the broad definition of publication and whether it extends primary liability too far.

239 *Ellis* v. *Sheffield Gas Consumers Co* (1853) 2 El and Bl 767; 118 ER 955 (*Ellis*).

open a road. PW had no lawful authority to do so and this constituted a public nuisance. A was liable for personal injury suffered by the plaintiff as a result of the authorised nuisance (she fell over the rubble). *Ellis* is not a case of vicarious liability; indeed, the court denied that liability would arise if a lawful task had merely been performed negligently.[240] The crux of liability was that PW was employed to do the very wrongful act amounting to a public nuisance and the accident was caused by the 'very thing done in pursuance of specific directions'.[241]

Liability seems clear enough in cases such as *Ellis* where the defendant has authorised the very *wrongful* acts, that is, the nuisance itself. More difficult to classify are cases of authorisation of *lawful* activities. An example is where an occupier authorises the playing of golf on its land and some players hit golf balls onto a C's premises.[242] Liability for authorised lawful activities is probably not accessorial in most cases,[243] unless perhaps the nuisance is a sufficiently predictable consequence of the authorised acts. The authorities use opaque language such as whether 'in the natural course of things, injurious consequences ... must be

[240] The 'contractee' would not have been liable for the negligent performance of the contracted tasks if such tasks were not themselves a nuisance, since there is no vicarious liability for the independent contractor.

[241] (1853) 2 El and Bl 767; 118 ER 955, 770 (Erle J).

[242] Where golf (e.g., *Lester-Travers* v. *City of Frankston* [1970] VR 2) or cricket balls (e.g., *Miller* v. *Jackson* [1977] QB 966 repeatedly land on a claimant's land, then accessory liability is not a plausible explanation. Presumably, if only one golf or cricket ball landed on the claimant's land, this would not constitute a nuisance (at most it is a trespass by the golfer). Liability appears primary, and perhaps only arises once the occupier knows or ought to have known of the nuisance (*Challen* v. *McLeod Country Club* (2004) Aust Torts Reports 81-760 (QCA)).

[243] Liability could be an example of primary liability or vicarious liability where the authorised parties are employees or, perhaps, even only licensees (e.g., *White* v. *Jameson* (1874) LR 18 Eq 303) or independent contractors who are acting in some representative or 'agency' capacity for the defendant. See, e.g., *De Jager* v. *Payneham & Magill Lodges Hall Inc* (1984) 36 SASR 498 (FC) 501–502 (liability of occupier for nuisances resulting from authorised uses, even where nuisance not inevitable, if 'special risk' or 'danger' of nuisance). Some cases have suggested a non-delegable duty arises in this context. See discussion in *Clerk and Lindsell*, [6–61], 388–389, and see also *McInnes* v. *Wardle* (1931) 45 CLR 548, and *Black* v. *Christchurch Finance Co* (1894) AC 48 (PC), some of the language in which suggests a non-delegable duty. Even if this were so, such duty in effect either extends notions of vicarious liability or is based on the genuine capacity by the occupier to control activities on its land, such that a failure to do so is a primary wrong. In *White* (authorised burning by licensee of bricks in kiln) the focus of Jessel MR's judgment (at 305) is on the capacity to control activities, by servants or contractors, on land – the land must be 'so used and managed that other persons are not injured'.

expected to arise',[244] but this obscures rather than enlightens. The more broadly that liability extends, the less likely an accessorial explanation holds.[245] Similar questions also arise with lessor's liability.

Liability for nuisance that is best characterised as accessorial arises in the context of lessors and tenants.[246] Clearly, tenants are not agents or representatives of the lessor, nor is the lessor in control of the way in which the tenant conducts itself. Nonetheless, cases have held lessors liable where they have authorised the tenant's nuisance.[247] In *Southwark London Borough Council* v. *Mills*,[248] Lord Millett stated that lessors 'must either participate directly in the commission of the nuisance, or they must be taken to have authorised it by letting the property'.[249]

As Lord Millett notes, the act may be authorised as a result of the grant of the lease itself, or as a result of acts or omissions subsequent to the grant.[250] In relation to the latter, liability for participating directly applies equally to persons other than lessors and raises merely a factual question of whether the nuisance has been 'authorised' or 'allowed' by A through his active participation. It requires a 'broad, common-sense judgment, based on the facts as a whole, as to whether there was such active

244 See *Bower* v. *Peate* (1876) LR 1 QBD 321, 326 (Cockburn CJ), though the broadly stated principles in that case are doubtful in Australia, in light of *Stoneman* v. *Lyons* (1975) 133 CLR 550 (HCA) 574, and generally 574–576. *Bower* involved the loss of support to an adjoining building as a result of a contractor's negligent building work. Responsibility for supporting the adjoining building had been delegated to the contractor, so the case looks like one of non-delegable duty, that is, an expanded vicarious liability.

245 If liability arises merely for the objectively foreseeable consequences of PW's conduct, then this is negligence liability and does not look to be accessorial. More than likely, these are cases in which onerous primary liability attaches because of the status of the defendant as occupier.

246 Supporting the characterisation of the issue as one of accessory liability is Lord Hoffmann in *Southwark London Borough Council* v. *Mills* [2001] 1 AC 1, 15 (HL): 'The primary defendant is the person who causes the nuisance by doing the acts.' See also *Winter* v. *Baker* (1887) 3 TLR 569.

247 Where the nuisance results from potentially harmful conditions on land that arose prior to a letting, the landlord is liable as a creator of the nuisance and continues to be liable. See, e.g., *Sampson* v. *Hodson-Pressinger* [1981] 3 All ER 710, 713-14 and authorities discussed in *Fleming's*, [21-190], 512-13.

248 [2001] 1 AC 1 (HL).

249 *Ibid.* 22. This is not to suggest that the mere letting of the property amounts to 'authorisation'. Indeed, the mere receipt of rents (even with knowledge of the nuisance) and a failure to intervene in the tenant's activities does not give rise to liability. See also *Coventry* v. *Lawrence (No 2)* [2014] UKSC 46; [2015] 1 AC 106; *Hussain* v. *Lancaster City Council* [2000] QB 1 [59].

250 *Coventry* v. *Lawrence (No 2)* [2014] UKSC 46; [2015] 1 AC 106 [11]–[13] (Lord Neuberger, Lord Clarke and Lord Sumption agreeing); [51] (Lord Carnwath, Lord Mance agreeing).

involvement by the landlord in the offending activities as to make him jointly responsible in law for their consequences'.[251]

In relation to liability from letting, the question is how likely must it be that a nuisance follows from the acts authorised by the letting? Lord Millett's statement avoids the issue – 'taken to have authorised it by letting the property' – as do references to 'impliedly' authorised. The law, contrary to the views of Lord Neuberger, is far from 'tolerably clear in terms of principle'.[252] The narrowest formulation of the liability rules is that the lessor must have authorised the wrong itself, or that it was at least certain or virtually certain to follow from the acts authorised by the grant of the lease.[253] For example, in Australia in *Peden* v. *Bortolazzo*, it was said that a lessor is not generally responsible for nuisances created by a tenant unless the premises were let:

> for a purpose calculated to cause a nuisance, that is, by express authorisation of the nuisance or the circumstances where the nuisance was certain to result from the purposes for which the property was let.[254]

In *Coventry* v. *Lawrence (No. 2)* (*Coventry*), the majority adopted the narrower approach endorsed in Australia, of virtual certainty or very high degree of probability,[255] whereas the dissentients[256] accepted and applied the broader test adopted by McNeill J in his detailed survey of the authorities in *Tetley* v. *Chitty*,[257] namely that the nuisance must be

[251] *Ibid.* [59], and see also [57]–[66] (Lord Carnwath). On participation, see *Malzy* v. *Eichholz* [1916] 2 KB 308, 315.

[252] *Coventry* v. *Lawrence (No. 2)* [2014] UKSC 46; [2015] 1 AC 106 [11].

[253] *Smith* v. *Scott* [1973] 1 Ch 314, 320–321; [1972]. The case was cited without disapproval in *Southwark London Borough Council* v. *Mills* [2001] 1 AC 1, 15 (HL), by Lord Hoffmann. Lords Slynn, Steyn and Clyde concurred with both Lord Hoffmann and Lord Millett's judgments.

[254] [2006] 2 Qd R 574 (CA) [29].

[255] *Coventry* [2014] UKSC 46; [2015] 1 AC 106 [12] (Lord Neuberger, Lord Clarke and Lord Sumption agreeing).

[256] *Ibid.* [54]–[55], though note the different wording adopted at [56] (Lord Carnwath dissenting, Lord Mance agreeing). This also reflects the position in Canada: *Banfai* v. *Formula Fun Centre Inc* [1984] OJ No 3444, 34 CCLT 171 (HCJ), cited in *Coventry* [2014] UKSC 46; [2015] 1 AC 106 [55]. On either test, the existence of a clause in the lease obliging the tenant not to commit a nuisance will not relieve a landlord from liability if the nuisance is otherwise authorised.

[257] [1986] 1 All ER 663, 668–671. This test itself, which McNeill J applied and held satisfied on the facts, came from *Harris* v. *James* (1876) 45 LJQB 545, 546, 547. This test was also applied in *Mayfair Ltd* v. *New Zealand Properties Ltd* [1940] NZLR 190, 198 (Myers CJ): landlord 'warned of the danger [of nuisance] and did not take steps completely to eliminate it'. McNeill J went further and expressed a preference for a less stringent test based on likelihood or objective foreseeability (council liable for nuisance created by

the 'ordinary and necessary' or 'natural and necessary' consequence of the authorised act. On neither test did liability arise, however. The differences of opinion in *Coventry* turned on whether there was participation post letting, with the dissentients holding the lessors liable for participating after the grant of the lease in the nuisance created by a speedway track.[258]

The 'virtual certainty' test probably equates with actual knowledge, that is, the lessor can predict that the wrong will almost certainly follow from the purposes for which the premises are leased. The difficulty with the 'ordinary and necessary' consequence test lies in its failure clearly to articulate a requisite mental state. The 'ordinary and necessary' consequences' test probably equates to a test that asks whether nuisance is substantially likely to follow from letting the premises and the lessor is recklessly indifferent to that risk. If so, this is probably an appropriately onerous test for liability. However, it could also merely be determined on a purely objective basis as to the likelihood of a nuisance, such that A's subjective knowledge is not relevant, in which case this seems unusually broad liability.

More generally, in all cases of secondary liability for nuisance, confusion about the extent of liability may arise, in part, from use of the term 'authorisation', which suggests authority on the part of the defendant,[259] and perhaps even some control over the activities of the 'authorised' party, such that she is treated in law as if a servant or agent. Arguably therefore, if the party committing the authorised acts is a genuine agent representing the defendant, then the courts may, in effect, be imposing vicarious liability for the ordinary consequences of

go-kart racing, having granted a licence and subsequently a lease to the operator for that express purpose). McNeill J did not consider that *Smith* v. *Scott* [1973] 1 Ch 314 was necessarily inconsistent with this, but the rule in *Smith* was stated in terms of express or implied authorisation of nuisance, and not in terms of probable results. That broader test has rightly been rejected by the Supreme Court in *Coventry* [2014] UKSC 46; [2015] 1 AC 106 [56] (Lord Carnwath), as 'insufficiently rigorous'. Since liability must be based on accessorial principles, negligence, and hence mere foreseeability of wrongdoing, is not a sufficient mental state to amount to wrongful involvement in another's tort [3.4.3]. A lessor's residual capacity via the contract of lease to control the tenant's activities does not justify such wide liability.

258 [2014] UKSC 46; [2015] 1 AC 106. See the factors set out at [21], which Lord Carnwath in dissent considered demonstrated active encouragement of the tenants' activities, and as going beyond the ordinary role of a landlord protecting his or her interests [64]. The dissenting conclusion is more persuasive on the facts.

259 *Cf. CBS Inc* v. *Ames* [1982] Ch 91, 106, cited with approval in *CBS Songs* [1988] AC 1013, 1054.

authorised acts.[260] This explanation does not, of course, apply to tenancy cases since *a tenant* of a lessor is clearly not an agent.

Importantly, the readiness of the courts to impose liability on occupiers and, to a lesser extent, lessors, on whatever basis, stems from the strict liability of the tort of nuisance, which in turn derives from the special status of an occupier/owner. It is for this reason, among others, that accessory liability principles are difficult to identify. It would aid analytical clarity if courts were to articulate clearly whether liability is primary (based on the defendant's status as occupier), vicarious, or accessory.[261]

5.5.4 Defamation cases

5.5.4.1 Publication as the essence of the tort

Defamation is the publication or communication of matters that are likely to damage the reputation of another.[262] The key conduct element that needs to be established is, therefore, that the defendant has *published* the defamatory material to someone other than the person defamed.[263] Material is 'published' if the defendant has conveyed by some means the defamatory sense of the material.[264] Although publication can be either intentional or negligent, the publisher need not know that the content of the published material is defamatory. The tort of defamation is, in this sense, strict.

[260] This could be an explanation of cases such as *Dalton* v. *Henry Argus and Co* (1881) 6 App Cas 740, and *Bower* v. *Peate* (1876) LR 1 QBD 321, in which landowners were held liable for independent contractors' failure to use sufficient support on a claimant's house when pulling down the defendants' buildings. See also the very broad obiter statement of Blackburn J in *Harris* v. *James* (1876) 35 LT 240, 241: 'where one person authorises and requests a person to do certain things, he is liable for any consequences that arise therefrom'.

[261] Further, if accessory liability is in fact being imposed, it would be useful for the courts to spell out both the requisite acts of involvement and the requisite state of knowledge of the actor necessary for determining liability.

[262] See generally, Patrick Milmo QC et al., *Gatley on Libel and Slander*, 11th edn (London, Sweet and Maxwell, 2010) 11 (*Gatley*); *Clerk and Lindsell*, Ch. 22; Patrick George, *Defamation Law in Australia*, 2nd edn (Australia, Butterworths LexisNexis, 2012).

[263] For a more detailed discussion of the matters here raised, see generally J. Dietrich, 'Clarifying the Meaning of "Publication" of Defamatory Matter in the Age of the Internet' (2013) 18 *Media and Arts Law Review* 88.

[264] *Webb* v. *Bloch* (1928) 41 CLR 331 (HCA) 363. As it was put in the Canadian Supreme Court decision of *Crookes* v. *Newton* [2011] SCC 47; [2011] 3 SCR 269 [55], [80], publication requires an act that makes the defamatory materials available in a comprehensible form to a third party who receives it in such a way that it is understood.

The broad definition of 'publication' means that a variety of very different means of conveying defamatory material may satisfy this requirement. The courts treat all such publishers as 'principals in the act of publication'.[265] Anyone who 'takes part' in the publication (with a sufficient nexus between its conduct and that of another publisher) is caught by the definition of publication.[266] This means that if D1 directs D2 to print and D3 to distribute defamatory material to retailers, all three are publishers of the work.[267] The question of accessory liability is therefore largely ignored in defamation law.[268]

However, the law's failure to distinguish between principal tortfeasors and accessory liability, and to treat even peripheral parties as principals leaves key conceptual questions unclear.[269] For example, it seems appropriate to describe the creator of defamatory matters as the publisher and a principal tortfeasor; but what about an innocent distributor? What is the relevance of knowledge as to the content of published matter in determining liability?

5.5.4.2 Knowledge of the content

Clearly, it is not necessary to prove that a 'publisher' is aware that material is itself defamatory, but must a 'publisher' know something of the nature or content of the work to be a publisher and therefore

[265] E.g., *Queen* v. *Cooper* (1846) 8 QB 533 536 (Lord Denman CJ): 'If a man request another generally to write a libel, he must be answerable for any libel written in pursuance of his request: he contributes to a misdemeanour and is therefore responsible as a principal.' See also *Crookes* v. *Newton* [2011] SCC 47; [2011] 3 SCR 269 [82].

[266] See David Lindsay, 'Liability for the Publication of Defamatory Material on the Internet' (Research Paper No. 10, University of Melbourne Centre for Media, Communications and Information Technology Law, 2000) 22, citing, among others, Sir Brian Neill and Richard Rampton, *Duncan and Neill on Defamation*, 2nd edn (London, Butterworths, 1983) [8.12]; Balkin and Davis, *Law of Torts*, 534.

[267] See, e.g., *Goldsmith* v. *Sperrings Ltd* [1977] 1 WLR 478 (Scarman and Bridge LJJ holding the distributors liable); but *cf.* the dissent of Lord Denning MR at 486–488: distributors are not prima facie publishers and proof that they knew or ought to have known of the defamatory content is required. And see [5.5.4.2]. See also *R* v. *Clerk* (1728) 1 Barn KB 304; 94 ER 207.

[268] However, the language of accessories is sometimes used. E.g., *R* v. *Paine* (1696) 5 Mod 163, 167; 87 ER 584, 587, and *Parkes* v. *Prescott* (1869) LR, 4 Ex 169, 173 (Giffard QC citing the rule in *Starkie on Libel*, 2nd edn, vol. ii, 225). Giffard QC's use of this description has likewise been cited many times: e.g., in *Webb* v. *Bloch* (1928) 41 CLR 331, 364; *Commisso* v. *United Telecasters Sydney Pty Ltd* [1999] NSWSC 51 [59]; *Zunter* v. *John Fairfax Publication Pty Ltd* [2004] NSWSC 696.

[269] This is not to suggest that accessorial principles would be simple to apply to defamation cases. If one sought to do so, who would be considered the primary tortfeasor: the creator of defamatory material, or the direct communicator of such matters?

potentially liable? The orthodox view is 'no',[270] though doubts have been expressed about this[271] (and in any case, in certain circumstances, innocent dissemination is a defence at common law or under statute).[272] It has been suggested that proof of knowledge is not required because certain persons are *deemed* to have knowledge of certain matters. For example, in *Commisso* v. *United Telecasters Sydney Pty Ltd*, Levine J stated 'that printers were traditionally encompassed in the *concerted action* because they were *considered to have known* the contents of the libel, it being fully composed at the time that the "printer clamped down the press"'.[273] But this conclusion is highly doubtful given that other innocent persons are not 'considered' or deemed to have such knowledge or to have so acted.[274]

Persons may even be liable as publishers by omission in some cases, for example, for failing to remove defamatory materials from a space

[270] It has previously been suggested that innocent dissemination of defamatory material 'does not amount to "publication at law"': George, *Defamation Law*, 476, citing the older English cases of *Emmens* v. *Pottle* (1885) 16 QBD 354, and *Vizetelly* v. *Mudie's Select Library Ltd* [1900] 2 QB 170, 179–180. If this were correct, then the definition of publication would involve knowledge of the nature of the published material and knowledge that it was likely to contain defamatory material (or the lack of such knowledge was negligent), so that an innocent disseminator would not require a defence at all. However, as George acknowledges, in *Thompson* v. *Australian Capital Television Pty Ltd* (1996) 186 CLR 574 (HCA) 587, Brennan CJ, Dawson and Toohey JJ suggest that the 'never published' analysis has created 'confusion' (citing *Gatley on Libel and Slander*, 8th edn (1981), 244, fn. 3). Their Honours seemingly approve the view that all disseminators 'publish' the defamatory material at law, but have available the defence of innocent dissemination (but *cf.* Gaudron J at 594–595).

[271] In English law, the issue is uncertain. The precise requirements of knowledge are unclear and some inconsistencies exist in the authorities. See the discussion in *Metropolitan International Schools Ltd* v. *Designtechnica Corporation and Ors* [2009] EWHC 1765 [49]. See, e.g., *Tamiz* v. *Google Inc* [2013] EWCA Civ 68 [26]. *Clerk & Lindsell* argue that someone who does not know the nature of a document (if he or she merely, say, delivers it) has not published it: 1447, [22–69]. The 11th edn of *Gatley* does not directly address this issue. See at 168 and 169.

[272] For a definition of innocent dissemination at common law, see *Emmens* v. *Pottle* (1885) 16 QBD 354, 357–358; adopted in *Thompson* v. *Australian Capital Television Pty Ltd* (1996) 186 CLR 574 (HCA) 586. In the UK, see s. 1(1) Defamation Act 1996, and see, e.g., *Godfrey* v. *Demon Internet* [2001] QB 201. In Australia, the defence is now contained in the (almost) uniform Defamation Acts (e.g., Defamation Act 2005 (Qld), s. 32).

[273] [1999] NSWSC 51 [64] (emphasis added).

[274] *Ibid.*, citing *Gatley on Libel & Slander*, 8th edn (1981) para. 237 ('it would be absurd . . . to suggest that the person who supplied alloy to the printer . . . could be regarded as having acted in concert . . ., unless there was evidence that that person intentionally supplied the alloy with the common design of publishing the libel').

over which they have control,[275] thereby continuing the defamation. In this context, however, the courts have held that there must be 'more than mere knowledge' of the presence of materials on the defendant's premises and the opportunity to remove them. The defendant must in some way have 'consented to', 'adopted' or 'ratified' the continued presence of materials, thereby accepting responsibility for them.[276] Given the secondary role that 'passive' publishers play it is particularly appropriate that some degree of knowledge and some concept of involvement in, or 'accepting responsibility' for, publication (through consent, authorisation etc.) be required if liability is to be extended to these parties.

Inevitably, the broad definition of 'publication' means that a clear delineation between the liability of defendants as primary wrongdoers and accessories is untenable. Although a dual analysis is possible, so that we could characterise the defendant as either a primary tortfeasor or an accessory, it is perhaps a more accurate conclusion to say that accessory liability is largely redundant.[277] One consequence, however, is that it has created an overbroad defamation law and some confusion as to the

[275] See, e.g., *Byrne* v. *Deane* [1937] 1 KB 818 (CA) (proprietor and secretary of club responsible for the publication of a lampoon of the plaintiff which someone had placed on an internal wall of the club premises; both had known for some days of the document); held to apply in *Tamiz* v. *Google Inc.* [2013] EWCA Civ 68 [27]–[36], to an internet service providing a platform for bloggers to post material, where notice of offending material had been given to it; *Urbanchich* v. *Drummoyne Municipal Council* (1991) Aust Torts Reports 81-127 (NSWSC); *Bishop* v. *State of New South Wales* [2000] NSWSC 1042. An interesting example is provided by a US case, *Hellar* v. *Bianco* (1952) 244 2d 757 (Dist CA, Cal) (proprietors of tavern held responsible for the publication in men's lavatory of a notice that imputed that the plaintiff was 'an unchaste woman who indulged in illicit amatory ventures', for failing to remove it within thirty minutes of being informed by plaintiff's husband). Contrast *Wolfson* v. *Syracuse Newspapers Inc* (1938) 4 NYS (2d) 640.

[276] *Urbanchich* v. *Drummoyne Municipal Council* (1991) Aust Torts Reports 81-127 (NSWSC), 69,193, 69,194; *Bishop* v. *State of New South Wales* [2000] NSWSC 1042 [21].

[277] However, it is possible for a party who does not fit within the broad definition of publication, nonetheless to participate in a common design, or to procure the tort, such that accessory liability may be imposed. For example, if A procures PW to create, print and distribute a defamatory article in PW's newspaper in order to destroy the reputation of a claimant, A is not likely to be considered a publisher.

One context in which the courts appear to be resorting to accessorial principles is when an original publisher is pursued as a joint tortfeasor for republication of the defamatory matter, as a further cause of action. An original publisher will only be liable for republication if he or she 'combined' with the subsequent publisher to publish it (*Habib* v. *Radio 2UE Sydney Pty Ltd* [2009] NSWCA 231 [203]), or authorised it (*Clerk and Lindsell,* [22-219]). The liability of the first publisher for republication is accessory liability – though the courts fail to call it that.

precise requirements of knowledge. 'Peripheral' parties to the wrongful conduct of others ought only to be liable if they are knowingly involved in that conduct.

Confusion over the meaning of publication and the role of knowledge has recently been brought into sharp focus in the context of claims against internet search engine providers, where a search term brings up defamatory material contained in a website over which the search engine provider has no control.[278] While these look like classic third-party cases, the courts have decided them on the basis of whether they involve 'publication' in the relevant sense. For example, in *Metropolitan International Schools Ltd* v. *Designtechnica Corporation*,[279] the English High Court held that Google Inc., the search engine provider, was not a publisher of such materials. It was held that the lack of input by Google Inc. into the search terms used or in the automatic (computer-generated) display of results meant that it merely facilitated communication by other persons, much like a telephone carrier or library catalogue identifying books.[280] Google Inc. did not *intend* to publish the materials.[281]

[278] See the excellent detailed discussion of defamation and the internet in Matthew Collins, *The Law of Defamation and the Internet*, 3rd edn (Oxford University Press, 2010) chs 2–6, who catalogues the range of scenarios that may arise.

[279] [2009] EWHC 1765; [2010] 3 All ER 548 [48]–[64]; *cf. Bunt* v. *Tilley* [2007] 1 WLR 1243 (internet service provider who did not host offending websites not a publisher: more than merely 'passive instrumental role in the process' required; there must be 'knowing involvement in the process of publication of *the relevant words*' [23], emphasis in original), criticised by Collins, *Defamation and the Internet*, 116–118. This conclusion is consistent with other European legislation and cases. See the summary of European decisions and legislation in *Metropolitan* [98]–[111] by Eady J.

[280] [2009] EWHC 1765; [2011] 1 WLR 1743 [40]–[41], [52].

[281] *Ibid.* [50]–[51]. Eady J's conclusions on the required intent [49], suggesting a requirement of knowledge of the content of the published material, involves a significant change from established authorities. *Tamiz* v. *Google Inc* [2013] EWCA Civ 68, supports this aspect of the case (Google Inc. did not publish offending materials on blogs that it hosted despite providing the platform and tools). See also *Crookes* v. *Newton* [2011] SCC 47; [2011] 3 SCR 269 [30]; see generally [25]–[30] (Abella J, Binnie, LeBel, Charron, Rothstein and Cromwell JJ concurring) (website that contains hyperlinks to other sites containing defamatory materials does not publish such materials as it does not communicate the content). *Cf.* the more open-ended approach of Deschamps J.

Further, it was held in *Metropolitan* in [54]–[64], that even where Google had notice of the offending material, given its limited capacity to remove material and the steps that it had already taken, it had not acquiesced to their publication. Contrast the conclusion in *Trkulja* v. *Google Inc and Anor (No 5)* [2012] VSC 533 [31]: where notice has been given, and there is a failure to remove materials where such power exists, it could be inferred that Google Inc. consented to publication. Eady J's decision on this point must be open to doubt, given the conclusion in *Tamiz* that Google Inc. as the provider of the

Even if a search engine assists in the republication or communication of defamatory material hosted by a website, they ordinarily do so without knowledge of the commission of a tort. The fact that a small percentage of identified materials may be defamatory does not equate with knowledge, any more than a salesperson of guns has knowledge of torts committed merely because a few gun purchasers use them for nefarious purposes. Only prior knowledge and a failure to ensure that the offending materials are not displayed for search upon certain terms would satisfy the knowledge requirement. Thankfully, English courts appear to have reached a common-sense solution.[282]

5.5.5 Negligence

Only a few cases have arisen in which courts have purported to hold a person liable as a joint tortfeasor to the tort of negligence on the basis of accessory liability principles. Perhaps the most famous case is that of *Brook* v. *Bool*.[283] A landlord and his tenant proceeded to look for a gas leak using a naked flame to do so. The tenant's light caused an explosion causing harm, but the plaintiff sued the landlord. The landlord was held liable on three grounds, the third (and most relevant) of which was that the parties had acted in concert and pursuant to a common enterprise. Undeniably, the two other grounds provided a sufficiently strong case for holding the landlord liable, but liability was not justified, we would suggest, on accessory principles. As Fleming stated, '[c]learly, the joint undertaking to discover the leak was not an agreement to engage in a negligent activity'.[284]

Although there are a few cases, other than *Brook* v. *Bool*, in which 'accessory liability' for negligence has been found, these cases are not

platform for blogs had published defamatory materials *after notice* had been given to it of offending materials that it hosted; though the court stressed that the facts of cases are important and therefore a search 'hit' and hosted blog may be entirely different things.

282 Contra *Trkulja* v. *Google Inc and Anor (No 5)* [2012] VSC 533 [18]–[30], regrettably likening a search engine to a newsagent selling newspapers; and see also *Rana* v. *Google Australia Pty Ltd* [2013] FCA 60.

283 [1928] 2 KB 578. See *MCA Records* [2001] EWCA Civ 1441; [2002] ECDR 37 [31]: '*Brook* v. *Bool* has engendered curiously little in the way of subsequent reported authority'.

284 John G. Fleming, *The Law of Torts*, 9th edn (Sydney, LBC Information Services, 1998) 289: 'the defendant's acquiescence, nay, the example he set in being the first to strike a match, coupled with his position of authority, was evidently the decisive factor in attracting joint liability.' The quote does not appear in the 10th edn of *Fleming's*.

inconsistent with the view that resort to accessory principles is unnecessary and that liability is better founded on primary liability for negligence.[285]

In our view, accessory liability to the tort of negligence is conceptually unconvincing.[286] Let us take a simple example. Passenger 'A' encourages PW to drive at 80 km/h through a school zone. The intentional acts of A to encourage PW to speed do not amount to the tort of negligence; however, nor does PW's careless driving. As was stated in another context, 'negligence in the abstract' is not actionable.[287] Only once PW runs over and injures a child is the tort committed, and what is relevant at that point is whether the act that caused the injury falls below the reasonable standard of care required by, and generated by, the foreseeable risk of such conduct. It is difficult to characterise the encouragement of the intentional act to drive at 80 km/h as *procuring* the commission of the tort, or entering into a common design to commit it, since no tort was thereby committed, and there was only a small chance that it would be.

Further, it is difficult to articulate what the requisite knowledge or 'mental element' ought to be in this context, since it is difficult to

285 *Fleming's*, 302, cites a number of cases but for the most part these can be explained on other grounds: *Mason* v. *Burke* (1968) 68 DLR 2d 19 (joint illegal enterprise as providing a defence to negligence); *McDonald* v. *Dalgleish* (1973) 35 DLR (3d) 486 (common enterprise in conducting a drag race, but decision could be better justified on the basis of a breach of duty by each of the parties). Difficult to explain away, however, is *Rogers* v. *RJ Reynolds Tobacco Co* 761 SW 2d 788 (Tex 1988). That case concluded that a 'conspiracy' to commit, and participate in, others' 'negligence' is actionable. The fraudulent nature of the defendants' conduct was noted in the reasons, however, and to the extent that negligence was the basis for the decision, the 'accessories' could have been found to owe a duty of care. It should be added that many courts in the US have, contrary to *Rogers*, found that conspiracy is *not* available as a basis of liability for the tort of negligence, given that conspiracy requires an intention to commit an unlawful purpose, so that one cannot agree or conspire to be negligent. See, e.g., *Juhl* v. *Arrington* 936 SW 2d 640, 644 (Tex 1996); *Wright* v. *Brooke Group Ltd* 114 F Supp 2d 797, 837 (N D Iowa, 2000); *Halberstam* v. *Welch* 705 F2d 472, 478 (DC Cir, 1983) ('it is difficult to conceive of how a conspiracy could establish vicarious [i.e. accessory] liability where the primary wrong is negligence'); and cases discussed by Combs, 'Civil Aiding', fn. 7.

More recent cases include *Morin* v. *Bonham and Brooks Ltd* [2003] EWCA Civ 1802; [2004] 1 Lloyd's Rep 702 (joint tortfeasorship for participation by a company in a subsidiary's negligent misstatement alluded to, but not addressed); and *Smith* v. *Amaca Pty Ltd and Anor* [2009] VSC 318 (Forrest J rejecting a statement of claim alleging accessory liability by one manufacturer of asbestos to another manufacturer's negligence on the basis of knowledge of the latter's activities and role in the market).

286 Peter Cane, '*Mens Rea* in Tort Law' (2000) *Oxford Journal of Legal Studies* 533, 546, fn. 44, agrees: 'There can be no accessory liability for tortious negligence.'

287 *Tabet* v. *Gett* [2010] HCA 12; 240 CLR 537, 577 [109] (Kiefel J).

conceptualise, other than in terms of A's failure to meet objective standards of care, the degree of knowledge that suffices to make someone an 'accessory' to negligence. If such carelessness exists and A owes a duty of care to the victim, liability in negligence follows. If, however, it is difficult to establish that A owes a duty of care (as with the passenger in the example) then accessory liability ought not to follow either.[288]

Contrary to the conclusions drawn above, US courts have repeatedly held[289] that it is possible to 'aid and abet' in the tort of negligence. Such cases are better explained on other grounds, by resort to concepts within the tort of negligence itself.[290] Similarly, in cases in which liability has *not been* imposed, the reasoning appears consistent with the absence of a *duty of care* on the part of the alleged 'accessory'.[291]

Negligence law already has the conceptual tools to impose liability on persons who are some steps removed from the actual conduct or person immediately responsible for the harm. There is no need to resort to accessory concepts.

[288] If A had no real control or authority over PW, but instead merely gave some assistance or encouragement, many of the elements of the tort of negligence would be difficult to satisfy. To take another example: the friend of a diver who encourages or helps the diver to dive carelessly off a bridge into water below while others are swimming nearby, is unlikely to be held liable when the diver jumps and injures a swimmer (probably contra if the aider is the father of a 14-year-old diver).

[289] See, e.g., *Re Temporomandibular Joint (TMJ) Implants Products Liability Litigation* 113 F3d 1484, 1495 (8th Cir, 1997), though no liability was found in that case.

[290] E.g., in *Cobb* v. *Indian Springs, Inc* 522 SW 2d 383, 387 (Ark 1975), a security guard employed by the defendant encouraged a young driver to speed on the defendant's premises. The court found that the guard could have foreseen an appreciable risk of harm to others. Despite the reference to 'aiding and abetting' principles, negligence reasoning predominates in the judgment, e.g., 522 SW 2d 383, 388–389 (Harris CJ and Fogleman J). Similarly, there are numerous cases involving public street drag races. See also, e.g., *Bierczynski* v. *Rogers* 239 A2d 218 (Del 1968) (two racers held concurrently liable in negligence). Wolcott CJ, Carey and Hermann JJ noted that the authorities have accepted rules of causation that all parties engaged in a race on a highway 'are wrongdoers acting in concert, and that each participant is liable for harm to a third person arising from the tortious conduct of the other, because he has induced and encouraged the tort'.

[291] E.g., in *Cecil* v. *Hardin* 575 SW2d 268 (Tenn 1978), one of the defendants was the passenger of a drunken and drug-affected driver who struck a cyclist on the road, yet failed to stop and give aid. It was argued that the passenger aided and abetted the defendant driver in committing a series of unlawful acts that resulted in the accident. Liability was denied. The reasoning is entirely consistent in terms of whether a duty is owed by a *passenger* to road users, when that passenger (unlike say, a driving instructor) has no right to control either the driver or vehicle. Contrast the facts of *Reilly* v. *Anderson* 727 NW 2d 102 (Iowa, 2001) (passenger jointly liable because he held the steering wheel while driver smoked marijuana pipe).

5.5.6 *Conclusion: no single test of accessory liability*

As the detailed discussion in this section demonstrates, the courts have approached questions of liability of accessories in different ways for different torts. This raises a general question. Is there one test or rule of accessory liability in tort law?[292] Given the approach of this book and the focus on the relevant analytical questions, we consider that it is desirable that we apply a consistent, albeit broad, analytical framework for all cases of accessory liability, but accept that there is no single determinative test of liability for private law as a whole.

Similarly, even within tort law, the scope of accessory liability may vary according to the tort committed.[293] For this reason, this book adopts a flexible approach to determining liability, which considers the nature of the wrong, the extent of involvement of A, and the extent and degree of A's knowledge. The formulation of liability in general terms is sufficiently flexible to take into account the specific (and very different) torts. The requisite content of knowledge of A (the essential matters that A needs to know) can factor in the specific tort that PW has committed and what must be proven against PW, and can be modified accordingly.

Such an approach is all the more necessary since even in the application of accessory liability to specific torts, the case law is often incoherent, uncertain and difficult to rationalise.

5.6 Defences to accessory liability

5.6.1 *Possible defences*

As a general rule, any defences that potentially justify a tort on the part of a primary tortfeasor will mean that there has been no breach of rights, such that C has no claim against anyone.[294] It is not necessary, therefore,

[292] *Cf.* the question raised by Mustill LJ in *Unilever Plc* v. *Gillette (UK) Limited* [1989] RPC 583, 608, in the context of IP torts, as to whether the two accepted grounds for liability ('procuring' and participation in a common design) 'are distinct ways of infringing, or different aspects of a single way' (Mustill LJ preferring the former view). Similarly, Lord Toulson in *Sea Shepherd* [2015] UKSC 10; [2015] 2 WLR 694 [19]–[20], describes them as different categories of liability.

[293] *Cf.* Foster, 'Personal Liability', 37–39, who notes that in the context of director's liability for company torts 'different tort areas may warrant different treatment'.

[294] Some defences may only be personal to a party and excuse what is otherwise a rights infringement. Such situations will be rare in tort law but mean that potentially, A could be liable where PW is excused. The distinction drawn is therefore one between justifying conduct, such that no wrong is committed at all, and excuses, that do not deny that a

to set out the detailed operation of specific defences; reference should be made to general works on tort law. The available defences are not limited, however, to defences that PW (or any other joint tortfeasors) can actually prove; that is, A can plead all defences *potentially* available to the parties, even where PW may not be able to establish all the elements of such defence. For example, if PW is disbarred from a defence because she has a certain state of mind, that state of mind does not defeat the defence of all other joint tortfeasors. This can be illustrated in the context of defamation law by the defence of qualified privilege, of which an absence of malice is an element.

In defamation law, the question has been asked as to whether the malice of one joint tortfeasor defeats a defence such as privilege pleaded by a non-malicious joint tortfeasor? Early authorities such as *Smith* v. *Streatfield* suggested that the malice of one would 'infect' all others.[295] More modern authorities have held otherwise, such as *Dougherty* v. *Chandler*[296] and *Egger* v. *The Viscount Chelmsford*,[297] in which Lord Denning MR concluded that *Smith* v. *Streatfield* was wrongly decided. As was stated obiter in *Cornwall* v. *Rowan*:

> where a state of mind . . . is an essential ingredient to be established, as in the case of express malice, in our view only those persons who have the necessary state of mind to defeat the plea of qualified privilege can be liable. To hold that a person who is not actuated by malice loses the protection of qualified privilege simply because another person who was party to the publication was activated by malice would offend the principle that except in cases where a person is vicariously liable for another's conduct, a person should not be held liable in tort for the conduct of another for whom he or she is not responsible.[298]

As the quote notes, this can be contrasted with the position of a vicariously liable employer: the employer *will* be affected by malice and therefore liable where the servant or agent was actuated by malice.[299]

wrong has been committed. See, e.g., John C. P. Goldberg, 'Tort Law's Missing Excuses' in Andrew Dyson, James Goudkamp and Frederick Wilmot-Smith, *Defences in Tort* (Oxford, Hart Publishing, 2015) 53-54. See also [3.6].

295 (1913) 3 KB 764: where two or more persons are sued in respect of a joint libel, proof that one was actuated by malice will defeat pleas of privilege by other defendants. See also *Webb* v. *Bloch* (1928) 41 CLR 331, particularly the judgment of Knox CJ; and *cf.* Isaacs J: liability based on principal and agent relationship.

296 (1946) 46 SR (NSW) 370, 375.

297 (1965) 1 QB 248, 265.

298 [2004] SASC 384 [452] (Bleby, Besanko and Sulin JJ).

299 *Ibid.*; see also *Egger* v. *The Viscount Chelmsford* (1965) 1 QB 248.

5.6.2 *Release by claimant of one joint tortfeasor*

The common law rule that the cause of action against joint tortfeasors is one and indivisible was abolished under legislative changes originally contained in s. 6 of the Law Reform (Married Women and Tortfeasors) Act 1935 (UK).[300] Under the old rule, there could only be one action and one judgment for the whole amount of damages to which C was entitled. Judgment against one joint tortfeasor, or release by one tortfeasor, barred further claims against other tortfeasors. Under the present law, therefore, a judgment against, or settlement with, one tortfeasor does not preclude a claim by C against another.[301] As a consequence of the abolition of this rule, the distinction between joint tortfeasors and several, concurrent tortfeasors has become largely irrelevant.

One significant distinction survives under English law, however. It has been held that despite the legislative changes and the abolition of the 'one and indivisible' rule, *release* by one joint tortfeasor still releases all other tortfeasors,[302] though it must be a release and not merely a covenant not to sue.[303] This conclusion has been rightly criticised by the High Court of Australia, which has held that release by one does not release other joint tortfeasors.[304] In England, release of one joint tortfeasor is therefore a valid defence to a claim against another tortfeasor, whereas in Australia it is not.

5.7 Remedies against accessories

5.7.1 *Damages*

In *Dougherty* v. *Chandler*, Jordan CJ stated:

> If a number of persons jointly participate in the commission of a tort, each is responsible, jointly with each and all of the others, and also severally, for

[300] *Thompson* v. *Australian Capital Television Pty Ltd* (1996) 186 CLR 574; *Wah Tat Bank Ltd* v. *Chan* [1975] AC 507 (PC), *Bryanston Finance Ltd* v. *de Vries* [1975] 1 QB 703. See now, e.g., s. 3 Civil Liability (Contribution) Act 1978 (UK).

[301] See, e.g., *Baxter* v. *Obacelo Pty Ltd* [2001] HCA 66; (2001) 205 CLR 635; *Cf. Jameson* v. *Central Electricity Generating Board* [2000] 1 AC 455.

[302] *Wah Tat Bank Ltd* v. *Chan* [1975] AC 507 (PC); applied by the Court of Appeal in *Bryanston Finance Ltd* v. *de Vries* [1975] 1 QB 703; the rule has been reaffirmed by the Privy Council on appeal from New Zealand in *New Zealand Guardian Trust Co Ltd* v. *Brooks* [1995] 1 WLR 96; [1995] 2 BCLC 242.

[303] *Bryanston Finance Ltd* v. *de Vries* [1975] 1 QB 703.

[304] *Thompson* v. *Australian Capital Television Pty Ltd* (1996) 186 CLR 574.

> the whole amount of the damage caused by the tort irrespective of the extent of his participation.[305]

As a general rule, C can sue all or some of the joint tortfeasors:[306] each is liable for the full damage caused.[307] Liability for the full damage arises even though different parties committed distinct torts as part of the common endeavour. A classic case is *Smithson* v. *Garth*, in which the court held that if parties have been charged 'jointly with the whole entire matter' 'being all done at one time' then each is liable for the whole damage, even if 'one of them committed the battery, another the imprisonment, another took the [silver] buttons'.[308] This means the defendant may be liable for all damage done by a group, even where he is only one of many tortfeasors. For example, in *Hume* v. *Oldacre*,[309] a defendant hunter was held liable in trespass for damage caused by the concourse of people accompanying him, as he was a 'co-trespasser'.[310]

Although earlier cases did not distinguish between parties' liabilities for 'aggregate' injury suffered from the conduct of the combined parties,[311] even where one party did 'greater wrong' than the other,[312] more recent Australian decisions have held otherwise in relation to aggravated and exemplary damages.

In *XL Petroleum (NSW) Pty Ltd* v. *Caltex Oil (Australia) Pty Ltd*,[313] the High Court of Australia had to consider the availability of exemplary damages against one of two joint tortfeasors. C (the appellant, XL) had acquired the right to occupy land that A (the respondent, Caltex) had formerly used. XL intended to commence business as a discount petrol station. Caltex employed an industrial plumber (PW) to spike the underground petrol tanks on the premises. The damage to the tanks and loss of profits resulting from the damage was assessed at $5,527, which was

[305] (1946) 46 SR (NSW) 370, 375.

[306] We do not consider remedies that are available *to* accessories, such as contribution from other joint tortfeasors. See, e.g., *Zunter* v. *Fairfax Publications Pty Ltd* [2004] NSWSC 696.

[307] E.g., *Mitchell* v. *Tarbutt and Others* (1794) 5 TR 649; 101 ER 362.

[308] (1691) 3 Lev 323, 324; 83 ER 711, 712.

[309] (1816) 1 Starke 351; 171 ER 494.

[310] *Clerk and Lindsell*, [4-04], 275, fn. 15, doubt whether there was concerted action towards a common end in that case, but the report merely asserts that they were co-trespassers and is too scant to indicate the relationship between the defendant and the co-trespassers, nor the circumstances.

[311] E.g., *Clark* v. *Newsam and Edwards* (1847) 1 Ex 130; 154 ER 55, a case of false imprisonment, though compare the headnote with some of the equivocal and cryptic statements of Pollock CB and Alderson B, at 140; 55, about aggravated damages based on the differing motive of the tortfeasors.

[312] *Heydon's Case* (1612) 11 Co Rep 5a, 5b; 77 ER 1150, 1151.

[313] (1985) 155 CLR 448.

awarded against both Caltex and the plumber; however, a sum of $150,000 exemplary damages was also awarded against Caltex. The High Court held that such a separate award was justifiable in the circumstances and the conclusion followed from the legislative changes relating to joint tortfeasors considered in [5.6.2]. Gibbs CJ considered that 'it does not seem . . . in the least impracticable to give separate judgments against two defendants'.[314] It has similarly been concluded that separate judgment sums can be awarded against different joint defendants to reflect 'differing amounts attributable to aggravated damages'.[315]

The position under English law is different; only one judgment is possible for a single sum against defendants all joined in the same action and therefore exemplary damages cannot be awarded against one joint tortfeasor only.[316] Such an inflexible approach may cause potential injustice to claimants[317] and is undesirable, especially since the legislature appears to have intended to abolish the single judgment rule in its entirety.[318]

It has been assumed by some commentators that accessory liability is a secondary liability and therefore parasitic or duplicative rather than merely derivative: the same remedies must apply to A as to PW.[319] As the Australian authorities demonstrate, this does not follow and nor is it desirable. There is no reason why the remedy against each joint tortfeasor should not be considered separately to reflect each tortfeasor's culpability. A's liability need not duplicate that of PW. This does not detract from the accessorial nature of liability. If anything, it is reflective of a general approach that uncouples remedy from the cause of action, requiring a separate assessment of remedial issues once liability, on whatever basis, has been established.

314 *Ibid.* 460.

315 *McFadzean* v. *CFMEU* [2004] VSC 289 [142] (Ashley J) and also [116], [141]. See also obiter in *Myer Stores Ltd* v. *Soo* [1991] 2 VR 597; (1981) Aust Torts Reports 81-077 (CA), and *De Reus* v. *Gray* [2003] VCA 84; (2003) 9 VR 432 [24]–[32].

316 See *Broome* v. *Cassell and Co.* [1972] AC 1027. The same rule may apply in relation to aggravated damages; see at 1063. It is unclear what the position would be if successive actions were brought against defendants.

317 *Broome* v. *Cassell and Co* [1972] AC 1027, held that exemplary damages must not be awarded if any of the defendants do not deserve a punitive award against them.

318 See *XL Petroleum (NSW) Pty Ltd* v. *Caltex Oil (Australia) Pty Ltd* (1985) 155 CLR 448, and *Thompson* v. *Australian Capital Television Pty Ltd* (1996) 186 CLR 574.

319 See, e.g., Stevens, *Torts*, 277.

The solidary principle that all joint tortfeasors are liable for the full extent of damage caused, such that the risk of non-payment of damages by one defendant rests with the other defendants, has been abolished by legislation in all Australian jurisdictions for economic loss and property damages in many categories of claims (with exceptions, for example, for consumer claimants). Claimants are therefore only entitled to a proportion of 'apportionable claims' against individual defendants. The proportionate liability legislation has 'dramatically' changed the law[320] and is very complex, riddled with potential uncertainties and difficulties of interpretation. It is outside the scope of this book to consider the legislation.

5.7.2 Injunctions

The types of circumstances that would warrant an injunction against a primary tortfeasor may also warrant an injunction against an accessory; for example, to prevent A's continued involvement in PW's ongoing nuisance, to prevent A's repeated procurement, etc., of infringements,[321] or even to prevent prospective infringements via *quia timet* injunctions.[322] Injunctions could be based on specific powers in legislation, such as s. 97A Copyright, Designs and Patents Act 1988 (UK) (CDPA)[323] or under general injunction powers. It may be more practical to bring claims for injunctive relief against accessories where they have allowed, through their activities, multiple and repeated infringements by multiple principal wrongdoers,[324] as the internet cases illustrate. Such attempts to indirectly curb infringements have often failed at the first hurdle, namely establishing that the provider is in fact an accessory, for example, in supplying high-speed recording equipment to breaches

320 *Yates* v. *Mobile Marine Repairs Pty Ltd* [2007] NSWSC 1463 [93].

321 See, e.g., the injunction granted in *Twentieth Century Fox Film Corporation* v. *Newzbin Ltd* [2010] EWHC 608; [2010] ECC 13.

322 The availability of such relief was accepted in *Roadshow* [2012] HCA 16; (2012) 248 CLR 42 [94], though no liability arose in that case. See also *Apotex Pty Ltd* v. *Les Laboratoires Servier (No 2)* [2012] FCA 748 [41]–[66].

323 In Australia, see s. 115(2) Copyright Act 1968 (Cth).

324 *Twentieth Century Fox Film Corporation* v. *Newzbin Ltd* [2010] EWHC 608; [2010] ECC 13.

of copyright,[325] providing search engines that locate defamatory material,[326] or running online sales sites on which goods are sold in breach of trademark.[327]

There have been some successful claims, however, including injunctions granted against various parties responsible for developing, marketing and supplying an internet file-sharing system, Kazaa, used to infringe copyright, albeit principally on the basis of authorisation of infringement.[328] In *Newzbin Ltd*[329] [5.5.2.2], [5.5.2.3.] the defendant provided an online service for indexing and locating films and television programmes allowing users readily to download and reassemble all the component parts of the original content, posted by other users. The English High Court granted an injunction in wide terms to prevent copying in breach of copyright of any materials contained in C's repertoire.[330] Mareva or freezing injunctions were also granted against parties associated with Newzbin Ltd[331] (perhaps as accessories to the accessory?).

Although the site was shut down, the same URL address was reactivated shortly thereafter by an unknown offshore provider against whom no feasible action could be brought.[332] Claims were therefore brought against one major internet service provider, British Telecommunications Plc, seeking injunctive relief for it to block access by its users to the offending website. The claim for relief was based on the application of s. 97A CDPA and not accessory liability principles. Relief was granted, requiring that technology be used to block or impede access.[333]

[325] *CBS Songs* [1988] AC 1013.

[326] *Metropolitan International Schools Ltd* v. *Designtechnica Corporation and Ors* [2009] EWHC 1765.

[327] *L'Oreal SA* v. *eBay International AG* [2009] EWHC 1094 (Ch) [2009] ETMR 53.

[328] See *Universal Music Australia Pty Ltd* v. *Sharman License Holdings Ltd* [2005] FCA 1242; (2005) 220 ALR 1. Mareva orders had also been granted at the end of the trial.

[329] [2010] EWHC 608; [2010] ECC 13.

[330] The court refused an injunction in the wider terms sought by the claimants (*ibid.* [135]), however, to extend to all infringements of any copyright material held by all copyright holders.

[331] See *Twentieth Century Fox Film Corporation* v. *Harris* [2013] EWHC 159 (Ch) [6].

[332] *Twentieth Century Fox Film Corporation* v. *British Telecommunications Plc* [2011] EWHC 1981 (Ch).

[333] Even despite the prospect of similar claims being brought against other internet service providers, *ibid.* [1], this will not be the end of similar infringing businesses.

5.7.3 Other remedies

Although a claim for an account of profits derived from an infringement of IP torts is available potentially even against an accessory,[334] profiting for example, by operating an internet service used by others to infringe, it has been held that this does not give rise to a *proprietary* claim (by means of a constructive trust) against any money or assets derived from such conduct.[335]

334 See, e.g., s. 96 CDPA. Given the lack of successful claims against accessories in general, such accounts appear to have been little used in that context.

335 *Twentieth Century Fox Film Corporation* v. *Harris* [2013] EWHC 159 (Ch).

6

Breach of contract

6.1 Overview

The tort of inducing breach of contract is committed when a defendant, A, induces or procures another (the contract breaker and primary wrongdoer, PW) to breach her contract with a claimant, C, causing damage. The acts constituting the inducement to breach must be done *with knowledge* of the contract, such that A *intended*, by his acts, to procure the breach. The tort owes its origins to the famous case of *Lumley* v. *Gye*,[1] decided in 1853, in which the defendant lured an opera star away from a rival opera house in order to contract with him, although the claim in *Lumley* itself ultimately failed at trial.[2] Examples of the tort include inducing a related company to terminate a contract with C to promote a sporting event;[3] paying moneys to workers to allow them to continue unlawful strike action;[4] a tenants' association urging tenants not to pay rents in order to achieve its objectives;[5] and a trade competitor engaging in unfair competition by poaching a rival's customers[6] or employees.[7] In this chapter, we use the label 'A' as our usual shorthand for accessory, albeit acknowledging that the accessorial nature of the inducing tort is disputed [6.2].

Some commentators question the need for a tort that further protects contracting parties, in addition to their contractual rights against breaching

[1] (1853) 2 E & B 216; 118 ER 749.

[2] See S. Waddams, 'Johanna Wagner and the rival opera houses' (2001) 117 *Law Quarterly Review* 431, 431 and 454–458; the defendant was able to prove that he honestly believed that the contracting party could lawfully terminate her contract with the plaintiff. For a successful claim on comparable modern facts, see *Fightvision Pty Ltd* v. *Onisforou* (1999) 47 NSWLR 473.

[3] *Zhu* v. *Treasurer (NSW)* [2004] HCA 56; (2004) 218 CLR 530 (*Zhu*).

[4] *Cf. Smithies* v. *National Association* [1909] 1 KB 310.

[5] *Camden Nominees* v. *Forcey* [1940] Ch 352.

[6] E.g., *Multinail Australia Pty Ltd* v. *Pryda (Aust) Pty Ltd* [2002] QSC 105, in which the defendant offered incentives and even guaranteed to subsidise the customer's damages.

[7] *Cantor Fitzgerald International* v. *Bird* [2002] IRLR 867.

parties.[8] Such a tort may stifle competition, for example,[9] and there is clearly the need to balance defendants' interests in freedom of action against claimants' interests in the security of their contracts. There is, however, widespread support for the tort, albeit on a number of different rationales. These rationales include the protection of quasi-proprietary rights, that is, that contract rights are 'a species of property'[10] protected by limited rights against non-contracting parties,[11] economic efficiency[12]

[8] See, e.g., H. Perlman, 'Interference with Contract and Other Economic Expectancies: A Clash of Tort and Contract Doctrine' (1982) 49 *University of Chicago Law Review* 61; D. Dobbs, 'Tortious Interference with Contractual Relationships' (1980) 34 *Arkansas Law Review* 335; W. Page Keeton et. al., *Prosser & Keeton on Torts*, 5th edn (St Paul, West Publishing Group, 1984) 978–979; contrast, in support, J. Danforth 'Tortious Interference with Contract: A Reassertion of Society's Interest in Commercial Stability and Contractual Integrity' (1981) 81 *Colorado Law Review* 1491, and W. Woodward, 'Contractarians, Community, and the Tort of Interference with Contract' (1996) 80 *Minnesota LR* 1103.

[9] D. Howarth, 'Against *Lumley* v. *Gye*' (2005) 68 *Modern Law Review* 195, 202. Apart from cases involving trade competitors, many of the older cases applying the tort (and establishing its boundaries) concern interferences in employment contracts during industrial disputes, instigated or supported by the defendants, often trade unions. One can question the suitability of the tort to resolving such disputes in today's social conditions (if it ever was suitable, as the classic case of *Hitchman Coal and Coke Co.* v. *Mitchell* 245 US 229 (1917) bears out). See also Howarth, at 224; but see 225. And see Keeton, *Prosser & Keeton*, 979, noting the tort's 'ominous beginnings as a tool to enforce compulsory labour and ... as a means of suppressing unions' (fn. omitted). Legislation reduces the capacity for the tort to operate in that context to varying degrees. See Howarth, 200, and Trade Union and Labour Relations (Consolidation) Act 1992 (UK), ss. 219–246.

[10] See Kitto J's analysis in *Attorney-General for New South Wales* v. *Perpetual Trustee Co. (Ltd)* (1952) 85 CLR 237 (HCA) 294–295 (also describing the rights as *in rem*), cited with approval in *Zhu* [2004] HCA 56; (2004) 218 CLR 530 [124]–[125].

[11] For commentary supporting a property-type rationale, see, e.g., C. E. Carpenter, 'Interference with Contract Relations' (1928) 41 *Harvard Law Review* 728; R. A. Epstein, 'Inducement of Breach of Contract as a Problem of Ostensible Ownership' (1987) 16 *Journal of Legal Studies* 1; Waddams, 'Johanna Wagner', 449–450. Roderick Bagshaw, 'Inducing Breach of Contract' in J. Horder (ed.) *Oxford Essays in Jurisprudence* (Fourth Series, Oxford, 2000) 131, does not use the label quasi-property, but considers that many of the arguments for protecting property interests against the world at large apply equally in this context (133–137). For case law adopting a property analogy, see the authorities discussed in *Zhu* [2004] HCA 56; (2004) 218 CLR 530 [124]–[135], especially the numerous US cases noted at fn. 65.

[12] In *Roadshow Films Pty Ltd* v. *iiNet Ltd* [2012] HCA 16; (2012) 248 CLR 42 [110], Gummow & Hayne JJ cite William M. Landes and Richard A. Posner, *The Economic Structure of Intellectual Property Law* (Harvard University Press, 2003) 118–119, supporting the proposition that liability for the tort of inducing breach of contract 'has been said to have an economic rationale ... namely a lower cost of prevention of breach of the primary obligation'.

and accessory liability principles.[13] Much of the academic debate about the need for the inducing tort and, if such need exists, its rationale and justifiable limits, has occurred in the US, where formulation of the tort in the *Restatement of Torts* is considerably wider than in Anglo-Australian law. The broad formulation in the *Restatement* leads to uncertainty: merely interfering with the 'performance' of a contract so as to cause the performance to be 'more expensive or burdensome' can give rise to liability, provided such interference is intentional and improper.[14] Obviously, therefore, this wide US liability rule requires a broader and even more uncertain defence of justification,[15] and a difficult balancing of interests,[16] to limit liability.

In the High Court of Australia, the most considered discussion of the inducing tort occurs in *Zhu* v. *Treasurer (NSW)* (*Zhu*) and supports a quasi-proprietary analysis;[17] but there is also support in recent decisions for an economic efficiency rationale[18] and for characterising liability as accessorial.[19] In the House of Lords in *OBG* v. *Allen* (*OBG*), an accessorial rationale received support.[20] As Lord Hoffmann stated, 'the person

[13] For an excellent summary of the competing rationales, see Hazel Carty, *An Analysis of the Economic Torts*, 2nd edn (Oxford University Press, 2010) 54–62, on which we have placed considerable reliance.

[14] See *Restatement (Second) of Torts* vol. 4, Ch. 37, §766A (American Law Institute, 1977). *Cf.* §766. Indeed, in some jurisdictions, even interference in 'prospective advantages' or expectancies may suffice. See §766B and *cf.* §766C; Keeton, *Prosser & Keeton*, 1005 ff.

[15] See generally *Restatement (Second) of Torts* vol. 4, Ch. 37, §§766–773. The *Restatement* requires that the defendant's conduct must be 'improper'. This also means that it is problematic to determine whether conclusions reached in some cases are based on the absence of the elements of the tort, or because prima facie the tort is established, but the defendant's conduct was justified. See examples provided in Francis B. Sayre, 'Inducing Breach of Contract' (1921) 36 *Harvard Law Review* 663.

[16] *Restatement (Second) of Torts* vol. 4, Ch. 37, §767, lists seven general factors, including freedom of action and contractual security, each party's interests and the defendant's motives, that need to be considered. An exercise of balancing such interests must be entirely unpredictable, we suggest.

[17] In *Zhu* [2004] HCA 56; 218 CLR 530[124]–[135], the joint judgment (Gleeson CJ, Gummow, Kirby, Callinan & Heydon JJ) strongly endorses a property analysis (above n. 10), though it notes that there is some element of 'circuity' [circularity] in the thesis [126] (the right to contract performance is protected because it is quasi-proprietary, but it is quasi-proprietary because it is protected against third-party interference).

[18] See above n. 12.

[19] *Zhu* [2004] HCA 56; (2004) 218 CLR 530 [121]–[122], in which the court describes the tort as another instance in which 'the law grants remedies against a third party who interferes in the legal relations between two other persons'. The court then proceeds to cite a number of examples of clearly accessory liability.

[20] [2007] UKHL 21; [2008] 1 AC 1. The issue is discussed below; it suffices here to say that there are numerous references to the tort being accessorial. See, e.g., Lord Hoffmann at [3], [5], [6], [8], [9], [16], [20], [21], [29], [32], [36], [37], [67], [69] and [86]; Lord

procuring the tort ... [is] liable as accessory to the liability of the contracting party'.[21] The contracting party must have committed a primary wrong (of breach).[22]

This book adopts the characterisation of the inducing tort as accessorial, though it is accepted that there may be more than one justificatory rationale for it and some commentators reject such characterisation; their views are critiqued in [6.2]. An analysis in terms of accessory liability, focusing on the wrong in question, the requisite acts of involvement and the requisite mental state, provides a useful and structured basis for resolving some of the uncertainties about the operation of the tort. At least one caveat applies, however: the tort does not share all of the common characteristics of other examples of accessory liability.

What is clear, however, is that irrespective of which rationales justify it, the inducing tort creates only a limited liability that does not capture all those persons who are in some way involved in breaches of contract by those who carry the primary responsibility to perform. The tort has been (and must be) narrowly confined,[23] despite the 'high store placed on compliance with contractual obligation by English law and by the common law systems derived from it'.[24] Indeed, the tort is one of the most limited forms of accessory liability, the elements having recently been confined by the House of Lords in *OBG*.[25] That decision has been widely

Nicholls at [172], [178] and [194]; and Lord Brown at [320]. The term 'secondary liability' is also used, by Lord Hoffmann at [32] and [44], by Lord Nicholls at [172] and by Lord Brown at [320]; the collation is from Simon Deakin and John Randall, 'Rethinking the Economic Torts' (2009) 72(4) *Modern Law Review* 519, fn. 116.

[21] *OBG* [2007] UKHL 21; [2008] 1 AC 1 [5].

[22] Query whether such breach need be actionable against PW [6.3.2].

[23] See, e.g., Carty, *Economic Torts*, 55–56, summarising some of the objections to the tort, in terms of its potential impact on commercial life and competition. Carty supports a very narrowly confined tort; see generally Ch. 3. See also discussion in Peter Cane, *Tort Law and Economic Interests* (Oxford, Clarendon Press, 1991) 129–130, who notes doubts about the tort but concludes that the tort may serve to provide remedies against unfair competition; and see Peter Cane, '*Mens* Rea in Tort Law' (2000) *Oxford Journal of Legal Studies* 533, 546, 554.

[24] This observation of the High Court in *Zhu* [2004] HCA 56; (2004) 218 CLR 530 [160], was made in the context of its support for a narrowly confined defence of justification (discussed below). That comment, however, must be seen in light of the fact that the *elements* of the tort are difficult to make out, at least accepting the restrictive approach in *OBG* [2007] UKHL 21; [2008] 1 AC 1. Consequently, it is justifiable to limit the defence of justification, otherwise the tort would be largely redundant. The Court's statement does not mean that the law gives wide protection to contracts via a broadly operating tort.

[25] [2007] UKHL 21; [2008] 1 AC 1.

approved, including in Australian authorities.[26] The confinement is achieved by the requirement that A must knowingly and intentionally procure through his acts a breach of PW's contract with C, that is, with subjective knowledge that the procured conduct amounts to a breach. These elements are elaborated upon in [6.3].

Importantly, in *OBG* the House of Lords reiterated, after considerable earlier uncertainty and contrary opinion, that inducing breach of contract is a separate tort and rejected the view that it is merely part of, or an example of, the broader tort of causing economic loss by unlawful means.[27] What is encompassed within unlawful means within that tort is the subject of debate, but a simple example is where a defendant assaults potential customers of C, preventing them from dealing with her. The tort of causing economic loss by unlawful means is firmly established in the UK; its acceptance in Australia remains open but one can assume that if it were accepted, it would be shaped by the House's reasoning in *OBG*.[28]

6.2 Liability as accessory liability

6.2.1 Liability in tort, not contract

The privity of contract rule stipulates that only parties to the contract may enforce the contractual obligations (that is, third-party beneficiaries are not able to enforce the contract) or be bound by those obligations.[29] There are statutory and common law exceptions to the rule[30] but they are

[26] See, e.g., Carty, *Economic Torts*, Ch. 3, and *Jaddcal Pty Ltd* v. *Minson (No 3)* [2011] WASC 362.

[27] The House rejected liability arising for mere *interference* with contract; as a result, earlier cases holding otherwise were either justifiable on the basis of the unlawful means tort or else wrongly decided. See [6.2.2].

[28] See, e.g., *Sanders* v. *Snell* (1998) 196 CLR 329 (HCA) 341–343; *Terry Cross Financial Services* v. *Misiti* [2008] NSWSC 1365; *Deepcliff Pty Ltd* v. *Council of the City of Gold Coast* [2011] QCA 342; *Qantas Airways Ltd* v. *Transport Workers Union of Australia* [2011] FCA 470; (2011) 280 ALR 503; *Ballard* v. *Multiplex* [2012] NSWSC 426. See further, Jason Neyers, 'Should the High Court of Australia follow *OBG* v. *Allan*' in J. Edelman, S. Degeling and J. Goudcamp (eds.), *Torts in Commercial Law* (Sydney, Thompson, 2011). R. Balkin & J. Davis, *Law of Torts*, 4th edn (Australia, LexisNexis Butterworths, 2009) 592 [21.4], state that since the earlier English decisions have never been accepted by the highest courts in Australia or New Zealand, one can assume that the principles in *OBG* will be accepted in those jurisdictions.

[29] See, e.g., *Dunlop Pneumatic Tyre Co. Ltd* v. *Selfridge & Co. Ltd* [1915] AC 847.

[30] See, e.g., N. Seddon, R. Bigwood and M. Ellinghaus, *Cheshire & Fifoot Law of Contract*, 10th Aust. edn (Australia, LexisNexis Butterworths, 2009) Ch. 7.

not relevant for present purposes and, importantly, they have not resulted in an abandonment of the common law's ongoing commitment to the rule. Further, the exceptions and associated cases tend to be concerned with the third-party beneficiary rule,[31] and not the aspect of the rule that is of relevance here, precluding non-parties from being bound by a contract.

In part because of the common law's acceptance of the privity rule and related bargain theory, it was conceptually and historically difficult for contract law to develop third-party liability principles within the doctrinal confines of contract itself, at least in 1853 when *Lumley* v. *Gye*[32] was decided. If the law was to provide protection to C against A's involvement in PW breaching her contract with C, then contract law itself could not develop those doctrinal tools, since non-parties could not be liable *as if* they themselves had breached the contract. Obviously, in *Lumley* v. *Gye*, the law did perceive a need for protection, at least against more egregious attacks on C's rights, to have the contract enforced. It is for that reason that the court resorted to tort law as the basis for liability, and the tort of inducing breach of contract developed.[33] It met the needs of claimants but did not directly impinge upon the privity rule,[34] since the obligation created against the world at large is not a positive one to perform the contract in question, but rather a negative one not to induce a breach. As such it was, and remains, compatible with the unity of contract doctrine.[35]

As explained in [2.7], wherever the formulation of the elements of a primary wrong creates legal or conceptual impediments as to who can be liable for the primary wrong, then accessory liability may provide a means of extending responsibility for the primary wrong. In the case of contract, those impediments precluded non-parties to the contract being liable as joint-contract breakers and also precluded the creation of any third-party liability within contract law itself.

It is as a result of these contract law restraints and the tort solution adopted to overcome them that the inducing tort has evolved as an

31 *Cf. ibid.* 285. 32 (1853) 2 E & B 216; 118 ER 749.

33 See *OBG* [2007] UKHL 21; [2008] 1 AC 1 [4].

34 Coleridge J in dissent in *Lumley* v. *Gye* (1853) 2 E & B 216; 118 ER 749, saw the tort as undermining privity of contract: remedies for breach of contract are confined 'by action to the contracting parties' (246; 760); 'the persuader has not broken and could not break the contract, for he had never entered into any; he cannot be sued upon the contract; and yet it is the breach of contract only that is the cause of damage' (249; 761).

35 See Bagshaw, 'Inducing Breach', 133.

independent wrong such that the accessory is never liable for the same wrong as PW.

6.2.2 *The accessorial rationale for liability*

Before considering whether inducing breach of contract is a form of accessory liability as it is described in this book, it is necessary to say something about the relationship between inducing breach and other economic torts. Inducing is the only economic tort, apart from conspiracy [5.3.2], that potentially falls within the broad ambit of accessory liability. This does not mean that there may not be overlapping claims. Other economic torts such as causing economic loss by unlawful means may be made out on the same facts that sustain the inducing tort,[36] for example, if assaults or batteries were committed against employees of C to prevent them performing their contractual obligations. This may be one reason that led to the treatment of inducing breach as an example of a broader, unified economic tort. That view has been rejected in the UK by *OBG*, in which the House of Lords stressed the key differences between the inducing and unlawful means torts.[37] Unlike inducing, the unlawful means tort is a stand-alone tort; that is, the liability arises as a result of A's conduct alone. There is no wrong committed by others to which A can be an accessory.[38] Although other parties may have been used as intermediaries to achieve A's ends, the liability of A arises irrespective of any claims against the intermediaries.[39] The tort is limited to the use of means that are unlawful in the sense that they must be actionable by the third party (that is, give rise to civil liability against A) or would have been actionable if they caused loss. Torts and breaches of contract are examples.[40] Acts that

36 *OBG* [2007] UKHL 21; [2008] 1 AC 1 [21] (Lord Hoffmann).

37 *Ibid.* [8]. See also the discussion by Lord Hoffmann of the unified theory and his ultimate rejection of it, [26]–[38]. Note, however, that Lord Hoffmann considered that '[i]t is not easy to point to cases which were wrongly decided because the court had adopted the unified theory rather than the two-tort analysis . . . ' [30].

38 *OBG* [2007] UKHL 21; [2008] 1 AC 1 [6] (Lord Hoffmann).

39 See *ibid.* [173] (Lord Nicholls); Carty, *Economic Torts*, 77.

40 See *OBG* at [45]–[64] (Lord Hoffmann); [270] (Lord Walker); [302] (Baroness Hale); [320] (Lord Brown). Contrast the approach of Lord Nicholls, concluding that unlawful means includes 'all acts a defendant is not permitted to do, whether by the civil law or the criminal law' [162], and see discussion [149]–[162]. For a discussion of further limitations placed on the 'actionable' requirement by the various judgments, see Carty, *Economic Torts*, 92–98. The House of Lord's narrow approach has been confirmed in Canada in *A I Enterprises Ltd* v. *Bram Enterprises Ltd* [2014] SCC 12, noted Pey-Woan Lee, 'The unlawful means tort in Canada' (2014) 130 *Law Quarterly Review* 559.

are criminal (without being tortious) do not qualify; nor do acts that are merely ultra vires or void.[41]

Turning to the inducing tort, in our view, it can usefully be analysed using the framework that we have adopted for all accessory liability. First, liability is dependent upon a wrong having been committed by another party. Secondly, the defendant's liability arises from the defendant's involvement in bringing about that wrong, with a requisite mental state. The defendant's (independently) wrongful conduct is linked to the commission of the wrong. The liability is accessorial. We are fortified in our conclusions by repeated statements in *OBG*, as well as a more tentatively expressed view by the High Court of Australia in *Zhu*, that liability can be described or characterised as accessorial (or 'secondary').[42]

Consistently with this view, the inducing tort reflects the themes of and rationales for accessory liability more generally [2.4]. First, the tort redresses the accessory's own wrongful conduct. Secondly, it vindicates Cs' rights and PWs' obligations by *extending* the protection of Cs via claims against parties *other than* PW. Importantly, the *scope* of that added protection depends very much on the specific wrong at issue. Finally, some judges support a property rationale for the inducing tort. This has obvious resonances in some other contexts; for example, the High Court has identified the need to protect equitable *property* interests as one further rationale for equitable accessory liability.[43]

As already noted, the inducing tortfeasor is always liable for a different wrong than PW, the contract breaker. Unlike joint tortfeasors, the inducing party and the contract breaker 'are not parties to the same wrong'.[44] Being liable for the same wrong as PW, as if a principal, is not, however, a universal characteristic of all examples of accessory liability and does not preclude inducing breach of contract from being analysed in those terms. Some other examples of liability that are in substance accessorial have developed as independent wrongs [2.3].

A number of commentators have rejected the substantive characterisation of liability as 'accessorial'. For example, Stevens notes specifically

[41] See, e.g., *Sanders* v. *Snell* (1998) 196 CLR 329 (pre-dating *OBG*: if unlawful means tort exists, it requires unlawful acts, not merely ones that are ultra vires or void (341–343)).

[42] [2004] HCA 56; (2004) 218 CLR 530. See [6.1].

[43] *Zhu* [2004] HCA 56; (2004) 218 CLR 530 [121].

[44] Carty, *Economic Torts*, 60, fn. 239. The inducer, of course, does not bear the contractual duty.

in relation to inducing breach of contract[45] that 'the wrongdoer is not held jointly liable as principal for breach of contract, but infringes a different right from the right to performance infringed by the party in breach'.[46] Of course, this distinction was accepted above, although arguably the point is largely semantic; for although the parties are not joint contract breakers, they can loosely be described as joint wrongdoers in relation to the contract.[47]

Further, Stevens correctly notes that the modes of participation may differ between inducing breach of contract (where a narrow test of inducement applies) and most other torts, where authorisation, or having a common design to commit a tort, suffices for liability.[48] This argument, however, amounts to little more than a rejection of the view that there is a single, uniform test of or for accessory liability, a view that we ourselves have rejected in Chapter 3. It is not an argument against the view that inducing breach is a form of accessory liability that can be analysed using the same framework as other instances of accessory liability.

Finally, Stevens notes that the remedies available against the inducing party differ from those available against PW, and indeed, there may be liability for the inducer where none falls upon the contracting party.[49] But tort law in some jurisdictions similarly allows for differing remedial outcomes [5.7.1] and in other areas of law where liability is undeniably

[45] More generally, Robert Stevens, *Torts and Rights* (Oxford University Press, 2007) rejects the view that joint tortfeasors are liable as accessories, analogously to criminal law accessories. See further, [5.1.3], where it was noted that they were mostly by the way.

[46] Stevens, *Torts*, 257, 276. The same point is made by Deakin and Randall, 'Rethinking the Economic Torts', 543, who correctly point out that for accessory liability in its usual manifestations, there is only one wrong, to which the defendant is an accessory, whereas in this context there are clearly two, one contractual and one tortious.

[47] As Deakin and Randall, 'Rethinking the Economic Torts', note at fn. 122, Erle J in *Lumley* v. *Gye* (1853) 2 E & B 216, 232; 118 ER 749, having stated the general principle that 'the procurement of the violation of a right is a cause of action in all instances where the violation is an actionable wrong', described a party who thus procures the wrong as 'a joint wrongdoer'. Whether one describes a given example of accessory liability as being a distinct wrong or 'secondary' to the same primary wrong is not important for the purposes of characterising the liability rule [2.3].

[48] Stevens, *Torts*, 276, and *cf.* 256–257, where Stevens draws the same distinction between accessory liability in criminal law and joint tortfeasors. Stevens further argues against assistance liability generally in tort (257), though he seems to consider it may suffice for the purposes of the inducing tort (276–277), a view that has been rejected in the cases [6.3.3].

[49] *Ibid.* 277: the contract may have excluded the secondary liability of the contracting party to pay damages.

accessorial, there is no prerequisite that A is always liable for the same remedies as PW or, indeed, that PW need be liable at all [2.6].

Stevens' conclusion that the basis for liability for the inducing tort is that 'contract rights carry with them a right good against everyone else that they do not induce the infringement of the contractual right'[50] does not help in answering questions such as what are the boundaries of such a 'right', how we determine when such a 'right' is infringed, and whether such a 'right' shares in common characteristics of other 'rights' that are similarly 'secondary' or 'accessory' (labels that Stevens himself uses).[51]

Deakin and Randall consider that the economic torts in general, and inducing breach of contract in particular, are not based on a theory of 'accessorial' or secondary liability. In their view, the use of such expressions is 'potentially misleading'[52] and 'doctrinally confusing and conceptually unnecessary, and should be rejected'.[53] Deakin and Randall's conclusion on the economic torts is correct for reasons already noted above. Their conclusion on the inducing tort, however, appears to be based on a view that describing the tort as accessorial necessarily means that liability must extend to merely facilitating breach;[54] this need not be so.

By way of contrast, Carty accepts that liability for the inducing tort follows the same *pattern* as joint tortfeasor liability, though it is not an example of it,[55] and that it is an example or form of 'secondary liability',[56] such that that label can therefore help 'elucidate' the framework of the tort.[57] However, Carty shares Deakin and Randall's concerns and is critical of the judges' use of the labels 'accessorial' and 'secondary', considering it as 'regrettable', because it can lead to the argument that facilitation could suffice for liability.[58] She states:

[50] *Ibid.* 281.

[51] *Ibid.* 281: 'The right is accessory because it has no existence independent of the contractual right to which it relates.' See also similarly at 334.

[52] Deakin and Randall, 'Rethinking the Economic Torts', 543, and see generally the discussion at 520, 542–544.

[53] *Ibid.* 544. Note at 543: liability is parasitic, 'but this is not the same thing as saying that it is accessorial'.

[54] See *ibid.*, e.g. at 542. 'Essentially the issue is this: should a defendant be liable for simply assisting or facilitating a legal wrong committed by another which deprives the claimant of an expected benefit?' Their conclusion that the answer is 'no' (at 543) is correct.

[55] See Carty, *Economic Torts*, 60–62, and see also 304–307.

[56] *Ibid.* 62, 306.

[57] *Ibid.* 305.

[58] *Ibid.* 62, 306. Compare also Pey-Woan Lee, 'Inducing Breach of Contract, Conversion and Contract as Property' (2009) 29 *Oxford Journal of Legal Studies* 511, 522: the tort 'may loosely be described as a form of … accessory liability … but this descriptor by itself neither justifies nor elucidates the tort'.

> The courts need to be wary, however, not to allow this *label*—'secondary liability'—to be seen as evidence of a wider *doctrine* of secondary civil liability where, for example, mere facilitation could suffice for liability.[59]

Certainly, there should be no liability for facilitating a breach of contract.[60] But one can accept that conclusion without rejecting an accessorial analysis, since it does not follow inherently from that analysis (or the label 'accessory') that liability automatically extends to assistance. We have stressed in Part I that wider or narrower liability rules or tests may be adopted for different wrongs to determine whether A is an accessory to another's wrong. The type of acts of involvement, and the particular mental state that satisfies the liability rules, differs according to the wrong in question.[61] As Carty correctly notes, the different examples of 'secondary' (accessory) liability 'reveal that different "links" to the primary wrongdoer are demanded by these separate examples of secondary liability'.[62]

6.3 The elements of the tort

6.3.1 Elements in general

Courts and commentators have formulated the elements of the tort in slightly varying ways; but the formulations generally all include, in some form, the need for (1) a breach of contract by PW, (2) as a result of an act of inducement or procurement by A, (3) done with the *intent* to induce or procure such a breach, that is, with *knowledge* of the existence of the contract and that the course of conduct will lead to a breach of it by PW, (4) that results in damage to C.[63] The formulations vary mostly around the relationship between knowledge and intent [6.3.4]. Before we turn to the central elements of procuring and the required mental state, however, it is worth saying a little more about the primary wrong that is at issue here.

59 *Ibid.* 62; see also 305–307. 60 *Ibid.* 307.

61 This could be so even where the wrongs are found within the same broad category, such as tort law.

62 Carty, *Economic Torts*, 306. See also at 307.

63 *Cf. Emerald Construction Co. Ltd* v. *Lowthian* [1966] 1 WLR 691, 703; [1966] 1 All ER 1013, 1019 (Diplock LJ): three essential elements, 'the act, the intent and the resulting damage'.

6.3.2 *The primary wrong: breach of contract*

The defendant's conduct must induce a breach of contract. Therefore, no tort is committed if the contract is void.[64] Similarly, merely inducing a party to avoid a voidable contract is not tortious,[65] but it is probably tortious to induce a breach of a contract that is unenforceable by reason of non-compliance with the Statute of Frauds.[66] Hindering or even seeking to prevent another's contractual performance does not suffice; there must be a breach of contract. The tort is not one of interference with contractual relations,[67] despite pre-*OBG* cases that stated it more broadly, particularly in the UK. Cases that have held otherwise[68] are, after *OBG*, either wrongly decided,[69] or else justifiable only on the basis of unlawful means being used to cause economic loss.[70] The breach of contract probably does not need to be actionable, for example, where PW is not liable because she has excluded the obligation to pay damages.[71] We would suggest, however, that it may be difficult in some circumstances to establish that damage has been suffered by C if the breach is not actionable.

64 *News Limited* v. *Australian Rugby Football League Ltd* (1996) 64 FCR 410, 516.

65 *Proform Sports Management Ltd* v. *Proactive Sports Management Ltd* [2006] EWHC 2903; [2007] 1 All ER 542 (contract voidable by minor); it was held that it does not matter that the inducement occurs when the contract has not yet been avoided, but causes the minor to 'breach' (i.e., avoid or rescind) the contract. Contrast *Building Workers' Industrial Union of Australia* v. *Odco Pty Ltd* (1981) 29 FCR 104, below n. 125, and the position in the United States, see below n. 66.

66 See the US cases discussed in Carpenter, 'Interference with Contract'. Indeed, even more serious defects may not preclude liability in the US. See Keeton, *Prosser & Keeton*, 995–996, in which the examples given would appear to be inconsistent with *Proform Sports Management Ltd* v. *Proactive Sports Management Ltd* [2006] EWHC 2903; [2007] 1 All ER 542, and the *Restatement (Second) of Torts* vol. 4., Ch. 37, 10 (1979).

67 Balkin and Davis, *Law of Torts*, 592 [21.4].

68 E.g., *Daily Mirror* v. *Gardner* [1968] 2 QB 762.

69 E.g., *Torquay Hotel Co. Ltd* v. *Cousins* [1969] 2 Ch 106, disapproved by Lord Nicholls in *OBG* [2007] UKHL 21; [2008] 1 AC 1 [181]–[187].

70 E.g., *Gdanska* v. *Latvian Shipping (No 3)* [2002] EWCA Civ 889 (company in breach of its contract with a third party withholding funds from subsidiary to prevent its performance of obligations with claimant); *Re The 'Kaliningrad' and 'Nadezhda Krupskaya'* [1997] 2 Lloyd's Rep 35; *GWK Ltd* v. *Dunlop Rubber Co. Ltd* (1926) 42 TLR 376, discussed by Lord Nicholls in *OBG* [2007] UKHL 21; [2008] 1 AC 1 [181]–[187].

71 See Stevens, *Torts*, 277, citing *Merkur Island Shipping Corp.* v. *Laughton* [1983] 2 AC 570; and Bagshaw, 'Inducing Breach', 149, arguing that where PW's conduct is not actionable by C because of a *force majeure* clause, then interference in PW's capacity to perform such contract is still tortious by A, though the argument is used to support liability for preventing performance, which is probably best seen as falling within the unlawful means tort.

Although the primary wrong of breach of contract is usually one of strict liability,[72] importantly, here the tort is fault-based. Indeed, it requires a high degree of fault when compared to other examples of accessory liability. Knowledge is central to the tort [6.3.4].

6.3.3 *Conduct: induce or procure*

There must be words or 'affirmative or positive' acts[73] of procurement by A directed at PW that seek to achieve or bring about a particular outcome, by means of 'inducement, incitement or persuasion',[74] money payments,[75] threats,[76] fraud,[77] or the like.[78] The acts used to incite, persuade, etc., may themselves be lawful.[79] Inducing a breach envisages success;[80] invitations or exhortations that do not achieve their aim are not actionable. Since some positive acts are required, merely omitting to take steps to prevent a breach does not suffice, such as where a holding company could have prevented a subsidiary from breaching a contract.[81] One unanswered question is whether the mere act of contracting with PW could suffice as inducement (absent any further inducement) such as where A provides PW with the means of escaping her contract with C by offering an alternative and thereby acquiesces in that breach.

The requirement of acts of inducement would generally only be satisfied by acts that seek to induce an individual infringer to carry out a

72 Frustration aside, the contracting party is generally liable for failing to perform the promised performance regardless of any fault or the reasons for that non-performance.

73 These terms are used in the statutory context in *ACCC* v. *SIP Australia Pty Ltd* [2002] FCA 824; (2002) ATPR ¶41–877 [112].

74 See Lord Templeman in *CBS Songs Ltd* v. *Amstrad Plc* [1988] 1 AC 1013, 1058.

75 *Cf. Smithies* v. *National Association* [1909] 1 KB 310, 335 (strike pay).

76 *Cf. Emerald Construction Co. Ltd* v. *Lowthian* [1966] 1 WLR 691.

77 See the US cases discussed in Carpenter, 'Interference with Contract'.

78 See also the dictionary definition used in *National Foods Milk Ltd* v. *McMahon Milk Pty Ltd* [2008] VSC 208 [277]. Indirect acts, not directed against PW but that may merely interfere, do not amount to inducement and are only actionable if they *are* unlawful and fall within another economic tort. Query whether acts of moral persuasion, not motivated by self-interest, could suffice, e.g., if A seeks to persuade PW to leave her employ as a tobacco company spokesperson.

79 *Independent Oil Industries Ltd* v. *Shell Co. of Australia* Ltd (1937) 37 SR (NSW) 394, 418–419.

80 *Cf. Trade Practices Commission* v. *Parkfield Operations Pty Ltd* (1985) 5 FCR 140; 59 ALR 489, in the context of restrictive trade practices under the Competition and Consumer Act 2010 (Cth).

81 *LMI Australiasia Pty Ltd* v. *Baulderstone Hornibrook Pty Ltd* [2003] NSWCA 74.

particular infringement, and not by acts directed at the public (or a segment of the public) at large.[82]

Since the procurer seeks a certain outcome – is the party that 'pulls the strings', so to speak[83] – he is generally the instigating force behind the breach by PW, and this means that there must be a sufficiently strong or close causal link between A's actions and the breach of contract. In this context, therefore, unusually and unlike in most other circumstances of accessory liability [3.3.3], it is probably necessary to show a 'but for' causal connection between PW's decision to breach and A's intentional conduct that sought to bring about such an outcome;[84] that is, that A's acts actually or successfully have procured PW's actions. As Lord Hoffmann stated in *OBG*:

> Did the defendant's [A's] acts of encouragement, threat, persuasion and so forth have a sufficient causal connection with the breach by the contracting party to attract accessory liability?[85]

Although this means that it is probably not stating it too highly that A's conduct generally needs to be a 'but for' cause of the breach rather than being merely *a* factor in the breach,[86] nonetheless, the courts may not

82 Carty, *Economic Torts*, 60, drawing parallels with the law of joint tortfeasors and relying on Lord Templeman's judgment in *CBS Songs* v. *Amstrad Consumer Electronics plc* [1988] AC 1013, 1058, as did Lord Hoffmann in *OBG* [2007] UKHL 21; [2008] 1 AC 1 [8], [36]. *Cf.* also T. Weir, 'Liability for Knowingly Facilitating Mass Breaches of Copyright' (1988) 47 *Cambridge Law Journal* 348, 349. Therefore, offering attractive terms to solicit business from a class of persons would not be tortious, despite knowledge that many of that class have existing contracts with competitors. See *Schindler Lifts Australia Pty Ltd* v. *Debelak* (1989) 89 ALR 275, 295 (Pincus J).

83 *Allen* v. *Flood* [1898] AC 1, 152 (Lord Macnaghten).

84 *Cf.* in the US, where it 'is a question of fact . . . whether the defendant has played a material and substantial part in causing the plaintiff's loss of the benefits of the contract'. See Keeton, *Prosser & Keeton*, 991.

85 *OBG* [2007] UKHL 21; [2008] 1 AC 1 [36]. *Cf.* at [191] Lord Nicholls: defendant liable because of intentional causative participation in third party's breach. Carty, *Economic Torts*, 36–37, considers that Lord Hoffmann's statement may lead to confusion, perhaps because it suggests *any* causative conduct may suffice. See also *Fightvision Pty Ltd* v. *Onisforou* (1999) 47 NSWLR 473, 534 (Scheller, Stein & Giles JJA): 'A finding of inducing breach of contract carries with it a finding that the defendant's actions caused the breach of contract and the loss which flowed. It does not matter that the contract breaker yields readily or [was,] before the inducement . . . willing to break the contract.' They cite *Woolley* v. *Durnford* (1972) 3 SASR 243, 290–291, and *Ansett Transport Industry (Operations) Pty Ltd* v. *Australian Federation of Air Pilots (No 2)* [1991] 1 VR 637, 659. Similarly, see *Multinail Australia Pty Ltd* v. *Pryda (Aust) Pty Ltd* [2002] QSC 105 [106]: irrelevant whether PW is 'predisposed' to breach; or whether 'determined' effort was required.

86 Contra Chris Bailey, 'Facilitation or manipulation: What conduct gives rise to liability for inducing or procuring a breach of contract?' (2014) 22 *Tort Law Review* 22, 24,

always insist upon proof of such causation. To a large extent causation must be inferred from the circumstances, including the temporal order of events, namely A's acts of incitement, persuasion, etc., and subsequent compliance by PW.[87] Causation may be established by inference (but not guesswork).[88] In many circumstances, forensic examination of the processes of deliberation by PW is not likely to be possible.[89]

Some cases have considered the question of whether liability can arise even in the absence of any active, causative, conduct by A that seeks to induce PW to breach, such as where PW decides to breach her contract by seeking out new contracting parties. This situation is often captured by the label 'inconsistent dealings'.[90] An example is where a manufacturer decides to sell goods to a (second) importer (A), in breach of its exclusivity agreement with the claimant importer;[91] the purchase by the second importer of itself means that PW (the manufacturer) must be in breach of its exclusive sales contract. Even if A knows of the original contractual obligations between PW and C, and that the transaction being entered into is inconsistent with those obligations, ought A to be liable? In our view, a merely passive, but willing, participant to a transaction that PW has of her own accord (that is, independently of A's persuasion) entered into ought as a general rule not to be liable.

Some earlier, probably now questionable, authorities pre-dating *OBG* considered that A need not have taken any positive act of inducement or initiative in order to be liable.[92] There are two difficulties, however, with the

concluding that statements in *Jaddcal Pty Ltd* v. *Minson (No 3)* [2011] WASC 362 that the defendant must have been 'instrumental in the decision to breach' should not be seen as supporting a 'but for' causal requirement, and *cf.* cases above at n. 85.

87 *Cf.* Bagshaw, 'Inducing Breach', 140–143. Note, however, Coleridge J's view in dissent in *Lumley* v. *Gye* (1853) 2 E & B 216, 247–248; 118 ER 749, 760–761, that breach (the 'hurtful act') 'is entirely and exclusively' the contract breaker's; 'there would be such a manifest absurdity in attempting to trace up the act of a free agent breaking a contract to all the advisers who may have influenced his mind, more or less honestly, more or less powerfully'. For similar views in early US case law, see Keeton, *Prosser & Keeton*, 990–991.

88 Admittedly, the dividing line between the two is uncertain: *Schindler Lifts Australia Pty Ltd* v. *Debelak* (1989) 89 ALR 275, 299.

89 See, however, *Multinail Australia Pty Ltd* v. *Pryda (Aust) Pty Ltd* [2002] QSC 105 [106]–[119], in which such a detailed examination occurs.

90 See *Jaddcal Pty Ltd* v. *Minson (No 3)* [2011] WASC 362 [193]–[198].

91 *Cf. World of Technologies (Aust) Pty Ltd* v. *Tempo (Aust) Pty Ltd* [2007] FCA 114; (2007) 71 IPR 307, and *LED Technologies Pty Ltd* v. *Roadvision Pty Ltd* [2012] FCAFC; (2012) 199 FCR 204.

92 See, e.g., *De Francesco* v. *Barnum* (1890) 63 LT 514, 515; obiter comment by Jenkins LJ in *A C Thomson & Co. Ltd* v. *Deakin* [1952] Ch 646, 694, and see the discussion of the authorities in Carty, *Economic Torts*, 45–50. *Against* liability in such circumstances, and

view that inconsistent dealing may give rise to liability. First, it is difficult to establish that such passive conduct alone by A, in entering into the transaction, is a sufficient act of inducement; that is, one that causes PW to breach her contract (the relevant discussion point for present purposes). The second is that, even if it can be seen as causative, it is difficult to conclude that A intended to cause that breach, rather than merely incidentally profiting from that breach (intention is discussed below).

The preferable view is that, in general, if PW intends to breach her contract (by seeking out an alternative party with whom to contract) then such minimal interference by A is generally not sufficient to render A liable, since A's conduct is not causal.[93] Such conclusions have been accepted in Australia by Le Miere J in *Jaddcal Pty Ltd* v. *Minson (No 3)*[94] as being in line with the limitations placed on the tort by *OBG*:

> Arguably, the only legitimate reason for adding tort liability to the contract breaker's already existing liability in contract is precisely because the defendant has played an important part in persuading the co-contractor to break his contract. It would appear justifiable to demand a causal link before facilitation could lead to liability. If the defendant has simply said 'yes' he is better regarded as the tool of the contract breaker, rather than vice versa.[95]

pre-dating *OBG*, is *Batts Combe Quarry Ltd* v. *Ford* [1942] 2 All ER 639, a case with very similar facts to *Jaddcal Pty Ltd* v. *Minson (No 3)* [2011] WASC 362. Australian cases that pre-date *OBG* either accepted or left open the possibility of inconsistent dealings giving rise to liability: see, e.g., *World of Technologies (Aust) Pty Ltd* v. *Tempo (Aust) Pty Ltd* [2007] FCA 114; (2007) 71 IPR 307, 335–336; *Polyaire Pty Ltd* v. *K-Aire Pty Ltd* [2003] SASC 41 [200]–[201]. *Cf.* the more cryptic statements in *Allstate Life Insurance Company* v. *Australia and New Zealand Banking Group Ltd* (1995) 58 FCR 26, 44–45; 130 ALR 469, 486, which Jessup J in *World of Technologies*, however, interpreted as supporting the possibility of liability on such basis.

93 *OBG* [2007] UKHL 21; [2008] 1 AC 1 is consistent with both the general conclusion, and also the possibility of some exceptions to the general conclusion. Carty, *Economic Torts*, 45–50, argues that cases suggesting that inconsistent dealings could give rise to liability are inconsistent with the need for intentional inducing, but she concedes (at 48), that in *Mainstream Properties Ltd* v. *Young* (one of the appeals decided in the *OBG* judgment), there was no inducing as such, a point not taken up by the litigants. Liability was rejected on the basis of lack of intention to induce a breach due to the defendant's belief that the conduct was consistent with PWs' contracts with C (as a result of lies told to the defendant by the PWs).

94 [2011] WASC 362.

95 *Ibid.* [195], citing Carty, *Economic Torts*. No liability arose in *Jaddcal* since the several defendants either did not know of the contracts that were breached, or of the particular obligations that were breached, or if they did know, had not engaged in acts of persuasion. *Cf. National Foods Milk Ltd* v. *McMahon Milk Pty Ltd* [2008] VSC 208, which appears to be an example of inducement but which Bailey, 'Facilitation', interprets as possibly only involving facilitation.

In short, passively profiting from another's conduct is not as a general rule tortious.[96] One possible exception might arise where A merely acquiesces to PW's desire to breach her contract with C, but A's act is nonetheless causative of PW's breach, for example, because PW clearly intimates that she will only breach her existing contract if A provides her with an alternative contract. A's offer may provide *the* reason for PW breaking her contract.

Another issue that arises is whether advising PW to breach her contract can amount to inducing a breach. In *James* v. *Commonwealth*, Dixon J noted that

> [t]here must be ... the intentional creation of some inducing cause or reason for the breach of contract; ... To induce a breach of contract means to create a reason for breaking it; to advise a breach of contract is to point out the reasons which already exist.[97]

But one can question whether this is a distinction that is so easily drawn.[98] Indeed, advice coupled with reasons supporting the advice is persuasion. To be sure, for the most part, an advisor may not seek a particular outcome, especially where the party seeking advice has already decided on a course of conduct. But some 'advice' may be given in order to dissuade PW from performing her contract.[99] The label attached to the conduct should not hide the substantive question.

Finally, agents (including company officers acting as agents) acting within the scope of their authority as agents, as well as company directors (officers) acting in their constitutional role, who cause their principals to breach their contract with third parties, are not liable for inducing breach

[96] Of course, if active inducement is disguised as passive conduct, then it is potentially an inducing *act*. This may be the real focus of the concern of Bagshaw, 'Inducing Breach', 144–145, who agrees that causation should do the work but argues, to the contrary to the conclusion above, that inconsistent dealings ought potentially to be a sufficient *act* of inducement, *if* they are *causative* of PW's decision to breach.

[97] (1936) 62 CLR 339, 371, citing Salmond, *Law of Torts*, 8th edn (1934) 391, though Dixon J introduced the quote with a tentative 'Apparently inducement is to be distinguished from advice or persuasion'.

[98] See *Camden Nominees* v. *Forcey* [1940] Ch 352, 366 (Simonds J): 'Advice which is intended to have persuasive effect is not distinguishable from inducement'; and Bagshaw, 'Inducing Breach', 144–145. Contrast *Qantas Airways Ltd* v. *Transport Workers Union of Australia* [2011] FCA 470; (2011) 280 ALR 503 [447]–[450], accepting the distinction.

[99] See A. Simester and Winnie Chan, 'Inducing Breach of Contract: One Tort or Two?' (2004) 63 *Cambridge Law Journal* 132, 160–161.

of contract.[100] The agent's and director's acts are those of the principal; if it were otherwise, the 'principal would be inducing a breach of its own contract'.[101] The principle is sometimes stated with an additional requirement of bona fides,[102] but this is doubtful.[103] Of course, an agent or director of a company who induces a third (corporate or other) party to breach its contract can be so liable.[104]

6.3.4 *Mental element: knowledge/intention*

6.3.4.1 The relationship between knowledge and intention

There is some debate and uncertainty about the relationship between the concepts of knowledge and intention, although we can with certainty make the trite observation that they are to a large extent intertwined.

100 *Said* v. *Butt* [1920] 3 KB 497; *O'Brien* v. *Dawson* (1942) 66 CLR 18 (obiter statements of principle have been treated as binding in Australia: see, e.g., *Tsaprazis* v. *Goldcrest Properties* (2000) 18 ACLC 285, 288); and see, e.g., *Ridgeway Maritime Inc.* v. *Beulah Wings Ltd* [1991] 2 Lloyd's Reps 611, and the detailed review of authorities in *Root Quality Pty Ltd* v. *Root Control Technologies Pty Ltd* (2000) 177 ALR 231). The principle extends to de facto directors: *Biscayne Partners Pty Ltd* v. *Valance Corp. Pty Ltd* [2003] NSWSC 874; *Mad Dog Pty Ltd (in liq.)* v. *Gilligan's Backpackers Hotel & Resort Pty Ltd* [2014] QSC 165. In the corporate context, the principle is based on the idea that the director is not in the position of an *outsider* influencing the independent volition of the company. The corporate entity (or principal) does not exercise its own volition: the volition of the director is that of the company. To hold otherwise would also undermine the limited liability principles of incorporation; a party to a contract with the company ought not to be able to shift the risk of corporate contract default onto the directors via tort. The principle has been followed in Canada: *Imperial Oil Ltd* v. *C & G Ltd* (1989) 62 DLR (4th) 261 (though director must have acted bona fide); *ADGA Systems International Ltd* v. *Valcom Ltd* (1999) 39 CCEL (2d) 163 (Ont CA). It has been suggested that the same principle also applies to holding companies, but there are contrary views. See, e.g., in support, *ASIC* v. *Adler* [2002] NSWSC 171 [62]; *Foxedon Pty Ltd* v. *IOOF Building Society Ltd* [2003] VSC 356 [329]; and *LMI Australiasia Pty Ltd* v. *Baulderstone Hornibrook Pty Ltd* [2001] NSWSC 886 [98], disapproved by Young CJ in Eq on appeal [2003] NSWCA 74, where Hodgson and Meagher JJA did not comment on the issue.

101 *Rustic Haven Sdn Bhd* v. *The Ravenswood Resort Pty Ltd (in liq.)* [2005] WASC 88 (Newnes M) [24]–[25]. Contrast the situation where an agent commits a wrong and where, as a result of attribution, the principal also commits that wrong; the agent is not absolved from liability. See Chapter 11.

102 Seemingly, e.g., in the Newfoundland CA decision of *Imperial Oil Ltd* v. *C & G Ltd* (1989) 62 DLR (4th) 261 [20], holding that non bona fide director may be liable 'upon affirmative proof that the dominating purpose of the director's act was aimed at depriving the aggrieved party of the benefits of the contract'.

103 See discussion in *Idoport Pty Ltd* v. *National Australia Bank Ltd* [2001] NSWSC 328, particularly at [65].

104 An example is *Multinail Australia Pty Ltd* v. *Pryda (Aust) Pty Ltd* [2002] QSC 105.

Some courts and commentators have focused on 'intention' as the central requirement of the tort. For example, in *Allstate Life Insurance Company* v. *Australia and New Zealand Banking Group Ltd* ('*Allstate*') Lindgren J in the Federal Court of Australia concluded that

> In my opinion, the authorities establish conclusively that the gravamen of the tort is intention. Although the requirement of knowledge of the contract is sometimes discussed as if it was a separate ingredient of the tort, it is in fact an aspect of intention. The requirement that the alleged tortfeasor have 'sufficient knowledge of the contract' is a requirement he have sufficient knowledge to ground an intention to interfere with contractual rights.
>
> Both this intention to interfere with contractual rights and the necessary supporting knowledge of the contract refer to the 'actual' or 'subjective' state of mind of the alleged tortfeasor.[105]

Other formulations place more emphasis on knowledge,[106] in some cases almost to the exclusion of intention, or consider knowledge and intention as dual requirements,[107] or as a connected, 'twofold' requirement,[108] or even as alternative means of establishing liability.[109]

The focus on knowledge in inducing cases is on its predictive sense, that is, the likelihood that PW will breach. That prediction is based on A's knowledge of existing facts. Applying this to the present context: we can know that a contract in particular terms exists and, armed with that

[105] (1995) 58 FCR 26, 43 (Lockhart and Tamberlin JJ agreeing); endorsed in *Fightvision Pty Ltd* v. *Onisforou* (1999) 47 NSWLR 473, 512 [171]. And see *Northern Territory* v. *Mengel* (1995) 185 CLR 307, 342. See also generally *OBG* [2007] UKHL 21; [2008] 1 AC 1, and in the US the *Restatement (Second) of Torts* vol. 4., Ch. 37, §§766–773 (1979).

[106] See, e.g., seemingly Bagshaw, 'Inducing Breach', 142, ('knowledge of the likelihood that conduct will bring about a breach' and persisting with that conduct despite such knowledge); *Short* v. *City Bank of Sydney* (1912) 15 CLR 148 (HCA) 160.

[107] *Cf.* Deakin and Randall, 'Rethinking the Economic Torts', 538–540, who suggest on the basis of *OBG* [2007] UKHL 21; [2008] 1 AC 1 that there are two requirements: to act intentionally, and to do so knowingly, i.e., with knowledge of the likelihood that breach of contract will follow.

[108] Carty, *Economic Torts*, 38 (concepts connected forming a 'twofold' requirement). This label is also used in *Merkur Island Shipping Corp.* v. *Laughton* [1983] 2 AC 570 (HL) 608 (knowledge of the contract and an intention to induce breach).

[109] Simester and Chan, 'Inducing Breach', 160, appear to consider the requirements of knowledge and intention as distinct ways of satisfying the mental element of persuasion (i.e., of procuring the outcome) for the tort: 'The mental element of persuasion is satisfied by *either* knowledge that what A encourages is inconsistent with [PW's] promise to P *or* an intention that [PW] should not perform as promised.' Liability follows on the first basis even if A merely undermines the 'status' of the promise and attempts to require a 'reconsideration' by PW of her promises and this leads to a breach by PW (at 159).

knowledge, we can aim to bring about certain outcomes, for example that PW will act in a certain way that will be a breach of her contract with C. It could also be said that we intend that outcome,[110] although we question below whether this last conclusion adds much.

From this, we hope, it is possible to make some uncontested propositions. First, absent knowledge of a contract that is still on foot, and at least sufficient knowledge of its general terms allowing A to conclude that PW's conduct would constitute breach, there can be no liability.[111] A need not know, however, of the precise term that is being breached.[112] As Jordan CJ stated in *Independent Oil Industries Ltd* v. *Shell Co of Australia Ltd*:

> It is necessary to establish that the third party knew of the contract, knew that the doing of a particular act by one of the parties to it would be a breach of it, and with that knowledge procured the party to do the act. . . . It may be that no tort is committed unless it is established that the doing of the act was procured either with intention to procure by its means the breach of the particular contract, or at least *with knowledge* that the doing of the act would necessarily and inevitably involve a breach of contract.[113]

[110] *Cf.* Peter Cane, '*Mens Rea*', 534. The word 'intend' is also used to refer to predicted outcomes that are aimed at as part of a plan. See also Cane, *Responsibility in Law and Morality* (Oxford, Hart Publishing 2002) 79, who notes the second meaning of 'intend', namely deliberate action; and see also Jim Evans, 'Choice and Responsibility' (2002) 27 *Australian Journal of Legal Philosophy* 97, 106. E.g., armed with the knowledge of the properties of metal and the fragility of the human body, if X forcefully swings a metal bar and hits Y on the chest we can conclude that X *intended* to cause serious harm to Y. Although X will have intended to harm Y, based on the high likelihood that the predicted harm will eventuate, X need not always succeed: e.g. if Y is wearing an armoured vest. Further, if X *knows* that Y is wearing the vest, then our conclusion that X *intended* to cause serious harm to Y is open to doubt.

[111] No liability would therefore arise if the inducer believes, honestly but wrongly, that the contract has been rescinded: see, e.g., *Short* v. *The City Bank of Sydney* (1912) 15 CLR 148, 160. But it is not sufficient merely that there may be some doubt about the validity of contract: *cf. Swiss Bank Corp.* v. *Lloyds Bank Ltd* [1979] Ch 548, 580.

Knowledge of a corporation includes knowledge of former officers and employees, such that the tort may be committed by a company acting through an officer who is unaware of a contract, but whose predecessor had such knowledge: *Fightvision Pty Ltd* v. *Onisforou* (1999) 47 NSWLR 473, 527–529 [244]–[251].

[112] *Allstate Life Insurance Company* v. *Australia and New Zealand Banking Group Ltd* (1995) 58 FCR 26, 43. Indeed, A may merely know that the term is a common one in that type of contract. *Cf. J T Stratford & Son Ltd* v. *Lindley* [1965] AC 307, 323–325, and *Cunard Steamship Co. Ltd* v. *Stacey* [1955] 1 Lloyd's Rep 247.

[113] (1937) 37 SR (NSW) 394, 415 (emphasis added), a statement endorsed by Gummow and Hayne JJ in *Roadshow Films Pty Ltd* v. *iiNet Ltd* [2012] HCA 16; (2012) 95 IPR 29 [110].

Jordan CJ posits the first requirement as essential, but he is more tentative in his second statement, formulating the tort in terms of either knowledge or intention. But even if the tort is stated in terms of intention, A cannot intend a breach without knowledge of the contract; knowledge is a prerequisite for intention. It is the cognitive platform upon which the higher mental state is built.

Secondly, whatever conduct A engages in in order to procure PW's conduct, such conduct must be intentional, in the sense of being deliberate and conscious;[114] but this adds little, since there is no realistic scope for non-deliberate or involuntary conduct in this context. This is because the act of involvement at issue, namely to induce or procure, already connotes within it the sense of deliberate conduct that seeks to achieve a particular outcome.

Finally, the courts have rejected any requirement of malice, that is, that A must intend to harm C,[115] despite early statements that included such an element.

Beyond that, it becomes difficult to posit any further clear conclusions. Although intention to breach has been stressed in many cases, on one view such an intention must surely be inferred in most cases. If there is evidence that A knew of the contract and that certain acts of PW are (likely) to be in breach of it, and A then proceeds deliberately to pursue such an outcome, then the court may conclude that A intended such a breach; but this is inferred from proof as to what A knew[116] and from the deliberate actions taken by A armed with that knowledge.[117] It is always

[114] See Cane, *Responsibility*, 79.

[115] Further, as Carty, *Economic Torts*, 41, puts it, there is no need to prove that *loss* was intended, beyond breach itself, although of course, there may be cases in which such intention exists. In most cases of inducing, A is focused on achieving gains for himself; the means of achieving such ends are not necessarily the primary focus of A's conduct (A is willing to pay PW a lot of money to sing for him; 'too bad' if she is contracted to C).

[116] Of course, in some cases, knowledge as to current facts may also be inferred, but it is much easier to prove what A knew by evidence. On inferring actual knowledge, see [3.4.3.3].

[117] See *Northern Territory* v. *Mengel* (1995) 185 CLR 307, 342, in which the High Court appears to draw the *conclusion* that the tort can be described as depending on intention 'for that is necessarily involved if a person knowingly interferes with the enjoyment . . . of a positive legal right'. See also in the context of the tort of misfeasance in public office the observation by Oliver LJ in *Bourgoin SA* v. *Ministry of Agriculture, Fisheries and Food* [1986] QB 716, 777: 'If an act is done deliberately and with knowledge of its consequences, I do not think that the actor can sensibly say that he did not "intend" the consequences.' This was interpreted by Lord Hutton in *Three Rivers DC* v. *Bank of England (No 3)* [2001] UKHL 16; [2003] 2 AC 1, 223, in terms that if a person 'acts deliberately, knowing that his action will injure another person, he *must be taken* to

difficult to prove precisely what A intended: for example, the outcome may be peripheral to A's objectives (and A would have preferred it not to happen).[118] If this is correct, then knowledge, both of current facts and as to the high level of predictability as to a future outcome that PW will breach her contract, if the defendant's inducements prove successful, is the essence of the tort.[119]

Perhaps the stress on 'intention' as a further requirement of the tort, above and beyond deliberate conduct engaged in with certain knowledge, reflects the need for there to be a *subjective* element, that is, that A must 'actually realise' 'the factual and *legal* effect of his actions'.[120] This means that the tort is narrower than most other examples of accessory liability in which A may be liable even absent any awareness that PW's conduct is unlawful [3.4.2.3], that is, of the legal characterisation of PW's conduct. A merely needs to know of essential matters of PW's act (that are wrongs). Yet in the tort of inducing breach of contract, A must satisfy the further subjective element of intending the wrong (breach), which is only possible if A knows enough to be able accurately to predict that PW will not comply with her obligations if A's inducement proves successful.[121] Therefore, a

intend the consequences and *is equated with* the person who acts with the intent to cause injury' (emphasis added).

118 See Peter Cane, '*Mens Rea*', 542. *Cf.* Bagshaw, 'Inducing Breach', 140–143.

Nonetheless, even if an outcome is peripheral, it must probably have been at least the means to an end. In the words of Lord Hoffmann in *OBG* [2007] UKHL 21; [2008] 1 AC 1 [43]: 'if the breach of contract is neither an end in itself nor a means to an end, but merely a foreseeable consequence, then in my opinion it cannot for this purpose be said to have been intended'. Hence also, the use of language such as C having been 'targeted' or 'aimed at'. There is a tension here, however; an outcome may not be a means or an end, and yet be more than merely foreseeable. It may be almost certain to follow from the course of conduct A pursues: collateral damage, so to speak. In the context of industrial actions, denying liability seems sensible where an outcome is near-certain but neither the means nor an end (see, e.g., *Barrett & Baird* v. *IPCS* [1987] IRLR 3). Outside of this context, realistic examples are difficult to find, however, and hence it is difficult to test the proposition whether near-certain side effects should found liability; although Philip Sales and Daniel Stilitz, 'Intentional Infliction of Harm by Unlawful Means' (1999) 115 *Law Quarterly Review* 411, 425–430, in the context of the unlawful means torts, argue for no liability for near-certain-to-materialise side effects.

119 On another view, it is perfectly accurate to say that if A knows that an opportunity 'belongs' to the claimant, and proceeds to obtain that opportunity for himself, that A *intends* to 'steal' it (*cf. OBG* [2007] UKHL 21; [2008] 1 AC 1 [167] (Lord Nicholls)). Again, however, this seems more by way of conclusion based on what A knew, including the inevitability of the likely outcomes of the course of conduct that A has pursued.

120 See Deakin and Randall, 'Rethinking the Economic Torts', 539, citing *OBG* [2007] UKHL 21; [2008] 1 AC 1 [39].

121 See Deakin and Randall, 'Rethinking the Economic Torts', 539–540.

mistaken belief as to the legal position, for example, that the result can be achieved without a breach,[122] or a genuine belief that PW's conduct would not amount to a breach,[123] will preclude a finding of liability. Similarly, if A seeks to have a contract between PW and C terminated, but such termination may be achieved lawfully without breach on PW's part, then A is not liable if it is left to PW to determine how to proceed.[124] This is at least so where A's conduct is consistent with such lawful conduct.[125] Although courts have sought to capture these conclusions by stressing 'subjective' intention, in all these examples A will also not genuinely have had subjective knowledge of sufficient facts about the contract and the options available to PW, from which to infer that A intended the breach. In short, if 'intention' is meant to capture this unusual subjective requirement, the same could be achieved by referring to subjective knowledge.

6.3.4.2 Degrees of knowledge

What if A seeks at all costs the termination of a contract between PW and C, irrespective of whether this could be achieved lawfully or not? Certainly, there is a strong case for liability in such circumstances even though it may be difficult to prove that A intended or knew that PW would breach.[126] In the absence of precise proof of what A actually knew,

[122] *Cf. Meretz Investments NV* v. *ACP Ltd* [2008] Ch 244 (legal advice that had right to engage in conduct); Carty, *Economic Torts*, 40. Contrast *Welsh Development Agency* v. *Export Finance Co. Ltd* [1992] BCLC 148, 179.

[123] *Mainstream Properties* v. *Young* [2007] UKHL 21; [2008] 1 AC 1 [39], [202]; *Short* v. *City Bank of Sydney* (1912) 15 CLR 148 (HCA) 160 (no liability if bona fide belief that conduct would not amount to breach, or that contract rescinded, or performance waived, or that certain act need not be performed); *British Industrial Plastics Ltd* v. *Ferguson* [1940] 1 All ER 479 (honest but foolish belief); Carty, *Economic Torts*, 39.

[124] See *Sanders* v. *Snell* [1998] HCA 64; (1998) 196 CLR 329, 339–340 in which a Minister directed his department to terminate an employment contract of the plaintiff at the 'earliest practicable date'; they did so by breaching contract, but could have done so lawfully by giving an appropriate notice.

[125] *Ibid.* The Minister had not asked that the department terminate summarily and therefore his direction could have been pursued lawfully. It would not matter if the 'alleged tortfeasor harboured an uncommunicated subjective desire that the contract would or might be breached': *ibid.* 339 (Gleeson CJ, Gaudron, Kirby and Hayne JJ). See also *Cleary* v. *Kocatekin & Seven Network (Operations) Ltd* [2012] NSWSC 692 [25] (no liability where confidentiality clause was breached by TV interview since A had no knowledge of the specific term and did not intend to breach whatever agreement was in place). *Cf. Building Workers' Industrial Union of Australia* v. *Odco Pty Ltd* (1981) 29 FCR 104, 141 onwards (wrong belief that a contract was attended by unlawful conduct did not preclude liability where A had intentionally induced breach of that agreement).

[126] *OBG* [2007] UKHL 21; [2008] 1 AC 1 [70] (Lord Hoffmann) seemingly endorsing the decision in *Greig* v. *Insole* [1978] 1 WLR 302, basing liability on indifference as to

courts have held that one way of proving actual knowledge/intention is if A 'turned a blind eye to the possibility' or 'made a conscious decision not to inquire into the existence of a fact in case [A] "discovered a disagreeable truth"'.[127] This is known as wilful blindness [3.4.3.3]. The more difficult question is whether 'reckless indifference' also suffices.[128] Recklessness has been usefully defined as 'awareness of a risk that certain consequences will result from conduct, and indifference to that risk'.[129] The risk must be so substantial, so as to have been an unreasonable one to take,[130] that is, there must be a 'conscious disregard of a substantial and unjustifiable risk'[131] [3.4.3.4].

Both 'wilful blindness' and 'reckless indifference' can refer either to what A knew about the contract, or of what A knew about the consequences of his deliberate actions, where A is wilfully blind or recklessly indifferent to those consequences, that PW will most likely breach.[132] Either way, the conclusion that A is 'wilfully blind' equates to a near certainty that PW will not comply with her contractual obligations, since it is a basis of inferring actual knowledge.[133]

whether contract breaches would occur. See also the approach of Diplock LJ in *Emerald Construction Co. Ltd* v. *Lowthian* [1966] 1 WLR 691, 703–704: defendant liable if intended that the party procured 'bring the contract to an end by breach of it if there was no way of bringing it to an end lawfully'. Contrast Carty, *Economic Torts*, 42.

127 *LED Technologies Pty Ltd* v. *Roadvision Pty Ltd* (2012) 287 ALR 1, 13 [54] (Besanko J, Mansfield and Flick JJ agreeing). *Cf. OBG* [2007] UKHL 21; [2008] 1 AC 1 [192].

128 Some judges have sought to state this as sufficient to meet the requirements of the tort. See, e.g., Denning LJ in *Emerald Construction Co Ltd* v. *Lowthian* [1966] 1 WLR 691: reckless indifference to whether there is a breach or not (presumably by showing reckless indifference to the existence of a contract or to specific terms, or to the options available to PW to comply with A's objects). Compare Diplock LJ, who uses the language of intention but notes that reckless indifference may be a means of proving that intention requirement. See discussion in *Allstate Life Insurance Company* v. *Australia and New Zealand Banking Group Ltd* (1995) 58 FCR 26, 43–44, approved in *Fightvision Pty Ltd* v. *Onisforou* (1999) 47 NSWLR 473, 510–512, [164]–[171]. Note, however, that Lord Hoffmann approved Lord Denning's formulation in *OGB* [2007] UKHL 21; [2008] 1 AC 1 [40]–[41].

129 See A. Ashworth, *Principles of Criminal Law*, 3rd edn (Oxford University Press, 1999) 184–185, cited in Cane, '*Mens Rea*', 535.

130 Cane, '*Mens Rea*', 535, and Cane, *Responsibility*, 80: the required knowledge of the actor is of a risk that, *because of the likelihood* of its outcome, is unreasonable to take; and see also Jim Evans, 'Choice and Responsibility' (2002) 27 *Australian Journal of Legal Philosophy* 97, 106.

131 *Imobilari Pty Ltd* v. *Opes Prime Stockbroking Ltd* [2008] FCA 1920 [28] (Finkelstein J).

132 E.g., *Cantor Fitzgerald International* v. *Bird* [2002] IRLR 867.

133 One needs to be cautious here, however. In criminal law, 'actual' knowledge of a crime merely requires that A had actual knowledge of PW's intended conduct, from which the

'Recklessness' suggests a high degree of predictability of breach, such that A is therefore not entitled to take that risk. In such circumstances, if A pursues an outcome, recklessly disregarding the substantial likelihood of breach, then the courts appear to be concluding that A predicted such breach and thereby intended it. It appears that in this context, at least, some courts are, unhelpfully it is suggested, defining 'recklessness' in very similar terms as 'wilful blindness' and therefore as satisfying the actual knowledge requirements. This is unhelpful because it merges two distinct degrees of knowledge and culpability.[134]

However we label the mental state, what is clear is that liability arises as a result of conduct pursued single-mindedly to achieve a goal where breach is a substantially likely outcome of such goal. As was stated obiter in *Allstate*:

> [T]here is an important distinction . . . between the essential elements of a cause of action and the evidence by which these elements may be proved. Although 'reckless indifference' and 'wilful blindness' are not synonymous with 'intention' or 'knowledge' . . ., they may, in the matrix of facts of a particular case, contribute to give rise to a finding of intention or knowledge . . .. But this does not signify that such terminology may be substituted for that of 'intention' if 'intention' is a necessary element of the tort.[135]

Similarly, as was stated in *LED Technologies Pty Ltd* v. *Roadvision Pty Ltd*:

> [B]earing in mind that the tort under consideration is an intentional tort and gross negligence is insufficient it seems to me that reckless indifference is something quite close to wilful blindness. It will be negated by an honest belief, even one exhibiting a high degree of credulity. It will be established only if the facts show affirmatively that the alleged tortfeasor,

crime need merely be likely to result. See [4.4.3]. This cannot be easily transferred into this context, since the issue is whether whatever PW does in response to A's inducing conduct will amount to a breach.

134 *Cf. World of Technologies (Aust) Pty Ltd* v. *Tempo (Aust) Pty Ltd* [2007] FCA 114; (2007) 71 IPR 307, 337 [110]–[111] (Jessup J): a defendant having the 'primary purpose' to have contract terminated ought to be liable; contrast the situation where A is not focused on the contract between PW and C at all, but the dealings merely have the effect of bringing the party into breach. 'In that context, to equate indifference, even "reckless" indifference, with intention would, I consider, be to denude the latter concept of any meaningful connotation.'

135 *Allstate Life Insurance Company* v. *Australia and New Zealand Banking Group Ltd* (1995) 130 ALR 469, 479. There was, however, clear evidence that the respondents knew of the contract (at 486). See also *Fightvision Pty Ltd* v. *Onisforou* (1999) 47 NSWLR 473, 512.

> faced with knowledge of at least a *substantial prospect* of a breach, proceeded not caring whether or not a breach, would occur.[136]

This means that for liability to arise, breach does not need to follow from A's conduct as a certainty, but rather may have been merely substantially likely, or a 'substantial prospect', or some similarly high threshold. It is not for A to claim that for all he knew/predicted, there may have been a lawful way of terminating the contract.[137] However, 'ignorance of the existence of a contract or of its terms born of inadvertence or negligence is not enough'[138] to sustain liability. In other words, the objective foreseeability that PW might breach does not equate with the subjective substantial likelihood that PW will breach if induced to act in a certain way.

To conclude on this element: beyond stating that knowledge and intention are connected, it is difficult to be more concrete as to the relationship between, and the respective roles of, those two concepts. Somewhat tentatively, however, we have suggested that, contrary to statements that intention is the gravamen of the tort, knowledge is the essential element. Knowledge, and deliberate conduct pursued with such knowledge in order to achieve certain outcomes, is the essence of the tort, provided one of the 'necessary', 'inevitable' or at least 'substantially' likely outcomes of the conduct pursued is breach. Intention may be little more than a conclusion that we draw where A acts deliberately to induce PW to achieve an outcome that, given A's actual knowledge of the facts, A could predict will certainly, or is substantially likely to, amount to a breach of contract by PW.[139]

[136] (2012) 287 ALR 1, 13 (Besanko J, Mansfield and Flick JJ agreeing), emphasis added. The quote was prefaced by the acknowledgement that reckless indifference is more difficult to describe in terms of content. This assumes that there is a difference between gross negligence and reckless indifference, but that distinction is obviously fine. Contrast the US Supreme Court (in the context of accessorial patent infringements) in *Globe-Tech Appliances, Inc.*, v. *SEB SA*, 131 S Ct 2060 (2011) 2070, where recklessness and negligence were equated with 'deliberate indifference'.

LED had an agreement with a manufacturer in Taiwan to make and exclusively provide certain lights for LED, and Roadvision and another company began buying those lights from that manufacturer in breach of the agreement. On the facts, there may have been negligence in not inquiring but there was no wilful blindness or reckless indifference (at 15).

[137] See, e.g., *Delphic Wholesalers Pty Ltd* v. *Elco Food Co. Pty Ltd* (1987) 8 IPR 545, particularly 553–554.

[138] *Fightvision Pty Ltd* v. *Onisforou* (1999) 47 NSWLR 473, 512. Similarly, see Cane, '*Mens Rea*', 546: 'Negligent interference with contract is not actionable in tort.'

[139] This is consistent with the second part of Jordan CJ's second formulation in *Independent Oil Industries Ltd* v. *Shell Co. of Australia Ltd* (1937) 37 SR (NSW) 394, 415, quoted above text to n. 113; Bagshaw, 'Inducing Breach', and *cf.* Simester & Chan, 'Inducing Breach'.

6.3.5 *Damage*

Damage is the gist of the action and must be proved by C.[140] It must be more than nominal, although damage may be inferred from the circumstances.[141] The breach of the contract is itself the harm, so there is no need to prove an intention to cause further harm. The damage suffered may be more than could be claimed against PW for breach of contract.[142] The tort claim can therefore give rise to an award of damages higher than could be awarded against PW. In many cases, however, the damages are congruent. When this is so, that is, PW and A are both liable for the same amount, judgment can be ordered against both jointly, although obviously there can be no double recovery.[143] If C has recovered full damages against PW, however, the claim against A would fail, as no damage could be shown.[144] C must show that A's conduct caused the breach and quantify the loss that flowed from the breach. If no claim is available against PW, then no loss has flowed; for example, breach of a voidable contract generally does not suffice.[145]

6.4 Defences

If PW has a defence against a claim by C, such that there is no breach of contract by PW at all, PW having lawfully terminated, or such that C cannot prove that A's conduct has caused C to suffer any damage, then no action will lie against A. Of course, if there is technically a breach by PW, but the contract excludes PW's obligation to pay damages, A might still be liable [6.3.2].

140 See, e.g., *Ansett Transport Industries (Operations) Pty Ltd* v. *Australian Federation of Air Pilots (No 2)* [1991] 2 VR 636, 645; *Goldsoll* v. *Goldman* [1914] 2 Ch 603, 615, (breach is one that 'must in the ordinary course of business inflict damage'), referred to with approval in *Palmer Bruyn & Parker Pty Ltd* v. *Parsons* [2001] HCA 69; (2001) 208 CLR 388, 412 [76].

141 In other words, proof of specific damage is not required. See, e.g., *Exchange Telegraph Co.* v. *Gregory & Co.* [1896] 1 QB 147 (CA) 153, 155–156, 158. Query whether purely non-pecuniary losses would suffice: see *Boase* v. *Seven Network (Operations) Ltd* [2005] WASC 269.

142 See the examples given in *Lumley* v. *Gye* (1853) 2 E & B 216, 233–234; 118 ER 749, 756.

143 *Fightvision Pty Ltd v. Onisforou* (1999) 47 NSWLR 473, 534, citing *Jones Bros (Hunstanton) Ltd* v. *Stevens* [1954] 1 QB 275, 283.

144 *Ibid.*, citing *Bird* v. *Randall* (1762) 3 Burr 1345, 1353–1354; 97 ER 866, 870–871.

145 *Proform Sports Management Ltd* v. *Proactive Sports Management Ltd* [2006] EWHC 2903; [2007] 1 All ER 542.

Where the contract has been breached, however, then the only defence that A may raise in this context, that of justification, is one that is not available to PW.[146] In Anglo-Australian law, justification has been restrictively interpreted. The defence was considered by the High Court in *Zhu*.[147] In *Zhu*, the Court noted that the defence has a 'confused genesis'[148] but held that the defence does not depend upon a discretionary 'balancing' of social and individual interests (unlike in the US) and instead, A must show[149] a superior statutory right[150] or superior interest that is either quasi-proprietary or proprietary.[151] It is not clear what 'quasi-proprietary' rights means, but a prior right to contractual performance may be an example.[152] An example of justification based on a proprietary right is where A induces an owner to breach a contract in order to protect the value of A's security interest

[146] Deakin and Randall, 'Rethinking the Economic Torts', 543, consider that the fact that a justification defence may be invoked under the tort but not as a possible defence for liability for breach of contract, supports the view that liability is not accessorial.

[147] [2004] HCA 56; (2004) 218 CLR 530. The court strongly endorsed and placed much reliance on obiter consideration of the defence by Jordan CJ in *Independent Oil Industries Ltd* v. *Shell Co. of Australia Ltd* (1937) 37 SR (NSW) 394.

[148] [2004] HCA 56; (2004) 218 CLR 530 [106].

[149] One exception arises perhaps in employment contracts and industrial disputes, e.g., the exceptional case of *Brimelow* v. *Casson* [1924] 1 Ch 302, applying a wider justification defence.

[150] Examples include *James* v. *The Commonwealth* (1939) 62 CLR 339, and probably *Stott* v. *Gamble* [1916] 2 KB 504.

[151] [2004] HCA 56; (2004) 218 CLR 530 [136] [139]. *Cf. Edwin Hill & Partners* v. *First National Finance Corporation Plc* [1988] 3 All ER 801 (EWCA): 'equal or superior legal right'. Consistently with *Zhu*, appeals to nebulous concepts such as performing a public service will not satisfy the defence: see *Camden Nominees* v. *Forcey* [1940] Ch 352 (tenants' association formed for purposes of pursuing grievances with landlord, induced tenants to withhold rent: no justification as tenants had remedies at law and it was not sufficient that they were performing a 'public service').

[152] Although the general statements *Zhu* [2004] HCA 56; (2004) 218 CLR 530 suggest that a quasi-proprietary right may suffice, later statements seem to imply that a superior right would need to be proprietary. Certainly a prior right to contractual performance (which is 'at most quasi-proprietary'), a 'temporal priority' of 'purely' or 'merely contractual rights', would not suffice (see, e.g., at [140], [145], [161]). Interestingly, where A contracts with B and C for the same performance, neither B nor C are liable in tort for insisting on performance: it appears to be because the elements of the tort are not made out, rather than because of an application of the defence of justification, but the High Court left open why this is so. See at [151]–[153]. This conclusion may go some way to addressing Paul S. Davies' criticism of *Zhu* that protecting equal rights ought to be justified: 'Defences and Third Parties' in Andrew Dyson, James Goudkamp and Frederick Wilmot-Smith (eds.) *Defences in Tort* (Oxford, Hart Publishing, 2015) 107, 115-116. *Cf.* also *Smithies* v. *National Association* [1909] 1 KB 310, 337, discussed and explained in *Zhu* [140]–[145].

over the property.[153] Given its limited scope, the defence rarely succeeds. Indeed, the Court noted that 'the absence in Anglo-Australian law of occasions where such a defence, however understood, has succeeded' is 'striking'.[154] Further, even if A has such a superior right, the actions taken must be reasonably necessary to protect that superior right.[155] The defence failed in *Zhu* as the defendant 'had no legal rights . . . of the kind alleged, but nevertheless attempted to vindicate the interests of itself . . . by the most direct means, independently of any concern for legality'.[156]

A narrow justification defence makes sense. Since the purpose of the inducing tort is to protect the security and integrity of contractual rights, interfering in the contractual relations of others is justified only if done in order to protect one's own superior contractual right, that is, a right that is proprietary or quasi-proprietary in nature.

6.5 Remedies

Remedies are awarded on tort principles, including the relevant tort remoteness rules, and therefore may differ in type and quantity to remedies available against PW.[157] Damages may be awarded in the form of a 'round sum based on the pecuniary loss proved'; this could include sums for inconvenience and unhappiness caused by the change of circumstances arising from the breach of contract.[158] Many of the cases involve claims for either final injunctions or interlocutory injunctions to prevent ongoing conduct of A that prevents performance by PW. Such remedies are not often available against the contract breakers in those same circumstances.[159] Further, mandatory injunctions have been

153 *Edwin Hill & Partners* v. *First National Finance Corporation Plc* [1988] 3 All ER 801 (EWCA).

154 *Zhu* [2004] HCA 56; (2004) 218 CLR 530 [160]. Similarly, see *Building Workers' Industrial Union of Australia* v. *Odco Pty Ltd* (1981) 29 FCR 104, 143 and 144, in which the Federal Court noted that a 'catalogue' of successful pleas 'would be a short one, there being a rarity of cases'. Contrast Howarth, 'Against *Lumley*', arguing for a wide application of the defence. For conduct not amounting to justification, see examples given in *Edwin Hill & Partners* v. *First National Finance Corporation Plc* [1988] 3 All ER 801.

155 [2004] HCA 56; (2004) 218 CLR 530 [162]. 156 *Ibid.* [111].

157 *Lumley* v. *Gye* (1853) 2 E & B 216, 233–234; 118 ER 749, 756.

158 *Rookes* v. *Barnard* [1964] AC 1129, 1221 (claimant not limited to damages available for wrongful dismissal if suing for inducing such dismissal). Sums are not limited to pecuniary losses: *Ansett Transport Industry (Operations) Pty Ltd* v. *Australian Federation of Air Pilots (No 2)* [1991] 1 VR 637.

159 The contract may be one of employment, so that remedies that have the effect of compelling performance are generally not available.

granted to require the tortfeasor to undo the consequences of its tort.[160] Similarly, exemplary damages are potentially available for the tort, but not against the contract breaker.[161] However, since intention – that is, deliberate conduct with knowledge – is always an element and therefore of itself is not a sufficient basis for exemplary damages, the conduct would need to be 'bordering on the malicious' to justify an award.[162]

6.6 Conclusion

The tort of inducing breach of contract is made out where a defendant's deliberate acts of procurement cause the contract breaker to breach her contract, in circumstances where the defendant subjectively knows that such breach is certain or substantially likely to follow from the defendant's conduct. The tort is accessorial in nature. The key elements of the defendant's knowing involvement in another's wrong are present, albeit that the elements are narrowly confined such that only a person who plays a significant causative role in the contract breaker's decision to commit the wrong, and who does so knowing the consequences of his actions, is an accessory. Outside of these circumstances, a claimant is limited to her rights against the primary wrongdoer who is in breach of contract.

160 See, e.g., *Esso Petroleum* v. *Kingswood* [1974] QB 142, 156 (subsidiary of PW required to re-transfer property to claimant as transfer was in breach of PW's contract); *Crestfort* v. *Tesco Stores* [2005] EWHC 805.

161 *Pratt* v. *British Medical Association* [1919] 1 KB 244, though this is now unlikely in the UK as inducing cases will rarely fall within the three categories in which exemplary damages are available under *Rookes* v. *Barnard* [1964] AC 1129; *Hospitality Group Pty Ltd* v. *Australian Rugby Union Ltd* [2001] FCA 1040 (Full Court).

162 *Hospitality Group Pty Ltd* v. *Australian Rugby Union Ltd* [2001] FCA 1040 [153].

7

Infringement of equitable property rights

7.1 Introduction

This chapter considers five doctrines that protect equitable property rights against interference by third parties and explains why they are not accessory liabilities, despite often being conceptually linked to accessory liability for procuring or assisting in a breach of trust. Each claim concerns the (often, but not always, wrongful) involvement, broadly speaking, of a third party, in a custodial relationship between a beneficiary and a trustee or fiduciary where that involvement relates to the property that is the subject of the trust or fiduciary relationship. Nearly all of these doctrines have at some time been grouped under the ubiquitous 'constructive trust' label [8.1.7].[1] It is challenging to disentangle them from accessory liability because they share similar rationales and elements to those of true equitable accessory liability and because none of them were necessarily conceived of with such classificatory concepts in mind. In particular, this chapter is concerned with one of the five doctrines considered, that is, equitable recipient liability: the personal fault-based liability that attaches to the recipient of property that is subject to a custodial fiduciary relationship and which has been received in breach of trust or fiduciary duty. Of the five doctrines, recipient liability is the one most closely related to accessory liability for procuring or assisting in a breach of trust. For that reason, its substantive content is discussed in Chapter 8 along with those accessory liabilities. Recipient liability is a contested doctrine; accordingly this chapter prepares the groundwork for Chapter 8 by explaining our understanding of recipient liability and why it should be considered in tandem with accessory liability.

[1] See, e.g., *Barnes* v. *Addy* (1874) LR 9 Ch App 244, 251–252, where trustees de son tort and those who 'receive and become chargeable with some part of the trust property' (now treated as inconsistent dealing and recipient liability, respectively) are described as 'constructive trustees'.

7.2 Trustee de son tort

A third party to a trust who has trust property vested in him or her, or has control over the trust property,[2] and who purports to act as a trustee in relation to that property, rather than as an agent or in a personal capacity, is accountable as though properly appointed as trustee.[3] The so-called 'trustee de son tort'[4] is a fiduciary who is subject to the usual duties of an express trustee and will hold all usual trustee powers.[5] The trusteeship arises prior to any breach of the trust.[6] As with express trustees, the trustee de son tort's liability for any ensuing breach of trust is strict; it is irrelevant whether he or she acted in good faith and without knowledge of the breach. There are few reported instances of successful trustee de son tort claims.[7]

Trustee de son tort liability reflects an 'ancient common law principle that a person who assumes an office or function which is not his, will be liable as if he had been properly appointed'.[8] Another, less convincing,

2 *In re Barney* [1892] 2 Ch 265, 273.

3 *Mara* v. *Browne* [1896] 1 Ch 199 (CA) 209–210 (AL Smith LJ); *Soar* v. *Ashwell* [1893] 2 QB 390, 394 (Lord Esher MR); *Selangor United Rubber Estates Ltd* v. *Cradock (No 3)* [1968] 1 WLR 1555 (Ch) 1579 (*Selangor*); *Dubai Aluminium Co Ltd* v. *Salaam* [2002] UKHL 48; [2003] 2 AC 366 [138] (Lord Millett) (*Dubai Aluminium*); *Williams* v. *Central Bank of Nigeria* [2014] UKSC 10; [2014] 2 WLR 355 [9] (Lord Sumption) (*Williams*). See generally, R. P. Austin, 'Constructive Trusts' in P. D. Finn (ed.), *Essays in Equity* (Sydney, Law Book Company Ltd, 1985) 196, 207–211; Charles Harpum, 'The Stranger as Constructive Trustee: Part I' (1986) 102 *Law Quarterly Review* 114, 127–130. Liability in this form also attaches to third parties assuming other fiduciary offices such as agency. See *Lyell* v. *Kennedy* (1889) 14 App Cas 437 (HL); *Phipps* v. *Boardman* [1965] Ch 992 (CA) 1017–1019 (Lord Denning MR affirming the reasoning of Wilberforce J at first instance); *English* v. *Dedham Vale Properties Ltd* [1978] 1 WLR 93 (Ch) 111; *Montrod Ltd* v. *Grundkotter Fleischvertriebs GmbH* [2002] CLC 499 (CA) 517. See also, Peter Watts, 'Self-appointed Agents – Liability in Tort' (2007) 123 *Law Quarterly Review* 519, 520.

4 The term appears in *Barnes* v. *Addy* (1874) LR 9 Ch App 244, 251, but had been coined earlier. It was borrowed from the common law concerning 'executors de son tort', although it did not mirror that liability. See *Pearce* v. *Pearce* (1856) 22 Beav 248, 251; 52 ER 1103, 1104; *In re Barney* [1892] 2 Ch 265, 272. Perhaps for that reason the term was not invariably used by the nineteenth-century lawyers.

5 A trustee de son tort will not necessarily hold further duties and powers conferred by any relevant trust instrument: *Jasmine Trustees Ltd* v. *Wells & Hind* [2007] EWHC 38; [2008] Ch 194, 213 (*Jasmine Trustees*).

6 *Selangor* [1968] 1 WLR 1555 (Ch) 1579.

7 Liability is most likely in relation to invalidly appointed express trustees who have acted in the mistaken belief that their appointment was valid (see, e.g., *Pearce* v. *Pearce* (1856) 22 Beav 248; 52 ER 1103; *Jasmine Trustees* [2007] EWHC 38; [2008] Ch 194 (Ch)) or in relation to laypersons assuming control over a deceased estate: see, e.g., *National Trustees Executors and Agency Co of Australasia Ltd* v. *Biffin* [1940] VLR 395 (VSC)).

8 *Phipps* v. *Boardman* [1965] Ch 992 (CA) 1017–1019 (Lord Denning).

explanation is that the third party's conduct in purporting to act as trustee amounts to a declaration of trust, the absence of any requisite writing being compensated for by the conduct in question.[9]

Historically, the liabilities of trustees de son tort, recipients, knowing dealers and accessories were intertwined in judicial discussion, the defendant was generally described as a 'constructive trustee' and was liable to account as though a trustee.[10] Despite these commonalities, however, trustees de son tort were always equated with express trustees for limitations purposes [8.6.3]. Trustee de son tort liability is now recognised as a distinct, non-accessorial liability.[11] It does not require a breach of duty by another (a primary wrong); indeed, there may be no properly appointed trustee at the relevant time.[12] The trusteeship arises prior to any breach of trust by the purported trustee, whereas an accessory becomes liable by virtue of his accessorial involvement in the breach of trust itself. Nor does it depend upon knowledge by the third party that he or she is in breach of the trust.[13] The trustee de son tort is a 'true trustee'[14] and, therefore, liability is primary.

[9] *Life Association of Scotland* v. *Siddal* (1861) 3 De G F & J. 58, 72; 45 ER 800 (CA in Ch) 805.

[10] The predominant nineteenth-century scenario concerned solicitors acting for trustees of family settlements and deceased estates who were involved in a breach of trust. Negligence claims were subject to the statutory limitations period and so were not always available. See, e.g., *Mara* v. *Browne* [1896] 1 Ch 199 (CA). A claim against the solicitors as 'mere' agents could not be brought by the cestui que trust. See, e.g., *Morgan* v. *Stephens* [1861] 3 Giff 226; 66 ER 392; *Lee* v. *Sankey* [1873] LR 15 Eq 204, 211. To avoid these procedural hurdles, it was often expedient to argue that the solicitors had exceeded their powers as agents and instead were 'assuming the position or duty of trustees' (trustee de son tort liability) and/or wrongfully intermeddling with the trust (accessory and recipient liability). See, e.g., *Morgan* v. *Stephens; Brinsden* v. *Williams* [1894] 3 Ch 185. The courts, however, were concerned to prevent solicitors from being unfairly saddled with the liabilities of impecunious trustee clients. See, e.g., *Morgan* v. *Stephens* at 236; 397; *Barnes* v. *Addy* (1874) LR 9 Ch App 244, 252 (Lord Selborne), 255 (James LJ); *Mara* v. *Browne* at 210.

[11] The judgment of Ungoed-Thomas J in *Selangor* [1968] 1 WLR 1555, 1579, has been influential in this respect. See also *Taylor* v. *Davies* [1920] AC 636 (PC) 651; *Paragon Finance* v. *DB Thakerar* [1999] 1 All ER 400 (CA) 408–410; *Dubai Aluminium* [2002] UKHL 48; [2003] 2 AC 366 [140] (where Lord Millett at [138] also suggested a more accurate description is that of 'de facto trustee'). See also *Williams* [2014] UKSC 10; [2014] 2 WLR 355 [9] (Lord Sumption).

[12] See, e.g., *Blyth* v. *Fladgate* [1891] 1 Ch 337. See also, *Lyell* v. *Kennedy* (1889) 14 App Cas 437 (HL).

[13] *In re Barney* [1892] 2 Ch 265, 272.

[14] *Williams* [2014] UKSC 10; [2014] 2 WLR 355 [9] (Lord Sumption).

7.3 Dealing inconsistently with trust property

An agent or other person who receives trust[15] property in a 'ministerial' capacity, rather than for personal benefit, but then knowingly deals with it in a manner that is contrary to the trust, will be liable to account in equity.[16] This is so whether the knowing dealer misappropriates the property for personal benefit or otherwise deals inconsistently with it[17] and whether or not the dealer acts in good faith.[18] Although knowing dealing has been authoritatively recognised as a distinct category of liability,[19] the cases are sparse.[20]

Inconsistent dealing liability extends to anyone holding trust property who knows at the time of receipt that it is trust property or later acquires such knowledge and who then deals with the property contrary to the trust or fiduciary obligation.[21] An example is a person who receives trust property as an innocent volunteer, but then learns of the trust and deals with the property inconsistently with that trust.

[15] Authorities are scarce, but it seems that, as with recipient liability, 'trust' property encompasses any property held pursuant to a custodial relationship governed by equity, whether or not it is subject to an express trust. See, e.g., *Locke* v. *Prescott* (1863) 32 Beav 261; 55 ER 103. On the meaning of trust property, see further [8.3.2.3].

[16] *Lee* v. *Sankey* (1873) LR 15 Eq 204; *Agip (Africa) Ltd* v. *Jackson* [1990] Ch 265, 391–392 (*Agip*). See generally, Harpum, 'The stranger as constructive trustee: Part I', 130–148; in relation to agents, see F. M. B. Reynolds and Michele Graziadei, *Bowstead and Reynolds on Agency*, 18th edn (London, Sweet & Maxwell, 2006) [9–131], [9–134].

[17] *Morgan* v. *Stephens* (1861) 3 Giff 226, 237; 66 ER 393, 397. This is clear in Millett J's statement of principle in *Agip* [1990] Ch 265, 391–392, referring to a third party who 'receives the trust property lawfully and not for his own benefit but who then *either misappropriates it or otherwise deals with it* in a manner which is inconsistent with the trust' (emphasis added).

[18] *Williams* v. *Williams* (1881) 17 Ch D 437.

[19] *Agip* [1990] Ch 265, 391–392. See also, *Koorootang Nominees Pty Ltd* v. *Australia and New Zealand Banking Group Ltd* [1998] 3 VR 16 (VSC) 79 (*Koorootang*).

[20] The leading nineteenth-century decision is *Lee* v. *Sankey* (1873) LR 15 Eq 204. In agency cases that consider inconsistent dealing, there is a concern not to unduly compromise an agent's contractual and statutory obligations to follow client instructions. Hence, the requisite culpability is high. See *Adams* v. *Bank of New South Wales* [1984] 1 NSWLR 285 (although the NSWCA did not explicitly address inconsistent dealing, the facts are most consistent with that doctrine); *Williams* v. *Williams* (1881) 17 Ch D 437; *Carl Zeiss Siftung* v. *Herbert Smith & Co (No 2)* [1969] 2 Ch 276 (CA) 304.

[21] See e.g., *Locke* v. *Prescott* (1863) 32 Beav 261; 55 ER 103: bankers held railway stock as security for a loan of £300. It was held that once the bankers received a letter from their customers referring to 'our principal' they were on notice that the stock belonged to another and they could not then use the secured property to satisfy amounts owed by their customers above the original loan of £300.

Inconsistent dealing is often coupled with recipient liability[22] in the case law. But although it involves a receipt of 'trust' property in the same sense as used for recipient liability [8.3.2.3], it is a conceptually distinct liability. In particular, it is the subsequent dealing, rather than the receipt of property, that founds liability.[23] Inconsistent dealing is also not an accessory liability because the dealer's liability is not dependent upon another's breach of duty (a primary wrong), even though sometimes the dealing may be in response to such a breach. In other words, the inconsistent dealing with the trust property need not have involved the trustee or fiduciary.[24]

It has been argued by Charles Harpum that where the dealing is not for personal benefit, the dealer's liability is accessory ('secondary') because '[t]he primary liability is ... that of the trustee who instructed [the dealer], and who thereby commits a breach of trust'.[25] But does this follow? It is the dealer's inconsistent dealing that generates liability: whether or not there is also a breach of duty by the trustee or fiduciary is immaterial.[26] Harpum acknowledges that the dealer's dealing may have been on his or her own initiative, rather than at the behest of the trustee or fiduciary, but says that in this case the dealer is a trustee de son tort.[27] But this does not necessarily follow either because the dealer's inconsistent dealing may not have been as a purported trustee.[28]

Conversely, where the dealer's inconsistent dealing *is* for personal benefit, Harpum considers that this is 'not secondary because [the dealer]

22 Lord Selborne LC in *Barnes* v. *Addy* (1874) LR 9 Ch App 244, 251–252, referred to those who 'receive and become chargeable with some part of the trust property', but Brightman J in *Karak Rubber Co Ltd* v. *Burden (No 2)* [1972] 1 WLR 602 (Ch) 633 (*Karak*), adopted 'as an admirable shorthand description' the subheading used in R. E. Megarry and P. V. Baker, *Snell's Principles of Equity*, 26th edn (London, Sweet & Maxwell Ltd, 1966) 202: 'knowing receipt or dealing'.

23 Reynolds and Graziadei, *Bowstead and Reynolds* [9–134].

24 See, e.g., *Williams* v. *Williams* (1881) 17 Ch D 437 (discussed in detail in *Karak* [1972] 1 WLR 602 (Ch) 637–639). See also, P. Finn, 'The Liability of Third Parties for Knowing Receipt or Assistance' in D. Waters (ed.), *Equity, Fiduciaries and Trusts* (Toronto, Carswell, 1993) 195, 209.

25 Charles Harpum, 'The Basis of Equitable Liability' in P. B. H. Birks (ed.), *The Frontiers of Liability: Volume 1* (Oxford University Press, 1994) 9, 16.

26 *Cf.* Reynolds and Graziadei, *Bowstead and Reynolds,* [9–134].

27 Harpum, 'The Basis of Equitable Liability', n. 89.

28 E.g., assume that D is an agent of a trustee and has control over the trust property in that capacity. D transfers the trust property to her son, S, knowing that S is not a trust beneficiary. The trustee did not instruct D to act in this way and was unaware of the distribution to S. D clearly is liable for inconsistent dealing in this situation, but it can only be a primary liability because there is no breach of duty by the trustee.

takes the property as his own. He does not merely deal with it on the instructions of his principal or bailor.'[29] This is consistent with our own analysis that the dealer's liability for inconsistent dealing is always a primary liability because liability rests on the dealing, rather than on another's primary wrong. It is 'the independent liability of a knowing "converter" of another's property'.[30]

7.4 The *Diplock* claim

Brief mention should be made of the strict liability personal claim against the recipient of a wrongful distribution from a deceased estate.[31] The '*Diplock* claim' has assumed significance beyond its specific context, and hence is discussed here, because it has been used to argue that strict personal receipt-based liability for breach of trust or fiduciary duty would not be unprincipled.[32] Indeed, the presence within equity of both the strict *Diplock* claim and fault-based recipient liability is argued (incorrectly, in our view: [7.6.4]) to be anomalous.

An unpaid creditor of the estate, a rightful beneficiary under the will or a rightfully entitled person under intestacy rules, may claim against the innocent recipient of a wrongful distribution where the distribution precluded the claimant (C) receiving their full entitlement.[33] The recipient will be strictly liable for the amount of the wrongly paid distribution, but only to the extent that the loss cannot be met by the personal representatives of the estate.[34] The liability is an example of a defendant's conscience being affected without knowledge of the flawed nature of the receipt.[35] The Court of Appeal in *Re Diplock* concluded that the claim, as

29 Harpum, 'The Basis of Equitable Liability', 20.

30 Finn, 'The Liability of Third Parties', 209.

31 *Re Diplock* [1948] 1 Ch 465 (CA); *Ministry of Health* v. *Simpson* [1951] AC 251 (HL). Such a distribution may be wrongful in part or in full.

32 Lord Nicholls, 'Knowing Receipt: The Need for a New Landmark' in W. R. Cornish, R. Nolan, J. O'Sullivan and G. Virgo (eds.), *Restitution: Past Present and Future* (Oxford, Hart Publishing, 1998) 231; Peter Birks, 'Receipt' in Peter Birks and Arianno Pretto, *Breach of Trust* (Oxford, Hart Publishing, 2002) 213, 237.

33 *Re Diplock* [1948] 1 Ch 465 (CA). Lionel Smith, 'Unjust Enrichment, Property, and the Structure of Trusts' (2000) 116 *Law Quarterly Review* 412, 439.

34 *Re Diplock* [1948] 1 Ch 465 (CA). See also *Hagan* v. *Waterhouse* (1992) 34 NSWLR 308 (NSWSC) 369–370. The historical support for this limitation has been questioned: S. J. Whittaker, 'An Historical Perspective to the "Special Equitable Action" in Re Diplock' (1983) 4 *Journal of Legal History* 3, 34–35.

35 *Cf. Bridgeman* v. *Green* (1757) Wilm 56; 97 ER 22. See also, Pauline Ridge, 'Third Party Volunteers and Undue Influence' (2014) 130 *Law Quarterly Review* 112, 120–122.

a matter of principle, precedent and jurisdictional history, applies only in the specific context of the administration of deceased estates.[36] Although explicable in its historical context, the claim may operate harshly because there is no change of position defence.[37]

The *Re Diplock* claim is not an accessory liability claim because, although it is dependent upon the commission of a primary wrong (the wrongful distribution), accessorial involvement through conduct is not an element of the liability [3.3]. Also telling against an accessory liability analysis is that the liability is strict.

7.5 The persisting property claim

Where a trustee misappropriates trust property and it or its traceable proceeds thereby comes into the hands of a third party who is not a bona fide purchaser for value of the legal interest, the beneficiaries of the trust may assert their prior, 'persisting'[38] equitable interest in the property held by the recipient third party by using the priorities rules[39] and, if

[36] [1948] 1 Ch 465 CA 488. See also, at 489, 492 and 503. The rationale and elements of the claim were attributed to the practice of the ecclesiastical courts' jurisdiction that was gradually taken over by Chancery. The former jurisdiction's practice of requiring legatees to provide security was reflected in Chancery's recognition of the weakness of the recipient's right to retain the distribution.

[37] A change of position defence should be recognised. There seems no reason to accord *Re Diplock* recipients a lesser status to that of other volunteer recipients of incorrectly paid funds. The defence seems particularly appropriate if formulated in equitable terms. See, e.g., *Australian Financial Services and Leasing Pty Limited* v. *Hills Industries Limited* [2014] HCA 14; (2014) 88 ALJR 552 (*Hills Industries*).

[38] The discussion in this section draws upon Joachim Dietrich and Pauline Ridge, '"The Receipt of What?": Questions Concerning Third Party Recipient Liability in Equity and Unjust Enrichment' (2007) 31 *Melbourne University Law Review* 47; Pauline Ridge, 'Constructive Trusts, Accessory Liability and Judicial Discretion' in Elise Bant and Michael Bryan (eds.), *Principles of Proprietary Remedies* (Sydney, Lawbook Co, 2013) 73. The term 'persisting property' comes from Charles Mitchell and Stephen Watterson, 'Remedies for Knowing Receipt' in Charles Mitchell (ed.), *Constructive and Resulting Trusts* (Oxford, Hart Publishing, 2010) 115. It is not a term used in the case law.

[39] E.g., if the trust property is shares and, in breach of trust, the trustee uses the shares as security for a loan by D, the priority rules determine whether C or D has better title to the shares. *Phillips* v. *Phillips* (1861) 4 De G F & J 208; 45 ER 1164, 1166; *Macmillan Inc* v. *Bishopsgate Investment Trust plc [No 3]* [1995] 3 All ER 747; *Koorootang* [1998] 3 VR 16 (VSC). See generally, R. Meagher, D. Heydon and M. Leeming (eds.), *Meagher Gummow and Lehane's Equity: Doctrine and Remedies,* 4th edn (Chatswood, Butterworths LexisNexis, 2002) Ch. 8. The rules of following may be needed to identify D, see Sarah Worthington, *Equity,* 2nd edn (Oxford University Press, 2006) Ch. 4. It is assumed here that no registration system overrides the operation of the equitable rules.

necessary, the tracing[40] rules.[41] The persisting property claim is defeated by the defence of bona fide purchaser of the legal interest for value without notice.[42] The provision of consideration and the absence of notice at the time of receipt means that the recipient's conscience is not affected and there is nothing else to attract equity's jurisdiction if the recipient holds a legal interest.[43] 'Notice' encompasses actual knowledge,[44] constructive notice (the knowledge that would have been gained by a reasonable person from reasonable and proper enquiries),[45] and imputed notice.[46] Thus, the beneficiaries' rights will prevail against a

[40] *Boscawen* v. *Bajwa* [1996] 1 WLR 328, 334–335; *Foskett* v. *McKeown* [2001] 1 AC 102 (HL) 128 (Lord Millett); *Robb Evans & Associates* v. *European Bank Ltd* (2004) 61 NSWLR 75 (NSWCA) 103; *Grimaldi* v. *Chameleon Mining NL (No 2)* [2012] FCAFC 6; (2012) 200 FCR 296 [251], [562]. The alternative remedies of constructive trust and lien are available: *Foskett* v. *McKeown* [2001] 1 AC 102 (HL) 130 (Lord Millett). The remedy is not discretionary, except in a weak sense that applies to all equitable remedies: *Foskett* v. *McKeown; Heperu Pty Ltd* v. *Belle* [2009] NSWCA 252; (2009) 76 NSWLR 230, 155.

[41] The claim is more pithily described in the *Restatement (Third) of Trusts (2012)* §108 (2): 'A third party who acquires an interest in trust property through a breach of trust is entitled to retain or enforce the interest to the extent the third party is protected as a bona fide purchaser.'

[42] The question of D's bona fides is relevant where D has no notice: see, e.g., *Nelson* v. *Larholt* [1948] 1 KB 339; *Midland Bank Trust Co Ltd* v. *Green* [1981] AC 513, 528. The bona fide purchaser defence extends to the purchaser of an equitable interest, but only where C's prior interest is a 'mere equity': *Phillips* v. *Phillips* (1861) 4 De G F & J 208, 218; 45 ER 1164, 1167 (Lord Westbury); *Latec Investments Ltd* v. *Hotel Terrigal Pty Ltd (in liq.)* (1965) 113 CLR 265 (HCA) 277–279. It has been persuasively argued that the protection of the bona fide purchaser doctrine should extend to purchasers of equitable interests generally: Austin Wakeman Scott, William Franklin Fratcher and Mark L. Ascher, *Scott & Ascher on Trusts,* 5th edn (Boston, Aspen Publishers, 2006) vol. 5, §29.1.2, citing *Restatement (Second) of Trusts* (1959) §285. See further concerning the bona fide purchaser doctrine, *Restatement (Third), Restitution and Unjust Enrichment* (2011) §§66–69.

[43] *Re Nisbet and Potts' Contract* [1905] 1 Ch 391, 398. The defence is 'an absolute, unqualified, unanswerable defence, and an unanswerable plea to the jurisdiction of this Court'. *Pilcher* v. *Rawlins* (1872) 7 Ch App 259, 269 (James LJ). See further, D O'Sullivan, 'The Rule in *Phillips* v. *Phillips*' (2002) 118 *Law Quarterly Review* 296.

[44] This includes 'wilful blindness' and 'contrived ignorance': *Macmillan Inc* v. *Bishopsgate Trust Plc [No 3]* [1995] 3 All ER 747, 769 (Millet J) and [3.4.3.3].

[45] *Ibid.* See also *English & Scottish Mercantile Investment Co Ltd* v. *Brunton* [1892] 2 QB 700 (CA) 707–708.

[46] Imputed notice is the actual or constructive notice acquired in the course of an agency by an agent acting for D where the information acquired is material to the transaction and the agent has a duty to pass it on. See *Espin* v. *Pemberton* (1859) 3 De G & J. 547, 554; 44 ER 1380, 1383; *Koorootang* [1998] 3 VR 16 (VSC) 115, discussing *Sargent* v. *ASL Developments Ltd* (1974) 131 CLR 634, 658. See also *Re Montagu's Settlement Trusts* [1987] Ch 264, 277. See also [11.2.2].

merely careless purchaser of the legal interest. This is a much more extreme and far-reaching mental state than that generally required for accessory liability [3.4.3.5].

Despite the beguiling logic underpinning the persisting property claim ('that is my property: give it back!'),[47] its impact upon a defendant is particularly severe where he or she is a volunteer recipient of the trust property without notice, or a bona fide purchaser of an equitable interest in the trust property without notice, who still holds the trust property or its traceable proceeds, but who has changed position in reliance on its receipt. The claim is probably not subject to a change of position defence, but in our view it should be.[48] Its harsh impact is exacerbated by the reach of the concept of constructive notice in this context.[49] The persisting property claim thus exhibits a strong property protection objective based upon the defendant's retention of the trust property.

Unlike recipient liability [8.3.2.3], the application of a persisting property claim is limited to property that is the subject of a trust,[50] rather than extending to property that is the subject of a non-trust, custodial fiduciary relationship. There are authorities to the contrary, but they contain little discussion of this point.[51] In recent Australian cases involving breach of fiduciary duty and misappropriated company assets, the persisting property claim has been limited to where 'trust property in the strict sense' was received by the defendant.[52] Limiting the scope of the persisting property claim in this way makes sense given its potentially severe impact upon recipients other than bona fide purchasers for value of a legal interest without notice. The persisting property and recipient

[47] *Cf. Foskett* v. *McKeown* [2001] 1 AC 102 (HL) 109 (Lord Browne-Wilkinson referring to 'hard-nosed property rights').

[48] *Cf. Gertsch* v. *Atsas* [1999] NSWSC 898; (1999) 10 BPR 18, 431 [22].

[49] *Cf.* the test of objective knowledge used in the context of equitable accessory liability [3.4.3.5], [8.3.4.3].

[50] This includes property impressed with a constructive trust. See, e.g., *United States Surgical Corporation* v. *Hospital Products International Pty Ltd* [1983] 2 NSWLR 157 (NSWCA) 247; *Grimaldi* v. *Chameleon Mining NL (No 2)* [2012] FCAFC 6; (2012) 200 FCR 296 (*Grimaldi*). See also, Heydon and Leeming, *Equity*, [2705]. See also *Black* v. *S Freedman & Co* (1910) 12 CLR 105; *Attorney-General for Hong Kong* v. *Reid* [1994] 1 AC 324 (PC) (constructive trust imposed over fiduciary's proceeds of bribery and traced into real properties held by fiduciary's wife and solicitor as volunteers).

[51] See, e.g., *Rolled Steel Products (Holdings) Ltd* v. *British Steel Corporation* [1986] Ch 246, 297–298. In Australia, see *Linter Group Ltd* v. *Goldberg* (1992) 7 ACSR 580; *Farrow Finance Co Ltd (in liq.)* v. *Farrow Properties Pty Ltd (in liq.)* [1999] 1 VR 584.

[52] *Grimaldi* [2012] FCAFC 6; (2012) 200 FCR 296 [254].

liability claims have different requirements in terms of knowledge[53] and onus of proof.[54] The wider scope of recipient liability is justified because it is fault-based and the relief is discretionary.

The persisting property claim is not an accessory liability even though it is triggered by another's primary wrong (the breach of trust). The holder of persisting property is not liable for 'involvement' [3.3] in that wrong (whether or not factually there was such involvement) but because C's property rights have priority. Further, the liability of the holder of persisting property is not dependent upon a particular mental state [3.4] except in a weak sense where he or she is a purchaser of a legal interest in the trust property who cannot prove bona fides or absence of notice. Instead, the rationale for liability is overwhelmingly concerned with the protection of C's equitable property rights.

7.6 Recipient liability

7.6.1 The dual character of recipient liability

Recipient liability is a personal fault-based liability that attaches to the recipient of property subject to a custodial fiduciary relationship that was knowingly received in breach of trust or fiduciary duty [Chapter 8]. Recipient liability incorporates both personal characteristics (the liability is not dependent upon retention of the subject property and does not usually attach to that property) and proprietary characteristics (the recipient defendant, D, must have received trust property to which C has a claim and the remedies relate to the value of that property). The claim operates at the intersection of personal and proprietary obligations and is amenable to different explanations according to where on a spectrum, ranging from personal to proprietary liability, it is positioned. Historically, its dual character was clear. Nineteenth-century cases often bundled it together with the property-related claims involving trustees de son tort, inconsistent dealing and tracing of persisting property rights, but it was also coupled with the personal claim of knowing assistance.[55]

[53] Contra *Crédit Agricole Corporation and Investment Bank v Papadimitriou* [2015] UKPC 13 [33]. See further, [8.3.4.4].

[54] In relation to the persisting property claim, D must prove absence of notice of the trust, whereas in relation to equitable recipient liability, C must prove that D had the requisite knowledge: Michael Bryan, 'The Liability of the Recipient: Restitution at Common Law or Wrongdoing in Equity?' in Simone Degeling and James Edelman (eds.), *Equity in Commercial Law* (Pyrmont, Lawbook Co, 2005) 331.

[55] See, e.g., *Barnes* v. *Addy* (1874) LR 9 Ch App 244.

The dominant rationale for recipient liability is D's culpable conduct (determined according to D's knowledge of the primary wrong), rather than the protection of C's property rights.[56] For this reason, in most jurisdictions a higher level of knowledge than for the persisting property claim is required.[57] A property-protection rationale is also present, but it does not determine the fault element for D's personal liability and cannot justify D's liability by itself.

7.6.2 *The relationship of recipient liability and accessory liability*

One of the most challenging aspects of our endeavour to identify and describe an organising principle of accessory liability that operates across private law has been the need to accommodate and respect the fact that equity traditionally did not organise the relevant law in terms of accessory and non-accessory liabilities (although there have been some moves in this direction[58]). It can be problematic to 're-classify' according to a concept that was not traditionally dominant in this area of law. The concept of accessory liability used in this book [Chapter 2] is influenced by common law notions of accessory liability. These focus upon A's accessorial 'involvement' in the wrong, that is A's conduct before or at the time of the commission of the primary wrong that contributes to it;

[56] Sir Robert Megarry VC's judgment in *Re Montagu's Settlement Trusts* [1987] Ch 264 is the leading authority. See *Bank of Credit and Commerce International (Overseas) Ltd* v. *Akindele* [2001] Ch 437 (CA) 452 (*Akindele*); *Grimaldi* [2012] FCAFC 6; (2012) 200 FCR 296 [368]–[369]. See further, Dietrich and Ridge, 'The Receipt of What?', 58–60. Two lines of case law had developed during the twentieth century. The first characterised recipient liability as the personal liability companion of a persisting property claim by C; both were concerned with 'rights of priority in relation to property': *Agip* [1990] 1 Ch 265, 292–293. That is, the rationale for intervention is property-protection. See also *El Ajou* v. *Dollar Land Holdings plc* [1993] 3 All ER 717, 738. According to this approach, liability depended on whether D made reasonable and appropriate enquiries to verify D's entitlement to the property; that is, objective notice, in the sense used in conveyancing-related claims, sufficed for liability [3.4.3.5]. Similarly, if D used an agent to do what was necessary on D's behalf, then the agent's actual or constructive notice would be imputed to D: see, e.g., *Powell* v. *Thompson* [1991] 1 NZLR 597. This approach was rejected in *Re Montagu's Settlement Trusts* where Megarry V-C preferred a fault-based rationale.

[57] *Akindele* [2001] Ch 437 (CA); *George Raymond Zage III* v. *Ho Chi Kwong* [2010] 2 SLR 589 (SCA) (*Zage*); *Grimaldi* [2012] FCAFC 6; (2012) 200 FCR 296. Contra Canada: *Citadel General Assurance Co* v. *Lloyds Bank Canada* [1997] 3 SCR 805; (1997) 152 DLR (4th) 411, 434 [49] (*Citadel*) (La Forest J: the knowledge required is the same, namely, 'knowledge of facts that would put a reasonable person on inquiry'). This is said to be because D's failure to make inquiry 'renders [D's] enrichment unjust'.

[58] See *Royal Brunei Airlines Sdn Bhd* v. *Tan* [1995] 2 AC 378 (PC) (*Royal Brunei Airlines*); [8.1.4.2].

[3.3], especially [3.3.4]. Equity, on the other hand, focuses not on the *timing* of D's conduct, but upon its fault-based and derivative nature.

The first and third elements of the analytical framework for accessory liability set out in Chapter 3 are also present in recipient liability. Recipient liability requires there to be a breach of trust or fiduciary duty by another (the primary wrong). Liability turns upon the recipient's knowledge of the primary wrong (the mental element). But the requisite conduct – the receipt of misappropriated property or its traceable product – occurs *after*, and potentially independently of, the commission of the primary wrong (the breach of trust or fiduciary duty). Hence, according to our explanation of the conduct element for accessory liability [3.3], recipient liability is not accessorial. D need not have been involved in the commission of the primary wrong: any subsequent recipient in a chain of recipients of trust property that remains traceable to that recipient, and who receives with knowledge of the breach of trust, is personally liable to C [8.3.3].

Factually speaking, of course, given that D must know of the primary wrong, it is possible, indeed quite likely, that the knowing receipt will be pursuant to a scheme that encompasses the primary wrong. If D has agreed to participate in a wrongful scheme, then the timing of D's receipt is by the way. D's agreement alone has facilitated the wrong. That is, D's receipt may well constitute accessorial involvement in the primary wrong by the primary wrongdoer (PW) and even suffice for a knowing assistance claim [3.3.4]. The closer D is in time and physical connection to the primary wrong, the more accessorial his or her behaviour becomes. Nonetheless, accessorial conduct is not an essential element of recipient liability and therefore it is not accessory liability.[59]

There is, however, an overlap in the rationale and objectives of recipient liability and equitable accessory liability. The rationale for recipient liability is that it is wrongful to knowingly interfere in the equitable relationship between C and PW for personal gain.[60] This is the most

[59] Another possible objection to treating recipient liability as accessorial concerns whether purely passive conduct suffices for accessory liability. See, e.g., *Zage* [2010] 2 SLR 589 (SCA) 608, where the two forms of liability were distinguished on this basis. See further, Pauline Ridge, 'Equitable Accessory and Recipient Liability in Singapore' (2013) *Singapore Journal of Legal Studies* 361, 375–376. If D's passive receipt occurred with the deliberate intention of furthering PW's breach of duty, then passive conduct in itself should not be a bar to accessory liability [3.3.6].

[60] See *Akindele* [2001] Ch 437 (CA) 455 (Nourse LJ): 'the recipient's state of knowledge should be such as to make it unconscionable for him to retain the benefit of the receipt'. It is difficult to find unambiguous statements in the case law because the persisting property claim, recipient liability and accessory liability are often not distinguished when courts

pervasive rationale for personal, fault-based equitable third-party liabilities in general [8.1.3]. The same fault-based rationale applies to accessory liability, but is expressed more broadly; it is wrongful to knowingly interfere (whether for gain or otherwise) with a relationship between C and PW that is governed by equity [8.1.3].[61] A factual scenario may satisfy the elements of knowing assistance in breach of fiduciary duty, for example, without the assistant having participated for personal gain.[62] On the other hand, advantage-taking does appear to be an essential rationale of recipient liability: D is liable *because* he or she has knowingly taken advantage of the primary wrong for personal gain; if there is no receipt for personal benefit, there is no recipient liability [8.3.2.3].

Until quite recently, courts applying equitable doctrine have not used 'accessory' terminology, instead grouping third-party personal fault-based liabilities more broadly. What is apparent from the commonalities in the elements of liability and rationales for both recipient liability and accessory liability is that the two can sensibly be grouped conceptually as distinct, but related, forms of liability for wrongful participation[63] in another's breach of equitable duty. There is support in equity jurisprudence for treating accessory liability and recipient liability for breach of trust or fiduciary duty as one, 'participatory liability' [8.3.5]. Accordingly, although recipient liability is not an accessory liability according to our analytical framework, we conclude that it nonetheless shares fundamental features with equitable accessory liability and should be considered in combination with it. Hence, we discuss the substantive principles of recipient liability in Chapter 8.

discuss the rationales for liability. See also *Consul Development Pty Ltd* v. *DPC Estates Pty Ltd* (1975) 132 CLR 373 (HCA) 397 (Gibbs J) (*Consul Development*) (where the comments were not specifically directed to recipient liability). In *Zhu* v. *Treasurer (NSW)* [2004] HCA 56; (2004) 218 CLR 530 [121], the Court referred to a property-protection rationale in relation to a 'third party who obtains trust property from a trustee in breach of trust' and a benefit-based rationale in relation to accessory liability. But a property-protection rationale cannot by itself justify recipient liability, nor is it clear whether the Court's comments were even directed to recipient liability, rather than the persisting property claim.

61 *Royal Brunei Airlines* [1995] 2 AC 378 (PC) 386–387.

62 E.g., accessory liability is imposed upon agents providing professional services regardless of whether a benefit (beyond professional remuneration) was received.

63 'Participation' here is not meant to imply involvement *in* the wrong as an accessory linked to the commission of the wrong [3.3.4]; it is intended to encompass liability that goes beyond 'involvement' before or during the commission of the primary wrong.

7.6.3 Recipient liability as a primary custodial liability

An alternative explanation of recipient liability is that it is a fault-based and 'distinctive, primary, custodial liability, which closely resembles the liability of express trustees to account for the trust property with which they are charged'.[64] On this view, the initial wrongful receipt operates to constitute the recipient a trustee of the received property; therefore, the remedies flow from the consequent trusteeship, rather than directly from the wrongful receipt.[65]

This explanation of recipient liability shifts attention away from the recipient's initial wrongdoing that generates liability, but why does that initial fault alone not justify and explain the imposition of liability? And why does the specific wrongdoing in question, namely knowing (unconscionable) receipt of misappropriated property, not explain the imposition of remedies that focus upon the loss of that property and the advantages gained by the recipient?[66] More simply, it could be argued that the recipient culpably received trust property in breach of trust or fiduciary duty and therefore is liable for the consequences. The explanation of recipient liability as a stand-alone, custodial liability is unnecessarily convoluted, given that an obvious rationale for liability – culpable receipt for personal gain – already exists.[67]

[64] Charles Mitchell and Stephen Watterson, 'Remedies for Knowing Receipt' in Charles Mitchell (ed.), *Constructive and Resulting Trusts* (Oxford, Hart Publishing, 2009) 115, 129. See also Steven B. Elliott and Charles Mitchell, 'Remedies for Dishonest Assistance' (2004) 67 *Modern Law Review* 16.

[65] This is rather like the liability of a trustee de son tort whose liability flows not from the assumption of trusteeship, but from a breach of the assumed duties [7.2]. Mitchell and Watterson, 'Remedies for Knowing Receipt', has been cited by the Privy Council (*Arthur* v. *Attorney General of the Turks and Caicos Islands* [2012] UKPC 30) and by the Federal Court of Australia (*Grimaldi* [2012] FCAFC 6; (2012) 200 FCR 296) in relation to the remedies for recipient liability, although these citations do not necessarily indicate endorsement of the overall thesis of that work.

[66] The additional step of subjecting D to a trusteeship appears to be considered necessary in order to justify the availability of accounting procedures and liabilities that, in Mitchell and Watterson's view, flow only from a trustee's duty to account for the trust fund. But even if this remedial view is correct (*cf.* [8.7.2]), could one not equally justify an accounting standard for assessing monetary remedies being available against D as culpable participant in PW's misappropriation of trust property? This, after all, seems to be the point of the historical labelling of a recipient or accessory as a 'constructive trustee', namely, that D is then liable to the full range of remedies available against an express trustee. See further [8.7].

[67] The persuasiveness of the custodial liability explanation is also undermined by its premise that true accessory liability must duplicate the primary wrongdoer's liability. Accessory liability is not a duplicative, but a derivative, liability. See further, Pauline Ridge,

7.6.4 Recipient liability and unjust enrichment liability

A more radical reimagining of recipient liability proposes unjust enrichment as the preferred explanation.[68] On this approach, fault-based recipient liability is an historical anomaly at odds with the common law's approach to receipt-based liabilities and with some equitable liabilities. The original resolution to this supposed anomaly, proposed by Peter Birks, was that recipient liability in its current form should be replaced by strict liability.[69] Specifically, the fault element of knowledge would be abolished, the remedy would be confined to restitution of the received 'enrichment', and the defence of change of position would be added to the bona fide purchaser defence. This requires a radical change to the existing law and has not occurred.[70]

A second proposed resolution[71] is a modified version of the first whereby the current recipient liability claim (with its fault requirement and greater range of remedies) is retained, but a strict liability claim is also recognised. The modified approach also requires radical changes to the current law. Notable proponents are Lord Nicholls[72] and Lord Millett.[73] In Lord Nicholls' view, a strict liability equitable personal

'Justifying the Remedies for Dishonest Assistance' (2008) 124 *Law Quarterly Review* 445; [2.6], [8.1.5].

68 'Unjust enrichment' is used here in the Birksian sense: if D was enriched at the expense of (by subtraction from) C and a legally recognised 'unjust factor' (e.g., a mistake by C) exists, D must restore the value of the enrichment to C unless the change of position defence applies or D is a bona fide purchaser for value without notice from C. It is a strict liability. See P. Birks, *An Introduction to the Law of Restitution* (Oxford, Clarendon Press, 1985). Contra *Citadel* [1997] 3 SCR 805; (1997) 152 DLR (4th) 411, where the Supreme Court of Canada accepted an unjust enrichment rationale for recipient liability, but held that D's enrichment is only unjust if D has constructive notice of PW's breach of duty. That is, the liability is fault-based.

69 See, e.g., Peter Birks, 'Misdirected Funds: Restitution from the Recipient' [1989] *Lloyd's Maritime and Commercial Law Quarterly* 296; 'Misdirected Funds' (1989) 105 *Law Quarterly Review* 352; *Restitution – The Future* (Sydney, Federation Press, 1992) Ch. 2. See also, Andrew Burrows, *The Law of Restitution*, 3rd edn (Oxford University Press, 2011) 424–431.

70 It was subsequently abandoned: P. Birks, 'Receipt' in P. Birks and A. Pretto (eds.), *Breach of Trust* (Oxford, Hart Publishing, 2002) 213.

71 This was accepted by Birks: *ibid.*

72 Lord Nicholls, 'Knowing Receipt: the Need for A New Landmark' in W. R. Cornish, R. Nolan, J. O'Sullivan and G. Virgo (eds.), *Restitution: Past Present and Future* (Oxford, Hart Publishing, 1998) 231. See also *Royal Brunei Airlines* [1995] 2 AC 378 (PC) 386, where Lord Nicholls had earlier distinguished recipient liability from dishonest accessory liability and noted that it was 'restitution-based'.

73 *Dubai Aluminium* [2002] UKHL 48; [2003] 2 AC 366 [87]. See also *Twinsectra Ltd* v. *Yardley* [2002] UKHL 12; [2002] 2 AC 164 [105].

claim is not anomalous and the *Re Diplock* claim [7.4] could be used as a starting point for developing the law. Other scholars have pointed to the strict liability of an innocent donee of a gift tainted by the undue influence of a third person to make the same point.[74]

Neither of these approaches has been adopted in ratio by the highest court in any jurisdiction.[75] The Supreme Court of Canada has noted that an 'enrichment' of D at the expense of C, by itself shows only that C has been unjustly *deprived* of the enrichment, but not necessarily that it is unjust for D to retain the enrichment. Accordingly, something more was required to show D's unjust enrichment, namely D's knowledge of the breach of duty by PW.[76] In 2000, Nourse LJ, giving judgment for the English Court of Appeal, cautioned against the acceptance of a strict liability unjust enrichment claim, suggesting that it would be 'commercially unworkable'.[77] He also actively discouraged any such move by preferring a higher threshold for fault than 'constructive knowledge' [8.3.4.4]. The High Court of Australia has emphatically rejected the unjust enrichment explanation of recipient liability. The Court noted that it would 'cut down traditional equitable protection' of D, and questioned 'how there was any justice in permitting restitution against a [D] who received trust property without notice of that fact'.[78]

It should also be noted that the analogies drawn with existing strict liabilities in equity are not compelling. The *Re Diplock* claim [7.4] is controversial and only explicable on historical grounds. The other equitable strict liability relied upon, namely, the liability of an innocent donee of a gift tainted by the undue influence of another, although

[74] A. Burrows, 'The Australian Law of Restitution: has the High Court lost its way?' in E. Bant and M. Harding (eds.), *Exploring Private Law* (Cambridge University Press, 2010) 67, 81; *The Law of Restitution,* 3rd edn (Oxford University Press, 2011) 426.

[75] In some jurisdictions this may be because a suitable claim has yet to arise. For judicial support, see *Grupo Torras SA* v. *Al Sabah* [2001] CLC 221 [122]–[123]; *Dubai Aluminium* [2002] UKHL 48; [2003] 2 AC 366 [87]; *Wee Chiaw See Anna* v. *Ng Li-Ann Genevieve* [2013] SGCA 36 (SCA). The conceptual reasoning of much unjust enrichment scholarship – that eschews consideration of policy – also impedes its judicial acceptance: *Wee Chiaw See Anna* [144].

[76] *Citadel* [1997] 3 SCR 805; (1997) 152 DLR (4th) 411, 435 [51] (La Forest J).

[77] *Akindele* [2001] Ch 437 (CA) 456. For reasons of *stare decisis* the court could not adjudicate on the issue. *Cf.* the obiter comments by the Court of Appeal in *Grupo Torras SA* v. *Al Sabah* [2001] CLC 221 [122]–[123].

[78] *Farah Constructions* [2007] HCA 22; (2007) 230 CLR 89 [153], [155]. The court also noted at [156] that there is no recognised 'unjust factor' justifying restitution in such circumstances.

uncontroversial, is explicable by way of a combination of factors that do not all apply to the quite different scenario of receipt of trust property.[79]

In our view, a strict liability unjust enrichment claim, as presently conceived, should not be recognised.[80] It unfairly shifts the risks and burdens of litigation from C to D, an innocent recipient who partakes of none of the benefits of the trust relationship between C and PW, and who has no opportunity to 'vet' PW's suitability as a trustee or fiduciary. It renders an innocent third party the unintentional insurer of C, yet offers no convincing explanation for why personal liability should be imposed in the absence of fault. Scenarios in which D could be an innocent volunteer who receives an indisputable windfall at C's expense are difficult to envisage and involve extreme circumstances.[81] A great deal of faith is placed in the ability of the change of position defence to remove any possible injustice to D from the consequences of a strict liability claim. But it is not possible to be confident that the change of position defence as currently formulated in some jurisdictions will adequately protect all innocent recipients.[82] Even where the defence is formulated more in accordance with equitable notions so as to accommodate a greater degree of judicial discretion, the vagaries of litigation mean that there still remains the risk that D will unjustly bear the liability.

An unjust enrichment strict liability claim would overly protect equitable property interests which, by their nature, are often less apparent to third parties and do not generally receive as strong protection as legal property rights.[83] A strong property-protection rationale exists where D retains true trust property or its traceable proceeds [7.5], but where D does not retain the property or it is not true 'trust' property [8.3.2.3], this rationale becomes far less persuasive. Instead, the most pervasive

[79] *Bridgeman* v. *Green* (1757) Wilm 56; 97 ER 22 (HL). See Ridge, 'Third Party Volunteers'. Strict liability is justified by a combination of factors, including the relatively mild impact of the remedy of rescission, absence of strong policy reasons for upholding D's security of receipt and the need to deter parties with influence from circumventing equitable protections.

[80] See Dietrich and Ridge, '"The Receipt of What?"' [81] *Ibid.* 82–85.

[82] Competing formulations of the defence are discussed in *Hills Industries* [2014] HCA 14; (2014) 88 ALJR 552 [78]. The inquiry under Australian law 'is directed to *who* should properly bear the loss and *why*. That inquiry is conducted by reference to equitable principles.' *Cf. Restatement (Third), Restitution and Unjust Enrichment*, §65 (American Law Institute Publishers, St Paul, 2011).

[83] Donovan W. M. Waters (ed.) and Mark R. Gillen (contributing ed.), *Waters' Law of Trusts in Canada*, 4th edn (Thomson Reuters Canada Ltd, 2008) 11.IIA.2(b). See further, L. D. Smith, 'Unjust Enrichment, Property and the Structure of Trusts' (2000) 116 *Law Quarterly Review* 412.

rationale for equitable personal third-party liability comes into play, namely, that it is wrong to *knowingly* take advantage of another's wrong-doing. A strict *personal* liability, based only upon a property-protection rationale, is far less defensible.

The unjust enrichment explanation for recipient liability, whether in substitution for, or in addition to, fault-based liability therefore cannot be accepted as it is currently formulated. Nonetheless, it is an important subtext in the modern case law that helps explain why recipient liability is so often conceptually distinguished from other participatory liabilities and why a lower standard of fault is sometimes accepted.

7.7 Conclusion

The infringement of equitable property rights by third parties in the context of fiduciary custodial relationships gives rise to primary liabilities (trustee de son tort and knowing dealing) and derivative liabilities (the *Re Diplock*, persisting property and recipient liability claims). Of the derivative liabilities, recipient liability is most closely related to equitable accessory liability for procurement and assistance in breach of equitable duties. Because of its positioning between property-based claims and fault-based claims, recipient liability is amenable to more than one plausible explanation. We argue that the best explanation is that it is a fault-based liability that prevents the recipient taking advantage of the primary wrong.

8

Breach of equitable duties

8.1 Introduction

8.1.1 Overview

The principles governing accessory liability for breach of an equitable duty are to be found within the broader principles that govern third-party participatory liability in equity. This chapter sets out the principles of accessory liability within that broader context, including recipient liability. The law governing accessory liability specifically, and participatory liability generally, is confused in some respects and differs across jurisdictions. The confusion is attributable in part to the extraordinary influence of one nineteenth-century Court of Appeal in Chancery decision, *Barnes* v. *Addy*, and specifically, Lord Selborne LC's *ex tempore* leading judgment.[1] *Barnes* v. *Addy* concerned claims against two solicitors who acted in relation to the appointment of a sole trustee to a testamentary trust. The beneficiaries sought redress against the solicitors for the trustee's misappropriation of the trust fund.[2] Lord Selborne was anxious to protect professional agents, particularly solicitors and bankers, acting honestly 'as the agents of trustees in transactions within their legal powers' and dismissed the beneficiaries' appeals.[3] His Lordship did not purport to change the law or to expound generally on the liability of third parties to breach of trust. Nonetheless, during the latter part of the twentieth century, his brief statement as to two exceptional circumstances in which agents of trustees would be liable for a trustee's breach of trust transmogrified into an inflexible

[1] *Barnes* v. *Addy* (1874) LR 9 Ch App 244.

[2] The bill charged that the solicitors 'being fully cognisant [of the trustee's fraud] aided and abetted the same, and were parties to the breach of trust, in conjunction and collusion with the [former and new trustees] ... '. *Barnes* v. *Addy* (1873) 21 WR 324 (Ch) 325. The beneficiaries were unsuccessful at first instance before Wickens VC: *Barnes* v. *Addy* (1873) 21 WR 324 (Ch).

[3] *Barnes* v. *Addy* (1874) LR 9 Ch App 244, 251.

template for equitable participatory liability generally, regardless of whether the participant was an agent or not and irrespective of the nature of the participant's conduct or the primary wrong in question.[4] A distinction was drawn between participants who were involved in the primary wrong through knowingly receiving trust property and those who assisted in egregious breaches of trust (later extended to breach of fiduciary duty more generally) without necessarily receiving property.[5] Little or no attention was paid to primary wrongs other than breach of trust and fiduciary duty. The so-called 'two limbs' of *Barnes* v. *Addy* were often applied in a formulaic and literal fashion. This need not have been so. In contrast to the jurisdictions focused upon in this chapter, the *Barnes* v. *Addy* template has not dominated the United States' jurisprudence on the topic.[6]

In recent times, there has been a move away from the *Barnes* v. *Addy* template in most jurisdictions, but with mixed results. Broadly speaking, there are currently two frameworks used to determine participatory liability for breach of trust and fiduciary duty. These largely involve accessory liability as we understand it, although the equitable

[4] Less attention was paid to the preceding statement that third parties 'actually participating in any fraudulent conduct of the trustee' would be liable: *ibid.*

[5] The original passage in *Barnes* v. *Addy ibid.* 251–252 from which this distinction derives is:

> Those who create a trust clothe the trustee with a legal power and control over the trust property, imposing on him a corresponding responsibility. That responsibility may no doubt be extended in equity to others who are not properly trustees, if they are found either making themselves trustees *de son tort*, or actually participating in any fraudulent conduct of the trustee to the injury of the *cestui que trust*. But, on the other hand, strangers are not to be made constructive trustees merely because they act as the agents of trustees in transactions within their legal powers, transactions, perhaps of which a Court of Equity may disapprove, unless those agents receive and become chargeable with some part of the trust property, or unless they assist with knowledge in a dishonest and fraudulent design on the part of the trustees.

[6] See, e.g., Austin Wakeman Scott, William Franklin Fratcher and Mark L. Ascher, *Scott & Ascher on Trusts*, 5th edn (Boston, Aspen Publishers, 2006) §30.6.4, where *Barnes* v. *Addy* is discussed without special emphasis. Of particular interest is that US law does not apparently single out accessory liability or *in personam* recipient liability as separate categories of liability. See, e.g., the *Restatement (Third) of Trusts* §108 (1) (2012): 'A third party is protected from dealing with or assisting a trustee who is committing a breach of trust if the third party does so without knowledge or reason to know that the trustee is acting improperly.' See further concerning the bona fide purchaser doctrine, *Restatement (Third), Restitution and Unjust Enrichment* §§66–69 (2011), especially Illustrations 12 and 13. Similarly, in *Scott & Ascher* recipient liability is subsumed into the bona fide purchaser doctrine: Ch. 29. See in relation to fiduciaries more generally, *Restatement (Second) of Torts* §874 Comment c (1979): 'A person who knowingly assists a fiduciary in committing a breach of trust is himself guilty of tortious conduct . . . '

principles did not develop by reference to accessory concepts or with such a classificatory scheme in mind. The traditional framework [8.1.4.1] differentiates procurement and knowing assistance and knowing receipt of trust property as instances of participatory liability to which similar elements apply. Culpability is determined according to the third party's knowledge of the primary wrong. The traditional framework holds most sway in Australia and still applies to an extent in Canada's common law courts. The reformed framework [8.1.4.2] on the other hand, combines liability for procurement and assistance and distinguishes liability for receipt of trust property. 'Dishonesty' [3.5.2] and 'unconscionability', rather than knowledge, are the respective culpability tests. The reformed framework was initiated by the Privy Council in the landmark case of *Royal Brunei Airlines Sdn Bhd* v. *Tan* (*Royal Brunei Airlines*).[7] It has been adopted by the English courts and jurisdictions that follow those courts. The requirements for recipient liability are unsettled and have yet to be fully articulated.

Regardless of jurisdictional differences, however, the same two questions dominate the case law. The first concerns the requisite culpable involvement of the third party [3.5.1]. This clearly turns upon the third party's knowledge of the primary wrong, but the courts have struggled to articulate criteria and a methodology that provide certainty for litigants as well as just outcomes. Secondly, although all jurisdictions to a greater or lesser extent differentiate third parties involved in the primary wrong through receipt of trust property and third parties involved in some other way, there is uncertainty as to the proper conceptualisation of recipient liability and its relationship to other instances of equitable third party liability [7.6].

Leaving aside *Barnes* v. *Addy*, the questions that beset participatory liability are policy-driven, rather than doctrinal. In particular, the circumstances in which agents providing professional services to trustees and fiduciaries should be liable for their principals' misconduct raises contested questions of policy. On the one hand, such agents are well placed to detect and deter such misconduct; on the other hand, the consequent liability, not to mention the cost to business, may be disproportionate to the degree of culpability. The issues are acute where it is unclear whether the agent was dishonest or simply incompetent. The complexity of such questions is exacerbated because the principles determining liability of professional agents tend to be indiscriminately

[7] [1995] 2 AC 378 (PC).

bundled together with those for determining the liability of third parties who are intimate with the primary wrongdoer, PW, such as corporate alter egos and spouses.

In this introductory part of the chapter, preliminary questions concerning equitable duties, the rationales of equitable accessory liability, the divergent frameworks and understandings of the liability and the terminology of constructive trusts are addressed. The second part of the chapter discusses the scope of equitable accessory liability, that is, whether it attaches to all equitable duties. The third part describes and evaluates the current law concerning accessory liability and recipient liability for breach of trust and fiduciary duty. The fourth and fifth parts consider, more briefly, accessory liability for breach of confidence and undue influence. The final two parts of the chapter deal with defences and remedies. As explained in [7.6.2], we regard recipient liability as closely related to accessory liability and hence include it in this chapter. For convenience and where it is not misleading, we use the terminology of 'A' to refer to a third party subject to recipient liability. The main focus of the chapter is upon Anglo-Australian law with reference to Canada, New Zealand, Singapore and Hong Kong as appropriate. The law in the US has developed separately from these jurisdictions. It is occasionally referred to in general terms where it provides a helpful point of comparison.[8]

8.1.2 *The primary wrong: equitable wrongs and 'wrongfulness'*

Breach of equitable duty falls within our concept of a primary wrong [3.2] and includes breach of trust, breach of fiduciary duty, breach of confidence and, perhaps, although this is contested, undue influence [8.5.1].

In any event, equity has a more expansive concept of 'wrongfulness' determined by reference to the conscience of the court as exemplified in equitable doctrine and principle.[9] This concept includes, but is not limited to,[10] conduct that is against good conscience whether or not it

[8] As to US sources of law on participation in breach of trust and fiduciary duty see generally, George Gleason Bogert, George Taylor Bogert, Amy Morris Hess, *Bogert's Trusts and Trustees* §§7, 901.

[9] See *Kakavas* v. *Crown Melbourne Limited* [2013] HCA 25; (2013) 250 CLR 292 [15]–[16], quoting John Norton Pomeroy and Spencer W. Symons, *A Treatise of Equity Jurisprudence*, 5th edn (Bancroft-Whitney Company, San Francisco, 1941) §57 (*Pomeroy's Equity*); D. Klinck, 'The Nebulous Equitable Duty of Conscience' (2005) 31 *Queen's Law Journal* 206.

[10] Only unconscionable conduct before or at the time of the primary wrong is relevant to accessory liability, although unconscionability can also arise later: *Tanwar Enterprises Pty*

constitutes breach of pre-existing duty to the claimant, C. Where unconscionability relates to a person's conduct and results in a cause of action being available to C, then, in principle, accessory liability may attach to that cause of action whether or not PW's unconscionable ('wrongful') conduct is conceived of as constituting breach of a duty. This would encompass undue influence if that doctrine is considered not to involve breach of a duty.[11] How accessory liability might attach to doctrines such as undue influence is discussed in [8.5].

It should also be noted for the sake of completeness that not all equitable claims against persons who owe equitable duties are based upon a breach of duty or even wrongful conduct in a wider sense.[12] Where this is so, there is no primary wrong at all and hence no accessory liability on the part of a third party can arise.[13]

8.1.3 The rationales for accessory liability and participatory liability

Equitable accessory liability is fault-based: the accessory's, A's, culpable involvement in the primary wrong grounds liability; see also

Ltd v. *Cauchi* [2003] HCA 57; (2003) 217 CLR 315 [25], citing *Redgrave* v. *Hurd* (1881) 20 Ch D 1, 12–15.

[11] *Cf.* Rick Bigwood, 'Contracts by Unfair Advantage: From Exploitation to Transactional Neglect' (2005) 25 *Oxford Journal of Legal Studies* 65, 67 n.10.

[12] E.g., an account of administration in common form can be claimed against trustees and fiduciaries administering a fund or property on another's behalf without the need to show breach of duty on their part. See *Glazier Holdings Pty Ltd* v. *Australian Men's Health Pty Ltd (No 2)* [2001] NSWSC 6; *Agricultural Land Management Ltd* v. *Jackson [No 2]* [2014] WASC 102; (2014) 285 FLR 121 [334]–[339]; *Ultraframe (UK) Ltd* v. *Fielding* [2005] EWHC 1638; [2006] FSR 17 [1513]–[1517] (*Ultraframe*); *Libertarian Investments Limited* v. *Hall* [2013] HKCFA 93 [166]–[172]; *AIB Group (UK) plc* v. *Mark Redler & Co* [2014] UKSC 58; [2014] 3 WLR 1367 [53] (*AIB Group*). See generally, R. Meagher, D. Heydon and M. Leeming (eds.), *Meagher Gummow and Lehane's Equity: Doctrine and Remedies*, 4th edn (Chatswood, Butterworths LexisNexis, 2002) Ch. 25.

[13] *Cf.* a claim for an account of administration on the basis of wilful default, which generally requires at least one instance of 'wilful default' (a breach of duty by the administrator which has caused something to be lost to the fund or not received by the fund when it should have been received). In an Australian case, a claim for account for wilful default was made against the three directors and an associated company of an insolvent trustee company (the primary wrongdoer). Both Austin J at first instance and Giles JA on appeal noted the fact and commented that the defendants' liability was presumably accessorial here (citing *Barnes* v. *Addy*): *Glazier Holdings Pty Ltd* v. *Australian Men's Health Pty Ltd (No 2)* [2001] NSWSC 6 [8]; *Meehan* v. *Glazier Holdings Pty Ltd* [2001] NSWCA 22; (2002) 54 NSWLR 146 [11], [65]–[66]. See also *Prudential Assurance Co Ltd* v. *Lorenz* (1971) 11 KIR 78 (Ch), in which interlocutory relief was given to restrain a trade union from inducing its members to breach a non-contractual duty to account to the plaintiff employer.

[2.4].[14] Culpability depends upon A's conduct (accessorial involvement), mental state (knowledge) and the consequent participation link to the primary wrong in question [3.5]. A's culpability is described in the cases in terms of two, overlapping rationales; the first such description is pervasive and applies to equitable participatory liability generally. Here, A's culpability is described in terms of A knowingly taking advantage of the equitable relationship between C and PW, for personal gain.[15] This rationale is used in relation to both accessory liability and recipient liability [7.6.2]. The second description of A's culpability has only been applied to accessories and does not require exploitative conduct as such. Thus, it has been said that the beneficiaries of trust and fiduciary relationships are entitled to expect that third parties will not deliberately *interfere* in those relationships.[16]

The fault-based rationale for equitable accessory liability is underpinned by pragmatic rationales that reflect the importance attached to equitable obligations of trust and confidence and the historically strong prophylactic and protective function of equity's jurisdiction over trusts and other fiduciary relationships.[17] One such pragmatic rationale is the courts' desire to deter participation in breach of trust or fiduciary duty, so lessening the risk of wrongdoing by trustees and fiduciaries.[18] Another rationale is to vindicate C's rights by providing

[14] In equitable terms, A's conduct is against good conscience. The legal norm at play here is that it is unconscionable to knowingly interfere with relationships and rights protected by equity. While awareness of the significance of one's actions is not the only norm informing conscience, it is a pervasive theme of equitable doctrines. See further, Klinck, 'The Nebulous Equitable Duty of Conscience', 250–257.

[15] See, e.g., *Consul Development Pty Ltd* v. *DPC Estates Pty Ltd* (1975) 132 CLR 373 (HCA) 397 (*Consul Development*); *Zhu* v. *Treasurer (NSW)* [2004] HCA 56; (2004) 218 CLR 530 [121] (*Zhu*). The same rationale is given in cases of breach of confidence (*Prince Albert* v. *Strange* (1849) 1 Mac & G 25, 44–45; 41 ER 1171, 1178–1179: a third party availing himself of 'a breach of trust, confidence or contract by another' will be injuncted) and undue influence (*Khan* v. *Khan* [2004] NSWSC 1189; (2004) 62 NSWLR 229 [21]). See also *Fyffes Group Ltd* v. *Templeman* [2000] 2 Lloyd's Rep 643 (QB) 669 (Toulson J) (*Fyffes*): 'although [A] owes no personal obligation of loyalty to [C], it is unconscionable for him dishonestly to suborn the loyalty of the agent [PW] and equally unconscionable for him to keep benefits which he has obtained by dishonestly abusing to his own advantage the position of [PW] whose duty was to [C]'.

[16] *Royal Brunei Airlines* [1995] 2 AC 378 (PC) 386–387 (drawing an analogy with the tort of inducing breach of contract). See also *Bogert's Trusts and Trustees*, §901.

[17] P. Finn, 'The Liability of Third Parties for Knowing Receipt or Assistance' in D. Waters (ed.), *Equity, Fiduciaries and Trusts* (Toronto, Carswell, 1993) 195, 197. The discussion in this section is based upon Pauline Ridge, 'Justifying the Remedies for Dishonest Assistance' (2008) 124 *Law Quarterly Review* 445, 446–447.

[18] See, e.g., *Zhu* [2004] HCA 56; (2004) 218 CLR 530 [121].

C with an alternative means of recourse, thereby increasing C's chances of a successful claim.[19] The pragmatic rationales underpinning equity's intervention can be seen most clearly in relation to professional agents of trustees and fiduciaries. Such agents generally receive no personal gain from the breach by PW other than remuneration for their services (hence, culpability in terms of the first description above cannot apply). Generally, they are related to PW only through the agency relationship. They are characteristically well placed to detect and expose trustee or fiduciary misconduct. Imposing accessory liability provides a strong incentive for such parties to minimise the opportunity for fiduciary misconduct and thus lessens the opportunities for such breaches.[20]

The pragmatic rationales that underpin equitable accessory liability are controversial because A becomes jointly and severally liable with PW for all of C's *losses* caused by the breach of trust or fiduciary duty [8.8.1]. Such an extensive liability may be disproportionate to A's involvement in the primary wrong.[21] Although this was historically explicable, there are signs in some jurisdictions of a desire to rein in the liability.[22]

8.1.4 Current frameworks for participatory liability, including accessory liability

8.1.4.1 The traditional framework

The traditional framework for determining equitable participatory – including accessory – liability comprises three overlapping categories. They refer to breach of trust and fiduciary duty:

> A's knowing receipt of, or inconsistent dealing with [7.3],[23] property in breach of trust or fiduciary duty;

[19] *Royal Brunei Airlines* [1995] 2 AC 378 (PC) 386–387.

[20] *Ibid.* See further, Simon Gardner, 'Knowing Assistance and Knowing Receipt: Taking Stock' (1996) 112 *Law Quarterly Review* 56, 79–83.

[21] This is of particular concern with respect to agents providing professional services, the group described by Lord Selborne in *Barnes* v. *Addy* where he was at pains to restrict their liability: (1874) LR 9 Ch App 244, 251–252. See also *Royal Brunei Airlines* [1995] 2 AC 378 (PC) 391.

[22] See in the US, e.g., the development of a 'modernized rule' – comment *d.* – of the *Restatement (Third) of Trusts* §108(3) (2012): 'In dealing with a trustee, a third party need not: (a) inquire into the extent of the trustee's powers or the propriety of their exercise; or (b) ensure that assets transferred to the trustee are properly applied to trust purposes.' See also *Uniform Trust Code* §1012(b).

[23] Lord Selborne LC in *Barnes* v. *Addy* (1874) LR 9 Ch App 244, 251–252, referred to those who 'receive and become chargeable with some part of the trust property', but Brightman J in *Karak Rubber Co Ltd* v. *Burden (No 2)* [1972] 1 WLR 602 (Ch) 633 (*Karak*), adopted

A's knowing assistance in a dishonest and fraudulent design on the part of the trustee or fiduciary;
A's procurement or inducement of any breach of trust or (probably) fiduciary duty.

The traditional framework is largely the product of the twentieth-century judicial distillation of the nineteenth-century authorities on third-party liability for breach of trust.[24] It was not conceived of as a framework for *accessory* liability per se, although it includes that form of liability; instead, broader descriptions such as 'participatory liability' or 'third-party liability' tend to be used.[25] There is little suggestion by courts applying the traditional framework that the three categories might be conceptually, as opposed to factually, distinct.[26] The traditional framework is settled law in Australia.[27] It also continues to inform the Canadian common law with respect to knowing assistance[28] and the New Zealand law with respect to

'as an admirable shorthand description' the sub-heading used in R. E. Megarry and P. V. Baker, *Snell's Principles of Equity*, 26th edn (London, Sweet & Maxwell Ltd, 1966) 202: 'knowing receipt or dealing'. The label is now almost always truncated to 'knowing receipt': *Farah Constructions Pty Limited* v. *Say-Dee Pty Limited* [2007] HCA 22; (2007) 230 CLR 89 [112] (*Farah Constructions*).

24 See especially, *Selangor United Rubber Estates Ltd* v. *Cradock (No 3)* [1968] 1 WLR 1555 (Ch) 1579–1580 (*Selangor*), where Ungoed-Thomas J described two categories of 'constructive trustee'. The first category ('[t]hose who, though not appointed trustees, take upon themselves to act as such and to possess and administer trust property for the beneficiaries ...') included trustees de son tort and those who 'receive and become chargeable with some part of the trust property'. The second category comprised those who participate or assist with knowledge in 'a dishonest and fraudulent design'. See also Brightman J's differently worded categories in *Karak* [1972] 1 WLR 602 (Ch) 633.

25 See also *Hasler* v. *Singtel Optus Pty Ltd* [2014] NSWCA 266; (2014) 101 ACSR 167 [72] (Leeming JA) (*Hasler*): 'ancillary liability'.

26 Indeed, in *Grimaldi* v. *Chameleon Mining NL (No 2)* [2012] FCAFC 6; (2012) 200 FCR 296 [247] (*Grimaldi*), they are grouped with further examples of equitable participatory liability for breach of trust or fiduciary duty that exhibit the same conceptual framework. But see *Hasler* [2014 NSWCA 266; (2014) 101 ACSR 167 [75]. See also the contrary Canadian position: below n. 39.

27 See *Consul Development* (1975) 132 CLR 373, where the High Court of Australia applied *Selangor* [1968] 1 WLR 1555, *Karak* [1972] 1 WLR 602, and *Carl Zeiss Stiftung* v. *Herbert Smith & Co (No 2)* [1969] 2 Ch 276 (*Carl Zeiss*), to a claim of participation in breach of fiduciary duty. See also *Farah Constructions* [2007] HCA 22; (2007) 230 CLR 89.

28 *Air Canada* v. *M & L Travel Ltd* [1993] 3 SCR 787; 108 DLR (4th) 592 (SCC) (*Air Canada*). See also Donovan W. M. Waters (ed.) and Mark R. Gillen (contributing ed.), *Waters' Law of Trusts in Canada*, 4th edn (Thomson Reuters Canada Ltd, 2008) 11.II.A.2.(a); Mysty S. Clapton, 'Gain-Based Remedies for Knowing Assistance: Ensuring Assistants Do Not Profit From Their Wrongs' (2008) 45 *Alberta Law Review* 989, 1004–1008.

knowing receipt, although this may change.[29] Although not a necessary corollary, the framework is associated with a literalist and formulaic methodology.[30]

The formulation of the traditional framework's first two categories derives from Lord Selborne's judgment in *Barnes* v. *Addy*. In conformity with a literal reading of that judgment, liability for assistance is confined to assistance in a 'dishonest and fraudulent design'. Until comparatively recently, the small number of nineteenth-century cases concerning procurement or inducement in breach of trust had escaped much attention.[31] Instead, scenarios involving procurement were dealt with within the 'assistance' category of liability.[32] The cases are now recognised as a third category of liability under the traditional framework.[33]

The traditional framework differs from the nineteenth-century case law in several respects relevant here. First, it applies Lord Selborne's judgment in *Barnes* v. *Addy* regarding agents of trustees to *all* third parties, whether agents or not. Consequently, courts applying the traditional framework have applied the two limbs of *Barnes* v. *Addy* as if they were a comprehensive formula for liability and have tended to ignore the much broader range of circumstances in which the nineteenth- and early-twentieth-century courts imposed participatory liability for breach

[29] *Westpac Banking Corporation* v. *Savin* [1985] 2 NZLR 41 (NZCA) (*Westpac* v. *Savin*), remains the leading authority, but the law is unsettled: *Equiticorp Industries Group Ltd* v. *Hawkins* [1991] 3 NZLR 700 (NZHC) 724–728; *Equiticorp Industries Group Ltd* v. *The Crown* [1998] 2 NZLR 481 (NZHC) 629–639; *Westpac Banking Corp.* v. *M. M. Kembla New Zealand Ltd* [2001] 2 NZLR 298 (NZCA). At the time of writing, the New Zealand Supreme Court has not had occasion to consider the leading English CA decision in *Bank of Credit and Commerce International (Overseas) Ltd* v. *Akindele* [2001] Ch 437.

[30] *Royal Brunei Airlines* [1995] 2 AC 378 (PC) 386. See also P. Finn, 'Knowing Receipt and Knowing Assistance: Balkanising Equity' (25th Annual Banking & Financial Services Law & Practice Conference, New Zealand, July 2008) 5; Pauline Ridge, 'Participatory Liability for Breach of Trust or Fiduciary Duty' in Jamie Glister and Pauline Ridge (eds.), *Fault Lines in Equity* (Oxford, Hart, 2012) 119, 126–127.

[31] *Fyler* v. *Fyler* (1841) 3 Beav 550, 49 ER 216 (*Fyler*); *Eaves* v. *Hickson* (1861) 30 Beav 136, 54 ER 840 (*Eaves*); *Alleyne* v. *Darcy* (1854) 4 I Ch R 199 (*Alleyne*). See also *Elders Trustee & Executor Co Ltd* v. *E.G. Reeves Pty Ltd* (1987) 78 ALR 193 (FCA) 238–239 (*Elders Trustee*) (Gummow J referring to Charles Harpum, 'The Stranger as Constructive Trustee: Part I' (1986) 102 *Law Quarterly Review* 114).

[32] The suggestion that a 'tort of procuring breach of trust' be recognised was nipped in the bud for this reason (as well as for others): *Metall und Rohstoff AG* v. *Donalson Lufkin & Jenrette Inc* [1990] 1 QB 391, 481.

[33] *Farah Constructions* [2007] HCA 22; (2007) 230 CLR 89 [161]. The same cases had been acknowledged by the Privy Council in *Royal Brunei Airlines* [1995] 2 AC 378 (PC). The Privy Council also cited *Attorney-General* v. *Corporation of Leicester* (1844) 7 Beav 176, 49 ER 1031.

of trust or fiduciary duty.[34] Secondly, the nineteenth-century cases primarily concerned express trusts, but under the traditional framework the categories of assistance and procurement apply to breaches of fiduciary duty generally, regardless of whether trust property, even of an extended description, is involved [8.3.1.3]. Finally, while the nineteenth-century courts appear not to have been troubled in applying the knowledge requirement for liability, the modern case law is marked by attempts to pin down this requirement. Thus, a notable feature of the traditional framework is its use of the five-level '*Baden* scale' of knowledge [8.3.4.3].

8.1.4.2 The reformed framework

Under the reformed framework, the three traditional categories (D's receipt, assistance and procurement/inducement) are reshaped into two, conceptually distinct, forms of fault-based liability for breach of trust or fiduciary duty:

> Dishonest procurement or assistance in a breach of trust or fiduciary duty;
> Unconscionable receipt of trust property.

Some features of this new framework can only be described in tentative terms because it derives from two leading cases that are not entirely reconcilable in their approaches and because it is heavily influenced by academic scholarship and extrajudicial commentary that is yet to be fully considered by the courts. The reformed framework has been adopted in England and Wales,[35] Singapore,[36] Hong Kong[37] and New

[34] This applies even to Lord Selborne's judgment itself, in that the comments regarding joint participation in 'any fraudulent conduct of the trustee to the injury of the cestui que trust' are largely ignored. *Barnes* v. *Addy* (1874) LR 9 Ch App 244, 251.

[35] *Twinsectra Ltd* v. *Yardley* [2002] UKHL 12; [2002] 2 AC 164 (*Twinsectra*); *Abou-Rahmah* v. *Abacha* [2006] EWCA Civ 1492; [2007] Bus LR 220 (adopting the further elucidation of dishonest accessory liability by the Privy Council in *Barlow Clowes International Ltd (in liquidation)* v. *Eurotrust International Ltd* [2005] UKPC 37; [2006] 1 WLR 1476 (*Barlow Clowes*).

[36] *George Raymond Zage III* v. *Ho Chi Kwong* [2010] 2 SLR 589 (SCA) (*Zage*). See also *Banque Nationale De Paris* v. *Hew Keong Chan Gary* [2000] 3 SLR (R) 686 (HC); *Caltong (Australia) Pty Ltd* v. *Tong Tien See Construction Pte Ltd (in liquidation)* [2002] 2 SLR (R) 94 (CA); *Bansal Hemant Govindprasad* v. *Central Bank of India* [2003] 2 SLR (R) 33 (CA). See also *Wee Chiaw Sek Anna* v. *Ng Li-Ann Genevieve* [2013] SGCA 36; [2013] 3 SLR 801. See further, Pauline Ridge, 'Equitable Accessory and Recipient Liability in Singapore' (2013) *Singapore Journal of Legal Studies* 361.

[37] *Peconic Industrial Development Ltd* v. *Lau Kwok Fai* [2009] HKCFA 17; [2009] 5 HKC 135 (*Peconic*) (dishonest assistance); *Thanakharn Kasikorn Thai Chamkat (Mahachon)* v. *Akai Holdings Limited (in liq.)* [2010] HKCFA 64; [2011] 1 HKC 357 (*Akai Holdings*)

Zealand[38] as well as in countries bound by the Privy Council. It is also broadly consistent with the Canadian common law.[39]

In relation to the first (accessory) category, procurement and assistance are grouped together and the traditional framework's requirement of assistance in a 'dishonest and fraudulent design' is discarded: the traditional framework's two distinct categories are combined. The fault element here is 'dishonesty' [3.5.2]. A's knowledge is an essential factor in determining whether A was dishonest, but is not the criterion for liability. Instead, there is an inquiry into first, the facts including A's knowledge and, second, whether A was dishonest in all the circumstances. The liability is generally, but inaccurately, referred to as 'dishonest *assistance*'.[40] Although foreshadowed in earlier decisions, the formulation of this first category in substitution for the traditional framework's second two categories was most authoritatively made in 1995 by Lord Nicholls of Birkenhead for the Privy Council in *Royal Brunei Airlines*.[41]

The second category of the reformed framework – recipient liability – in its current form is very similar to that of the traditional framework, namely, knowing receipt of trust property in breach of trust or fiduciary

(unconscionability test for recipient liability stated in *Bank of Credit and Commerce International (Overseas) Ltd* v. *Akindele* [2001] Ch 437 (*Akindele*) assumed to apply in Hong Kong).

38 In relation to dishonest assistance, see *US International Marketing Ltd* v. *National Bank of New Zealand Ltd* [2004] 1 NZLR 589 (NZCA) (*US International Marketing*); *Westpac New Zealand Limited* v. *MAP & Associates Limited* [2011] NZSC 89; [2011] 3 NZLR 751; *Fletcher* v. *Eden Refuge Trust* [2012] NZCA 124; [2012] 2 NZLR 227. The law concerning recipient liability is unsettled. While fault-based, a lower standard than dishonesty suffices. There have been some suggestions that liability should be strict. At the time of writing, *Akindele* [2001] Ch 437 has not been considered in New Zealand. See *Westpac* v. *Savin* [1985] 2 NZLR 41 (NZCA); *Equiticorp Industries Group Ltd* v. *Hawkins* [1991] 3 NZLR 700 (NZHC) 724–728; *Equiticorp Industries Group Ltd* v. *The Crown* [1998] 2 NZLR 481 (NZHC) 629–639; *Westpac Banking Corp.* v. *M. M. Kembla New Zealand Ltd* [2001] 2 NZLR 298 (NZCA).

39 The Canadian Supreme Court adheres to the *Barnes* v. *Addy* two-limb formulation of knowing assistance and knowing receipt, but draws a strong conceptual distinction between the former (which is conscience-based and requires actual knowledge by A) and the latter (which is unjust enrichment-based, although not a strict liability, and which requires constructive knowledge by A). See *Air Canada* [1993] 3 SCR 787; 108 DLR (4th) 592 (SCC); *Gold* v. *Rosenberg* [1997] 3 SCR 767; 152 DLR (4th) 385 (SCC); *Citadel General Assurance Co.* v. *Lloyds Bank Canada* [1997] 3 SCR 805; 152 DLR (4th) 411 (SCC) (*Citadel*).

40 It is even sometimes referred to as 'knowing assistance': *Jyske Bank (Gibraltar) Limited* v. *Spjeldnaes* (CA, 29 July 1999).

41 [1995] 2 AC 378 (PC).

duty.[42] The recipient's knowledge must be 'such as to make it unconscionable for [the recipient] to retain the benefit of the receipt'.[43] The liability is referred to interchangeably as 'unconscionable receipt', 'knowing receipt' and 'recipient liability'. The reformed framework with respect to recipient liability, particularly whether the liability is fault-based, is not yet settled.[44]

8.1.5 *Equitable accessory liability is a secondary ('derivative') and independent liability*

Equitable participatory (including accessory) liability is a 'secondary' liability in the sense that it is dependent upon the commission of a primary wrong by PW [2.3].[45] Nonetheless, A's liability is in respect of his own wrongdoing.[46] It has been suggested by others that the secondary nature of liability for procurement or assistance should be understood in a stronger sense of being duplicative of PW's liability.[47] Once a 'causal nexus' is established between A's conduct and the principal wrong, it is argued, A is treated as though he were a primary wrongdoer.[48] That is, A *becomes* the primary wrongdoer for remedial purposes.

42 See *Akindele* [2001] Ch 437 (CA). As with the traditional framework, the distinct liability of inconsistent dealing with trust property is included: see [7.3].

43 *Ibid.* 455; *Charter plc* v. *City Index Ltd* [2007] EWCA Civ 1382; [2008] Ch 313 (*Charter*).

44 Leave to appeal was refused by the Court of Appeal in *Akindele* [2001] Ch 437 (CA). The Supreme Court has not yet had the opportunity to fully consider recipient liability. But see *Criterion Properties plc* v. *Stratford UK Properties LLC* [2004] UKHL 28; [2004] 1 WLR 1846 [4](*Criterion Properties*); *Twinsectra* [2002] UKHL 12; [2002] 2 AC 164 [105].

45 *Royal Brunei Airlines* [1995] 2 AC 378 (PC) 382; *Vestergaard Frandsen A/S* v. *Bestnet Europe Ltd* [2013] UKSC 31; [2013] 1 WLR 1556 [26]. See further, Ridge, 'Justifying Remedies for Dishonest Assistance'.

46 *Michael Wilson & Partners Ltd* v. *Nicholls* [2011] HCA 48; (2011) 244 CLR 427 [106] (*Michael Wilson*).

47 Steven B. Elliott and Charles Mitchell, 'Remedies for Dishonest Assistance' (2004) 67 *Modern Law Review* 16. Cited with approval in *Ultraframe* [2005] EWHC 1638 (Ch); [2006] FSR 17 [1600]. The argument was subsequently revised in Charles Mitchell and Stephen Watterson, 'Remedies for Knowing Receipt' in Charles Mitchell (ed.), *Constructive and Resulting Trusts* (Oxford, Hart Publishing, 2009) 115, 150–153. Elliott and Mitchell drew upon Philip Sales, 'The Tort of Conspiracy and Civil Secondary Liability' (1990) 49 *Cambridge Law Journal* 491. See also Charles Harpum, 'Knowing Receipt: The Need for a New Landmark: Some Reflections' in W. R. Cornish, R. Nolan, J. O'Sullivan and G. Virgo (eds.), *Restitution: Past Present and Future* (Oxford, Hart Publishing, 1998) 247, 248.

48 In equity, the causal nexus was said (in accordance with the prevailing fault element) to be A's *knowing* procurement of, or assistance in, the primary wrong: Sales, 'The Tort of Conspiracy', 508 n. 58.

If considered purely in terms of loss-based remedies,[49] the 'duplicative liability' thesis might explain why A is liable for all losses flowing from the primary wrong with no separate enquiry undertaken into whether A's conduct was a cause of those losses and why A is generally held to be jointly and severally liable with PW [8.8].[50] But there are other equally credible explanations for these principles. For example, a claimant-favouring approach to remedy that dispenses with a 'but for' causation inquiry is consistent with the pragmatic rationales underpinning accessory liability for breach of trust and fiduciary duty. It is only in relation to C that questions of causal responsibility for C's losses are ignored; as between A and PW such issues are relevant and go to the question of contribution [8.8.3]. Furthermore, the duplicative liability thesis does not explain why, if A's liability is duplicative of PW's liability, A should be liable for gain-based remedies in relation to A's *own* gain.[51] Conversely, duplicative liability logically encompasses A's liability for PW's gains and yet the justice of this is not at all self-evident.[52] Thus, equitable participatory (including accessory) liability is an independent wrong that is derivative in that it is dependent upon the commission of a primary wrong, but that is not duplicative of PW's liability; see further [2.6].[53]

8.1.6 An equitable tort?

Perceived similarities between accessory liability for assisting breach of an equitable duty and some torts have led to suggestions that there is a

[49] This was done in Sales' original article. The duplicative liability theory with respect to loss-based remedies has attracted some support. See, e.g., Graham Virgo, *The Principles of Equity and Trusts* (Oxford University Press, 2012) 697–699, 709–711.

[50] It is also argued that the procedure of account can only be taken against a custodian of the trust fund, namely PW, and hence cannot be available against A unless A's liability is duplicative of PW's liability. A's liability 'duplicates the trustee's primary liability for substitutive performance of his custodial duties': Mitchell and Watterson, 'Remedies for Knowing Receipt', 153. But this view of account and its relationship to equitable compensation is disputed: see [8.7.2].

[51] This was acknowledged by Elliott and Mitchell: 'Remedies for Dishonest Assistance', 40.

[52] *Michael Wilson* [2011] HCA 48; (2011) 244 CLR 427 [106]. See further, Ridge, 'Justifying Remedies for Dishonest Assistance'; Gardner, 'Knowing Assistance and Knowing Receipt', 72–73.

[53] *Michael Wilson ibid.* See also, Lord Nicholls, 'Knowing Receipt: the Need for A New Landmark' in Cornish, Nolan, O'Sullivan and Virgo (eds.), *Restitution*, 231, 244.

general tort of knowing assistance that could subsume some of equitable accessory liability.[54] These suggestions have been rejected.[55]

8.1.7 *The terminology of constructive trusts*

Traditionally, the liability of an accessory or other third party to breach of an equitable duty is described as being that of a 'constructive trustee'. Although the term 'constructive trust' originated in the late seventeenth century,[56] its use to describe the personal liability of an accessory who did not necessarily hold trust property (a 'constructive *trusteeship*') is harder to pin down. The change appears to have happened without express acknowledgement by the courts and as the logical consequence of finding that third-party participants should be treated in the same way as trustees for the purposes of liability.[57] 'Constructive trustee' denoted that A was to be subject to the same liability as the express trustee even though not

[54] See e.g., M. Jones (general ed.) *Clerk & Lindsell on Torts*, 20th edn (London, Sweet & Maxwell, 2010) 1623, but *cf.* 1621, and generally 1619–1624; in *OBG* v. *Allen* [2007] UKHL 21; [2008] 1 AC 1 [189], Lord Nicholls left open such a possibility. The tort is unnecessary, since equitable principles of accessory liability adequately cover the field. See, e.g., *Metall und Rohstoff AG* v. *Donaldson Lufkin & Jenrette Inc.* [1990] 1 QB 391 (*Metall und Rohstoff*), and Robert Stevens, *Torts and Rights* (Oxford University Press, 2007) 283. Such suggestions have been made for strategic reasons so as to come within the wording of court rules concerning service outside a jurisdiction (as in *Metall und Rohstoff*) or to attract vicarious liability (*Credit Lyonnais Bank Nederland NV* v. *Export Credits Guarantee Department* [2000] 1 AC 486).

[55] *Metall und Rohstoff* [1990] 1 QB 391 (CA) 474; *Credit Lyonnais Bank Nederland NV* v. *Export Credits Guarantee Department* Bank [1998] 1 Lloyd's Law Rep 19 (CA) 46. However, similarities between the fault-based nature, and compensatory remedies, of equitable liability and tort claims generally have been noted. See, e.g., *Grupo Torras SA* v. *Al-Sabah* [2001] CLC 221 (CA) 255–256.

[56] The use of the term is attributed to the influence of Lord Nottingham both in his judicial capacity and as draftsman of s. 8 of the Statute of Frauds 1677 (referring to trusts which 'arise or result by implication of construction of law'). Lionel Smith, 'Constructive Trusts and Constructive Trustees' (1999) 58 *Cambridge Law Journal* 294, 297–298. It referred to a trust construed from the circumstances and imposed upon property.

[57] See, e.g., *Fyler* (1841) 3 Beav 548, 561; 49 ER 216, 221, where Lord Langdale MR said of solicitors alleged to have procured a breach of trust for personal benefit, 'the Court ought to impute to them the duty of seeing to the due application of this trust money; in other words, will impute to them the character of trustees'. See also *Rolfe* v. *Gregory* (1865) 4 De G J & S 576, 579; 46 ER 1042, 1043–1044. One explanation for the terminology is that it overcame the rule that trust beneficiaries could not sue anyone other than a trustee. Smith, 'Constructive Trusts', 300. A similar suggestion is that because equity did not generally award monetary remedies, it was necessary to draw upon an established source of such relief, namely the trustee's obligation to account: William Swadling, 'The Fiction of the Constructive Trust' (2011) *Current Legal Problems* 399, 412.

appointed as such.[58] The procedural ramifications of this designation (particularly in relation to statutory limitations periods [8.6.3]) and the confusion generated by applying it to all third parties, whatever the basis of liability, were not settled during the nineteenth century and continue to cause some problems.

Constructive trust terminology has become controversial or, at the least, is said to be 'sometimes unhelpful'.[59] The terminology can be misleading in the context of third-party liability and ideally should be avoided because, generally, the third party is not a fiduciary and does not hold property.[60] They are simply 'accountable in equity'; that is, the liability is for an independent wrong [2.3.3].[61] Ungoed-Thomas J's statement that the term is no more than a 'formula for equitable relief' is widely accepted.[62] An historical understanding of the terminology of constructive trusts is still crucial to understanding the current law, however, given its continuing presence in legislation.[63]

8.2 The scope of accessory liability

The frameworks of equitable accessory liability refer to breach of trust without further elaboration when describing the primary wrong in question.[64] The liability also attaches to breaches of fiduciary duty by non-trustees, although the extent to which this is so is obscured by a lack of consensus as to the meaning of 'fiduciary duty' [8.3.1.2]. For example, it is

58 *Soar* v. *Ashwell* [1893] 2 QB 390 (CA) 405 (Kay LJ): '[T]he stranger is not expressly appointed a trustee. He becomes bound by the trust by the construction which the law puts upon his dealings with the trust property.'

59 *Grimaldi* [2012] FCAFC 6; (2012) 200 FCR 296 [242].

60 *Dubai Aluminium Co Ltd* v. *Salaam* [2002] UKHL 48; [2003] 2 AC 366 [141] (*Dubai Aluminium*). Lord Browne-Wilkinson's suggestion in *Westdeutsche Landesbank Girozentrale* v. *Islington London Borough Council* [1996] AC 669, 705 (*Westdeutsche*), that in this instance a trust arises without the need for property has not been accepted: Elliott and Mitchell, 'Remedies for Dishonest Assistance', 21.

61 *Dubai* [2002] UKHL 48; [2003] 2 AC 366 [142]. It has been queried whether even 'accountable' is a necessary description of D's liability: Swadling, 'The Fiction of the Constructive Trust', 415.

62 *Selangor* [1968] 1 WLR 1555, 1582; *Paragon Finance* v. *DB Thakerar* [1999] 1 All ER 400 (CA) 408–409 (*Paragon*); *Dubai Aluminium* [2002] UKHL 48; [2003] 2 AC 366 [140].

63 See, e.g., in relation to statutory limitation periods, *Williams* v. *Central Bank of Nigeria* [2014] UKSC 10; [2014] 2 WLR 355 (*Williams*). Some courts retain the terminology of constructive trusts in the sense of 'a personal liability to account in the same manner as that of an express trustee': *Giumelli* v. *Giumelli* [1999] HCA 10; (1999) 196 CLR 101 [4].

64 See, e.g., *Barnes* v. *Addy* (1874) LR 9 Ch App 244; *Royal Brunei Airlines* [1995] 2 AC 378 (PC).

unclear whether accessory liability attaches to breach of some of the (possibly non-'fiduciary') equitable duties held by non-trustee fiduciaries; this is discussed below in relation to the duties that regulate the exercise of a company director's discretionary powers [8.3.1.2].

Returning to the scope of accessory liability more generally, the grounds for such liability in relation to any equitable duty are strongest where A's involvement consists of procurement of the primary wrong. Liability for procuring the violation of another's right is recognised across private law [3.3.5]. Furthermore, the rationales for *equitable* liability [8.1.3] have the greatest force here. This may be so even where the primary wrong is breach of an equitable duty of care. For example, if a solicitor, A, procures a breach of trust by advising a trustee client, PW, to make an (imprudent) investment of trust funds that will benefit A, accessory liability should arise given A's intentional exploitation of the trust relationship for personal benefit. There is case law to support liability for procurement of breach of trust, including non-fiduciary trust duties.[65]

The possibility of accessory liability that extends much beyond the trust, agency and corporate contexts has received little attention, perhaps because it is easier outside those contexts for a third party involved in equitable wrongdoing to become subject to the same principal liability as the original wrongdoer [2.7], [8.4.1]. Hence, accessory liability has less practical significance. The equitable duty of confidence is an example of where accessory liability may arise [8.4], but will not often be necessary.[66] The equitable duties of a mortgagee are another example of where accessory liability is available in principle.[67] There seems no reason why accessory liability cannot apply to such duties.[68] The doctrine of

[65] See, e.g., *Fyler* (1841) 3 Beav 550; 49 ER 216; *Alleyne* (1854) 4 I Ch R 199. See also *City of Atascadero* v. *Merrill Lynch* 80 Cal Rptr 2d 329, 68 Cal App 4th 445 (1998) (California Court of Appeal), where it was claimed that a financial broker and adviser to a statutory investment trustee procured breaches of the trustee's duty to invest. The trustee engaged in a highly imprudent investment programme. The claim for inducement or participation in a breach of trust was recognised, although it was necessary that A acted 'for personal gain or in furtherance of his or her own financial advantage'; this was satisfied on the alleged facts.

[66] On whether the duty of confidence is fiduciary, *cf.* P. D. Finn, *Fiduciary Obligations* (Sydney, Law Book Company, 1977); M. Conaglen, *Fiduciary Loyalty* (Oxford, Hart Publishing, 2010) 236–244.

[67] See *Downsview Nominees Ltd* v. *First City Corporation Ltd* [1993] AC 295 (PC). See also P. Young, C. Croft and M. Smith, *On Equity* (Sydney, Lawbook, 2009) [9.80], describing the mortgagee as a 'quasi-fiduciary'.

[68] R. P. Austin, 'Constructive Trusts' in P. D. Finn (ed.) *Essays in Equity* (Sydney, Law Book Company, 1985) 196, 200 ('liability of a third party who benefits from an abuse of power by a mortgagee'). But mortgagees may also attract core fiduciary duties, breach of which

undue influence and other doctrines that focus upon vitiation of transactions raise particular questions that are discussed in [8.5].

Instances of equitable duties, arising without there being a fiduciary or a fiduciary-like relationship, are limited. A clear example concerns the duties governing the exercise of a power of appointment over a trust fund by a non-trustee donee ('appointer') of the power.[69] The exercise of a power of appointment is subject to the doctrine of fraud on the power.[70] A fraud on the power renders an appointment of trust property invalid.[71] A common instance of fraud on a power is where an appointer arranges with one of the objects of the power to appoint to that person who will then transfer some of the property back to the appointer or to a stranger.[72]

The conduct of the object of the power here could be characterised as accessorial involvement (through assistance) in a primary wrong (the fraud on the power committed by the appointer), but is it necessary to do so? An appointment will still be invalid absent such involvement if a fraud on the power is committed.[73] Nor is it necessary that the object know of the fraud: the usual requisite mental element for accessory liability is not required. In other words, all the elements of accessory liability may be *factually* present, but they are not legally necessary where it is possible to restore the subject matter of the invalid appointment to the trust.

Where it is not possible to restore the trust property, the remedial consequences of the fraud are visited upon the appointer (and, in some circumstances, upon a trustee who carried out the appointer's instructions) on the current law, but not upon the object of the power.[74] That is, the 'liability' of the object of the power appears to be limited by the extent to which rescission of the appointment is possible. It is here that accessory liability could, as a matter of principle, have a role to play.

can engage accessory liability: see *Bofinger* v. *Kingsway Group Limited* [2009] HCA 44; (2009) 239 CLR 269 [49]–[51].

69 See generally, Geraint Thomas, *Thomas on Powers*, 2nd edn (Oxford University Press, 2012) Ch. 10.

70 See *Vatcher* v. *Paull* [1915] AC 372 (PC) 378 (Lord Parker) (*Vatcher*): the doctrine operates where 'the power has been exercised for a purpose, or with an intention, beyond the scope of or not justified by the instrument creating the power'. See generally, Thomas, *Thomas on Powers*, Ch. 9.

71 *Ibid.*

72 *Ibid.* See, e.g., *Aleyn* v. *Belchier* (1758) 1 Eden 132; 28 ER 634 (power of jointure); *Daubeny* v. *Cockburn* (1816) 1 Mer 626; 35 ER 801; *Birley* v. *Birley* (1858) 25 Beav 299; 53 ER 651. See also Young, Croft and Smith, *On Equity*, [8.880].

73 *Vatcher* [1915] AC 372 (PC) 378.

74 See Thomas, *Thomas on Powers*, [9.119], [9.121].

8.3 Accessory and recipient liability for breach of trust and fiduciary duties

8.3.1 The primary wrong

8.3.1.1 Breach of trust

Equitable accessory liability attaches to the breach of any express trust, including charitable[75] trusts. The liability also attaches to constructive trusts[76] and to so-called *Quistclose* trusts, whether considered to be express or resulting trusts.[77] It has been suggested that constructive trustees do not owe fiduciary duties where the trust is simply a remedial device for transferring title to property and, hence, accessory liability cannot attach to 'breach' of such a constructive trust,[78] but this cannot be correct in relation to breaches of such a trust that involve the trust property.[79]

Practically speaking, it is difficult to envisage scenarios where A might be culpably involved in breach of any of a trustee's duties of care, unless A has procured the trustee's carelessness [8.2], or has knowingly received trust property as a result of such carelessness. Accessory or recipient liability should apply in those instances, but otherwise – assuming such a scenario could arise at all[80] – it is not immediately apparent why equitable liability should attach for *assistance* in PW's carelessness given the contrary position at common law with respect to accessory liability for breach of duties of care [5.5.5]. Such liability could be supported on the

75 See, e.g., *Fletcher* v. *Eden Refuge Trust* [2012] NZCA 124; [2012] 2 NZLR 227.

76 In relation to assistance-based liability, see, e.g., *Grupo Torras SA* v. *Al-Sabah (No.5)* [1999] CLC 1469 (QB), and the cases discussed in Charles Mitchell, 'Assistance' in Peter Birks and Arianna Pretto (eds.), *Breach of Trust* (Oxford, Hart Publishing 2002) 139, 166–168. In relation to recipient liability, see, e.g., *K & S Corporation Ltd* v. *Sportingbet Australia Pty Ltd* [2003] SASC 96; (2003) 86 SASR 312 (stolen money); *Wambo Coal Pty Ltd* v. *Stuart Karim Ariff* [2007] NSWSC 589; (2007) 25 ACLC 809 (mistaken payment); *Armstrong DLW GmbH* v. *Winnington Networks Ltd* [2012] EWHC 10; [2013] Ch 156 (*Armstrong*) (fraudulently transferred carbon emission allowance).

77 *Twinsectra* [2002] UKHL 12; [2002] 2 AC 164; *George* v. *Webb* [2011] NSWSC 1608 [282].

78 *Nicholson* v. *Morgan [No 3]* [2013] WASC 110 [55] (*Nicholson*).

79 See *CGU Insurance Limited* v. *One.Tel Limited (in liq.)* [2010] HCA 26; (2010) 242 CLR 174 [36]: 'One obligation of a trustee which exists by virtue of the very office is the obligation to get the trust property in, protect it, and vindicate the rights attaching to it.' See also L. Smith, 'Constructive Fiduciaries?' in P. Birks (ed.), *Privacy and Loyalty* (Oxford, Clarendon Press, 1997) 249, 262–267. Mitchell, 'Assistance', 166.

80 It probably cannot arise under the traditional framework given the requirement that assistance be in a 'dishonest and fraudulent design' by PW [8.3.1.4].

basis that *all* trust duties are fiduciary in nature, but this is not a widely accepted view.[81]

Property under the control of a fiduciary is treated as trust property for the purposes of recipient liability.[82] For example, breaches of fiduciary duty by company directors in relation to company assets are considered breaches of trust for the purpose of recipient liability on the basis that the company's property is analogised to trust property [8.3.2.3].

8.3.1.2 Breach of fiduciary duty

There has been a shift of emphasis in case law and commentaries since the nineteenth century from 'fiduciary' as the descriptor of an office-holder whose equitable[83] duties were thereby all imbued with fiduciary characteristics to 'fiduciary' as the descriptor of particular duties, most notably the proscriptive duties not to engage in a conflict of interest and not to profit from the fiduciary position.[84] There is now a body of judicial opinion that not all equitable duties held by a fiduciary are 'fiduciary' duties.[85] There is also disagreement as to whether 'fiduciary' is the appropriate descriptor of a relationship of confidence or of undue influence.[86] Such questions, while beyond the scope of this book, are relevant to it because it is sometimes assumed that only fiduciary duties (or, alternatively, only trust and fiduciary duties) attract accessory liability, a view with which we disagree.

Accessory liability clearly attaches to the fiduciary duties concerning conflict of interest and profiting from the fiduciary position. It is not as clear whether it attaches to other equitable duties that regulate the exercise of a fiduciary's discretionary powers. There is an immense body of law governing the exercise of such powers by trustees, company directors and other fiduciaries; consequently, it is dangerous to

[81] See generally, Antony Goldfinch, 'Trustee's Duty to Exercise Reasonable Care: Fiduciary Duty?' (2004) 78 *Australian Law Journal* 678. See also Thomas, *Thomas on Powers*, [1.46]–[1.49].

[82] *Russell* v. *Wakefield Waterworks Co* (1875) LR 20 Eq 474 (Ch). For a recent example, see *Statek Corporation* v. *McNeill Alford* [2008] EWHC 32 (Ch).

[83] Of course, a fiduciary will generally hold common law duties as well.

[84] See, e.g., *Bristol and West Building Society* v. *Mothew* [1998] Ch 1 (*Bristol*); *Breen* v. *Williams* (1996) 186 CLR 71 (HCA).

[85] See, e.g., *LAC Minerals Ltd* v. *International Corona Resources Ltd* (1989) 61 DLR (4th) 14 (SCC) 28; *Breen* v. *Williams* (1996) 186 CLR 71 (HCA); *Bristol* [1998] Ch 1. *Contra.* Hon. Dyson Heydon QC, 'Modern Fiduciary Liability: the Sick Man of Equity?' (2014) 20 *Trusts & Trustees* 1006.

[86] *Cf.* Finn, *Fiduciary Obligations*; Conaglen, *Fiduciary Loyalty*, 236–244. See also [8.5].

generalise.[87] Broadly speaking, the duties encompass duties to exercise such powers in good faith and for proper purposes, as well as duties of care in relation to specific powers. Breach of such duties may involve a breach of the conflict or profit prohibitions[88] (in which case, accessory liability attaches), but not necessarily. Generally, breach of a duty governing the exercise of a fiduciary's discretionary power renders the exercise of the power voidable; that is, the relevant doctrines have a vitiating function and accessory liability questions simply do not arise.[89] On the other hand, it tends to be assumed that accessory liability attaches to all breaches of duty by a trustee.[90]

The question of whether accessory liability may attach to the breach of duties regulating the exercise of fiduciary powers by company directors, not involving the conflict and profit rules, was raised, albeit not by the pleadings, in the Australian case of *Westpac Banking Corporation* v. *Bell Group Ltd (in liq.)*.[91] The issue was formulated as whether directors' duties to act in the best interests of the company and for proper purposes were 'fiduciary' so as to attract accessory liability. Several lower court decisions had assumed this to be so.[92] The case concerned refinancing transactions entered into between the appellant banks and the directors of the Bell group of companies at a time when the Bell group was insolvent. The banks thereby became secured, rather than unsecured, creditors of the group and obtained full repayment of their loans in the subsequent insolvencies of the group. The directors were held to have breached duties to act bona fides in the best interests of each company and to exercise their powers for proper purposes, but not to have breached the conflict and profit duties. The litigation focused upon whether the banks could be liable as accessories. A majority in the West Australian Court of Appeal held that the relevant duties were fiduciary and the banks were so liable; leave to appeal was

87 See generally, the specialist text, Thomas, *Thomas on Powers*, especially Chs. 9–10.

88 *Moulin Global Eyecare Holdings Ltd (in liq.)* v. *Lee* [2014] HKCFA 63 [36].

89 *Cf.* [8.2] (the doctrine of fraud on a power) and [8.5] (undue influence and similar doctrines).

90 Subject to the traditional framework's 'dishonest and fraudulent design' requirement for knowing assistance: [8.3.1.4].

91 [2012] WASCA 157; (2012) 44 WAR 1. See further, the Hon. T. F. Bathurst and Sienna Merope, 'It Tolls for Thee: Accessory Liability after *Bell* v. *Westpac*' (2013) 87 *Australian Law Journal* 831; Pauline Ridge, 'Equitable Accessory Liability: Moving Beyond *Barnes* v. *Addy*' (2014) 8 *Journal of Equity* 28 (the discussion in this section draws upon this article).

92 See, e.g., *Linter Group Ltd* v. *Goldberg* (1992) 7 ACSR 580 (VSC); *Farrow Finance Co Ltd (in liq.)* v. *Farrow Properties Pty Ltd (in liq.)* [1999] 1 VR 584 (VSC) (*Farrow*); *Kalls Enterprises Pty Ltd (in liq.)* v. *Baloglow* [2007] NSWCA 191; (2007) 63 ACSR 557.

granted by the High Court, but the parties settled before the hearing. The underlying question of principle that remains is whether accessory liability should attach to such duties, regardless of their labelling.

A principled approach is to determine whether accessory liability in relation to a particular duty is consistent with the equitable rationales for liability,[93] coherent when viewed in the broader private law context, including analogous statutory regimes,[94] and consistent with good policy.[95] But even this approach is likely to yield different outcomes because the policy issues in the corporate context are contested.[96] There is, however, a substantial consensus against equitable accessory liability for breach of an equitable duty of care, other than in cases of procurement [8.2].

93 See [8.1.3]; *Westpac Banking Corporation* v. *Bell Group Ltd (in liq.) No. 3* [2012] WASCA 157; (2012) 44 WAR 1 [2148] (*Westpac* v. *Bell*).

94 See, e.g., the Australian statutory regime in the Corporations Act 2001 (Cth) ss. 79, 180–183. The Act provides for accessory liability for 'involvement' (s. 79) in the breach of some duties of directors and company officers (e.g. the duty to 'exercise their powers and discharge their duties: (a) in good faith in the best interests of the corporation; and (b) for a proper purpose': s. 181; see also ss. 182–183), but not for breach of the statutory duty of care and diligence (s. 180). This has been relied upon by analogy to support equitable accessory liability in relation to equitable duties other than the duty of care: Hon. W. Gummow, 'The Equitable Duties of Company Directors' (2013) 87 *Australian Law Journal* 753. See also Ridge, 'Moving beyond *Barnes* v. *Addy*', 40–43. *Contra.* J.D. Heydon, 'Are the Duties of Company Directors to Exercise Care and Skill Fiduciary?' in Simone Degeling and James Edelman (eds), *Equity in Commercial Law* (Pyrmont, Lawbook Co, 2005) 185, 235, and 'Modern fiduciary liability', 1011–1012. The English statutory regime in the Companies Act 2006 (UK) does not as readily lend itself to this form of legal reasoning because the statutory duties replace a director's equitable duties: s. 170(3). The statutory duties are to 'be interpreted and applied in the same way as common law rules or equitable principles, and regard shall be had to the corresponding common law rules and equitable principles in interpreting and applying the general duties': s. 170(4). On the other hand, the duties contained in ss. 171–177, except the 'duty to exercise reasonable care, skill and diligence' in s. 174, are said to be 'enforceable in the same way as any other fiduciary duty owed to a company by its directors': s. 178(2). A literal reading of s. 178 suggests that accessory liability applies to all statutory duties regulating the exercise of directors' fiduciary powers, other than the duty of care.

95 See, e.g., Bathurst and Merope, 'It tolls for thee', 834: limiting accessory liability to breach of the conflict and profit duties of company directors appropriately balanced 'the right of the company and through it, its members and creditors, to be protected against improper and improvident transactions and the rights of third parties dealing with the company'. See also *Westpac* v. *Bell* [2012] WASCA 157; (2012) 44 WAR 1 [3060]–[3066] (Carr AJA).

96 *Cf.* Gummow, 'The Equitable Duties of Company Directors' and Bathurst and Merope, 'It tolls for thee'.

8.3.1.3 Must there be a misapplication of trust property?

Recipient liability obviously requires that there be a misapplication of trust property, but is this also a requirement for accessory liability? In Australia and Canada, knowing assistance liability for breach of trust or fiduciary duty can arise whether or not the primary wrong involves trust property.[97] The law is not as clear in the English courts in relation to dishonest procurement or assistance in breach of trust or fiduciary duty. Judgments in the House of Lords and Supreme Court have implied, without direct consideration of the issue, that the primary wrong must involve a misapplication of trust property.[98] The issue has been addressed in the English Court of Appeal on a number of occasions[99] where the opposite view now prevails:

> [I]n a case for accessory liability there is no requirement for there to be trust property. Such a requirement wrongly associates accessory liability with trust concepts ... Accessory liability does not involve a trust. It involves providing dishonest assistance to somebody else who is in a fiduciary capacity [and] has committed a breach of his fiduciary duties.[100]

This must be correct. It is the culpability of A's knowing involvement in the primary wrong that grounds A's liability. While the trust is the

[97] Neither of the two leading cases on knowing assistance in Australia involved trust property: *Consul Development* (1975) 132 CLR 373; *Farah Constructions* [2007] HCA 22; (2007) 230 CLR 89. The Canadian courts do not appear to require a misapplication of trust property; see Waters and Gillen, *Waters' Law of Trusts,* 11.II.A(2) (c). Although there is no case on point, this must also be true of procurement liability in those jurisdictions. On the other hand, both jurisdictions require that the breach of trust be 'dishonest and fraudulent' for knowing assistance liability: [8.3.1.4].

[98] See, e.g., *Twinsectra* [2002] UKHL 12; [2002] 2 AC 164 [107]; *Barlow Clowes* [2005] UKPC 37; [2006] 1 WLR 1476 [28]; *Williams* [2014] UKSC 10; [2014] 2 WLR 355 [9] (Lord Sumption JSC, Lord Hughes JSC agreeing): dishonest assistance and knowing receipt described as both involving 'participation in the unlawful misapplication of trust assets'. For a discussion of the Singapore cases on this point, see Ridge, 'Equitable Accessory and Recipient Liability in Singapore', 365–366.

[99] See, e.g., *Satnam Investments Ltd* v. *Dunlop Heywood & Co Ltd* [1999] 3 All ER 652 (CA) 671 (*Satnam*) (apparently of the view that for either dishonest accessory liability or recipient liability 'there must be trust property or traceable proceeds of trust property'); *Petrotrade Inc* v. *Smith* [2000] 1 Lloyd's Rep 486 (dishonest assistance claim rejected for lack of a trust); *Goose* v. *Wilson Sandford & Co.* [2001] Lloyd's Rep PN 189 (CA) [86]–[88] (querying *Satnam*).

[100] *Novoship (UK) Limited* v. *Yuri Nikitin* [2014] EWCA Civ 908 [92] (Longmore, Moore-Bick and Lewison LJJ), quoting *JD Wetherspoon Plc* v. *Van de Berg & Co Ltd* [2009] EWHC 639 (Ch) [510]–[520] (Peter Smith J). *Cf. Fiona Trust & Holding Corporation* v. *Yuri Privalov* [2010] EWHC 3199 (Comm) [61]. See also *Brown* v. *Bennett* [1999] 1 BCLC 649 (CA) 657–659.

paradigm of a relationship protected by equity, and hence the pragmatic rationales supporting accessory liability are very strong, these are not restricted to protection of C's property interests [8.1.3].

8.3.1.4 Must there be a dishonest and fraudulent design?

An issue that differentiates the traditional and reformed frameworks for liability is whether an egregious breach of trust or fiduciary duty – 'a dishonest and fraudulent design' – is required if A's accessory conduct is by way of assistance, rather than procurement.[101] The 'dishonest and fraudulent design' requirement was jettisoned by the Privy Council in *Royal Brunei Airlines* on the grounds that it had no basis in principle.[102] Whether PW acted fraudulently was not a logical precondition for A to have acted culpably.[103] Conversely, the High Court of Australia has retained the 'dishonest and fraudulent design' requirement for the time being.[104] The Court held that the phrase 'was to be understood by reference to equitable principles', but did not elaborate further.[105]

In a comprehensive judgment in the NSW Court of Appeal, Leeming JA has explained that, when viewed in its historical context, Lord Selborne's use of the words 'dishonest and fraudulent' was deliberate clarification that more (namely, dishonesty) was required than equitable, as opposed to common law, fraud.[106] Such clarification was a necessary precaution as the meaning of 'fraud' was contested in the late nineteenth century. According to Leeming JA, a design will be dishonest and fraudulent where it transgresses 'ordinary standards of honest behaviour'.[107] The 'dishonest and fraudulent design' requirement has also been retained

[101] *Barnes* v. *Addy* (1874) LR 9 Ch App 244, 251–252.

[102] [1995] 2 AC 378 (PC). It was said to be the result of a formulaic application of Lord Selborne's fact-specific statement in *Barnes* v. *Addy*.

[103] Lord Nicholls drew on the nineteenth-century cases concerning procurement of a breach of trust to support this position: in those cases any breach of trust sufficed. See *Fyler* (1841) 3 Beav 550, 49 ER 216; *Eaves* (1861) 30 Beav 136; 54 ER 840; *Attorney-General* v. *Corporation of Leicester* (1844) 7 Beav 176; 49 ER 1031.

[104] *Farah Constructions* [2007] HCA 22; (2007) 230 CLR 89 [161]–[163], [179]–[184](albeit in obiter).

[105] *Ibid.* [181]. In *Westpac* v. *Bell* [2012] WASCA 157; (2012) 44 WAR 1 [2112]–[2125] (Drummond AJA), [1099] (Lee AJA), the majority interpreted *Farah Constructions* as requiring only that 'the breach of duty is more than a trivial breach and is also too serious to be excusable because the fiduciary has acted honestly, reasonably and ought fairly to be excused' [2112]. This was rejected by the NSW CA as 'plainly wrong': *Hasler* [2014] NSWCA 266; (2014) 101 ACSR 167 [102] (Leeming JA). See also *Nicholson* [2013] WASC 110; 8 ASTLR 277, 292 [59]; *Alexander* v. *Burne* [2013] NSWSC 1953 [18] (Young AJ): 'There must be a plan or intention to defraud the beneficiary.'

[106] *Hasler* [2014] NSWCA 266; (2014) 101 ACSR 167 [122]–[123]. [107] *Ibid.* [124].

by the Supreme Court of Canada[108] and is interpreted to mean 'the taking of a risk to the prejudice of another's rights, which risk is known to be one which there is no right to take'.[109]

Lord Selborne's objective in *Barnes* v. *Addy* was to contain the liability of professional agents within reasonable limits. An egregious, premeditated breach of trust was required in that setting to counteract the fact that the agent was a mere assistant who did not benefit personally from the breach of trust.[110] The culpability of an accessory who knowingly assists a dishonest trustee is of a greater magnitude and the rationale for accessory liability is strongly engaged. Whether there was a dishonest and fraudulent design is therefore a relevant consideration.[111] It will be particularly relevant where the third party is an agent providing only professional services to the trustee or fiduciary. Consistently with Lord Nicholls' legitimate concerns regarding the formulaic application of *Barnes v. Addy*, dishonest and fraudulent conduct is better addressed by treating the egregiousness of the primary wrong as part of the factual context in which A's culpability is assessed. This accords with the Federal Court of Australia's methodology in *Grimaldi* in which 'the nature of the actual fiduciary or trustee wrongdoing in which the third party was a participant' is identified as one of three elements to be weighed up in determining A's liability.[112]

8.3.2 The accessorial involvement or the receipt

8.3.2.1 Procurement and inducement

In scenarios of procurement and inducement, the accessory is a cause of PW's decision to breach an equitable duty, rather than assisting or facilitating it [3.3.3]. This could be through A's corporate control,[113]

[108] *Air Canada* [1993] 3 SCR 787; 108 DLR (4th) 592 (SCC). Iacobucci J's leading judgment canvassed the competing lines of Canadian case law and concluded that the requirement should be retained. McLachlin J in a separate judgment preferred not to deal with the issue until a suitable case came before the Court.

[109] *Ibid.* 618 (Iacobucci J).

[110] *Westpac* v. *Bell* [2012] WASCA 157; (2012) 44 WAR 1, 378–379 [2103].

[111] See also, in the context of statutory limitation periods, *Williams* [2014] UKSC 10; [2014] 2 WLR 355 [157] (Lord Mance JSC in dissent).

[112] [2012] FCAFC 6; (2012) 200 FCR 296 [247]. See also [3.5.3].

[113] See, e.g., *Elders Trustee* (1987) 78 ALR 193, 238–239 (procurement not found); *Australian Securities Commission* v. *AS Nominees Limited* (1995) 62 FCR 504 (FCA) 523 (procurement not found). See also the scenario discussed in *Grimaldi* [2012] FCAFC 6; (2012) 200 FCR 296 [243]. Such scenarios have tended to be treated as assistance,

deception,[114] manipulation,[115] inducement (by bribery, secret commissions or otherwise),[116] encouragement[117] or simple request[118] of PW.[119] In such circumstances, A tends to be the main player with respect to the ensuing primary wrong, but this does not necessarily mean that PW was unwilling to be prevailed upon.

On the whole, 'procurement' and 'inducement' are used interchangeably by the courts. Lord Nicholls in *Royal Brunei Airlines* referred only to 'procurement' when describing this form of accessory conduct.[120] On the other hand, the High Court of Australia appeared to recognise a distinction in its reference to 'knowingly induced or immediately procured'.[121] 'Induce' is perhaps a more appropriate characterisation of A's conduct in situations requiring persuasion of PW on the part of A,[122] whereas 'procure' is appropriate where A controls PW and simply causes PW to commit the principal wrong. These semantic considerations have no bearing on the applicable principles.

Nor is it relevant that A's conduct was not undertaken for personal gain.[123] Finally, cases in which this form of accessory conduct is

rather than procurement: see, e.g., *NCR Australia* v. *Credit Connection Pty Ltd* [2004] NSWSC 1.

114 See, e.g., *Eaves* (1861) 30 Beav 136; 54 ER 840.

115 As where a solicitor engineers a breach of trust by an unsuspecting trustee for the solicitor's benefit: *Fyler* (1841) 3 Beav 550, 49 ER 216 (not made out on the facts); *Alleyne* (1854) 4 I Ch R 199.

116 See, e.g., *Syrimi* v. *Hinds* (1996) 6 NTLR 1 (NTCA), where A offered PW options for units in a secret unit trust in return for the breach of fiduciary duty to C; *Regnery* v. *Meyers*, 679 NE2d 74, 223 Ill Dec 130, 248 Ill App3d 354, cert. denied, 686 NEe.2d 1173, 227 Ill.Dec. 17, 174 Ill.2d 594 (1994), where A, a company executive, 'initiated the idea of the sale' at an under-value of voting trust shares in the family-controlled company to himself and his brother (a trustee of the voting trust and also executive of the company), 'proposed such sale' to the company's board and 'fully participated' in the sale.

117 See, e.g., *Crawley Borough Council* v. *Ure* [1996] QB 13 (CA): claim that a council 'advised and indeed encouraged' PW's alleged breach of trust in relation to the joint tenancy of a council flat.

118 See, e.g., the facts, but not the reasoning of *George* v. *Webb* [2011] NSWSC 1608 [283], where A instructed the trustees to distribute trust funds for his personal benefit.

119 See, generally, Harpum, 'The Stranger as Constructive Trustee: Part I', 141–144.

120 *Royal Brunei Airlines* [1995] 2 AC 378 (PC) 392.

121 *Farah Constructions* [2007] HCA 22; (2007) 230 CLR 89 [161].

122 But see *Fiona Trust & Holding Corporation* v. *Yuri Privalov* [2010] EWHC 3199 [61] (Comm), where Andrew Smith J describes procurement in terms of 'persuasion' of a fiduciary.

123 See, e.g., *Eaves* (1861) 30 Beav 136; 54 ER 840; *Midgley* v. *Midgley* [1893] 3 Ch 282 (CA). See also Harpum, 'The Stranger as Constructive Trustee: Part I', 142–143.

considered are relatively sparse; instead, facts suggesting procurement or inducement more often are treated as assistance.

8.3.2.2 Assistance

Lord Selborne's comments in *Barnes* v. *Addy* with respect to 'knowing assistance' concerned the provision of professional services that enabled trustees to commit breaches of trust. 'Participation' in a trustee's fraudulent conduct was also described as a form of accessorial conduct.[124] 'Participation' is most apt to describe scenarios in which A and PW act in concert to design and implement the primary wrong.[125] Nonetheless, 'assistance' is now the preferred descriptor of any facilitative actions of any third party involved in a breach of trust and fiduciary duty.[126] This has led to unnecessary straining of the concept of assistance.[127] It can also be noted that, as the receipt of trust property may constitute assistance in the primary wrong, the receipt and assistance categories of participatory liability overlap.[128]

Whether there has been assistance is 'a simple question of fact'[129] and has not greatly occupied the courts' attention.[130] Assistance generally connotes active, rather than passive, conduct; indeed, it has been suggested that this is essential:

> [A]ssistance should 'make a difference' and forward or advance the primary breach or misconduct in some way. Mere passive acquiescence in the breach would not, in the ordinary case, suffice to establish liability

124 (1874) LR 9 Ch App 244, 251. See, e.g., *Colour Control Centre Pty Ltd* v. *Ty* (NSWSC, 24 July 1995) (*Colour Control*); *Super 1000* v. *Pacific General Securities* [2008] NSWSC 1222; (2008) 221 FLR 427 [133].

125 A common scenario is where PW is employed by C and, in breach of PW's fiduciary duty to C, PW and A divert C's business or a business opportunity to a corporate entity created to compete in business with C. PW and A may also be in an intimate relationship. See, e.g., *Timber Engineering Co Pty Ltd* v. *Anderson* [1980] 2 NSWLR 488 (NSWSC); *Colour Control* (NSWSC, 24 July 1995); *Dyson Technology Ltd* v. *Curtis* [2010] EWHC 3289 (Ch).

126 Harpum's observation in 1986 that '[s]ituations in which it is necessary to allege knowing assistance are in fact likely to be rare' has not been borne out: 'The stranger as constructive trustee: Part I', 116.

127 *Grimaldi* [2012] FCAFC 6; (2012) 200 FCR 296 [243]–[246].

128 See *Baden* v. *Société Générale pour Favoriser le Développement du Commerce et de l'Industrie en France SA* [1993] 1 WLR 509 (Ch) 572–573 (*Baden*). Only liability for assistance can apply if the receipt was ministerial, rather than for personal benefit: *Re-Engine Pty Ltd (in liq.)* v. *Fergusson* [2007] VSC 57; (2007) 209 FLR 1 [117] (*Re-Engine*).

129 *Baden* [1993] 1 WLR 509 (Ch) 574.

130 See *Re-Engine* [2007] VSC 57; (2007) 209 FLR 1. See further, Mitchell, 'Assistance', 171–187.

> on the ground of assistance. Further, it appears clear that assistance must take the form of some activity or conduct over and above mere knowledge of the fiduciary's breaches.[131]

But, in our view, if A has actual knowledge of the primary wrong and intends to assist, then mere presence during the commission of the primary wrong might be judged sufficient accessorial conduct for there to be liability: [3.3.6]. This is how the findings in *Brinks Ltd* v. *Abu-Saleh (No 3)* (*Brinks*) could be understood.[132] A woman, A, accompanied her husband by car on his money-laundering trips to Switzerland. It was not proved to Rimer J's satisfaction that either she or her husband had intended her presence to act as a cover to her husband's illegal activities by giving the false appearance of a family holiday. But if she had intended her presence to divert suspicion from him, then her intentional presence alone could have constituted assistance.[133] That is, passive conduct in intentional furtherance of PW's wrong may constitute assistance in exceptional circumstances. This conclusion accords with our analytical framework for accessory liability: the weighting of the conduct and mental elements should be determined relative to each other and in relation to the primary wrong [3.5.3].

US case law in the context of claims against attorneys advising trustees supports the view that an omission to act will not be considered sufficient participation or assistance unless A was under a legal duty to act. Thus, where a firm of attorneys was hired to do specific, due diligence tasks in relation to a proposed investment by the trustees, there was no duty to ensure that the investment was prudent and hence the attorneys were not liable for aiding and abetting a breach of trust through their alleged omission to advise C that the investment was imprudent.[134]

131 *Re-Engine* [2007] VSC 57; (2007) 209 FLR 1 [120] (Dodds-Streeton J). See also *Nightingale Finance Ltd* v. *Scott* (Ch D, 18 November 1997) (Carnwath J): A 'must be an active participant in the breach of trust'.

132 [1996] CLC 133 (Ch).

133 The nature of the primary wrong is not spelt out in the judgment. It appears to have been breach of a constructive trust over gold bullion stolen in breach of a fiduciary duty by C's employee. The assistance was argued to be in relation to a breach of 'trust'. A separate issue in the case concerned the requisite mental element for accessory liability: [8.3.4.2].

134 See, e.g., *KPERS* v. *Kutak Rock* 44 P.3d 407, 273 Kan 481 (2002). See also *Bogert's Trusts and Trustees*, §901 and the cases cited therein:

> Mere knowledge by a third person that a breach of trust is in progress, coupled with a failure to notify the beneficiary or to interfere with the action of the trustee, does not amount to participation in a breach. Such conduct is inaction which may be reprehensible under the highest standards of ethics, but no legal duty has been violated.

8.3.2.3 Beneficial receipt of trust property

The requisite conduct for recipient liability is receipt of 'trust' property or its traceable proceeds for personal benefit by the recipient, A, as a consequence of PW's breach of trust or fiduciary duty. It is not necessary that A continue to hold the property or its traceable proceeds. A's receipt may also constitute assistance in, PW's breach.

Property The concept of property is not immutable; its meaning is shaped by the legal context in which the concept operates. The characteristics identified by Lord Wilberforce in *National Provincial Bank Ltd* v. *Hastings Car Mart Ltd* have been relied upon in the context of recipient liability:

> Before a right or an interest can be admitted into the category of property, or of a right affecting property, it must be definable, identifiable by third parties, capable in its nature of assumption by third parties and have some degree of permanence or stability.[135]

An example of the contextual nature of the property designation concerns information acquired in circumstances importing an equitable obligation of confidentiality. Clearly, information can be the subject of statutory or non-statutory proprietary rights and those rights can be the subject of a breach of trust and a recipient liability claim.[136] But confidential information per se is not treated as property for the purposes of recipient liability.[137]

'Trust' property Recipient liability applies to property to which legal or equitable title is held on trust for another, whether express, resulting or constructive.[138] 'Trust property' is a misnomer, however, for the liability extends to any property under the control of PW pursuant to a custodial relationship governed by equity.[139] Accordingly, a company's assets are

135 [1965] AC 1175 (HL) 1247–1248. Applied in *Armstrong* [2012] EWHC 10; [2013] Ch 156 [50]; *Westpac* v. *Bell* [2012] WASCA 157; (2012) 44 WAR 1 [2154].

136 See generally, *Smith Kline & French Laboratories (Aust.) Limited* v. *Secretary, Department of Community Services and Health* (1990) 22 FCR 73 FCA 119–122 (*Smith Kline*).

137 *Farah Constructions* [2007] HCA 22; (2007) 230 CLR 89 [116]–[120]. See also, *Ultraframe* [2005] EWHC 1638; [2006] FSR 17 [1525]; *OBG Ltd* v. *Allan* [2007] UKHL 21; [2008] AC 1, 76–78 [275]–[277]. On accessory liability for breach of confidence, see [8.4].

138 See, e.g., *Armstrong* [2012] EWHC 10; [2013] Ch 156: property in electronic form stolen by PW is subjected to a constructive trust at the point of theft and is therefore received as trust property by A regardless of the speed of the respective transactions.

139 There may not be a true trust here: *In Re Lands Allotment Company* [1894] 1 Ch 616, 631.

considered to be trust property in the hands of the company's directors.[140] The principle extends to others in control of the company's assets if they owe fiduciary duties to the company.[141] Nor is the principle confined to company assets; it applies whenever a fiduciary has property of the principal under his or her control.[142]

If property held by A is a *product* of the breach of fiduciary duty, but cannot be traced from PW to A, recipient liability cannot apply.[143] For example, property acquired as a result of the disclosure of information, such as a business opportunity, by PW in breach of fiduciary duty is not trust property.

Receipt Trust property is received when there is a transfer of the legal title to, or an equitable interest in, the trust property from PW to A. Such transfer could be absolute (for example, by way of gift or contract of sale[144] or loan) or by way of security.[145] The transaction's 'mere form cannot stay the hand of equity'.[146] Recipient liability also applies to the receipt of the traceable proceeds of the trust property.[147] Whether A received property pursuant to a security transaction depends upon the terms of the transaction and the nature of the chose in action or other proprietary interest thereby created.[148] Even if there is no receipt of

140 *Russell* v. *Wakefield Waterworks Co* (1875) LR 20 Eq 474, 479; *In Re Lands Allotment Company* [1894] 1 Ch 616; *Selangor* [1968] 1 WLR 1555 (Ch) 1574–1577; *Belmont Finance Corporation* v. *Williams Furniture Ltd [No. 2]* [1980] 1 All ER 393 (CA) 405 (*Belmont Finance [No. 2]*).

141 *Agip (Africa) Ltd* v. *Jackson* [1990] Ch 265 (Ch) 290 (*Agip*).

142 See, e.g., *Foley* v. *Hill* (1848) 2 HL Cas 28, 35–36; 9 ER 1002, 1005–1006; *Russell* v. *Wakefield Waterworks Co* (1875) LR 20 Eq 474; *In re Land Allotment Co* [1894] 1 Ch 616; *Belmont Finance [No. 2]* [1980] 1 All ER 393; *Rolled Steel Products (Holdings) Ltd* v. *British Steel Corporation* [1986] Ch 246, 297–298 (*Rolled Steel*); *El Ajou* v. *Dollar Land Holdings Plc* [1994] 2 All ER 685, 700. Despite some caution expressed in *Farah Constructions* [2007] HCA 22; (2007) 230 CLR 89 [113], this continues to be so in Australia: see *Westpac* v. *Bell* [2012] WASCA 157; (2012) 44 WAR 1 [2132]–[2137].

143 *Satnam* [1999] 3 All ER 652 (CA) 671. See also *Ultraframe* [2005] EWHC 1638; [2006] FSR 17 [1525].

144 See, e.g., *Zage* [2010] 2 SLR 589 (SCA).

145 See, e.g., *Westpac* v. *Bell* [2012] WASCA 157; (2012) 44 WAR 1.

146 *Robins* v. *Incentive Dynamics Pty Ltd (in liq.)* [2003] NSWCA 71; (2003) 175 FLR 286 [65] (Mason P) (*Robins*).

147 *Ibid.* [69].

148 See *Westpac* v. *Bell* (2012) 44 WAR 1 [2158]–[2162]. On whether a guarantee supported by a collateral mortgage is trust property, see the conflicting positions taken in *Gold* v. *Rosenberg* [1997] 3 SCR 767; 152 DLR (4th) 385 (SCC) [54] (Iacobucci J, dissenting) and [70]–[72] (Sopinka J).

property pursuant to the security transaction itself, there may be a subsequent receipt if and when the security is realised.[149]

There are conflicting authorities on whether contractual rights created by an executory contract for the transfer of property from PW to A constitute property received by A.[150] Can the chose in action that is comprised of A's contractual rights, rather than the proprietary subject matter of the contract, that is yet to be transferred, constitute trust property received by A so as to satisfy a recipient liability claim where PW's contracting was in breach of duty to C? In our view, it cannot. Although the creation of an executory contract clearly confers contractual rights upon A and such rights are themselves property for certain purposes, they are not relevant 'trust property' because they do not effect a subtraction from the trust property under PW's control. It is only if the contract is performed by PW that there will be a transfer of the trust property in breach of trust.[151]

Receipt, contracts and agents[152] Difficult issues regarding 'receipt' arise at the intersection of the principles governing agency, contract and equity. If PW, acting as C's agent and in breach of PW's fiduciary duties, purports to secure a contract between C and A whereby trust property is transferred[153] to A, does A 'receive' the trust property for the purposes of a recipient liability claim? There is a range of possible outcomes here depending upon the subject matter of the contract, whether PW had authority to contract on C's behalf and whether C brings a claim at common law or in equity. A further complication is that, while the common law looks to the time of contract formation to determine PW's authority to bind C to the contract, equity considers the time of receipt of the trust property in determining A's recipient liability. The effect of the contract might be to transfer the property immediately or at a later date.

[149] *Akai Holdings* [2011] 1 HKC 357 [143] (HKCFA).

[150] *Cf. Criterion Properties* [2004] UKHL 28; [2004] 1 WLR 1846 [27]; *Westpac* v. *Bell* (2012) 44 WAR 1 [2154].

[151] *Criterion Properties* [2004] UKHL 28; [2004] 1 WLR 1846 [27].

[152] Receipt of property pursuant to a contract with a breaching *trustee*, rather than a fiduciary agent, is also discussed in Matthew Conaglen and Richard Nolan, 'Contracts and Knowing Receipt: Principles and Application' (2013) 129 *Law Quarterly Review* 359, 360–363.

[153] For the purposes of discussion, it does not matter whether such transfer is absolute or way of security.

There is Australian authority that a breach of equitable duty by PW can still be within PW's actual authority.[154] If so, a contract for the transfer of property entered into between C and A in breach of PW's duty to C is binding at common law, but not in equity. The contrary, perhaps preferable, view is that the breaching PW cannot have acted within her actual authority in entering the contract.[155] According to this view, the contract is only valid if PW acted with ostensible authority. If PW acted with ostensible, rather than actual, authority as C's agent in entering the contract, but was in breach of duty in so doing, the contract is valid at common law, but voidable in equity.[156]

Property passes under a contract that is valid at common law, but voidable in equity; hence, there will be a receipt of the subject matter of the voidable contract when the contract is performed. A recipient liability claim is available in principle at that point.[157] Where the property has been transferred immediately, scenarios in which A would *not* be put on inquiry as to PW's lack of actual authority (and thus be able to rely on PW's ostensible authority), yet have sufficient knowledge for recipient liability, must be rare if not non-existent, given that the requisite facts for establishing A's recipient liability are the same as, or very similar to, the facts required to refute A's reliance on PW's actual or ostensible authority.[158] Thus, although a recipient liability claim is available in principle when there has been an immediate receipt of trust assets pursuant to the contract, it is unlikely to succeed in practice.

Where the contract is performed at a later date, so that the dates of the contract's formation and the receipt of trust property do not coincide, it

[154] *Richard Brady Franks Ltd* v. *Price* (1937) 58 CLR 112 (HCA) 142 (*Richard Brady*); *Greater Pacific Investments Pty Ltd (in liq.)* v. *Australian National Industries Ltd* (1996) 39 NSWLR 143 (NSWCA) 149; *Grimaldi* [2012] FCAFC 6; (2012) 200 FCR 296 [254].

[155] F. M. B. Reynolds and Michele Graziadei, *Bowstead and Reynolds on Agency*, 18th edn (London, Sweet & Maxwell, 2006) [3–008]–[3–009], citing *Lysaght* v. *Falk Bros & Co Ltd* (1905) 2 CLR 421 (HCA) 430.

[156] *Richard Brady* (1937) 58 CLR 112 (HCA) 142; *Grimaldi* [2012] FCAFC 6; (2012) 200 FCR 296 [254]; *Rolled Steel* [1986] Ch 246. See also Peter Watts, 'Authority and Mismotivation' (2005) 121 *Law Quarterly Review* 4, 5.

[157] *Contra.*, Conaglen and Nolan, 'Contracts and Knowing Receipt', 365, arguing that no recipient liability claim is possible here and that 'the agent's breach of duty is a matter solely between him and his principal'.

[158] See Reynolds and Graziadei, *Bowstead* [8–051]–[8–052] concerning the requisite notice for A not to be able to rely on PW's apparent authority. Recipient liability clearly would not apply if the tests determining an agent's ostensible authority and culpability under recipient liability respectively were to be assimilated as proposed in *Akai Holdings* [2011] 1 HKC 357 [135] (HKCFA).

is possible that PW may have had ostensible authority in relation to the contract's formation, but by the time of receipt of trust property, A has acquired sufficient knowledge of PW's breach of duty for recipient liability. C is not precluded, as a matter of principle, from relying on the equitable recipient liability claim, rather than upon common law rights arising from PW's lack of authority even where a valid contract governs the receipt of trust property and may found a counterclaim.[159]

Where A is precluded from relying upon either PW's actual or ostensible authority concerning the contract between C and A, the contract will be void at common law. Whether A receives property under a void contract depends upon the nature of the property and the terms of the contract, including whether it is executed or executory.[160] If property has passed under the void contract, then there has been a 'receipt' for the purposes of recipient liability. The leading cases view a recipient liability claim and a common law claim as alternative vehicles by which C obtains redress against A in such scenarios.[161]

Finally, it may be possible on the facts of a particular case to argue that the purported contract entered into on behalf of C by PW was a fiction and that, in effect, the trust property was stolen rather than contractually transferred.[162] Here, a receipt of the property can be established without reference to the contract.

Beneficial receipt The receipt of trust property must be for A's personal benefit.[163] Accordingly, recipient liability is unlikely to apply to an agent who receives misappropriated trust property in the course of their agency.[164] Millett J has explained the personal benefit requirement in normative terms as limiting A's liability to where 'the receipt is relevant

159 *Cf.* Watts, 'Authority and Mismotivation', 8. See also Rebecca Lee and Lusina Ho, 'Reluctant Bedfellows: Want of Authority and Knowing Receipt' (2012) 75 *Modern Law Review* 78, 95. *Contra.*, Conaglen and Nolan, 'Contracts and Knowing Receipt', 364.

160 The specific rules concerning the transfer of title are beyond the scope of this book, however, it cannot be assumed that property will never pass under a void contract. See further, Ji Lian Yap, 'Knowing Receipt and Apparent Authority' (2011) 127 *Law Quarterly Review* 350, 351; Lee and Ho, 'Reluctant Bedfellows'.

161 See, e.g., *Rolled Steel* [1986] Ch 246, 297–298 (Slade LJ). See also, at 306–307 (Browne-Wilkinson LJ), although it is not clear whether his Lordship is referring to recipient liability or a 'persisting property' claim: [7.5].

162 See *Robins* [2003] NSWCA 71; (2003) 175 FLR [83].

163 *Agip* [1990] Ch 265, 291–292; *Evans* v. *European Bank Ltd* [2004] NSWCA 82; (2004) 61 NSWLR 75 (*Evans*).

164 Agents who deal with the trust property inconsistently with the trust may be liable for 'knowing dealing': see [7.3]. Accessory liability for assistance may also arise.

to the loss'.[165] It also goes to the heart of the rationale for participatory liability, namely, A's exploitation for personal gain of a relationship governed by equity. In *Gray* v. *Johnston*, the requirement was seen by Lord Cairns LC as having probative value in helping to establish that 'the bankers [A] are in privity with the breach of trust which is about to be committed'.[166] Lord Westbury's explanation in the same case reflects both the evidential and principled reasons for the requirement: '[A] has at once not only abundant proof of the breach of trust, but participates in it for his own personal benefit'.[167]

Particular rules apply to beneficial receipt of trust funds by banks. Under the general law the banker–customer relationship is one of debtor–creditor, rather than agent–principal, and therefore 'money placed in the custody of a banker is, to all intents and purposes, the money of the banker, to do with it as he pleases'.[168] This would suggest that a bank receiving funds from a PW customer always receives beneficially, but this is not so for recipient liability purposes. A bank receiving and paying out money in the ordinary course of business for its customer is treated as not receiving a personal benefit,[169] instead acting in 'the ministerial role of a "mere depository" or "channel"'.[170] Spigelman CJ, in the NSW Court of Appeal, has speculated that 'this special treatment of banks ... may be an application of the maxim that equity looks to the intent not to the form'.[171]

Conversely, there is a beneficial receipt where the bank uses the trust funds to reduce PW's overdrawn account (other than where the account operates continuously in such fashion).[172] This appears counter-intuitive,[173] but perhaps is less so in circumstances

165 *Agip* [1990] Ch 265, 292. 166 (1868) LR 3 HL 1, 11. 167 *Ibid.* 14.

168 *Foley* v. *Hill* (1848) 2 HL Cas 28, 36; 9 ER 1002, 1005–1006 (Lord Cottenham LC).

169 *Gray* v. *Johnston* (1868) LR 3 HL 11, 16; *Agip* [1990] Ch 265, 292.

170 *Evans* [2004] NSWCA 82; (2004) 61 NSWLR 75 [175] (Spigelman CJ) quoting from *Cigna Life Insurance New Zealand Ltd* v. *Westpac Securities Ltd* [1996] 1 NZLR 80 (NZHC) 87 (Greig J). The law was explained by Millett J in *Agip* [1990] Ch 265 on the basis that the bank is acting as the customer's agent, but this seems inconsistent with the general law position that agency and debt relationships can coexist. See Lionel Smith, 'W (h)ither knowing receipt?' (1998) 114 *Law Quarterly Review* 394, 397.

171 *Evans* [2004] NSWCA 82; (2004) 61 NSWLR 75 [166].

172 *Agip* [1990] Ch 265, 292; *Citadel* [1997] 3 SCR 805; 152 DLR (4th) 411 (SCC) 422–433. Spigelman CJ in *Evans* [2004] NSWCA 82; (2004) 61 NSWLR 75 [167] refers to this as a 'definitive reduction of the overdraft'.

173 *ANZ* v. *Westpac* (1988) 164 CLR 662 HCA 681. See further Michael Bryan, 'When Does a Bank Receive Money?' (1996) *Journal of Business Law* 165.

of impending insolvency, which may explain why equity assumes a beneficial receipt.[174]

It has been suggested that 'a bank which culpably receives trust property should be potentially liable no matter the state of the account'.[175] As is suggested by the judgments in *Gray* v. *Johnston*, however, the rules perform a gatekeeper role in limiting claims to where there is most likely to be culpability.[176] There is still uncertainty, however, as to which receipts other than reduction of overdrafts, could amount to personal receipt.[177]

Receipt in breach of trust or fiduciary duty A's receipt of the trust property or its traceable proceeds must occur in breach of the trust or fiduciary duty by PW.[178] This distinguishes recipient liability from the persisting property claim [7.5]. The latter claim is founded upon C's stronger proprietary entitlement to the trust property, not upon PW's breach of duty as such, whereas recipient liability 'responds to the mismanagement of property'.[179] It is not necessary that PW's breach of duty be fraudulent.[180]

8.3.3 The causal or other link between A's conduct and the primary wrong

If A procured PW's decision to breach, a causal nexus between A's conduct and PW's decision is embedded in the conduct itself. A's conduct is, at the least, a factual cause of PW's breach of duty because it contributed to that outcome.[181] It should not matter whether PW had a propensity to act fraudulently and would have breached her duty in any

174 See, e.g., *Westpac* v. *Savin* [1985] 2 NZLR 41 (NZCA); *Citadel* [1997] 3 SCR 805; 152 DLR (4th) 411 (SCC) 422–425.

175 Smith, 'W(h)ither knowing receipt?', 397.

176 (1868) LR 3 HL 11.

177 See, e.g., *Polly Peck International Plc* v. *Nadir (No 2)* [1992] 4 All ER 769 (CA) 777 (*Polly Peck*) (currency exchange from Turkish lira to sterling by a bank on a fiduciary's instructions held to be a receipt for personal benefit because the bank thereby 'became entitled to the sterling not as banker . . . but in its own right'. But, with respect, this is not self-evident). See also *Uzinterimpex JSC* v. *Standard Bank plc* [2008] EWCA Civ 819; [2008] 2 CLC 80 [40].

178 *Akindele* [2001] Ch 437 (CA) 448. See further, *Evans* [2004] NSWCA 82; (2004) 61 NSWLR 75 [160]–[161].

179 Conaglen and Nolan, 'Contracts and Knowing Receipt, 378.

180 *Agip* [1990] Ch 265 (CA) 292.

181 It is a 'cause in fact' in the sense of historical involvement in PW's wrongdoing: Jane Stapleton, 'Cause-in-fact and the Scope of Liability for Consequences' (2003) 119 *Law Quarterly Review* 388.

event. That is, while a 'but for' causal link will generally be present, it is sufficient that A's conduct is a contributing cause [3.3.3].

Where A has merely assisted PW in the primary wrong, it need not be shown that PW would not have, or could not have, gone ahead but for A's assistance.[182] Although the courts explicitly require that A's conduct have a 'causative effect', a 'but for' causal link is not necessary.[183] Such causal effect must be more than of 'minimal importance'.[184] It must '"make a difference" and forward or advance the primary breach or misconduct in some way'.[185]

Self-serving conduct by A, that takes advantage of a breach of duty by PW in which A was not involved, is not a cause of that breach and is therefore not assistance.[186] Where more than one breach of duty has been committed by PW in an ongoing course of conduct, A will only be liable for losses resulting from the particular breaches of duty in which he assisted. Thus, 'it is necessary to identify what breach of trust or duty was assisted and what loss may be said to have resulted from that breach of trust or duty'.[187]

It is clear that A's involvement need not be a 'but for' cause of the breach of trust or fiduciary duty, or even a 'contributing' cause, with respect to recipient liability, in order to render A liable.[188] In relation to recipient liability, a strong proprietary link (established through following and tracing) between the trust property and A is required, but this is not expressed in terms of causation: 'causal questions do not arise. Where [A] has received trust property ... with notice, the cause of action is complete without having to examine causal questions.'[189] The link is

[182] *Grupo Torras SA* v. *Al-Sabah* [2001] CLC 221 (CA) 255, endorsing Mance J at first instance: 'In this context, as in conspiracy, it is inappropriate to become involved in attempts to assess the precise causative significance of the dishonest assistance in respect of either the breach of trust or fiduciary duty or the resulting loss.'

[183] *Brown* v. *Bennett* [1999] 1 BCLC 649 (CA) 659 (Morritt LJ).

[184] *Baden* [1993] 1 WLR 509 (Ch) 575 (Peter Gibson J). See also Harpum, 'The stranger as constructive trustee: Part I', 116 ('significant assistance'); Elliott and Mitchell, 'Remedies for Dishonest Assistance', 20, '[A] has dishonestly assisted ... in such a way that his actions or omissions have at least made the commission of the breach easier than it would otherwise have been ... '.

[185] *Re-Engine* [2007] VSC 57 [120] (Dodds-Streeton J).

[186] E.g., if Company A is created after PW's breach of duty, but benefits from the consequences of the breach by being able to buy C's business at an advantageous price, A has not assisted in the prior breach of duty: *Brown* v. *Bennett* [1999] 1 BCLC 649 (CA).

[187] *Grupo Torras SA* v. *Al-Sabah (No.5)* [1999] C.L.C. 1469 (Ch) 1667 (Mance J); *Grupo Torras SA* v. *Al-Sabah (No 5)* [2001] CLC 221 (CA) 255.

[188] The terminology is taken from Jane Stapleton, 'Unnecessary Causes' (2013) 129 *Law Quarterly Review* 39. See [3.3.3].

[189] *Farah Constructions* [2007] HCA 22; (2007) 230 CLR 89 [199].

strengthened through the requirement that the receipt be for A's *personal* benefit. This is said to limit liability to situations where 'the receipt is relevant to the loss' and explains why A's receipt should be visited with legal liability.[190]

In *Brown* v. *Bennett*, Morritt LJ held that the receipt of trust property must be 'the direct consequence of the alleged breach of trust or fiduciary duty of which [A] is said to have notice'.[191] This is in addition to following or tracing the trust property into A's hands. To illustrate his point, Morritt LJ described a scenario involving a sale of trust property (a house) after it had fallen into disrepair due to previous trustees' breaches of trust. The purchaser is a neighbour who watched the property's decline and who paid a fair price. Morritt LJ concluded that there would be no recipient liability even though the neighbour knew of the previous breaches of trust because he 'was not in any way responsible for them and he paid the full value for what he received from the new trustees'.[192] This is clearly correct, but the 'direct consequence' requirement suggested by Morritt LJ is superfluous.[193] The breaches of trust involved no misappropriation of the property to which the neighbour could have become a party through receipt. The neighbour's later receipt of the trust property is in pursuance of the lawful actions of the new trustees. It is not a receipt *in* breach of trust.

8.3.4 The mental state of the accessory or recipient

8.3.4.1 Overview

Accessory liability and recipient liability turn upon A's knowledge of the circumstances constituting the primary wrong coupled with A's accessorial conduct in relation to that wrong. Formulating the requisite knowledge has proved difficult. There is a broad consensus that actual knowledge of the primary wrong is desirable, given the personal, conscience-based nature of equity's jurisdiction, but minds differ as to which lesser degrees of 'knowledge' will suffice for liability.[194]

190 *Agip (Africa) Ltd* v. *Jackson* [1990] Ch 265, 292 (Millett J).

191 *Brown* v. *Bennett* [1999] 1 BCLC 649 (CA) 655. 192 *Ibid.*

193 See Virgo, *Principles of Equity and Trusts*, 684.

194 The US commentaries describe the requisite mental element of knowledge in very broad terms. See, e.g., Bogert, §901: 'knowledge at the time that the transaction amounted to a breach of trust, or the legal equivalent of such knowledge'; *Restatement (Third) of Trusts* §108(1) (2012): 'knowledge or reason to know that the trustee is acting improperly'.

Courts using the traditional framework frame their inquiry in terms of A's knowledge but with reference to the equitable concept and terminology of 'notice'. Courts using the reformed framework instead consider a general descriptor of A's overall culpability to determine whether the requisite mental element is present. In relation to procurement and assistance liability, the question is whether in all the circumstances, including, but not limited to, A's knowledge of the primary wrong, A's conduct was 'dishonest'. In relation to recipient liability, the question is whether A's knowledge made A's conduct 'unconscionable'.

Policy considerations inform the content of the requisite mental element under both frameworks. Explicit concerns of the courts include the danger of disrupting the operation of commercial dealings by imposing impracticable, inefficient procedural burdens upon professional agents[195] and financiers,[196] the potential injustice of disproportionate liabilities being imposed upon such third parties,[197] and the importance of ensuring coherence with statutory regulatory schemes, particularly in the corporate insolvency context.[198]

The following discussion begins with some general questions concerning the content of A's knowledge. We then describe the current law according to the traditional and reformed frameworks for liability.

8.3.4.2 The content of A's knowledge

An aspect of the mental element that does not often receive attention concerns the requisite 'content' of A's knowledge.[199] Recipient liability can be dealt with quickly; in relation to breach of an express trust: A must know that the property received is trust property and that its receipt is in breach of the trust.[200] In relation to receipt of 'trust property' in the wider sense of property under the control of a fiduciary, A must know that the property is subject to the fiduciary duty and its receipt is in breach of the

195 E.g., through imposing a duty to inquire: *Royal Brunei Airlines* [1995] 2 AC 378 (PC) 387; *Akindele* [2001] Ch 437 (CA) 456.

196 See, e.g. *Baden* [1993] 1 WLR 509 (Ch) 585; *US International Marketing* [2004] 1 NZLR 589 (NZCA).

197 *Farah Constructions* [2007] HCA 22; (2007) 230 CLR 89 [179].

198 *Westpac* v. *Bell* [2012] WASCA 157; (2012) 44 WAR 1 [3062]–[3063] (Carr AJA, in dissent).

199 See generally, Mitchell, 'Assistance', 195–200.

200 See *Akindele* [2001] Ch 437 and the cases discussed therein. In Australia, see *Bell Group Ltd* v. *Westpac Banking Corporation (No 9)* [2008] WASC 239; (2008) 39 WAR 1 [4746] and the cases discussed therein. *Cf. Sino Iron Pty Ltd* v. *Palmer (No 3)* [2015] QSC 94.

fiduciary duty.[201] That is, A must know of the 'essential matters' that constitute the wrong *and* their legal complexion, see [3.4.2.2]–[3.4.2.3]. These requirements appear not to have been questioned.[202]

The requisite content of A's knowledge in relation to accessory liability, however, is far less clear, as is now discussed.

Knowledge of the primary wrong and of C's identity For accessory liability, must A simply know the essential matters [3.4.2.2] (howsoever determined) that constitute the primary wrong or must it also be shown that A appreciates their legal significance [3.4.2.3]? Furthermore, must A appreciate their *precise* legal significance?

The question arose in a simple form before the House of Lords in *Twinsectra* in the context of a dishonest assistance claim against a solicitor, A, with respect to his client's breach of a '*Quistclose*' trust.[203] Was it 'sufficient that [A] was aware of the arrangements which created the trust or must he also have appreciated that they did so?'[204] Lord Hoffmann in the majority held that that there need not be a 'full appreciation of the legal analysis of the transaction. A person may dishonestly assist in the commission of a breach of trust without any idea of what a trust means.'[205] This seems unexceptional; A must know of the facts constituting the trust or fiduciary relationship and the breach of duty, but cannot be expected to appreciate their precise legal significance.[206] To hold otherwise would unduly limit liability to those with sufficient legal training.[207] What is not clear, however, is whether there must still be *some* appreciation of the legal significance of the known facts. The Privy Council in *Barlow Clowes* arguably required this in holding that A must know or suspect that he is 'assisting in a misappropriation of money'.[208]

201 *El Ajou* v. *Dollar Land Holdings plc* [1994] 2 All ER 685 (CA) 700.

202 Similar questions to those discussed next could be raised.

203 [2002] UKHL 12; [2002] 2 AC 164. 204 *Ibid.* [52] (Lord Millett).

205 *Ibid.* [24]. Lord Millett was in agreement on this point: [135].

206 *Cf. Yeshiva Properties No. 1 Property Ltd* v. *Marshall* [2005] NSWCA 23; (2005) 219 ALR 112 [22] (Bryson JA) (*Yeshiva Properties*), where the question is formulated in terms of objective knowledge [3.4.3.5]: 'it is not necessary that the fraudulent scheme or purpose of [PW] should be fully known, or should be understood in any detail at all; the test is complied with if the known facts would communicate to a reasonable person a general understanding that there was a fraud, breach of trust or breach of fiduciary duty.' *Contra., United States Surgical Corporation* v. *Hospital Products International Pty Ltd* [1983] 2 NSWLR 157 (NSWCA) 253. See also *Australian Super Developments Pty Ltd* v. *Marriner* [2014] VSC 464 [302] (Sloss J): '[A] must be aware of the nature of the funds in question: that is, that the funds are trust funds. . .'.

207 Austin, 'Constructive Trusts', 236–237.

208 *Barlow Clowes* [2005] UKPC 37; [2006] 1 WLR 1476 [28].

'Misappropriation' connotes wrongfulness; it is not a normatively neutral term.[209]

The solicitor in *Twinsectra* knew facts (that funds borrowed for a property development were being paid out contrary to instructions) indicating the general nature (misappropriation of money) of the primary wrong (breach of trust) and that the victim was C. More difficult scenarios arise where A knows that PW's conduct is wrongful, but is mistaken as to the type of wrong and/or the identity of the victim. The cases so far turn upon their own facts. In *Agip*, for example, Millett J was unimpressed with an argument by two chartered accountants that they thought that they were assisting their clients to evade foreign exchange controls, rather than assisting in a dishonest and fraudulent breach of trust; that is, that they were involved in criminal wrongdoing and that the victim was the Revenue, rather than a private individual.[210] His Honour held that, '[i]t is not necessary that [A] should have been aware of the precise nature of the fraud or even of the identity of [A's] victim'.[211] The implication is that A must still have some general appreciation of the wrongfulness of his conduct.

The decision in *Agip* must be read in light of the fact that the case concerned professional agents providing 'the services of nominee companies for the purpose of enabling their clients to keep their activities secret'.[212] Millett J made it quite clear that imposing liability upon these professionals performed an essential regulatory function in deterring future misconduct by professional agents and their clients and encouraging whistle-blowing.[213]

It was also suggested in *Agip* that a third party who is mistaken as to the nature of the primary wrong and/or the intended victim has assumed the risk of liability for a wrong with more serious remedial consequences.[214] But this must surely depend upon the nature of the primary wrong and the accessorial conduct in question. The consequences of equitable personal liability may be quite disproportionate to the penalty or remedy that A thought was at stake. It also does not necessarily follow that if A

209 There is a danger in placing too much weight on subtle nuances in language, however, and it must be conceded that the statement in *Barlow Clowes ibid.* is perhaps ambiguous. *Cf. Consul Development* (1975) 132 CLR 373 (HCA) 397 (Gibbs J referring to knowledge of 'improper' conduct and 'impropriety').

210 [1990] 1 Ch 265. 211 *Ibid.* 295. 212 *Ibid.*

213 *Cf. Abou-Ramah* v. *Abacha* [2006] EWCA Civ 1492; [2007] Bus LR 220 [37] (in relation to the prevention by banks of money laundering).

214 [1990] 1 Ch 265, 295. See also Mitchell, 'Assistance', 198.

was prepared to assist in a fraudulent activity such as tax evasion, A would equally have assisted in a breach of trust or fiduciary duty or even that A took the risk that this might be so. In some scenarios, such as those involving professional agents, it may be entirely appropriate to expect A to bear the costs of reckless conduct, but not in all. The accountants in *Agip*, for example,

> were at best indifferent to the possibility of fraud [by PW]. They made no inquiries of [C] because they thought that it was none of their business.[215]

The fact-specific nature of such questions helps explain the decision of Rimer J in *Brinks*.[216] The evidence suggested that A believed her husband was assisting a friend's tax evasion whereas he was involved in money laundering of funds stolen in breach of fiduciary duty and, consequently, impressed with a trust. Her misunderstandings as to the primary wrong and the identity of C were similar to those of the accountants in *Agip*, yet it is questionable whether her knowledge should suffice for liability. Rimer J held, inter alia, that A was not liable because she did not know the facts constituting the trust, that is, that the funds were stolen.[217] The reasoning in *Brinks* has been doubted,[218] but is correct in our view. The wife was not a professional agent to whom the policy considerations in *Agip* might apply, she had not assumed the risk of a breach of trust, and she was not aware of the essential matters constituting the primary wrong. Furthermore, her alleged involvement in the primary wrong was minimal [8.3.2.2]. What is still not clear, however, from these and other cases, is whether A must know the victim's identity,[219] although in our view this is not essential and must be considered in

215 *Ibid.* 295 (Millett J). 216 [1996] CLC 133 (Ch). 217 *Ibid.* 151.

218 See, at first instance, *Grupo Torras SA* v. *Al-Sabah (No.5)* [1999] CLC 1469 (QB) (Mance J disagreeing with the reasoning, but not the outcome, in *Brinks*). In Mance J's view, the question was whether A's dishonesty was 'towards [C] in relation to property held or potentially held on trust or constructive trust, rather than in the introduction of a separate criterion of knowledge of any such trust'. The CA in *Grupo Torras SA* v. *Al-Sabah (No 5)* [2001] CLC 221 indicated agreement with Rimer J in *Brinks* without reaching a conclusion on the question. The Privy Council in *Barlow Clowes* [2005] UKPC 37; [2006] 1 WLR 1476 [28] disagreed with the reasoning in *Brinks*, apparently on the basis that knowledge of the trust is not necessary where A knows or suspects that there is a misappropriation of property. It does not appear that the Privy Council engaged with the further complication in *Brinks* that A did not know or suspect any wrongdoing *in relation to C*.

219 *Cf. Agip* [1990] 1 Ch 265, 295; *Grupo Torras SA* v. *Al-Sabah (No.5)* [1999] CLC 1469 (QB); *Nicholson* v. *Morgan (No 3)* [2013] WASC 110; 8 ASTLR 277 [62]–[65] (Edelman J): A must know the identity of the particular trust beneficiaries, rather than of 'a breach of trust to a third party generally' [64].

light of the nature of A's involvement and 'the extent of [A's] knowledge or, assumption of the risk of, or indifference to, actual, apprehended or suspected wrongdoing by [PW]'.[220]

Knowledge of a claim by C If A knows only that C *claims* that PW is breaching an equitable duty to C, is this sufficient for A's liability? In such scenarios the courts consider how A should have acted in response to C's claim and, in particular, whether A should have taken further steps to ascertain its veracity; see also [9.4.3.2]. There is a legitimate reluctance to impose a duty to inquire upon professional agents such as solicitors[221] and bankers.[222] Outside these contexts, if C's claim is detailed and consistent with the surrounding circumstances, there is time to make an informed decision as to the claim's veracity before pursuing A's own interests further, and A will not suffer any detriment from so doing, A may be fixed with knowledge of the primary wrong [3.4.2.5].[223]

8.3.4.3 The necessary mental state under the traditional framework

The nineteenth-century courts considered the necessary mental element in terms of A's 'cognition',[224] 'knowledge', 'suspicion', 'notice' and the like, but with no particular emphasis or apparent difficulty.[225] Particularly in the context of recipient liability, the courts looked beyond actual knowledge to what A could have learnt through inquiry.[226] As is well known, Equity developed a concept of 'notice' to describe mental states and that operated largely in the context of conveyancing-related claims to equitable property interests in old

220 *Grimaldi* [2012] FCAFC 6; (2012) 200 FCR 296 [247] (Finn, Stone and Perram JJ).

221 See, e.g., *Carl Zeiss* [1969] 2 Ch 276; *Adams* v. *Bank of New South Wales* [1984] 1 NSWLR 285 (NSWSC).

222 See, e.g., *US International Marketing* [2004] 1 NZLR 589 (NZCA) [6]; *Nicholson* [2013] WASC 110; 8 ASTLR 277 [67].

223 See, e.g., the facts of *United States Surgical Corporation* v. *Hospital Products International Pty Ltd* [1983] 2 NSWLR 157 (NSWCA) 258.

224 *Lee* v. *Sankey* (1873) LR 15 Eq 204, 211 (Sir James Bacon VC).

225 See, e.g., references to both knowledge and suspicion by Lord Selborne in *Barnes* v. *Addy* (1874) LR 9 Ch App 244 (CA). The 'apparent tendency to unguarded language [in the earlier cases] was doubtless due to there often being no need upon the particular facts of the case under consideration either to distinguish between "notice" and "knowledge" or to examine their precise meaning in the context of those facts': *Carl Zeiss* [1969] 2 Ch 276 CA 296 (Sachs LJ).

226 See, e.g., *Mayor, Aldermen and Burgesses of the Borough of Berwick-Upon-Tweed* v. *Murray* (1857) 7 De G M & G 497, 512–513; 44 ER 194 (Ch) 200–201; *Selangor* [1968] 1 WLR 1555 (Ch) 1584–1590.

system land, see [3.4.3.5], [7.5].[227] Notice for such purposes includes actual notice, constructive notice and imputed notice. Actual notice includes A's proven knowledge of facts as well as actual knowledge inferred from A's 'wilful blindness' or 'contrived ignorance'; see also [3.4.3.3].[228] Imputed notice is the actual or constructive notice acquired in the course of an agency by an agent acting for D where the information acquired is material to the transaction and the agent has a duty to pass it on.[229] It is uncontroversial here.

Constructive notice, in the conveyancing sense of the knowledge a reasonable person making reasonable inquiries would have gained,[230] was avoided by the twentieth-century judges that took up *Barnes* v. *Addy*.[231] But some – although not all[232] – interpreted the nineteenth-century cases as allowing a modified form of constructive notice where A had actual knowledge of facts that imposed a duty to inquire further.[233] In relation to knowing assistance in a dishonest and fraudulent design, for example, it was said that A must have either

> knowledge of circumstances which would indicate to an honest, reasonable man that such a design was being committed or would put him on inquiry, which [A] failed to make, whether it was being committed.[234]

Neither of these scenarios involves 'true' constructive notice because they operate upon A's actual knowledge of the circumstances, rather than what a reasonable person would have known.

[227] *Macmillan Inc* v. *Bishopsgate Investment Trust plc* [No 3] [1995] 3 All ER 747 (*Macmillan*). See generally, Michael Bryan, 'Notice and Knowledge in Private Law Claims' (2009) 3 *Journal of Equity* 204.

[228] *Macmillan* [1995] 3 All ER 747, 769 (Millett J).

[229] See, e.g., *Espin* v. *Pemberton* (1859) 3 De G & J 547, 554; 44 ER 1380, 1383; *Re Montagu's Settlement Trusts* [1987] Ch 264, 277. See also [11.2.2.2].

[230] *Macmillan* [1995] 3 All ER 747, 769. See also *The English & Scottish Mercantile Investment Co Ltd* v. *Brunton* [1892] 2 QB 700, 707–708.

[231] An exception was when recipient liability was treated as the in personam companion to a priorities claim: see [7.5]. See also on the avoidance of true constructive notice, *Kakavas* v. *Crown Melbourne Limited* [2013] HCA 25; (2013) 250 CLR 392 [152].

[232] See, e.g., *Carl Zeiss* [1969] 2 Ch 276 (CA) 298 (Sachs LJ), 300–301 (Edmund Davies LJ); *Consul Development* (1975) 132 CLR 373 (HCA) 412 (Stephen J noting Jacobs P's view in the NSW CA that constructive notice sufficed for knowing recipient liability, but otherwise actual knowledge was necessary so that A 'can truly be described as a participant in that fraudulent dishonest activity' [1974] 1 NSWLR 443 (NSWCA) 459).

[233] See further on the modified sense of constructive notice, Bryan, 'Notice and Knowledge'.

[234] *Selangor* [1968] 1 WLR 1555 (Ch) 590 (Ungoed-Thomas J). See also *Karak* [1972] 1 WLR 602 (Ch) 639. But see *Carl Zeiss* [1969] 2 Ch 276 (CA).

In 1968 in *Baden* v. *Société Générale pour Favoriser le Développement du Commerce et de l'Industrie en France SA (Baden)*,[235] Peter Gibson J adopted counsel's summary of the modern case law and recognised five degrees of knowledge as being sufficiently culpable for knowing assistance liability, with the caveat that courts should be very slow to find that a duty of inquiry arose for the purposes of level (v):

(i) actual knowledge;
(ii) wilfully shutting one's eyes to the obvious;
(iii) wilfully and recklessly failing to make such inquiries as an honest and reasonable man would make;[236]
(iv) knowledge of circumstances which would indicate the facts to an honest and reasonable man;[237] and,
(v) knowledge of circumstances which would put an honest and reasonable man on inquiry.[238]

The '*Baden* scale' incorporates the concept of actual knowledge (explained in [3.4.3.3]) in levels (i) to (ii)[239] and, in level (iii), recklessness (explained in [3.4.3.4]). Levels (iv) and (v) involve degrees of 'objective knowledge' (see [3.4.3.5]). They depend upon what A should have recognised (iv) or discovered through further inquiry (v), as an honest and reasonable person with A's actual knowledge. Neither equates to constructive notice in the strict conveyancing sense.[240]

The *Baden* scale, although criticised,[241] is used to determine both knowing assistance and recipient liability under the traditional

[235] [1993] 1 WLR 509 (Ch).

[236] See *Belmont Finance Ltd* v. *Williams Furniture (No 1)* [1979] Ch 250, 267. See also J. D. Heydon and M. J. Leeming, *Jacobs' Law of Trusts in Australia*, 7th edn (Sydney, LexisNexis Butterworths, 2006) [1335].

[237] See *Consul Development* (1975) 132 CLR 373 (HCA) 398 (Gibbs J), 412 (Stephen J). See also Heydon and Leeming, *Jacobs' Law of Trusts*, [1335].

[238] *Baden* [1993] 1 WLR 509 (Ch) 575–576.

[239] Level (ii) is sometimes referred to as 'Nelsonian' or 'blind eye' knowledge. '[It] requires an amalgam of suspicion that certain facts may exist and a decision to refrain from taking any step to confirm their existence.' *Manifest Shipping Co Ltd* v. *Uni-Polaris Insurance Co Ltd* [2001] UKHL 1; [2003] 1 AC 469 [112] (Lord Scott). See also *Twinsectra* [2002] UKHL 12; [2002] 2 AC 164 [22].

[240] See Gardner, 'Knowing Assistance and Knowing Receipt', 57–58.

[241] It has been described as the 'zenith of complexity': Heydon and Leeming, *Jacobs' Law of Trusts* [1335] and as encouraging a 'formulaic' approach to determining A's culpability: *Grimaldi* [2012] FCAFC 6; (2012) 200 FCR 296 [260] (Finn, Stone and Perram JJ). The Privy Council held that it was 'best forgotten': *Royal Brunei Airlines* [1995] 2 AC 378 (PC) 392.

framework.[242] Level (v) does not suffice for either form of liability. A must have actual knowledge of the breach of trust or fiduciary duty - levels (i) to (ii), be recklessly indifferent as to whether it occurs - level (iii) - or, exceptionally, have actual knowledge of facts from which an honest and reasonable person would deduce the breach - level (iv).[243] Level (iv) is said to capture the 'morally obtuse' third party who did not recognise 'an impropriety that would have been apparent to an ordinary person applying the standards of such persons'.[244] The Federal Court of Australia has explained the link between level (iv) objective knowledge and actual knowledge thus:

> It is, in essence, an understandable, objective, default rule designed to prevent a third party setting up his or her own "moral obtuseness" as the reason for not recognising an impropriety that would have been apparent to an ordinary person ... It is the surrogate of actual knowledge.[245]

The mental element for procurement of a breach of trust or fiduciary duty is only beginning to receive attention.[246] In recent cases, the courts have dealt with the question by analogy to the knowledge required for knowing assistance.[247] The requisite mental state for procurement is discussed more generally in [3.4.3.6].

8.3.4.4 The necessary mental state under the reformed framework

Knowledge of the primary wrong remains at the core of the mental state for liability under the reformed framework. But, critically, this is expressed at a higher level of generality - 'dishonesty' and 'unconscionability' respectively - that involves a normative judgment upon A's conduct in all the circumstances, including A's knowledge.

[242] *Farah Constructions* [2007] HCA 22; (2007) 230 CLR 89.

[243] *Ibid.*; *Grimaldi* [2012] FCAFC 6; (2012) 200 FCR 296 [267].

[244] *Farah Constructions* [2007] HCA 22; (2007) 230 CLR 89 [177]. See also *Consul Development* (1975) 132 CLR 373, 398.

[245] *Grimaldi* [2012] FCAFC 6; (2012) 200 FCR 296 [261] (Finn, Stone and Perram JJ).

[246] In *Fyler* (1841) 3 Beav 550, 668, 49 ER 216, 224 the mental element was framed in terms of actual knowledge.

[247] See, e.g., *Marriner* v. *Australian Super Developments Pty Ltd* [2012] VSCA 171 [152]–[162]; *Australian Super Developments Pty Ltd* v. *Marriner* [2014] VSC 464 [301]-[305] (on remitter from the VSCA). See also *Macedonian Orthodox Community Church St Petka Inc* v. *Metropolitan Petar* [2013] NSWCA 223.

The criterion of dishonesty in relation to liability for assistance and procurement Lord Nicholls' judgment in *Royal Brunei Airlines* remains the most authoritative and helpful statement of the test for dishonesty.[248] Lord Nicholls sets aside criminal law definitions of 'dishonesty' before explaining what the term meant in relation to accessory liability:

> acting dishonestly, or with a lack of probity, which is synonymous, means simply not acting as an honest person would in the circumstances. This is an objective standard. At first sight this may seem surprising. Honesty has a connotation of subjectivity, as distinct from the objectivity of negligence. Honesty, indeed, does have a strong subjective element in that it is a description of a type of conduct assessed in the light of what a person actually knew at the time, as distinct from what a reasonable person would have known or appreciated. Further, honesty and its counterpart dishonesty are mostly concerned with advertent conduct, not inadvertent conduct. Carelessness is not dishonesty. Thus for the most part dishonesty is to be equated with conscious impropriety. However, these subjective characteristics of honesty do not mean that individuals are free to set their own standards of honesty in particular circumstances. The standard of what constitutes honest conduct is not subjective.[249]

The passage following made it clear that A's knowledge is of crucial relevance to the dishonesty inquiry; this resonates with the traditional framework:

> Honest people do not intentionally deceive others to their detriment. Honest people do not knowingly take others' property. Unless there is a very good and compelling reason, an honest person does not participate in a transaction if he knows it involves a misapplication of trust assets to the detriment of the beneficiaries. Nor does an honest person in such a case deliberately close his eyes and ears, or deliberately not ask questions, lest he learn something he would rather not know, and then proceed regardless.[250]

Nonetheless, in his Lordship's view, knowledge was 'better avoided as a defining ingredient of the [dishonesty] principle, and in the context of this [dishonesty] principle the *Baden* scale of knowledge is best forgotten'.[251] In addition to considering A's knowledge, the court 'will also have regard to personal attributes [of A], such as [A's] experience and intelligence, and the reason why [A] acted as [A] did'.[252]

[248] *Royal Brunei Airlines* [1995] 2 AC 378 (PC) 387. [249] *Ibid.* 389. [250] *Ibid.*
[251] *Ibid.* 392. [252] *Ibid.* 391.

In further explaining the dishonesty test, Lord Nicholls identified two problematic scenarios as being where A's conduct was either reckless or careless. The recklessness, or risk-taking, scenario was framed in terms of an agent assisting a trustee where there was doubt as to whether the trustee's actions were in breach of trust. In such situations, the court's inquiry must be framed broadly:

> The only answer to these questions lies in keeping in mind that honesty is an objective standard. The individual is expected to attain the standard which would be observed by an honest person placed in those circumstances. It is impossible to be more specific.[253]

Where A's lack of awareness of the breach of trust was due to, what Lord Nicholls termed, 'negligence' (A 'would have become aware [of the breach of trust] had he exercised reasonable diligence'), this would not suffice for liability.[254]

After some initial confusion,[255] it is now clear that dishonesty is determined according to an objective standard; it is not necessary that A appreciate that his conduct is dishonest according to ordinary standards.[256] The dishonesty test laid down in *Royal Brunei Airlines* and subsequently reiterated by the Privy Council in *Barlow Clowes*[257] has been adopted in England,[258] New

[253] *Ibid.* 390. The phrasing of the question in *Cowan de Groot Properties Ltd* v. *Eagle Trust Plc* [1992] 4 All ER 700 (Ch) 761 (Knox J) was referred to with approval: whether A was 'guilty of commercially unacceptable conduct in the particular context involved . . . '.

[254] *Royal Brunei Airlines* [1995] 2 AC 378 (PC) 391–392.

[255] Confusion was generated by *Twinsectra* [2002] UKHL 12; [2002] 2 AC 164. In a brief passage agreeing with Lord Hutton, Lord Hoffmann [20] considered that *Royal Brunei Airlines* required 'a dishonest state of mind, that is to say, consciousness that one is transgressing ordinary standards of honest behaviour'. Similarly, Lord Hutton [27] viewed dishonesty as combining both objective and subjective features. *Contra.*, Lord Millett.

[256] *Barlow Clowes* [2005] UKPC 37; [2006] 1 WLR 1476 [15]–[16]. Any 'ambiguity' arising from *Twinsectra* was removed by holding that the dishonesty test 'did not require that [A] should have had reflections about what [the] normally acceptable standards [of honest conduct] were'.

[257] *Ibid.*

[258] See *Jyske Bank (Gibralter) Limited* v. *Spjeldnaes* (CA, 29 July 1999); *Abou-Rahmah* v. *Abacha*. [2006] EWCA Civ 1492; [2007] Lloyd's Rep 115 [66]–[69]; *Sinclair Investments (UK) Ltd* v. *Versailles Trade Finance Limited (in administration)* [2011] EWCA Civ 347; (2012) Ch 453 [74]. But see Leveson LJ in *Starglade Properties Ltd* v. *Nash* [2010] EWCA Civ 1314; [2011] Lloyd's Rep FC 102 [42] in obiter, expressing concern 'if the concept of dishonesty for the purposes of civil liability differed to any marked extent from the concept of dishonesty as understood in the criminal law'. It is not clear whether Leveson LJ considered that change was needed in the criminal concept of dishonesty or the civil concept of dishonesty. For the reasons given by Lord Millett in *Twinsectra* [2002] UKHL

Zealand,[259] Singapore[260] and Hong Kong.[261] There appears to be no significant uncertainty as to the content or methodology of the dishonesty test. It appears to work well in the context of non-agent accessories.[262] In particular, the normative dimension of the dishonesty inquiry is well-accepted and that it may involve the court sending a message to the commercial community as to the propriety of certain common forms of conduct.[263]

One scenario that continues to be challenging for courts is that of the agent whose professional services have assisted a (generally fraudulent) breach of trust or fiduciary duty, but who is not proved to have had actual knowledge of the primary wrong. Distinguishing between A turning a blind eye to suspicions of impropriety (dishonesty) and A simply failing, however incompetently, to see any impropriety (not dishonesty), has proved difficult.[264] This is, of course, unsurprising. It is the question that has bedevilled the courts in various guises since the beginning of the modern cases.[265] The merit of the reformed framework's test of dishonesty is that it makes explicit the normative and contextual nature of the inquiry: dishonesty is determined by A's mental state and conduct in all the circumstances. The remarks of Aldous LJ are apt in this context:

> Once the facts have been found, the judge has to decide, according to the standards of right thinking members of society, whether the act or omission was due merely to incompetence or to dishonesty . . . It may not be an easy question to answer, but it is the sort of question that judges and juries throughout the country answer every day without needing to analyse a large number of authorities.[266]

12; [2002] 2 AC 164 [115]–[117] the criminal law conception of dishonesty is inappropriate. See also Virgo, *Principles of Equity and Trusts*, 708.

[259] *Royal Brunei Airlines*, as a pre-2004 Privy Council decision, bound the New Zealand courts. The Privy Council's clarification of the dishonesty test in *Barlow Clowes* [2005] UKPC 37; [2006] 1 WLR 1476 was followed in *Westpac New Zealand Ltd* v. *MAP & Associates Ltd* [2011] NZSC 89.

[260] See, e.g., *Caltong (Australia) Pty Ltd* v. *Tong Tien See Construction Pte Ltd (in liq.)* [2002] 2 SLR (R) 94 (SCA); *Bansal Hemant Govindprasad* v. *Central Bank of India* [2003] 2 SLR (R) 33 (CA); *Zage* [2010] 2 SLR 589.

[261] *Peconic* [2009] HKCFA 17; [2009] 5 HKC 135.

[262] See, e.g., *Starglade Properties Ltd* v. *Nash* [2010] EWCA Civ 314; [2011] Lloyd's Rep FC 102.

[263] *Ibid.*

[264] See, e.g., *Attorney General of Zambia* v. *Meer Care and Desai* [2008] EWCA Civ 1007; [2008] Lloyd's Rep FC 587.

[265] See, e.g., *Selangor* [1968] 1 WLR 1555 (Ch); *Karak* [1972] 1 WLR 602 (Ch).

[266] *Mortgage Express Ltd* v. *S Newman & Co* [2000] Lloyd's Rep PN 745 [40].

It is an interesting question whether the difference in the requisite mental element of the traditional and reformed frameworks leads to different outcomes here. Certainly, there is consensus that the burden on professional agents to protect the interests of beneficiaries to fiduciary relationships should be restrained.[267] Different outcomes are possible in the exceptionally difficult cases where it cannot be proved that A had actual knowledge or notice of the principal wrong and yet a reasonable person in A's position would have been alerted to that possibility. But in such cases, the line between preliminary fact-finding as opposed to a conclusory application of law becomes blurred and it is very difficult to predict how the differing fault elements will apply. Nonetheless, the automatic inclusion of situations of 'moral obtuseness' under the traditional framework may make liability more likely than under the reformed framework.

The criterion of unconscionability in relation to recipient liability The mental element for recipient liability under the reformed framework requires A's knowledge of the primary wrong to be, in all the circumstances, 'such as to make it unconscionable for [A] to retain the benefit of the receipt'.[268] This test was laid down in 2000 by Nourse LJ for the English Court of Appeal in *Akindele*.[269] His Lordship endorsed a conscience-based approach to recipient liability,[270] but rejected the *Baden* scale of knowledge as unhelpful.[271] Instead, a two-stage inquiry, similar to that for dishonest assistance, is undertaken. First, A's knowledge of the breach of trust is ascertained. Second, a normative judgment is made as to whether A's conduct, given A's knowledge, is unconscionable. His Lordship noted that this approach would enable 'commonsense decisions in the commercial context'.[272]

[267] See also in the US, the 'modernized rule' in *Restatement (Third) of Trusts* §108(3) (2012) and Comment *d*; and similarly, *Uniform Trust Code* §1012(b). See also Scott, Fratcher and Ascher, *Scott & Ascher*, §30.6.6: 'It seems plainly inappropriate … to compel third persons to supervise the fiduciary's conduct and to hold them liable for failing to do so. Indeed, the possibility of such liability over the years has made it dangerous to deal with trustees and interfered with proper administration.'

[268] *Akindele* [2001] Ch 437 (CA) 455.

[269] *Ibid*. In *Criterion Properties* [2004] UKHL 28; [2004] 1 WLR 1846 [4] Lord Nicholls incorrectly suggested that recipient liability did not arise on the facts of *Akindele*. See further, Conaglen and Nolan, 'Contracts and Knowing Receipt'.

[270] [2001] Ch 437 (CA) 452. See further [7.6.1].

[271] *Ibid*. [455] (although opining that the *Baden* scale was helpful in determining dishonesty for knowing assistance).

[272] *Ibid*. 455 (Nourse LJ).

Extrapolating from the discussion in *Akindele* of the earlier case law, it seems that, generally, actual knowledge is required, but that 'there must be cases where there is no justification on the known facts for allowing a commercial man who has received funds paid to him in breach of trust to plead the shelter of the exigencies of commercial life'.[273] The implication is that something less than actual knowledge may suffice, but perhaps does not go as far as the traditional framework for knowing receipt which assumes that the knowledge that an honest and reasonable person would deduce from A's actual knowledge will *always* suffice for liability [8.3.4.3]. A contextual approach to the inquiry, which allows A to be liable with less than actual knowledge, has been supported in the Singapore Court of Appeal[274] and by the English Court of Appeal.[275]

Conversely, in the Hong Kong Court of Final Appeal decision, *Akai Holdings*, Lord Neuberger NPJ interpreted the *Akindele* test by reference to the common law principles for determining whether A could rely on the apparent authority of C's agent, PW, in enforcing a contract made with C.[276] Equity should 'follow the law' in this respect.[277] This led him to conclude that only actual knowledge suffices for recipient liability.[278] This did not mean, however, that recipient liability could be assimilated with dishonest accessory liability, because the test for determining an agent's apparent authority incorporated 'irrationality' as well as dishonesty.[279]

With respect, the reasoning in *Akai Holdings* is difficult to follow. There is no necessary connection between an agent's authority to enter

[273] *Ibid.* 454 quoting from *Westpac* v. *Savin* [1985] 2 NZLR 41 (CA) 53 (Richardson J).

[274] See *Zage* [2010] 2 SLR 589, 606 (SCA concluded that *Akindele*-type unconscionability was not limited to where A had actual knowledge. Instead, '[t]he test of unconscionability should be kept flexible and be fact centred'. The SCA approved of Cheung JA's concurring judgment in *Akai Holdings Ltd (in liq)* v. *Thanakhan Kasikorn Thai Chamkat (Mahachon)* [2010] 3 HKC 153 (HKCA). Cheung JA concluded [266] that: 'it is precisely because of the broad approach when unconscionability is adopted as the underlining test of knowledge that one should not confine the examination only to the actual knowledge of the recipient and exclude constructive notice in its wider sense.' But see *Yong Kheng Leong* v. *Panweld Trading Pte Ltd* [2013] 1 SLR 173 [81]: SCA instead required 'actual knowledge or the wilful avoidance of knowledge'. Similarly, the HKCFA in *Akai Holdings* [2011] 1 HKC 357 [134]–[137] required actual knowledge without addressing the view of Cheung JA in the CA.

[275] *Criterion Properties plc* v. *Stratford UK Properties LLC* [2002] EWCA Civ 1783; [2003] 1 WLR 2108 [32], [40]. See also *Niru Battery Manufacturing Co* v. *Milestone Trading Ltd* [2003] EWCA Civ 1446; [2004] QB 985. The case concerned the change of position defence at common law, but referred by analogy to *Akindele* unconscionability. The CA agreed with Moore-Bick J at first instance who did not require actual knowledge.

[276] [2010] HKCU 2362 [128]. [277] *Ibid.* [135]. [278] *Ibid.* [134]–[137].

[279] *Ibid.* [134].

a contract and the receipt of trust property that would require the principles for determining liability to be the same.[280] Nor does the maxim 'equity follows the law' apply.[281] The finding that A must have actual knowledge for recipient liability is contrary to the reasoning and, we suggest, the spirit of, *Akindele*. Nor is it consistent with how other courts have interpreted the *Akindele* test.[282]

The UK Supreme Court has not yet had the opportunity to consider the mental element for recipient liability.[283] In 2012 the Privy Council in an appeal from the Turks and Caicos Islands Court of Appeal, in which the *Akindele* test was not challenged, equated unconscionability in the *Akindele* sense with 'equitable fraud'[284] and noted that it was 'a classic example of lack of bona fides'.[285]

8.3.5 *Shortcomings of the two frameworks and a preferred approach*

The two dominant frameworks for equitable accessory and recipient liability both have shortcomings. Accessory liability is imposed in a broader range of circumstances and often in a less formulaic fashion than such frameworks concede. In particular, both frameworks are unwieldy in relation to corporate, rather than trust, breaches of duty. The leading cases take as their paradigm scenario A's involvement in breach of an express trust and formulate liability in those terms.[286] Yet much of the modern case law concerns the corporate context, particularly breach of directors' fiduciary duties. Where, for example, A is the corporate vehicle for PW's breach of duty and is fully or substantially under PW's control, both frameworks prove cumbersome.[287]

[280] Ji Lian Yap, 'Knowing receipt and apparent authority' (2011) 127 *Law Quarterly Review* 350.

[281] See Meagher, Heydon and Leeming, *Equity*, [3–035]–[3–045]. *Cf. Farah Constructions* [2007] HCA 22; (2007) 230 CLR 89 [153].

[282] See, e.g., *Zage* [2010] 2 SLR 589 (SCA); *Criterion Properties plc* v. *Stratford UK Properties LLC* [2002] EWCA Civ 1783; [2003] 1 WLR 2108.

[283] But see the references to 'knowing receipt' in *Williams* [2014] UKSC 10; [2014] 2 WLR 355. The Singapore CA has noted that the law is 'still in a state of *flux*'. *Wee Chiaw See Anna* v. *Ng Li-Ann Genevieve* [2013] SGCA 36 [144] (Andrew Phang Boon Leong JA).

[284] *Arthur* v. *Attorney General of the Turks and Caicos Islands* [2012] UKPC 30 [36] (*Arthur*).

[285] *Ibid.* [40].

[286] See, e.g., *Royal Brunei Airlines* [1995] 2 AC 378, and the consequent uncertainty, discussed at [8.3.1.3], as to whether a misappropriation of trust property is required for accessory liability.

[287] See *Grimaldi* [2012] FCAFC 6; (2012) 200 FCR 296 [243]. See also *Air Canada* [1993] 3 SCR 787, 824; 108 DLR (4th) 592 (SCC), 617. See further Chapter 11. Another scenario

The formulation of the traditional framework may render it more prone to a rigid and formulaic application. The methodology of the reformed framework, whereby A's conduct and mental state are considered contextually, is preferable in this respect, but the same result could be achieved without the complication of dishonesty or unconscionability labels. In our view, such labels are unnecessary, given an otherwise sufficient methodology; see also [3.5.2]. This is supported by Lord Millett's dissenting comments in *Twinsectra* challenging the premise of *Royal Brunei Airlines* that 'dishonesty' provides a clearer criterion of fault than knowledge:

> [T]he introduction of dishonesty is an unnecessary distraction, and conducive to error ... If the condition of liability is intentional wrongdoing and not conscious dishonesty as understood in the criminal courts, I think that we should return to the traditional description of this head of equitable liability as arising from "knowing assistance".[288]

Unfortunately, these concluding remarks have not received serious attention, perhaps because of the controversy generated by the majority's distortion of the dishonesty test in that case.[289]

A further shortcoming of the reformed framework, in our view, is that while its differentiation of accessory liability and recipient liability is analytically correct, there is a danger that the very real commonalities between the two forms of liability are lost in the process.[290] Given that recipient liability (and, sometimes, equitable vitiating doctrines [8.5]) share rationales and similar elements to liability for procurement or assistance in breach of equitable duties, it is questionable whether they should be separated by an exclusively accessorial classificatory scheme.

There is substantial support in equity jurisprudence for treating procurement, knowing assistance and recipient liability for breach of trust or fiduciary duty as one, participatory liability, regime, given the significant overlap and commonalities of the types of liability. On this approach,

which courts sometimes treat as outside the two frameworks is where PW, a fiduciary, solicits a bribe or secret commission from A, or accepts one that is offered by A, to secure a transaction between C (PW's principal) and A. See, e.g., *Logicrose Ltd* v. *Southend United Football Club Ltd* [1988] 1 WLR 1256 (Ch) 1261 (*Logicrose*) (Millett J noting the 'close parallel with the cases on knowing assistance in a breach of trust ... [T]he difference ... lies not in the factual background but in the remedy sought ... '. See also *Grimaldi* [246] citing *Grant* v. *Gold Exploration and Development Syndicate* [1900] 1 QB 233 (CA) 249; *Daraydan Holdings* Ltd v. *Solland International Ltd* [2004] EWHC 622; [2005] Ch 119 [53].

288 *Twinsectra* [2002] UKHL 12; [2002] 2 AC 164 [134]. 289 See nn. 255–258 above.

290 The same can be said of undue influence and similar doctrines discussed at [8.5].

'receipt' after the primary wrong becomes merely another means of participation in the wrongdoing. This understanding reflects the law in Australia.[291] It is also supported by high authority in England.[292] It is less evident in other jurisdictions.[293] In light of the shortcomings of the traditional framework specifically, the Federal Court of Australia in *Grimaldi* concluded that a flexible approach by which three broad elements determining liability are considered in a context-specific fashion and given varying weight accordingly, was to be preferred. The Court's conclusion is one that we share:

> [P]articipatory liability as it evolved in equity in cases prior and subsequent to *Barnes* v. *Addy* was not based on inflexible formulae. Given the variety of circumstances in which, and bases on which, a third party could be characterised as a wrongdoer in equity . . . varying importance has been given to three matters: (i) the nature of the actual fiduciary or trustee wrongdoing in which the third party was a participant; (ii) the nature of the third party's role and participation, e.g., as alter ego, inducer or procurer, dealer at arm's length, etc.; and (iii) the extent of the participant's knowledge or, assumption of the risk of, or indifference to, actual, apprehended or suspected wrongdoing by the fiduciary.[294]

291 See *Farah Constructions* [2007] HCA 22; (2007) 230 CLR 89, in which the High Court of Australia retained the traditional *Barnes* v. *Addy* liability framework of two limbs (knowing receipt of trust property and knowing assistance in a dishonest and fraudulent design by the trustee or fiduciary); *Grimaldi* [2012] FCAFC 6; (2012) 200 FCR 296. See also the extra-judicial writings of one member of the Court in *Grimaldi*: Paul D. Finn, 'The Liability of Third Parties for Knowing Receipt or Assistance' in Donovan W. M. Waters (ed), *Equity, Fiduciaries and Trusts* (Carswell, 1993) 195.

292 See *Williams* [2014] UKSC 10; [2014] 2 WLR 355 [9], Lord Sumption referring to:

> persons who never assumed . . . the status of a trustee, whether formally or informally, but have exposed themselves to equitable remedies by virtue of their participation in the unlawful misapplication of trust assets. Either they have dishonestly assisted in a misapplication of the funds by the trustee, or they have received trust assets knowing that the transfer to them was in breach of trust . . . These can conveniently be called cases of ancillary liability.

The statement is framed only in terms of misapplication of trust funds. See also *Dubai Aluminium Co Ltd* v. *Salaam* [2002] UKHL 48; [2003] 2 AC 366, 391; Lord Nicholls, 'Knowing Receipt: the Need for A New Landmark' in W. R. Cornish, R. Nolan, J. O'Sullivan and G. Virgo (eds.), *Restitution: Past Present and Future* (Hart Publishing, Oxford, 1998) 231, 243: recipient liability and dishonest assistance are 'two instances of similarly wrongful conduct: dishonest participation by third parties in a breach of trust'.

293 In the context of Singapore and Hong Kong, see Ridge, 'Equitable Accessory and Recipient Liability in Singapore', 374–378.

294 *Grimaldi* [2012] FCAFC 6; (2012) 200 FCR 296 [247]. The comments extended to breach of confidence and undue influence.

These 'three matters' and the accompanying methodology closely parallel our general framework for accessory liability [Chapter 3].

8.4 Accessory liability for breach of confidence

8.4.1 When does accessory liability arise?

A duty of confidentiality ('confidence') may arise in equity or pursuant to a contract. The two jurisdictions overlap as do the accompanying accessory liabilities.[295] The equitable duty of confidence is more simply acquired than a trust or fiduciary duty and, hence, it is easier for A to become a primary wrongdoer in his own right. The question considered here is when equitable accessory – rather than primary – liability for breach of confidence arises.[296] The question is of practical significance given that many breach of confidence claims are made against a third party to the original breach of confidence (for example, the publisher of confidential material acquired by another in breach of confidence) rather than against the original PW. Notwithstanding the prevalence of such claims, there is uncertainty as to when and why they are allowed.[297] Three scenarios involving a third party, A, to an initial breach of confidence by PW must be distinguished when considering the possibility of accessory liability.

8.4.1.1 Scenario 1: A, knowing of a breach of confidence by PW, receives the confidential information

A may be liable as a primary wrongdoer for breach of confidence, even if A is not the original primary wrongdoer in the chain of events comprising an actionable breach of confidence, if A subsequently received and dealt with the confidential information.[298] This will be

295 See, e.g., *Printers & Finishers Ltd* v. *Holloway* [1965] RPC 239 (Ch).

296 The law in England and Wales post-1998 has diverged from other jurisdictions due to the influence of the Human Rights Act 1998: see *Campbell* v. *MGN Ltd* [2004] UKHL 22; [2004] 2 AC 457, but there does not yet appear to be any difference in the treatment of accessories. For the circumstances in which a duty of confidence arises, see generally Tanya Aplin, Lionel Bently, Phillip Johnson and Simon Malynicz, *Gurry on Breach of Confidence*, 2nd edn (Oxford University Press, 2012).

297 *Johns* v. *Australian Securities Commission* (1993) 178 CLR 408, 460 (*Johns*); *Hunt* v. *A* [2007] NZCA 332; [2008] 1 NZLR 368 [69]. On third-party liabilities for breach of confidence generally, see Tanya Aplin, Lionel Bently, Phillip Johnson and Simon Malynicz, *Gurry on Breach of Confidence*, 2nd edn (Oxford University Press, 2012) [7.103]–[7.142].

298 *Abernethy* v. *Hutchinson* (1825) 1 H & TW 28, 39–40; 47 ER 1313, 1317–1318; *Prince Albert* v. *Strange* (1849) 1 Mac & G 25; 41 ER 1171; *Attorney-General* v. *Guardian*

so where A 'knew or ought to have known' of the confidential nature of the information.[299] There is no need to resort to accessory liability here because the elements of breach of confidence (the primary wrong itself) can be met in relation to A.[300] In some such cases, A will not be involved in the original breach of confidence by PW at all, in which case accessory liability cannot arise in any event. For example, if A seeks to take advantage of an earlier breach of confidence that A did not instigate or participate in, and that is not ongoing, A is not accessorily involved.[301]

Nonetheless, there is commentary and case law that conceptualises scenario 1 in accessorial terms. In this respect the extrajudicial views of Lord Toulson have been influential.[302] The English Court of Appeal in *Thomas* v. *Pearce* adopted the following passage from his text, *Confidentiality*:

> Where the third party receives information knowing that it has been disclosed by his informant in breach of confidence, he will himself owe a duty of confidence to the confider. This principle is derived from the doctrine that it is equitable fraud in a third party knowingly to assist in a breach of trust, confidence or contract by another . . .[303]

This led the court to apply the dishonesty test used to determine accessory liability for breach of trust in order to determine primary liability for breach of confidence.[304] The passage in *Confidentiality* conflates primary

Newspapers Ltd (No 2) [1990] 1 AC 109; *Australian Broadcasting Corporation* v. *Lenah Game Meats Pty Limited* [2001] HCA 63; (2001) 208 CLR 199 [39](*Lenah Game Meats*); *Cadbury Schweppes Inc* v. *FBI Foods Ltd* (1999) 167 DLR (4th) 577 (SCC) 588.

299 *Campbell* v. *MGN Ltd* [2004] UKHL 22; [2004] 2 AC 457 [14] (Lord Nicholls of Birkenhead); *Lenah Game Meats* [2001] HCA 63; (2001) 208 CLR 199 [39] (Gleeson CJ): 'the manner in which the information was obtained'. Sometimes the criterion is formulated in terms of notice by A of the breach of confidence by PW (see, e.g., *Force India Formula One Team Limited* v. *Malaysia Racing Team Sdn Bhd* [2012] EWHC 616; [2012] RPC 29 (Ch) [224] (*Force India*).

300 *Attorney-General* v. *Guardian Newspapers Ltd (No 2)* [1990] 1 AC 109 (HL) 281; *Force India* [2012] EWHC 616 (Ch) [248].

301 *Attorney-General* v. *Guardian Newspapers Ltd* [1987] 1 WLR 1248 (Ch) 1264 (newspapers sought to capitalise on a prior breach of confidence by the author and publishers of a book).

302 R. G. Toulson, *Confidentiality* (London, Sweet & Maxwell, 1996) [7.02]–[7.03]. See also, R. G. Toulson and C. M. Phipps, *Confidentiality*, 2nd edn (London, Sweet & Maxwell, 2006) [3–051]; *Confidentiality*, 3rd edn (London, Sweet & Maxwell, 2012) [3.068]–[3.075].

303 *Thomas* v. *Pearce* [2000] FSR 718 (CA) 720–721.

304 PW provided her new employer, A, with a confidential list of her former employer, C's, clients. The CA determined A's liability according to whether she was 'dishonest' in her

liability with accessory liability. It is not necessary to rely upon accessory liability where A possesses the relevant information and knows or ought to know that it is confidential, for A has thereby become a primary wrongdoer.[305] This is not to deny that C could plead accessory liability in the alternative where the facts are amenable to that analysis on the basis, for example, that A procured or assisted in PW's breach of confidence.[306]

8.4.1.2 Scenario 2: A innocently receives confidential information from PW

Here, a bona fide third party innocently receives confidential information from PW (for example, pursuant to a contract with PW[307] or inadvertently from PW[308]) but subsequently learns of its confidential nature (most often through C bringing a claim for injunctive relief). It is generally accepted that (primary) liability will arise;[309] however, the courts differ as to the relevant considerations. The better view is that once the third party is put on notice of the breach of confidence by PW, C is prima facie entitled to relief, but that the court has a discretion as to the terms of such relief and whether it should be refused taking into account all the circumstances.[310]

receipt of the confidential information, applying the test in *Royal Brunei Airlines* [1995] 2 AC 378. Some cases have uncritically accepted this approach. See, e.g., *Campbell* v. *MGN Ltd* [2002] EWCA Civ 1373; [2003] QB 633 [66] (except that the dishonesty test was held to be inappropriate in a non-commercial context); this was not discussed on appeal: *Campbell* v. *MGN Ltd* [2004] UKHL 22; [2004] 2 AC 457.

305 See Paul Stanley, *The Law of Confidentiality: A Restatement* (Oxford, Hart Publishing, 2008) 27–30; Aplin, Bently, Johnson and Malynicz, *Gurry* [7.106]–[7.110]; Richard Arnold, 'Circumstances Importing an Obligation of Confidence' (2003) 119 *Law Quarterly Review* 193, 198–199. This does not, in itself, resolve the problem with which the Toulson text is concerned, namely, the requisite mental element for *primary* liability.

306 Stanley, *Law of Confidentiality*, 28 n. 20. But see [8.4.2] regarding differences in the requisite mental element that may make an accessory claim less attractive.

307 See, e.g., *Wheatley* v. *Bell* [1982] 2 NSWLR 544 (NSWSC).

308 See, e.g., *Director of Public Prosecutions (Commonwealth)* v. *Kane* (1997) 140 FLR 468 (NSWSC).

309 *Johns* (1993) 178 CLR 408 (HCA) 460; *Cadbury Schweppes* (1999) 167 DLR (4th) 577 (SCC) 588; *Vestergaard Frandsen A/S* v. *Bestnet Europe Ltd* [2013] UKSC 31; [2013] 1 WLR 1556 [25] (*Vestergaard).*

310 *Retractable Technologies* v. *Occupational and Medical Innovations* [2007] FCA 545; (2007) 72 IPR 58 [70]–[87] (*Retractable Technologies*). See further, Aplin, Bently, Johnson and Malynicz, *Gurry*, [7.119]–[7.142]. If the third party was a bona fide purchaser for value without notice in entering a contract which involves a breach of confidence, this is a factor to be taken into account. The defence cannot operate directly

Some situations involving innocent recipients of confidential information are susceptible to a dual analysis of primary and accessory liability. On one view, the liability of A should then be analogised with knowing assistance for breach of trust and fiduciary duty.[311] Thus, on appropriate facts, once A is given notice of the breach of confidence by PW, '[i]f he then persists in continuing [in a project with PW] he should be restrained as participating in a dishonest and fraudulent design in breach of a duty of confidence'.[312]

The Queensland Supreme Court decision of *Franklin* v. *Giddins*[313] provides an example. In that case, an orchardist stole budwood cuttings from C's nectarine trees and propagated them in breach of confidence. He was convicted of theft. From the time of this conviction, the orchardist's wife, A, knew of his breach of confidence. C sought orders against both the orchardist and A for delivery up of the wrongfully propagated trees. In relation to A, the court held that, given her subsequent notice of the breach, it was 'unconscionable for her to derive any benefit from the trees, and she too infringes C's rights'.[314] This suggests that A became subject to her own duty of confidence. But the case has been subsequently explained in accessorial terms:

> Since [A] jointly conducted the orchard with her husband . . . and became after knowledge of her husband's conduct an active participant in the continued use of [C's] stolen trade secret, she became an accessory to the primary conduct and thus susceptible to an injunction . . . and delivery up of the trees.[315]

The explanation of A's liability as accessorial is convincing given that there was an ongoing breach of confidence in which she participated.[316]

because confidential information is not property: *Wheatley* v. *Bell* [1982] 2 NSWLR 544 (NSWSC) 549–550; *Moorgate Tobacco Co Ltd* v. *Philip Morris Ltd (No 2)* (1984) 156 CLR 414 (HCA) 438; *Breen* v. *Williams* (1996) 186 CLR 71 (HCA) 129.

311 Meagher, Heydon and Leeming, *Equity*, [41–110]. No analogy can be drawn with recipient liability for breach of trust or fiduciary duty because A's receipt of confidential information is not a receipt of property: *Farah Constructions* [2007] HCA 22; (2007) 230 CLR 89; [8.3.2.3].

312 Meagher, Heydon and Leeming, *Equity* [41–110].

313 [1978] QR 72 (QSC).

314 *Ibid.* 81 (Dunn J).

315 *Retractable Technologies* [2007] FCA 545; (2007) 72 IPR 58 [79] (Greenwood J).

316 See also *Lancashire Fires Limited* v. *SA Lyons & Company Limited* [1996] FSR 629, 677 (CA): 'Knowledge of the [confidential information] came to [A] by reason of what has been held to be a breach of confidence by [PW]. It came to her not as a third party new to the scene but as one who had been employed by the company whose confidence had been breached by [PW] and who was involved with him in setting up the rival business.' Injunctive relief was awarded against A.

And this suggests that sometimes the accessory liability analysis is a more accurate vehicle for pleading A's liability.[317] But the accessorial analysis cannot explain all situations in which a third party innocently receives confidential information, for that party will not always have been involved in the primary wrong, whereas it will always be possible to characterise the liability as primary once the third party has notice of the confidentiality of the information acquired innocently.

8.4.1.3 Scenario 3: A does not receive the confidential information at all

Accessory liability is only essential if A is involved in a breach of confidence by PW without becoming privy to the confidential information in circumstances imparting a duty of confidence.[318] The clearest example is where A does not become privy to the confidential information at all. The facts of *Vestergaard Frandsen A/S* v. *Bestnet Europe Ltd* suggest how this might occur.[319] Two ex-employees of C and a former consultant to C established a business in competition with C. In so doing, the consultant breached his obligation of confidentiality to C in relation to trade secrets concerning C's products. One of the ex-employees, Mrs S, was never privy to the confidential information, but was nonetheless instrumental in establishing and managing the rival business. It was held that she could be accessorily liable for assisting in the breach of confidence if she knew that the consultant was misusing information that had been acquired by him in circumstances of confidence.[320]

8.4.2 *The elements of accessory liability for breach of confidence*

Of the three broad elements required for accessory liability (a primary wrong, accessorial conduct and the requisite mental state) the first two are uncontentious. Clearly there must be a breach of confidence by PW in which A is accessorily involved by way of procurement or assistance.[321]

317 See, e.g., the alleged facts in *Vestwin Trading Pte Ltd* v. *Obegi Melissa* [2006] SGHC 107 (overturned on appeal for other reasons: *Obegi Melissa* v. *Vestwin Trading Pte Ltd* [2008] 2 SLR 540 (SCA)). A, a judgment creditor of C, procured PW, a private investigator, to search for financial records in relation to C's affairs. PW obtained the documentation in breach of confidence. A was liable for breach of confidence, but could have been treated as an accessory to PW's breach, having procured it.

318 *Force India* [2012] EWHC 616 (Ch) [248].

319 [2013] UKSC 31; [2013] 1 WLR 1556.

320 *Ibid.* [26]. The claim failed on the facts.

321 Receipt of confidential information is not a receipt of property and thus cannot in itself be accessorial conduct: *Farah Constructions* [2007] HCA 22; (2007) 230 CLR 89.

But there is considerable confusion in the cases and commentaries between the requisite mental elements for primary liability and for accessory liability.[322]

As a third party to an initial breach of confidence by another, A will come under a *primary* duty of confidence if A 'knew or ought to have known' that the information was confidential.[323] This goes beyond A's actual knowledge to notice 'objectively assessed by reference to a reasonable person standing in [A's] shoes'.[324] It is a form of objective knowledge [3.4.3.5] and its focus is upon the information in question. Conversely, equitable accessory liability requires that A know of the breach of duty by PW, rather than simply that the information is confidential. That is, the basis of A's liability and the focus of the knowledge inquiry are different: it does not necessarily follow, therefore, that the requisite knowledge should be the same as for primary liability.

In *Vestergaard*, Lord Neuberger applied the dishonesty standard used to determine accessory liability for breach of trust or fiduciary duty under the reformed framework.[325] He has been criticised for doing so on the basis that the dishonesty standard requires actual knowledge, whereas the knowledge test for primary liability for breach of confidence does not.[326] But such criticisms are misguided, given that the only possible basis for liability in *Vestergaard* was accessorial. The only relevant question is whether the primary wrongs in question – breach of trust, fiduciary duty and confidence – are sufficiently similar for accessory liability purposes that the same mental element should apply.[327] Of course, if

322 See also the discussion of *Thomas* v. *Pearce* [2000] FSR 718 (CA) above [8.4.1.1].

323 *Campbell* v. *MGN Ltd* [2004] UKHL 22; [2004] 2 AC 457 [14] (Lord Nicholls); *Lenah Game Meats* [2001] HCA 63; (2001) 208 CLR 199 [39].

324 *Force India* [2012] EWHC 616; [2012] RPC 29 (Ch) [224] (Arnold J). It is not necessary to explore more precisely here what is meant by 'notice'.

325 [2013] UKSC 31; [2013] 1 WLR 1556 [26] (applying *Royal Brunei Airlines* [1995] 2 AC 378 (PC) 390–391). Contra *Force India* [2012] EWHC 616; [2012] RPC 29 (Ch) [245]–[251] (finding that an accessory to an equitable breach of confidence should be liable as a joint tortfeasor).

326 See, e.g., Chris D. L. Hunt, '"Mens Rea", Breach of Confidence and the Implications for England's Privacy "Tort"' (2013) 72 *Cambridge Law Journal* 504. See also the similar criticism of *Thomas* v. *Pearce* [2000] FSR 718 (CA) in Aplin, Bently, Johnson and Malynicz, *Gurry* [7.110].

327 The authors of *Gurry* argue that they are not: 'the courts have developed a separate notion of confidence at the root of the breach of confidence action which is to be distinguished from equity's other creation, the trust.' Aplin, Bently, Johnson and Malynicz, *Gurry* [7.110]. Of course, there is a further question as to which of the current tests (under the traditional and reformed frameworks) should be preferred if the analogy to trust and fiduciary obligations is considered appropriate.

the requisite mental element for accessory liability is indeed set at a higher level than for primary liability this will effectively rule out such claims in scenarios 1 and 2. But accessory liability continues to be necessary wherever A is accessorily involved in another's breach of confidence without becoming privy to the confidential information (scenario 3).

8.5 Undue influence and related doctrines

8.5.1 Introduction

Does accessory liability attach to equitable[328] doctrines concerned primarily with the vitiation of transactions, such as undue influence, misrepresentation,[329] the related *Etridge* doctrine[330] or any residual category[331] of 'equitable fraud'? Such doctrines will vitiate a gift or contract between C and a defendant, D, that resulted from wrongful (unconscionable) conduct by another person (X) (scenario 1).[332] Is D's liability accessorial to X's wrongdoing here? Alternatively, could a non-transacting third party D be liable as an accessory for procuring or assisting X's wrongful conduct (scenario 2)? The following discussion uses the doctrine of undue influence to explain why D's liability in scenario 1 is not accessorial and to consider whether accessory liability might arise in scenario 2.

328 Duress could be included in this list despite being largely common law in origin. See *Australian Competition and Consumer Commission* v. *CG Berbatis Holdings Pty Ltd* [2003] HCA 18; (2003) 214 CLR 51 [45]. See also, N. C. Seddon, R. A. Bigwood and M. P. Ellinghaus, *Cheshire and Fifoot Law of Contract*, 10th Aust. edn (Australia, LexisNexis Butterworths, 2012) [13.3]; H. G. Beale (gen. ed.), *Chitty on Contracts*, 31st edn (London, Sweet & Maxwell, 2012) [7-053].

329 Some forms of misrepresentation attract more extensive remedies at common law. The equitable doctrine encompasses innocent misrepresentation. In Australia, the common law and equitable doctrines are rendered less relevant because of statute. See Seddon, Bigwood and Ellinghaus, *Cheshire and Fifoot*, Ch. 11.

330 *Royal Bank of Scotland plc* v. *Etridge (No 2)* [2001] UKHL 44; [2002] 2 AC 773 (*Etridge*). Conversely, neither the similar doctrine developed in Australia (see *Garcia* v. *National Australia Bank Ltd* (1998) 194 CLR 395 (HCA)), nor the related doctrine of unconscionable dealing (see, e.g., *Commercial Bank of Australia Ltd* v. *Amadio* (1983) 151 CLR 447 (HCA)), are relevant here because neither requires wrongful conduct by X (although it may be present on the facts).

331 See Young, Croft and Smith, *On Equity* [5.10].

332 Vitiating doctrines such as mistake, accident and surprise cannot attract accessory liability for they do not require wrongful conduct by another person.

8.5.2 *Undue influence*

In bare outline, the doctrine of undue influence comprises two categories: actual and presumed undue influence.[333] In the first category, it must be proved that the gift or contract made by C with X or D 'was the outcome of such an actual influence [by X] over the mind of [C] that it cannot be considered his free act'.[334] In the second category, a court may presume, because of the nature of the relationship between C and X, that undue influence was exerted by X over C to secure a transaction between C and X, or C and D, where such a transaction would not normally be expected.[335]

If the transaction is a gift from C to D and there is actual undue influence or the presumption of undue influence is not rebutted, D's liability is strict.[336] If the transaction is a contract between C and D and there is actual undue influence or the presumption is not rebutted, D's liability turns on whether D had knowledge of the relationship of influence between X and C (or, less commonly, whether X acted as D's agent in the transaction).[337] D must have actual knowledge[338] of the features of the relationship between C and X that render it one of influence.[339] If direct evidence of D's knowledge is unavailable,[340] the court may infer actual knowledge from the facts known by D.[341] Although reference is

[333] See generally, Beale (gen. ed.), *Chitty on Contracts*, Ch. 7 (England); Seddon, Bigwood and Ellinghaus, *Cheshire and Fifoot* Ch. 14 (Australia). The Australian courts treat actual undue influence and presumed undue influence as distinct categories with separate rationales. The English courts treat presumed undue influence as a 'forensic tool' for determining actual undue influence. See *Etridge* [2001] UKHL 44; [2002] 2 AC 773 [16] (Lord Nicholls). See also at [161] (Lord Scott). Such doctrinal variations do not affect the discussion in this section.

[334] *Johnson* v. *Buttress* (1936) 56 CLR 113 (HCA) 134 (Dixon J). See also *Allcard* v. *Skinner* (1887) LR 36 Ch D 145 (CA) 181; *Etridge* [2001] UKHL 44; [2002] 2 AC 773 [8].

[335] *Allcard* v. *Skinner* (1887) 36 Ch.D 145 (CA) 185; *Johnson* v. *Buttress* (1936) 56 CLR 113 (HCA) 134–135. See also *Goldsworthy* v. *Brickell* [1987] 1 Ch 378 (CA) 401; *Etridge* [2001] UKHL 44; [2002] 2 AC 773 [156]. See also Beale (gen. ed.), *Chitty on Contracts* [7–090].

[336] *Bridgeman* v. *Green* (1757) Wilm 56, 64–65; 97 ER 22 (HL) 25.

[337] A true agency relationship will be a 'rare occurrence': *Barclays Bank plc* v. *O'Brien* [1994] 1 AC 180 (HL) 195. See further, Ridge, 'Third Party Volunteers' 119–120.

[338] This is despite some references to 'constructive' notice: see, e.g., *Etridge* [2001] UKHL 44; [2002] 2 AC 773 [40]. Constructive notice in the strict, conveyancing law sense does not suffice: [145]; see also at [144]–[146]; *Kakavas* v. *Crown Melbourne Limited* [2013] HCA 25; (2013) 250 CLR 292 [152]–[155].

[339] *Bainbrigge* v. *Browne* (1881) 18 Ch D 188, 197. *Cf.* the 'essential matters' approach to content of knowledge: [3.4.2.2].

[340] See, e.g., the facts of *Bank of New South Wales* v. *Rogers* (1941) 65 CLR 42 (HCA).

[341] See, e.g., *ibid.*, 55. See also *Kakavas* v. *Crown Melbourne Limited* [2013] HCA 25; (2013) 250 CLR 292 [155]–[156].

sometimes made to D not having made further inquiries (which is suggestive of objective knowledge [3.4.3.5]),[342] this is only for the purpose of proving D's wilful ignorance (see [3.4.3.3]) and, hence, actual knowledge.[343]

The remedies for undue influence, of which rescission is the most common, focus on the effect of the transaction upon C.[344] Because of this, the remedies are generally directed towards the counterparty to the transaction. Whether remedies are available against X where the transaction is between C and D has received little attention.[345]

8.5.3 Scenario 1: D is party to the transaction tainted by X's undue influence

Establishing the first element of accessory liability, namely a primary wrong [3.2], is problematic in scenario 1 because the rationale of undue influence and, specifically, whether it is wrong-based at all is contested.[346] We consider that it is concerned with X's actual or presumed wrongdoing.[347] Therefore, our starting point for analysis is that undue

[342] See, e.g., *Maitland* v. *Irving* (1846) 15 Sim 437; 60 ER 688; *Bank of New South Wales* v. *Rogers* (1941) 65 CLR 42 (HCA) 71–72.

[343] See, e.g., *Owen and Gutch* v. *Homan* (1853) 4 HL Cas 997, 1035; 10 ER 752, 767.

[344] In relation to remedies other than rescission, see, e.g., *Mahoney* v. *Purnell* [1996] 3 All ER 61 (QBD) (equitable compensation for the actual value of the property less the amount received); *Haywood* v. *Roadknight* [1927] VLR 512 (account against D for the proceeds of sale of the subject property); *McCulloch* v. *Fern* [2001] NSWSC 406 (remedial constructive trust upon subject property to reflect contributions by C); *Hartigan* v. *International Society for Krishna Consciousness Inc* [2002] NSWSC 810 (account for the proceeds of sale of the subject property). See also *Treadwell* v. *Martin* (1976) 67 DLR (3d) 493, 13 NBR (2d) 137 (NBCA) ('damages'); *Dusik* v. *Newton* (1985) 62 BCLR 1 (BCCA) ('damages' in lieu of rescission); *Rick* v. *Brandsema* (2009) 303 DLR (4th) 193 [66]–[68].

[345] But see *Smith* v. *Glegg* [2004] QSC 443; (2005) 1 Qd R 561.

[346] For a helpful introduction to the extensive literature concerning whether undue influence is a wrong, see V. J. Vann, 'Equitable Compensation when Rescission is Impossible' (2003) 17 *Trust Law International* 66. The seminal work denying that undue influence is fault-based is Peter Birks and Chin Nyuk Yin, 'On the Nature of Undue Influence' in Jack Beatson and Daniel Friedmann (eds.), *Good Faith and Fault in Contract Law* (Oxford, Clarendon Press, 1995) 57. We do not take this approach, nor is it supported by the cases in our view. See further, Bigwood, 'Undue Influence: "Impaired Consent" or "Wicked Exploitation"?' (1996) *Oxford Journal of Legal Studies* 503; 'Contracts by Unfair Advantage: From Exploitation to Transactional Neglect' (2005) 25 *Oxford Journal of Legal Studies* 65; Mindy Chen-Wishart, 'Undue Influence: Vindicating Relationships of Influence' (2006) 59 *Current Legal Problems* 231.

[347] We also incline to the view that the doctrine of undue influence is a fiduciary doctrine. See e.g., *Tate* v. *Williamson* (1866–67) LR 2 Ch App 55; *Johnson* v. *Buttress* (1936) 56

influence involves either an actual or presumed primary wrong in the sense of X's breach of a pre-existing duty or primary wrongfulness in the broader equitable sense of unconscionable conduct by X [8.1.2].

The second element of accessory liability, namely involvement through conduct in X's actual or presumed undue influence [3.3], is also problematic. Accessorial involvement may well be present on the particular facts, as is clear from the leading Australian authority concerning undue influence and contracts between C and D, *Bank of NSW* v. *Rogers*.[348] A plausible reading of that case is that the bank (D) procured an insolvent debtor (X) who had no prospect of reversing his fortunes to exert undue influence over his adult niece to whom he was in *loco parentis* (C) in order to obtain a guarantee for his debts secured by her assets. The High Court of Australia held that the bank could not enforce the guarantee because it had knowledge of the relationship of influence.[349]

It has been suggested that D's liability in such instances contains the same elements as 'participatory' liability for breach of trust or fiduciary duty[350] or 'secondary liability based on knowing participation'.[351] Nonetheless, such cases cannot be examples of accessory liability. In the surety undue influence cases exemplified by *Bank of NSW* v. *Rogers*, the courts' concern was that creditors were indeed procuring debtors to abuse their influence over relatives, but proof of such procurement was never required, nor was it presumed.[352] Deterrence of accessorial conduct is clearly one of several reasons why equity assumes a prophylactic role in relation to relationships of influence and third parties, but active involvement is never required. All that is necessary is that D has entered

CLR 113 (HCA) 135. See further, L. S. Sealy, 'Fiduciary Relationships' [1962] *Cambridge Law Journal* 69; Finn, *Fiduciary Obligations*, Ch. 16; David Tiplady, 'The Limits of Undue Influence' (1985) 48 *Modern Law Review* 579; P. D. Finn, 'The Fiduciary Principle' in T. G. Youdan (ed.), *Equity, Fiduciaries and Trusts* (Carswell Law Book Co, Toronto, 1989), 42, 43–48; Robert Flannigan, 'The Fiduciary Obligation' (1989) 9 *Oxford Journal of Legal Studies* 285; Rick Bigwood, '"Impaired Consent or Wicked Exploitation"?'; 'Undue Influence in the House of Lords: Principles and Proof' (2002) 65 *Modern Law Review* 435. It is not necessary to resolve that issue here.

348 (1941) 65 CLR 42 (HCA). 349 *Ibid.*, especially at 51.

350 *Grimaldi* [2012] FCAFC 6; (2012) 200 FCR 296 [247]. See also Austin, 'Constructive Trusts', 200 citing *Lancashire Loans Ltd* v. *Black* [1934] 1 KB 380 (CA). See also Finn, 'The Liability of Third Parties', 204.

351 *Khan* v. *Khan* [2004] NSWSC 1189; (2004) 62 NSWLR 235 [21] (Barrett J citing *Royal Brunei Airlines* [1995] 2 AC 378 (PC)).

352 See, e.g., *Sercombe* v. *Sanders* (1865) 34 Beav 382, 385; 56 ER 682, 683; *Maitland* v. *Irving* (1846) 15 Sim 437; 60 ER 688; *Bainbrigge* v. *Browne* (1881) 18 Ch D 188; *Bank of New South Wales* v. *Rogers* (1941) 65 CLR 42 (HCA).

the subject contract or, in the case of a gift, accepted the transfer.[353] If the gift is by way of a deed of settlement, D need not even have been alive at the time of the settlement's execution.[354]

It could be argued that D's entry into the contract or acceptance of the gift completes X's wrong, so to speak, and therefore constitutes facilitative involvement in a weak sense. The argument perhaps has some weight given that undue influence is not actionable until a tainted transaction eventuates, although it strains the concept of accessorial conduct. It is, however, more consistent with a participatory liability explanation for D's liability.[355]

The third element of accessory liability concerns D's mental state. Here, it becomes clear that the liability of a volunteer D is most unlikely to be accessorial because it is strict, rather than fault-based (see [3.4.1]).[356] Instead, D's strict liability is explicable by a combination of factors, including the mild impact of rescission upon D compared with other equitable remedies, the lack of strong policy reasons for upholding gifts in circumstances where the gift is tainted by a vitiating factor, and because it is seen as against good conscience for D to retain the gift in such circumstances.[357] Conversely, where D is the counterparty to a contract with C, D's liability is fault-based, and the requisite mental element is the same as that required for both equitable accessory and participatory liability: knowledge of the relationship of influence [8.5.2].

Thus, D's liability is not accessory liability in scenario 1. This is clearest if D is a donee because accessorial involvement is unnecessary and the liability is strict. If D is a contracting party, D's liability may well be a form of participatory liability, but it is not accessorial because involvement in X's wrongdoing is not required.

8.5.4 *Scenario 2: D is not a party to the transaction tainted by X's undue influence*

The second scenario in which accessory liability might arise is where C has entered a transaction with X or another party that is tainted by X's

[353] In relation to contracts see, e.g., *Khan* v. *Khan* [2004] NSWSC 1189; (2004) 62 NSWLR 229 [18], citing Meagher, Heydon and Leeming, *Equity* [15–150]. In relation to gifts, see *Bridgeman* v. *Green* (1757) Wilm 56, 64–65; 97 ER 22 (HL) 25.

[354] *Cf. Gibbon* v. *Mitchell* [1990] 1 WLR 1304 (Ch) (vitiating factor of mistake). See also *Giarrantano* v. *Smith* (1985) NSW Conv R 55267 (trust for X's living grandchildren).

[355] *Cf.* the discussion of recipient liability at [7.6.2].

[356] *Bridgeman* v. *Green* (1757) Wilm 56, 64–65; 97 ER 22 (HL) 25.

[357] See further, Pauline Ridge, 'Third Party Volunteers and Undue Influence' (2014) 130 *Law Quarterly Review* 112.

actual or presumed undue influence and where X's undue influence was procured or facilitated by D.

The same comments regarding the presence of a primary wrong by X apply as in scenario 1 [8.5.3], but A's accessorial involvement is much clearer here. The requisite mental element, by analogy with established categories of equitable accessory liability, would be actual knowledge of the primary wrong, although a limited form of objective knowledge might be countenanced [8.3.4.3].

There are no cases directly supporting such liability, although an embryonic form of accessory liability for undue influence did exist in the eighteenth and nineteenth centuries.[358] Much depends upon one's understanding of the doctrine of undue influence and its purposes and values. Furthermore, if the doctrine's function is primarily to obviate the effects of the tainted transaction, then the need for relief against non-transacting parties is not great. The presumptive, prophylactic nature of the doctrine, in its traditional form at least, may also cast doubt on the wisdom of extending liability too far. If, however, undue influence is viewed as a subset of fiduciary law, then recognition of accessory liability would be principled.

8.6 Defences

8.6.1 Introduction

An accessory may rely upon any of the general equitable defences to defeat C's claim or to preclude the award of particular remedies.[359] The

[358] See, e.g., *Bennet* v. *Vade* (1742) 2 Atk 324; 26 ER 597. See also *Beadles* v. *Burch* (1839) 10 Sim 332; 59 ER 642, and the cases referred to in that case. The cases concern whether a solicitor who prepared documents tainted by equitable fraud or undue influence should be liable for the costs of proceedings to set aside or rectify the tainted transaction. Liability was recognised where the solicitor personally benefitted from the transaction (other than by way of legal fees: *Maw* v. *Pearson* (1860) 28 Beav 194; 54 ER 340) or was accessorily involved in PW's fraudulent conduct. See, e.g., *Harvey* v. *Mount* (1845) 8 Beav 439; 50 ER 172. The question for the court at 453; 178 (Lord Langdale MR) was whether A 'wilfully and designedly conspired with [X]' or whether 'he was a willful partaker in any fraud intended to be practiced upon [the influenced party, C]'.

[359] Broadly speaking, these defences are grounded in concepts of waiver, delay or unlawfulness on the part of C. They include statutory defences that apply directly or by analogy. See further, Michael Spence, 'Equitable Defences' in Patrick Parkinson (ed.), *The Principles of Equity*, 2nd edn (Sydney, Lawbook Co, 2003) 997. In *Corporacion Nacional del Cobre de Chile* v. *Sogemin Metals Ltd* [1997] 1 WLR 1396 (Ch) 1402, Carnwath J held that the common law defence of contributory negligence or 'its equivalent in equity' did not apply to a dishonest assistance claim. But at 1403 His

mental element required for accessory liability and recipient liability necessarily precludes the operation of defences that depend on lack of notice. For example, A cannot rely upon the defences of bona fide purchase or change of position in relation to recipient liability.[360] The following discussion notes specific issues that have arisen regarding defences and accessory liability.

8.6.2 Is it a defence that PW is not liable?

Should A be liable for the primary wrong if, in the particular circumstances, PW has a defence? Examples of such a scenario are where C has undertaken not to sue PW, PW has been excused by the court pursuant to exculpatory legislation, or PW has been released from liability by C.

In all these scenarios, PW's prima facie liability can be established; thus, it cannot be argued that a necessary element of A's liability, namely the primary wrong, is not present. Conversely, where C has consented to, or acquiesced in,[361] the primary wrong, PW is not even prima facie liable. If C has consented to, or acquiesced in, the primary wrong, this will therefore also preclude A's accessory liability.[362]

Where PW is prima facie liable, but has a defence personal to herself, is it inequitable for A to bear (perhaps sole) responsibility for the primary wrong, such that the undertaking, exculpation or release also constitutes a defence to A? The principles concerning joint and several liability and contribution have some bearing on these questions and are discussed further in [8.8].

Honour left open the possibility that C's failure to protect its own interests might affect the measure of equitable compensation. See also *Equiticorp Industries Group Ltd (in stat. man.)* v. *R (No 47)* [1998] 2 NZLR 481 (NZHC) 659–661, in which Smellie J reduced the amount of equitable compensation payable by A for knowing assistance by 2.5% due to C's failure to discover the breaches of fiduciary duty and intervene.

360 *Grupo Torras SA* v. *Al-Sabah (No.5)* [1999] CLC 1469 (QB).

361 'Acquiescence' here means 'the contemporaneous and informed ("knowing") acceptance or standing by which is treated by equity as "assent" (i.e. consent) to what would otherwise be an infringement of rights … '. *Orr* v. *Ford* (1989) 167 CLR 316 (HCA) 337 (Deane J). In most instances, consent is treated as a defence, rather than as precluding prima facie liability. See further, Young, Croft and Smith, *On Equity* [17.150], [17.180].

362 *Blackwood* v. *Borrowes* (1843) 4 Dr & War 441; 65 RR 729 (*Blackwood*). Affirmation of the primary wrong is also a defence: see *Jyske Bank (Gibralter) Limited* v. *Spjeldnaes* (CA, 29 July 1999). The same reasoning applies if PW relies upon an exemption clause in a trust deed or other foundational document, the primary wrong will not have been made out and A cannot be liable. This also precludes accessory liability for *attempted* procurement or inducement of a primary wrong.

An undertaking not to sue PW does not extinguish the substantive liability of either PW or A.[363] Thus, A has no defence here, but may still claim contribution against PW where that is otherwise available. Similarly, whether PW has been excused from liability by the court pursuant to exculpatory legislation has no necessary bearing upon A's liability and does not constitute a defence.[364]

Whether A has a defence where C has released PW from liability is not as clear and is influenced by whether A's liability is several or joint and several [8.8]. Where A's liability is several only (for example, A has made a gain) then it should not be a defence that PW is released from liability in relation to the primary wrong. Thus, if C releases PW (who would otherwise be jointly and severally liable with A for C's losses), C may still claim against A in relation to A's gains for which A is severally liable.[365]

If C has received valuable consideration through an accord and satisfaction with PW, this should be taken into account in assessing A's liability and ensuring that C does not receive double recovery.[366] Some such adjustment may be necessary even where the remedy that is sought is only available against A. For example, in *Yeshiva Properties* the issue was whether A, who made a short-term loan at high interest rates to Company C, could enforce the loan contract.[367] Company C argued that its directors (the PWs) had breached fiduciary duties in entering the contract on its behalf and that A was an accessory. Company C had released the directors from liability.[368] If A were liable, the obvious

363 See, e.g., *Brinks* [1996] CLC 133 (Ch) 146. See further, Alison Gurr, 'Accessory Liability and Contribution, Release and Apportionment' (2010) 34 *Melbourne University Law Review* 481, 509–510; Mitchell, 'Assistance', 208–209.

364 *Farah Constructions* [2007] HCA 22; (2007) 230 CLR 89 [184] n. 264. E.g., where A procures an innocent breach of duty by PW, the court may well excuse PW, while finding A liable.

365 *Cf. Coulton* v. *Coulton* [2008] NSWSC 910. C and PW were in partnership. C released PW by deed from liability, but claimed that A, PW's wife, knowingly participated in a breach of fiduciary duty by PW and other partners. McLaughlin AJ at [51] rejected a strike-out application: 'I am far from being persuaded that the inevitable consequence of the release of [PW] is that [A] . . . is also thereby released from the consequences of her such knowing participation.'

366 See in the context of accessory liability, *Michael Wilson* [2011] HCA 48; (2011) 244 CLR 427 [100]–[110], and the cases cited at [101]. It is clear that A has an 'equity . . . to prevent enforcement of an award or judgment ... where to do so would lead to double recovery': [101].

367 [2005] NSWCA 23; (2005) 219 ALR 112.

368 The directors were released from potential liabilities owed to the group of companies in question when the group was in provisional liquidation.

remedy was rescission of the loan contract, which would require Company C to repay the principal sum, plus an interest component (at market rates). A would not be able to enforce the contract provisions for default interest. Bryson JA considered that any value received by Company C pursuant to the deed of release should be taken into account in assessing the remedy available against A. This must be the correct outcome to avoid double recovery by Company C.

Where A is jointly and severally liable with PW the position is less clear because PW's release from liability could mean that A bears the full remedial consequences of the primary wrong, depending upon whether any right to contribution from PW survives. The previous common law rule was that 'a release given to, and an accord and satisfaction effected with, one of a number of parties jointly or jointly and severally liable, contractually discharges the others'.[369] There are conflicting authorities on whether this rule should apply to co-trustees[370] and further uncertainty as to whether it should apply as between trustees and accessories. The better view is that it does not apply in either scenario;[371] thus, with respect to accessory liability, A remains liable.[372] In a detailed study of this question, Alison Gurr has proposed in relation to loss-based remedies for breach of trust or fiduciary duty that the courts:

> treat releases of [PW] as extinguishing their own liability and reducing [A's] liability by [PW's] share of the [compensation]. This 'share' would be the greater of:
>
> (i) The amount paid by [PW] in settling with [C];
> or
> (ii) The amount that the court would otherwise have allowed the remaining wrongdoers [A] to recover from the released [PW].[373]

[369] *Thompson* v. *Australian Capital Television Pty Limited* [1996] 186 CLR 574 (HCA) 608 (Gummow J). See also [3.6] and [5.6.2].

[370] *Ibid.* 608–609. Gummow J referred to *First & Merchants National Bank* v. *Bank of Waverley* (1938) 197 SE 462, which held that a release of one co-trustee automatically discharges the other co-trustees by analogy with the rules governing joint tortfeasors, and contrasted this with the approach in the Irish case of *Blackwood* (1843) 4 Dr & War 441, 475; 65 RR 729, 745–744 (deciding that the release of one trustee may, but need not, discharge the other trustees depending upon the 'substance and merits of the case').

[371] *Contra.*, Mitchell, 'Assistance', 208.

[372] The reasoning in *First & Merchants National Bank* v. *Bank of Waverley* (1938) 197 SE 462 has been rejected on the basis that the liability of co-trustees is joint and several, rather than joint: *Coulton* v. *Coulton* [2008] NSWSC 910 [47]–[51]. See further, Gurr, 'Accessory Liability, 504–505.

[373] Gurr, 'Accessory Liability', 507. If this proposal is not accepted, she suggests, at 508, that the courts '(i) take into account any advantage received by [C] in respect of the release;

8.6.3 *Statutory limitation periods*

Whether A can rely upon the expiry of a statutory limitation period as a defence is, of course, a question of statutory interpretation.[374] Nonetheless, there are commonalities because limitation legislation in many jurisdictions is based upon the nineteenth-century seminal English legislation and its successors.[375] It must therefore be interpreted in the context of that broader legislative history and the judicial interpretations thereof, as well as with equity's understanding of participatory liability in mind. Complicating the matter is that the legislative history is contested, the nineteenth-century cases were not consistent in their treatment of 'constructive trustees',[376] including accessories, and the leading cases[377] on the application of statutory limitation periods to equitable accessories cannot all be

and (ii) allow contribution'. *Cf. Yeshiva Properties* [2005] NSWCA 23; (2005) 219 ALR 112 [80].

374 The following discussion focuses upon common questions, using the English law as its focus; it does not purport to provide a specialist treatment. In other jurisdictions, see generally, Meagher, Heydon and Leeming, *Equity*, Ch. 34 (Australia); Waters and Gillen, *Waters' Law of Trusts*, 25.IV.C. (Canada); *Yong Kheng Leong* v. *Panweld Trading Pte Ltd.* [2012] SGCA 59 (Singapore); Andrew S. Butler (gen. ed.), *Equity and Trusts in New Zealand*, 2nd edn (Wellington, Thomson Reuters, 2009) [38.1.2]–[38.1.3] (New Zealand); *Peconic* [2009] HKCFA 17; [2009] 5 HKC 135 (Hong Kong).

375 Trustee Act 1888, 51 & 52 Vict, c 59. Section 8(1) introduced a limitation period for claims against trustees except where: 'founded upon any fraud or fraudulent breach of trust to which the trustee was party or privy' or 'to recover trust property, or the proceeds therefor still retained by the trustee, or previously received by the trustee and converted to his use'. 'Trustee' included 'a trustee whose trust arises by construction or implication of law': s. 1(3). The English law is less relevant in much of Canada where there has been substantial reform of statutory limitation schemes: Waters and Gillen, *Waters' Law of Trusts*, 25.IV.C.4. It is also necessary to be alert to jurisdiction-specific changes to the English statutory template. See, e.g., the wording of s.11(1) *Limitation Act 1969* (NSW): '[t]rust includes express implied and constructive trusts, whether or not the trustee has a beneficial interest in the trust property, and whether or not the trust arises only by reason of a transaction impeached . . . ' and NSW Law Reform Commission, *First Report on the Limitation of Actions*, October 1967 (LRC 3) [80]; *Queensland Mines* v. *Hudson* (1976) CLC ¶40–266 (NSWSC) [28709]-[28710].

376 Generally, the limitation period applied to third-party participants in breach of trust other than trustees de son tort, but this was not always so. See Austin, 'Constructive Trusts', 205 citing *Wilson* v. *Moore* (1834) 1 My & K 337; 39 ER 629; *Bridgman* v. *Gill* (1857) 24 Beav 302; 53 ER 374; *Soar* v. *Ashwell* [1893] 2 QB 390.

377 *Soar* v. *Ashwell* [1893] 2 QB 390 (CA); *Taylor* v. *Davies* [1920] AC 636 (PC); *Clarkson* v. *Davies* [1923] AC 100 (PC); *Selangor* [1968] 1 WLR 1555 (Ch); *Paragon Finance* [1999] 1 All ER 400 (CA); *Dubai Aluminium* [2002] UKHL 48; [2003] 2 AC 366.

reconciled.[378] Although the topic of limitation periods may appear peripheral to a work on accessory liability, the legal questions involved have raised fundamental questions regarding the nature of A's liability.

The core question is whether A's liability as a 'constructive trustee' [8.1.7] should be equated with that of an express trustee for the purpose of determining which provisions of relevant limitation legislation apply to C's claim. This is important because in many jurisdictions no limitation period at all applies to claims against an express trustee involving fraudulent breach of trust or to recover trust property.[379] There is also a subsidiary question concerning the ambit of the wording of such provisions.[380] The UK Supreme Court in *Williams* considered these two questions in relation to the application of s. 21(1)(a) of the Limitation Act 1980 (UK) to claims for dishonest assistance and knowing receipt in breach of trust.[381] A majority of the Court answered both questions in the negative, namely: was A to be considered a 'trustee' and were claims against a dishonest assistant 'in respect of a trustee's fraud'.[382] Thus, a 6-year limitation period applied and C's claim was barred.

Williams cannot be regarded as settling these issues for other jurisdictions with similar legislation for several reasons.[383] First, the majority in *Williams* was persuaded by the reasoning in a series of twentieth-century cases that distinguished constructive trustees according to whether 'a trust arose before the occurrence of the transaction impeached' (for example, trustees de son tort) or 'only by reason of that transaction' (accessories).[384]

378 The complexity of the statutory interpretation exercise is strikingly illustrated by the opposing judgments of Lord Sumption (majority) and Lord Mance (dissenting) in *Williams* [2014] UKSC 10; [2014] 2 WLR 355.

379 See, e.g., Limitation Act 1980 c.58 (UK) s. 21(1).

380 See, e.g., Limitation Act 1980 c.58 (UK) s. 21(3): 'Subject to the preceding provisions of this section, an action by a beneficiary to recover trust property or in respect of any breach of trust, not being an action for which a period of limitation is prescribed by any other provision of this Act, shall not be brought after the expiration of six years from the date on which the right of action accrued.'

381 [2014] UKSC 10; [2014] 2 WLR 355.

382 *Ibid.* The majority consisted of Lord Sumption and Lord Neuberger (Lord Hughes agreed with both judgments). Lord Mance dissented; Lord Clarke dissented in relation to the second question.

383 But see in Hong Kong: *Peconic* [2009] HKCFA 17; [2009] 5 HKC 135. Lord Hoffmann's leading judgment was approved by the majority in *Williams* [2014] UKSC 10; [2014] 2 WLR 355 [28] (Lord Sumption JSC), [63]–[64] (Lord Neuberger), but was heavily criticised by Lord Mance [154] and Lord Clarke [180]–[181].

384 *Taylor* v. *Davies* [1920] AC 636 (PC) 650–651, 653 (Viscount Cave); *Clarkson* v. *Davies* [1923] AC 100 (PC); *Selangor* [1968] 1 WLR 1555 (Ch); *Paragon Finance* [1999] 1 All ER 400 (CA); *Dubai Aluminium* [2002] UKHL 48; [2003] 2 AC 366.

Statutory limitation periods applied to the latter form of trustee. This distinction was said to be based upon the nineteenth-century case law, but not all judges accept this interpretation of the nineteenth-century cases.[385] Secondly, the outcome in *Williams* was said to reflect a principled distinction between fiduciaries on the one hand and dishonest assistants and knowing recipients on the other.[386] But Lord Mance offered an alternative, plausible explanation for finding that a dishonest assistant should be grouped with a dishonest trustee for limitation purposes: 'to equate a third person, who dishonestly joins with a dishonest trustee to defraud the trust, with the dishonest trustee for limitation purposes is entirely natural'.[387] This explanation particularly resonates with the traditional framework's knowing assistance in a dishonest and fraudulent design [8.3.1.4]. Finally, although all the judgments in *Williams* engaged with the complex legislative history of the Limitation Act 1980, it cannot be said that those of the majority were more persuasive than the dissentients.[388]

In the unusual event that no statutory limitation period applies directly to an equitable accessory liability claim, one may still apply by analogy.[389]

8.6.4 Statutory indefeasibility of title

Questions arise as to whether it is a defence to recipient liability that A has registered title to the received trust property pursuant to a Torrens, or

385 See, e.g., *Williams* [2014] UKSC 10; [2014] 2 WLR 355. See also Austin, 'Constructive Trusts', 203–207.

386 *Williams* [2014] UKSC 10; [2014] 2 WLR 355 [118]. Other rationales include that the evidential basis for establishing a constructive trusteeship may be more fragile (*Soar* v. *Ashwell* [1893] 2 QB 390 (CA) 400, citing *Beckford* v. *Wade* 17 Ves Jun 87, 34 ER 34) and that equity acts in its concurrent jurisdiction in cases of accessory liability and therefore the limitation period for a common law action for fraud should apply to the concurrent equitable action (*Paragon Finance* [1999] 1 All ER 400 (CA) 409–410).

387 *Williams* [2014] UKSC 10; [2014] 2 WLR 355 [157] (see also [129]).

388 See James Lee, 'Constructing and Limiting Liability in Equity' (2015) 131 *Law Quarterly Review* 39.

389 E.g., in Australia, the limitation period in the *Corporations Act 2001* (Cth) s. 1317K could apply by analogy to an accessory claim concerning breach of a director's fiduciary duties: *cf. Gerace* v. *Auzhair Supplies Pty Ltd* [2014] NSWCA 181; (2014) 100 ACSR 465 (concerning equitable claims for breach of fiduciary duty by directors). *Gerace* contains an extensive discussion of the relevant principles in the context of equity's exclusive jurisdiction and their relationship to the doctrine of laches. See also Justice Mark Leeming, 'How Long is Too Long for an Equitable Claim?' (2014) 88 *Australian Law Journal* 621.

other, system of land registration.[390] The answer in any particular case must depend upon the terms and effect of the relevant registration scheme in question;[391] the objective of the legislation, the rationale for recipient liability and the *in personam* nature of its remedies will also be relevant. The High Court of Australia has stated in obiter that a knowing recipient who has a registered interest in land pursuant to Torrens legislation may rely on statutory indefeasibility of title as a defence to C's claim except where (referring to interpretation of the specific legislation under consideration)[392] there is 'actual fraud or moral turpitude'.[393] That is, the *in personam* exception to indefeasibility of title did not apply to recipient liability.[394] In the Court's view, this was because a knowing recipient was 'a party who merely had notice of an earlier interest or notice of third party fraud'.[395]

The obiter comments in *Farah Constructions* were made in relation to a proprietary remedy for knowing receipt.[396] It has been suggested, in the context of the English land registration system, that the same approach should apply to personal remedies for recipient liability; that is, a recipient liability claim is not available where the trust property is registered land.[397] The suggestion relies upon the rationale for recipient liability being the vindication of C's property rights, rather than the redress of A's wrongdoing per se.[398] Conversely, we would argue that it is precisely

390 See Matthew Harding, '*Barnes* v. *Addy* Claims and the Indefeasibility of Torrens Title' (2007) 31 Melbourne University Law Review 343. Harding argues that *Barnes* v. *Addy* claims even those with 'proprietary consequences' do not present a special threat to the principle of indefeasibility of title in the Australian land registration schemes.

391 *Arthur* [2012] UKPC 30 [15]. 392 *Real Property Act 1900* (NSW) s. 42(1).

393 *Farah Constructions* [2007] HCA 22; (2007) 230 CLR 89 [192].

394 *Ibid.* [193] (approving the reasoning of *Macquarie Bank Ltd* v. *Sixty-Fourth Throne Pty Ltd* [1998] 3 VR 133, 156–157, which was followed in *LHK Nominees Pty Ltd* v. *Kenworthy* (2002) 26 WAR 517 and *Tara Shire Council* v. *Garner* [2003] 1 Qd R 556 [34]). But see *Super 1000* v. *Pacific General Securities* [2008] NSWSC 1222; (2008) 221 FLR 427 [215]–[232] (*Super 1000*); Harding, '*Barnes* v. *Addy* Claims'.

395 *Farah Constructions* [2007] HCA 22; (2007) 230 CLR 89 [195], quoting from *LHK Nominees Pty Ltd* v. *Kenworthy* [2002] WASCA 291; (2002) 26 WAR 517 [289] (Pullin J).

396 *Super 1000* [2008] NSWSC 1222; (2008) 221 FLR 427 [235] (White J considered that personal remedies were therefore available).

397 Matthew Conaglen and Amy Goymour, 'Knowing Receipt and Registered Land' in Mitchell, *Constructive and Resulting Trusts*, 159. The authors acknowledge that their argument is contrary to the Law Commission report that led to the enactment of the relevant legislation: Law Commission, *Land Registration for the Twenty-First Century* (Law Com. No.254, 1998) [3.48]–[3.49].

398 This appears to have been rejected by the Privy Council, which instead emphasised that unconscionable receipt is 'not merely absence of notice but unconscionable conduct

because the rationale for recipient liability is the redress of A's wrongdoing, rather than the vindication of property rights, that personal remedies may persist against a registered owner of land [7.6.1]. It is only when the remedy sought is a trust over the land itself that the two schemes come into conflict. In the same way that registered title would not be a defence to a dishonest assistance claim where the assistance was in transferring registered title to trust property, personal remedies for recipient liability should not be precluded.[399]

8.7 Remedies

8.7.1 Introduction

A culpable third party to breach of an equitable duty, including an accessory, is exposed to the full range of equitable remedies available against an express trustee.[400] While A's wrongdoing is different in kind to that of PW,[401] it can be equally unmeritorious.[402] Although parallels can be drawn with the tort of inducing breach of contract, for which gain-based remedies are not available,[403] the nature of the primary wrongs in contract and equity that accessory liability is designed to protect are qualitatively different. It is entirely appropriate that more extensive remedies are available where necessary to meet the different objectives of the equitable liability.[404] Gain-based remedies, for example, are easily justified if A has profited from culpable interference with a relationship

amounting to equitable fraud. It is a classic example of lack of bona fides.' *Arthur* [2012] UKPC 30 [39]. See also at [38].

399 Conaglen and Goymour accept that a dishonest assistance claim will prevail against the registered proprietor because the rationale is redress of wrongdoing: 'Knowing Receipt and Registered Land', 177–181.

400 *Grimaldi* [2012] FCAFC 6; (2012) 200 FCR 296 [667]; *Novoship* [2014] EWCA Civ 908 [82]. A is said to be accountable as a constructive trustee or more simply, 'accountable in equity'. The discussion in [8.7] further develops arguments first presented in Ridge, 'Justifying the Remedies for Dishonest Assistance' and 'Constructive Trusts, Accessory Liability and Judicial Discretion' in Elise Bant and Michael Bryan (eds.), *Principles of Proprietary Remedies* (Sydney, Lawbook Co, 2013) 73. For a useful review of the US case law on remedies for participation in breach of trust, see *Bogert's Trusts and Trustees* §868.

401 There is no pre-existing obligation of loyalty, for example.

402 *Fyffes* [2000] 2 Lloyd's Rep 643 (QB) 669.

403 See *Royal Brunei Airlines* [1995] 2 AC 378 (PC) 386–387; *Sinclair Investment Holdings SA v. Versailles Trade Finance Ltd* [2007] 2 All ER (Comm) 993 [132]. But note *Novoship* [2014] EWCA Civ 908 [72].

404 Ridge, 'Justifying the Remedies for Dishonest Assistance', 451–452.

between C and PW that is protected by equity.[405] Further justifying the range of remedies for accessory liability is that equitable remedies are never available as of right. They are awarded at the court's discretion[406] and are fashioned to fit the particular factual and legal scenario.[407] Relevant factors in determining relief include the rationale for A's liability, the nature of the primary wrong[408] and the egregiousness of A's conduct. In most instances, however, it is the consequences of PW and A's wrongdoing for C and A, respectively, that will determine the remedy or remedies available against A.[409]

There are jurisdictional differences concerning the availability of some equitable remedies, the principles by which they are determined and the permissible scope of judicial remedial discretion. Such questions are discussed here only where relevant to accessory liability. Most judicial discussion concerning remedies has occurred in the context of accessories to breach of trust and fiduciary duty; however, the same principles apply in relation to breach of confidence.

8.7.2 Loss-based remedies

The loss-based remedy of equitable compensation is the most common remedy for accessory liability.[410] A will be jointly and severally liable with PW for C's losses resulting from the primary wrong (rather than from A's accessory conduct directly) [8.8.1]. In the case of recipient liability, on the other hand, the remedy focuses upon A's culpable receipt and requires A

405 *Consul Development* (1975) 132 CLR 373 (HCA) 397; *Michael Wilson* [2011] HCA 48; (2011) 244 CLR 427 [106]; *Novoship* [2014] EWCA Civ 908.

406 See, e.g., *Grimaldi* [2012] FCAFC 6; (2012) 200 FCR 296 (constructive trust refused); *Novoship* [2014] EWCA Civ 908 [119] (account of profits refused if 'disproportionate in relation to the particular form and extent of wrongdoing').

407 *Warman International Ltd* v. *Dwyer* (1995) 182 CLR 544 (HCA) 559 (*Warman* v. *Dwyer*). Equitable remedies can be awarded on terms: see, e.g., *Ninety Five Pty Ltd (in liq.)* v. *Banque Nationale de Paris* [1988] WAR 132.

408 In relation to breach of confidence, see *Vercoe* v. *Rutland Fund* [2010] EWHC 424; [2010] Bus LR D [344].

409 'It is the case that, in many instances and for many types of equitable wrong, the remedy that is most appropriate will self select absent unusual circumstances.' *Grimaldi* [2012] FCAFC 6; (2012) 200 FCR 296 [503] (Finn, Stone and Perram JJ).

410 Indeed, sometimes it is incorrectly implied that this is the *only* remedy. See, e.g., *Royal Brunei Airlines* [1995] 2 AC 378 (PC) 392 (but note *Novoship* [2014] EWCA Civ 908 [73]–[74]); *Twinsectra* [2002] UKHL 12; [2002] 2 AC 164 [107]. See also Mitchell and Elliott, 'Remedies for Dishonest Assistance', 24.

to compensate on a restorative basis in the same manner as for a custodial breach of trust.

No jurisdiction has yet established a comprehensive, coherent and settled jurisprudence concerning equitable compensatory remedies. This is unsurprising given that the availability of such remedies outside the context of trusts was not widely recognised until the twentieth century.[411] Nonetheless it is clear that, as with the different measures of compensation available at common law, the calculation of C's loss will vary according to the equitable wrong or wrongs in question.[412] There are two bodies of law[413] that inform loss-based remedies for accessory liability: that concerning compensation for breach of fiduciary duty[414] and that concerning the monetary orders and procedures that accompany a custodial fiduciary's duty to account (by way of either an account in common form or an account for wilful default).[415] The interrelationship of these two bodies of law is not yet fully settled,[416] although the UK Supreme Court has now held that the same compensatory principles apply whether the remedy eventuates from an account

411 *Nocton* v. *Lord Ashburton* [1914] AC 932 (HL) (*Nocton*) is the landmark case. See also *McKenzie* v. *McDonald* [1927] VLR 134 (VSC); *Canson Enterprises Ltd* v. *Boughton & Co* [1991] 3 SCR 534; 85 DLR (4th) 129 (*Canson*). Unresolved questions include the weight to be given to common law principles for calculating compensation and the extent to which equity's procedurally driven jurisdiction with respect to a trustee's duty to account applies, either directly or indirectly, to the compensatory remedy for non-trustee wrongs.

412 *AIB Group* [2014] UKSC 58; [2014] 3 WLR 1367 [92]–[93].

413 *Lord Cairns' Act* damages are not considered here, but according to some authorities may be awarded in relation to equitable wrongs: see, e.g., *Giller* v. *Procopets (No 2)* [2009] VSCA 72; (2009) 24 VR 1.

414 See, e.g., *Nocton* [1914] AC 932 (HL); *McKenzie* v. *McDonald* [1927] VLR 134 (VSC); *Canson* [1991] 3 SCR 534; 85 DLR (4th) 129.

415 See further, *Agricultural Land Management Ltd* v. *Jackson [No 2]* [2014] WASC 102; (2014) 285 FLR 121 [334]–[339]; *Ultraframe* [2005] EWHC 1638; [2006] FSR 17 [1513]–[1517]; *Libertarian Investments Limited* v. *Hall* [2013] HKCFA 93 [166]–[172]; *AIB Group* [2014] UKSC 58; [2014] 3 WLR 1367 [53].

416 The pace of the case law has not matched that of the commentaries, resulting in perplexing differences between judicial and scholarly explanations of relief for breach of trust. There is a reliance upon the nature of the traditional procedure of account in the secondary literature – and a consequent differentiation between wrong-based claims for compensation and claims to enforce primary, debt-like, obligations in the case of an account in common form (see, e.g., Charles Mitchell, 'Equitable Compensation for Breach of Fiduciary Duty' (2013) *Current Legal Problems* 1; Lionel Smith, The Measurement of Compensation Claims Against Trustees and Fiduciaries' in Elise Bant and Matthew Harding (eds.), *Exploring Private Law* (Cambridge University Press, 2010) 16).

or a direct claim for compensation.[417] 'Equitable compensation' is the more common description for equitable 'loss'-based remedies, although 'account' is also used in this context.

In a scenario where neither the primary wrong nor A's accessorial wrongdoing involves a breach of trust or a misappropriation of property,[418] the remedy engaged is that of equitable compensation for losses resulting from the primary wrong and the relevant jurisprudence is that following the House of Lords decision in *Nocton* v. *Lord Ashburton*.[419] There are some unresolved questions concerning the particular rules for assessing the compensation for which A and PW are then jointly and severally liable.[420]

In a scenario where the primary wrong is a breach of trust that does not involve beneficial receipt of misappropriated trust property by A,[421] a compensatory order may follow an account for wilful default against the trustee or compensation may be sought directly, depending upon the circumstances.[422] Whatever procedure is followed, the same principles apply to assessment of the compensation for breach of trust.[423] Again, A is liable for losses resulting from the primary wrong.

The principles for assessing compensation for breach of trust apply in relation to recipient liability. The courts use the language of 'account' here in the sense that A is liable to restore the value of the property at the time of its receipt, plus interest.[424] Even where the remedy is described as 'compensation', the measure of such compensation is the amount

[417] *AIB Group* [2014] UKSC 58; [2014] 3 WLR 1367 [62] (Lord Toulson JSC); [90]–[91], [133]–[135] (Lord Reed JSC).

[418] E.g., PW and A exploit a business opportunity in breach of PW's fiduciary duty to C. C may seek compensation for the loss of business opportunity: *Colour Control* (NSWSC, 24 July, 1995).

[419] [1914] AC 932.

[420] Discussion of these questions is beyond the scope of this book. See, e.g, *Ramsay* v. *BigTinCan Pty Ltd* [2014] NSWCA 324; (2014) 101 ACSR 415. A knowingly assisted PW, a director of C, in PW's breach of fiduciary duty. Matters in dispute regarding compensation included: the relevant causation test for breach of fiduciary duty, whether common law principles concerning damages for loss of a chance applied, and assessment of the value of a lost chance. Special leave to appeal to the HCA was refused.

[421] E.g., where A assists in the money laundering of trust funds by a fiduciary.

[422] *AIB Group* [2014] UKSC 58; [2014] 3 WLR 1367 [90]–[91]. See above n. 13 with respect to accessory liability attaching to an account for wilful default.

[423] *Ibid.* See also, in the context of knowing assistance, *Hasler* [2014] NSWCA 266; (2014) 101 ACSR 167 [152].

[424] See, e.g., *Akindele* [2001] Ch 437 (CA); *Charter* [2007] EWCA Civ 1382; [2008] Ch 313; *Williams* [2014] UKSC 10; [2014] 2 WLR 355 [31] (Lord Sumption): A may be accountable for 'any profit that would have been made or any loss that would have been avoided

necessary to restore the trust fund.[425] Compensation for recipient liability has been awarded in conjunction with a proprietary remedy where this was necessary to make up a shortfall between the value of the property received and the (lesser) value realised on sale of the property or its traceable product.[426]

8.7.3 *Gain-based remedies*

8.7.3.1 Introduction

Relevant gain-based remedies include the account of profits, constructive trust and lien.[427] The availability of proprietary relief depends upon whether the jurisdiction in question recognises the remedial constructive trust or lien.[428] There are clear pragmatic justifications for gain-based remedies. The relationship between A and PW sometimes means that both will derive a benefit regardless of which party actually holds the gain in question. This will clearly be the case where A is the corporate alter ego of PW; see further [11.2.1].[429] Courts sometimes speak of the fiduciary obligation having been 'transmitted' to A here. What is meant is that the principled reasons that dictate the availability of relief in relation to PW apply equally to A because the two parties are indistinguishable in terms of their culpability.[430] The same considerations may also apply where the interests of PW and A are closely intertwined even though PW does not 'control' A as such.[431]

if the assets had remained in the hands of the true trustees and had been dealt with according to the trust'.

425 See, e.g., *Grimaldi* [2012] FCAFC 6; (2012) 200 FCR 296 [559]. See also *Arthur* [2012] UKPC 30; [2012] All ER (A) 164 [37].

426 *Farrow* [1999] 1 VR 584 (VSC) 636–637.

427 On liens in this context, see Harding, '*Barnes* v. *Addy* Claims' 364–365. A lien is often used to secure an award of a personal remedy: see, e.g., *Morlea Professional Services Pty Ltd* v. *Richard Walter Pty Ltd (in liq.)* [1999] FCA 1820; (1999) 96 FCR 217 [36] (compensation plus compound interest for recipient liability secured by a 'charge' over A's assets); *Warman* v. *Dwyer* (1995) 182 CLR 544 (HCA) 570 (equitable charge to secure an account of profits).

428 The English courts do not recognise remedial constructive trusts or liens for breach of fiduciary duty: *FHR European Ventures LLP* v. *Cedar Capital Partners LLC* [2014] UKSC 45; [2015] AC 250 [47].

429 See, e.g., *Cook* v. *Deeks* [1916 AC 554; *Fyffes* [2000] 2 Lloyd's Rep 643, 669–670.

430 See, e.g., *Bli Bli No 1 Pty Ltd* v. *Kimlin Investments Pty Ltd* [2008] QSC 289 [48].

431 See, e.g., *Timber Engineering Co Pty Ltd* v. *Anderson* [1980] 2 NSWLR 488; *Colour Control* (NSWSC, 24 July, 1995). A common scenario is where PW, a fiduciary, and A, the intimate companion/s of PW, divert a business opportunity from C. See, e.g., *Warman* v. *Dwyer*

Pragmatic considerations of tax minimisation, insolvency protection, secrecy, convenience and the like, may mean that A, rather than PW, holds property referable to the breach of fiduciary duty. In these circumstances, if a gain-based remedy for PW's equitable wrong is warranted at all, it can only be sought from A. Thus,

> Equity avoids the inequitable result of a fiduciary retaining a profit (albeit indirectly through an accessory in which it has a shareholding) merely because it was shrewd enough to have a third party, rather than itself, obtain the profit.[432]

Gain-based remedies are not limited to such scenarios, however, and are available against an accessory who is completely independent of PW.[433]

8.7.3.2 Account of profits

An account of profits may be awarded against an accessory who procures or assists the primary wrong.[434] Like all equitable remedies, it is not available as of right.[435] The account may be secured by a lien over assets acquired by A through A's accessory involvement.[436] The account of profits is a highly utilised remedy for accessory liability for breach of confidence.[437] It is also available in relation to recipient

(1995) 182 CLR 544 (HCA) 559; *Andrews Advertising Pty Ltd* v. *David Andrews* [2014] NSWSC 318; *Dyson Technology Ltd* v. *Curtis* [2010] EWHC 3289 (Ch).

432 *Club of the Clubs Pty Limited* v. *King Network Group Pty Limited (No 2)* [2007] NSWSC 574 [58] (Bergin J).

433 See, e.g., *Consul Development* (1976) 132 CLR 373 (HCA); *United States Surgical Corp* v. *Hospital Products International Pty Ltd* [1983] 2 NSWLR 157 (overturned on appeal on other grounds); *Fyffes* [2000] 2 Lloyd's Rep 643 (QB).

434 The remedy is more recognised in Australia (see, e.g., *Michael Wilson* [2011] HCA 48; (2011) 244 CLR 427 [106]), but has recently been recognised by the English Court of Appeal: *Novoship* [2014] EWCA Civ 908. See also *Cook* v. *Deeks* [1916] AC 554 (PC); *Fyffes* [2000] 2 Lloyd's Rep 643; *Ultraframe* [2005] EWHC 1638 (Ch); [2006] FSR 17 [1589]–[1601].

435 See, e.g, *Fyffes* [2000] 2 Lloyd's Rep 643 (account of profits available, in principle, against the briber, A, of PW, but refused because it was 'highly probable' that C would have entered the contract with A in any event. Any '"ordinary" profit element' was not caused by the bribery and, if the contract price was inflated due to the bribe, C was protected by damages or equitable compensation); *Novoship* [2014] EWCA Civ 908 [119] (account of profits refused if 'disproportionate in relation to the particular form and extent of wrongdoing').

436 See, e.g., *US Surgical Corporation* v. *Hospital Products International Pty Ltd* [1982] 2 NSWLR 766 (NSWSC) 812 ; *Warman* v. *Dwyer* (1995) 182 CLR 544 (HCA) 570.

437 See, e.g., Toulson J's analysis of *Attorney-General* v. *Guardian Newspapers (No 2)* [1990] 1 AC 109 in *Fyffes* [2000] 2 Lloyd's Rep 643 (QB) 670. At [8.4.1.1] we suggest that it is

liability,[438] in which case, any increase in the value of the received property in A's hands may be taken into account.[439]

The 'profits' must have been made by A, rather than PW.[440] It must be shown that the profits are referable to A's wrongdoing.[441] It has been suggested that common law rules of causation should apply by analogy here, although it is not clear which rules would apply given that the common law does not award gain-based remedies.[442] Furthermore, in cases where A and PW are very closely linked (such as where the fiduciary obligation is said to be 'transmitted' to A), the courts are clearly applying the same causation approach to both A and PW.

Grimaldi provides an illustration of the fact-specific, discretionary process of determining an account of profits for participatory (here, recipient) liability.[443] Simplifying the facts somewhat, the court was required to determine what proportion of the profits made, over seven years or so, by a large mining company, A, were attributable to an initial injection of capital (the trust property) received by A through PW's breach of fiduciary duty. The court indicated that the account should be determined in the following manner:

> [T]he benefit/profit to which [C] was entitled was its proportionate share in the net profits (providing the proportion itself was identifiable) from ore found, extracted, transported and marketed and sold which had been, or would be, extracted over the life of the Project less the costs of finding, etc. that ore and, arguably, less any such allowance as [A] would be allowed for its skills and risk-taking and for its exertion in finding, etc., the ore. We merely suggest that that benefit, if [C] elects to pursue it, may best be reflected in a royalty-like payment on ore extracted.[444]

unnecessary to resort to an accessory analysis here, but this does not affect the point concerning remedy.

438 *Charter* [2007] EWCA 1382; [2008] Ch 313, 337–339; *Williams* v. *Central Bank of Nigeria* [2014] UKSC 10; [2014] 2 WLR 355, 371 [31]; *Grimaldi* at 415 [555] (Finn, Stone and Perram JJ, stating that 'it is uncontroversial'). See also the authorities referred to in Mitchell and Watterson, 'Remedies for Knowing Receipt' 142.

439 See Virgo, *Principles of Equity and Trusts*, 689.

440 *Grimaldi* [2012] FCAFC 6; (2012) 200 FCR 296 [609]–[614]; *Michael Wilson* [2011] HCA 48; (2011) 244 CLR 427 [106]. See also *Restatement (Second) of Torts* §874 (1979) Comment c: '[A] is responsible only for harm caused or profits that he himself has made from the transaction, and he is not necessarily liable for the profits that the fiduciary has made nor for those that he should have made.'

441 See generally, *Warman* v. *Dwyer* (1995) 182 CLR 544 (HCA).

442 See *Novoship* [2014] EWCA Civ 908 [94]–[115].

443 [2012] FCAFC 6; (2012) 200 FCR 296.

444 *Ibid.* [740] (Finn, Stone and Perram JJ). The Court drew upon the judgment of Learned Hand J in *Primeau* v. *Granfield* 184 F 480 (1911).

In reaching this conclusion, the court exercised its discretion not to award a constructive trust over a proportionate share of the mining tenements held by company A and also emphasised that the profits of A and a related company that acquired shares in A, also an accessory defendant in the proceedings, should be distinguished for the purposes of the account.

8.7.3.3 Gain-based proprietary remedies

Some jurisdictions, such as Australia and Canada, recognise the courts' discretion to impose a remedial constructive trust where appropriate and according to settled principles. On this approach, proprietary relief may – but need not – be awarded in relation to any form of equitable accessory wrongdoing.[445] English courts are averse to the judicial alteration of property rights by way of discretionary proprietary relief, including in relation to dishonest accessory liability.[446] Proprietary relief is generally only permissible if an 'institutional', as opposed to a 'remedial', constructive trust arises.[447] There is, however, English authority that a discretionary constructive trust is available for procuring an equitable breach of confidence.[448]

[445] There is Australian case law and commentary recognising a remedial constructive trust even where property is not traceable from C to A. See, e.g., *DPC Estates Pty Ltd* v. *Grey* [1974] 1 NSWLR 443 (NSWCA) 459–461; 469–472 (knowing assistance) (overturned on appeal on other grounds); *Timber Engineering Co Pty Ltd* v. *Anderson* [1980] 2 NSWLR 488 (NSWSC) (approved by Mason J in *Hospital Products Ltd* v. *United States Surgical Corp* (1984) 156 CLR 41 (HCA) 115–116); *United States Surgical Corp* v. *Hospital Products International Pty Ltd* [1983] 2 NSWLR 157 (overturned on appeal on other grounds); *Disctronics Ltd* v. *Edmonds* [2002] VSC 454. See also *Say-Dee Pty Ltd* v. *Farah Constructions Pty Ltd* [2005] NSWCA 309: overturned by the High Court without querying the availability in principle of a constructive trust for knowing receipt. See also, Heydon and Leeming, *Jacobs Law of Trusts,* [1338]. See, perhaps *contra., Giumelli* v. *Giumelli* (1999) 196 CLR 1010 (HCA) 112 [4]: 'some constructive trusts create or recognise no proprietary interest . . . An example of a constructive trust in this sense is the imposition of personal liability upon one "who dishonestly procures or assists in a breach of trust or fiduciary duty".' The Federal Court has noted that there is no 'presumptive rule' that a (non-recipient) assistant is liable to proprietary relief: *Grimaldi* [2012] FCAFC 6; (2012) 200 FCR 296 [510] (Finn, Stone and Perram JJ). For an evaluation of the Canadian law, see Clapton, 'Gain-Based Remedies'.

[446] *Polly Peck* [1998] 3 All ER 812, 831–832; *Dubai Aluminium* [2002] UKHL 48; [2003] 2 AC 366 [141]–[142].

[447] *Westdeutsche* [1996] AC 669 (HL) 714–715 (Lord Browne-Wilkinson).

[448] *Ocular Sciences Ltd* v. *Aspect Vision Care Ltd* [1997] RPC 289, 411–416 (Laddie J). His Honour refused this relief for practical reasons, including the difficulty of determining how decisions relating to the property would then be made. See also *United Pan-Europe*

We support the availability of discretionary proprietary relief for equitable accessory liability.[449] It allows for transparent judicial reasoning that addresses both principled and policy-driven rationales for the liability as well as fact-specific matters such as the interests of innocent third parties, and it allows for relief tailored to the particular circumstances. The discretionary nature of such relief and the fact that it appears to be quite difficult to obtain in practice makes it a preferable solution to recognising institutional constructive trusts. The all or nothing aspect of the latter approach, while superficially more 'certain' than that of the former approach, is a blunt instrument that does little to meet the concerns of those opposed to judicial alteration of property rights.

Proprietary relief for recipient liability is less controversial in England[450] because a proprietary link between C and property held by A is established through following or tracing. Thus, irrespective of whether a persisting property claim is also available [7.5] (as is generally the case), the custodial nature of A's recipient liability is said to require A to restore the trust property in specie if possible.[451]

As discussed in [7.5], in Australia, C cannot rely on a persisting property claim to received property or its traceable product in A's hands if C's original interest was legal, rather than equitable, even though such property is treated as traceable trust property for the purposes of establishing a receipt of property. Proprietary relief *is* available for recipient liability here, but on a discretionary basis only. In *Grimaldi*, the Federal Court decided that a constructive trust for knowing receipt should not be awarded automatically on the basis of a persistent property/tracing claim over certain assets of a corporation, noting that the culpability of the corporate accessory was different in kind to the fiduciary on the particular facts.[452] One relevant

Communications NV v. *Deutsche Bank AG* [2000] 2 BCLC 461 (CA); Matthew Conaglen, 'Thinking about Proprietary Remedies for Breach of Confidence' (2008) *Intellectual Property Quarterly* 82.

449 See further, Ridge, 'Constructive Trusts, Accessory Liability and Judicial Discretion'.

450 *Contra*. Andrew Burrows, *The Law of Restitution*, 3rd edn (Oxford University Press, 2011) 418.

451 Mitchell and Watterson, 'Remedies for Knowing Receipt', 132. On this view, and depending on whether the trust is ongoing or not, A must either reconstitute the trust fund or transfer it to the fully entitled beneficiaries. This has also been accepted by the Privy Council in relation to property subject to a non-trust, custodial fiduciary duty. *Arthur* [2012] UKPC 30 [37].

452 *Grimaldi* [2012] FCAFC 6; (2012) 200 FCR 296 [674].

factor was that the corporate accessory had changed significantly in composition and wealth base since the receipt of trust property. Thus, '[t]his is not a simple case of wrongdoers continuing knowingly to perpetuate their own wrongs to their own advantage behind a corporate form'.[453] It would be inappropriate to visit the consequences of proprietary liability upon subsequent investors in the company who had not been responsible for the accessory conduct.[454] This was so even though property was traceable to the accessory.

A complication in the Australian law on recipient liability concerns the relevance of a valid, but voidable, contract that governs the subject matter of the claimed proprietary relief and is inconsistent with it.[455] Must any such contract be rescinded before a constructive trust is imposed?[456] Any such contract is voidable because of the primary wrong and A's culpable involvement in it; however, rescission may not always be possible given the lapse of time.[457] As a matter of principle and assuming that proprietary relief may be awarded on terms, rescission should not be a necessary requirement for a discretionary constructive trust. The court takes the contract into account in fashioning the proprietary remedy; the functions of rescission in ensuring third-party rights are protected and future enforcement of the contract is precluded[458] are thereby accommodated in other ways. What appears to have caused the confusion is that there are, in fact, two alternative means by which a constructive trust may arise in such scenarios. The first is where a constructive trust arises as an automatic 'consequence of the effective avoidance or rescission of the transaction' so that A holds the property as constructive trustee 'ab initio'.[459] The second, more recently

[453] *Ibid.* [675] (Finn, Stone and Perram JJ). [454] *Ibid.* [677].

[455] The contract may be void, rather than voidable, due to statutory contraventions: see *Belmont Finance [No 2]* [1980] 1 All ER 393, discussed in *Hancock Family Memorial Foundation Ltd* v. *Porteous* [2000] WASCA 29; (2000) 22 WAR 198 [198]–[201]. Alternatively, the contract may be a sham: *Robins* [2003] NSWCA 71; (2003) 175 FLR 286, 303 [83].

[456] Rescission was required in *Greater Pacific Investments Pty Ltd (in liq.)* v. *Australian National Industries Ltd* (1996) 39 NSWLR 143, 153 (*Greater Pacific*); *Hancock Family Memorial Foundation Ltd* v. *Porteous* (2000) 22 WAR 198, 210–220; *Robins* [2003] NSWCA 71; (2003) 175 FLR 286 [72]–[74]; [82]–[83]. The rescission requirement was doubted in *Robins* at [65] and *Grimaldi* [2012] FCA 1129; (2012) FCR 296 [273]–[281], [342].

[457] A's culpability tends to be a given in such scenarios because A will be PW's corporate alter ego.

[458] *Robins* [2003] NSWCA 71; (2003) 175 FLR 286, 302–303 [82].

[459] *Greater Pacific* (1996) 39 NSWLR 143, 153.

recognised, means to a constructive trust is by way of a discretionary remedy. In the latter scenario, rescission is not required if justice can otherwise be done by the imposition of terms. Importantly, even if rescission is not available, the second means to a constructive trust may still apply.

8.7.4 Other remedies

Pre-judgment interest at compound rates is available for recipient liability where that would better reflect either an actual loss to the trust fund or a gain made by A.[460] The trust property must have been used in the course of A's business for commercial, profit-making purposes.[461] Compound interest can be capped to avoid the possibility that A might indirectly benefit from the interest award.[462] Little needs to be said regarding other forms of equitable relief, other than to note their availability where appropriate.[463] Specific relief may be especially appropriate in relation to breach of confidence where C's objective is to ensure that exploitation of the confidential material ceases.[464] If A's accessorial involvement results in C entering a contract with A, then C is entitled to rescind.[465] If rescission is unavailable, then C may still treat the contract as at an end as to the future.

460 *Belmont Finance (No 2)* [1980] 1 All ER 393, 419; *Grimaldi* [2012] FCA 1129; (2012) FCR 296 [547]–[552], [753].

461 *Belmont Finance (No 2)* [1980] 1 All ER 393, 419.

462 *Ninety Five Pty Ltd (in liq)* v. *Banque Nationale de Paris* [1988] WAR 132 (WASC).

463 In relation to ongoing accessorial conduct see, *Prudential Assurance Co Ltd* v. *Lorenz* (1971) 11 KIR 78 (Ch), in which interlocutory relief was given to restrain a trade union from inducing its members to breach a non-contractual duty to account to their employer, C.

464 E.g., A may be ordered to deliver up for destruction property in which the confidential material resides as well as being enjoined from further breaches. See, e.g., *Prince Albert* v. *Strange* (1849) 2 De G & Sm 651; 64 ER 293; 1 Mac & G 25; 41 ER 1171; *Franklin* v. *Giddins* [1978] QR 72.

465 *Panama and South Pacific Telegraph Co* v. *India Rubber, Gutta Percha, and Telegraph Works Co* (1875) LR 10 Ch App 515; *Grant* v. *Gold Exploration and Development Syndicate Limited* [1900] 1 QB 233; *Logicrose* [1988] 1 WLR 1256. In accounting for benefits received under the contract, C need not return any money paid to A that was recovered by C: *Logicrose* 1264 (Millett J). If C elects not to rescind, C can recover any 'specific sum over and above what must be taken as between the parties to be the real [consideration]' by a claim for money had and received: *Grant* 249 (Collins LJ); *Logicrose* 1263.

8.8 Apportioning liability

8.8.1 Joint and several liability for losses

An accessory who assists in the primary wrong is jointly and severally liable with PW for C's losses.[466] Conversely, one might have assumed that A would be liable only for losses caused by A's own wrong,[467] but this is not the case with respect to loss-based remedies for knowing or dishonest assistance at least.[468] Instead, A's liability is determined on exactly the same basis as that of PW once a connection between A's conduct and the primary wrong, rather than between A's conduct and C's loss, is established [8.3.3].

Concerns that A's liability might be disproportionate to the extent of A's culpable involvement are most likely to arise where A has merely assisted PW (for example, through the provision of professional services). But joint and several liability for C's losses flowing from the primary wrong is still consistent with the strong rationales for equitable accessory liability [8.1.3]. Crucially, it is only in relation to C that questions of relative responsibility are ignored; as between A and PW such issues are relevant and go to the questions of apportionment. In this way, the risks associated with a potentially difficult evidential inquiry into relative responsibility are shifted from C to the two wrongdoers, A and PW. Nevertheless, the potentially onerous and disproportionate consequences of joint and several liability for losses to a knowing or dishonest assistant are a reason for caution in finding A liable in the first place. This is especially the case when liability is sought to be imposed upon 'strangers' to the relationship between C and PW, such as professional agents.

Whether an accessory who *procures* the primary wrong is jointly and severally liable is not as clear due to the paucity of case law. There are two possibilities apparent in the cases. First, A could be severally liable for the full losses resulting from the primary wrong and PW would be liable for whatever could not be recovered from A or through other means.[469] This would be appropriate, for example, where PW was duped by A into

466 *Blyth* v. *Fladgate* [1891] 1 Ch 337; *Cowper* v. *Stoneham* (1893) 68 LT 18; *Trustor AB* v. *Smallbone (No 3)* unreported, 9 May 2000, CA [97] (Scott VC); *Ultraframe* [2005] EWHC 1638; [2006] FSR 17 [600]. In Australia, see *Grimaldi* [2012] FCAFC 6; (2012) 200 FCR 296 [558].

467 *Target Holdings Ltd* v. *Redferns* [1996] 1 AC 421 (HL) 432.

468 Graham Virgo argues that A, a dishonest accessory, and PW should never be jointly and severally liable for C's losses: *Principles of Equity and Trusts*, 710–711.

469 See, e.g., *Eaves* (1861) 30 Beav 136; 54 ER 840.

committing the primary wrong.[470] Alternatively, where A and PW jointly participate in a primary wrong that was instigated by A, liability should be joint and several.[471] If, for example, A is intimately related to PW and engaged in a common enterprise constituting PW's wrong or has procured the primary wrong, then it seems appropriate for A to be visited with the full losses referable to that wrong.

It is also not clear whether a knowing recipient is jointly and severally liable with PW or simply severally liable to restore the trust fund by way of compensation plus interest. In *Grimaldi*, the Full Federal Court of Australia intimated that the liability was several, without deciding the point.[472] Early authorities suggest that the liability is joint and several with that of the trustee.[473]

8.8.2 *Joint and several liability for gains*

It is often said that A and PW should not be jointly and severally liable for each other's gains resulting from the primary wrong.[474] This is sometimes explained on the basis that equity's jurisdiction is not penal.[475] It also follows from the fact that A's liability is grounded in A's own, independently wrongful, conduct: the remedies available against A should be directed to the consequences of A's wrongdoing.[476] Where, however, the facts suggest that the gains made by one party in fact will benefit both parties, a principled case may be made for joint and several liability. Thus, if PW is simply the vehicle for A's enrichment and A is the instigator of the primary wrong, joint and several liability for PW's gains is appropriate.[477] There may sometimes be other ways to deal with such

470 Although presumably PW may be exculpated in such circumstances.

471 See further Alison Gurr, 'Accessory Liability and Contribution, Release and Apportionment' (2010) 34 *Melbourne University Law Review* 481, 486 n. 30. *Cf. George* v. *Webb* [2011] NSWSC 1608 [331]–[332] (Ward J considering apportionment of liability).

472 *Grimaldi* [2012] FCAFC 6; (2012) 200 FCR 296 [559].

473 *Wilson* v. *Moore* (1833) 1 My & K 125,142–143; 39 ER 629, 635; *Rolfe* v. *Gregory* (1865) 4 De GJ & S 576; 46 ER 1042; *Cowper* v. *Stoneham* (1893) 68 LT 18. See also Glanville L. Williams, *Joint Obligations* (London, Butterworth & Co, 1949) 159.

474 See, e.g., *Ultraframe* [2005] EWHC 1638 (Ch); [2006] FSR 17 [600]. See also, in Australia, *Glandon Pty Ltd* v. *Tilmunda Pastoral Company Pty Ltd* [2008] NSWSC 218; [2008] ASAL [55–186] [108]. See generally in relation to joint and several liability for gains, Ridge, 'Justifying the Remedies for Dishonest Assistance', 459–460.

475 *Ultraframe* [2005] EWHC1638 (Ch); [2006] FSR 17.

476 *Michael Wilson* [2011] HCA 48; (2011) 244 CLR 427 [106].

477 *Grimaldi* [2012] FCAFC 6; (2012) 200 FCR 296 [556], citing *Green & Clara Pty Ltd* v. *Bestobell Industries Pty Ltd (No 2)* [1984] WAR 32, 40; *Gencor ACP Ltd* v. *Dalby* [2000] 2 BCLC 734 (Ch).

scenarios. For example, in a corporate setting, where A has a substantial interest in PW Co, removing the gains of PW Co may have the indirect consequence of withholding or removing gains from A.[478]

A further scenario in which joint and several liability for gains is justified is where A and PW have jointly participated in the primary wrong. The court in *Grimaldi* suggested, without needing to decide the question, that

> If [PW] and the third party assistant or recipient *act in concert* to secure a mutual benefit . . . they are jointly and severally liable to [C] to restore the trust or to account for the profits made . . . One can readily understand why, when wrongdoers so entangle their affairs, that the law as a matter of legal policy might wish to make it their responsibility – and not [C's] – to untangle them for accountability purposes.[479]

8.8.3 *Contribution*

Because PW and A bear joint and several liability for C's losses resulting from the primary wrong, C may sue either wrongdoer for the full sum. As between PW and A, however, the party who discharged the liability may seek contribution from the other.[480] A detailed treatment of the equitable and statutory contribution rules in relation to accessory

[478] See, e.g., *Warman* v. *Dwyer* (1995) 182 CLR 544 (HCA) 563–564. The Court noted that an account of profits against Co A would indirectly achieve a similar result to an account of profits or constructive trust in relation to PW's shareholding in Co A.

[479] *Grimaldi* [2012] FCAFC 6; (2012) 200 FCR 296 [558] (Finn, Stone and Perram JJ) citing inter alia *CMS Dolphin Ltd* v. *Simonet* [2002] BCC 600 (Ch); *Green & Clara Pty Ltd* v. *Bestobell Industries Pty Ltd (No 2)* [1984] WAR 32. See also Charles Mitchell, *The Law of Contribution and Reimbursement* (Oxford University Press, 2003) [8.28]. A line of Canadian cases supports A's joint and several liability for PW's gains on the wider basis that A is in the same position as a co-trustee or fiduciary: *Canada Safeway Ltd* v. *Thompson* [1951] 3 DLR 295, 323; [1952] 2 DLR 591, 592; *A'Amore* v. *Macdonald* (1973) 32 DLR (3d) 543, 549; *Abbey Glen Property Corp* v. *Stumborg* (1976) 65 DLR (3d) 235; *Macdonald* v. *Hauer* (1976) 72 DLR (3d) 110, 130. These decisions, along with *MacMillan Bloedel Ltd* v. *Binstead* (1983) 22 BLR 255 (BCSC) and *Glenko Enterprises Ltd* v. *Keller* 2000 MBCA 7, 150 Man R (2d), are defended in Clapton, 'Gain-Based Remedies', 1009–1010, as necessary to 'safeguard the relationship of trust and confidence' between C and PW: 1010. But the cases do not address the application of contribution rules to co-trustees and contain little by way of principled analysis. They have been not been followed in other jurisdictions. See, e.g., *Ultraframe* [2005] EWHC 1638; [2006] FSR 17 [595]–[600]; *Grimaldi* [557].

[480] Arden LJ has suggested that equitable contribution should also be available in relation to an account of profits: *Charter* [2007] EWCA 1382; [2008] Ch 313 [71].

liability is not attempted here; however, the following general points can be noted.[481] Where equity's contribution rules continue to apply, the rules concerning contribution by co-trustees should not necessarily apply to accessories, although this is sometimes assumed to be the case.[482] Instead, the general rules for equitable contribution should apply. There is an open question in Australia as to whether the general rules allow for proportionate, rather than equal contribution to be ordered.[483] The better view is that proportionate contribution is permissible.[484] The strongest case for this is where A procured PW's breach: here, PW may have a right of indemnity under the general rules.[485]

In some jurisdictions, statutory contribution schemes also apply to equitable claims.[486] In England, for example, section 2(1) of the Civil Liability (Contribution) Act 1978 has been held to apply to claims for dishonest assistance[487] and unconscionable receipt[488] and provides that ' . . . the amount of the contribution recoverable from any person shall be such as may be found by the court to be just and equitable having regard to the extent of that person's responsibility for the damage in question'.

Finally, a controversial development in relation to apportioning liability has been the introduction in some jurisdictions of statutory proportionate liability.[489] Such schemes remove joint and several liability and allow a party to be made liable only for the proportion of the

481 For an excellent analysis in the context of Australian law, see Gurr, 'Accessory Liability and Contribution, Release and Apportionment'.

482 See, e.g., *MacDonald* v. *Hauer* (1977) 72 DLR (3d) 110 (Saskatchewan CA) 134–135; *Westpac* v. *Savin* [1985] 2 NZLR 41 (NZCA) 54; *Equiticorp Industries Group Ltd* v. *Hawkins [No. 4]* (1992) 5 PRNZ 484, 491; *McNally* v. *Harris* [2008] NSWSC 659 [150]–[154]. See further, Gurr, 'Accessory Liability and Contribution, Release and Apportionment', 491–493.

483 For a discussion of the Australian authorities, see Gurr, 'Accessory Liability and Contribution, Release and Apportionment', 497–499.

484 *George* v. *Webb* [2011] NSWSC 1608 [339]–[354] (Ward J concluding in obiter that the 'loss should be apportioned pro rata': [354]). See also, Gurr, 'Accessory Liability and Contribution, Release and Apportionment', 497, 499; Mitchell, *The Law of Contribution* [4.21] fn. 89.

485 *George* v. *Webb* [2011] NSWSC 1608 [353] citing *Burke* v. *LFOT Pty Limited* [2002] HCA 17; (2002) 209 CLR 282 [19]).

486 But see Mitchell, *Law of Contribution*, [1.32].

487 See, e.g., *Dubai Aluminium* [2002] UKHL 48; [2003] 2 AC 366.

488 See, e.g., *Charter* [2007] EWCA 1382; [2008] Ch 313.

489 See Mitchell, *Law of Contribution*, [8.34]–[8.35].

loss caused by that party. The application of such legislation to equitable accessorial claims is still unclear.[490]

[490] See, e.g., *George* v. *Webb* [2011] NSWSC 1608: Ward J considered the application of the *Civil Liability Act 2002* (NSW) to A's liability for knowing assistance and knowing receipt in breach of trust. The Act applies to '(a) a claim for economic loss or damage to property in an action for damages (whether in contract, tort or otherwise) arising from a failure to take reasonable care...': s. 34(1). Ward J concluded at [325] that the particular breach of trust (payment out contrary to the terms of the trust) was not 'predicated on or arising from a failure to take reasonable care' and, hence, the Act did not apply. See further, Gurr, 'Accessory Liability and Contribution, Release and Apportionment', 511–517. See generally on the undesirability of proportionate liability, Mitchell, *Law of Contribution*, [8.36]–[8.37].

9

Infringement of statutory intellectual property rights

9.1 Introduction

9.1.1 Overview

This chapter considers rules imposing accessory, and accessory-like, liability to remedy infringements of intellectual property (IP) rights. We have already considered accessory liability for IP infringements via the application of generic tort accessory principles in Chapter 5. However, persons may also be liable on the basis of specific statutory provisions. This chapter considers such provisions under the following three headings:

(1) **Authorisation of infringements.** Copyright and design law in the UK and Australia, and patents and trademarks law in Australia, provide that right holders have the rights to do the acts or exploit the rights contained within the relevant IP, and that these rights include the right to 'authorise' such use or exploitation [9.2]. Any 'authorisation' by a person, A, of a primary infringement by another, primary wrongdoer (PW), without the consent of the right holder therefore itself infringes those rights. The general concept of 'authorisation' is therefore central to establishing accessory liability.

(2) **Other accessory liability rules.** This chapter briefly notes some minor and specifically targeted statutory doctrines that create accessory liability [9.3].

(3) **Non-accessorial 'indirect' infringements.** A number of different, specifically targeted, statutory provisions create precise sources of liability, variously labelled in the legislation and commentary as 'secondary', 'contributory' or 'indirect' infringement. Even though some of these labels suggest accessory liability, for the most part, these provisions do not impose what is conceptually accessory

liability (excepting those just noted in (2)), despite having considerable affinity with accessory liability [9.4].[1]

9.1.2 *Competing policies in IP accessory law*

Accessory liability based on a party's wrongful involvement in another's primary wrong is a narrowly confined basis for liability. The goals of deterring primary infringement and vindicating rights face serious challenges in IP law if third parties are only liable on the basis of such narrowly confined liability rules. In part, these challenges come from technological innovations, particularly on the internet, that enable widespread and repeated infringements of rights by numerous individual infringers. Examples include mass copying of copyrighted materials or worldwide marketing by persons selling goods that infringe trademarks. It may be practically impossible to deter such infringements or remedy their consequences by pursuing individual primary infringers, and this has the potential to significantly diminish the value of IP proprietary interests.[2] From IP rights holders' perspectives, therefore, it is desirable to extend liability to 'intermediaries' who can act as 'gatekeepers',[3] 'based on who is in the best position to prevent the harm in question'.[4] As noted in [2.4.4], such deterrence rationales may be supported on economic

1 In US law, since 'contributory infringement' in part originates from tort law, that concept obviously overlaps with aiding and abetting liability. See Adams, 'Indirect Infringement', 635–636. See also *Metro Goldwyn Mayer Studios Inc* v. *Grokster Ltd* 545 US 913, 934–935 (2005); 64 IPR 645: courts should turn to common law tort principles to further evaluate contributory infringement in IP. Many of the US cases dealing with IP infringements are discussed both here and in Chapter 5.

2 As to the nature of IP rights as negative in character, giving a power of exclusion, see *JT International* v. *Commonwealth* [2012] HCA 43; (2013) 250 CLR 1 [31] (French CJ), and [137] (Gummow J): the right to 'relax that exclusivity in favour of licencees [etc.] . . . may properly be regarded as proprietary in nature'.

3 See generally, Renier Kraakman, 'Gatekeepers: The Anatomy of a Third Party Enforcement Strategy' (1986) 2 *Journal of Law, Economics and Organisation* 53.

4 Katja Weckström, 'Liability for Trademark Infringement for Internet Providers' (2012) 16 *Marquette Intellectual Property Law Review* 1, 39: liability is treated as a question of 'cost allocation'. See *Metro Goldwyn Mayer Studios Inc* v. *Grokster Ltd* 545 US 913, 929–930 (2005); 64 IPR 645, noting that the impossibility of effectively enforcing rights against direct infringers may mean that the only practical alternative is to pursue parties for 'secondary' liability. For economic analysis of the liability of intermediaries in the IP context, particularly focusing on internet-related issues, see, e.g., Douglas Lichtman and William Landes, 'Indirect Liability for Copyright Infringement: An Economic Perspective' (2003) 16 *Harvard Journal of Law and Technology* 395; Douglas Lichtman and Eric Posner, 'Holding Internet Service Providers Accountable' (2006) 14 *Supreme Court Economic*

efficiency grounds. Since, however, IP right holders' interests are only some of many competing interests that need to be balanced,[5] there need to be strong policy reasons to impose gatekeeper duties on persons, at least in the absence of some fault on their part. An appropriate policy balance needs to be set and this is best achieved via legislation.

The competing interests at stake have created tensions in the law. For example, Anjanette Raymond argues that recent decisions of the courts in the United Kingdom and the European Union (EU)[6] have expanded liability for intermediaries and thereby shifted the burden of protecting rights from right holders onto both internet service providers (ISPs) and right holders as a shared burden. Raymond argues that the parameters of this shared burden are uncertain and that achieving the right balance is difficult, given the competing interests. The expanding liability that Raymond notes is partly a result of the application of existing accessory liability rules, and partly a result of legislative provisions having a prophylactic purpose of preventing infringement. Attempts by policy-makers in the EU to balance competing interests are outside the scope of this work.[7] In any case, as has been noted in an English case, even where such provisions apply, the question of accessory liability for past infringements is still primarily a matter for national law.[8] Similarly, this chapter does not consider detailed and specially targeted legislative schemes that seek to regulate the digital communication industry, for example, by involving ISPs in processes aimed to 'prevent or deter'

Review 221; and Jonathan Zittrain, 'A History of Online Gatekeeping' (2006) 19 *Harvard Journal of Law and Technology* 253.

5 See Weckström, 'Trademark Infringement', arguing that it is not efficient or justifiable to hold internet intermediaries liable for trademark infringements facilitated by internet technology. See also Anjanette H. Raymond, 'Intermediaries' Precarious Balance Within Europe' (2013) 11 *Northwestern Journal of Technology & Intellectual Property* 359, and 'Heavyweight Bots in the Clouds: The Wrong Incentives and Poorly Crafted Balances That Lead to the Blocking of Information Online' (2013) 11 *N. W. J. of T. & I.* 473, on the difficulties of balancing the competing interests in the internet context.

6 Raymond, 'Intermediaries', discussing the European Court of Justice's decision in *Scarlett Extended* v. *SABAM* Case C-70/10 2011 ECR-I 0000, and the UK cases, *Twentieth Century Fox Film Corporation* v. *Newzbin Ltd* [2010] EWHC 608; [2010] ECC 13 (*Newzbin*) [9.2.6.4], and *Twentieth Century Fox Film Corporation* v. *British Telecommunications Plc* [2011] EWHC 1981 (Ch) [9.5.1].

7 Consequently, this chapter does not consider the detailed rules on IP infringement and enforcement contained in EU law, such as the Electronic Commerce Directive and Trade Marks Directive. Some of these are considered, e.g., in *L'Oreal SA* v. *eBay International AG* [2009] EWHC 1094 (Ch) [2009] ETMR 53.

8 *Ibid.* [344].

unlicensed peer-to-peer file sharing.[9] Such legislative schemes do not generally impact on liability for past infringements.

To the extent, however, that established doctrines (concerned with identifying accessories to infringements that have occurred) are used to meet the legal challenges posed by modern technologies, the case law evidences the ongoing tensions created by competing interests and values. For example, in the copyright context, the potential to seek relief against an 'authoriser' or other 'secondary' infringer enhances the means by which copyright owners can protect their rights. As Gummow and Hayne JJ in *Roadshow Films Pty Ltd* v. *iiNet Ltd* (*Roadshow*) noted:

> Liability as a secondary infringer of copyright has been said to have an economic rationale similar to that of the tort of inducing breach of contract, namely a lower cost of prevention of breach of the primary obligation.[10]

By way of contrast, French CJ, Crennan and Kiefel JJ in the same case stated that the decision that no authorisation had occurred, 'shows that the concept and the principles of ... authorisation ... are not readily suited to enforcing the rights of copyright owners in respect of widespread infringements occasioned by peer-to-peer file sharing'.[11] In short, fault-based accessorial concepts may not be adequate for the task of meeting the many challenges thrown up by the internet, at least from rights holders' perspectives.

The same tensions are particularly evident in the US where much of the commentary on these issues has occurred. In that jurisdiction, what we would call accessory liability for IP infringement is encompassed by the generic concept of 'contributory infringement' (or 'indirect infringement') derived from common law principles.[12] This broad concept has

[9] See, e.g., Digital Economy Act 2010 (UK), considered in Kevin Garnett, Gillian Davies and Gwilym Harbottle, *Copinger and Skone James on Copyright*, 16th edn (London, Sweet & Maxwell, 2011) vol. 1, [21–288]–[21–367] 1217–1247, (quote from 1217) (*Copinger*). This includes requiring ISPs to adopt 'graduated responses' against customers using internet services to infringe. See, e.g., Rebecca Giblin, 'Evaluating Graduated Responses' (2014) 37 *Columbia Journal of Law & the Arts* 147.

[10] [2012] HCA 16; (2012) 248 CLR 42 [110]; they cite Landes and Posner, *The Economic Structure of Intellectual Property Law* (2003), 118–119.

[11] *Ibid.* [79].

[12] In patents law, where accessory liability rules are found in statute, 'indirect' (or 'inducing') and 'contributory' infringement are distinct concepts. The Patent Act, 35 USC §271 (b)-(c), divides liability into two heads, for contributory infringement of a seller of materials (para. (c)) and for inducing infringement (para. (b)). Outside the patents context, varying usage by courts and commentators means that it is not entirely clear

been applied across patents, copyright and trademarks law, though it has developed differently in each of those areas.[13] There are two necessary elements for liability, namely that a defendant has (1) materially contributed to the direct (primary) infringement, (2) with some knowledge or culpable mental state.[14]

For present purposes, it should be noted that this fault-based liability has been expanding and, further, US law has developed non-fault-based liability.[15] Almost certainly, economic efficiency rationales in part underlie[16] the expansion of liability. The effect of these rules may be to require intermediaries such as ISPs to undertake a gatekeeper role in order to curb infringements, but the tensions created by competing policy factors

whether 'indirect' or 'inducing' infringement is a sub-set of, a synonym for, or a separate, but related, head of liability to, contributory infringement. See, e.g., Mark Bartholomew and Patrick F. McArdle, 'Causing Infringement' (2011) 64 *Vanderbilt Law Review* 675, 689–690, who characterise inducement as a type of contributory infringement, though other commentators make a division between inducing and contributory infringement, consistently with the patent statutory scheme.

[13] Charles W. Adams, 'Indirect Infringement from a Torts Law Perspective' (2008) 42 *University of Richmond Law Review* 635, 635. Problematically, perhaps, 'contributory infringement' does the work that in Anglo-Australian law is done by a combination of concepts: joint tortfeasor liability, statutory authorisation liability, and more specific statutory provisions some of which are not truly accessorial in nature.

[14] Bartholomew and McArdle, 'Causing Infringement', 683.

[15] In particular, the misleadingly labelled 'vicarious liability' in IP law applies even outside of the employment and agency contexts, 'where a defendant has the right and ability to supervise the infringing activity and has also a direct financial interest in such activities': *Gershwin Publishing Corp* v. *Columbia Artists Management, Inc* 443 F2d 1159, 1162 (2d Cir 1971). *Cf.* the obiter definition in *Metro Goldwyn Mayer Studios Inc* v. *Grokster Ltd* 545 US 913, 930 (2005); 64 IPR 645. See also *Shapiro, Bernstein & Co* v. *HL Green Co,* 316 F2d 304, 308 (2d Cir 1963), and Mark Bartholomew, 'Copyright, Trademark and Secondary Infringement after Grokster' (2009) 32 *Columbia Journal of Law & the Arts* 445, 461 onwards and fn. 26. Vicarious liability was broadly defined and considered potentially to apply in *A & M Records Inc* v. *Napster, Inc* 239 F3d 1004 (9th Cir 2001), and *Perfect 10, Inc.* v. *Cybernet Ventures, Inc.,* 213 FSupp 2d 1146, 1171–1172 (CD Cal 2002) but failed in cases such as *Tiffany, Inc.* v. *eBay Inc.,* 576 FSupp 2d 463 (SDNY 2008) (affirmed *Tiffany (NJ) Inc.* v. *eBay Inc.,* 600 F3d 93 (2nd Cir 2010) vicarious liability not discussed), and *Perfect 10 Inc.* v. *Amazon.com Inc.,* 508 F3d 1146 (9th Cir 2007).

According to Bartholomew, both vicarious liability and contributory infringement are applied more broadly in the context of copyright than trademarks, and see *Shapiro, Bernstein & Co.* v. *HL Green Co,* 316 F2d 304, 309 (2d Cir 1963), citing *Sony Corp. of America* v. *Universal City Studios Inc.,* 464 US 417, 439 n. 19 (1984). See also Weckström, 'Trademark Infringement'.

[16] Even where liability is denied, economic efficiency reasons may be influential. See Bartholomew and McArdle, 'Causing Infringement', 679, 711–712, discussing *Tiffany, Inc* v. *eBay, Inc* 576 FSupp 2d 463 (SDNY 2008).

may explain why US law has been described as '"uncertain", "contradictory" and "incoherent"'.[17]

9.1.3 Statutory accessory liability compared to similar concepts

Since authorisation is a statutory 'tort' as explained in [9.2.1], there are 'linkages' between statute and common law.[18] One such linkage is that litigants have sought to argue, and the courts have applied, common law (joint tortfeasor) principles of accessory liability in the same broad factual circumstances as raise statutory-based authorisation claims.[19] A person liable for authorisation will 'often' be liable as a joint tortfeasor as well [Chapter 5].[20] In copyright litigation in Australia, the focus of litigation has tended to be on the interpretation of 'authorisation',[21] perhaps because authorisation may be easier to establish than common law accessory liability.[22] In the UK, claimants (Cs) have relied on both 'authorisation' and the common law in the same factual context in many cases.[23] Cases that apply common law tort principles in the context of infringements of IP rights are generally discussed in Chapter 5.

The concept of 'authorising' infringement has a long judicial history and a considerable body of jurisprudence. Further, the law on IP infringements and accessories thereto is strongly influenced by policy considerations – both the broader ones noted above, as well as the more specific factors relevant to specific IP rights. Partly for this reason, it is difficult to make sense of this area of law. Consequently, this book considers the

17 See Bartholomew and McArdle, 'Causing Infringement', 678, citing various scholars.

18 *Roadshow* [2012] HCA 16; (2012) 248 CLR 42 [107] (Gummow and Hayne JJ).

19 Interestingly, in the US, although copyright legislation contains the exclusive rights 'to do and to authorize' the activities enumerated (s. 106 Copyright Act 1976), this has not led to a jurisprudence on 'authorize' as the source of accessory liability. Instead, general tort accessory principles are used to impose liability.

20 See *Copinger*, [7–146], 518.

21 For the most part in copyright litigation in Australia, the focus has been on the interpretation of the statutory term 'authorisation' of a breach of copyright. E.g., in *Roadshow* [2012] HCA 16; (2012) 248 CLR 42 [100], the plaintiff did not bring action against the defendant on the basis of tort accessory principles. *Cf.*, e.g., *Apotex Pty Ltd* v. *Les Laboratoires Servier (No 2)* [2012] FCA 748 where common law principles were considered alongside statutory-based claims (for patent infringements).

22 A similar assumption seems implicit in *Cooper* v. *Universal Music Australia Pty Ltd* [2006] FCAFC 187; (2006) 156 FCR 380 [81] (Branson J, French J agreeing) (*Cooper*).

23 See, e.g., *CBS Songs Ltd* v. *Amstrad Ltd* [1988] AC 1013 (*CBS Songs*); *Newzbin* [2010] EWHC 608; [2010] ECC 13; *Dramatico Entertainment Ltd* v. *British Sky Broadcasting Ltd* [2012] EWHC 268 (Ch); [2012] 3 CMLR 14.

statutory rules on IP accessories separately from more generic statutory accessory rules, discussed in Chapter 10.

One specific context in which questions of accessory liability have arisen is where directors are sought to be made liable for companies' infringements of IP rights. This topic is considered separately as part of a broader discussion of directors' liability in Chapter 11.

9.2 Authorisation of infringements

9.2.1 Statutory sources of liability

The difficult concept[24] of authorisation of another's infringement is an important basis for establishing 'secondary' liability in the law of copyright, where much of the case law has arisen, although more recently, authorisation has been incorporated into other IP rights. Section 16 of the Copyright, Designs and Patents Act 1988 (UK) (CDPA) states (emphasis added): 'Copyright in a work is infringed by a person who without the licence of the copyright owner does, *or authorises another to do*, any of the acts restricted by the copyright.' The authorisation without consent of the doing of the acts within copyright (as well as design rights) is therefore itself an actionable infringement.[25] The same authorisation principle applies in Australia in copyright law,[26] and more recently, designs,[27] trademarks[28] and patents law. Under patents law, for example, the owner of a patent has the 'exclusive rights, during the term of the

[24] The authorities on authorisation have been described as a 'mire': see Cowdrey J in *Roadshow Films Pty Ltd* v. *iiNet Ltd* [2010] FCA 24; (2010) 83 IPR 430 [358], at first instance. Academic commentary also generally decries the current state of affairs. See, e.g., Yee Fen Lim, '"Bound to infringe": the forgotten child of the doctrine of authorisation of copyright infringement' (2011) 33(2) *European Intellectual Property Review* 91; Brendan Scott, 'Authorisation under copyright law and "the nature of any relationship"' (2011) 22 *Australian Intellectual Property Journal* 172; Javier J. Forrester and Eddy D. Ventose, 'Authorization and Infringement of Copyright on the Internet' (2010) 14(6) *Journal of Internet Law* 3; Michael Napthali, 'Unauthorised: Some thoughts upon the doctrine of authorisation of copyright infringement in the peer-to-peer age' (2005) 16 *AIPJ* 5; Sydney Birchall, 'A doctrine under pressure: The need for rationalisation of the doctrine of authorisation of infringement of copyright in Australia' (2004) 15 *AIPJ* 227.

[25] A similar approach has been adopted for registered design rights in the UK: see s. 226(3) CDPA.

[26] In Australia, the law draws a distinction between copyright in 'works' and in relation to subject matter other than works. See s. 36(1) and s. 101(1) Copyright Act 1968 (Cth), respectively. A 'work' is a literary, dramatic, musical or artistic work (s 10(1)); the other matter comprises film, television and sound recordings, and published editions of works (Pt IV).

[27] See Designs Act 2003 (Cth), s. 10.

[28] See Trade Marks Act 1995 (Cth), s. 20(1).

patent, to exploit the invention and to authorise another person to exploit the invention',[29] such that authorisation of another's exploitation[30] without consent is actionable. These developments suggest an expanding role for 'authorisation'.[31]

The term 'authorise' is not defined in any of the legislation. However, the Copyright Act 1968 (Cth) lists a number of relevant factors to be taken into account when determining whether a person has authorised an infringement. These factors are noted in [9.2.3]. It is likely that the meaning of 'authorise' will be the same in all the various manifestations of its use.[32] Any possible differences as to its meaning under specific legislation do not affect the general points being made here. Of course, in the UK, since no authorisation provision exists in patents or trademarks law, a claimant will need to rely on either the specific indirect liability provisions, or common law principles to establish liability.[33]

9.2.2 Is authorisation accessory liability? The need for a primary wrong

'Direct' acts of infringement of IP rights are statutory 'torts' committed by the primary infringer. Similarly, the *authorisation* of the doing of any acts comprised within those rights (without the licence of the owner) is also itself a 'statutory tort' and a separate act of infringement that is 'distinct from primary infringement', as the joint judgment of French CJ, Crennan and Kiefel JJ in the High Court of Australia in *Roadshow*[34]

[29] See Patents Act 1990 (Cth), s. 13(1).

[30] 'Exploit' is defined in Schedule 1 to the Patents Act 1990 (Cth).

[31] Some patents litigation has arisen since the insertion of 'authorising' into the legislation. There appear to be few cases on trademarks. Indeed, common law tort accessory principles have been used in this context: see, e.g., *Ward Group Pty Ltd* v. *Brodie and Stone plc* [2005] FCA 471; (2005) 143 FCR 479, in which authorisation was potentially arguable.

[32] It has been held that the use of the term authorise in patents law has the same meaning as it does under the Copyright Act. See, e.g., *Bristol-Myers Squibb Co* v. *FH Faulding & Co Ltd* (2000) 97 FCR 524, 559 [97] (FCAFC); *Inverness Medical Switzerland GmbH* v. *MDS Diagnostics Pty Ltd* [2010] FCA 108; (2010) 85 IPR 525, 568 [194]; *Apotex Pty Ltd* v. *Les Laboratoires Servier (No 4)* [2010] FCA 1202 [14]; *Rescare Ltd* v. *Anaesthetic Supplies Pty Ltd* (1992) 25 IPR 119, 155 (FCA). On this view, presumably, the factors identified in the Copyright Act would be equally relevant to consider under patents law.

[33] E.g., that A is an accessory to the statutory tort of infringing patents or trademarks, or else to the tort of passing off (as in *Lever* v. *Goodwin* (1887) 4 RPC 492).

[34] [2012] HCA 16; (2012) 248 CLR 42 [42]. See also at [8]; and at [107] (Gummow and Hayne JJ), citing S. Ricketson and C. Creswell, *The Law of Intellectual Property: Copyright, Designs & Confidential Information* (2002) §9.10, §13.160. See also *ABKCO Music & Records Inc* v. *Music Collection International Ltd* [1995] RPC 657. The fact that authorisation is an independent wrong does not detract from its accessorial nature, see [2.3].

notes. Nonetheless, it has been repeatedly affirmed that authorisation is a form of 'secondary' (meaning accessory) liability that is *dependent* on proof of a primary infringement having occurred.[35] On this view, even if an act of 'authorisation' takes place, if there is no subsequent primary infringement, such 'authorisation' alone is not actionable.[36]

The identification of authorisation as a separate tort has led to doubts in the UK as to whether such a claim is, in fact, dependent on a 'primary' infringement having occurred. In *MCA Records Inc* v. *Charly Records Ltd*, Rimer J suggested that authorisation 'is complete when the authorisation is effected'.[37] The comment was made in the context of a determination of the start of the statutory limitation period, and whether such period commenced at the time of the grant of a licence (the act of authorisation) or at the time of any (and for each) subsequent infringements. It was held that the date of licence was the appropriate commencement date. The comment can be confined to that context and ought not to be accepted as a general principle.[38] It has, however, received the support of some

[35] *Roadshow* [2012] HCA 16; (2012) 248 CLR 42 [8], where French CJ, Crennan and Kiefel JJ put the matter most clearly on the facts of that case: communicating copyrighted materials by making available online is the primary infringement, authorising the making available online is the 'secondary' infringement. Similarly, at [110], Gummow and Hayne JJ describe the authoriser's liability as 'liability as a secondary infringer'; the concept's purpose is to make 'prevention of breach of the primary obligation' more cost-effective. See also, e.g., *Performing Right Society Ltd* v. *Mitchell & Booker (Palais de Danse) Ltd* [1924] 1 KB 762, 773; *RCA Corporation* v. *John Fairfax & Son Ltd* [1981] 1 NSWLR 251; [1982] RPC 91 (NSWSC); *Australasian Performing Right Association Ltd* v. *Jain* (1990) 18 IPR 663, 667 (FCAFC); *WEA International Inc* v. *Hanimex Corp Ltd* (1987) 17 FCR 274; (1987) 10 IPR 349, 359; *ABKCO Music & Records Inc* v. *Music Collection International Ltd* [1995] RPC 657, 660 (authorised act must itself be an infringement); *Heinz Wattie's Ltd* v. *Spantech Pty Ltd* (2005) 67 IPR 666, 670 [23] (NZCA).

If the elements of the primary wrong can be established against a party, then she is liable as primary wrongdoer, though the boundaries between primary and accessorial infringement are not always clear. E.g., in *National Rugby League Investments Pty Ltd* v. *Singtel Optus Pty Ltd* [2012] FCAFC 59, the Full Court reached a different conclusion to that of the trial judge, and concluded that the defendant had committed a primary infringement of copying a broadcast. See [39] onwards. Had the court concluded otherwise, then issues of authorisation or other accessory liability may have arisen.

[36] This does not mean, however, that a *quia timet* injunction may not be available where *the prospect* of (an authorised) primary infringement occurring exists [9.5.1].

[37] [2000] EMLR 743, 807 [179]. The issue was not taken up in the Court of Appeal: *MCA Records Inc* v. *Charly Records* [2001] EWCA Civ 1441; [2002] FSR 26. Supporting authority may be found in *Fenning Film Service* v. *Wolverhampton, Walsall and District Cinemas* [1914] 3 KB 1171.

[38] See discussion in *Copinger*, [7–151], 524, which is critical and points out that the comment is, in any case, probably obiter. Also critical is Dickens, 'When is an authorisation an authorisation?' (2000) 22(7) *European Intellectual Property Review* 339.

commentators. The authors of *Laddie*, for example, support the view that an 'authorisation right' is not dependent on an act of infringement occurring.[39] This conclusion leads to some potentially undesirable consequences. The cause of action would be complete where a party, without consent of the true owner, grants a purported licence or authority to someone to copy works, but then revokes the 'authority', even if no infringing copying takes place.[40] We would argue that authorisation is dependent on proof of primary infringement and is thus a form of accessory liability. It should be noted, however, that *Laddie's* conclusion that where a primary infringement *does take* place, an authoriser could be liable even if the primary infringer can avail herself of a defence personal to her,[41] is consistent with the conceptualisation of accessory liability as not being duplicative [2.6].

If authorisation of infringement is an example of accessory liability, but is also a separate statutory tort, is it possible to be an accessory to an authoriser, or an accessory to an accessory, as it were? The authors of *Laddie* assert that it is possible for a person to 'procure' an authorisation, or to enter into a common design to authorise jointly with another.[42] In the Federal Court of Australia, however, it has been doubted whether there is any liability such as authorising an authoriser.[43] There are good reasons to doubt. The possibility of someone being an 'accessory' to an accessory stretches responsibility too far and is a conceptually unnecessary step.[44] There is no reason why someone cannot authorise via an

39 M. Vitoria et al., *Laddie, Prescott & Vitoria, The Modern Law of Copyright and Designs*, 4th edn (UK, LexisNexis, 2011) (*Laddie*), [19.6]–[19.8], who consider the statement in *MCA* [2000] EMLR 743, 807 [179] to be correct.

40 Such a right seems unjustifiable and, presumably, pointless since, in any case, no damage would surely arise.

41 *Laddie*, [19.8]. 42 *Ibid.* [19.1].

43 *Cooper* [2006] FCAFC 187; (2006) 156 FCR 380 [12] (Branson J, French J agreeing). *Cf.*, Kenny J, at [163] (with whom French J also agreed), who held that a director had authorised his company's conduct under the deeming provisions of s. 101(1) Copyright Act 1968 (Cth) [164]. But Her Honour also held that the director had 'directed and procured' the company's authorisation, i.e., was an accessory to it. (Branson J held that the director had authorised the infringement [65].) Note, also, the confusion in *Australasian Performing Right Association Ltd* v. *Metro on George Pty Ltd* [2004] FCA 1123; (2004) 210 ALR 244, as to whether the director was liable on the basis of authorising the infringements, or of having procured his company's authorisation of infringements, e.g., at [79]–[80]. *Cf.* also Christopher Wood, 'Liability of directors as joint tortfeasors in intellectual property matters' (2010) 21 *Australian Intellectual Property Journal* 164, 178 onwards, on the interaction between authorisation and procurement.

44 Similarly in the US, it has been held in the context of trademarks that if A sells to B who sells to C in the US, thereby infringing US patents, A is not liable (*Baden Sports, Inc*

intermediary, that is, there need not be direct acts from the authoriser to the primary infringer.[45] Similarly, a 'procurer' of an authorisation, or joint conspirator with another authoriser, either authorises the primary infringement, or ought not to be liable. Where a company is the authorising party, the liability of directors is best determined on the basis that they have also personally authorised the infringement, via the company.[46]

9.2.3 *Definitions of 'authorise'*

In the UK, the courts have defined authorisation fairly narrowly,[47] focusing on the definition of Atkin LJ in *Falcon* v. *Famous Players Film Co*, that to authorise in law means to 'grant or to purport to grant to a third party the right to do the act complained of'.[48] This generally requires that the person seeking to authorise has or purports to have some authority,[49] and does not include the acts of someone who 'merely enables or possibly assists . . . but does not purport to have any authority which he can grant to justify doing the act'.[50] Although a broader

v. *Kabushiki Kaisha Molten* No CO6-21OMJP (US Dist 2007), cited by Bartholomew, 'Copyright', 457. The facilitator of a facilitator is too indirectly involved to have materially contributed to the trademark infringement, though as Bartholomew notes, the position in the context of copyright is not so clear-cut.

45 *Cf. Ash* v. *Hutchinson & Co (Publishers) Ltd* [1936] 1 Ch 489 (CA), and see *Applera Corp* v. *MJ Research, Inc* 297 FSupp 2d 459, 462–463 (D Conn 2004) (Arterton J): 'So long as proof of direct [IP] infringement is causally connected to the [corporate officer's] conduct, the interposition of a controlled intermediary does not necessarily relieve a corporate officer of liability as an infringer for actively inducing patent infringement.'

46 See, however, conflicting authorities discussed above n. 43 and generally Chapter 11.

47 Interestingly, before the introduction of the proscription against authorisation (in the UK, under the Copyright Act 1911 (UK); and in Australia, under the Copyright Act 1905 (Cth)) previous copyright law had proscribed 'causing' an infringement, but this was interpreted very restrictively. The term 'authorise' was therefore deliberately chosen to broaden liability. For a discussion of the history of the concept, see *WEA International Inc* v. *Hanimex Corp Ltd* (1987) 10 IPR 349, 356–360 (FCA). For a detailed summary of the law on 'authorisation' pursuant to s. 101 of the Copyright Act 1968 (Cth), see *Roadshow Films Pty Ltd* v. *iiNet Limited (No 3)* [2010] FCA 24 at first instance, particularly [357]–[423].

48 *Falcon* v. *Famous Players Film Co* [1926] 2 KB 474, 499 (*Falcon*), approved in *CBS Songs* [1988] 1 AC 1013, 1054, holding that providing someone with the means to copy materials in infringement of copyright does not grant such persons or purport to grant such persons the right to do so.

49 It would generally be 'purporting' to have authority, since the authoriser does not generally own the right or hold a licence.

50 *CBS Inc* v. *Ames Records & Tapes Ltd* [1982] Ch 91, 106 (Whitford J), approved in *CBS Songs* [1988] 1 AC 1013, 1054.

dictionary definition of authorise by Bankes LJ in the same case – 'to sanction, approve and countenance'[51] – has also been cited in English cases, and the House of Lords in *CBS Songs Ltd* v. *Amstrad Plc*[52] (*CBS Songs*) considered that definition of some relevance, the House clearly preferred Atkin LJ's formulation as the legal definition.[53] This narrow approach in the UK has led Scott to describe the legal position on authorisation as 'comparatively straightforward as a result',[54] though other commentators have pointed out that this 'narrow formulation is itself uncertain'.[55] It has been stressed, for example, that the meaning of authorise cannot be limited to an authoriser purporting to be in a position to grant a right under the copyright, such as to grant a licence, and must include a person who purports to grant a right to do restricted acts (such as copy).[56]

In Australia, the position is perhaps even less straightforward. The broader, dictionary definition of Bankes LJ in *Falcon* has been frequently cited as authoritative, albeit in the most recent High Court decision in *Roadshow*,[57] alongside other definitions, including the narrower formulation of Atkin LJ. Indeed, although in the Full Court of the Federal Court, Kenny J asserted that Australian case law has rejected the narrower English approach,[58] *Roadshow* suggests that there are now signs of qualification. As Gummow and Hayne JJ stated, the difficulties associated with the term 'authorise' 'are unlikely to be resolved merely by recourse to a dictionary'.[59] It would be wrong to take one element of the definition, such as 'countenance', 'and by fixing upon the broadest dictionary meaning of that word to seek to expand the core notion of "authorise"'.[60]

51 *Falcon* v. *Famous Players Film Co* [1926] 2 KB 474, 491. In some formulations, 'or' has been used instead of 'and': see *Roadshow* [2012] HCA 16; (2012) 248 CLR 42 [43]–[44].

52 [1988] 1 AC 1013. 53 *Ibid.* 1054.

54 Brendan Scott, 'Authorisation under copyright law and "the nature of any relationship"' (2011) 22 *Australian Intellectual Property Journal* 172, 175.

55 *Laddie*, [19.3], [19.4]–[19.5] 800, 802–804. 56 *Ibid.* [19.5] 804,

57 [2012] HCA 16; (2012) 248 CLR 42 [43]–[44], [121]–[130]; *University of New South Wales* v. *Moorhouse* (1975) 133 CLR 1 (HCA) (*Moorhouse*).

58 *Cooper* [2006] FCAFC 187; (2006) 156 FCR 380 [116], [140] (French J agreeing). Similarly, see *Australasian Performing Right Association Ltd* v. *Metro on George Pty Ltd* [2004] FCA 1123; (2004) 210 ALR 244. *Moorhouse* (1975) 133 CLR 1 (HCA) is usually cited as supporting the rejection of the UK approach, but Scott, 'Authorisation', 187–190, questions the validity of this interpretation.

59 *Roadshow* [2012] HCA 16; (2012) 248 CLR 42 [117]. See also at [68] (French CJ, Crennan and Kiefel JJ).

60 *Ibid.* [125] (Gummow and Hayne JJ), and see at [122]: authorise *includes* purporting to authorise, to 'clothe with authority'.

Gummow and Hayne JJ considered that there 'is force' in the statement of Herring CJ in *Winstone* v. *Wurlitzer Automatic Phonograph Co of Australia Pty Ltd*:

> As the acts that may be complained of as infringements of copyright are multifarious, so, too, the conduct that may justify an inference of authorisation may take on an infinite variety of differing forms. In these circumstances any attempt to prescribe beforehand ready-made tests for determining on which side of the line a particular case will fall, would seem doomed to failure.[61]

This sentiment aligns with the observation, which courts in numerous cases have stressed, that establishing liability is a question of fact and requires a close analysis of the facts.[62] But such statements hide more fundamental questions, namely what is it that we are seeking from the facts (other than, unhelpfully, whether A has 'authorised' an infringement)? If our understanding of accessory liability is accepted as the basis for liability here, then the question becomes easier to formulate. It is whether A, the authoriser, is knowingly *involved* in PW's primary infringement, so that A's conduct itself is wrongful such as to justify liability. Liability turns on what the parties knew when they engaged in certain conduct and the case law is consistent with both conduct and knowledge requirements being relevant [9.2.6]. Nonetheless, in our view, the fact that 'authorisation' does not expressly and separately allude to these elements has led to uncertainty: it is an opaque concept. Certainly, it is fair to say that Australian courts have struggled to contain the concept.[63]

Amendments inserted in 2000 into the Copyright Act 1968 (Cth)[64] identify relevant factors that must be taken into account in establishing

[61] [1946] VLR 338, 345, cited in *Roadshow* [2012] HCA 16; (2012) 248 CLR 42 [125].

[62] See, e.g., *Roadshow* [2012] HCA 16; (2012) 248 CLR 42 [63] (French CJ, Crennan and Kiefel JJ); *Cooper* [2006] FCAFC 187; (2006) 156 FCR 380 [72], [142]. See Scott, 'Authorisation', 175: 'one thing that all the authorities agree on is that authorisation is a question of fact'.

[63] Attempts to do so have focused on notions of 'power to prevent' and 'control'. For an excellent attempt to rationalise the doctrine of authorisation, albeit on a very different basis to that suggested here, see Birchall, 'A doctrine under pressure'.

[64] These were inserted into the Act by the Copyright Amendment (Digital Agenda) Act 2000 (Cth). Section 36(1A) concerns works and s. 101(1A) concerns subject matter other than works. The sections are almost identical and no distinction is drawn, even though s. 101(1A), but not s. 36(1A), contains the word 'other' in para. (c). See S. Birchall, 'Authorisation of Copyright Infringement: Is the Word "Other" an Impostor in Section 101(1A)(c)?' (2006) 66 *Intellectual Property Forum* 34.

whether a person has authorised an infringement of any act comprised in a copyright. Under s. 101(1A), these factors are:

(a) the extent (if any) of the person's power to prevent the doing of the act concerned;
(b) the nature of any relationship existing between the person and the person who did the act concerned;
(c) whether the person took any other reasonable steps to prevent or avoid the doing of the act, including whether the person complied with any relevant industry codes of practice.

Applying these factors involves 'an element of judgment'.[65] Other relevant considerations can also be taken into account.[66] The factors all loosely relate to the conduct element [9.2.4] and do not allude to any knowledge requirements [9.2.5]. These factors are discussed below in the course of the consideration of the case law [9.2.6]. Briefly, factor (a) (power to prevent or, presumably, deter) is also labelled as 'control', and focuses on whether there is power to prevent the specific act of infringement, but A abstains from taking reasonable steps to do so.[67] It is therefore closely related to the reasonable steps factor (c) and whether any steps could have been taken, and whether any steps that were taken were adequate.

It has been accepted that these factors partially codify the relevant principles existing at common law in relation to authorisation,[68] and therefore these factors may also be relevant and useful to UK law, as it has been suggested in the cases.[69] We proceed on the assumption that these factors are equally relevant in UK law, albeit noting the narrower definition of authorisation in that jurisdiction,[70] and further, that there are some differences in the outcomes of earlier cases in the UK and Australia [9.2.6.2]. In the UK, perhaps the central feature of many of the cases is the status of the authoriser and its relationship with the authorised party, suggesting a purported right or authority of the

65 *Cooper* [2006] FCAFC 187; (2006) 156 FCR 380 [15]. 66 *Ibid.* [14], [135].

67 *Roadshow* [2012] HCA 16; (2012) 248 CLR 42 [47]–[51], [128]. 68 See *ibid.* [22].

69 See *Newzbin* [2010] EWHC 608; [2010] ECC 13 [90]–[95], and in particular the passage quoted in [9.2.6.4] at n. 129, in which those factors are applied.

70 In the US, control or capacity to control another's infringing conduct, based on the relationship between the accessory and primary infringer, are also relevant considerations for determining contributory infringement. See, e.g., *Sony Corp of America* v. *Universal City Studios Inc* 464 US 417 (1984), and Bartholomew and McArdle, 'Causing Infringement', 691.

former to authorise the latter or purport to do so.[71] More recently, decisions (both denying liability in Australia, and imposing it in the UK) appear to suggest a greater alignment [9.2.6.4].

9.2.4 *Conduct that amounts to authorisation*

It has been said that in order for authorisation to exist, there must be 'immediacy . . . of the relationship between the primary infringement and the secondary infringement'.[72] This statement is cryptic, but such immediacy suggests some causal link between the authorisation and the act of primary infringement. As Scott summarises,[73] the need for such causal link has been expressed in a number of cases in terms of the primary infringement being 'sufficiently caused'[74] by, or 'consequent upon',[75] the authorisation; or that the authorised party must have 'acted upon' the authorisation.[76] Consistently with other types of accessory liability [3.3.3], however, it is doubtful that this requires that 'but for' causation is established.

Putting aside the need for some causative link, as the definitions in the case law demonstrate, authorisation does not spell out specifically what sort of conduct it encapsulates, that is, what acts of involvement are required. Indeed, the term is open to varying interpretations. Authorisation generally involves situations where the authorising party has close control over either the means of infringement,[77] or else some authority or control over the person doing the infringement.[78] Many of the cases involve persons procuring or directing others to commit certain acts, sometimes as a result of some position of authority, but not always. Clearly, the concept is not limited to cases of principals authorising

[71] This factor is much less prominent in Australian law. See Scott, 'Authorisation', 175. The existence of a relationship makes it more likely that A's conduct is akin to procuring infringement.

[72] *Roadshow* [2012] HCA 16; (2012) 248 CLR 42 [127] (Gummow and Hayne JJ).

[73] Scott, 'Authorisation', 173. [74] *Moorhouse* (1975) 133 CLR 1 (HCA) 23 (Jacobs J).

[75] *RCA Corporation* v. *John Fairfax & Son Ltd* [1981] 1 NSWLR 251; [1982] RPC 91 (NSWSC) 100 (Kearney J).

[76] *WEA International Inc* v. *Hanimex Corp Ltd* (1987) 17 FCR 274, 288; (1987) 10 IPR 349 (FCA) 364 (Gummow J).

[77] *Moorhouse* (1975) 133 CLR 1 (HCA); *Australian Tape Manufacturers Association Ltd* v. *Commonwealth* [1993] HCA 10; (1993) 176 CLR 480, 498; *Roadshow* [2012] HCA 16; (2012) 248 CLR 42 [127]–[130]. In the UK, this concept has also been stressed: *CBS Songs* [1988] 1 AC 1013, particularly at 1054.

[78] *RCA Corporation* v. *John Fairfax & Sons Ltd* [1981] 1 NSWLR 251; [1982] RPC 91 (NSWSC) 100. *Cf.* the discussion of 'permitting' an infringement [9.3.2].

agents: 'authorisation is wider than authority'.[79] However, as the cases discussed below demonstrate [9.2.6], liability has extended to conduct that amounts merely to acquiescence in wrongdoing in contexts where the acquiescent party has some capacity to control the activities of PW. Even facilitation of wrongs absent control may suffice where it is targeted at widespread infringement [9.2.6.4].

This is not to suggest that liability may arise for mere omissions by A, which might be suggested by the relevant factors identified in statute and common law in determining whether A has, indeed, authorised an infringement (power to prevent, etc. [9.2.3]). Instead, these focus on identifying whether and to what extent A needs to be active to prevent infringement, *after* some initial facilitation of it.

9.2.5 *Mental element: the role of knowledge*

Accessory liability in general requires knowledge by A of the acts of infringement: the essential matters or features of PW's conduct (that is infringing). However, the definitions of authorise do not expressly allude to the requisite mental element that needs to be established and 'knowledge' is not included in the factors set out in s. 101(1A) Copyright Act 1968 (Cth) (supposedly reflecting the common law). The cases demonstrate, however, that knowledge is critical to establishing liability; more specifically, what precisely A must know (and to what degree) relates to the level of A's activity in bringing about the wrong.

The relevance of knowledge has expressly been acknowledged in some cases. For example, Gibbs J stated in *University of New South Wales* v. *Moorhouse*:

> [T]he word 'authorize' connotes a mental element and it could not be inferred that a person had, by mere inactivity, authorized something to be done if he neither knew nor had reason to suspect that the act might be done.[80]

In our view, knowledge is a centrally important concept and is the basis for explaining and rationalising at least some of the seemingly

[79] *Moorhouse* (1975) 133 CLR 1 (HCA) 20 (Jacobs J, McTiernan ACJ agreeing), cited with approval in *Roadshow* [2012] HCA 16; (2012) 248 CLR 42 [124].

[80] (1975) 133 CLR 1 (HCA) 12–13. See also *Roadshow* [2012] HCA 16; (2012) 248 CLR 42 [110]–[111].

inconsistent decisions.[81] These conclusions are further justified below after a consideration of the cases and an analysis of their outcomes.

One of the complicating factors in IP cases on authorisation is that the primary wrongs being infringed are often strict: PW is liable even if she is unaware of the existence of copyright over the matter, or the patent or trademark that is infringed. Consequently, the case law struggles with the question of whether A must have knowledge of the existence of the infringed right in order to be liable. The cases are confused and not entirely consistent. We have argued in Chapter 3 that outside some cases of procurement, A must generally have a culpable mental state and know that PW is committing an act that is wrongful. Authorising may involve procuring conduct, but it may not. We conclude in [9.2.7] that, overall, the results of the cases are broadly consistent with the approach adopted in Chapter 3, that the more active A is in bringing about an outcome, the less A needs to know about the specific details of PW's infringement. Indeed, A may be liable even where A's conduct is not blameworthy, A being unaware of the existence of the IP right and therefore that PW is committing a wrong. Such liability ought to be exceptional, however. In most cases, where A is less active in bringing about PW's infringement, the more A will need to know in order to be liable, including that PW's conduct actually infringes existing rights [9.2.7].

9.2.6 Cases of authorisation

9.2.6.1 Express request or direction

The most straightforward cases of authorisation are those falling within the narrow definition of purporting to grant a right to do the restricted act. An authoriser may have expressly requested or directed certain actions that amount to infringements. In other words, there may be 'express or formal permission or sanction'[82] of the particular infringing conduct. For example, in *Evans* v. *E Hulton & Co Ltd*,[83] Tomlin J held that 'a man having a manuscript the copyright in which does not belong to him' but who 'sells to another some right in relation to it with a view to that other producing it', has authorised the ensuing production. A person who hires out a film to be screened authorises such screening and the

[81] Contrast Birchall, 'A doctrine under pressure', who seeks to rationalise 'authorisation' but considers that 'knowledge' has only a limited role to play in that doctrine (at 235).

[82] *Moorhouse* (1975) 133 CLR 1 (HCA) 12 (Gibbs J).

[83] [1923–28] MacG Cop Cas 51, 60.

performance of the work in which copyright is held.[84] It is in the contexts of these types of case that the comment of Lord Templeman that the conduct 'was bound to infringe'[85] is most apt.

Such request, direction, or purported giving of authority to do the acts, can be by way of supply of an article, if such supply amounts to the authorisation 'in physical form' that the supplied article be used in its intended way.[86] The seller of a digital key, the use of which automatically infringes by accessing copyrighted material, authorises such infringement;[87] where a record is sold, it can be assumed that it will be played and therefore the seller authorised such playing;[88] and the shop proprietor who installs on its premises a jukebox that plays records when money is inserted, infringing performance rights, has authorised each playing.[89] Liability is clear since the use of the physical object for its sole or only real purpose leads to infringement. More questionable is the situation where the physical object could be used for other purposes but infringement is 'almost' inevitable.[90]

[84] See *Falcon* [1926] 2 KB 474. There is a purported grant of the right to show the film. Similarly, a person who places an order with a manufacturer to make copies of works is authorising the subsequent infringements. See *Standen Engineering Ltd* v. *A Spalding & Sons Ltd* [1984] FSR 554; *Widen Pump & Engineering Co* v. *Fusfeld* (1983) 8 IPR 250.

[85] [1988] 1 AC 1013, 1053, referring to *Evans* v. *E Hulton & Co Ltd* [1923-28] MacG Cop Cas 51 and the object of the sale, namely publication. In the United States, the phrase 'good for nothing else' but infringement has been used in the patents context but also translated to copyright cases: see *Metro Goldwyn Mayer Studios Inc* v. *Grokster Ltd* 545 US 913, 932 (2005); 64 IPR 645. For a discussion of the relevance of 'bound to infringe' see Lim, 'Bound to infringe', albeit taking an unjustifiably broad approach to what might be encompassed by this phrase, including, e.g., cases such as *Cooper* [2006] FCAFC 187; (2006) 156 FCR 380; 71 IPR 1, which case does not readily fall within this description; see [9.2.6.4].

[86] *Football Association Premier League Ltd* v. *QC Leisure* [2008] EWHC 1411 (Ch) [379].

[87] *Ibid.*: decoder cards used to access copyrighted transmissions of football matches; suppliers liable for authorising infringements by their customers as card 'has one purpose only' and is therefore 'authorisation in physical form . . . to use the cards for the purpose for which they are supplied'. The court distinguished *CBS Songs* [1988] AC 1013 [9.2.6.2].

[88] See obiter in *Monckton* v. *Pathé Frères Pathepone Ltd* [1914] 1 KB 395, 403.

[89] *Vigneux* v. *Canadian Performing Right Society Ltd* [1945] AC 108 (PC), in obiter. So too the owner of the jukebox who hires it out to the shop proprietor authorises it to be used for its intended use (to play records), at least on the preferable authority: *Winstone* v. *Wurlitzer Automatic Phonograph Company of Australia Pty Ltd* (1946) VLR 338, distinguishing *Vigneux* at 123, which had concluded there is no authorisation in such a case, based on the lack of control over the use of the machine and whether it was made available to customers.

[90] See Kearney J in *RCA Corporation* v. *John Fairfax & Sons Ltd* [1981] 1 NSWLR 251; [1982] RPC 91 (NSWSC) 100, approving a statement in Laddie, Prescott and Vitoria, *The*

9.2.6.2 Providing mechanical means of copying

A number of cases have considered whether authorisation can be implied from conduct in the form of supplying or making available the mechanical means of making infringing copies (compare the internet cases [9.2.6.4]).[91] One such case is *CBS Songs*[92] in which a supplier supplied high-speed recording equipment that could be used by purchasers for the purposes of making pirate copies and which made this much easier. The House of Lords held that providing persons with the means to copy materials does not 'grant or purport to grant' them the right to do so, particularly since the equipment was capable of use for legitimate purposes and the seller had no further impact on or control over the activities of the users.[93]

Although the outcome of that case is correct, the case does not appear to accept (as other cases do) that there can ever be authorisation in making available to others the means of infringement. It therefore does not further consider what knowledge is required when engaging in such conduct.

A decision to similar effect is *Australian Tape Manufacturers Association Ltd* v. *Commonwealth,*[94] in which the High Court of Australia held that there is no authorisation by the seller of blank tapes, of any infringing copies made with those tapes, since the seller has no control over purchasers' use. Mason CJ and Brennan, Deane and Gaudron JJ distinguished[95] between the mere sale of an article, such as a blank tape or a video recorder, which is likely to be used for infringing purposes, and the circumstances of *Moorhouse.*[96]

In *Moorhouse*, the High Court held that a university that provided photocopiers in the library was liable for infringing copying that took place on the premises. Notices in the library that told readers of their responsibility to obey the law were inadequate and were not focused on

Modern Law of Copyright, 1980 edn, 403. This proposition was disapproved by Lord Templeman in *CBS Songs* [1988] AC 1013, 1055, as being stated 'much too widely'.

91 On Australian and US cases concerning the liability of the suppliers of technology, see M. Jackson and M. Shelly, 'Black Hats and White Hats: Authorisation of Copyright Infringement in Australia and the United States' (2006) 14 *International Journal of Law and Information Technology* 28.

92 [1988] AC 1013. 93 *Ibid.* 1054–1055. 94 (1993) 176 CLR 480 (HCA).

95 (1993) 176 CLR 480 (HCA) 497–498. Their Honours noted that in *Moorhouse* (1975) 133 CLR 1 (HCA) the University not only failed to take steps to prevent infringement; it provided potential infringers with both the copyrighted material and the means by which it could be copied.

96 (1975) 133 CLR 1 (HCA).

preventing infringements by users. Therefore the university was held to have authorised the copying, though the reasoning differed between Gibbs J and Jacobs J (with whom McTiernan ACJ agreed). Gibbs J emphasised the University's control over both the books and the means to infringe, the knowledge or reason to suspect on the part of the university that '*any one of a number* of particular acts [of infringement] is likely to be done',[97] and the failure to take reasonable steps to prevent such infringement.[98] In the circumstances, it was not necessary that there be knowledge or reason to suspect that '*the particular act* of infringement is likely to be done'.[99] Jacobs J also focused on the supply of both the books and the machines, and the lack of reasonable steps to prevent such use, but viewed this as an implied invitation to infringe. Jacobs J therefore did not consider knowledge of the likelihood of infringement as critical.[100]

Certainly, if it were a realistic factual conclusion that the university impliedly invited library users to breach copyright, then the decision in *Moorhouse* may be justifiable; it is, however, a questionable interpretation of the facts.[101] Is putting a photocopier next to books really an invitation to copy works that are copyright, in excess of any lawful limits or defensible copying?[102]

A contrary decision on almost identical facts is *CCH Canadian Ltd* v. *Law Society of Upper Canada*,[103] in which the Supreme Court of Canada expressly disapproved *Moorhouse*. The unanimous judgment considered that that case's 'approach to authorisation shifts the balance in copyright too far in favour of the owner's rights and unnecessarily interferes with the proper use of copyrighted works for the good of society as a whole'.[104] The court considered that '[c]ourts should presume that a person who authorizes an activity does so only so far as it is in

[97] *Ibid.* 13, emphasis added.

[98] *Ibid.* 13–14, 17. It was considered that putting up notices next to photocopiers that mislead as to the effect of copyright law are not reasonable steps.

[99] *Ibid.* 13 emphasis added.

[100] *Ibid.* 21–22; *cf.* at 22: 'Knowledge could become important if the invitation were qualified in such a way as to make it clear that the invitation did not extend to the doing of acts comprised in copyright and if nevertheless it were known that the qualification to the invitation was being ignored.'

[101] In any case, surely one cannot *impliedly* invite infringing conduct unless one has some knowledge or reason to believe that infringing conduct is taking place.

[102] At the time of *Moorhouse*, a defence of 'fair dealing' existed in s. 40 Copyright Act 1968 (Cth), albeit one without any guidelines as to what it included. Attempts to provide greater guidance were included in s. 40 after the decision in *Moorhouse*.

[103] [2004] SCC 13; [2004] 1 SCR 339.

[104] *Ibid.* [41].

accordance with the law'.[105] Perhaps relevant to that presumption was the fact that the copier was held in the Law Society's library. Such presumption is perhaps untenable when the photocopier is supplied to university students!

With respect, the decision in *Moorhouse*[106] is questionable and should preferably be seen as falling on the non-infringing side of the line.[107] Although providing the means of infringement can in limited circumstances give rise to liability, as recent internet cases have correctly held [9.2.6.4], it should only do so where there is sufficient knowledge [9.2.7]. Where the 'authoriser' does not have control over the users, and they can put the equipment to both infringing and non-infringing use, then knowledge of the inevitability or at least substantial likelihood of numerous repeated infringements (probably backed by knowledge of past infringements) ought to be required. To passively condone is not to authorise, even if one has made the means available.

9.2.6.3 Live performance on premises

A number of cases have considered the liability of operators of premises on which infringing performances of copyrighted works occur, often the playing of live music. Liability has generally been found on the basis of authorisation where the operators know that infringing works will be performed or are substantially likely to be performed and respond with indifference. The strongest case for liability is where the fact of past infringement has been brought to the attention of the defendant, as in *Australasian Performing Right Association Ltd* v. *Jain* (*Jain*).[108]

105 *Ibid.* [38], and see, [43], noting that it was plausible that patrons using machines did so in a lawful manner.

106 (1975) 133 CLR 1 (HCA).

107 Support for this conclusion can be found in the legislature's swift response after *Moorhouse* that sought to minimise the impact of the decision on libraries. See s. 6 of the Copyright Amendment Act 1980 (Cth) (inserting a new s. 39A) and Copyright Amendment Act 1989 (Cth) including Pt VB (ss. 135ZB-135ZZH), which allows for a scheme of equitable remuneration (ss. 153C, 153D) for authors. There are also some signs of disapproval of *Moorhouse* in the judgment of Gummow and Hayne JJ in *Roadshow* [2012] HCA 16; (2012) 248 CLR 42 [127]. See also [126], [129]–[132]. Further, although the House of Lords in *CBS Songs* [1988] 1 AC 1013, 1054, did not expressly disapprove of *Moorhouse*, one senses some unease about that decision.

108 (1990) 18 IPR 663, 667 (FCAFC) (Sheppard, Foster and Hill JJ). Despite the defendant having been given express notice of repeated past infringements, he did nothing to obtain licences; instead, he took 'a studied and deliberate course of action ... to ignore the appellant's rights and to allow a situation' (at 671). He must have known that infringement was likely.

Similarly, in *Australasian Performing Right Association Ltd* v. *Metro on George Pty Ltd*,[109] the corporate operator of a live music venue was held to have authorised the playing of copyrighted works in C's repertoire without relevant licences having been obtained by the promoters of the music. The operator had control over the venue (but not the content of performances) and was indifferent to the fact that promoters were not obtaining licences.[110] Justice Bennett concluded:

> Metro knew or had reason to anticipate or suspect that the infringing act, . . . was to be or was likely to be done (Metro conducted the advertising), had the power to prevent it (by not allowing the performance or by insisting in advance that a licence be obtained by the promoter), made default in some duty of control . . . (continuing to facilitate the performance) and thereby failed to prevent it.[111]

The more difficult question is whether the defendants in these cases would have been liable prior to the notices of past infringements, given that in *Jain*, for example, it seemed 'unlikely' that any non-copyright material would be played. Some earlier English cases have gone so far as to impose liability for failing to take precautions against infringements, even in the absence of any past infringement or, seemingly, knowledge that infringements will occur.[112] These cases are

Scott, 'Authorisation', appears to consider this and similar cases to be wrongly decided, given the absence of a sufficient relationship between the defendant and infringer suggesting to the infringer that the defendant is in any position to grant or purport to grant a right to do the act. Given, however, the knowledge of past and therefore of likely future infringements, and the control over the activities on the defendants' premises, liability is justified in these cases.

In the US, similar factual scenarios have often led to vicarious liability that is not based on any fault on the part of the proprietors of the premises. See Adams, 'Indirect Infringement', who is critical of such instances of liability.

109 [2004] FCA 1123; (2004) 210 ALR 244. 110 *Ibid.* [52], [56], [57].

111 *Ibid.* [57]. Similarly, see *Australian Performing Right Association Ltd* v. *Canterbury-Bankstown League Club Ltd* [1964–65] NSWR 138, 140; (1964) 5 FLR 415 (club had previously been alerted to infringements).

112 See, e.g., *Monaghan* v. *Taylor* (1885) 2 TLR 685: liability arose where the defendant was present while the infringing performance took place, and took 'no precautions to prevent' the infringement. See also *Performing Right Society Ltd* v. *Bray UDC* [1930] AC 377 (PC), where approval of a performance of a playlist which included two copyrighted works was considered to amount to authorisation of such performance.

Copinger, [7–149], 520, fn. 916, rightly considers that such cases must be 'regarded with caution'. The decisions can be criticised. Where generic conduct is permitted (e.g., the playing of music) and the party authorising that conduct does not know that it infringes or that infringement is substantially likely to follow, including because of a lack of knowledge about the subsistence of copyright over the works, then that ought to preclude a finding of authorisation. See [9.2.7] (2).

questionable given the lack of knowledge and also in light of *CBS Songs*.[113]

9.2.6.4 Internet cases

A number of recent cases have involved the provision of internet services that are used repeatedly to infringe copyright. In such cases, it may often be impractical to sue the individual infringers, so that there is considerable benefit to suing the service providers. The ISPs are not liable as primary infringers for communicating copyright materials,[114] but have they *authorised* infringement? The liability of ISPs is further complicated by certain exemptions from liability created by specific statutory provisions. In both the UK and Australia, these preclude awards of damages and accounts of profits against service providers on certain conditions being met.[115] Such 'safe-house' provisions limit liability once found to exist: they do not preclude such liability.

The High Court of Australia decision in *Roadshow*[116] involved a claim against iiNet Ltd ('iiNet'), who provided internet services to a range of private and business users. *Some* of the users were using peer-to-peer file-sharing software to infringe copyright. The plaintiffs, including Roadshow Films Pty Ltd, brought specific examples of such infringement to the attention of iiNet, and asked it to terminate such users' accounts. The High Court held that failure to terminate such accounts did not amount to authorisation. It noted that iiNet had no control over the users' activities other than by means of terminating their accounts (in which case, of course, they could take their business elsewhere); and thus no reasonable steps were available to it to prevent infringement.[117] Even if there was indifference to the infringement, which was questionable, iiNet could legitimately consider that it could not investigate nor take at face value every allegation of

113 [1988] AC 1013.

114 See s. 22(6) and (6A) Copyright Act 1968 (Cth). See also s. 112E. *Cf.* in the UK the defences of 'mere conduit', 'hosting' and 'caching' discussed, e.g., *Copinger*, 1125–1131, [21-105]–[21-118].

115 On the UK legal position, see, e.g., *Laddie*, Ch. 37. In Australia, see Div. 2AA of Part V Copyright Act 1968 (Cth) (ss. 116AA-116AI).

116 [2012] HCA 16; (2012) 248 CLR 42.

117 The only relationship that existed was that of customer/provider, which existed in relation to both infringing and non-infringing activities. The court accepted, however, that a relevant relationship can arise from one that generates commercial profits and advantages: *Roadshow* [2012] HCA 16; (2012) 248 CLR 42 [150]; see also *Cooper* [2006] FCAFC 187; (2006) 156 FCR 380 [48].

infringement.[118] Omissions rarely amount to authorisation unless the person 'authorising' has the power to prevent the specific act and abstains from taking reasonable steps to do so.[119]

Roadshow can be compared to *Cooper* v. *Universal Music Australia Pty Ltd* (*Cooper*),[120] finding liability on the part of a proprietor of a website, as well as the companies providing a platform and technical assistance to that website, set up specifically for the purpose of allowing peer-to-peer file sharing by its users. They did not provide the file-sharing software. The defendant, Cooper, had registered a domain and operated a website 'MP3s4FREE' that contained hyperlinks to other websites containing music files which were thereby able to be downloaded. Claims were also brought against the companies that hosted Cooper's website, the director who was the controlling mind of those companies, and an employee of one of the companies who provided technical assistance to Cooper in establishing and operating of the website. The court held that all parties, other than the employee,[121] authorised infringements of copyright occurring in Australia[122] by users of Cooper's website. The liable defendants had control[123] over

[118] In any case, *indifference* to the acts of infringements of others will rarely amount to authorisation, unless it reaches such a degree that authorisation may be inferred. *Roadshow* [2012] HCA 16; (2012) 248 CLR 42 [47]–[51], [128].

[119] As was concluded by Gummow and Hayne JJ, '[t]he progression urged by the appellants from the evidence, to "indifference", to "countenancing", and so to "authorisation", is too long a march.' *Ibid.* [143]. *Cf. Ellison* v. *Robertson,* 357 F3d 1072 (9th Cir 2004), leaving open the possibility of liability of an ISP.

[120] [2006] FCAFC 187; (2006) 156 FCR 380. The decision can be compared with *Universal Music Australia Pty Ltd* v. *Sharman License Holding Ltd* [2005] FCA 1242; (2005) 65 IPR 289, which held that the providers of software that enabled peer-to-peer file-sharing authorised the infringements of the claimants' copyright resulting from the software's intended and predominant use for copying.

[121] The *employee*, however, had no authority or managerial role and hence no control over activities and nor was there a duty to compel his employer to take steps to close the website down. [2006] FCAFC 187; (2006) 156 FCR 380 [71] and [166]–[167]. An employee is not required to disobey his employer's instructions.

[122] Section 101(1) has a geographic limit: although acts of authorisation need not occur in Australia, the primary infringements must do so. See *Cooper* [2006] FCAFC 187; (2006) 156 FCR 380 [10]–[12], [175]–[176]. The same geographic limitation applies in the UK. See s. 16(1) CDPA.

[123] It was suggested that the burden of the Australian decisions is that power or control does not require control over the person engaging in the infringing conduct or the place where the infringement takes place. Instead, the focus is on power in the sense of making available the means of infringement rather than the capacity to control what can be done with those means by individual users: *Cooper* [2006] FCAFC 187; (2006) 156 FCR 380 [30]–[32]. As Scott, 'Authorisation', 182–183, has pointed out, however, this wide meaning is not really about power *to prevent*, or capacity to control at all, but rather

the use of the website.[124] The defendants did not take steps to prevent infringements and the inclusion of some disclaimers was 'merely cosmetic'.[125]

Cooper seems to go beyond the confines of the narrower definition and application of authorisation liability in the UK in *CBS Songs*.[126] In *Cooper*, the defendants did little more than provide the means of infringement, which *CBS Songs* expressly stated was not a sufficient basis for liability. There was no purported authority of, nor suggestion by, the defendants that they had some right or capacity to allow the infringers' conduct. Despite this, the English High Court in *Twentieth Century Fox Film Corporation* v. *Newzbin Ltd* (*Newzbin*)[127] considered that *Cooper* was consistent with UK law, while still purporting to apply *CBS Songs*.

In *Newzbin,* an internet search engine for 'Usenet' (an internet message board) provided sophisticated indexing to movies and television programmes, and provided users with the means to download and reassemble the multiple digital component parts (files) of infringing materials posted by other users. The provider of the search engine was held liable as authoriser of the multiple infringements by the users of the search engine. The defendant, the search engine service provider, profited considerably from these activities. Although attempts were made to conceal the purpose of the search engine and to warn users against illegal acts, these were 'entirely cosmetic and . . . neither intended to be nor in fact acted upon'.[128] Kitchin J sought to justify the decision in terms of a purported grant to do the relevant acts which may:

about a so-called 'power' not to facilitate. This is a valid criticism as it defines 'power' in artificial terms. This does not mean that facilitation (making means available) may not in some contexts amount to authorisation.

In other cases, courts have focused more on the capacity to control the activities of the infringers themselves, e.g., *CBS Songs* [1988] 1 AC 1013, and *CCH Canadian Ltd* v. *Law Society of Upper Canada* [2004] SCC 13; [2004] 1 SCR 339 [45], finding that there was a clear lack of control in the circumstances where the means of infringing were merely made available (discussed in [9.2.6.2]).

124 It did not matter that the website operated automatically, as that was the result of a deliberate choice. *Cooper* [2006] FCAFC 187; (2006) 156 FCR 380 [43].

125 *Ibid.* [49] (Branson J); see also at [151] and at [149] (Kenny J: Mr Cooper was not merely indifferent to the use made of the website).

126 [1988] AC 1013.

127 [2010] EWHC 608; [2010] ECC 13. *Cf.* also *Dramatico Entertainment Ltd* v. *British Sky Broadcasting Ltd* [2012] EWHC 268 (Ch); [2012] 3 CMLR 14, applying *Newzbin* in what were, factually, even stronger examples of authorising the infringements of users by the operators of a 'pirate' copying website.

128 [2010] EWHC 608; [2010] ECC 13 [42].

> ... be express or implied from all the relevant circumstances. In a case which involves an allegation of authorisation by supply, these circumstances may include the nature of the relationship between the alleged authoriser and the primary infringer, whether the equipment or other material supplied constitutes the means used to infringe, whether it is inevitable it will be used to infringe, the degree of control which the supplier retains and whether he has taken any steps to prevent infringement.[129]

As *Newzbin*[130] demonstrates, if the service provider actively facilitates breaches by others, then liability will follow, even where it is not possible to point to specific identifiable infringements by identifiable infringers.[131]

The difference between *Cooper* and *Newzbin* on the one hand, and *Roadshow* (and earlier cases such as *CBS Songs*) on the other, is between providing the means by which some persons may infringe, and providing means whose primary, perhaps even sole, commercial purpose and very design, are intended to encourage infringement.[132] Important to reconciling the decisions is the extent to which substantial non-infringing use could be made of the service; but it is also critical to focus on the knowledge of the defendant when making available the means of infringement [9.2.7].

9.2.7 The interaction between A's conduct and mental state

One reason why authorisation is such a difficult concept is because a wide variety of conduct can conceivably be, and has been held to be, encompassed within it. We have sought to group some of this conduct within four different types of cases, albeit potentially overlapping and not entirely distinct, and being conscious of the warnings about the futility of prescribing 'ready-made tests for determining' whether authorisation exists. The determination of whether liability arises in each type of case can be interpreted as following from the combination of the nature of A's conduct and his knowledge of the likelihood of PW infringing as a result of that conduct. There must be 'immediacy' in the relationship between the primary and accessory wrongdoing. That relationship ought to be

[129] *Ibid.* [90]. [130] [2010] EWHC 608; [2010] ECC 13.
[131] This was because the defendant did not keep records. *Ibid.* [111].
[132] See also *Dramatico Entertainment Ltd* v. *British Sky Broadcasting Ltd* [2012] EWHC 268 (Ch); [2012] 3 CMLR 14.

considered flexibly, consistently with this book's suggested approach to determining liability [3.5].

As the 'categories' identified below suggest, central to establishing immediacy is the variable of A's conduct and mental state. In short, the more directly an 'authoriser' seeks to bring about a particular outcome, the less relevant are questions of knowledge (and also control); the less that an authoriser's conduct is directed to achieving particular outcomes, the more relevant knowledge and control become. The following types of case may go some way to clarifying the operation of 'authorisation'. The 'categories' are not intended to be mutually exclusive or absolute.

(1) Express request or direction to infringe *Conduct.* An authoriser may have expressly requested or directed certain actions that amount to infringements. The act of authorisation may involve a granting of a purported right to do certain acts (perhaps cloaked with some authority). In other words, there may be an 'express or formal permission or sanction'[133] of the particular conduct that is infringing. This is the very essence of what is sought to be captured by the narrower definition applied in the UK [9.2.2]. These cases demonstrate authorisation of the most unequivocal type. References to 'implied' requests also perhaps fall within this class of case.[134]

Mental element. Where an authoriser requests, directs or expressly or formally sanctions, the courts have not considered the knowledge of A and whether A knew that infringing conduct would follow, since A must have clearly intended the requested act and its inevitable consequences.[135] It is in this category that references to acts that are 'bound to infringe' are most apt. Liability should generally therefore follow even

[133] *Moorhouse* (1975) 133 CLR 1 (HCA) 12 (Gibbs J).

[134] Implied request could mean that there is in fact a request or permission through conduct, that is, a genuine invitation to do the infringing act. In this case, the conduct is essentially similar as for express requests. 'Implied' authorisation could also mean that someone has made the means of infringement available to others; in other words, it could be a label attached to merely facilitating conduct (cases of type (2) and (3) below) in order to give it the appearance of coming within the narrower confines of the UK definition. Perhaps *Newzbin* [2010] EWHC 608; [2010] ECC 13 [9.2.6.4] is an example. *Winstone* v. *Wurlitzer Automatic Phonograph Company of Australia Pty Ltd* (1946) VLR 338 could also be considered in the same light.

[135] In the context of contributory infringements of patents, Souter J stated in *Metro Goldwyn Mayer Studios Inc* v. *Grokster Ltd* 545 US 913, 932 (2005); 64 IPR 645, 653: 'one who makes and sells articles which are only adapted to be used in a patented combination *will be presumed to intend the natural consequences of his acts*' that 'they shall be used in combination of the patent'; cited by French J in his dissenting judgment in *Collins*

in the absence of knowledge of what the user does with the materials,[136] and even in the absence of any control or power over the actual acts of infringement.[137]

Not only is knowledge as to whether and how copying (or other infringements) take place unnecessary in such cases, the directing or requesting party also need not know that copying amounts to infringement, that is, that copyright subsists.[138] The relevant authorisation is to copy, not to infringe copyright.[139] A may therefore not necessarily have a culpable state of mind. In part, this may be so because the authoriser intends that copying (or performance, etc.) takes place and copying a protected work automatically infringes. As Rantanen has stated, 'intent to cause copying of a protected work is the same as intent to cause copyright infringement'.[140] The situation is different where a party merely facilitates another to engage in generic conduct that could be lawful or unlawful ((2) and (3)). In such cases, unless the requesting party

v. *Northern Territory* (2007) 161 FCR 549 [42], [62], whose decision ultimately prevailed on appeal. Emphasis added.

136 Support can be found in *EMI Songs Australia Pty Limited* v. *Larrikin Music Publishing Pty Ltd* [2011] FCAFC 47; (2011) 191 FCR 444 [238]–[253]; particularly at [243]. Special leave to appeal to the High Court was refused: [2011] HCATrans 284. *Cf.* also Jacobs J in *Moorhouse* (1975) 133 CLR 1 (HCA): 'If general permission or invitation may be implied it is clearly unnecessary that the authorizing party have knowledge that a particular act . . . will be done.'

137 See Lim, 'Bound to infringe', arguing that control is not a relevant factor in 'bound to infringe' cases.

138 See, e.g., *Kimberley-Clark Australia Pty Ltd* v. *Arico Trading International Pty Ltd* (1998) 42 IPR 111, 129: if the defendant directs that certain acts be carried out, then ignorance that they are infringing is no excuse.

139 *Heinz Wattie's Ltd* v. *Spantech Pty Ltd* (2005) 67 IPR 666 (NZCA) [33]–[34], in which instructions to a party contracting to construct a building for Heinz Wattie's Ltd included that the specifications were to be essentially the same as for the previous buildings (constructed by the claimant). The court held that if following the specifications and instructions necessarily resulted in an infringing copy, the copying, having been directed by Heinz, had been authorised by it. The mistaken belief that there could be no breach of copyright (since the builder had so represented) was clearly no excuse.

140 As Jason A. Rantanen, 'An Objective View of Fault in Patent Infringement' (2011) 60(6) *American University Law Review* 1575', 1604, fn. 163, has noted, since copying necessarily constitutes infringement, the fault requirement may be readily satisfied. Rantanen appears to be saying that the infringement is a necessary consequence of the intended actions and absence of knowledge as to whether a work is protected or not does not preclude liability. Arguably, lack of knowledge of whether a work is protected or not shades into ignorance of, or a mistake as to, the law of copyright itself, which offers no excuse. Having said that, in the US, whether an inducer is liable absent knowledge of infringement, e.g., because of a bona fide belief that the conduct of the infringer is a fair use of copyright or that a patent is invalid, is not settled. See Adams, 'Indirect Infringement', 365; and see n. 148 below.

knows that the other is performing its tasks in an infringing way, there should be no liability.

(2) Making available means of infringement and control over such means *Conduct.* Particularly in Australia, liability has been imposed in circumstances going beyond conduct in the form of purported grants of rights, requests or directions. Such conduct is 'not essential to constitute an authorisation'.[141] Therefore, authorisation may involve the making available of facilities or means of infringing, such as by providing the mechanical means of copying [9.2.6.2], or making available the premises in which infringements take place [9.2.6.3].

Mental Element. In this category, the defendant generally needs specific knowledge that what the parties are doing infringes or that infringement is substantially likely to follow; further, whether the defendant has the means to prevent the infringement becomes critically relevant to determining liability. As the live music venue cases show [9.2.6.3], the defendant would generally need to have notice of past infringements in order to be alerted to the likelihood of future infringements.[142] Knowledge that infringement will occur, or is substantially likely to follow, that is, reckless indifference to infringement, generally is required.[143] Absent such knowledge, liability does not and ought not generally to arise.[144]

In this type of case, it is probably necessary that the defendant also needs to know that copyright subsists in the relevant matter and that no licences have been granted; it ought not to be sufficient that the defendant merely knows that copying/performance etc. is taking place. An 'innocent' alleged authoriser ought not to be liable even though the primary infringer is strictly liable for the 'authorised' act. Knowledge of *infringing* conduct ought to be required. The cases are perhaps broadly consistent with this conclusion,[145] but the issue has

141 *Moorhouse* (1975) 133 CLR 1 (HCA) 12 (Gibbs J).

142 Armed with such knowledge and given some relationship of power or control over the infringing party and/or place of infringement, indifference may give rise to liability.

143 Merely requiring that infringement 'may' follow sets the requirement too low: see Gibbs J in *Moorhouse* (1975) 133 CLR 1 (HCA) 13.

144 E.g., *Microsoft Corp* v. *Marks* (1995) 33 IPR 15, 27 (FCA) (employer not liable for authorising acts of employees as he had advised them of the importance of not copying materials and he was not aware that infringements were taking place).

145 Note, however, the further complicating factor in the IP context where directors are sought to be made liable for their companies' infringements [Chapter 11].

rarely been addressed.[146] In the US, broadly the same approach appears to be taken. Although the courts have variously formulated the requisite mental states for contributory infringement,[147] importantly, liability is generally seen as fault-based, even where primary liability is strict.[148]

(3) Making available means of infringement absent control *Conduct.* Where A makes available the means of infringement, but does not have any power or control over the users, or the place of use – that is, the means are made available generally – then both infringing and non-infringing conduct is possible. Consequently, knowledge by A of the likelihood of infringing conduct by PW becomes critically important. This is the most problematic area, and internet cases fall within this category, as does *CBS Songs*. The cases suggest that liability only arises if the authoriser has targeted its services towards infringement (as in

[146] If A allows or invites PW to perform music on A's premises, which could include both infringing and non-infringing conduct, then knowledge ought to include some awareness that the works to be performed are subject to copyright. Liability ought not to be strict since A has not authorised the *specific* act (that is an infringement). See cases discussed in [9.2.6.3]. Contrast this scenario with authorised conduct that is 'bound to infringe' (type 1 cases), e.g., if A tells PW, 'play Song Z', and PW does so, thereby infringing. A has authorised that infringement, even if A quite innocently believes that no copyright subsists. *Brintons Ltd* v. *Feltex Furnishings of New Zealand Ltd* [1991] 2 NZLR 677 (HC) lends support to the first proposition. The owner of a hotel being built asked a designer to carry out interior design; the designer did so after discussions with a carpet manufacturer, and submitted a design to the owner that, unbeknownst to it, infringed the plaintiff's copyright. The claim against the owner was dismissed. Hillyer J considered that unless the owner knew that the carpets to be made were a copy of another's design, there could be no authorisation of breach. The decision has been criticised (see *Copinger*, 518, [7–149], fn. 913); in particular because the reasoning includes a statement that the primary infringer 'can only be copying if the infringer knows he is copying' (at 681). Certainly, the criticism of *this* statement as being incorrect is valid. Nonetheless, the ultimate conclusion in the case is correct. Authorisation should therefore not be characterised as a strict liability wrong in all types of cases (contrary to Jennifer E. Stuckey, 'Liability for Authorizing Infringement of Copyright' (1984) 7 *University of New South Wales Law Journa*l 77, 87, who considers that proposition 'uncontroversial').

[147] See, e.g., Rantanen, 'An Objective View', on the many ways in which mental states have been formulated by the courts.

[148] See *ibid.*, generally, and citing numerous articles supporting fault-based liability at fn. 9. See also Bartholomew and McArdle, 'Causing Infringement', 686: 'Although liability for direct infringement has historically been a strict liability offense, contributory infringement has traditionally been viewed as an inappropriate candidate for . . . liability without evidence of a culpable mental state.'

Newzbin[149]) and has not merely provided a general service (as in *Roadshow*[150] and *CBS Songs*[151]).

Mental element. Clearly, it is not necessarily possible for A to know of prospective specific infringements by specific infringers, nor necessarily even of specific past infringements.[152] If it is accepted that liability can arise from such general facilitation, then it can only do so in limited circumstances and close attention must be paid to the requisite knowledge of A. The degree of knowledge must generally be high – the cases are consistent with liability based on actual knowledge (including wilful blindness [3.4.3.3]) – and the content of A's knowledge must generally be of inevitable, numerous and repeated infringements. In such circumstances, we can infer that A intends such infringements. If the very attraction of the service is that it allows for infringement and the service is targeted to maximising infringement, then this is little different to the situation in category (1) cases, namely, to request that infringing conduct takes place.[153] This is especially so where A is seeking to benefit commercially. If A knows merely of the possibility of infringements, or even of their substantial likelihood, A ought not generally to be liable (absent some control over users). Even if the 'facilitator' is alerted to the fact that users, such as buyers of high-speed recorders, are using them to infringe, this does not mean that the sellers cannot sell such equipment.

(4) Non-targeted assistance or facilitation *Conduct*. Non-targeted assistance or facilitation provided to assist another to infringe does not amount to authorisation even if provided with knowledge. This follows from the absence of any request or direction to do the acts; and because there is no status or power on the part of the assister to exercise control over the infringement (as in the category (2) cases). 'Non-targeted' means that A does not intend to maximise the scale of infringements (usually for its own benefit).

To summarise, it follows that different knowledge requirements apply, depending on the precise conduct of A. The more or less active a defendant is, and taking into account the likelihood that non-infringing

[149] [2010] EWHC 608; [2010] ECC 13. [150] [2012] HCA 16; (2012) 248 CLR 42.
[151] [1988] 1 AC 1013. [152] *Cf.* the requirements of *CBS Songs* [1988] 1 AC 1013.
[153] *Cf. Dramatico Entertainment Ltd* v. *British Sky Broadcasting Ltd* [2012] EWHC 268 (Ch); [2012] 3 CMLR 14.

conduct may also result from his conduct, the more or less he must know about the infringement. How active the defendant is in the primary infringement will depend in part on his relationship with PW and any control that he has over her.[154] A similar phenomenon can be seen in the US, with at times more or less detailed knowledge being required for liability, albeit without any consistency as to how knowledge is evaluated and applied.[155] The lack of consistency is perhaps unavoidable, however, and supports a flexible approach to considering the effects of A's conduct and mental state when deciding whether, as a whole, A's conduct is wrongful.

9.3 Other accessory liability provisions

9.3.1 Introduction

A number of more specific provisions in IP legislation, in addition to authorisation, also impose accessory liability as we conceive it. This section briefly outlines some of these from copyright and trademarks law. This section also explains why the liability can be characterised as accessorial.

9.3.2 Permit premises to be used for performance

In the UK, s. 25 CDPA creates the 'secondary infringement' of permitting the use of premises for an infringing performance (at a place of public entertainment). The person permitting such performance is 'liable for the infringement unless when he gave permission he believed on reasonable grounds that the performance would not infringe copyright'.[156]

In Australia, s. 39(1) Copyright Act 1968 (Cth) is in very similar terms to s. 25 CDPA. Where a person for profit[157] permits the performance in public of a work, such person is liable unless 'he or she was not aware, and had no reasonable grounds for suspecting, that the performance would be an infringement of the copyright'.[158]

154 *Cf.* Bartholomew and McArdle, 'Causing Infringement', 691–692.

155 See *ibid.* 689–690. See also Paul M. Janicke, 'Do We Really Need So Many Mental and Emotional States in United States Patent Law?' 8 *Texas Intellectual Property Law Journal* 279 (2000).

156 See subsection (1). 157 See s. 39(2)(b).

158 See subsection (2)(a). See also s. 26 CDPA, supply of apparatus used for infringement.

Liability under these sections is accessorial. A primary infringement must occur and liability is based on knowing involvement by A in such infringement.

The concept of 'permit' is obviously closely related to authorisation,[159] but do 'permit' and 'authorise' mean the same thing? Some cases have suggested they are largely synonymous,[160] but this is questionable, as 'permit' does not include within it any sense of having or purporting to have authority to allow the permitted act, unlike 'authorise'.[161] In any case, the provisions place a positive onus on parties giving permission to show that they believed on reasonable grounds that no infringement would take place.[162] 'Permit' therefore appears to be a broader concept than 'authorise'.[163]

There are, however, only a few, mostly early twentieth-century, cases on 'permitting'.[164] Perhaps inconsistently with the above conclusions, the most authoritative case took a fairly restrictive approach to the scope of liability. In *Adelaide Corporation* v. *Australasian Performing Right Association Ltd*,[165] the defendant Council had let out the Town Hall for performances. At the time it entered into the contract to hire out the premises, it did not have any knowledge or awareness of prospective infringements. After entry into the contract, one advertised performance included on the programme a song in which the plaintiff held copyright.

159 Indeed, some recent cases involving public performance have been decided on the basis of authorisation even where the 'permit' provisions would have been available [9.2.6.3].

160 See, e.g., *Performing Right Society Ltd* v. *Ciryl Theatrical Syndicate Ltd* [1924] 1 KB 1, 9; *Moorhouse* (1975) 133 CLR 1 (HCA) 12–13, citing *Adelaide Corporation* v. *Australasian Performing Right Association Ltd* (1928) 40 CLR 481, 497–498, 503. There are some statements in *Roadshow* [2012] HCA 16; (2012) 248 CLR 42 [47]–[48] that appear to accept such equation. Scott, 'Authorisation', 184–186, argues, correctly we would submit, that *Adelaide Corporation* at least is not authority for treating the terms as synonymous. Similarly, see Birchall, 'A doctrine under pressure', 236–238.

161 *Cf.* Birchall, 'A doctrine under pressure', 236–238, arguing that 'permit' has a wider meaning than 'authorise'.

162 *Adelaide Corporation* v. *Australasian Performing Right Association Ltd* [1928] HCA 10; (1928) 40 CLR 481 (A must exculpate himself).

163 *Laddie* [20.30] agree. The structure of the UK Act suggests that the person granting permission must establish positive facts to sustain a conclusion of reasonableness.

164 *Adelaide Corporation* v. *Australasian Performing Right Association Ltd* (1928) 40 CLR 481 (HCA) and *Performing Right Society Ltd* v. *Ciryl Theatrical Syndicate Ltd* [1924] 1 KB 1 are cases based on similarly worded earlier versions of the modern provisions. In *Performing Right Society Ltd* v. *Mitchell & Booker (Palais de Danse) Ltd* [1924] 1 KB 762, a claim based on permission was abandoned.

165 (1928) 40 CLR 481 (HCA) (Higgins, Gavan Duffy and Starke JJ, Knox CJ and Isaacs J dissenting).

Prior to the performance, the plaintiff informed the defendant of this fact (and that infringements had taken place during previous performances). The High Court of Australia held that the defendant had no right or power to prevent the performance of the infringing song and had not specifically permitted singing of that song when it entered into the agreement. There was nothing that the defendant was required reasonably to do. In the view of the majority, the relevant power must relate to the specific infringing act, such as having control over the hirer of the hall or the concerts being given, and not to some general capacity to alter its legal relations to acquire such power, for example, by termination of the contract.[166]

9.3.3 Trademarks

Under the UK Trade Marks Act 1994, a primary infringement of a trademark occurs where a defendant uses a sign identical or similar to the trademark in the course of trade.[167] A person who engages in accessorial infringing conduct is also liable for infringement. Section 10(5) provides:

> (5) A person who applies a registered trademark to material intended to be used for labelling or packaging goods, as a business paper, or for advertising goods or services, shall be treated as a party to any use of the material which infringes the registered trademark if when he applied the mark he knew or had reason to believe that the application of the mark was not duly authorised by the proprietor or a licensee.

[166] *Ibid.*, e.g., 503, (Gavan Duffy and Starke JJ): 'some power or authority to control the act to be done'. Similarly, Higgins J stressed the need for the defendant to have some direct power to prevent the specific act, the singing of the song, rather than merely indirect power (such as by ending the whole relationship of lessor and lessee) to achieve a result (at 499). Contrast Isaacs J.

The High Court relied on the English Court of Appeal decision in *Performing Right Society Ltd* v. *Ciryl Theatrical Syndicate Ltd* [1924] 1 KB 1, which on its facts is more straightforward. The defendant was the managing director of a company that had engaged a band to play music at a theatre leased by it. During the managing director's absence overseas, and without his knowledge, the band infringed the plaintiff's copyright. It was held that in the absence of knowledge, or control over the activities of the band, the director had not permitted the performance. See at 12–13 (Scrutton LJ); Atkin LJ agreed that the permission must relate to the 'work the performance of which is complained of . . . [and] is not to be inferred from a merely general authority to use a theatre for . . . performance' (at 15).

[167] See s. 14 and s. 10(1)–(4) Trade Marks Act 1994 (UK). Under s. 120, the sign must be 'deceptively' similar to the trademark.

Importantly, liability is accessorial since no infringement arises at all until the primary infringing use of the trademark has occurred and there is an involvement in that infringement (applying a trademark to labels etc.) with knowledge. The section has had limited judicial consideration.[168]

The section requires that the person knew or had reason to believe that any use of materials would not be authorised. Presumably, this requires knowledge that the trademark is registered to another party, since a belief that the person using the trademark owns it would mean that any use was authorised. The section therefore very precisely identifies the content of knowledge before liability attaches: in effect, knowledge that the use was not authorised and therefore would be infringing.

The defendant must have had 'reason to believe' that the conduct was not authorised. Cases discussed under the heading of '"Constructive" knowledge' under copyright are therefore relevant here [9.4.3.2].[169]

9.4 Non-accessorial 'indirect' infringements

9.4.1 Introduction

IP statutes contain specific provisions creating 'indirect' infringements. The label 'indirect' infringement is the most accurate, since it does not necessarily connote accessory liability; and many of these indirect infringements are not accessorial in nature, despite the labels 'secondary' and 'contributory' also being applied in the legislation or by commentators. The statutory rules do not impose accessory liability since the commission of a primary infringement is not a prerequisite to liability,[170] but they have affinity with accessory liability. The justification for the particular characterisation of the provisions is given below. Liability under these provisions is fault-based, generally requiring actual or 'constructive' knowledge by 'A' of the likelihood of primary infringement

168 See, however, *Beautimatic International Ltd* v. *Mitchell International Pharmaceuticals Ltd and Alexir Packaging Limited* [1999] ETMR 912 (section does not have extra-territorial operation).

169 As discussed in [9.4.3.2.], mere negligence, in failing to make inquiries, ought not to suffice. Section 10(5) is therefore unlikely to lead to a different outcome to that in *Paterson Zochonis & Co Ltd* v. *Merfarken Packaging Ltd* [1986] 3 All ER 522, noted [5.4.3.3] n. 155.

170 See, e.g., the discussion in *Grimme Maschinenfabrik GmbH & Co KG* v. *Scott* [2010] EWCA 1110 [87]–[90] (*Grimme*).

occurring or of primary rights existing, though the precise mental elements are variously formulated [9.4.3.2].

9.4.2 'Contributory' infringement of patents

At common law, courts took a restrictive approach when applying general tort law accessory principles to patent infringements. As Dixon J summarised the position in *Walker* v. *Alemite Corp*,[171] this 'narrow ... view' as to what 'constitutes participation' in another's infringement is based on the policy that an unpatented item can be lawfully sold for whatever purpose it may be used by the purchaser: 'whatever is not included in the monopoly granted is publici juris and may be freely used as of common right'.[172] In part as a response to this restrictive interpretation and limited applicability of joint tortfeasor principles [Chapter 5], the legislatures in both the UK and Australia amended the statutory regimes to broaden liability by creating 'contributory' infringements of patents. In the UK, principles of contributory infringement were introduced under the Patents Act 1977 because of the common law's 'great reluctance to treat as a "contributory infringer" someone who assisted in preparation for acts within the [patented] claims, but did not himself perform the acts'.[173] In Australia, the Industrial Property Advisory Committee recommended that patents legislation be amended to overcome 'the uncertainty surrounding the doctrine of contributory infringement under the common law'.[174] This resulted in s. 117 of the Patents Act 1990 (Cth). One of the significant consequences of allowing a

[171] (1933) 49 CLR 643 (HCA) 657–658 (McTiernan J concurring), references to cases omitted.

[172] *Ibid.* 658. This was cited with approval by Crennan J in *Northern Territory* v. *Collins* [2008] HCA 49; (2008) 235 CLR 619 [104] (*Collins*).

[173] See W. Cornish, D. Llewelyn and T. Aplin, *Intellectual Property: Patents, Copyright, Trade Marks and Allied Rights*, 7th edn (London, Sweet and Maxwell, 2010) [6-17] 277. The principles that were adopted are similar to those applicable in other European jurisdictions and as a result of European conventions.

[174] See A. Stewart, P. Griffith and J. Bannister, *Intellectual Property in Australia*, 4th edn (Australia, LexisNexis Butterworths, 2010) [14.12] 462. See also Crennan J in *Collins* [2008] HCA 49; (2008) 235 CLR 619 [103]–[104]: 'The limitations of the common law position ... [meant that the] legislatures of Australia ... and the United Kingdom ... considered it necessary to intervene'; and M. J. Davison, A. L. Monotti and L. Wiseman, *Australian Intellectual Property Law*, 2nd edn (Melbourne, Cambridge University Press, 2012) [15.5.7], 569: 'The uncertain boundaries of tortious accessory liability for infringement combined with its limitations were catalysts for enacting statutory liability for contributory infringement.'

claim for contributory infringement is 'the capacity to suppress competition in an unpatented article.'[175]

To simplify considerably, a contributory infringement occurs where a supplier supplies, on certain conditions, an unpatented product or method that can be used to produce a patented product or as part of a patented method.

Contributory infringements are not strictly speaking accessory or 'secondary' liability as we define that liability, since they arise even in the absence of a primary infringement by those persons to whom the materials are supplied. It is the supply alone of the product that attracts liability. The product need not even have been used to infringe as part of a method patent, or been used to construct a patented invention. Indeed, since the UK provision applies even to 'offering' a product for sale, this is really an unarguable point.[176] In Australia, s. 117 Patents Act 1990 (Cth) does not extend to offers to supply, but nonetheless it is unlikely that s. 117 requires proof of a primary infringement, though there is no authoritative decision.[177]

Nonetheless, contributory infringement has considerable conceptual affinity with accessory liability for at least two reasons. First, primary infringement will almost inevitably occur in most cases as a result of the supply of relevant materials.[178] The purpose of the sections is to deter primary infringements occurring and to provide a further mechanism to protect patent holders from such infringements. Secondly, although proof of primary infringement is not essential, these sections do require knowledge of *likely* infringements, and therefore if the evidence is that the product supplied would not be used to infringe except in unusual or maverick circumstances, then such knowledge will not exist.[179]

[175] *Collins* [2008] HCA 49; (2008) 235 CLR 619 [113] (Crennan J).

[176] See *Grimme* [2010] EWCA 1110 [87]–[90].

[177] See Stewart et al., *Intellectual Property*, [14.12] 462–463, who agree. This is borne out by the language of s. 117, which states that infringement occurs if a product's use 'would' infringe a patent and, in some circumstances, if there is reason to believe that a person 'would put it to that use'.

[178] In the UK, since a claimant can bring action against someone for merely offering a product for sale, this is less likely.

[179] Claimants would need to be able to show that a product will likely be put into effect by some users. See *Grimme* [2010] EWCA 1110 [112], [116], excluding maverick or 'freak' use.

'Contributory' infringement therefore has considerable similarity to the tort of passing off and specifically, the liability of a party for enabling passing off by others. One context in which the tort is committed is where a manufacturer or importer, for example, puts an 'instrument of fraud' or deception into hands of others, such as a retailer, if this

Contributory infringement has received relatively little attention in Australia and the UK,[180] unlike in the US.[181] In the latter jurisdiction, patents statutory 'contributory' liability is potentially wider, based on a widely drafted inducement provision that allows for liability in circumstances extending beyond the supply of materials used to infringe.[182]

Section 60 of the Patents Act 1977 (UK) defines infringement and relevantly provides for contributory infringement where a person supplies (or offers to supply) a person with:

> (2) . . . any of the means, relating to an essential element of the invention, for putting the invention into effect when he knows, or it is obvious to a reasonable person in the circumstances, that those means are suitable for putting, and are *intended* to put, the invention into effect in the United Kingdom [emphasis added].
>
> (3) Subsection (2) above shall not apply to the supply or offer of a staple commercial product unless the supply or the offer is made for the purpose of inducing the person supplied or, as the case may be, the person

enables the retailer to make a false representation. See the classic statement of principle in *Singer* v. *Loog* (1880) 18 Ch D 395, 412. This is another example of a difficult to classify liability rule, but it is probably best viewed as primary and not accessory liability. The tort is committed even if the retailer is not deceived (and therefore no wrong has been committed against the retailer) and even if, ultimately, no purchasers are deceived, because the retailer takes steps to guard against deception or does not on-sell. See generally Christopher Wadlow, *The Law of Passing-Off*, 4th edn (London, Sweet & Maxwell, 2011) [5-134], [5-140]–[5-174]; and David Kitchin et al., *Kerly's Law of Trademarks and Trade Names*, 14th edn (London, Sweet & Maxwell, 2005) [15-201]–[15-203].

180 See, however, e.g., Justin Wheelahan, 'Contributory infringement under s. 117 of the Patents Act 1990 (Cth): What suppliers need to know' (2009) 20 *Australian Intellectual Property Journal* 53; Graham Burnett-Hall, 'Court of Appeal Delivers Key Judgment on Contributory Patent Infringement' (2011) 6(5) *Journal of Intellectual Property Law and Practice* 282; Wayne Condon and Justin Lambert, 'The Vexed Issue of Therapeutic Combinations and Contributory Patent Infringement in Australia' (2012) 9(4) *Journal of Generic Medicines* 207.

181 See, e.g., Bartholomew and McArdle, 'Causing Infringement'; Heinz Goddar, 'Cross-Border Contributory Patent Infringement' (2011) 7(2) *Washington Journal of Law, Technology and the Arts* 135; Rantanen, 'An Objective View'; Corinne Langinier and Philippe Marcoul, 'Contributory Infringement Rule and Patents' (2009) 70(2) *Journal of Economic Behavior and Organization* 296; Mark Bartholomew, 'Cops, Robbers and Search Engines: The Questionable Role of Criminal Law in the Contributory Infringement Doctrine' (2009) 4 *Brigham Young University Law Review* 783; Adams, 'Indirect Infringement'; Paul A. Braier and Azza M. Jayaprakash, 'Indirect patent infringement in the US: Points to consider for generic and API manufacturers' (2007) 4(4) *Journal of Generic Medicine* 287.

182 The Patent Act, 35 USC §271(b).

> to whom the offer is made to do an act which constitutes an infringement of the patent by virtue of subsection (1) above.

Two sources of liability are created: knowledge-based liability (subsection (2), which does not apply to staple commercial products) and inducing infringing conduct (subsection (3)).[183]

The English section has been discussed at length by the Court of Appeal in *Grimme Maschinenfabrik GmbH & Co KG* v. *Scott*.[184] In that case, the defendant supplied potato sorting machines that were sold either with rubber rollers or with steel rollers. The machines sold with rubber rollers infringed the plaintiff's patent; the machine with steel rollers did not. The machines were designed so that the rollers were readily interchangeable, which was one of their selling points. The Court held that the sale of the machine with steel rollers was a contributory infringement of patent.

The Court considered that the relevant intention referred to in subsection (2) is that of some prospective users and need not be a settled present intention;[185] indeed, such intention will generally arise later. The court stated the requisite knowledge in the following terms:

> In short, the knowledge and intention requirements of . . . section 60(2) are satisfied if, at the time of supply or offer of supply, the supplier knows, or it is obvious in the circumstances, that ultimate users will intend to put the invention into effect. . . . [This] is likely to be the case where the supplier proposes or recommends or even indicates the possibility of such use in his promotional material.[186]

This sets out what it is that the seller or supplier must know, that is, the content of knowledge. In relation to the requisite degree of knowledge, the meaning of 'obvious to a reasonable person' is considered below, under the related heading of 'constructive' knowledge relevant to 'indirect' infringements of copyright [9.4.3.2]. It is assumed that the knowledge requirement will be defined similarly here.

183 One issue under subsection (3) is that 'staple commercial product' is not defined in the Act and is capable of a variety of meanings, but it is outside the scope of this book to consider that concept. There are few judicial authorities on point. It is discussed in Australia in *Collins* [2008] HCA 49; (2008) 235 CLR 619. See also Condon and Lambert, 'Therapeutic Combination'.

184 [2010] EWCA 1110; [2011] FSR 7. For a more detailed summary of the facts and issues, see Burnett-Hall, 'Court of Appeal'. The case was applied in, e.g., *KCI Licensing Inc* v. *Smith & Nephew Plc* [2010] EWCA 1260; [2011] FSR 8.

185 See the set of questions the court posited at [2010] EWCA 1110; [2011] FSR 7 [107].

186 *Ibid.* [131]. See also [70].

Applying these principles to the facts of the case, the supply of machines with steel rollers was a contributory infringement because the supplier knew, or it was obvious in the circumstances, that ultimate users would put the machine into effect in a way that infringed patent by interchanging the steel and rubber rollers.[187]

In Australia, s. 117 was inserted into the Patents Act 1990 (Cth)[188] and deals with 'Infringement by supply of products'. It provides:

(1) If the use of a product by a person would infringe a patent, the supply of that product by one person to another is an infringement of the patent by the supplier unless the supplier is the patentee or licensee of the patent.
(2) A reference in subsection (1) to the use of a product by a person is a reference to:
    (a) if the product is capable of only one reasonable use, having regard to its nature or design – that use; or
    (b) if the product is not a staple commercial product – any use of the product, if the supplier had reason to believe that the person would put it to that use; or
    (c) in any case – the use of the product in accordance with any instructions for the use of the product, or any inducement to use the product, given to the person by the supplier or contained in an advertisement published by or with the authority of the supplier.

Section 117 effectively creates three (albeit potentially overlapping) sources of liability, which Hayne J in *Collins* summarises in terms of 'only use' (para. (a)), 'known use' (para. (b)) and 'instructed use' (para. (c)).[189] This contrasts with the two heads of liability in the UK. The UK Act does not have an equivalent liability to para. (a).

Under s. 117, if the product is a staple commercial product, then even if the supplier knows or believes that it will be used to infringe patent, no

[187] *Ibid.* [70].

[188] One of its purported aims was to harmonise the law with Australia's trading partners, including the US and the UK. However, s. 117 is expressed in very different terms to other contributory infringement provisions such that Crennan J stated in *Collins* [2008] HCA 49; (2008) 235 CLR 619 [110] that '[t]here is, therefore, only limited assistance to be gained from considering the expressed desire for harmony with major trading partners'. See also at [49] (Hayne J).

[189] *Ibid.* [35].

liability arises unless the supplier instructs or induces users to use it in an infringing way (para. (c)).

The approach in s. 117 has some similarity to the approach that this book considers appropriate to accessory liability more generally, namely that the requisite knowledge may vary according to how active a role the accessory has had in bringing about the primary infringement. In the circumstances encompassed in para. (a), in which infringement is inevitable, knowledge has no role because a supplier can be considered to intend the use of a product capable of only one reasonable use.[190] In relation to para. (c), although knowledge is not expressly alluded to, to induce or instruct someone to engage in certain conduct clearly encompasses an intention that they so act (and therefore implicitly knowledge that they will do so);[191] it appears, however, that knowledge of the existence of the patent is not necessary.[192] Where, however, a product can be used in a variety of ways (para. (b)), knowledge of likely acts that are infringing becomes necessary, though 'constructive' knowledge suffices [9.4.3.2].

9.4.3 Copyright

9.4.3.1 'Secondary' or 'indirect' infringement liability

Certain types of conduct are treated as infringements of copyright only upon the establishment of some 'guilty knowledge' on the part of the 'secondary' infringer:[193] the common feature of such infringements is the requirement of proving actual or 'constructive' knowledge that the conduct relates to infringing works. In the UK, such infringements have been described in the statute as 'secondary' infringements, but the label is apt to mislead, since that term is more generally often used to describe accessory liability.[194] The Australian description (in the commentary but not in the copyright legislation itself) of 'indirect' infringement is

[190] See French J in *Collins* v. *Northern Territory* (2007) 161 FCR 549 [42], [62], noted above n. 135.

[191] *Cf.* Wheelahan, 'Contributory infringement', 61–63, who asserts, somewhat cryptically, that knowledge is relevant but does not clearly spell out in what way it is relevant.

[192] An innocent infringer, however, would only be subject to more limited relief by way of injunction and not for damages or accounts of profit: s. 123 Patents Act 1990 (Cth).

[193] *Copinger* [8-01], 525.

[194] This conclusion adds further weight to our rejection, in [1.5], of the label 'secondary' liability as a descriptor of accessory liability, since it is used to describe liability that is not accessorial.

preferable, since the liability created under these provisions is in most cases not accessorial.

A number of provisions in both the UK and Australia create indirect liability for the importation of or dealing with (selling etc.) copyrighted work.[195] The sections create liability that is not accessorial for at least two reasons. First, although the label 'secondary' is used in the UK, because the acts 'generally depend upon a primary act of infringement having first taken place',[196] this is not always the case. In some circumstances, no primary infringement has taken place at all, nor need it even be likely to occur.[197] An example is where 'secondary' infringement relates to copies of works made overseas by someone who is not infringing copyright (having a licence or ownership of the copyright in that territory) and where the defendant imports such item into the relevant jurisdiction in which C holds the copyright or licence.[198] The importation is in fact the only act of infringement and the remedies are a means of protecting the copyright owner's rights in the jurisdiction into which the defendant is importing.

195 In the UK, a person who imports (other than for private use) (s. 22 CDPA), or possesses or deals with (by way of sale, hire, etc.) (s. 23), 'an article which is, and which he knows or has reason to believe is, an infringing copy of the work', has committed a 'secondary' infringement. In Australia, see ss. 37, 38, 102 and 103 Copyright Act 1968. These provisions are subject to numerous complex exceptions and defences that limit the reach of those provisions in relation to certain types of copyrighted materials. See ss. 44A, 44C, 44D, 44E, 44F, 112A, 112C, 112D, 112DA Copyright Act 1968 (Cth).

196 *Copinger* [8-01], 525; although it appears that 'first' is being used chronologically, such use of the terms 'primary' and 'secondary' is unusual. 'Secondary' as it is ordinarily used, as a label for accessory liability, refers to its derivative status, not to the order in which infringements occur. 'Secondary' (accessorial) infringements generally occur at or before the time of 'primary' infringement.

197 See also s. 24(1) of the CDPA which imposes liability on various persons who knowingly provide or possess in the course of business articles specifically designed for making infringing copies, with the requisite knowledge. See also subsection (2) (transmission of work by means of a telecommunications system). The liability created by s. 24(1) has considerable affinity to accessory liability, since it is obviously intended to curb acts that will almost invariably lead to primary infringement and, where infringements do occur, the defendant's conduct will have contributed to, and therefore amounts to some act of involvement in, those primary infringements. However, it is *not necessary* that primary infringement has taken place. Section 24 is likely to have only limited operation, since it requires an article to be specifically designed for the making of copies of *particular* works. It is therefore unlikely to overcome the decision of the House of Lords in *CBS Songs* [1988] 1 AC 1013, [9.2.6.2]. See *Laddie*, [20.28], 825. Nor does the section apply if the equipment is exported overseas: *Kabushiki Kaisha Sony Computer Entertainment Inc* v. *Ball* [2004] EWHC 1738 (Ch); [2005] FSR 9 [19]–[22].

198 See the variety of possible circumstances in *Copinger* [8-05], 527.

Secondly, even where primary infringements have taken place, in many cases the 'secondary' acts occur after that initial infringement and, therefore, such acts are not a wrongful involvement in the commission of the primary wrong; that is, 'secondary' is not a reference to accessory (or derivative) liability.[199] The effect of the provisions is therefore to protect more extensively the right holders against further harm to their interests caused by the 'secondary' acts.

Critical to the operation of these liability rules is the meaning of 'constructive' knowledge, which is also relevant to other specific statutory infringements and is a central concept to some circumstances of accessory liability more generally; consequently, the relevant cases are considered in [9.4.3.2].

9.4.3.2 'Constructive' knowledge: objective knowledge

Indirect infringement requires some knowledge on the part of the infringer before liability arises. Something less than actual knowledge suffices for this purpose. Although the requisite knowledge is often described in general terms, somewhat misleadingly, as 'constructive' knowledge, in fact the legislation uses a variety of terms. The required level of knowledge is variously described as 'obvious to a reasonable person';[200] that the person 'ought reasonably to have known';[201] having 'reason to believe';[202] or 'no reasonable grounds for suspecting',[203] or negatively, that the person 'believed on reasonable grounds that' the conduct would *not* infringe.[204] It is not clear whether the slight differences in terminology are intended to create slight distinctions in meaning.

We prefer the more neutral and accurate label of objective knowledge to constructive knowledge, and take that concept to mean a state of mind attributed to A that is determined according to an objective standard – that of the reasonable person – from the facts that A actually (subjectively) knew; that is, it captures the 'morally obtuse'. 'Constructive' knowledge ought not to be interpreted as determined purely by a negligence standard of what persons may have discovered had they made

199 Indeed the defendant may have no relationship or direct dealing with the primary infringer at all and may only be opportunistically using the infringing materials for his or her own purposes.

200 See s. 60 Patents Act 1977 (UK).

201 See ss. 37, 38, 102, 103 Copyright Act 1968 (Cth).

202 See ss. 22, 23, 24, 26 CDPA; s. 10(5) Trade Marks Act 1994 (UK); s. 117 Patents Act 1990 (Cth).

203 See s. 39 Copyright Act 1968 (Cth).

204 See s. 25 CDPA.

reasonable inquiries [3.4.3.5]. That would set the bar for liability at too low a level of culpability, absent any standardised practice or procedure for making the inquiries that are appropriate in the particular context.[205]

The authorities for the most part accord with a test of objective knowledge in the sense of obvious to a reasonable person and with a rejection of 'negligence'-based liability, but not entirely so and they are in a confused state. It has been said that mere suspicion does not suffice: facts from which a reasonable person 'might suspect the relevant conclusion cannot be enough' to amount to constructive knowledge and therefore to give rise to knowledge-based liability.[206] Therefore, a party who merely fails to make inquiries, because of some suspicions, does not meet the requirement.[207] This suggests that something must be obvious to a reasonable person from that person's actual knowledge of facts. Conversely, someone who wilfully shuts his or her eyes to the obvious will clearly be liable, since in any case this is one means of establishing actual knowledge [3.4.3.3].[208]

'Objective' knowledge is therefore only subtly different to a concept of reckless indifference to infringement. As we have defined the former concept, it extends to objectively determinable risks based on a person's subjective factual knowledge. The only difference is that recklessness suggests an easily avoidable high risk; that is, a *reckless disregard* of the *substantial likelihood* of infringement,[209] whereas objective knowledge need not necessarily do so.

205 See the discussion of 'true' constructive notice in equity, which is premised on standard conveyancing practices and procedures in relation to old system land [8.3.4.3].

206 See *LA Gear Inc* v. *Hi-Tec Sports Plc* [1992] FSR 121, 129 (Morritt J), upheld by the Court of Appeal in the same report; cited with approval in, e.g., *Linpac Mouldings Ltd* v. *Eagleton Direct Export Ltd* [1994] FSR 545, 549 (EWCA).

207 Note, however, in *Raben Footwear Pty Ltd* v. *Polygram Records Inc* (1997) 37 IPR 417, a case concerning s. 103 Copyright Act 1968 (Cth), Tamberlin J equates 'constructive knowledge' with the neglect of a careful person to inquire, but this is clearly contrary to the usual meaning of the term and contrary to Burchett J's approach in that case, Lehane J agreeing, at 433 onwards (constructive knowledge requires abstention from pursuing plain indication). In *Pioneer Electronics Australia Pty Ltd* v. *Lee* [2000] FCA 1926; (2001) 108 FCR 216 [36], Sundberg J, however, accepted Tamberlin J's definition, and stated that constructive knowledge 'focuses on the reasonableness of the conduct of the alleged infringer, and is concerned with whether, acting reasonably, the infringer ought to have made further inquiries that would have led to it acquiring the relevant knowledge'.

208 See, e.g., *Laddie*, [20.4] 810; *Copinger*, [8-09] 530; *ZYX Music GmbH* v. *King* (1997) 38 IPR 139, 153 and 154; contrast *Husqvarna Forest & Garden Ltd* v. *Bridon New Zealand Ltd* (1997) 38 IPR 513, 523.

209 In the US, Rantanen, 'An Objective View', has argued in the context of the knowledge requirements for contributory infringements across different IP rights that an objective

One further complicating factor is whether the objective assessment of knowledge includes within it some subjective characteristics of the person in question (other than the person's knowledge). In the UK, for the purposes of ss. 22 and 23 CDPA, the relevant test of whether a person had 'reason to believe' that products being imported were infringing copies of C's drawing has been held to be entirely objective in *LA Gear Inc* v. *Hi-Tec Sports Plc*.[210] However, the Full Court of the Federal Court of Australia, in *Raben Footwear Pty Ltd* v. *Polygram Records Inc*,[211] considered that some subjective element may be relevant. Burchett J stated that the term 'ought reasonably to have known' *nevertheless* allows 'regard to be had of the knowledge, capacity and circumstances of the particular defendant. An objective assessment is to be made as to whether he, rather than some other person, "ought reasonably to have known".'[212] The inconsistency may be more apparent than real. Even under the UK test the position and status of the defendant is clearly relevant to determining knowledge: that is, the reasonable person must be one in the position of the defendant (and therefore, presumably, having such objective knowledge and experience etc. – for example, a 'reasonable music distributor'[213] – as well as any specific information that the defendant had).[214]

At times, an issue that arises is how a defendant must respond to *allegations* of infringement [3.4.2.5]. It is important to note that in determining a defendant's objective knowledge, he or she must be given the opportunity and sufficient time, if need be,[215] to evaluate and seek further information about C's assertions of copyright and of the

test of recklessness applies, irrespective of variations in how the requisite mental state is formulated. As Rantanen states, 'the fault element of indirect infringement should be articulated as an objective, risk-based inquiry, asking whether a high risk that the relevant conduct infringed a patent would have been obvious to a person in the' defendant's place (1581). Rantanen argues that the decisions apply such an objective test in practice, even where stated in terms of intention or knowledge of infringement.

210 [1992] FSR 121. In other words, the question of the defendant's state of knowledge is one for the court, namely whether reasonable persons would have formed a belief from the information available to them.

211 (1997) 37 IPR 417 (*Raben*). The case concerned ss. 102 and 103 Copyright Act 1968 (Cth), the language of which 'quite closely parallels' that of ss. 22 and 23 CDPA.

212 *Ibid.* 420 (Lehane J agreeing).

213 *ZYX Music GmbH* v. *King* (1997) 38 IPR 139. Indeed, *Copinger*, [8-10], 531, does not draw a distinction and cites statements in *Raben* as consistent with the principles in UK law and with *ZYX*.

214 Admittedly, the reference to 'capacity' in *Raben* (1997) 37 IPR 417 is more problematic. See also *Laddie*, [20.7]–[20.8] 810–811, supporting a more subjective approach.

215 E.g., *Nouveau Fabrics Ltd* v. *Voyage Decoration Ltd* [2004] EWHC 895 (Ch); [2004] All ER (D) 288 [47], [53].

defendant's infringement of such rights. A party does not have to accept at face value mere allegations. In *Van Dusen* v. *Kritz*,[216] in the context of a claim concerning an exhibition of copyrighted material that to the exhibitor's 'knowledge' infringed copyright, it was held that liability would only arise if the exhibitor had deliberately continued to exhibit *after* a reasonable opportunity to investigate the claim. Nonetheless, it has also been said that suspicion can become an objective 'reason to believe' if no sensible inquiries are carried out and the defendant does nothing in response to assertions of copyright.[217]

Objective knowledge would generally require defendants to have reason to know that the goods that they are dealing with are, indeed, *infringing* goods.[218] This would require knowledge of facts suggesting the absence of, for example, a licence to copy materials, or that copyright still subsists.[219] However, ignorance of, or mistakes as to, the law of copyright are no excuse.[220]

9.5 Remedies

9.5.1 Injunctions

The types of circumstances that would warrant an injunction against a primary infringer may also warrant an injunction against an accessory; for example, to prevent an accessory's continued authorisation of primary infringements; to prevent accessories repeated authorisation etc. of infringements;[221] or even to prevent prospective authorisation of infringements via *quia timet* injunctions.[222] Injunctions could be based on

[216] [1936] 2 KB 176, 182.

[217] *Nouveau Fabrics Ltd* v. *Voyage Decoration Ltd* [2004] EWHC 895 (Ch); [2004] All ER (D) 288 [53]. *Laddie*, [20.8] 811, rightly states that this cannot be correct if it imposes a duty to make inquiries: there would need to be sufficient information available to the defendant that would lead a reasonable person's suspicions to harden into belief, after sufficient time for evaluation.

[218] *Cf. Copinger*, [8-10] 531; *Laddie*, [20.12] 815.

[219] This means that where a person lacks knowledge, it may be necessary for the claimant to give notice of the facts to the defendant to alert him or her to the claimant's claim of copyright, such that further dealings will therefore infringe, as in *LA Gear Inc* v. *Hi-Tec Sports Plc* [1992] FSR 121.

[220] *Husqvarna Forest & Garden Ltd* v. *Bridon New Zealand Ltd* (1997) 38 IPR 513, 524.

[221] See, e.g., the injunction granted in *Newzbin* [2010] EWHC 608; [2010] ECC 13.

[222] The potential availability of such relief was accepted in *Roadshow* [2012] HCA 16; (2012) 248 CLR 42 [94]. For an unsuccessful attempt to obtain a *quia timet* injunction, for an alleged authorisation of a prospective patent infringement, see *Apotex Pty Ltd* v. *Les Laboratoires Servier (No 2)* [2012] FCA 748 [41]–[66].

specific powers in legislation, such as s. 97A CDPA[223] or on general court powers to grant injunctions. It may be more practical to claim injunctive relief against authorisers rather than against primary infringers where they are said through their activities to have allowed, usually on the internet, multiple and repeated infringements by multiple, perhaps unknown, PWs.[224] The forms of orders for injunctions and declaratory relief can be detailed and wide-ranging, in order to capture the difficulties of restraining the wide-ranging conduct that may be at issue.[225] Alternatively, injunctions might be in simple terms, for example, merely restraining the defendant from infringing a particular patent.[226] Anton Piller orders may be granted for purposes of seizing, for example, records, data and statistics of internet usage.[227]

There have been some successful claims for injunctions on the basis of authorisation of infringement by ISPs, including injunctions granted against various parties responsible for developing, marketing and supplying an internet file-sharing system, Kazaa, used to infringe copyright.[228] In *Twentieth Century Fox Film Corporation* v. *Newzbin Ltd*,[229] the English High Court granted an injunction in wide terms, to prevent copying of any materials contained in C's repertoire.[230] Mareva or freezing injunctions were also granted against parties associated with Newzbin Ltd.[231]

Newzbin illustrates, however, the inherent difficulties in attempts to curb unlawful internet activities. Although the site was shut down, the same URL address was reactivated shortly thereafter by an unknown offshore provider against whom no feasible action could be brought.[232]

223 This does not create liability for past primary infringements for ISPs but nonetheless allows for injunctions against providers whose services are used to infringe copyright. In Australia, see s. 115(2) Copyright Act 1968 (Cth).

224 *Newzbin* [2010] EWHC 608; [2010] ECC 13.

225 See, e.g., *Cooper* [2006] FCAFC 187; (2006) 156 FCR 380 [23]–[24].

226 See, e.g., *Grimme* [2010] EWCA 1110 [134].

227 See, e.g., *Cooper* [2006] FCAFC 187; (2006) 156 FCR 380[100].

228 See *Universal Music Australia Pty Ltd* v. *Sharman License Holdings Ltd* [2005] FCA 1242; (2005) 65 IPR 289. Mareva orders had also been granted at the end of the trial.

229 [2010] EWHC 608; [2010] ECC 13.

230 The court refused an injunction in the wider terms sought by the claimants (*ibid.* [135]), however, to extend to all infringements of any copyright material held by all copyright holders.

231 Were they accessories to the accessory, perhaps? See *Twentieth Century Fox Film Corporation* v. *Harris* [2013] EWHC 159 (Ch) [6].

232 *Twentieth Century Fox Film Corporation* v. *British Telecommunications Plc* [2011] EWHC 1981 (Ch).

Claims were therefore brought against one major ISP, British Telecommunications Plc, seeking injunctive relief against it under s. 97A CDPA (and not on principles of authorisation) to block access by its users to the offending website.[233]

9.5.2 *Damages*

Damages are available for authorisation and other accessory liability. Such damages are assessed by reference to the loss caused by the primary infringements. In many circumstances, particularly in the modern context of mass primary infringements that are the result of a defendant's accessory or indirect conduct, it may be difficult to assess how much primary infringement has occurred and therefore what loss flowed from the defendant's conduct. In the context of 'contributory' infringement of patents, it has been suggested that one method of assessment, albeit difficult to quantify, may be to determine what proportion of sales of a defendant are attributable to users who have adapted or intend to adapt the device to infringe. Alternatively, the court might determine how much the defendant augmented his or her sales by virtue of the contributory infringement.[234] For some types of 'indirect' infringement, damages are not available in all circumstances under the legislative regimes.

[233] The relief granted required that technology be used to block or impede access, with the prospect of similar claims being brought against other ISPs. *Ibid.* [1].

[234] See, e.g., *Grimme* [2010] EWCA 1110 [137].

10

Other statutory wrongs

10.1 Introduction

Some statutory schemes create obligations, contraventions of which are civilly enforceable under the statute; for example, in the contexts of consumer protection and the regulation of wrongdoing by corporate officers. There are at least two broad ways in which parties suffering harm as a result of statutory infringements may obtain relief: either via claims initiated by regulators, but allowing for orders to be made for the benefit of individuals, as is more commonly the case in the UK; or else directly, by means of statutory causes of action commenced by private claimants. The direct approach is prominent in Australia, where statutory causes of action are used to create sources of private law obligations. Such obligations have had a major impact on the legal landscape, especially the statutory prohibition against misleading or deceptive conduct.

As part of statutory liability schemes, civil liability may expressly[1] be imposed on accessories to the contraventions of the statutory obligations. This chapter considers accessory liability regimes that provide remedies, such as compensation orders, that are available to benefit individuals.[2] It does not focus on accessory liability for civil penalties[3] or for crimes.

[1] In the US, courts have held that privately enforceable statutory rights of action for infringements may also impliedly extend private rights to actions against accessories, depending on the wording and policy of the statute. In the securities fraud area, such developments were rejected by the Supreme Court in *Central Bank of Denver* v. *First Interstate Bank of Denver, NA* 511 US 164 (1994), but courts continue to imply private rights of action against accessories in the context of other statutes. See, e.g., *Boim* v. *Quranic Literary Institute* 291 F3d 1000 (CA 7th Cir 2002) in the context of terrorism statutes; and the discussion in Charles W. Adams, 'Indirect Infringement from a Torts Law Perspective' 42 *University of Richmond Law Review* 635 (2008).

[2] This chapter does not consider statutory accessory liability schemes that are tailored to the protection of IP rights discussed in Chapter 9.

[3] Civil penalties encompass monetary and other sanctions imposed for contraventions of regulatory schemes, on civil standards of proof. Civil penalty cases are relevant, however, where the tests for accessory liability are the same under the legislation being considered.

In Australia, the legislative schemes adopted to extend liability to accessories are largely uniform. The legislative schemes generally proceed by creating liability for those 'involved in a contravention' and then enumerate four circumstances that amount to involvement. The uniformity in approach is somewhat surprising, since the primary obligations to which the accessory liabilities attach vary considerably. The primary obligations range from strict liability for engaging in misleading conduct to the liability of officers of corporations for conduct that may also constitute breaches of proscriptive fiduciary duties[4] (leading to potential overlap with equity's accessory liability regime).

In the UK there is much less statutory activity in the private law field than in Australia. There are relatively few statutes that create sources of private obligations and none of these are as wide-ranging in their scope as Australia's misleading conduct prohibition. Obviously, this means that there are even fewer examples of statutory accessory liability regimes supporting civil claims. In the limited circumstances in which UK statutes impose obligations on primary wrongdoers and, correspondingly, extend liability to accessories, the UK legislation uses the broad concept of persons 'knowingly concerned' in a contravention or other shorthand formulations. Importantly, unlike the position in Australia, 'knowingly concerned' has been left undefined and there is a dearth of judicial authority on its meaning.

This chapter outlines, with some examples from Australia and the UK, general legislative approaches that are adopted to frame the civil liability of accessories pursuant to statutory liability regimes. We draw a number of conclusions that are of relevance and importance to understanding accessory liability more generally:

1. Statutory accessory liability regimes adopt an analytical structure that is consistent with the approach in this book [Chapter 3]. Once a primary wrong has been established, the rules focus on the twin requirements of a conduct element, namely some acts of involvement in the primary wrong, coupled with a requisite mental element, namely knowledge [10.3], [10.4.4].

This chapter does not deal with legislative regimes creating obligations to which no accessory liability attaches, such as product safety liability (e.g., the Consumer Protection Act 1987 (UK) expressly creates an action for breach of statutory duties relating to unsafe products: s. 41(1)).

4 See ss. 181(1)(a) and (b), 182(1)(a) and (b) and 183(1)(a) and (b) of the Corporations Act 2001 (Cth).

2. The Australian statutory schemes illustrate that a very broad approach to the types of involvement that satisfy the conduct element does not lead to broad accessory liability. Instead, a rigorously and narrowly interpreted knowledge requirement limits accessory liability [10.4.4].
3. The statutory approaches highlight that the focus of much of the inquiry is on the narrow factual question of whether A had actual knowledge of the essential matters of the statutory contravention [10.4.4].

10.2 Legislative frameworks

10.2.1 United Kingdom

In the UK there is little statutory intervention in private law in the form of obligations that create rights, and corresponding remedies, for individual claimants who are aggrieved as a result of a contravention of a *statutory* obligation.[5] For the most part, financial services, corporate law and consumer protection statutes create criminal offences or civil penalties enforced by regulators. The legislative schemes rely on a continuation of common law actions to allow private parties who have suffered loss to enforce their rights. For example, s. 178 Companies Act 2006 (UK) provides for the continued enforcement via common law and equitable remedies against directors of the statutory duties under the Act (ss. 171–177); indeed, the duties are stated to be enforceable as fiduciary duties.[6] The effect is to preserve the general law and there is no remedial scheme in the Act itself.[7] Similarly, in the context of consumer protection, J. K. Macleod has concluded that, for the most part, civil proceedings will continue to be in contract or tort.[8] There are

[5] For an interesting exception see s. 16 Directors Disqualification Act 1986 (UK).

[6] See s. 178(2); the exception is s. 174 (duty to exercise reasonable care, skill and diligence), which is not so enforceable (and see also below text to nn. 24–27, on the Australian position). See also Chapter 8, n. 94.

[7] Further, accessory liability applies generally only for criminal offences under the Companies Act 2006, e.g. s. 549 ('knowingly contravenes'); s. 993(1). One exception, however, is s. 579(3): a director who 'permits or authorises' a contravention of s. 578, prohibiting the allotment of shares in certain circumstances, is personally liable for losses incurred by the allottee as a result.

[8] See J. K. Macleod, *Consumer Sales Law*, 2nd edn (London, Routledge-Cavendish, 2007) [3.21]–[3.22]. This is borne out by the Enterprise Act 2002, which regulates conduct in the supply of goods and services to consumers. The underlying approach is to give powers to regulators under the Act to stop ongoing infringing conduct; the purpose of the Act is not

therefore even fewer legislative examples extending civil obligations to accessories.[9]

One exception in which a statute potentially creates means to remedy losses of private individuals is the Financial Services and Markets Act 2000 (FSMA), regulating the provision of financial advice. For example, ss. 380, 382 and 384 give powers to regulators (s. 384) and courts (ss. 380 and 382) to make remedial orders and restitution orders for *any* contraventions of any of the requirements under the FSMA.[10] Importantly, these sections also allow for orders to be made against parties who are 'knowingly concerned in the contraventions'. However, enforcement is only by the regulator, not by private action and therefore proceedings are more in the nature of disciplinary rather than civil action.[11]

Sections 380 and 382 were broadly interpreted in *Financial Services Authority* v. *Martin*,[12] which appears to be one of the few cases in which remedial orders were made against accessories to compensate for losses suffered by consumers. The Court of Appeal allowed claims against an individual solicitor, as well as the firm of which he was a partner, in a case in which the solicitor had been actively involved in the administration of an investment scheme carried on by an unauthorised person.[13] It was

to provide remedies to individual consumers. See Pt 8 Enterprise Act 2002; and Macleod, 230 [6.07]. There are limited exceptions: see s. 211(2).

9 Where a criminal prosecution occurs, there is potential scope for criminal compensation orders to be made under s. 130 Powers of Criminal Courts (Sentencing) Act 2000, thereby indirectly providing a potential remedy for losses incurred by victims of wrongdoing against both primary wrongdoers and accessories. See Macleod, *Consumer Sales Law*, [3.20], 101–102. Macleod, [4.02] 122, fn. 23, states in the context of offences under the Trade Description Act 1968 [now mostly displaced by offences in the Consumer Protection from Unfair Trading Regulations 2008] that the power was 'fairly widely used'.

10 The FSMA distinguishes claims against persons who provide financial services while unauthorised and between breaches of rules by authorised persons. In relation to the latter, s. 150 (1) is available to remedy losses incurred by private persons not acting in the course of business; and see also, e.g., ss. 20(3), 71, 202(2), 241. As Eva Lomnicka, 'The future of consumer credit regulation: a chance to rationalise sanctions for breaches of financial services regulatory regimes?' (2013) 34(1) *Company Lawyer* 13, 16–17, fn. 75, has noted, this breach of statutory duty action 'has proved a very useful addition' to private actions in contract or tort. Section 150 does not apply to claims against accessories.

11 See Lomnicka, *ibid.*

12 [2005] EWCA 1422; [2006] PNLR 11, noted in Joanna Gray, 'Court of Appeal rules on solicitor's liability to make redress to investors' (2006) 14(2) *Journal of Financial Regulation and Compliance* 210–216.

13 The solicitor's actions assisted with implementing the scheme in ways 'which were not peripheral but key elements'. The firm received the investors' money and assisted in the

held that the solicitor was 'knowingly concerned' in the contravention (the meaning of which is discussed below).[14]

The extension of liability under the FSMA to those who are 'knowingly concerned' in a contravention clearly is aimed at spreading the net of obligation beyond conduct of the primary wrongdoers committing the primary contravention, thereby enhancing the protection of victims. Beyond the liability being accessorial, the rationale for the liability is unclear.[15]

10.2.2 *Australia*

One of the most significant sources of private obligations arises in the regulation of business conduct and consumer protection, namely laws that allow claimants to claim for damage suffered as a result of misleading or deceptive conduct in trade or commerce under the uniform Australian Consumer Law (ACL). These were adopted by the Commonwealth in the Competition and Consumer Act 2010 (Cth) (CCA) and by all states and territories[16] (and were previously contained in the Trade Practices Act 1974 (Cth) (TPA)). Section 18 ACL (previously s. 52 TPA) imposes, in seemingly short and simple terms, a norm of conduct. Section 18(1) provides: 'A person must not, in trade or commerce, engage in conduct that is misleading or deceptive or is likely to mislead or deceive.' The title 'Australian Consumer Law' is misleading, however, since the prohibition in s. 18 is not limited to persons acting in trade or commerce *towards consumers* and has therefore been used by business parties in dispute. Breach of s. 18 allows C to pursue remedies under specific sections of the ACL, including claiming

purchase of the shares to be sold to the investors. See at first instance: [2004] EWHC 3255 [33]–[34] (Alton J).

14 Importantly, the court made the orders despite subsection (4) of s. 380, which states that an order cannot be made unless a transaction has been entered by the person 'concerned'. This was interpreted to mean that a transaction was entered with the contravener, not necessarily with the person against whom the orders were being made (in this case, the accessory). See [2005] EWCA 1422; [2006] PNLR 11, particularly [55]–[56].

15 See Eva Lomnicka, '"Knowingly Concerned"? Participatory Liability to Regulators' (2000) 21(4) *Company Lawyer* 120, 121, quoted [2.4.1].

16 E.g., Fair Trading Act 1987 (NSW) Part 3, Division 2, inserted by the Fair Trading Amendment (Australian Consumer Law) Act 2010 (NSW). New Zealand has also adopted the key elements of the Australia's approach to accessories in consumer protection law, including for misleading conduct. See Fair Trading Act 1986 (NZ) s. 9 (misleading conduct) and s. 43 (remedies available against persons aiding, abetting etc. contraventions).

damages as of right under s. 236 ACL (also s. 82 CCA) for loss suffered 'because' of the conduct of another in contravention of s. 18.

The impact of the misleading conduct provisions (and to a much lesser extent, other obligations in the consumer protection and business context) as sources of obligation is nothing short of revolutionary in Australian law.[17] Conduct is misleading if it leads others astray or into error.[18] The obligation that is imposed is strict – C need not show that the defendant knew that its conduct was misleading, or even that it had been careless in engaging in the misleading conduct[19] – and therefore the section has largely displaced more difficult to prove claims.[20] It has 'become a staple of civil litigation in Australian courts at all levels. Its frequent invocation, in cases to which it is applicable, reflects its simplicity relative to the torts of negligence, deceit and passing off'.[21]

Importantly for our purposes, in support of the claim against parties contravening the legislative prohibitions, the ACL and CCA remedial sections also impose civil liability on accessories, that is, parties involved in the contravention of various provisions of the ACL and CCA.[22] The phrase 'involved in' is defined in s. 2 of the ACL:[23]

[17] Consumer protection and standards in business conduct are reinforced by prohibitions against more specifically defined types of misleading conduct (Ch. 3 ACL) and prohibitions against, e.g., unconscionable conduct (ss. 20–22). The Australian Securities and Investments Commission Act 2001 (Cth) ('ASIC Act') concerning financial services contains equivalent provisions to those in the ACL.

[18] See, e.g., *Johnson Tiles Pty Ltd* v. *Esso Australia Ltd* [2000] FCA 1572; (2000) 104 FCR 564.

[19] *Hornsby Building Information Centre Pty Ltd* v. *Sydney Building Information Centre Ltd* (1978) 140 CLR 216 (HCA) 228; *Parkdale Custom Built Furniture Pty Ltd* v. *Puxu Pty Ltd* (1982) 149 CLR 191 (HCA) 197. Note, although 'deceptive' requires a dishonest state of mind, the disjunctive 'or' means that parties need not prove such element, making the second half of the phrase largely redundant.

[20] In Australia, therefore, cases pleaded solely as a negligent misrepresentation claim are exceptional, arising, e.g., because the representor was not engaged in conduct in trade or commerce: see, e.g., *Tepko Pty Ltd* v. *Water Board* [2001] HCA 19; (2001) 206 CLR 1; *Falls Investment* v. *New South Wales* [2007] NSWCA 18.

[21] *Miller & Associates Insurance Broking Pty Ltd* v. *BMW Australia Finance Ltd* [2010] HCA 31; (2010) 270 ALR 204 [5] (French CJ and Kiefel J).

[22] Accessory liability is imposed by s. 236 ACL (and s. 82 CCA) and ss. 237, 238 (compensation and associated orders) (and s. 87 CCA) including relevantly for contraventions of Ch. 2 and 3 of the ACL; most importantly, including s. 18. Injunctions are also available against parties 'involved in' conduct 'that constitutes or would constitute' a contravention or attempted contravention (s. 232). The definition contained in s. 2 has been incorporated into s. 232 itself.

[23] It is also defined in various other sections of the CCA.

> A person is involved, in a contravention of a provision of [the ACL] or in conduct that constitutes such a contravention, if the person:
>
> (a) has aided, abetted, counselled or procured the contravention;
> (b) has induced, whether by threats or promises or otherwise, the contravention;
> (c) has been in any way, directly or indirectly, knowingly concerned in, or party to, the contravention; or
> (d) has conspired with others to effect the contravention.

The meaning of these provisions has been the subject of much litigation (under the corresponding TPA provisions) and yet uncertainties as to their meaning remain.

Other sources of accessory liability are found in corporate governance provisions. The significant civil duties of directors and other corporate officers are contained in ss. 180–183 of the Corporations Act 2001 (Cth) for which a range of statutory remedies are available.[24] Persons are said to have contravened ss. 181(1) if they were 'involved in' a failure of officers to act in 'good faith in the best interests of the corporation' (subsection (2)(a)) and 'for a proper purpose' (para. (b)). The same applies to ss. 182 and 183 (improper use of position, or of information, respectively, for self-gain or to harm the corporation).

Accessory liability provisions apply only to breach of some of the duties.[25] Significantly, accessory liability does not apply to contravention of s. 180(1), which imposes the duty of care and diligence. This is consistent with the general principle that accessory principles generally do not apply to negligence-based primary wrongs.[26] As an important aside, this also supports the conclusion that equity's accessory rules generally ought not to be applied to breach of equitable duties to take care.[27]

[24] The Act preserves the rights of private litigants (s. 179) to commence proceedings under general law, governed by the relevant general law principles, for the same conduct that constitutes a contravention of the regulatory laws. For a detailed discussion of the liability of accessories to civil penalties and other orders and remedies for corporations law infringements, see Tom Middleton, *ASIC Corporate Investigations and Hearings* (Australia, Thomson Reuters, 2012) [8.1940]–[8.2115].

[25] It may be easier for the Australian Securities and Investments Commission (ASIC) to argue that a person is liable as a PW, rather than as an A, on the basis that they are 'deemed' directors. See Middleton, *ASIC*, [2.180]. By contrast, for persons who are not deemed directors, liability must be by the more circuitous routes of accessory liability (*ASC* v. *AS Nominees Ltd* (1995) 62 FCR 504; 133 ALR 1, 53).

[26] See also Chapter 8 n. 94. But note, however, the few exceptional cases in torts, critiqued at [5.5.5].

[27] See W. M. C. Gummow, 'The equitable duties of company directors' (2013) 87 ALJ 753, 758. See *Contra*. J. D. Heydon, 'Are the Duties of Company Directors to Exercise Care and

10.3 The meaning of 'knowingly concerned' in the UK

UK legislation uses the broad concept of 'knowingly concerned' without further definition, suggesting that the legislature is intending the law to be open-ended to allow the courts to develop the concept on a case-by-case basis. There are, however, very few cases on the meaning of this phrase in the civil context. Although the phrase is also often used in the criminal context, here too there appears to be little judicial exposition of its meaning, presumably because 'knowingly concerned' is usually left as a jury question.[28]

What is clear is that 'knowingly concerned' consists of two conceptual elements, namely some conduct (act of involvement or 'concern' in the relevant contravention) and a requisite mental state (knowledge).[29] As Alton J stated in the High Court in *Financial Services Authority* v. *Martin* (*Martin*),[30] one of the few cases to consider the meaning of 'knowingly concerned': 'Knowledge is insufficient without that involvement and vice versa.' Similarly, in *SIB* v. *Pantell SA (No 2)*, it was stated that '[m]ere passive knowledge will not be sufficient: actual involvement in the contravention must be established'.[31]

In *Martin*, Alton J went on to state: 'So far as the question of the matter of concern is concerned, there is no guidance as to the level of the necessary involvement within the statute or in the cases.'[32] Similarly, there has been little judicial discussion of the knowledge requirement. Actual knowledge is required,[33] though one would expect that something in the nature of wilful blindness could justify inferring actual

Skill Fiduciary' in Simone Degeling and James Edelman, *Equity in Commercial Law* (Australia, Lawbook Co, 2005) 185, particularly 235. The issue is discussed in [8.3.1.1] and [8.3.1.2] and see [8.2] as to whether *procuring* a breach of duties of care ought to give rise to accessory liability.

28 In any case, even if there are useful criminal law decisions, this raises the question of whether the criminal cases are analogously relevant. They clearly are in Australia [10.4.2] but this is more doubtful in the UK (see more generally [4.1]).

29 *Financial Services Authority* v. *Martin* [2004] EWHC 3255 (Ch) [32]–[33]. On the facts of the case, noted above, it was held that the solicitor was sufficiently concerned with the contravention. Similarly, the court was readily able to find knowledge [48], [49].

30 *Ibid*. The concept was discussed at more length in the High Court than in the Court of Appeal, which dismissed an appeal: [2005] EWCA 1422; [2006] PNLR 11.

31 [1993] Ch 256, 283 (Scott LJ). 32 [2004] EWHC 3255 (Ch) [32]–[33].

33 *SIB* v. *Scandex Capital Management A/S* [1998] 1 WLR 712 (*Scandex*) (successful claims against the managing director and shareholder of the first defendant for being knowingly concerned in its unauthorised investment scheme). *Scandex* was applied in *FSA* v. *Asset LI Inc (t/a Asset Land Investment Inc)* [2013] EWHC 178 (Ch).

knowledge.[34] It was further held in *SIB* v. *Scandex Capital Management A/S* that a person must have knowledge of 'ingredients of the contravention' since the accessory must have been 'knowingly concerned in the *contravention*' not just knowingly concerned in the carrying on of the unauthorised business.[35] However, as is generally the case in other areas of law,[36] mistakes as to, or ignorance of, the law are no excuse.[37] As Neville J stated in *Burton* v. *Bevan*

> I think that 'knowingly' means with knowledge of the facts upon which the contravention depends. I think it is immaterial whether [A] had knowledge of the law or not. I think he is bound to know what the law is, and the only question is, did he know the facts which made the act complained of a contravention of the statute?[38]

10.4 The meaning of involved in a contravention in Australia

10.4.1 Liability as primary wrongdoer or accessory?

As a preliminary matter and before we consider the meaning of 'involved' in a contravention in Australian law, it is necessary to consider precisely the circumstances in which a party may be liable as a primary wrongdoer ('principal' in this context), or as an accessory, or both, in the highly litigated context of misleading conduct.[39]

A corporation may be liable for misleading conduct as a PW where conduct by directors, employees or agents of the corporation, acting within the scope of their 'actual or apparent authority' is deemed ('taken') to have been engaged in also by the body corporate.[40] A corporation (or a natural person) may also be liable for misleading conduct even where it has not made direct representations (through its employees, etc.) to the party or parties misled (or potentially misled). It will be liable if it merely used an intermediary as the means of conveying

[34] Similarly, but in a different and criminal context, *R* v. *Chargot Ltd* [2008] UKHL 73 [8], knowingly turning a blind eye suffices for 'consent or connivance'. And see [3.4.3.3].

[35] *Scandex* [1998] 1 WLR 712, 717 (CA, Millett LJ, Otton and Hobhouse LJJ agreeing). This is comparable to the test in Australia looking at the 'essential elements' of, or the essential matters that go to make up, the contravention

[36] See [3.4.2.3].

[37] *Financial Services Authority* v. *Fradley (Trading as Top Bet Placement Services)* [2004] EWHC 3008 (Ch).

[38] [1908] 2 Ch 240, 247.

[39] Section 18 *ACL*. There have, however, also been numerous cases brought under the Corporations Act 2001 (Cth) in recent years. See, e.g., *ASIC* v. *Adler* [2003] NSWCA 131 and Middleton, *ASIC*.

[40] Section 139B *CCA*; see also s. 84.

information or representations.[41] The party who engages in conduct only indirectly towards the parties misled (by supplying information, endorsing misleading conduct and so on) will be liable if, taken as a whole, its conduct is misleading.[42]

Conversely, a party who engages in conduct directly towards others, the content of which conduct is misleading, may merely be passing on information supplied by another. If an intermediary is a mere conduit of information received from another and passes it on merely 'for what it is worth and without any belief in its truth or falsity', it will not be liable as a principal for misleading or deceptive conduct.[43] However, if the misleading information appears to have been adopted by it, or if by its conduct, it appears to be affirming the truth of the information or otherwise misstating its position,[44] then the intermediary will be engaging in mislead-

[41] See, e.g., *Barton* v. *Croner Trading Pty Ltd* (1984) 3 FCR 95, 107 (Bowen CJ, Beaumont and Wilcox JJ) (defendant liable for representations written on goods supplied by it for sale by W, having used W merely as the 'vehicle for the purposes of communication with the public'); and *Downey* v. *Carlson Hotels Asia Pacific Pty Ltd* [2005] QCA 199.

[42] If nothing in the party's conduct associates it with representations made to the public, then although there may be misleading conduct, it will not be by that party: e.g., where an advertising agency creates advertisements for another, but does not place the advertisements or associate its name with them. See *Cassidy* v. *Saatchi & Saatchi Australia Pty Ltd* (2004) ATPR 41-980 (advertisements subject to final approval of the client). *Cf. Medical Benefits Fund of Australia Ltd* v. *Cassidy* (2003) 205 ALR 402, in which only the accessory liability of the advertising company was argued. See generally B. Sweeney, 'Advertising Agencies: Their Role in Consumer Protection' (2004) 12 *Competition and Consumer Law Journal* 1, and S. Ng, 'Accessorial Liability of Advertising Agency For Misleading and Deceptive Conduct' (2004) 12 *Trade Practices Law Journal* 223.

[43] *Butcher* v. *Lachlan Elder Realty Pty Ltd* [2004] HCA 60; (2004) 218 CLR 592, 611 [64] (Gleeson CJ, Hayne and Heydon JJ). For discussion, see P. Gillies, 'Misleading and Deceptive Conduct: Immunising the Intermediary – the Conduit Defence' (2006) 14 *Trade Practices Law Journal* 209, and S. Appleton and B. McCabe, 'In the Wake of Butcher: Decisions Affecting the Liability of Agents and Third Parties in Proceedings for Misleading or Deceptive Conduct' (2006) 14 *Trade Practices Law Journal* 46. See also *Google Inc* v. *ACCC* [2013] HCA 1; (2013) 249 CLR 435, in which it was held that the Google search engine provider was merely passing on for what 'they were worth' various sponsored advertisers' links that were misleading, generated by Google searches. Google had no control over a user's choice of search terms or the advertiser's choice of keywords and the advertiser determined all aspects of the sponsored links. This indicated that the source was the advertiser [66]–[70].

[44] Obviously, this suggests that fine lines may be drawn at times: someone who *merely* passes on information may be a mere conduit and therefore not liable but, alternatively, if in some way endorsing the information, may be liable for the primary wrong. See, e.g., the different conclusions reached by the High Court in *Google Inc* v. *ACCC* [2013] HCA 1; (2013) 249 CLR 435 to that of the Full Court of the Federal Court [2012] FCAFC 49; (2012) 201 FCR 503 overturned on the appeal.

ing conduct.[45] This means that some persons whose conduct may seem largely participatory may be caught, not as accessories, but rather as principals.[46]

Since it is much simpler for C to proceed against a party as a PW, as confirmed in the High Court decision in *Houghton* v. *Arms*,[47] this is one reason why the accessory liability provisions have been of limited use in misleading conduct cases. In *Houghton* v. *Arms*, misleading conduct was engaged in by the employees on behalf of their corporate employer. It was alleged that the employees had themselves breached the primary obligation not to engage in misleading conduct.[48] The High Court allowed the claim, deciding that the requirement that persons engage in misleading conduct in 'trade or commerce' does not require the conduct to be in their *own* business, so long as their conduct is in the course of *another's* trade or commerce.[49] The effect of this decision is that a person[50] making statements on behalf of a corporation can be liable both as a PW – indeed, can be so liable even where the corporation is also potentially liable as a PW[51] – and also as

[45] See *John G Glass Real Estate Pty Ltd* v. *Karawi Constructions Pty Ltd* (1993) ATPR 41–249 (FCAFC) 41,358–41,359, and *Argy* v. *Blunts & Lane Cove Real Estate Pty Ltd* (1990) 26 FCR 112.

[46] In a note on the Federal Court's decision in *ACCC* v. *Google Inc* [2012] FCAFC 49; (2012) 201 FCR 503, finding Google liable, Megan Richardson, 'Why Policy Matters: *Google Inc* v. *Australian Competition and Consumer Commission*' (2012) 34 *Sydney Law Review* 587, 592, saw Google's liability as 'operating in a kind of legal grey area that the provision's [s. 52 *TPA*, now s. 18 *ACL*] broad wording permits; not quite so parasitical as full accessory liability, albeit one step removed from standard scenarios of a party engaged in misleading or deceptive conduct under s. 52'.

[47] [2006] HCA 59; (2006) 225 CLR 553. See J. Dietrich, 'The (almost) redundant civil accessory liability provisions of the *Trade Practices Act*' (2008) 16 *Trade Practices Law Journal* 37.

[48] This would have been under the previous s. 9 of the Fair Trading Act 1999 (Vic). Although initially the claims against the employees were based on accessory liability, on an amended application, that claim was abandoned.

[49] See [2006] HCA 59; (2006) 225 CLR 553 [34], and [40]–[47]. The fact that the corporation is itself only liable because the conduct of the defendant employees was deemed to be that of the corporation, (s. 84(2) of the TPA and now s. 139B CCA) did not preclude such liability. See to similar effect, e.g., *CH Real Estate Pty Ltd* v. *Jainran Pty Ltd* [2010] NSWCA 37 [93], [99]–[100], [103]–[104].

[50] Under the previous TPA regime, natural persons were not caught by the Act because of jurisdictional limits on the TPA (with some limited exceptions under s. 6 TPA, see, e.g., *ACCC* v. *Kaye* [2004] FCA 1363). However, natural persons were caught by some States' Fair Trading Acts. Both corporations and natural persons are now caught by the ACL.

[51] It is interesting that the 'trade or commerce' of a corporation will be 'imputed' onto persons acting on its behalf, whereas the business of an agent, hired by a principal to facilitate a private transaction, will not be imputed onto the principal. See S. Corones and

an accessory, albeit the latter course is a more onerous means of getting at a defendant.[52] Indeed, given the wide approach to primary liability and the restrictive interpretation of the knowledge required for accessory liability (below), the accessory provisions of the ACL have much less potential sphere of operation and may be largely redundant.[53]

10.4.2 Intentional wrongdoing

Perhaps surprisingly, little commentary[54] has been published on the TPA and the ACL accessory provisions. One thing that is clear from the litigation and commentary, however, is that it is difficult to prove accessory liability. This may seem surprising: since much of the litigation concerns misleading conduct, liability for which is far-reaching and strict, one might expect potentially wide accessory liability. However,

S. Christensen, 'Vicarious and Ancillary Liability for Misleading Conduct under the Trade Practices Act' (1996) 4 *Current Commercial Law* 99, 105–106.

[52] They can be liable as accessories because the question of 'whether a natural person can be an accessory to a corporate principal whose liability arises from the act of that person' (*Wright* v. *Wheeler Grace & Pierucci Pty Ltd* (1988) ATPR ¶40-865, 49,376 (French J)) has been answered clearly in the affirmative: *Hamilton* v. *Whitehead* (1988) 166 CLR 121; *Wheeler Grace & Pierucci Pty Ltd* v. *Wright* [1989] FCA 127; (1989) ATPR ¶40-940 (FCAFC). The primary contraveners need not be sued in order for the accessories to be liable: see, e.g., *ACCC* v. *Kaye* [2004] FCA 1363; *World Class Alpacas Pty Ltd* v. *Ostrich Farms (Cook Islands) Ltd* [1997] 1193 FCA. Conversely, in the corporate law context, where a director is the primary contravener of a provision of the Corporations Act 2001 (Cth) and the director is the 'guiding mind' of the company, that company may be liable as an accessory to that director's contravention. See *Re Krypton Nominees Pty Ltd* [2013] VSC 446 [13], [290], in the context of misleading and deceptive conduct under s. 1041H of the Act.

[53] In some previous decisions, natural persons unsuccessfully sought to be made liable as accessories could have been pursued as primary contravenors under some state Fair Trading Acts. See, e.g., *Crocodile Marketing* v. *Griffith Vintners* (1992) 28 NSWLR 539, and *Hatt* v. *Magro* [2007] WASCA 124, in which pursuit of a claim for accessory liability and not for direct liability may have been fatal to C's chances of success.

[54] One notable exception is the excellent article by Michael Pearce, 'Accessorial Liability for Misleading or Deceptive Conduct' (2006) 80 *Australian Law Journal* 104. See also Corones and Christensen, 'Vicarious and Ancillary Liability', 106–108; Dietrich, 'Civil accessory liability'; M. Brent, 'Must An Accessory Be A Know-It-All?' (2010) 18 *Trade Practices Law Journal* 234. Textbooks tend only briefly to discuss the case law. See, e.g., J. W. Carter, *Contract Law in Australia*, 6th edn (Australia, LexisNexis Butterworths, 2013) [19–15]; N. Seddon, R. Bigwood and M. Ellinghaus, *Cheshire & Fifoot Law of Contract*, 10th Aust. edn (Sydney, Butterworths, 2012) [11.110]. But see the quite extensive discussion in Ray Steinwall, *Annotated Competition and Consumer Legislation*, 2013 edn (Australia, LexisNexis) 565–570, [11, 585], and C. Lockhart, *The Law of Misleading or Deceptive Conduct*, 3rd edn (Australia, LexisNexis, 2011) 253–259.

given that the derivation of the scheme of accessory liability adopted in the legislation is 'found in the criminal law',[55] the interpretation adopted by the High Court[56] is that an accessory must have actual knowledge of the misleading or deceptive nature of the principal's conduct. The obvious tension created by this approach is that the accessory liability is based on wrongdoing, that is, requires 'intent based upon knowledge, notwithstanding that the statutory provision creating the principal' contravention imposes strict liability.[57]

Australian law sets out alternative ways in which one may participate in a breach of the ACL, that is, be involved in a contravention. Although the legislation delineates the type of conduct that amounts to sufficient accessorial participation – the acts of involvement – it does so without expressly indicating the requisite mental state for each, apart from the phrase 'knowingly concerned' (para. (c)). Nonetheless, the High Court in *Yorke* v. *Lucas*[58] in relation to the four differently worded paragraphs has held that they all import an element of knowledge. In relation to para. (a) (aid, abet, etc.), the court noted that the words are derived from the criminal law and require intentional participation. The court considered that notwithstanding the liability operated as an 'adjunct' to civil liability:

> To form the requisite intent [the accessory] must have knowledge of the essential matters which go to make up the offence whether or not he knows that those matters amount to a crime.[59]

Consequently, the court held in relation to paragraphs (b), (c) and (d) that all three imported 'intent based upon knowledge', the relevant knowledge being 'knowledge of the essential elements of the contravention'.[60]

Given that the High Court has described the liability as being based on intent, it has therefore been said in some cases that intention is an essential element of all the forms of accessorial conduct.[61] But as the

55 See *Yorke* v. *Lucas* (1985) 158 CLR 661 (HCA) 669 (Mason CJ, Wilson, Deane and Dawson JJ) (*Yorke*); and, e.g., *Caple* v. *All Fasteners (WA) (a firm)* [2005] FCA 1558 [19].

56 This is based on cases on the previous s. 75B TPA.

57 See *Yorke* (1985) 158 CLR 661 (HCA) 668.

58 (1985) 158 CLR 661.

59 *Ibid.* 669 (Mason CJ, Wilson, Deane and Dawson JJ).

60 *Ibid.* 670. *Cf.* at 667 'essential matters which go to make up the offence'. See also, e.g., *ACCC* v. *Universal Sports Challenge Ltd* [2002] FCA 1276 [45].

61 See, e.g., *Compaq Computer (Aust) Pty Ltd* v. *Merry* (1998) 157 ALR 1; *Bray* v. *F Hoffman-La Roche Ltd* [2002] FCA 243; (2002) 118 FCR 1 [162]; *Cassidy* v. *NRMA Health Pty Ltd* [2002] FCA 1228; (2002) ATPR 41-891 [73].

High Court itself stressed, such an intention is based on knowledge. Indeed, we would suggest that the term 'intention' adds little beyond the fairly obvious requirement that the accessory's conduct needs to be deliberate (which in only very rare cases it would not be).[62] Once the court concludes that the particular conduct was engaged in with knowledge of the essential elements of the contravention,[63] a conclusion of intention follows. What is clear, however, is that liability is based on the accessory's culpable conduct.

10.4.3 Involvement

Although the legislation sets out in detail the different types of conduct that constitute acts of involvement, or participation, in another's contravention, this has not been a significant focus of much dispute.[64] As in the criminal law, the courts do not draw any real distinctions as between the types of involvement. Although courts have at times sought to define some of the terms used, the cases have not turned on such definitions.[65] The purpose of the legislation seems to have been to cast a very wide net over all types of possible acts of participation.[66] Quite minor acts of involvement, facilitating some aspects of others' wrongdoing[67] (albeit before or contemporaneously with the contravention),[68] will satisfy the conduct element.[69]

62 *Cf. New Zealand Bus Ltd and Infratil Ltd* v. *Commerce Commission* [2007] NZCA 502 [119].

63 *Yorke* (1985) 158 CLR 661 (HCA) 670, 677.

64 *Cf. Rafferty* v. *Time 2000 West Pty Ltd (No 4)* [2010] FCA 725 [315] (Besanko J): 'There is not a great deal of authority on the level of involvement required in order to establish that a party was [directly or indirectly] "knowingly concerned in" or "party to" a contravention.' In any case, these phrases appear to be catch-alls that seemingly capture the three circumstances enumerated in the other paragraphs.

65 E.g., *Yorke* v. *Lucas* (1983) 49 ALR 672, 681, defining 'inducing' and 'incite'; *Trade Practices Commission* v. *Service Station Assn Ltd* (1992) 109 ALR 465; (1992) ATPR 41–179, 40456 ('procure').

66 *Cf. Yorke* (1985) 158 CLR 661 (HCA) 677 (Brennan J): the term 'a party to' adds little to the specific terms used but 'ensures that none is omitted from the net of . . . liability whom the common law [on criminal accessories] would include'. See also *R* v. *Kelly* (1975) 12 SASR 389, 400 (SASC FC); *R* v. *Lam* (1990) 46 A Crim R 402, 405 (NSWCCA).

67 Query whether conspiring to contravene the *Act* requires some act to give effect to the agreement to be carried out by the co-conspirator, as in tort law.

68 Knowledge acquired after a contravention has been completed cannot give rise to liability. See, e.g., *ASIC* v. *Australian Investors Forum Pty Ltd (No 2)* [2005] NSWSC 267; (2005) 53 ACSR 305 [114]–[118].

69 Certainly, the width of paras. (a) and (c) in the definition means that there is no real need to prove some causative impact from A's conduct. The low threshold test from criminal law applies, as to whether A's conduct or words do something to render more likely the

Importantly, however, the fact that wide-ranging conduct is encompassed by being 'involved' in a contravention does not equate with broad accessory liability. It is the mental element that is key to establishing wrongdoing on the part of A such as to warrant liability and that restrains accessory liability to prevent overreach.[70] Statutory accessory liability is in fact narrow and restricted because of a high threshold of knowledge requirement. This means that concerns expressed by judges and commentators in the context of tort law, that joint tortfeasor liability ought not to extend to parties who merely assist or facilitate a tort, is therefore unfounded,[71] provided such assistance is carried out with sufficient requisite knowledge.

One ongoing difficulty as to the meaning of 'involved in' a contravention is whether mere passive conduct suffices. It has been held that a party who passively stands by while false information is conveyed by another may be liable as an accessory, *if* such standing by is done with knowledge of the falsity.[72] Presumably, the silent party would need to have some authority or status in the proceedings such that the standing by amounted to an endorsement of the statements.[73] Interestingly, in the US, in the context of the liability of accessories for securities frauds, the courts have

> struggled over the question of whether silence and inaction alone can qualify as 'substantial assistance'. . . . The range of judicial responses to claims based on silence and inaction in the face of knowledge or fraud extends from unqualified acceptance to outright rejection; in between are holdings that silence or inaction may create liability where there is a duty

contravention. See *Giorgianni* v. *R* (1985) 156 CLR 473, 492, cited in *ASIC* v. *Camelot Derivatives Pty Ltd (in liq)* [2012] FCA 414 [55].

70 *Cf. New Zealand Bus Ltd and Infratil Ltd* v. *Commerce Commission* [2007] NZCA 502 [118]–[119] (Hammond J, Wilson J agreeing, in the context of pecuniary penalties for anti-competitive mergers): since even peripheral players may be captured as being involved and this does not restrict liability, '[r]ather, the protection of the innocent "must lie in the mental element"'.

71 See Chapter 5. It is the lack of focus on the knowledge element, and what precisely it is that a joint tortfeasor must know in order to be liable, that makes tort law unstable.

72 See *Sutton* v. *A J Thompson Pty Ltd* (1987) 73 ALR 233, particularly at 241 (Forster, Woodward and Wilcox JJ): an accountant, by remaining silent, withheld vital information while accepting joint responsibility, by being part of the discussion, for false statements made by the vendor. Admittedly, the accountant had also engaged in some positive conduct and the court stated that the issue was to be considered as a course of conduct, as a whole (at 242).

73 *Ibid.* The accountant's failure to produce the books, on the basis of an excuse that was entirely unconvincing, nonetheless satisfied the claimants, 'perhaps because of the trust they placed in him.'

to disclose, or where it is proved that the silence was *consciously intended* to aid the securities violation.[74]

It must be said that, absent a duty to disclose,[75] the notion that one can be passive and silent and yet have 'consciously intended' to aid in a violation is difficult to grasp.[76]

10.4.4 Knowledge

The courts have often stated that an accessory must have 'knowledge of the essential elements of the contravention',[77] but what precisely does this mean? There are two (overlapping) questions encompassed by the issue of knowledge: (1) the content of the knowledge, that is, the factual question of *what* it is precisely that the defendant must have known, and (2) the degree of knowledge [3.4]. It is in relation to the former question, in particular, that different views have been expressed.

10.4.4.1 Content of knowledge

What A must know in order to be held liable depends, factually, on the terms of the obligation that has been contravened.[78] A number of propositions can be made with certainty in relation to this question[79] (and see generally [3.4.2]).

[74] See *Halberstam* v. *Welch* 705 F2d 472 (DC Cir 1983) 485 fn. 14, emphasis added, citing *Woodward* v. *Metro Bank of Dallas* 522 F.2d 84, 96–97 (5th Cir 1975). See also, e.g., *Metge* v. *Baehler* 762 F2d 621, 624–625 (8th Cir. 1985) (most courts agree on a duty to disclose where a duty is owed to C, but in the absence of such a duty, it is necessary to show something like that A '*consciously* intended to assist in perpetration of wrongful act' or that A had 'knowledge of underlying fraud and intent to aid and abet wrongful act'); *Armstrong* v. *McAlpin* 699 F2d 79, 91 (CA 2d Cir 1983) ('designed intentionally to aid the primary fraud'); and P. J. McNulty and D. J. Hanson, 'Liability for Aiding and Abetting by Silence or Inaction: An Unfounded Doctrine' (1993) 29 *Tort & Insurance Law Journal* 14.

[75] E.g., as a result of A's status, such as where he has inside information or is a member of a profession holding special obligations. See *Cleary* v. *Perfectune* 700 F2d 774, 777 (CA 1st Cir 1983).

[76] It appears that, at the least, this would require something in the nature of a gain to A as a result of PW's ongoing fraudulent activities, e.g., prolonging an ongoing business to maximise the likely returns of A on securities or debts. See, e.g., *Metge* v. *Baehler* 762 F2d 621, 624–625 (8th Cir 1985).

[77] *Yorke* (1985) 158 CLR 661 (HCA) 670 (Mason ACJ, Wilson, Deane and Dawson JJ) and 677 (Brennan J).

[78] *Rafferty* v. *Madgwicks* [2012] FCAFC 37 [253].

[79] Compare the observations made by Pearce, 'Accessorial liability', 106–107.

First, A need not know or 'appreciate'[80] that the conduct amounts to infringing conduct: it suffices that A knows *of the* conduct that amounts to the infringement.[81] To the extent that liability is formulated in terms of intention, A need not intend to infringe; that is, A need not know that conduct is unlawful[82] since lack of knowledge of the law is no excuse.[83] As the High Court stated in *Rural Press Ltd* v. *ACCC* 'it is not necessary to know that those facts [known to the alleged accessory] are capable of characterisation in the language of the statute'.[84]

Secondly, in many cases of misleading conduct, knowledge may be a straightforward matter of whether A knew of the falsity of a statement,[85] but the more complex the prohibition or contravention in question,[86] the more difficult it may be to determine the 'essential elements of' the contravention.[87] Indeed, it has been suggested in the context of New Zealand pecuniary penalty provisions applying to anti-competitive mergers, that where the infringements are not constituted by simple facts, but 'conclusions, predictions, and judgments that must be deduced from facts and that reasonable people may disagree on',[88] then the knowledge of the essential elements test may be (too) difficult to apply.[89] It is in

80 *ACCC* v. *Grant* [2000] FCA 1564 [13].

81 It does not necessarily involve actual subjective knowledge of a contravention. It is 'conceivable' that an accessory can still be acting in good faith. See *Dimension Data Australia Pty Ltd* v. *Kepper* [2000] FCA 218 (FCAFC). See also *Wheeler Grace and Pierucci Pty Ltd* v. *Wright* [1989] FCA 127; (1989) ATPR ¶40-940, 50,255–50,257 (FCAFC).

82 *Council of the City of Sydney* v. *Goldspar Pty Limited* [2004] FCA 568 [155].

83 Contrast the exceptional position for inducing breach of contract where A must generally appreciate the legal consequence that PW's conduct will amount to a breach: see [3.4.2.3] and Chapter 6.

84 *Rural Press Ltd* v. *ACCC* [2003] HCA 75; (2003) 203 ALR 217 [48] (Gummow, Hayne and Heydon JJ; Gleeson CJ and Callinan J agreeing). To similar effect is *ACCC* v. *Grant* [2000] FCA 1564 [13] and *AMI Australia Holdings Pty Ltd* v. *Bade Medical Institute (Aust) Pty Ltd (No 2)* [2009] FCA 1437; (2009) 262 ALR 458 [93].

85 See, e.g., *ACCC* v. *Grant* [2000] FCA 1564 (director of a corporation liable as accessory, having had knowledge of the falsity of the statements he made *on behalf of* the corporation).

86 For the elements of a contravention of a director's breach of duty not to make improper use of position, see *ASIC* v. *Doyle* [2001] WASC 187; (2001) 38 ACSR 606 [212]–[215]: must know of the purpose of PW to make a gain or to cause detriment to the corporation.

87 *Rafferty* v. *Madgwicks* [2012] FCAFC 37 [253].

88 *New Zealand Bus Ltd and Infratil Ltd* v. *Commerce Commission* [2007] NZCA 502 [124] (Hammond J, Wilson J agreeing). See also [122] and [262]–[267] (Arnold J).

89 *Ibid.*, particularly [117]–[161]. Hammond J considered that a more global approach, of whether the participants have put their knowledge to dishonest use [152], may be more appropriate: see [141]–[161]. Wilson J agreed, but Arnold J was not attracted to Hammond J's approach (at [266]–[267]).

similar contexts (that is, predictions to be deduced from facts) that Australian courts have also disagreed; but that controversy is a very narrow one[90] and does not alter the restrictive approach that generally requires that A must actually know of the conduct that infringes.[91]

Finally, as an aside, there is some uncertainty as to the applicability of accessory liability for 'misleading' statements made by PW as to future matters, and as to the requisite content of knowledge, but that matter is by the way for present purposes.[92]

[90] Different views have been expressed as to whether an 'accessory' must *always* know of the misleading character or falsity of the conduct engaged in by PW or merely know of the elements of the contravention, where it consists of conduct that merely is 'likely to mislead', rather than that which actually misleads. The difference is expressed in the judgments of Moore J (Mansfield J agreeing), on the one hand, and Stone J, on the other, in *Medical Benefits Fund of Australia Ltd* v. *Cassidy* [2003] FCAFC 289 (*MBF*). That controversy has not been stilled by subsequent decisions. See, e.g., favouring the majority opinion in *MBF*, cases such as *Propell National Valuers (WA) Pty Ltd* v. *Australian Executor Trustees Ltd* (2012) 202 FCR 158 (Collier J, with whom Stone J, seemingly irreconcilably with her contrary opinion in *MBF*, agreed); contra *Quinlivan* v. *Australian Competition & Consumer Commission* [2004] FCAFC 175 [10] and *ACCC* v. *TF Woollam & Son Pty Ltd* [2011] FCA 973; (2011) 196 FCR 212 [120]. See also *McGrath* v. *HNSW Pty Ltd* [2014] FCA 165 [11]–[24].

[91] Even if it were to be accepted, the broader test of knowledge in *MBF* [2003] FCAFC 289 does not mean that it will be easy to establish accessory liability, as that case demonstrates. On the facts of *MBF*, it appears difficult to accept that experienced advertisers who prepare the contents of advertisements do not intend their advertisements to give rise to certain, predicted, likely impressions and effects. As Ng, 'Accessorial Liability', at 226, asks, 'how could they not know?' They ought therefore to be liable even absent knowledge that the campaign was 'likely' to mislead, since such knowledge can never positively be had (provided the advertiser also knew the information that rendered the perceptions inaccurate). Similarly, Sweeney, 'Advertising agencies', at 9, concludes that 'it seems somewhat hollow for the agency to be protected by a claim that it was not aware of a message conveyed by its own creation. Indeed, it makes one wonder why good money would be spent to hire an advertising agency.' We agree. See the detailed discussion in Dietrich, 'Civil accessory liability'.

[92] Under s. 4 ACL a person who makes representations as to future matters (for example, as to the likely future profitability of an investment) may be taken to have engaged in misleading conduct if the person cannot establish 'reasonable grounds for making the representation' (s. 4(1)(b); 4(2)). Under the previously formulated provision under the TPA (s. 51A), it was held that s. 51A TPA did not apply to accessories: e.g., in *Quinlivan* v. *ACCC* [2004] FCAFC 175 and *ACCC* v. *Universal Sports Challenge Ltd* [2002] FCA 1276 [44]. With the introduction of the ACL, one of the stated purposes of the changes made on the issue of future matters, included an intention to extend the s. 4 evidential onus of proof to accessories. See Trade Practices Amendment (Australian Consumer Law) Bill (No 2) 2010, Explanatory Memo., [2.22]. It is not clear, however, that the section has achieved its aim and, even if it has, Seddon et al. rightly conclude that it would seem to require A to prove that *he or she* had reasonable grounds for a statement

10.4.4.2 Degrees of knowledge

The second question on knowledge, albeit one that overlaps with the *content* question above (and hence, perhaps, tends to be conflated with it), is the degree of knowledge that the party must have of a given fact, or of the misleading character of conduct, as the case may be (and see generally [3.4.3]).

For the purpose of accessory liability, it has been authoritatively affirmed that actual knowledge is necessary for liability.[93] It may, however, be difficult to prove of such consciousness in a given case, for example, by conclusively proving that A subjectively knew the falseness of the representation. In response to this problem, the courts have held that wilful blindness [3.4.3.3] of a fact may suffice as a basis for inferring 'actual knowledge',[94] allowing the courts to fill evidentiary gaps. Essentially, 'wilful blindness' is a conclusion that, surely, A really does know.[95] As Mason CJ, Deane, Dawson, Toohey and Gaudron JJ concluded in *Pereira* v. *Director of Public Prosecutions*, a criminal law case, but a conclusion that equally applies to civil claims:[96]

> [A]ctual knowledge ... may be established as a matter of inference from the circumstances surrounding the commission of the alleged offence. ... [I]n such cases the question remains one of actual knowledge: ... the fact remains that a combination of suspicious circumstances and failure to make inquiry may sustain an inference of knowledge of the actual or likely existence of the relevant matter.[97]

about future matters 'actually made by someone else (which could be nonsensical)'. See Seddon et al., *Cheshire*, [11.110] 600–601; [11.117] 615–616.

93 See, e.g., *Yorke* (1985) 158 CLR 661.

94 *Zipside Pty Ltd* v. *Anscor Pty Ltd* [2004] QSC 33 [42]. See also Stone J in *MBF* [2003] FCAFC 289 and *ASIC* v. *Somerville* [2009] NSWSC 934 [40]. *Cf.* references to 'dishonest ignorance' of the truth or 'ignorance being dishonestly and deliberately maintained', e.g., *Crocodile Marketing* v. *Griffith Vintners* (1992) 28 NSWLR 539, 545–546 (Cole J). This concept appears to be the same as 'wilful blindness'. As Cole J concluded, it may be regarded as not ignorance at all (at 546). In *Rafferty* v. *Madgwicks* [2012] FCAFC 37 [261], the court referred both to 'wilful blindness' and 'dishonest or deliberate ignorance' without spelling out whether these were being used synonymously or as different tests. But conceptually, surely there cannot be a difference, at least if one assumes that the court meant dishonest *and* deliberate ignorance. Deliberate ignorance without dishonesty may be something different.

95 *Cf.* Lord Sumner in *The Zamora No 2* (1921) 1 AC 801, 812–813, and see the extensive discussion of the phrase 'wilful blindness' in *Richardson & Wrench (Holdings) Pty Ltd* v. *Ligon No 174 Pty Ltd* [1994] FCA 1222; (1994) 123 ALR 681.

96 The statement has been cited in misleading conduct cases, e.g., *Richardson & Wrench (Holdings) Pty Ltd* v. *Ligon No 174 Pty Ltd* [1994] FCA 1222; (1994) 123 ALR 681.

97 (1988) 63 ALJR 1, 3. See also *Bahri Kural* v. *The Queen* [1987] HCA 16; (1987) 162 CLR 502, 507; *Giorgianni* v. *R* (1985) 156 CLR 473, 507–508.

Nonetheless, wilful blindness is not easily inferred.[98] And any lesser level of awareness, such as reckless indifference or objective knowledge, does not equate to knowledge.[99]

The requirement of actual knowledge appears appropriate in the context of liability for misleading conduct for at least two reasons. First, since the liability of PW is itself wide-ranging and readily established, caution in extending the range of liability even further via a broader accessory liability is warranted. Secondly, the criminal origins of the definition of accessories suggest that this is consistent with the legislature's intentions.[100]

Having said that, in exceptional cases, even the burdensome actual knowledge requirement has been satisfied, for example, in the successful civil penalty claim in *ASIC* v. *Somerville*[101] against an accessory to a breach of directors' duties by directors engaged in asset stripping of a company. In that case, a solicitor gave various advices to assist in establishing new companies and recommended transactions that breached the sections in question, such that there was a direct causal connection between the solicitor's conduct and the breaches of directors' duties that occurred.[102] Although the judge accepted that in a 'normal case' 'it would be extraordinary if a solicitor just giving advice became liable', such liability was justified because the advice was 'given by a solicitor to carry out an improper activity and the solicitor [did] all the work involved in carrying it out'.[103]

[98] *Australian Competition and Consumer Commission* v. *Kaye* [2004] FCA 1363 [189].

[99] See, e.g., *Inchcape Financial Services (Aust) Pty Ltd* v. *Classic Automobiles Ltd* [1999] NSWSC 895 [98]–[118]. This is sometimes put in terms of 'constructive knowledge' being insufficient (e.g., *Compaq Computer (Aust) Pty Ltd* v. *Merry* (1998) 157 ALR 1, 5) but that phrase is not helpful: see [3.4.3.5].

[100] Although most cases on knowledge concern the ACL, specific issues also arise for corporate wrongdoing. Despite the conclusion above, limiting liability to accessories with actual knowledge in the context of company directors' wrongdoing is problematic for several reasons, as Tom Middleton argues in 'ASIC's regulatory powers – interception and search warrants, credit and financial services licences and banning orders, financial advisers and superannuation: Problems and suggested reforms' (2013) 31 *Company & Securities Law Journal* 208, particularly 221–222, on accessory liability, and 228, noting the advantages of suing in equity rather than using the statutory remedies, either against primary wrongdoers or accessories. Nonetheless, given the accepted jurisprudence on the statutory definitions of accessories, it is only through legislative changes that coherence between the principles applicable – to the same conduct – in both equity and under statute, is achievable.

[101] [2009] NSWSC 934. [102] *Ibid.* [48]. [103] *Ibid.* [49].

10.4.5 *Conclusion on Australian statutory accessory liability*

Statutory accessory liability has been restrictively applied in Australia and has had limited impact, despite the wide-ranging conduct that the statutes identify as acts of involvement. The restraint is the result of the courts' insistence on proof of actual knowledge of a contravention. Such an approach is consistent with liability that is founded on accessory's culpable conduct. This means that it will not be easy to establish accessory liability. Indeed, as the law currently stands, persons found liable as primary wrongdoers may not be found liable as accessories even for the same conduct.[104] However, some liberalisation in approach may be justified. It has been suggested in other statutory contexts that less than actual knowledge may indicate a sufficiently culpable state of mind.[105]

[104] E.g., *Australian Competition and Consumer Commission* v. *Kaye* [2004] FCA 1363 [186].
[105] *Cf.* reference to 'participatory dishonesty' as capturing the essential requirement of some wrongful involvement in another's wrong, in *New Zealand Bus Ltd and Infratil Ltd* v. *Commerce Commission* [2007] NZCA 502 [155].

11

Wrongs involving companies

11.1 Introduction

11.1.1 Overview

A company, although a separate legal entity, can only operate through human actors. Both the company's mental state and its conduct and, therefore, its primary or accessory liability, can only be determined by reference to the state of mind and conduct of those actors. But equally, the same state of mind and conduct of those human actors can generate primary liability or accessory liability on their part. Whereas in a non-corporate scenario, there is a direct interaction between a human accessory and the person committing the primary wrong, in the corporate context there is an element of circularity: a director ('D')[1] may be accessorily involved in the affairs of the corporate primary wrongdoer, PW Co, which in turn has only committed a wrong because of the acts of its employees and agents, perhaps including D himself or herself. When D pursues his or her objectives through the medium of a corporate vehicle (itself acting through its employees and agents), or a corporate group, an analysis in terms of accessory principles becomes complicated and, possibly, artificial. Legal analysis is sometimes also obscured by the metaphorical language of going behind, 'piercing' or 'lifting' the 'corporate veil'.[2]

1 The shorthand of 'director' or 'D' is used to encompass any officers to whom directors' duties will attach as a consequence of their management or control function in relation to a company. This may include persons in control of a company without holding formal office. There are significant differences in this respect between the Australian and English companies legislation. See *Grimaldi* v. *Chameleon Mining NL (No 2)* [2012] FCAFC 6; (2012) 200 FCR 296 [53]-[58] (*Grimaldi*). A further complication is that in England, but not Australia, a director may be a company: *Grimaldi* [53].

2 *Prest* v. *Petrodel Resources Limited* [2013] UKSC 34; [2013] 2 AC 415 [106] (*Prest*) (Lord Walker of Gestingthorpe): 'piercing the corporate veil' is a description of when 'some rule of law produces apparent exceptions to the principle of the separate juristic personality of a body corporate'. Examples may be the result of 'a statutory provision, or from joint liability in tort, or from the law of unjust enrichment, or from principles of equity and the law of trusts'.

This chapter considers some particular questions concerning accessory liability that arise in the corporate context because of the sui generis nature of the company/human actor relationship[3] (although some of these questions also arise more generally for principals and agents). It does not attempt a comprehensive resolution of these questions, nor does it deal with the various statutory regulatory schemes;[4] that would require a much more detailed treatment of company law and policy that is beyond the scope of this book. Instead, some particular problems are noted and some possible solutions suggested.

First, this chapter introduces and compares the general law tools of attribution and vicarious liability that are used to determine a company's liability [11.1.2]. Secondly, it considers the application of attribution principles to determine the accessory liability of companies (whether to primary wrongs committed by directors, other companies or third persons). Equitable accessory liability is used here to illustrate the application of attribution principles [11.2.2]. The third section of the chapter focuses upon D as accessory to his or her company's primary wrong [11.3]. A director's accessory liability usually depends upon the same general law and statutory principles as apply to non-directors, but in the context of torts and statutory intellectual property (IP) infringements by companies the courts have not always clearly iterated whether D's potential liability is primary or accessory and when it arises: [11.3.3]. Questions specific to the corporate context also have arisen in relation to the mental state required for D's accessory liability where the company's liability is strict: [11.3.4]; D's accessory liability for a company's breach of contract: [11.3.5]; and whether there can be accessory liability where directors act in a constitutional role: [11.3.6]. Finally in [11.3.7], there is a brief discussion of the accessory liability of directors of trustee companies.

11.1.2 The general law tools of attribution and vicarious liability

Attribution refers to

> the process of legal reasoning by which the conduct or state of mind of one or more natural persons (that is, human beings) is treated as that of a non-natural person (that is, a company) for the purposes of determining the

[3] Many of the issues canvassed here are discussed by Justice Ashley Black, 'Directors' Statutory and General Law Accessory Liability for Corporate Wrongdoing' (2013) 31 *Companies & Securities Law Journal* 511.

[4] This chapter does not discuss statutory accessory liability schemes in company law; see generally Chapter 10.

> company's legal liability or rights in civil proceedings ... or its criminal liability.[5]

In the case of agents (including D when acting as an agent), the agent's conduct and knowledge is attributed to the company,[6] so that it is also personally or 'directly liable for' the conduct of its agent.[7] Attribution of mental state and conduct is used not only to establish a primary wrong against a company, but also to establish the accessory liability of a company. The application of the principles of attribution is discussed further in the context of equitable accessory liability in [11.2.2].

Attribution is a different mechanism to that of vicarious liability. If all the elements of a primary wrong are made out against an employee or an agent acting in the course of employment or within the scope of authority, then the company is vicariously liable for the primary wrong jointly with the employee or agent.

There are, however, factual scenarios in which it is difficult to establish all the elements of a wrong against any individual and the company is the only primary wrongdoer (PW). For example, where a company purchases and purports to obtain title to a claimant's (C's) goods, the conversion may only have been carried out by it.[8] Indeed, in some cases, 'the delict cannot be done by a person *other* than the

[5] *Moulin Global Eyecare Trading Ltd* v. *Commissioner of Inland Revenue* [2014] HKCFA 22 [61] (Lord Walker NPJ) (*Moulin Global Eyecare*). The UK Supreme Court has comprehensively reviewed the general law rules of attribution and the relevant case law in *Bilta (UK) Ltd (in liq)* v. *Nazir* [2015] UKSC 23; [2015] 2 WLR 1168 (*Bilta UKSC*).

[6] See generally *Meridian Global Funds Management Asia Ltd* v. *Securities Commission* [1995] 2 AC 500 (PC) (*Meridian Global Funds*) on primary, general and special rules of attribution; *Moulin Global Eyecare* [2014] HKCFA 22 [61] onwards, especially [106]. See also Jennifer Payne, 'The Attribution of Tortious Liability Between Director and Company' (1998) *Journal of Business Law* 153, 160, drawing a distinction between attribution of liability for a state of mind and of acts. On the attribution of agents' knowledge, or imputing knowledge, generally, see Peter Watts, 'Imputed Knowledge in Restitutionary Claims—Rationales and Rationes' in Simone Degeling and James Edelman (eds.), *Unjust Enrichment in Commercial Law* (Australia, Thomson Reuters, 2008) 429.

[7] *Moulin Global Eyecare* [2014] HKCFA 22 [64] (Lord Walker NPJ), and see *Bilta (UK) Ltd* v. *Nazir (No 2)* [2013] EWCA Civ 968; [2014] Ch 52 (*Bilta CA*). In the view of Peter Watts, the direct liability is a result of the company being deemed a wrongdoer because of the acts of its agents: 'Corrupt Company Controller, their Companies and their Companies' Creditors: Dealing with Pleas of *Ex Turpi Causa*' [2014] *Journal of Business Law* 161, 166. Liability is not vicarious: *Hamilton* v. *Whitehead* [1988] 166 CLR 121 (HCA); *Bilta CA* [2013] EWCA Civ 968; [2014] Ch 52 [27].

[8] *Johnson Matthey (Aust) Ltd* v. *Dascorp Pty Ltd* [2003] VSC 291; (2003) 9 VR 171. Contrast the facts of *Wah Tat Bank Ltd* v. *Chan Cheng Kum* [1975] AC 507, 514–15, in which D had personally committed all the acts of conversion.

company itself',[9] such as where a company imports or sells infringing goods in breach of copyright.[10]

The interrelationship between attribution and vicarious liability is not entirely clear, but to simplify somewhat, where an employee in the course of employment (or agent within scope of authority) commits a wrong, such as where she negligently drives over C, then PW Co is vicariously liable; there is no need to rely on attribution.[11] If, for example, however, a number of different employees develop a technology in breach of patents, then PW Co is liable as a primary wrongdoer based on the attribution of the aggregated acts and knowledge of the *various* employees [11.2.2.5]. Knowledge that is aggregated can even extend to that of former employees.[12] If no individual employees have committed a wrong, then PW Co cannot be vicariously liable, since none of the employees have committed the tort.

In all these examples, the company is liable either vicariously, or by attribution, for the primary wrong. It is not an accessory.[13] If liability then is sought to be imposed upon a director of PW Co, then such director could only be liable as an accessory.

11.2 Company liability

11.2.1 Distinguishing accessory from primary liability

Sometimes, it is difficult to determine whether a court has found a company liable as a primary wrongdoer or as an accessory. Where, for example, a company is 'the corporate creature, vehicle, or alter ego of

[9] *Keller* v. *LED Technologies Pty Ltd* [2010] FCAFC 55; (2010) 185 FCR 449 [384] (Jessup J) (*Keller*) (emphasis added). This category of case is most troubling since D cannot have committed the primary wrong, nor procured any individual employee to do so; and D may have been carrying out his or her managerial and constitutional functions in directing PW Co's activities as a whole.

[10] E.g., *Sporte Leisure Pty Ltd (ACN 008608919)* v. *Paul's International Pty Ltd (ACN 128 263 561) (No 3)* [2010] FCA 1162; (2010) 88 IPR 242 [105] (*Sporte Leisure (No 3)*).

[11] See the discussion of the difference between vicarious liability and attribution in *Bilta UKSC* [2015] UKSC 23; [2015] 2 WLR 1168 [185]-[186] (Lord Toulson and Lord Hodge), concluding as follows:

> Such vicarious liability is indirect liability; it does not involve the attribution of the employee's act to the company. It entails holding that the employee has committed a breach of a tortious duty owed by himself, and that the company as his employer is additionally answerable for the employee's tortious act or omission.

[12] *Cf. Fightvision Pty Ltd* v. *Onisforou* (1999) 47 NSWLR 473 (*Fightvision*).

[13] The exception is where a company is vicariously liable for an employee's accessory liability: *cf. Dubai Aluminium Co Ltd* v. *Salaam* [2002] UKHL 48; [2003] 2 AC 366 (*Dubai Aluminium*) (partnership vicariously liable).

wrongdoing fiduciaries who use it to secure the profits of, or to inflict the losses by, their breach of fiduciary duty'[14] the company's liability is not always clearly distinguished from that of the wrongdoing fiduciary (generally the company's director).

Corporate accessories are, of course, ubiquitous in the equitable accessory liability cases.[15] Often the company is within the fiduciary's complete control: an alter ego that, for all intents and purposes, is indistinguishable from the fiduciary and which is used to execute the breach of fiduciary duty and hold property acquired as a consequence.[16] Sometimes courts explain such accessory liability decisions as 'lifting the corporate veil',[17] but the liability extends to where the company is not within the fiduciary's sole control, so long as other third parties with interests in the company are also implicated in the breach.[18] Other courts reject the corporate veil approach and treat the company as having 'jointly participated in the breach of trust'[19] or as having a 'transmitted' fiduciary obligation.[20] The latter analysis is misleading because it suggests that the company becomes a primary wrongdoer in its own right.

Perhaps one reason for the disparity in descriptions of a company's liability is that it is 'rather artificial' here to use the template for accessory liability set by *Barnes* v. *Addy*, and that was formulated with human actors (solicitors and other professional agents) in mind; see [8.1.1], [8.3.5].[21] Nonetheless, once one accepts that equitable accessory (or

[14] *Grimaldi* [2012] FCAFC 6; (2012) 200 FCR 296 [243].

[15] *Ibid.* citing *Cook* v. *Deeks* [1916] 1 AC 554 (PC); *Gencor ACP Ltd* v. *Dalby* [2000] 2 BCLC 734 (Ch) (*Gencor*); *CMS Dolphin Ltd* v. *Simonet* [2002] BCC 600 (Ch) (*CMS Dolphin*); *Queensland Mines Ltd* v. *Hudson* (1975–76) ACLC 28 (NSWSC) 658; *Timber Engineering Co Pty Ltd* v. *Anderson* [1980] 2 NSWLR 488 (NSWSC); *Green & Clara Pty Ltd* v. *Bestobell Industries Pty Ltd (No 2)* [1984] WAR 32 (WASC) (*Green*). This paragraph is taken from Pauline Ridge, 'Constructive Trusts, Accessory Liability and Judicial Discretion' in Elise Bant and Michael Bryan (eds.), *Principles of Proprietary Remedies* (Sydney, Lawbook Co, 2013) 73, [5.70], and is reproduced with permission of Thomson Reuters (Professional) Australia Ltd.

[16] See, e.g., *Cook* v. *Deeks* [1916] 1 AC 554.

[17] See, e.g., *Gencor* [2000] 2 BCLC 734 (Ch) [26] (Rimer J).

[18] See, e.g., *Green* [1984] WAR 32 (WASC).

[19] See, e.g., *CMS Dolphin* [2002] BCC 600 [98]–[104] (Collins J); *Fyffes Group Ltd* v. *Templeman* [2000] 2 Lloyd's Rep 643, 669–70 (Toulson J).

[20] The term is used in *John* v. *Dodwell & Company Limited* [1918] AC 563 (PC) 569 (Viscount Haldane) in the context of a partnership; followed by the Supreme Court of NSW in *Queensland Mines* v. *Hudson* (1975–76) CLC 40–266. See also *Club of the Clubs Pty Limited* v. *King Network Group Pty Limited (No 2)* [2007] NSWSC 574 [58].

[21] *Grimaldi* [2012] FCAFC 6; (2012) 200 FCR 296 [243] (Finn, Stone and Perram JJ) quoting *CMS Dolphin* [2002] BCC 600 [104] (Collins J).

more broadly participatory: [8.1.1]) liability is an independent liability to which the full range of equitable remedies attaches, then identifying the company's liability as accessorial is not problematic. It is not apparent that there are any unjust outcomes that would warrant overriding the separate legal personality of the company.[22]

11.2.2 Companies as accessories

11.2.2.1 Attribution of conduct and mental states for the purposes of accessory liability

In order to determine a company's accessory liability it will be necessary to determine its conduct and mental state. Using equitable participatory liability as an example, the company may be linked to C and PW by several alternative relationships. For example, the company may have participated, through procurement, assistance or receipt of trust property, in an unrelated PW's breach of trust or fiduciary duty to C. The attribution question here is whether knowledge of PW's breach of duty that is held by a director or agent of the company can be attributed to it so as to satisfy the requisite mental element for the company's accessory or recipient liability.[23] The parties may be more closely related, such as where PW is a director of the company or, as is often the case, where the company and C Co belong to a corporate group controlled by one individual, PW.[24] Here, more difficult questions arise concerning the circumstances in which the knowledge of PW may be attributed to one or both companies for the purposes of a claim by C Co.[25]

11.2.2.2 General rules of attribution

Attribution of both conduct and a state of mind may occur in relation to the same set of facts for the purposes of establishing the elements of

22 *Cf. Prest* [2013] UKSC 34; [2013] 2 AC 415.

23 See, e.g., *El Ajou* v. *Dollar Land Holdings plc* [1994] 2 All ER 685 (*El Ajou*). See also *Grimaldi* [2012] FCAFC 6; (2012) 200 FCR 296, citing as an example *John* v. *Dodwell & Co* [1918] AC 563 (PC) 569; *Bilta UKSC* [2015] UKSC 23; [2015] 2 WLR 1168.

24 See, e.g., *Belmont Finance Corporation* v. *Williams Furniture Ltd (No 2)* [1980] 1 All ER 393; *Robins* v. *Incentive Dynamics Pty Ltd (in liq.)* [2003] NSWCA 71; (2003) 175 FLR 286.

25 Attribution questions may also arise in relation to a company's primary wrongdoing, of course, but – because liability for breach of trust or fiduciary duty is strict – tend to concern the company's conduct, rather than its state of mind. See, e.g., *Royal Brunei Airlines Sdn Bhd* v. *Tan* [1995] 2 AC 378 (PC) (*Royal Brunei Airlines*). An example of where a state of mind must be attributed to a PW Co is the requirement for knowing assistance liability of a 'dishonest and fraudulent design' by PW [8.3.1.4].

accessory liability or it may be the case that attribution of conduct occurs, but attribution of knowledge is not permitted.[26] The focus of much of the equitable accessory liability case law, however, is on attribution of an agent's state of mind, rather than the agent's conduct.

The courts use two methods of attribution in determining a company's state of mind for accessory liability purposes.[27] One method is to apply the so-called 'general rules of attribution',[28] namely the general principles of agency law. Accordingly, within certain constraints, the knowledge of its agents will be imputed to the company. For example, if the company was under a duty to investigate a matter then the knowledge of its agent in relation to that matter is imputed to the company.[29] If the company's agent has actual or ostensible authority to receive information on the company's behalf in relation to a matter, then knowledge or notice of any such information will be imputed to the company.[30] But if the agent had a duty to disclose information to the company and did not do so, it will not be imputed with knowledge of that information unless it was under a duty to investigate.[31]

11.2.2.3 The company's directing mind and will

The concept of the company's 'directing mind and will' is the second method used to determine the state of mind of a company for accessory liability purposes. According to this approach, a natural person may be considered 'the very ego and centre of the personality of the corporation', that is, the company itself, rather than merely its agent.[32] If so, then the mind of its human alter ego is the mind of the company

[26] See *Moulin Global Eyecare* [2014] HKCFA 22 [99] (Lord Walker NPJ) citing the findings in *Belmont Finance Corporation Limited* v. *Williams Furniture Limited* [1979] Ch 250 as an example. See generally on the general rules of attribution, *Bilta UKSC* [2015] UKSC 23; [2015] 2 WLR 1168.

[27] The distinction between the two methods (use of agency law and the directing mind and will theory) can be seen in the leading case of *El Ajou* [1994] 2 All ER 685.

[28] The terminology is that of the Privy Council in *Meridian Global Funds* [1995] 2 AC 500. The Privy Council also referred to the 'primary rules of attribution' that are to be found either expressly stated in a company's constitution or implied by company law. The primary rules tend to focus upon a company's conduct, rather than its state of mind.

[29] *El Ajou* [1994] 2 All ER 685, 702–702.

[30] *Ibid.* 703.

[31] *Ibid.* See further on the principles of agency law, P. Watts and F. M. B. Reynolds, *Bowstead and Reynolds on Agency*, 19th edn (London, Sweet & Maxwell, 2010).

[32] *Lennard's Carrying Company Limited* v. *Asiatic Petroleum Company Limited* [1915] AC 705 (HL) 713 (Viscount Haldane LC). See also, *Hamilton* v. *Whitehead* [1988] 166 CLR 121 (HCA).

for the purposes of establishing the company's accessory liability.[33] Depending upon the circumstances, the human alter ego in his or her personal capacity may be the primary wrongdoer. The converse also applies; that is, the company may be the primary wrongdoer and its human alter ego the accessory.[34] That is, two, distinct liabilities may be grounded in the one person's state of knowledge or notice.[35]

The simplest scenario to which the directing mind and will theory applies is that of a small company with one controlling director. Where this is not the case, the question of who is the directing mind and will is determined in respect of the impugned transaction, rather than as a general question, and by reference to the company's articles of association and what the person was expressly or impliedly authorised to do on behalf of the company.[36] '[I]t would be wrong to suppose that the same person or persons (not being the full board of directors) must perform this function for each and every one of a company's activities.'[37]

Recent judicial discussions of the directing mind and will theory have cautioned against treating it as an exercise in metaphysics.[38] Lord Walker NPJ in the Hong Kong Court of Final Appeal has gone so far as to suggest that 'it might be better if it were to fade away as a general concept'.[39] Instead, the question is one of construction of the relevant statutory or common law liability rule in the specific factual context in order to identify the officer or employee whose state of mind is relevant.[40] One must look to the 'terms and policies of the substantive rule': context is everything.[41]

11.2.2.4 The 'fraud' exception to attribution

The importance of construing the rules of attribution within the particular accessory liability context is illustrated in relation to the so-called 'fraud exception' of agency law.[42] The rule, in broad terms, is that

33 See, e.g., *Farah Constructions Pty Ltd* v. *Say-Dee Pty Ltd* [2007] HCA 22; (2007) 230 CLR 89 [128].

34 *R* v. *Goodall* (1975) 11 SASR 94 (SASC) 100.

35 *Hamilton* v. *Whitehead* [1988] 166 CLR 121 (HCA). 36 *El Ajou* [1994] 2 All ER 685.

37 *Moulin Global Eyecare Trading Ltd* [2014] HKCFA 22 [66] (Lord Walker NPJ).

38 *Meridian Global Funds* [1995] 2 AC 500 (PC); *Moulin Global Eyecare* [2014] HKCFA 22 [61]–[72], [106].

39 *Moulin Global Eyecare* [2014] HKCFA 22 [106].

40 *Ibid.; Bilta (UKSC)* [2015] UKSC 23; [2015] 2 WLR 1168 [41], [202].

41 *Meridian Global Funds* [1995] 2 AC 500 (PC) 512 (Lord Hoffmann). See also 507.

42 It has been suggested by Lord Neuberger that the terminology of 'fraud exception' be abandoned because the principle to which it refers is neither limited to fraud, nor an

'knowledge is not attributed to the principal where it is acquired by an agent who is defrauding the principal in the same transaction'.[43] But this rule does not apply in proceedings by C against a company (Co A) for accessory liability in relation to a breach of trust or fiduciary duty owed to C by Co A's agent (PW). That is, the knowledge of PW in respect of the breach of duty towards C will be imputed to Co A, as PW's principal, even though the breach may also constitute fraudulent conduct towards Co A. This is because, in relation to C, Co A is not viewed as a 'victim' of PW's fraud. The rationale has been explained in this way:

> As between the company and the defrauded third party, the former is not to be treated as a victim of the wrongdoing on which the third party sues but one of the perpetrators. The consequences of liability are therefore insufficient to prevent the actions of the agent being treated as those of the company. The interests of the third party who is the intended victim of the unlawful conduct take priority over the loss which the company will suffer through the actions of its own directors.[44]

This rule of attribution for the purposes of accessory liability does not apply to, or preclude a claim by, Co A against PW in relation to any wrong committed against it.[45] In other words: '[w]here the purpose of attribution is to apportion responsibility between a company and its agents so as to determine their rights and liabilities to each other, the result will not necessarily be the same as it is in a case where the purpose is to apportion responsibility between the company and a third party'.[46]

exception to the general principles concerning attribution. See *Bilta (UKSC)* [2015] UKSC 23; [2015] 2 WLR 1168 [9]. See also [181] (Lord Toulson and Lord Hodge).

43 *Bowstead & Reynolds* [8-207]. The authors go on to qualify this statement at [8-213]. See also the discussion in *Grimaldi* [2012] FCAFC 6; (2012) 200 FCR 296 [282]-[283] (and the cases cited therein) where the exception is also qualified. The court in *Grimaldi* at [284] (Finn, Stone and Perram JJ) also noted that the 'fraud' exception has been applied in Australia to an agent's knowledge of breach of fiduciary duty 'at least where the fiduciary's conduct is morally reprehensible' (quoting *Aequitas Ltd* v. *AEFC Leasing Pty Ltd* [2001] NSWSC 14; (2001) 19 ACLC 1,006 [306] (Austin J)).

44 See *Bilta CA* [2013] EWCA Civ 968; [2014] Ch 52 [42], [34] (Patten LJ). An appeal to the UKSC was dismissed. See also *Moulin Global Eyecare* [2014] HKCFA 22. See also the discussion in *Grimaldi* [2012] FCAFC 6; (2012) 200 FCR 296 [286].

45 *Bilta (UKSC)* [2015] UKSC 23; [2015] 2 WLR 1168.

46 *Ibid.*, [92] (Lord Sumption).

11.2.2.5 Aggregation of conduct and mental states for the purposes of attribution

Some questions surround the extent to which the knowledge of various company personnel can be aggregated when attributing conduct and mental state to a company for the purposes of accessory liability.[47] It is clear that aggregation of conduct and knowledge is possible for some legal liability purposes.[48] To hold otherwise would drastically reduce the circumstances in which companies could be liable. Conversely, to allow aggregation of the conduct and knowledge of any company personnel would have 'potentially alarming consequences for large, multi-function, corporations'.[49] It has been suggested that aggregation of knowledge between two or more human actors for the company will be permitted – absent any evidence of a deliberate intention to maintain the disaggregation of knowledge – where one has a duty to communicate his or her knowledge and the opportunity to do so, but that the particular liability context in which aggregation of knowledge is argued will have a significant bearing on whether it is permissible.[50]

More generally in relation to aggregation of knowledge and conduct, the knowledge and conduct of the different employees or agents of a company can be combined and are attributed to it for the purposes of the tort of inducing breach of contract.[51] Such liability may also arise from the disparate knowledge and conduct of different directors and officers, such that the company is liable but an individual director will not necessarily be liable.[52]

[47] This comment and the following discussion are not intended to apply to the example of a company acting through a valid board resolution or the general meeting.

[48] *Krakowski* v. *Eurolynx Properties Ltd* (1995) 183 CLR 563 (HCA).

[49] *Australian Competition and Consumer Commission* v. *Radio Rentals Ltd* [2005] FCA 1133; (2005) 146 FCR 292 [181] (Finn J).

[50] *Ibid.* [179], [182]–[183], citing *Re Chisum Services Pty Ltd* (1982) 7 ACLR 641, 649–650 and *Macquarie Bank Ltd* v. *Sixty-Fourth Throne Pty Ltd* [1998] 3 VR 133, 161–162. *Cf.* Uniform Trust Code (2000) §104(b):

> An organization that conducts activities through employees has notice or knowledge of a fact involving a trust only from the time the information was received by an employee having responsibility to act for the trust, or would have been brought to the employee's attention if the organization had exercised reasonable diligence. ... Reasonable diligence does not require an employee of the organization to communicate information unless the communication is part of the individual's regular duties or the individual knows a matter involving the trust would be materially affected by the information.

[51] *Cf. Fightvision* (1999) 47 NSWLR 473.

[52] *Cf. Daniels (formerly practising as Deloitte Haskins & Sells)* v. *Anderson* (1995) 37 NSWLR 438, 574–5; 16 ACSR 607, 730, and R. P. Austin and I. M. Ramsay, *Ford's Principles of Corporations Law*, Online edition (Australia, LexisNexis, 2013) [16.080.3]: contributory negligence of a

11.3 Directors as accessories

11.3.1 Distinguishing accessory liability from primary liability

If PW Co has committed a primary wrong, a question arises for common law wrongs as to whether D can also be liable as a primary wrongdoer or else as an accessory. The same problem has not arisen in equity, where D cannot generally be liable as a primary wrongdoer where the equitable duty in question is held by the company.

For common law wrongs, the issue is complicated by the fact that PW Co may have committed the wrong because of D's own conduct such that PW Co is liable on the basis of either vicarious liability or attribution.[53] Some judges and commentators have relied on the fact of attribution to support the view (which we consider illogical)[54] that D, when acting as an agent, cannot be liable for his or her own acts, since these have been attributed to PW Co.[55] This argument is especially made when attribution is based on the concept of

company can be based on the attribution of conduct and knowledge of all persons who are its directing mind and will and on acts and omissions of all those for whom the company is vicariously liable. See also *Bowstead and Reynolds*, [8–186].

53 Austin and Ramsay, *Ford's*, [16.080.3].

54 One does not lose one's legal identity when acting for a company. There is no reason in principle why such a person cannot be personally liable for his or her acts. See Stefan H. C. Lo, 'Liability of directors as joint tortfeasors' (2009) *Journal of Business Law* 109, 127 and following. Nonetheless, some authorities, albeit conflicting and mostly historical, suggest that where a company acts by deed, this is the act of the company itself and not the consequence of the attribution of agents' acts. See P. Watts, N. Campbell and C. Hare, *Company Law in New Zealand* (Wellington, LexisNexis, 2011) [11.2.2], rejecting this analysis. In any case, it is not clear what impact this analysis could have on the liability of directors for their acts.

55 See, e.g., *Trevor Ivory Ltd* v. *Anderson* [1992] 2 NZLR 517, 520 (Cooke P) (*Trevor Ivory*); Christopher Wood, 'Liability of Directors as Joint Tortfeasors in Intellectual Property Matters' (2010) 21 *Australian Intellectual Property Journal* 164. See also R. Grantham and C. Rickett, 'Directors' "Tortious" Liability: Contract, Tort or Company Law?' (1999) 62 *Modern Law Review* 133, 133, whose arguments are unconvincing, e.g., in asserting without reasons that there is a 'primacy inherent in the rules of company law'. A more detailed defence is mounted by Grantham in 'The Limited Liability of Company Directors' [1997] *Lloyd's Maritime and Commercial Law Quarterly* 362, and see also 'Attributing Responsibility to Corporate Entities: A Doctrinal Approach' (2001) 19 *Company and Securities Law Journal* 168, 178–9. This assumption also seems to underlie many of the cases supporting the 'make the wrong his own' test (discussed [11.3.3.3]).

In our view, therefore, there is no 'clash of legal principle giving rise to a very difficult question of policy', contrary to J. Farrar, 'Personal Liability of Director for Torts of Company' (1997) 71 *Australian Law Journal* 20, 20. Farrar's conclusion that there should be a 'presumption of no personal liability' (22) is misconceived. Where all the elements of the wrong are established against D, liability must follow. Where they are not, then liability can only be accessorial, though such liability is in any case not easily established.

identifying D as the company itself or as its directing mind and will [11.2.2.3].[56] This 'disattribution heresy'[57] has, for the most part, been rejected in modern law.[58] The fact that an agent's acts are attributed to the principal, corporate or otherwise, does not mean that the agent's acts are somehow privileged. To hold otherwise is not, contrary to the view of some commentators, 'to deny the company's very existence'.[59] As Campbell and Armour have concluded, 'as a matter of principle, there is no convincing reason why the company being liable should exclude or immunise the agent from being liable'.[60] Similarly, the House of Lords in *Williams* v. *Natural Life Health Foods* (*Williams*) stated:

> the issue is not peculiar to companies. Whether the principal is a company or a natural person, someone acting on his behalf may incur personal liability in tort as well as imposing vicarious or attributed liability upon his principal.[61]

This means that D can be liable either for his or her own acts as a primary wrongdoer, or alternatively, as an accessory to PW Co's wrong,[62] but not both. Whether D is liable for committing the primary wrong is determined by application of the rules of civil liability relevant to the wrong in question[63] and by whether all the elements of that wrong can be made out

[56] The directing mind and will concept is seen to be particularly applicable to the acts of boards of directors. See, e.g., *Brooks* v. *New Zealand Guardian Trust Co Ltd* [1994] 2 NZLR 134 (CA), criticised by Watts, Campbell and Hare, *Company Law*, [2.4.2]. The point was not discussed on appeal: [1995] 1 WLR 96 (PC).

[57] N. Campbell and J. Armour, 'Demystifying the civil liability of corporate agents' (2003) 62 *Cambridge Law Journal* 290, 292, and see also the discussion 292–296.

[58] The authorities are too numerous to mention, but see, e.g., *Standard Chartered Bank* v. *Pakistan National Shipping Corporation (No 2)* [2003] 1 AC 959 [22], [40]; *C Evans & Sons Ltd* v. *Spritebrand Ltd* [1985] 1 WLR 317; *Johnson Matthey (Aust) Ltd* v. *Dascorp Pty Ltd* [2003] VSC 291; (2003) 9 VR 171, 227 [198] (Redlich J): 'Both in Australia and in England a director is in no different position to an agent who, whilst binding their principal may also be liable for their tortious acts.' See also Peter Watts, 'The Company's Alter Ego – a Parvenu and Imposter in Private Law' (2000) *New Zealand Law Review* 137, and an early statement by Cairns LJ in *Ferguson* v. *Wilson* (1866–67) LR 2 Ch App 77, 89–90. In a statutory context, see *Houghton* v. *Arms* [2006] HCA 59; (2006) 225 CLR 553.

[59] Grantham and Rickett, 'Directors', 139.

[60] Campbell and Armour, 'Demystifying', 295–296. See also Peter Watts, '*Trevor Ivory* v. *Anderson*: Reasoning from Outer Space' (2007) *New Zealand Law Journal* 25.

[61] [1998] 1 WLR 830, 835.

[62] If D has not committed the primary wrong, then liability must be on accessory principles and cannot be based merely on D's status as director. PW Co is not the agent of D, as a result only of D's status as director. See, e.g., *British Thomson-Houston Co Ltd* v. *Sterling Accessories Ltd* [1924] 2 Ch 33; (1924) 41 RPC 311; but see also text to n. 65–69.

[63] See Campbell and Armour, 'Demystifying', 298–29.

against D. In *O'Brien* v. *Dawson*, in the High Court of Australia, Starke J stated:

> [I]t does not follow that a director of a company would escape personal liability under cover of the company's responsibility if he himself became an actor and invaded the plaintiff's rights, as by trespassing on his land or seizing his goods and so forth.[64]

One concept for making a director liable, though probably of very limited use, is that of 'piercing the corporate veil'. A company may merely be 'the cat's paw' or alter ego of directors or shareholders[65] and liabilities and remedies may be enforced against the parties controlling such company. 'Piercing the veil' seeks to identify the circumstances in which one ignores the company's separate legal personality so that the company is identified with its shareholders (or controllers).[66] The existence of the company may, in essence, be ignored. Where a company is controlled by wrongdoers, and is used as a device or façade to conceal their wrongdoing,[67] then 'the court will pierce the veil . . . to provide a remedy for the particular wrong which those controlling the company have done'.[68] Whatever the conceptual basis for sheeting home liability to the controllers, such liability is not accessorial – the controllers are treated as primary wrongdoers.[69]

A number of tests have been suggested as being appropriate specifically for determining the liability of directors. All of these tests have been

64 (1942) 66 CLR 18, 32.

65 *TS & B Retail Systems Pty Ltd* v. *3Fold Resources Pty Ltd (No 3)* [2007] FCA 151; (2007) 239 ALR 117 [187] (Finkelstein J); *Townsend* v. *Haworth*, reported as a note to *Sykes* v. *Haworth* (1875) 48 LJ Ch (NS) 770, 772.

66 Robert Miles and Eleanor Holland, 'Shams and Piercing the Corporate Veil' in Edwin Simpson and Miranda Stewart (eds.) *Sham Transactions* (Oxford University Press, 2013) [11.03].

67 *VTB Capital Plc* v. *Nutritek International Corp* [2013] UKSC 5; [2013] 2 AC 337 [128] (*VTB Capital*), though Lord Neuberger (Lord Wilson agreeing) left open whether such general jurisdiction exists [130]; *cf.* in the Court of Appeal, [2012] 2 Lloyd's Rep 313 [80] (Lloyd LJ): D's wrongdoing must be 'an independent wrong that involves the fraudulent or dishonest misuse of the corporate personality of the company for the purpose of concealing the true facts'. Note also the limited scope given to such concept in *Prest* [2013] UKSC 34; [2013] 2 AC 415, discussed at length in Miles and Holland, 'Shams', Ch. 11.

68 *VTB Capital* [2012] EWCA Civ 808; [2012] 2 Lloyd's Rep 313 [78] (Lloyd, Rimer and Aikens LJJ), citing *Ben Hashem* v. *Ali Shayif* [2008] EWHC 2380 (Fam); [2009] 1 FLR 115. Importantly, questions of conflating a company with its shareholders are not relevant to situations in which directors act as agents: 'construing the agency situation as involving corporate veil considerations misses the point.' See Miles and Holland, 'Shams', [11.13].

69 See generally Miles and Holland, 'Shams'.

applied to determine liability for common law and statutory wrongs, and have not been influential in equity. One of these tests, that D 'assumes responsibility' for the wrong, has generally been recognised as a test of primary liability. It goes to the question of whether a duty of care in negligence arises on the part of a director,[70] and is not considered any further here.[71]

One of the tests considered in this chapter, namely, whether D 'makes the tort [or the tortious act or wrong] "his" own',[72] does not spell out whether it is determinative of D's liability as a primary wrongdoer having personally committed all of the elements of the tort,[73] or as an accessory. That fundamental distinction must always be kept in mind.[74] A second test, the 'direct and procure' test, has been recognised to be a test of accessory liability. As tests of accessory liability, however, neither test sets out clearly what acts of involvement are included within it and may potentially give rise to liability. More importantly, neither test acknowledges the importance of the knowledge of D in determining liability. One of the intractable problems in the cases stems from a failure to identify

[70] It is not therefore appropriate as a test of liability for other primary wrongs, a point that was forgotten in *Standard Chartered Bank* v. *Pakistan National Shipping Corporation (No 2)* [2000] 1 Lloyd's Rep 218 (CA), in which the court applied 'assumption of responsibility' to a case of fraud. The error was corrected by the House of Lords [2003] 1 AC 959.

[71] It should be noted, however, that in some cases, it is not clear whether the test is advocated as a *general* test of directors' liability. This is particularly so in New Zealand. See the Court of Appeal in *Trevor Ivory* [1992] 2 NZLR 517, applying the test in circumstances in which it was not entirely clear whether it was more generally applicable. See also *Livingston* v. *Bonifant* (1995) 7 NZCLC 96-658; [1994] BCL 1024 (NZ HC) and *Banfield* v. *Johnson* (1994) 7 NZCLC 260 [140].

[72] It is also called the '*Mentmore*' test after the Canadian case in which it was formulated: *Mentmore Manufacturing Co Inc* v. *National Merchandising Manufacturing Co Inc* (1978) 89 DLR (3rd) 195 (*Mentmore*). There are a number of linguistic variations on this test, but for convenience, the non-gender neutral description of 'makes the wrong "his" own' will be used.

[73] *Fairline Shipping Corporation* v. *Adamson* [1974] 2 All ER 967 and *Allen Manufacturing Co Pty Ltd* v. *McCallum & Co Pty Ltd* (2001) 53 IPR 400 are examples. A failure by judges to spell out which distinct basis for liability is being applied can lead to confusion. See, e.g., *Microsoft Corporation* v. *Auschina Polaris Pty Ltd* [1996] FCA 1069; (1996) 71 FCR 231; (1996) 36 IPR 225 which seemingly is treated in *Sydneywide Distributors Pty Ltd* v. *Red Bull Australia Pty Ltd* [2002] FCAFC 157; (2002) 55 IPR 354 [160] as a case of D being liable as primary wrongdoer, but the exact opposite characterisation is adopted by Jessup J in *Keller* [2010] FCAFC 55; (2010) 185 FCR 449 [384]: D was only liable as an accessory since the company was the relevant seller and importer that infringed.

[74] See Campbell and Armour, 'Demystifying', who succinctly and persuasively draw the same distinctions. These distinctions are also drawn, e.g., in *MCA Records Inc* v. *Charly Records Ltd* [2001] EWCA Civ 1441; [2002] FSR 26, [26], [53] (*MCA Records*).

when D's knowledge of the wrongfulness of PW Co's conduct is essential and when it is not. That is explored further in [11.3.4].

11.3.2 *General principles of accessory liability*

Where D has not committed all the elements of the primary wrong, D may nonetheless be liable on the application of ordinary accessory principles. Importantly, if liability is determined on accessory principles, this means that the status of D as director is not critical as such. For example, an employee can also be liable as an accessory, where the employee uses the company as a vehicle to commit wrongs.[75]

Importantly, the accessory liability rules may vary depending on the primary wrong in question. For example, where D is sued as an accessory to a breach of PW Co's contract, then we need to resort to the law of the tort of inducing breach of contract. That law is relatively certain and liability is generally denied [11.3.5].[76] Similarly, infringements of IP rights will be assessed on the relevant IP accessory principles (e.g., authorisation [9.2]);[77] tort liability on tort principles;[78] and breach of trust or other equitable duties by PW Co on the relevant equitable principles [Chapter 8].[79]

11.3.3 *D's liability for PW Co's torts and statutory IP infringements*

11.3.3.1 Overview

When considering the question of the personal liability of directors and officers of a company for the company's torts, Gummow J stated in obiter in *WEA International Inc* v. *Hanimex Corporation Ltd*:[80]

[75] See *Keller* [2010] FCAFC 55; (2010) 185 FCR 449 [407].

[76] This is based on D's status as agent. Interestingly, despite the relative security of D from liability, this scenario is often highlighted by judges and commentators when decrying the dangers of holding D liable. See, e.g., *Keller* [2010] FCAFC 55; (2010) 185 FCR 449 [402].

[77] *Cf. MCA Records* [2001] EWCA Civ 1441; [2002] FSR 26 [51].

[78] For a detailed discussion of the relevant principles in one specific context, see Neil Foster, 'Personal Civil Liability of Company Officers for Company Workplace Torts' (2008) 16 *Torts Law Journal* 20.

[79] *Cf.* Campbell and Armour, 'Demystifying', 299.

[80] (1987) 17 FCR 274, 283 (1987) 10 IPR 349, 359; approved in *Microsoft Corporation* v. *Auschina Polaris Pty Ltd* [1996] FCA 1069; (1996) 71 FCR 231; (1996) 36 IPR 225, 233, a case that, unlike *WEA*, concerned that question. Redlich J in *Johnson Matthey (Aust) Ltd* v. *Dascorp Pty Ltd* [2003] VSC 291; (2003) 9 VR 171 [105]–[107], endorses Gummow J's statement, but goes on to state that directors' liability is probably accessorial and determined by joint tortfeasor principles.

> Where the infringer is a corporation questions frequently arise as to the degree of involvement on the part of directors necessary for them to be rendered personally liable. Those questions are not immediately answered by principles dealing with 'authorisation' or joint tortfeasance. Rather, recourse is to be had to the body of authority which explains the circumstances in which an officer of a corporation is personally liable for the torts of the corporation.

The assumption that special rules need to be applied to determine the liability of directors – that directors' liability 'is constrained by the doctrines of company law'[81] – underlies many key cases in New Zealand,[82] Canada[83] and Australia.[84] Overarching concerns about preserving the separate legal personality of corporations and not unduly sheeting personal responsibility upon directors have intruded here.[85] Some cases in the UK have also invoked the status of the corporate legal personality in support of the need for special rules.[86] However, the law in that jurisdiction is that liability is determined by resort either to the principles relevant to establishing the liability of D as a primary wrongdoer, or to accessory liability principles, rather than to distinct rules.[87]

[81] R Grantham and C Rickett, 'Directors' "Tortious" Liability: Contract, Tort or Company Law?' (1999) 62 *Modern Law Review* 133, 133.

[82] E.g., *Trevor Ivory* [1992] 2 NZLR 517.

[83] E.g., *Mentmore* (1978) 89 DLR (3rd) 195 (FCA).

[84] E.g., *King* v. *Milpurrurru* (1996) 66 FCR 474, 495–501; *Root Quality Pty Ltd* v. *Root Control Technologies Pty Ltd* [2000] FCA 980; (2000) 177 ALR 231 (*Root Quality*); *Keller* [2010] FCAFC 55; (2010) 185 FCR 449.

[85] It has also been said that the need for special rules arises from the limited liability of shareholders for corporate liabilities (see, e.g., *Trevor Ivory* [1992] 2 NZLR 517, 523-4 (Cooke P) and also extra-judicially, Lord Cooke of Thorndon, *Turning Points of the Common Law* (London, Sweet & Maxwell, 1997) 18). But this principle protects shareholders and not directors. See, e.g., J. Farrar, 'Personal Liability of Director for Torts of Company' (1997) 71 *Australian Law Journal* 20, 21, and S. Watson, 'Who Hides Behind the Corporate Veil? Finding a Way out of "The Legal Quagmire"' (2002) 20 *Company and Securities Law Journal* 198, 205. Even where directors are major shareholders, there are no policy reasons or economic arguments for limiting liability, according to Lo, 'Liability of directors, 120 onwards. Contrast *Keller* [2010] FCAFC 55; (2010) 185 FCR 449 [403].

[86] See, e.g., *White Horse Distillers Ltd* v. *Gregson Associates Ltd* [1984] RPC 61.

[87] See, e.g., *MCA Records* [2001] EWCA Civ 1441; [2002] FSR 26, and the summary of the English legal position in *Handi-Craft Company* v. *B Free World Ltd* [2007] EWHC B10 (Pat) [181] (*Handi-Craft*). In *MCA Records*, D's *status* as controller of the company did not appear significant in determining liability: see at [41]. Nonetheless, cases specifically on directors' liability were central to the reasoning of the court. At least in the *application* of those accessory liability principles, therefore, the company/director factual matrix is important and, further, policy may still exert some influence. See, e.g., *Società Esplosivi Industriali SpA* v. *Ordnance Technologies (UK) Ltd (No 2)* [2007] EWHC 2875 (Ch);

English law can be identified with relative certainty and appears settled for common law wrongs and statutory torts, in which contexts much of the case law arises: D is either personally liable as a primary wrongdoer, if all the elements of the specific wrong alleged can be established; or else is liable as an accessory based on application of general accessory principles,[88] either because D authorised, directed or procured the wrong,[89] or was a party to a common design to commit the wrong.[90] Nonetheless, English courts have also struggled at times to articulate what the joint tortfeasor principles precisely require and how they are applied in the specific factual contexts. For example, the role of knowledge has not been clearly articulated; indeed in many cases it has been sidelined.

Most of the recent cases in Australia view the competition in the authorities as between 'two relevant lines of authority'[91] that determine

[2008] 2 All ER 622 [87] (Lindsay J): 'this is an area of the law that raises an elusive question and a very difficult question of policy'. In Australia, *Johnson Matthey (Aust) Ltd* v. *Dascorp Pty Ltd* [2003] VSC 291; (2003) 9 VR 171 (see below n. 118) appears to come closest to the English approach.

88 *MCA Records* [2001] EWCA Civ 1441; [2002] FSR 26 [41]. As Lo, 'Liability of directors', 136 points out, the UK position has also been accepted in Hong Kong, in *Yakult Honsha* v. *Yakuda* [2004] 1 HKC 630; *Tai Shing* v. *Maersk* [2007] 2 HKC 23. See also David Debenham, 'Return to the Beaten Path? Directors' and Employees' Liability for Intellectual Property Torts after Mentmore' (2003) 16 *Intellectual Property Journal* 527, who argues that this approach should also be adopted in Canada, contrary to the current vague *Mentmore*-based approaches to liability.

89 Although statements that D may be liable for having 'made the wrong his own' have received support (e.g., *White Horse Distillers Ltd* v. *Gregson Associates Ltd* [1984] RPC 61, 91), that test has been rejected.

90 It is worth noting briefly that in the UK (e.g., in *Handi-Craft* [2007] EWHC B10 (Pat)) courts applying joint tortfeasor principles have at times applied the common design test, alongside direct or procure. Applying that test seems an artificial and indeed, a conceptually unsound basis for liability, however, if the common design between D and PW Co is based on the attribution of D's knowledge and conduct to PW Co. To engage in such reasoning is to hold D liable for a common design entered into with himself or herself (as appeared to be done in *Handi-Craft* [214]). The artificiality is acknowledged in *Societa Esplosivi Industriali SpA* v. *Ordnance Technologies (UK) Ltd (No 2)* [2007] EWHC 2875 (Ch); [2008] 2 All ER 622 [96]. Nonetheless, 'common design' was applied alongside the direct or procure test. In any case, common design is often implied, so that there is artificiality in concluding that there was a genuine agreement or meeting of minds.

Seemingly to a lesser extent, the same test has also been applied in Australia. See, e.g., *LED Technologies Pty Ltd* v. *Elecspess Pty Ltd* [2008] FCA 1941; 80 IPR 85, 128-9 [171]–[175], in which Gordon J concluded that the directors had a common design with the company. The decision on the directors' liability was overturned on appeal: *Keller* [2010] FCAFC 55; (2010) 185 FCR 449.

91 E.g., *Cooper* v. *Universal Music Australia Pty Ltd* [2006] FCAFC 187; 156 FCR 380 [160] (Kenny J, French J agreeing). See also *Allen Manufacturing Co Pty Ltd* v. *McCallum & Co*

D's liability for corporate wrongs, usually in the contexts of tort liability and IP (statutory) infringements. These are that D directs or procures the company to commit the wrong, or 'makes the wrong his own' as distinct from it being the company's act. As Sundberg J in the Federal Court noted in *Pioneer Electronics Australia Pty Ltd* v. *Lee*,[92] after summarising the 'uncertain state' of the law in Australia, 'the clear preponderance of authority, especially in this Court, favours the [direct or procure] approach'.[93] Arguably, however, the preference in the authorities for the 'direct or procure' test supports the view that Australian courts are moving away from treating directors' liability as raising distinct policy concerns requiring special treatment, and are instead simply applying accessory principles.[94]

We will briefly consider the meaning of the two main competing tests here: 'direct or procure' and 'makes the wrong his own'. It should be

Pty Ltd (2001) 53 IPR 400 and *Sydneywide Distributors Pty Ltd* v. *Red Bull Australia Pty Ltd* [2002] FCAFC 157; (2002) 55 IPR 354.

It has been suggested in some recent cases (e.g. *Inverness Medical Switzerland GmbH* v. *MDS Diagnostics Pty Limited* [2010] FCA 108 [179]) that a further test may also be relevant, namely the statement of principle by Finkelstein J in *TS & B Retail Systems Pty Ltd* v. *3Fold Resources Pty Ltd (No 3)* [2007] FCA 151; (2007) 239 ALR 117 [185]–[187] and *Root Quality* [2000] FCA 980; (2000) 177 ALR 231, 268 [146]: 'The director's conduct must be such that it can be said of him that he was so personally involved in the commission of the unlawful act that it is just that he should be rendered liable.' It is not clear, however, that Finkelstein J saw this as a distinct test, or merely a further elaboration of the 'make the wrong his own' test; the latter seems more likely (see *Root Quality* at [146]).

92 [2000] FCA 1926; (2001) 108 FCR 216. In fact, Sundberg J identified three competing tests for liability (as well as one limitation on liability) as having judicial support. The third test was whether D has assumed responsibility for the company's acts [45]. This 'assumption of responsibility' test has not received significant support and, as concluded above, is not a test of accessorial liability. In *Oakley Inc* v. *Oslu Import and Export Pty Ltd* [2001] FCA 385 [7], however, Finn J adopted Sundberg J's summary and appeared to consider the tests as determining the liability of directors *as accessories*. See also *Oakley* [2000] FCA 700; (2000) 48 IPR 32, 39 [35].

93 [2000] FCA 1926; (2001) 108 FCR 216 [46]. See also *Universal Music Australia Pty Ltd* v. *Sharman License Holdings Ltd* [2005] FCA 1242; (2005) 65 IPR 289 [433] (Wilcox J) (the authorities are in 'some disarray'). The Australian position remains open, however, and many cases apply the two tests in the alternative. E.g., *AMI Australia Holdings Pty Ltd* v. *Bade Medical Institute (Australia) Pty Ltd (No 2)* [2009] FCA 1437; (2009) 262 ALR 458; *Inverness Medical Switzerland GmbH* v. *MDS Diagnostics Pty Limited* [2010] FCA 108 [179]–[192]; *Hoath* v. *Connect Internet Services* [2006] NSWSC 158.

94 See Lo, 'Liability of directors', 131. After engaging in a comprehensive overview of the competing authorities in *Johnson Matthey (Aust) Ltd* v. *Dascorp Pty Ltd* [2003] VSC 291; (2003) 9 VR 171, Redlich J adopted conclusions that are broadly consistent with those in the UK and that are adopted in this chapter.

noted that on either test, there must be some positive act of involvement by D; mere inaction cannot suffice.[95]

11.3.3.2 Direct or procure

The direct or procure test is derived from statements by Atkin LJ (as he then was) in *Performing Right Society Limited* v. *Ciryl Theatrical Syndicate Ltd* (*Ciryl*),[96] relying on earlier authorities as supporting the following principle:

> Prima facie a managing director is not liable for tortious acts done by servants of the company unless he himself is privy to the acts, that is to say unless he ordered or procured the acts to be done. ... If the directors themselves directed or procured the commission of the act they would be liable in whatever sense they did so, whether expressly or impliedly.[97]

In *Microsoft Corporation* v. *Auschina Polaris Pty Ltd*, Lindgren J said of this test:

> The 'procured or directed' test, sometimes referred to as the 'authorised, procured or directed' test, focuses attention on the relationship between the director's intention and the *particular* corporate conduct which the law characterises as tortious.... where a particular human being involved and responsible to an appropriate extent [in a company's tortious conduct] can be identified, he should, as a matter of policy, be liable. [98]

The test requires some deliberate course of conduct on the part of D that furthers, via the corporate vehicle, the commission of the wrong, but the courts have not spelt out what precise acts of involvement might satisfy the test. It is not limited to procuring, that is, to seeking to bring about the very act that is a wrong. The concept of 'direct' is potentially much broader.[99] The liability does not follow merely from the relationship of

95 *King* v. *Milpurrurru* (1996) 66 FCR 474, 480-81; 136 ALR 327); *cf. Societa Esplosivi Industriali SpA* v. *Ordnance Technologies (UK) Ltd (No 2)* [2007] EWHC 2875 (Ch); [2008] 2 All ER 622 [95]–[102](coming close to suggesting liability for a mere omission, but ultimately finding positive encouragement and procurement of the infringing conduct).

96 [1924] 1 KB 1.

97 *Ibid.* 14-15. This passage was approved by the Privy Council in *Wah Tat Bank Ltd* v. *Chan Cheng Kum* [1975] AC 507, 514-15. *Ciryl* was a case concerning copyright, and Wood, 'Liability', has questioned the basis for applying tort principles to statutory IP infringements; but the body of authority is now too well established to be challenged.

98 [1996] FCA 1069; (1996) 71 FCR 231, 243-4; (1996) 36 IPR 225, 237 (emphasis in original).

99 Although some statements of the test posit it as the 'direct and procure' test, the two limbs are disjunctive.

D with PW Co and the degree of control that D has over PW Co's affairs.[100] The preponderance of authority rejects the view that D must know of the infringement where the primary wrong in question is one of strict liability [11.3.4]. Indeed, in some cases it appears to be assumed that applying the direct or procure test automatically leads to liability where D merely directs certain specific acts (that are, or lead to, infringements), as opposed to directing certain infringements.[101] In other words, the test is applied literally without reference to any mental state.

This approach may be correct in those circumstances where D directs and procures the employees and agents of PW Co to perform specific acts that amount to strict liability infringements, where the employees have no real choice as to how to go about their tasks. In other words, our requirement, set out in Chapter 3, that D must generally be knowingly involved in a wrong, knowing of the essential qualities of the wrong, is not applicable where PW Co commits a strict liability wrong and where D uses the corporate vehicle in a purely instrumental way to achieve specific objectives that amount to wrongs [11.3.4]. The conduct that D has procured is actionable according to its character. Where, however, D gives merely broad instructions, liability for 'directing or procuring' should be interpreted consistently with the underlying accessory principles to require that there is culpable conduct on D's part. In other words, D must knowingly direct or procure *an infringement* and not merely direct or procure certain actions that, absent knowledge of some essential matter, appear innocent. The results of the authorities, if not their reasoning, are for the most part consistent with this conclusion [11.3.4].

If the direct or procure test is interpreted to include a mental element, then it becomes a much more limited basis for liability – D must generally knowingly direct – and doubts expressed about that test in cases supporting the 'makes the wrong his own' test are adequately addressed.

[100] *C Evans & Sons Ltd* v. *Spritebrand Ltd* [1985] 1 WLR 317, 329A-C; *PLG Research Ltd* v. *Ardon International Ltd* [1993] FSR 197, 238 and 239 (Aldous J): 'in every case . . . it is necessary to examine with care what part [D] played personally in regard to the act or acts complained of'; *Johnson Matthey (Aust) Ltd* v. *Dascorp Pty Ltd* [2003] VSC 291; (2003) 9 VR 171, 227 [198].

[101] See, e.g., *Sporte Leisure (No 3)* [2010] FCA 1162; (2010) 88 IPR 242 [109]. Most cases that prefer the 'make the wrong his own' test seem to make the same assumption about the direct or procure test.

11.3.3.3 'Makes the wrong his own' test

The 'makes the wrong his own' test originated in the Canadian Federal Court of Appeal case of *Mentmore Manufacturing Co Inc* v. *National Merchandising Manufacturing Co Inc*[102] (*Mentmore*), concerning claims against D for patent infringements by D's company. The test has received some support in UK and Australian law.[103] It is unclear from the shorthand formulation what needs to be proved in order for the test to be satisfied, above and beyond the direct or procure test. The test fails to explicitly separate out the necessary conduct by D and the requisite mental state when so acting, such that without further elaboration, it is fair to conclude that it is 'indeterminate and possibly circular'.[104] Its supporters have conceded that it is not an easy test to apply.[105] Finkelstein J in *Root Quality Pty Ltd* v. *Root Control Technologies Pty Ltd* supported the test but noted the difficulty of applying it and that D is not rendered liable merely for deciding that PW Co carry out acts that result in infringement. He went on to state:

> Where the boundary lies, between the non-tortious conduct of a director who acts bona fide within the course of his authority and the tortious conduct of a director who acts deliberately and maliciously to cause harm, cannot be stated with any precision.[106]

In *Mentmore* itself, Le Dain J (jointly with Urie and Rich JJ) suggested that there needs to be something in the nature of a 'deliberate, wilful and knowing pursuit of a course of conduct that was likely to constitute infringement or reflected an indifference to risk of it'.[107] This suggests a focus on a high state of knowledge, but earlier, Le Dain J also stated that:

102 (1978) 89 DLR (3rd) 195.

103 See, e.g., *White Horse Distillers Ltd* v. *Gregson Associates Ltd* [1984] RPC 61, 91; *King* v. *Milpurrurru* (1996) 66 FCR 474, 495–501; 136 ALR 327, 346–51; *Keller* [2010] FCAFC 55; (2010) 185 FCR 449, e.g., at [405]; *Sporte Leisure (No 3)* [2010] FCA 1162; (2010) 88 IPR 242.

104 J. Farrar, 'The Personal Liability of Directors for Corporate Torts' (1997) 9 *Bond Law Review* 102, 108. Indeed, in Canada, the acceptance of *Mentmore* has led to even more vague statements of the relevant test, by determining from all the circumstances whether 'as a matter of policy, they call for personal liability' – see *Pater International Automotive Franchising Inc* v. *Mr Mechanic Inc* [1990] 1 FC 237, 242 – discussed by Debenham, 'Return to the Beaten Path?'

105 The commonly made, but unhelpful, statement that it is a 'question of fact to be decided on the circumstances of each case' (*Mentmore* (1978) 89 DLR (3d) 195, 203 (Le Dain J)) does not address these inadequacies.

106 *Root Quality* [2000] FCA 980; (2000) 177 ALR 231 [146].

107 *Mentmore* (1978) 89 DLR (3d) 195, 204-5. Further, Le Dain, Urie and Ryan JJ stated: 'It is unnecessary for him to know, or have the means of knowing, that the act or conduct is tortious. It is enough if he knows or ought to know that it is likely to be tortious.'

> I do not think we should go so far as to hold that the director or officer must know or have reason to know that the acts which he directs or procures constitute infringement. That would be to impose a condition of liability that does not exist for patent infringement generally.[108]

It is contradictory, however, to suggest on the one hand that D must engage in a 'deliberate, wilful and knowing' pursuit of conduct that is likely to constitute infringement, and yet to state that D need not 'know or have reason to know' that the acts D procures are infringing.[109] There is an obvious tension here, one that needs to be resolved in favour of an explicit knowledge requirement. Certainly, it has been stated that the *Mentmore* test is a 'more stringent' or 'stricter' or 'higher' test,[110] that 'requires some further involvement'[111] than direct or procure. In the view of White J in *Hoath* v. *Connect Internet Services*, that extra requirement is one of knowledge. The director must 'not only procure the commission of the tort, but act deliberately, knowing that the conduct infringed the plaintiff's rights, or with reckless indifference as to whether it did'.[112] This is a persuasive statement of the appropriate level of required knowledge, but could and should equally be incorporated into the direct or procure test rather than within the Delphic 'make the wrong his own' test.[113]

11.3.4 Liability for strict liability common law wrongs

We have concluded in [3.4.3.7] that some difficulties arise when applying accessory liability principles to strict liability wrongs, but that as a general

108 *Ibid.* 204.

109 As Nourse LJ noted in *White Horse Distillers Ltd* v. *Gregson Associates Ltd* [1984] RPC 61, 91, it is not very easy to reconcile all the passages in *Mentmore*.

110 Lo, 'Liability of directors', 111, 132: 'stricter approach', 'more difficult to satisfy'; *Hoath* v. *Connect Internet Services* [2006] NSWSC 158 (White J): 'more stringent', 'stricter' approach [88], a 'higher test' [92]. See also *White Horse Distillers Ltd* v. *Gregson Associates Ltd* [1984] RPC 61, 91-92.

111 *Sydneywide Distributors Pty Ltd* v. *Red Bull Australia Pty Ltd* [2002] FCAFC 157; (2002) 55 IPR 354 [161] (Weinberg and Dowsett JJ). See also *TS & B Retail Systems Pty Ltd* v. *3Fold Resources Pty Ltd (No 3)* [2007] FCA 151; (2007) 239 ALR 117 [185] (Finkelstein J): the comment that the differences are more apparent than real 'goes too far'.

112 [2006] NSWSC 158 [88].

113 A number of recent cases have suggested that the differences between the direct or procure and *Mentmore* tests may be 'more apparent than [real]': *Allen Manufacturing Co Pty Ltd* v. *McCallum & Co Pty Ltd* [2001] FCA 1838; (2001) 53 IPR 400 [43]. This conclusion is not correct unless it assumes that both tests contain a knowledge requirement, that D knowingly directs an *infringement*. This is the knowledge approach we advocate, but is contrary to express statements in a number of the 'direct or procure' authorities, although not necessarily in their outcomes.

rule, A needs to know of the essential elements of PW's conduct that make it a wrong, even where PW is strictly liable. In other words, A ought not generally be liable if he believes that PW's conduct is innocent.

In the corporate context, however, where D merely uses a corporate vehicle (or its employees and agents) to achieve his or her ends, it could be argued that it would be unfair if an innocent 'agent' of D is liable, whereas D is not. This conclusion is consistent with cases that have focused on D using PW Co as D's instrument to achieve targeted and specific outcomes. It is precisely these sorts of examples that are highlighted, for example, in Slade LJ's observation, based on an attractive appeal to fairness, in *C Evans & Sons Ltd* v. *Spritebrand Ltd*:

> In my judgment, it would offend common sense if . . . the law of tort were to treat the director of the company any more kindly than the servant, who took his orders from the director; . . . if one postulates the case of a servant of a company who in all innocence has trespassed on another's land . . . on the specific orders of a director who was present on the spot when the trespass occurred, though he did not cross the boundary but was equally innocent. Since this is a tort of absolute liability, the employee must be liable. Why should the director himself escape scot-free, even if he was unaware that his order would give rise to a trespass?[114]

The imposition of potentially strict liability has been justified partly on the basis that the accessory's knowledge merely needs to be commensurate with, or parallel, that of the primary infringer.[115] Many IP infringements are strict liability wrongs and it is in that context that many of the cases have arisen.[116] Particularly in that context, the predominant view

114 [1985] 1 WLR 317; [1985] 2 All ER 415, 425.

115 *Ibid.* 424:

> I would accept that if the plaintiff has to prove a particular state of mind or knowledge on the part of the defendant [the primary tortfeasor] as a necessary element of the particular tort alleged, the state of mind or knowledge of the director [the accessory] who authorised or directed it must be relevant if it is sought to impose personal liability on the director merely on account of such authorisation or procurement; the personal liability of the director in such circumstances cannot be more extensive than that of the individual who personally did the tortious act. If, however, the tort alleged is not one in respect of which it is incumbent on the plaintiff to prove a particular state of mind or knowledge (eg, infringement of copyright) different considerations may well apply.

116 The infringer may not know that copyright subsists in a work, or that the infringer's own product does not differ sufficiently from the claimant's patent, design or trademark. Liability is not strict for all IP infringements; see, e.g., ss. 37 and 38 Copyright Act 1968 (Cth) (a knowledge requirement for primary infringement).

appears to be that D need not necessarily know that PW Co's conduct is wrongful, in other words, that it is tortious or infringing.[117]

Such an approach, however, only appears justified if D has procured that very act or outcome, for which PW Co is liable. In other words, PW Co is, in effect, an 'agent' of D and knowledge that the acts are wrongful is not required.[118] In *MCA Records Inc* v. *Charly Records Ltd* (*MCA Records*), for example, the party had exercised control over PW Co and induced PW Co 'to ensure those acts were done'. Liability was therefore justified even in the absence of knowledge of infringement.[119]

[117] As Lindgren J stated in *Microsoft Corporation* v. *Auschina Polaris Pty Ltd* [1996] FCA 1069; (1996) 71 FCR 231; (1996) 36 IPR 225, 235, the proposition seems to be uncontroversial. Even cases such as *Mentmore* (1978) 89 DLR (3rd) 195 appear to accept this, albeit in the context of seemingly contradictory statements. Slade LJ's view has been followed in many cases, e.g., in *Handi-Craft* [2007] EWHC B10 (Pat), but also rejected in others, e.g., in *Root Quality* [2000] FCA 980; (2000) 177 ALR 231 [136].

[118] Even in this scenario, strict liability can lead to harsh outcomes, where, e.g., the primary liability is particularly wide-ranging, capturing wholly innocent parties. E.g., in *Johnson Matthey (Aust) Ltd* v. *Dascorp Pty Ltd* [2003] VSC 291; (2003) 9 VR 171, in which two directors of a small company under their control, were liable as accessories for the tort of conversion committed by the company, even in the absence of evidence that they were aware of the thief's defective title. Redlich J at 227 [200]–[201] saw no reason to require

> . . . that a director who, by virtue of their level of involvement and control is found to have procured or directed the commission of the acts should not be liable unless the director knew or was indifferent as to whether the acts were unlawful or likely to cause loss or damage to the true owner of the goods.
>
> . . . For a tort such as conversion that does not require a particular intention, a director is liable for the tortious acts of the corporation which he or she directed or procured regardless of the director's state of mind. The level of involvement and the degree of control which a director exercises will determine whether it can be said that the acts have been directed or procured by the director.

One of the difficulties with the case is that it was concluded that the directors had not exercised sufficient possession or control over the goods such as to have personally committed conversion (rather than as accessories). Although the company was the vehicle by which the Ds committed the acts, in the absence of any employees to carry out Ds' wishes, however, the accessory liability characterisation merges the company with its directors and again suggests that any liability should perhaps be primary or not arise at all.

[119] [2001] EWCA Civ 1441; [2002] FSR 26 [61]; see also [54]–[55]: party exercised control over company and used powers to ensure that infringing conduct occurred. In *Keller* [2010] FCAFC 55; (2010) 185 FCR 449, one of the directors ought to have been held liable given his very active role in PW Co's infringement and that he had actually designed the infringing products and had knowledge of C's designs. He ought to have been held liable as if he had personally done all the infringing acts rather than while acting through and for an intermediary, i.e., even absent knowledge that the designs

Critical is whether D has procured the very acts that turn out to be strict liability wrongs, or else procured merely some general objective or tasks, leaving the employees and agents of PW Co the choice as to how to achieve those objectives. In the latter type of case, knowledge ought to be critical and strict liability is not justified. The reasons of policy that may support imposing liability on an innocent PW do not apply equally to A, who has not committed the wrongful acts [3.4.3.6]; [3.4.3.7]. If D's involvement falls short of procuring, then involving oneself in acts that D believes are innocent is not wrongful.[120] The difficulty with the 'direct or procure' test is that it is not necessarily limited in its operation to parties who have sought that very (wrongful) outcome.

Despite general statements that D should be strictly liable where PW Co (through its employees and agents) is strictly liable, and the preponderance of authority supporting the view that knowledge is not required, in many of the cases, absence of knowledge was not in fact an issue. D either knew precisely of the infringements,[121] or that they were substantially likely to follow,[122] or the question of knowledge was a hypothetical one.[123] Further, in many cases in which D did not know some essential matters going to PW Co's infringement, courts have rejected liability.[124] As Nicholas J stated in the Federal Court of Australia, after noting that D will need to have done something more than causing or directing PW Co to perform acts:

> The extent of the director's personal involvement in the commission of the infringing acts is no doubt critical. But his or her state of mind is itself an important aspect of that involvement. That does not mean that

actually infringed. See Besanko J at [292], whose judgment, dissenting on this point, is to be preferred.

120 Of course, D need not know the law; e.g., D will be liable if D believes there is no such thing as copyright or trademark protection.

121 E.g., *Microsoft Corporation* v. *Auschina Polaris Pty Ltd* [1996] FCA 1069; (1996) 71 FCR 231; (1996) 36 IPR 225, 240; *Oakley Inc* v. *Oslu Import and Export Pty Ltd* [2001] FCA 385; seemingly *Handi-Craft* [2007] EWHC B10 (Pat) (although knowledge is not directly averted to in many of the factual findings).

122 *Cf.* state of knowledge of D in *Societa Esplosivi Industriali SpA* v. *Ordnance Technologies (UK) Ltd (No 2)* [2007] EWHC 2875 (Ch); [2008] 2 All ER 622, particularly at [95].

123 *C Evans & Sons Ltd* v. *Spritebrand Ltd* [1985] 1 WLR 317 (strike-out application).

124 See, e.g., *Root Quality* [2000] FCA 980; (2000) 177 ALR 231, in which a bona fide belief by a director that the manufacturing and sale of a product did not infringe patents was fatal to a claim; and *Mentmore* (1978) 89 DLR (3rd) 195, 205, liability denied because of uncertainty as to the scope and application of claimant's patent claim. In *Keller* [2010] FCAFC 55; (2010) 185 FCR 449, knowledge was given a critical role, even if not a determinative one, in all three judgments.

> knowledge that the relevant acts are infringing is a prerequisite to liability. The authorities are clear in holding that it is not. Even so, a finding that a director who held an honest belief that the acts which he or she directed or procured were not unlawful is a significant consideration telling against the director's liability [and in this case decisive].[125]

Apart from the procuring of specific acts, knowledge that PW Co's conduct is wrongful ought to be required. Knowledge that infringement is substantially likely to follow would also suffice.[126]

The conclusions reached above support a more general observation, namely, that the more active D is in seeking to bring about a result, the less D needs to know about whether PW Co's conduct is wrongful. The lesser a role that D has, then the more D's knowledge becomes critical, and D should not be liable absent knowledge of the infringing nature of the corporate acts unless D has procured that very outcome.

11.3.5 Liability of D for PW Co's breach of contract

If the primary wrong committed by PW Co is a breach of contract, then the courts will not directly or indirectly enforce that obligation against D other than in exceptional circumstances. The courts will not directly enforce the contract against D unless D expressly guarantees the performance of the contract, or otherwise has contracted personally rather than on behalf of PW Co.[127] If such liability does arise, it is not accessorial; D is liable as a party to the contract. Certainly, where the company's name appears on any written contractual documents, it is difficult to argue that D has contracted personally.[128] D as agent has not, according to the rules of contract law itself, contracted with C and

[125] *Sporte Leisure (No 3)* [2010] FCA 1162; (2010) 88 IPR 242 [118]. The finding of no liability for the director was not the subject of the unsuccessful appeal in *Paul's International Pty Ltd (ACN 128 263 561)* v. *Sporte Leisure Pty Ltd (ACN 008608919) (No 3)* [2012] FCAFC 51; (2012) 91 IPR 151.

[126] We reject the notion that a further requirement is necessary, apart from knowledge, that D 'stand apart' from PW Co, directing or procuring it as a 'separate entity' (whatever, with respect, that may mean): *Keller* [2010] FCAFC 55; (2010) 185 FCR 449 [88] (Emmett J), and [404] (Jessup J).

[127] See, e.g., *Re International Contract Company* (1871) 6 Ch App 525; *VTB Capital* [2013] UKSC 5; [2013] 2 AC 337. In *Fairline Shipping Corporation* v. *Adamson* [1974] 2 All ER 967, arguments that the contractual obligations had passed to D by novation failed.

[128] See generally Lexa Hilliard QC, 'Liabilities of Directors to Third Parties', Ch. 24 in Simon Mortimore (ed.), *Company Directors, Duties, Liabilities and Remedies*, 2nd edn (Oxford University Press, 2013) [24.04]–[24.08], and on pre-incorporation contracts, [24.09] onwards.

therefore is not liable.[129] Further, the courts will not indirectly enforce such a contract against D, by imposing liability in tort for inducing breach of contract. It has been repeatedly held that D is not liable in that tort for decisions that result in PW Co breaching its contracts [6.3.3]. Although some cases have criticised this view,[130] to hold otherwise would be to undermine completely the principle that only the company is liable for the breach of the company's contractual obligations.[131] The inducing tort 'cannot be used to sidestep important contract principles'[132] nor, it should be added, principles of separate corporate personality. These limitations play no role when the imposition of liability for wrongs unrelated to the contract is at issue, since claimants seeking to impose such liability have not chosen to have dealings with the company.[133]

11.3.6 *Liability of directors acting in their constitutional role*

Courts in the common law context have often raised the important 'policy' of needing to protect directors from the dangers of a broad liability regime, under which liability may be imposed on directors for merely fulfilling their constitutional roles, for example, by voting at board meetings.[134] At times, this is stated almost as a prohibition on liability. For example, in *MCA Records* Chadwick LJ stated:

> [A] director will not be treated as liable with the company as a joint tortfeasor if he does no more than carry out his constitutional role in the governance of the company—that is to say, by voting at board meetings.

[129] In some cases, statute may impose direct liability on a director in relation to the company's breach of contract. E.g. Corporations Act 2001 (Cth) Pt 5.7B, especially s. 588G, makes a director liable in relation to company's debts incurred while insolvent.

[130] See, e.g., doubts expressed in *Welsh Development Agency* v. *Export Finance Co Ltd* [1992] BCLC 148 (CA), 173 (Dillon LJ), 179 (Ralph Gibson LJ) and 191 (Staughton LJ), though ultimately, the authority of *Said* v. *Butt* [1920] 3 KB 497 was accepted.

[131] *Root Quality* [2000] FCA 980; (2000) 177 ALR 231. Note, however, the attempt to indirectly enforce the contract against the directors in *Tsaprazis* v. *Goldcrest Properties* (2000) 18 ACLC 285, 288, in which an argument that they owed a duty of reasonable care to ensure the company fulfilled its contract failed; although the door was left open to a successful claim if a director took positive steps that would lead to greater losses to a claimant should the company breach.

[132] Wood, 'Liability', 172.

[133] *Johnson Matthey (Aust) Ltd* v. *Dascorp Pty Ltd* [2003] VSC 291; (2003) 9 VR 171, 227 [199].

[134] E.g., *TS & B Retail Systems Pty Ltd* v. *3Fold Resources Pty Ltd (No 3)* [2007] FCA 151; (2007) 239 ALR 117.

> That, I think, is what policy requires if a proper recognition is to be given to the identity of the company as a separate legal person. . . . if all that a director is doing is carrying out the duties entrusted to him as such by the company under its constitution, the circumstances in which it would be right to hold him liable as a joint tortfeasor with the company would be rare indeed.[135]

If the courts were to adopt the approach as to knowledge advocated in this chapter, namely, that as a general rule, D must have actual knowledge of, or be recklessly indifferent to, the qualities of PW Co's acts that make it a wrong, then the perceived problems in applying accessory liability to directors acting in their constitutional role largely fall away. If D merely votes at a board meeting, absent any knowledge of specific infringements, D will clearly not be liable. Directing the carrying on of a business is not directing infringement.[136] The exceptional circumstance in which liability should be imposed, even in the absence of knowledge, is not enlivened when D merely votes at a board meeting on a new direction or strategy, for example. In such a case, D is merely a cog in a larger organisational wheel. PW Co is not D's instrument (even if it *is* the board's instrument) nor is D using his or her authority to procure PW Co and its employees to perform specific acts. D should be able to deliberate on the merits of decisions without fear of unknown liability. However, this does not mean that D is immune from liability.[137] For example, if D, with members of the board, pursues a deliberate strategy of *knowingly* stealing a rival's IP rights, then D's knowledge satisfies the mental element. The fact that D is merely one of many, and that the strategy is a group strategy, should not matter. An example is *T Oertli AG* v. *EJ Bowman (London) Ltd (No 3)*,[138] in which all the directors of a company were held liable for the company's passing off, having acted in concert to adopt a 'deliberate' policy of engaging their business to that end.[139] But such circumstances, as Chadwick LJ rightly stated in *MCA*, quoted above, 'would be rare indeed'.

[135] [2001] EWCA CIV 1441; [2002] FSR 26 [49], see also [50].

[136] This is all the more so where the company engages in a range of activities, only some of which may infringe.

[137] See Lo, 'Liability of directors', 137–138, who argues that D may be liable for Board decisions where the Board authorises or directs *specific* infringing acts, such as a tortious policy.

[138] [1956] RPC 282 Ch D.

[139] *Ibid.* e.g., at 288, 292, 298 (Roxburgh J). The decision's persuasiveness is lessened since it was overturned on appeal on the basis that there was no passing off: [1959] RPC 1 (HL),

11.3.7 Accessory liability of directors of company trustees

It is very common for a company to be a trustee.[140] Corporate trusts are highly utilised in a range of commercial and non-commercial contexts. But generally a company trustee[141] need not have a minimum capital, unless required to do so by statute in order to obtain particular privileges or do certain acts.[142] Therefore, if there is a breach of trust by the company trustee, there may be little point in pursuing the company itself.[143] For this reason, the question of whether the directors of the company trustee may be liable for a breach of trust and, if so, the form of such liability is of immense importance.[144]

The fundamental principle is that a director of a company trustee is not liable as a primary wrongdoer for a breach of trust by the company. A director owes duties to the company, including fiduciary duties,[145] but (unless such duties are imposed by statute)[146] a director does not owe duties directly to the beneficiaries of the trust.[147] Specifically, a director

without any discussion of the merits of the claim against the directors if passing off by the company had been established (see at 6).

140 In Australia, corporate trustees are also subject to detailed legislative and regulatory frameworks under Ch. 5C and 5D of the Corporations Act 2001 (Cth). Consideration of these frameworks is beyond the scope of the discussion here.

141 Bearing in mind that confusion may well result from the use of either 'company trustee' or 'trust corporation' (given that those terms are used in some statutory contexts), we have opted for 'company trustee' to refer to *any* company acting as a trustee.

142 See in Australia, e.g., Trustee Companies Act 1964 (NSW), and in England, Law of Property Act 1925. For discussion of when a company trustee of a pension scheme might nonetheless be worthless, see Henry Legge, 'Pension Schemes' in Simon Mortimore (ed.), *Company Directors: Duties, Liabilities, and Remedies* (Oxford University Press, 2009) 797 [26.62]–[26.63].

143 See, e.g., the facts of *Gregson* v. *HAE Trustees Ltd* [2008] EWHC 1006; [2008] 2 BCLC 542 (*Gregson*).

144 See Richard Nolan, 'Shopping for Defendants: Worthless Trust Companies and Their Directors' (2008) 67 *Cambridge Law Journal* 472. Legislation in some jurisdictions renders directors liable in relation to the debts of company trustees, but not in relation to breaches of trust per se. See, e.g., s. 197 Corporations Act 2001 (Cth) and the interpretation of a predecessor to that section in *Young* v. *Murphy* [1996] 1 VR 279 (VCA).

145 See, generally, *Australian Securities Commission* v. *AS Nominees Ltd* (1995) 62 FCR 504 (FCA).

146 See, e.g., s 601FD(1) Corporations Act 2001 (Cth).

147 *Bath* v. *Standard Land Co Ltd* [1911] 1 Ch 618; *Gregson* [2008] EWHC 1006; [2008] 2 BCLC 542 [27]–[69]; *McEwen* v. *Combined Coast Cranes Pty Ltd* [2002] NSWSC 1227; (2002) 44 ACSR 244 [54] (*McEwen*) and the cases discussed therein. See also H. A. J. Ford and I. J. Hardingham, 'Trading Trusts: Rights and Liabilities of Beneficiaries' in P. D. Finn (ed.), *Equity and Commercial Relationships* (Sydney, Law Book Company Limited, 1987) 48.

does not 'owe a direct duty to safeguard the assets of a trust of which [its trustee company] is trustee'.[148]

Attempts to circumvent this fundamental principle by the use of a 'dog leg' claim by trust beneficiaries against directors have been comprehensively rejected by the courts.[149] Although rights of action against third parties that are acquired by a corporate trustee on behalf of the trust are trust property (and hence, in some circumstances, can be enforced by the beneficiaries directly: a dog leg claim), a corporate trustee's right of action against a director for breach of a duty owed to it, and that is linked to a breach of trust by the company itself, is not considered trust property in this sense.[150]

Although a director of a trustee company is not generally a primary wrongdoer in relation to a breach of trust by the company, he or she may undoubtedly be liable as an accessory to such primary wrong by the company:

> [accessory] liability is one of no little significance to the directors of a trust company for the very reason that, often enough, it will be their own conduct in exercising the powers of the board which causes their company to commit a breach of trust. They are, in other words, peculiarly vulnerable to this rule.[151]

Leading cases on equitable accessory liability bear this out.[152] An example, if any is needed, is *Royal Brunei Airlines*: a director's conduct was imputed to his trustee company for the purposes of the company's

[148] *Gregson* [2008] EWHC 1006; [2008] 2 BCLC 542 [46]. The fundamental principle is not always expressed in unqualified terms; see, e.g., *McEwen* [2002] NSWSC 1227; (2002) 44 ACSR 244 [54]. A possible exception concerns the self-dealing rule that precludes trustees purchasing trust property. see *Clay* v. *Clay* [2001] HCA 9; (2001) 202 CLR 410 [51]–[52]. It has been held that this rule applies also to the directors of the trustee company: *Re James* [1949] SASR 143 (SASC) 146. See also, Ford and Hardingham, 'Trading Trusts', 60; J. Mowbray, L. Tucker, N. Le Poidevin and E. Simpson, *Lewin on Trusts*, 17th edn (London, Sweet & Maxwell, 2000) [20-74]; Austin Wakeman Scott, William Franklin Fratcher and Mark L. Ascher, *Scott & Ascher on Trusts*, 5th edn (Boston, Aspen Publishers, 2006), §30.6.3.

[149] See *Young* v. *Murphy* [1996] 1 VR 279 (VCA); *Gregson* [2008] EWHC 1006; [2008] 2 BCLC 542.

[150] *Young* v. *Murphy* [1996] 1 VR 279 (VCA); *Gregson* [2008] EWHC 1006; [2008] 2 BCLC 542 [27]–[69]. See also, Nolan, 'Shopping for Defendants'. Contra Scott, Fratcher and Ascher, *Scott & Ascher*, §30.6.4 noting that such a claim is 'arguable', but without reference to the comprehensive analysis in the Anglo-Australian cases.

[151] *Australian Securities Commission* v. *AS Nominees Ltd* (1995) 62 FCR 504 (FCA) 523 (Finn J).

[152] See, e.g., *Royal Brunei Airlines* [1995] 2 AC 378 (PC); *Air Canada* v. *M & L Travel Ltd* [1993] 3 SCR 787; 108 DLR (4th) 592 (SCC) (*Air Canada*).

primary liability for breach of trust, the director being held accessorily liable (on the basis of his conduct and mental state) for dishonest assistance in that breach of trust. Similar concerns to those regarding the artificiality of a *Barnes* v. *Addy*-style template being used in relation to a company's accessory liability [11.2.1] have been expressed in relation to the determination of a director's accessory liability,[153] although the liability itself is not questioned.[154]

11.4 Conclusion

The discussion in this chapter leads us to conclude that the same principles that determine the liability of human actors as either primary wrongdoers or accessories apply equally to directors of companies and to the companies themselves. Although concerns about the dangers of imposing liability on directors too readily are legitimate, these concerns can be addressed by the application of the relevant accessory principles which, if properly understood, include identifying what acts of involvement potentially give rise to liability, as well as a transparent consideration of any knowledge requirement (which ought to be more rigorous than some case law currently suggests). There are no cogent reasons why company directors deserve special immunity from liability for wrongs, nor why the principles of accessory liability should not provide just outcomes.[155] In essence, the scheme adopted in this book applies equally to determining the accessory liability of directors and of companies.

This is not to say that in some circumstances the status of companies as separate, but artificial, legal entities managed by directors, does not impact on the *application* of the relevant principles.[156] One of those circumstances, the limited liability of D in contract, is not the result of

[153] See, e.g., *Air Canada* [1993] 3 SCR 787, 824; 108 DLR (4th) 592 (SCC), 617 (Iacobucci J noting that a director differs from other company agents).

[154] See Ford and Hardingham, 'Trading Trusts', 64 fn. 68a: the extensive US case law and commentary concerning accessory liability of directors of company trustees may be of assistance in developing more tailored accessorial rules. See Scott, Fratcher and Ascher, *Scott & Ascher*, §30.6.3; George Gleason Bogert, George Taylor Bogert, Amy Morris Hess, *Bogert's Trusts and Trustees*, §901 and the cases discussed at fn. 10. On the relevance of the US law, see *Australian Securities Commission* v. *AS Nominees Ltd* (1995) 62 FCR 504 (FCA) 523.

[155] See Lo, 'Liability of directors', particularly at 110.

[156] *Cf. Keller* [2010] FCAFC 55; (2010) 185 FCR 449 [403] (Jessup J.): the answer to directors' liability 'lies in the application of the conventional rules of law as to joint liability to the particular circumstance where the primary wrongdoer is an artificial person who can act only by human agency'.

D's status as director, but of D's status when acting as an agent for a principal. Further, D's actions as a director are a relevant factual circumstance that establishes D's role in the decision-making of the company and in the commission of the wrong; this is especially so where D's conduct involves no more than carrying out his or her constitutional role of voting at board meetings [11.3.6].

PART III

12

Conclusion

This book has explored the circumstances in which a person will be found liable in private law as an accessory to another's wrong. It has also sought to explain this liability. Why must an 'accessory' remedy the consequences of another's wrongdoing even though he did not personally commit the wrongful act? The answer, broadly speaking, is that knowing involvement in another's wrong is sometimes considered legally wrongful in itself. The accessory is liable for his own wrongdoing.

Accessory liability is a narrow basis of liability. This is, perhaps, unsurprising given the potentially onerous nature of the liability. Nor is accessory liability the sole basis for imposing liability on persons who participate in another's wrongdoing; consequently, the book has also explored the boundaries between accessory liability and such related liabilities.

This book does not argue that there is a single cause of action for accessory liability. The legal rules that determine accessory liability across private law are too complex and varied, even as to the form of liability itself, for that to be the case. Nonetheless, accessory liability in its various manifestations shares a deceptively simple analytical framework. Liability depends upon three factors: the commission of a wrong by another party; the accessory's involvement, through conduct, in the wrong; and the accessory's mental state at the time of such involvement. The content of the conduct and mental elements – and, consequently, the reach of liability – is a function of the purposes, values and historical development of the primary wrong. These three factors are legally significant in all instances of accessory liability, whether or not they are explicitly averted to.

Furthermore, the analytical framework is not static, but operates in a dynamic fashion. The normative question of whether a person is sufficiently linked to a wrong committed by another depends on the relative weight of, and interplay between, the three elements. The relational interplay of the elements can be discerned in the doctrinal formulation of specific liability rules and, sometimes, in their judicial application. In particular, it is the accessory's conduct and mental state, considered in combination and relative to each other, that may create a sufficiently strong participation link to the primary wrong for the accessory to be considered culpable in relation to that primary wrong.

The analysis in Part II of the legal rules that determine accessory liability for torts, breach of contract, equitable wrongs and statutory wrongs yields some interesting general observations. First, procuring another to commit a wrong is universally condemned by the law. This scenario offers the strongest case for liability no matter in which context it occurs. Secondly, legislation is a very important source of accessory liability. Although it is challenging to present a generalised account of its operation, it is necessary to do so given its enormous practical relevance and its symbiotic relationship with the common law. The third observation is related to the second. The relationship of company and director, particularly where this involves an alter ego, raises quite specific questions with respect to accessory liability. We have identified some of these, but at the expense of a detailed treatment of their legislative context. The topic deserves more extensive analysis than has been possible within the scope of this book. A fourth and final observation is that, while analytical frameworks have their place, an understanding of accessory liability is greatly enhanced by an appreciation of its context; that is, by a treatment of the various liability rules with which it interacts and overlaps. Accordingly, we hope that this book has provided transparent analytical tools for understanding a truly fascinating form of legal liability, without shying away from the complexity and richness of the law itself.

INDEX

For EU product safety concerns, contact us at Calle de José Abascal, 56–1°, 28003 Madrid, Spain or eugpsr@cambridge.org.

www.ingramcontent.com/pod-product-compliance
Lightning Source LLC
LaVergne TN
LVHW020325220926
848484LV00001BB/241